triomf

triomf

MARLENE VAN NIEKERK

Translated from the Afrikaans by Leon de Kock

THE OVERLOOK PRESS
Woodstock & New York

This edition first published in the United States in 2004 by
The Overlook Press, Peter Mayer Publishers, Inc.
Woodstock & New York

WOODSTOCK:
One Overlook Drive
Woodstock, NY 12498
www.overlookpress.com
[for individual orders, bulk and special sales, contact our Woodstock office]

NEW YORK:
141 Wooster Street
New York, NY 10012

⊗The paper used in this book meets the requirements for paper
permanence as described in the ANSI Z39.48-1992 standard.

Library of Congress Cataloging-in-Publication Data

Van Niekerk, Marlene.
Triomf / by Marlene van Niekerk ; translated by Leon de Kock.
p. cm.
I. De Kock, Leon. II. Title.
PT6592.32.A545T75 2004   839.3'636—dc22   2003063977

Printed in the United States of America
ISBN 1-58567-500-8
10 9 8 7 6 5 4 3 2 1

Removing the heat from inside a refrigerator is somewhat like removing water from a leaking canoe. A sponge may be used to soak up the water. The sponge is held over the side, squeezed and the water is released overboard. The operation may be repeated as often as necessary to transfer the water from the canoe into the lake.

Modern Refrigeration and Airconditioning, Althouse, Turnquist & Bracciano, 1988. South Holland, Illinois: The Goodheart-Willcox Company Inc.

CONTENTS

1. The Dogs, 1
2. The Witnesses, 23
3. Knitting, 42
4. Polishing the Brass, 57
5. Sweet is the Day, 75
6. Oh, It's a Saturday Night, 99
7. Running Repairs, 125
8. Pest Control, 141
9. Coughing, 162
10. The Never-Ending Painting, 179
11. The Saving Perspective
    Meat, 190
    This One's For You, 195
    Tether, 200
    Fruit Salad, 206
12. Dog's Heaven, 213
13. Lucky Finds, 228
14. Fifth of November
    From Dream to Dream, 258
    Blow High the Flame, 258
    Watermelon, 272
    Happy Guy Fawkes, 276
    Overload, 286
    Bath, 288
    Man of Stars, 295
    To Sleep, 298
15. Urban Angel, 300

16. The Queen of England
    Fence, 324
    Second of September, 331
    Christmas, 337
    Also Just Human, 343
17. Peace on Earth, 345
18. Triomf Trials
    Family Bible, 365
    Jesus' Blood Never Failed Me Yet,
    371
    Tickey, 373
    Multiple Choice, 379
19. The Miracle of the Fridges
    The First Miracle: Tiny Bubbles, 394
    The Second Miracle: Shock
    Treatment, 397
20. Sunrise, Sunset
    Finishing Touches, 401
    Sermons on the Mount, 416
    Lambertus and Cleopatra, 434
    Reportback, 457
21. North No More
    Parallel Parking, 487
    Wonder Wall, 496
    Family Secrets, 502
    Guy Fawkes, 514
Glossary 525

Thank you to Leon de Kock for accepting and persevering with the mammoth task of translating this book; and for the ingenuity, sensitivity and thoroughness with which he did it. Thank you to the editors, Sally Abbey, Sarah Shrubb and Andrew Gordon and the other members of the Little, Brown team who were involved in the production of Triomf in the UK; Hettie Scholtz and Dineke Volschenk; to Pippa Lange for making this possible.

Thank you to Wendy Matthews for her sustained empathy throughout; to Ena Jansen for advice and support; to John Miles and Gerrit Olivier; and especially to Cobus Nothnagel for firm backing during the writing process. And for his freshwater pearls! Without him and without Wendy – and without the Old South Africa – *Triomf* would not have been possible.

1

~

THE DOGS

It's late afternoon, end of September. Mol stands behind the house, in the backyard. As the sun drops, it reaches between the houses and draws a line across the middle button of her housecoat. Her bottom half is in shadow. Her top half feels warm.

Mol stares at all the stuff Lambert has dug out of the earth. It's a helluva heap. Pieces of red brick, bits of smooth drainpipe, thick chunks of old cement and that blue gravel you see on graves. Small bits of glass and other stuff shine in the muck. Lambert has already taken out most of the shiny things – for his collection, he says. He collects the strangest things.

Gerty's at Mol's feet, sniffing at the heap. Must still smell of kaffir, she thinks. Gerty drags out something from between two bits of cement and drops it at Mol's feet.

'What is it, Gerty? Hey? What you got there? Show the missus!'

Mol picks it up. It's a flat, rusted tin. Looks like a jam tin. Kaffir jam! Sis, yuk! She throws it back on to the heap.

She picks up Gerty and looks across the length of the bare yard. The yellow lawn stretches all the way up to the wire fence in front. Lambert says it's just rubble wherever you dig, here where they live. Under the streets too, from Toby right through to Annandale on the other side. Rubble, just rubble.

*   *   *

The kaffirs must've gotten the hell out of here so fast, that time, they didn't even take their dogs with them.

A lot of their stuff got left behind. Whole dressers of crockery. You could hear things breaking to pieces when the bulldozers moved in. Beds and enamel basins and sink baths and all kinds of stuff. All of it just smashed.

That was quite a sight.

The kaffirs screamed and shouted and ran up and down like mad things. They tried to grab as much as they could to take with when the lorries came.

And those kaffirdogs cried and yelped as they ran around, trying to get out of the way of all that stuff falling and breaking everywhere.

Mol remembers the day very well; when they took away the first bunch of kaffirs. It was raining. February '55. She and Pop and Treppie stood at the top end of Ontdekkers, on the other side, watching the whole business, 'cause Treppie had heard the Department of Community Development wanted to build houses here for 'less privileged whites' – here where Sophiatown used to be.

Triomf, they were told, would be the new suburb's name.

Just for whites. They said they'd start building in 1960.

'From Fietas to Triomf!' Treppie said – and he didn't want to hear any of them complaining they weren't going up in the world.

Fietas was also flattened in later years. Not long after they got out.

Ja, it was also a right royal mixed-up lot there in Vrededorp – that was now supposed to be Fietas' proper name.

Gerty squirms in Mol's arms. She puts her down. The little dog turns around and looks at the heap again. God alone knows how much deeper that hole in his den must still go. Lambert says it's for petrol; he wants to store petrol in there. It's for when the shit starts flying after the election, he says. That's the kind of rubbish Treppie talks into his head.

Gerty wants attention. She digs with both her front paws in the rubble, poking her nose in the clods that are still red from all the old bricks. Then she pricks her ears and looks up at Mol – she wants to play. Ag shame, the poor little thing, not much chance to play around here.

Mol goes and sits heavily on the old Dogmor tin next to the house. She puts her hand into her housecoat pocket, takes out a cigarette and lights up.

The kaffirs weren't very impressed with the whole business, that's for sure.

She and Pop and Treppie stood on the side of the road, watching them stone the buses. The trams too.

In those days there was a tram that ran all the way to Roodepoort.

Treppie was very worked up about the bulldozing. Some days he used to go there after work, riding up and down in the trams so he could check things out for himself. And sometimes, when he worked the night shift, he'd first walk all the way to Sophiatown before going to work. Then, later, he'd come home and make them long speeches, for hours on end, about everything he'd seen there, 'there where our future lies', he'd say, 'where we're going to make a new start in life', cackling through that crooked mouth of his. In those days, she never understood what that laugh of his meant, but she's learnt in the meantime. As for their lives here in Triomf – there's nothing funny about that. Here it just buggers on. And these days the buggering's getting rough.

When they were bulldozing that time, there was a skinny priest in a long, black dress who used to run up and down behind the bulldozers, trying to help the kaffirs with all their things.

The kaffirdogs all knew him. They used to jump up at him as he ran around, and after a while that black dress of his started looking a real mess from all the dusty paw marks.

But he could do nothing for them. The dogs, that is. And their kaffirs.

He was an English priest. A real kaffirlover, by the name of Huddleston. Treppie used to call him Muddlemouth or old Meddlebones, 'cause he was one of those holier-than-thou big-mouths from overseas who came here to interfere with stuff.

His church still stands today, just behind them, but these days not much goes on there. It's the PPC of Triomf now. The Pentecostal Protestant Church. Those Protestants look a poor bunch to her. There are not many more than there are of the Members in Christ. And the Members

3

all fit into a single Kombi. She sees the pastor driving past sometimes, going up Martha Street to pick people up. MEMBERS IN CHRIST, it says in big, blue letters on one side. Here one, there one, he picks them up. Chicken feed.

Here in Triomf they've got the PPCs, the Members, the Apostolics and the Jehovah's Witnesses. There's also an NG church across the road from Shoprite, but it's always empty, except when they've got a bazaar going. Right next to the NG, in front of the police flats, she's seen a white noticeboard with DAY SPRING CHRISTIAN CHURCH written in pink letters. And guess what, they actually go there, those policemen, with their little wives and all. Must be a nice church, that. But as for priests in dresses, you don't see many of them around here any more. Except right down in Annandale at the tail-end of Triomf, on the Martindale side. They saw a priest there one day, but he was wearing a white dress, not a black one. That's another mixed lot. One day she and Pop and Treppie – Lambert wasn't with them – were coming back from the panelbeaters when they saw the mixed-up congregation coming out – it must have been a wedding or something – and there stood the priest at the door, greeting kaffirs and Hotnots and whites all together. All smiles. And all with the same hand.

Treppie says it's a Roman church. He says it's foreign to our nation's interest to greet different nations like that, and then he laughs like the devil himself. He says there's a world of difference separating the two nations in that sentence. But in Triomf they know it's actually just Ontdekkers that separates them. 'Cause across the road it's Bosmont, and in Bosmont it crawls with nations.

Not that they have much trouble with them, here in Triomf. It's only at the Spar in Thornton that the Hotnot children stand around and beg. Pop gives them sweeties sometimes when he takes Toby and Gerty to the little veld behind the Spar. But when the piccanins play with the dogs, Toby and Gerty don't want to. All they want is to chase those big kaffirs who play soccer there. Young, wild kaffirs with strong, shiny legs and angry faces. And they play rough. Toby got his wind kicked right out one day when he tried to bite one of them on the leg. Pop says it's 'cause Toby's a white

4

dog – although kaffirs are quite fond of dogs in general. Then Treppie says that may be the case, but it really depends how hungry the kaffir is. And then he starts telling that old story about Sophiatown's dogs again.

When everything was flattened – it took almost three years – the dogs who'd been left behind started crying. They sat on heaps of rubble with their noses up in the air and they howled so loud you could hear them all the way to Mayfair.

Treppie says he saw some of the kaffirs come back one night with pangas, and then they killed those dogs of theirs. After a while, he says, you couldn't tell any more who was crying, the kaffirs or their dogs. And then they took the dead dogs away in sacks.

Treppie says he's sure they went and made stew with those dogs, with curry and tomato and onions to smother the taste. For eating with their pap. A little dog goes a long way, he says, and those kaffirs must've been pretty hungry there in their new place.

Some of the dogs died on their own, from hunger. Or maybe from longing for their kaffirs. And then their bodies just lay there, puffing up and going soft again, until the flesh rotted and fell right off the bones. Then, later, even the bones got scattered.

Even now Lambert finds loose dog bones when he digs.

Treppie says the ghosts of those dogs are all over Triomf.

Sometimes he wakes up at night from all their barking. It starts at the one end of Triomf and then it goes right through to the other end before coming back again. Like waves, breaking and splashing out, going back in and then breaking again. It sounds like the end of all time. Then she, Mol, waits for the earth to open up and the skeletons' bones to grow back together again, so they can be covered with flesh and rise up under the trumpets.

That's why she says to Lambert he must rather leave those bones there where he finds them. Lambert says he doesn't believe in the resurrection. He takes the bones and tins and things, even faded old marbles and knobkieries with carved heads, and then he hangs them up around the paintings on his walls. He says it's his museum, and one day future generations will be grateful someone preserved it. Even if it is just kaffir rubbish. He says Treppie says old kaffir rubbish has suddenly become quite valuable these days.

If Lambert takes after anyone, then it's Treppie. That's what she always says. They play the fool like their lives depend on it, and they've both got a talent for the horries. It's just that Treppie's a cleverer fool than Lambert and Lambert's horries are worse than Treppie's. Then Pop says she shouldn't talk like that about her own flesh and blood. All they have is each other and the roof over their heads. If there's one thing she must never forget, he says, it's that.

Well, maybe, but she's still got Gerty.

Mol bends over and scratches Gerty between the ears. Gerty stares back at her with big eyes.

Gerty knows what she knows. And she's had the dog's luck of landing up with them. A long history of dog's luck.

Gerty is Old Gerty's granddaughter. All the Gertys – Old Gerty and Old Gerty's only child, Small Gerty, and now Gerty – have seen their share of luck. It's in this dog-family's blood, she always says. Luck.

The dog business started one day when she and Pop and Treppie went walking around Sophiatown. They wanted to see where they'd come to live, 'cause Treppie had applied to the municipality for a house, one of those they said Community Development was going to build here. And of course Treppie had lots to say about it all.

'Look,' he said, 'this is now what you call white man's luck. Just as we're about to go kaffir there in Vrededorp, the Red Sea opens before us.'

They were walking up and down the streets, Miller, Tucker, Good, Martha, through Southlink and then into Gerty, when they heard a cry coming from under a rusted old piece of zinc.

That little priest was there too, in his black dress, walking through the piles of smoking rubbish, the burst pipes and the pools of dirty water. All the dogs were traipsing after him, as usual. Every now and again he'd stop, and then he'd write down something in a little notebook.

'I bet he's making notes so he can go complain to the Queen of England,' Treppie said. 'Cause if he understood correctly, the Queen was in charge of all the churches. But he couldn't understand what was bothering that priest, 'cause there his church still stood. No one had even touched it.

Treppie tried to stop her and Pop from looking under the rubbish to see what was crying like that. The priest would think they were stealing kaffir rubbish, he said.

But she kept on at him, and in the end they found a little dog there. It was still a tiny puppy with the cutest little looking-up eyes. Ag shame.

'You better just leave that kaffirdog alone, Mol,' Treppie said. 'All she's good for is stew. I don't want that worm-guts in our house.'

'It's for Lambert,' she said.

Pop's heart was soft. He said, yes, it was true, a boy needed a dog. Maybe it would calm Lambert down a bit.

Then Treppie said it would take more than a dog to make that piece of shit pipe down, and the next thing she had to jump between Pop and Treppie to stop them from smashing each other up right there in the middle of Sophiatown's rubbish. And all the time that priest just stood there, watching them.

Then she wrapped the little dog up in her jersey and carried her all the way back home. When they got to Vrededorp, she decided to call her Gerty, after the name of the street where they found her. Two years later, when they eventually moved to their new house in Triomf, Old Gerty came with them, and that same street was still there.

'So now you're back in your old hometown again, hey, Gerty,' she still said. The Benades had come to live here in Martha Street, just one behind Gerty. She could have sworn that little dog, with her heartsore eyes, knew very well where she was, even though all the houses were brand new and the old ones were gone, 'cause she walked around sniffing everything for days on end. Old Gerty was always a strange, nervous little dog. Lambert never had any time for her. She was Mol's dog. And when Old Gerty got pregnant, she feared for her. Not for nothing, 'cause three of her puppies were stillborn, and only the smallest one survived. Dead or alive, it was just too much for Old Gerty – she gave up the ghost right there, just as the last puppy was coming out.

That was a terrible day. Treppie wanted to throw away all the puppies, the living one too, but she wouldn't let him. Pop also stood between him and the dogs, and that's how they came to raise Small Gerty with a play-play bottle from a lucky packet.

Treppie kept on telling them they must fix Small Gerty up, 'cause he didn't want to be stuck with a brood of kaffirdog descendants here on his property. He needed the space for his fridges, he said. The fridge business came with them from Fietas, and in those days Treppie still had big ideas. Watch carefully, he said, Triomf was the place where they'd still get rich.

But they never did, and they never fixed Small Gerty either.

And now Gerty – the daughter of the daughter of Sophiatown's Old Gerty – now even Gerty is over the hill.

Before they fixed Gerty, she had Toby, who was the size of three dogs in one. They usually kept Gerty inside when she went on heat, but one day she slipped out and a policeman's Alsatian cornered her. The Alsatian got stuck inside her so bad that Pop had to pull them apart. Gerty was screaming like a pig.

The Alsatian's policeman still lives just one street away, in Toby Street. And that's also how Gerty's puppy got his name.

From the start, Toby was a rough beast who suckled for too long and then wanted to get fresh with his mother before he even had hairs on his chest.

So they eventually decided to get Gerty fixed up.

But what about Toby? she still asked, and then Treppie said no, a dog without balls wouldn't go chasing after kaffirs, and the way things were going they needed all the protection they could get. Then Lambert said yes, he agreed. So in the end she left it.

Mol's glad Toby came along, and that they kept him, balls and all, 'cause he keeps them young. He's a jolly dog, even if he does pee in the house sometimes. And he's also good company for Gerty, although he still tries to mess around with her, as old as she is. Dogs need dogs, she thinks. People are not really enough for them.

People also need dogs.

That's 'cause people aren't enough for people. She and Pop and Treppie and Lambert aren't nearly enough for each other. They're too few, even for themselves. Without Toby and Gerty they'd be much worse off. Dogs understand more about hard times than people. They lick sweat. And they lick up tears.

When Lambert gets so dangerously quiet in his den, then she can say to the others that she's just quickly going to look where Toby's got to and why he's so quiet today. Just to put her mind at rest, 'cause with Lambert you never know.

And when there's too much going on in her head and she can't get her thoughts up and running, then she can say to Gerty, so, Gerty, what you think, old girl, will Pop make it to Christmas? You think we'll be okay after he's gone? And when I go, one of these days, you think Treppie will look after Lambert, or will he leave him to make or break as he pleases, without checking that he doesn't bite off his tongue?

It doesn't matter that Gerty never answers. She's just a dog and she's happy to play her little part, and at least Mol gets to think things through a bit, with that little dog-breath right here next to her. And those little eyes looking at her with so much dog's love. Shame.

Sometimes, when things get too much for her in the lounge, or when Treppie's had too much Klipdrift and his shoulder begins twitching so, and he starts looking for trouble again, or when Lambert gets wild about something, or there's another one of those speeches on TV, and people start shooting, this side and that side and all over the place, with bullet holes in cars and blood on the seats, then a person can just say: I'm taking Gerty outside quickly; or, It looks to me like that Toby wants to pee against the wall again. Come, Toby!

It's easy. And no one thinks anything funny's going on.

Then you're outside on the lawn, under the stars, and you can take a couple of deep breaths, or smoke a few cigarettes. Or you can look up and down Martha Street to see what's going on. Even if you see nothing, just the lights in the dark, it still helps. Or when she's not in the mood to see the inside of Shoprite, all the trolleys and shelves and people who can't make up their minds 'cause there's just too much stuff, or the light's too bright and the music sounds like asthma buzzing in her ears; when just the thought of that Shoprite fish-smell mixed with Jeyes fluid makes her feel sick to the stomach, then she can say to Pop, after he's finished parking on that parking lot with stripes, no, you and Treppie go, I'll stay in the car with Gerty and Toby.

Then she can quietly light up a smoke and watch everything with the dogs, ears pricked as the shoppers go inside with empty hands and then come out again with bags full of stuff, back and forth, back and forth, in and out of the different doors of Triomf's shopping centre: the café, the chemist, the material shop and the Roodt Brothers Forty Years Meat Tradition.

Mol lights another cigarette.

'You think I'm talking a lot of rubbish, hey, Gerty?' Gerty looks at Mol and wags her tail once or twice.

'Let's go inside and see what everyone else's doing, hey, Gerty. Let's ask them to take us for a ride, hey, how's that sound for a change?'

Gerty knows the word ride. And Mol says it in a way that Gerty understands. The little dog gets up, takes a step backwards, then a step forwards and then she starts wagging her whole body along with her tail. Her ears are pricked and her eyes glitter.

'Yes, Gerty, ride, ride, ride! You like a ride, hey! Just let the missus quickly finish her smoke here, then we can ride!'

Gerty goes and sits down again, right next to Mol's feet. Mol is sitting on the old Dogmor tin, leaning her elbows on her knees. She looks at the yard. Winter has made the grass look like straw. There's only one patch of green, right next to the kitchen drain.

She won't be able to keep up with the mowing again one of these days when the rains begin to fall. She wonders if the lawn-mower's been fixed yet. There's always so much trouble with that thing, God alone knows. She stands up and moves away from the house. Some of the roof's corrugated strips have come loose. Every year a few more. She's going to have to put down empty tins and buckets all over the show again. Leaks. Just leaks all over the place.

And then there's also the overflow that keeps on dripping. So bad, all the wood's peeling off. Here and there the wood's rotted through completely. Loose pieces hang from the roof.

At least the fig tree behind the house is still standing. She told them to leave it when it first started growing, 'cause it was the only shade Toby and Gerty could find. And that's the only reason the tree was allowed to grow.

Mol walks around the house to the front, with Gerty here under her feet all the time. 'Oops!' she says to her.

That's the other thing about dogs. When something's broken or missing, or if something's dangling or dripping or it's causing a lot of trouble and you want something done about it, but you also don't want to start something you can't finish, then you can say: Hell, Toby, just listen to that overflow dripping on to our roof again tonight; or, Gerty, where do you think the missus's bath plug has got to again?; or, Come now, Toby, don't lean against that sideboard, it's only got three legs and the fourth is a brick, and that brick's got a crack in it; or, Calm down, you two, not so wild here in the kitchen, the missus is just getting the empties together, so many empties, we mustn't leave them lying all over the floor like this, hey?

Then everyone gets to hear what's bothering you and they can do something about it. And then, if they say what rubbish are you talking now, you can just say, no, it's nothing, you're talking to the dogs and they must mind their own business.

Mol's at the front now, looking into the postbox. Lambert's postbox. When they go out in the Volkswagen they always put the key for the gate inside the postbox. Then it's easy to find again.

Here comes the Ding-Dong. The Ding-Dong's also a Kombi, like the Members' one. It sells soft-serve, with a stretched tape that plays false notes, the same little song over and over again, up and down the streets of Triomf.

There it goes faster now, around the bottom corner. When it goes faster, the tune plays higher notes. Treppie has different words for that tune, depending on what kind of mood he's in.

Most of the time his words go like this:

11

Oh the sun it rises up,
and it sinks again into its pit
and then the bloody lot of us
sink deeper in the shit

Oh the sun comes up and sinks again
into its goddamn pit
and then the bloody lot of us
dissolve like ice cream in the dirt.

Sometimes it goes like this:

Oh the dogs they're sitting in a ring
it's 'cause they know here comes a thing
oh the dogs they're crying in a ring
it's cause bad news to them you bring.

There's no end to Treppie. Once he gets going, you can't get a word in sideways. Only he can stop himself – when he's had enough or when he runs out of rhymes.

Here comes Toby now, running from behind the house.

'Whoof! Whoof!' he says. Old yellow thing with a curly tail.

'Whoof!' Mol replies. 'You also want to go for a ride, hey, Toby?'

Toby and Gerty run in circles on the grass. Then Toby lifts his leg and pees against the fence.

When Toby comes charging out like this, Mol knows it's actually Pop who's looking for her. She stands quietly at the wire fence with a little smile on her face. She knows exactly what's going to happen next.

'Oh, so here's the missus, hey. We were just wondering where's the missus now, and meanwhile she's out here all the time,' Pop calls out from behind her.

He puts his hand on her shoulder.

'So what's the missus doing out here, hey? What's so interesting here in Martha Street today?'

Toby's jumping up against them. Gerty sits at Mol's feet, shivering.

When people tune in their voices to the dogs like this, the dogs know they're part of the company. That's a nice thing for a dog to know. And it's nice for people too.

'So, Gerty,' Pop says, 'tell me why the missus is spending so much time here in the yard today. Tell the old man.'

'Gerty's wondering if she's going to get a soft-serve today.'

Pop smiles like he knows something they don't. He feels in his back pocket.

'The Kombi went round this way,' she says, pointing to where it's busy turning at the bottom of Martha Street.

Pop turns and walks to the Volksie parked under the little side roof next to the front door. Lambert calls it the carport.

'Get in!' Pop says, opening the driver's door for the dogs.

Mol signals with her eyes to the lounge: what about them?

Ag, let's not worry about them, Pop signals back.

'We're taking a chance, hey – it could mean trouble,' Mol says softly.

But Pop shakes his head. She mustn't worry. He gets into the car.

Pop starts the car. Mol opens the gate.

Toby jumps into the dicky at the back. 'Swish-swish-swish' goes his tail as he wags it against the seat. Then he jumps out of the dicky again, on to the back seat, and then back into the dicky. In and out, in and out.

'Sit still, Toby, you're going to piss in your pants if you carry on like this!' Pop says gruffly. Toby quietens down. Gerty sits on Mol's seat in front, shivering and pawing.

Pop swings out and waits for Mol to close the gate. He wants to drive down Martha and then turn up into Gerty so he can catch up with the Ding-Dong.

Mol gets in and shouts: 'Go!'

But it's too late.

'Hey! Where d'you think you're going? Hey, wait!'

It's Lambert. He's standing on the little stoep in front, in his green T-shirt, which is stretched over his fat belly, and his black boxer shorts, which keep falling down his backside. He's up to his elbows in dirt from digging his hole.

'What did I tell you,' Mol says to Pop.

Pop turns down his window. 'Bring me a litre Coke and twenty Paul Revere,' Lambert shouts.

'Okay,' shouts Pop.

'Okay,' shouts Mol.

'Whoof!' barks Toby through the window, right next to Pop's head. Gerty jumps up and down on Mol's lap to see what's going on.

Here comes Treppie too. He marches across the lawn towards the little front gate. His back is stiff and there's a spring in his step. A stiff spring. When Treppie walks like this you know there's shit to play.

Mol rubs Gerty's back.

'There goes our soft-serve,' she says.

'What was that, hey, Mol? Hey? Hey?' Treppie's past the gate now. He shoves his head through Pop's window.

'I was just talking to the dog,' she says.

'So why you sneak out like this without even asking a person if he wants anything, hey?'

'What is it you want, Treppie?' says Pop.

'I said, why you sneaking out like you're on a secret mission or something, hey?'

'Kaboof!' Treppie thumps his fist on the Volksie's roof. 'Whoof!' says Toby.

'Ee-ee-ee,' says Gerty.

'Just going for a little ride,' says Pop.

Pop lets go of the wheel and takes his cigarettes out of the top pocket of his khaki shirt. He lights up. The Volksie goes 'zicka-zicka-zicka-zicka' as they all wait there in the hot sun.

Toby licks Pop's ear. Pop reaches back and scratches Toby's head. 'Just going for a little ride, not so, my old doggies,' he says, looking straight ahead. 'Just a little afternoon ride, hey, just for a few blocks.'

Treppie straightens up next to the car. He lights up. He's taking his time.

The sound of the Ding-Dong gets fainter and fainter down the streets of Triomf.

Mol looks straight ahead.

This could go on forever.

Nothing to be done.

Just wait and see, that's all.

She looks at the big old tree at the bottom of Martha Street. It's the only shady tree in the whole of Martha Street, indeed in the whole of Triomf. Pop says it's an oak tree.

He says he thinks that tree's easily three hundred years old. Much older than him. He says it's very interesting that they left it alone when they bulldozed Sophiatown. Oaks are special trees. They're supposed to live for hundreds of years. Pop says it must have taken a special kind of person to plant that tree, someone with a feeling for the future generations. And it must've been a special kind of resettlement officer, Pop says, who told his men to leave that tree alone – someone with a feeling for trees.

'Switch off,' says Treppie. 'I'm standing here in the fumes. Sis!' He waves his hand in front of his nose. Pop switches off.

'So, Gerty, what you think Treppie wants, hey? Hey, Gerty, what does he want us to get him from the café?' she asks.

Treppie sticks his head through Pop's window again.

'Peppermints,' he says. 'Wilsons Extra Strongs. Two packets.' He holds up two fingers.

'Right!' says Pop. 'Two.' He starts the car.

Pop reverses Molletjie's tail slowly out into the street while Treppie walks alongside. When Pop pulls away, Treppie slams the roof – 'kaboof!' – one more time.

'Whoof! Whoof! Gharrr!' Toby snarls at Treppie.

'Grrr!' says Gerty.

'That's it, tell him,' Mol says to Gerty. 'Let him have it, old girl.'

'Tell him his backside, yes, tell him,' Pop says to Toby. 'Treppie's backside. Him and his sulphur breath. All he needs is a pair of horns!'

Pop revs the Volksie hard through first and second, looking back in the mirror as he takes the turn at the bottom of Martha Street, just past the oak tree. Mol turns round.

There stands Treppie in the middle of the road, with his hands on his hips, glaring at them. Lambert too. He's standing at the front gate, also with his hands on his hips, for all the world to see how dirty he is.

Pop sticks his arm out of the window and slams the roof – 'kaboof!' – just for fun.

Mol smiles. Pop's in a jolly mood today.

'Where you think that Ding-Dong's gone?' she asks.

'We look till we find it!' says Pop.

They drive up and down Triomf's streets, looking for the Ding-Dong. Up Gerty, down Bertha, up Meyer, down Gold, up Millar, down Smithsen, right to the end of Triomf, past the PPC church.

'Maybe it was that priest who got all mixed up with the kaffirs here,' Mol says.

'Maybe it was what about him, Mol?'

'Maybe it was him who planted the oak tree at the bottom of our street.'

'No, Molletjie, you've got your sums all wrong, old girl. That priest must be about the same age as me, but that tree . . . that tree's as old as Adam.'

'Or Jan van Riebeeck?'

'Ja, Jan van Riebeeck!' Pop takes her hand and smiles. He turns back into Thornton.

'Sorry, old girl, it looks like our luck's out. That Ding-Dong's gone with the wind.'

'No ice cream for you today,' Mol says to Gerty.

She always eats her soft-serve three-quarters of the way down and then lets Gerty lick-lick with her little pink tongue until it's completely flat. Then she gives her the cone, too. But Toby also wants some, so Pop has to give Toby his cone. Pop likes the cone, so all Toby gets is the little piece at the bottom without any ice cream.

Lambert and Treppie eat theirs all the way to the end. Stingy bastards. No heart for a dog.

Now there's no soft-serve for anyone today.

They stop at Ponta do Sol. A blackboard outside says DISCOUNT ON

VIDEOS FOR POLICEMEN. It's the kind of café that's got just about every-thing.

'Coke, Paul Revere, Wilsons,' Mol says, as they stand at the counter where it reeks of fish and chips.

'We still got bread?' Pop asks. Suddenly he feels hungry.

'Better get some,' she says. 'Polony too.'

'And you, Molletjie,' Pop says to her, 'you want anything?'

She can see Pop's feeling sorry for her 'cause she missed out on the Ding-Dong.

'Ag, don't worry,' she says.

'You sure?' Pop asks.

'Mmm.' She wants out. There's a woman looking at them as if the cat dragged them in. Must be a policeman's wife. Her arms are full of videos.

Pop thinks she can't see him, but she sees – he's buying her a Snickers, after all. It's a new kind. He knows she likes trying out new kinds.

When they get back into the car, she asks, 'Did you get *two* packets of Wilsons?'

'Oh shucks!' Pop says. 'Just as well you reminded me.'

'You'd better,' she says.

She eats the Snickers while Pop buys the Wilsons. Good old Pop. Gerty gets little bites from her Snickers. Toby also gets a piece.

'So, how was your drive, then?' Treppie asks as soon as they walk back into the house.

He's sitting on his crate in the lounge with an old *Star* in his hands. Every other Monday, when those two across the road put out their old papers for recycling, he goes and takes them. Treppie says they think they're big news there across the road. Those two girlies act like larnies, he says, like they're making a big statement or something, putting out their newspapers for the green lorry. All it shows is how out of touch they are with Triomf. 'Cause in Triomf everything gets recycled, from kitchen cupboards to exhaust pipes, for ages already. And nobody makes a show out of it. He's one to talk, this Treppie. He makes a show out of everything, recycled or not. Mind you, Lambert always phones from across the road, and he also says those two are up to something. He says it's just books wherever you look in that house, and they play funny music with women who bleat like goats. One of their cars is also a Volkswagen. Lambert says it's in even worse condition than their own two.

Treppie holds out his hand for the Wilsons.

'Ka-thwack!' go the packets as Mol slaps them into his open hand.

Treppie snaps his hand shut very quickly, almost catching her fingers in his hard, bony grip.

'Watch it, man!' she says, pulling her hand away.

Treppie says it's not fresh news he's after in the papers. The same things just keep happening over and over again, he says. You must be able to spot the 'similarities'.

Well, Treppie sees more 'similarities' than she does. Mind you, he sees more of everything.

And he also remembers everything. If he doesn't remember something, he makes it up. Just like that.

Pop says Treppie's got a 'photographic memory'. Ever since he was a boy. But she has her doubts. He remembers what he wants to, and for the rest he makes up things to torment them with. It's just Lambert who's impressed with Treppie's nonsense. But Lambert's not right in his top storey.

'Don't you even say thank you, hey, Treppie?' she asks.

'Just check this out,' he says, pretending not to hear. '"Pit bull terriers in Triomf. Policeman's cruel game. Illegal backyard betting. Shocked vets keep sewing up mangled dogs",' he reads. 'So, that's what we keep hearing at night, Mol! It's got nothing to do with Sophiatown's ghosts. It's blood and money – and those two together make a terrible racket. Trapped between walls, with bared teeth and ghost eyes, blood spewing from their veins.'

Treppie opens his one hand and closes it, open, close, open, close, to show how the blood spews out of the dogs' veins.

'It's worse than ghosts,' he says. 'Much worse. If I understand correctly, you could say the whole of Jo'burg is one big pit bull terrier fight.'

Treppie closes his paper and folds it up, as if what he's just read is no surprise, 'cause he knew it all along.

He opens one of his Wilsons packets and puts a big white peppermint into his mouth. His shoulder twitches.

'So then,' he says. 'I said, how was your drive? Don't you even answer a person?'

He makes a loud sucking noise with his tongue on the peppermint.

Pop sits down quietly in his chair and lights up. Mol too. That's the best. Sit nice and quietly.

'Hey, Toby, so how was your drive, hey? See lots of other dogs?' Treppie asks.

'And you, Gerty old girl, how does Triomf look to you today, hmmm?'

Suddenly Treppie slips off his crate and slides down on to his heels. He pretends he's walking on his back paws, like a trained poodle. Toby and Gerty run around him, jumping up and down.

Then he goes down on his knees, stretching his arms out in front of him with his knuckles on the floor. And then he lifts his nose up into the air, letting out a long dog-wail.

'Ag Christ no, Treppie,' Mol says. 'Don't start that nonsense now. Just now we get into trouble with next door again.'

But it's too late.

Treppie's crying like the dogs.

Toby and Gerty's barking gets higher and thinner, until their voices break and they too give in to the crying. They sit next to Treppie with their front legs stretched out in front of them, their snouts lifted up into the air, just like him. The way they cry, all three of them, you'd swear they were in a little choir together.

Lambert comes in from the back. He smiles when he sees what's going on.

Then Lambert joins in too, wailing like a dog. He knows this game of Treppie's, and he likes it. It's a long time since they last played like this. He thinks it's big fun, this game. If they carry on long and hard enough, then all the dogs will eventually join them. Martha Street's dogs and the other streets' dogs, until the dogs are crying all the way to Ontdekkers and beyond.

'Ag Jesus no, you two, stop this now, just now someone calls the police again and then all hell breaks loose.' Mol motions to Pop. He must do something.

Leave them, Pop shows with his hands, it'll pass. That's the quickest way, with the least pain and misery, is what he means. It's like a clock's alarm that you have to let run all the way to the end.

'Oowhoooeee-oowhooooeee!' wails Treppie.

'Oowhoooeee-oowhooooeee!' cries Lambert.

'Ee-ee-ee-ee-eeee!' wails Gerty.

'Whoof-whoof-whoof-whoeee!' shouts Toby.

Treppie comes slowly to his feet. Now he pretends he's holding a microphone, swaying his hips like Elvis. He got a frown on his face like he's hot for something but he doesn't know what. Mol thinks she can guess.

He signals with his other hand to Lambert, he must join in. Lambert plays along. He's also holding a microphone. Now they're a duet. They're singing the great sadness of dogs, to the tune of 'Pass me not, Oh gentle Saviour', stretching out the notes as far as they can.

It's like they're on stage, Mol thinks. Now all they need are some lights.

Treppie and Lambert signal to Mol and Pop to join in.

But they just sit and watch.

Treppie makes as if he's pulling the microphone cord through his fingers, like he's got the Elvis' shakes. Then he pulls the cord out from under his feet, shuffling from one foot to the other.

Up and down the lounge he walks, like that Rolling Stone on TV the other night. He points a long finger up into the air. Lambert stands to one side with his eyes closed. He sways his body as he cries for the gentle Saviour that's passing him by. His face is turned upwards like he's waiting for rain on his cheeks after a long drought.

'Bow-ow-owww-oeee!' cries Treppie.

'Wha-owwww-ooeee!' answers Lambert.

Toby and Gerty provide the accompaniment.

Mol just sits. These two are working themselves up nicely again. Where will it all end tonight? There's Treppie's bottle of Klipdrift on the sideboard.

Must've been at it since late afternoon already. She looks at Pop. No, he doesn't know either.

But Pop looks like he wants to smile. He lifts his finger to one side, holding his head at an angle. She must listen, outside. She listens.

Oh yes, there goes next door's woolly-arsed dog. Treppie says it's a husky who's got too much pedigree for Triomf. That lot next door also think they're high and mighty.

Now Mol begins to smile too.

Pop points with his finger to the other side. There go the fish-breeder's five Malteses.

Well, well. Here we go again.

The Benades have got Triomf in the palm of their hands again.

Treppie goes out the front door, wailing his Saviour song, with Lambert on his heels. Lambert winks at Mol and Pop, they must come too. They go and sit on the edge of the little stoep. It's almost dark now.

Lambert and Treppie stand on the lawn, with Toby and Gerty between them. They've all got their noses up in the air.

Treppie and Lambert push up the revs.

'Wild dogs!' says Pop.

'Jackals and wolves!' says Mol.

Now all the neighbourhood dogs are crying, big dogs and small dogs, all wailing together.

Each time Treppie and Lambert let out a few nice wails of their own, they cock their heads to one side, and then they listen.

They stand facing each other, and when they start up again, they both take a deep breath, bend their bodies slightly forward, sag down a bit and then, as they take in air for another wail, tilt their necks over backwards, with mouths pouting up into the sky. As if they're sucking the sound up through their bodies, from deep under the ground, from the hollows of Triomf.

Treppie learnt this game from Old Pop when they still lived in Vrededorp. Shame, Old Pop also just did his best.

Mol remembers, there were just as many dogs on that side.

That's how Old Pop used to amuse them when he felt jolly. There wasn't much entertainment in Vrededorp in those days, specially in their house. 'You're teaching the children bad things, Lambertus,' Old Mol always said to their father, but even she couldn't help smiling a bit.

Of the three of them, only Treppie really caught on how to make the dogs cry.

And now Treppie's teaching Lambert. The way things are going, it looks like Lambert's a natural.

Mol gets a funny feeling in her stomach all of a sudden, listening to the dogs crying out there in the dusk, near and far.

They're in good form now. The dogs are almost at the point where they don't need Treppie and Lambert any more. They've got their own front-criers leading them and giving them the notes, and the others pick them up and run with them, the high notes and the low notes and the ones in the middle.

The sound of dogs crying echoes further and further through the streets. Then, suddenly, on the western side, there's a barking noise that sounds louder and different.

'Those must be the pit bulls,' says Pop.

'Do you remember when Old Pop used to do this?' Mol asks.

'Jaaa,' says Pop. Pop must be able to hear from her voice what she's thinking. He always knows what she's thinking, old Pop.

'Shame, Pop,' Mol says. 'Who will Lambert teach how to make the dogs cry, one day?'

Pop has no answer. Mol picks up Gerty and presses her tightly to her chest.

'Who, Gerty?' she asks. 'Who will Lambert have to teach?'

2

~

THE WITNESSES

I t's ten o'clock in the morning. Lambert feels hot. It should rain but it
won't. The sun-filter curtains, which he ripped down last night, hang
over the pelmet in tatters, where Treppie chucked them afterwards.
The window's open, but the curtains don't move. Yesterday it wanted to
rain but it didn't. Dust and flies swim around in the broad strip of sun
slanting into the room.

Everyone's in the lounge. It's Sunday and they're listening to the
Witnesses of Triomf. A Boeing flies overhead and the house trembles.
As the plane passes, the Witness who's reading keeps moving her lips
but they can't hear a word she's saying. Then the Boeing passes by and
they can hear again. It drones further and further away. Must be heading
for Jan Smuts.

'"Blessed is he that readeth, and they that hear the words of this
prophecy, and keep those things which are written therein: for the time
is at hand".'

Lambert tries not to look at the Witness as she reads. He looks at
his hands, at the lines on his palms, his fingers and his three missing
fingertips. They got caught in the escalator when he was six years old.
He didn't actually see Treppie doing it, but he's always known it was
Treppie who pushed him. On purpose. Now he lifts his head and looks
past the Witness in the pink dress at Treppie. Treppie's sitting on a beer
crate, squinting at the big aerial photo of Jo'burg that hangs from the

23

wall just above Mol's head. It was on a calendar he brought home with him one day. Must've been another thing he got from the Chinese.

'But it's last year's calendar,' his mother still said. 'What rubbish is this now?'

'It's for the picture,' Treppie said, 'so we make no mistake where we live.' Then he took a hammer out of the toolbox and started banging a nail into the wall.

'You'll crack the plaster,' Pop said.

'Then let it crack,' said Treppie, hanging up the calendar on its hard little plastic loop. His mother later cut off the part with the dates on. Now the bottom edges are curling up.

Lambert narrows his eyes to slits so he can see the little crosses Treppie made on the picture. A cross for Triomf, where they live now, and one for Vrededorp, where they used to live. No, it was him who made the crosses, with a red ball-point. Treppie showed him where, pointing with the sharp end of his pocket-knife. 'Here!' he said. 'There!'

Vrededorp wasn't there any more, not the part where they used to live. And he couldn't, not for the life of him, make out from above, on such a small photo, where Vrededorp ended and Triomf began – it was somewhere in the area of Westdene and Pageview and Newlands and Bosmont. Everything just started swimming before his eyes.

Treppie shifts on his crate. He takes out his pocket-knife and slowly opens it up. Lambert can see Treppie's checking out the Witness. He, Lambert, also can't help looking at her, even when he tries not to. She's wearing a smooth, shiny, pink petticoat that shows right through her cotton print dress. The dress is full of red and purple roses. They also show through. In front, where her knees come together, he can see the petticoat. He can also see it along the side where the roses got scrunched up as she sat down in Pop's chair, the petticoat pulling tightly around her thighs.

He drops his eyes and looks past his knees, at the floor. Then he sees a lost ant. It runs first this way, then that. Lost. He looks for the others, but they're on the far side of the room, in a line on the wall. When ants get lost like this, you know it's going to rain. Lambert cups his hand in front of his crotch. Then he pulls his toes into an arch and slowly lifts up the balls of his feet. Loose wooden blocks from the parquet floor stick to the bottom of his feet. They go 'click' as he lifts them up. He could at least have washed his feet. Just look how dirty they are. But that doesn't help either. Dirty feet or not. Lost ants or ants marching in a row. It cuts no ice, as Treppie always says, 'cause he's already got a hard-on. When he looks up, he catches his mother looking at him.

The Witness reads: '"Behold, he cometh with clouds; and every eye shall see him, and they also which pierced him: and all kindreds of the earth shall wail because of him. Even so, Amen."'

Treppie says that the girl they're going to get for him won't be wearing a petticoat. Her kind don't wear petticoats. Or rather, he says, petticoats are *all* they wear. He must remember to tell Treppie he doesn't mind petticoats. Or dresses with petticoats. As long as it's not overalls, or a 'housecoat', as his mother calls it. He hates the sight of housecoats.

He sticks a match into his mouth and frowns, like the cowboys on videos do as they pull their horses around when they get up the hills, so they can check where the Indians are, far below on the plains.

He looks at the lounge and everything in it.

Pop's sitting on a crate with his back against the wall. Toby lies between Pop's feet. His eyebrows and ears twitch as he listens to the Witness. Pop's braces hang over his knees. His white hair stands up in little tufts on his head and his mouth hangs open. Any minute now he'll fall asleep again. Pop's almost eighty, and the closer he gets to his birthday, the more he sleeps. Treppie says Pop's different to all the other old people he knows. They lie wide awake, he says, waiting for death.

His mother says Pop's tired. They must just leave him alone. Next to Pop is the sideboard with its bandy legs: three bandy legs and one brick. He can't remember which night it happened, but there was a mega fuck-around here again. Last night's glasses are still on the half-piece of tray on top of the sideboard. It's been like that for a long time now. Ever since he broke the thing over Pop's chair that time.

It was Treppie who started the whole thing, over stuff in the sideboard's top drawer that he, Lambert, isn't supposed to see or know anything about.

Then there's his mother's library books from the Newlands library. Next to them is the china cat without a head. When it broke, his mother went and fetched a plastic yellow rose from the bunch on her dressing table and stuck it into the cat's hollow neck.

'There, that's a little better,' she said. That was a year ago.

His father might be old, but his mother's over the hill. Completely. She sits with her legs wide apart under her housecoat. In-out, in-out, she moves her false tooth. She's sitting there with Gerty on her lap. Gerty's mouth hangs open. Above their heads he can see the coloured-in photo of her and Pop and Treppie. She's holding a bunch of roses. Yellow, touched-up roses. All you see are teeth, the way they're smiling. When she was in her prime, she used to sell roses. That's after she stopped working at the factory. She sold them at bioscopes and restaurants.

'Better days,' she says every time she straightens the portrait following another earth tremor.

These days she swallows all the time, and the skin around her throat is beginning to shrivel. Now she's staring at the bits of curtain in front of the window.

Treppie suddenly jerks forward on his crate and starts cleaning his nails with his pocket-knife. The knife goes 'grr-grr' as it scrapes under his nails. His face is blue from not shaving and he looks live, like an open electric wire. His shoulder twitches. Lambert's not sure whether it's him or Treppie giving off the Klipdrift fumes that he can smell all over the room. From last night, when the curtains came down. When Treppie started taunting him about his birthday again. They mustn't taunt him. He gives as good as he gets.

The other Witness is a man. He clears his throat, preparing to take over the reading. His cheeks look like they've been planed down, and his hair's oiled. Smooth, like Elvis. He's wearing a brown suit with a pale blue sheen. He smells of mothballs and peppermints and shaving cream.

The smell makes Lambert feel sick to his stomach. It's a strange feeling, the heat and the hardness all at the same time. He tries to look out of the window, just past the little carport where the Volla's standing. He wants to see if his postbox that he welded on to the gate yesterday is still there.

But all he sees are molehills. The heads of the two Witnesses are in his way. The tips of the sun-filter curtains hang down behind their heads and shoulders. From the front, it looks like wings are growing out of them: sloppy, faded old wings full of holes. Growing and growing, like dusty old cloths that keep stringing out and rising up into the warm air, up, up from their innermost insides.

Pink Dress looks at Elvis. She's reading the last sentence of her turn.

'"I am Alpha and Omega, the beginning and the ending, saith the Lord, which is, and which was, and which is to come, the Almighty."'

Lambert grabs his knees in front and squeezes his buttocks together. He must just hold it now, hold it tight, just think of his postbox that he made all on his own. From pieces of plate his father fetched for him at Roodepoort Steel's scrapyard. That was after the fridge business went bankrupt. After Guy Fawkes. Pop went to fetch the steel on the day before Guy Fawkes, 'cause his mother had said: 'Pop, you'd better do something to keep Lambert busy. He'll be the end of me yet.' He'd been out of school for two years by then. Eighteen years old.

A house looks better with a postbox in front in any case. It says: People live here and they've got an address. This is where you'll find them if you want them. It helps, 'cause the houses in Triomf all look much the same, anyway.

So he took the steel plates, cut them to size and welded them together. He made a little silver house with a V-roof and a slot for letters and a round hole in front. He made it nicely, with a double row of welding spots all round the edges, and with their number, 127, in front. Nice and black in lead so you could see it from the street. Then he put it up on a nail against the prefab wall, just inside the gate so the postman-kaffir could lean over and put in the letters, 'cause they always lock the gate in front. But since then, every time Treppie turns Molletjie into the gate at the end of the month, he knocks that postbox right off the wall again. Molletjie's been panelbeaten and spray-painted to death from driving into that postbox. So in the end he just took the thing and chucked it into his den. It was always full of junk anyway. Adverts and pamphlets and the *Western Telegraph*. That kind of thing doesn't need a postbox. You just pick it up off the lawn. There's nothing to read in that paper in any case, except the flying squad's emergency numbers and all the new stuff in the by-laws. About making a racket, 'noise pollution', as Treppie calls it.

The postbox stayed in his den until yesterday, when he suddenly clicked: nowadays a person needs a decent postbox here in Triomf. Easily visible, and within reach of the pavement, so you can get the pamphlets, so you can keep up with what's going on, so you can keep ahead, so you don't wake up one morning to find that the kaffirs have already taken over, right under your nose. So they can be ready – Molletjie's points grinded just right, and her front boot and roof-rack loaded with bags of petrol, for the great road to the North.

'No, shit, I'm going to weld that postbox on to the gate now. It's now or never,' he said. That was yesterday.

'But the rain's coming, Lambert,' his mother said.

'If I don't do it now, I'll never do it,' he said, making them run around under the blue lightning to bring his tools: the welding box, his helmet, his hammers, his pliers and his level. Rain or no rain, when a thing's got to be done, it's got to be done. Otherwise there's always a fuck-around. When he, Lambert, wants a thing to work, then it must work. Come hell or high water.

But his mother was slow on the uptake, as usual. She gets like that sometimes, her head all haywire. He had to send her back to his den three times to get the level. First she came out with a monkey wrench, then the crowbar, till he finally told her it was the fucken plank with the fucken bubble in it!

He swears, she's driving him nuts.

And then those fuckers from next door peeped at them over the prefab wall, as they stood there, struggling with that damn postbox 'cause it kept fucking off the pole. Till at last he figured he must actually just weld a flat plate on to the pole, and then fix the postbox on to the top of the plate. Then it worked. He, Lambert, can tell you all about never giving up. In the end, he gets everything fixed. Postboxes, lawn-mowers, taps, overflow pipes, geysers, you name it. Fridges and washing machines too.

And Molletjie. He services her all the time. Drains her oil, greases her, grinds her points, the works.

It's just his mother that he can't get fixed up. You can still fool Pop. And Treppie needs the occasional smack on the head, then he's okay again. But his mother is his fucken end.

Treppie's his mother's brother, but even he's given up on her. No matter how much he carries on with her, she just takes it lying down, like a scared little dog. Never backchats. And the day she does open her mouth, then it's to say the same thing he's just said to her. Like a blarry echo machine.

Treppie says she's their 'valley of echoes'. And when he really lets her have it, your ears start burning, 'cause Treppie can say mean, bad things.

Like the day they went to buy the car. They first wanted to trade Flossie in, but the man there said no, she's too far gone, they must rather keep her for spares. Then Treppie winked, with those slit-eyes of his. That devil's wink of his, when you know he's up to something.

Treppie said to Pop, right in his face, right there next to that garage man, they should name the new Volla after his brother-in-law's 'dear little wife'.

Mol, he said, should be the little car's name, and then he started pushing Pop around. What for, Lambert still doesn't know.

'Old, but game!' Treppie said, and Pop pointed his finger at him. He must go slowly now, but Treppie just fucked along.

'For a man to *come* with, to the place where he needs to *come*!'

Still it wasn't enough; Treppie went and fetched his mother from where she was standing among the scrapheaps and the write-offs, and he put his arm around her in an off kind of way, half-soft, half-hard, and then he said, still in front of the garage man, she wouldn't mind, of course, 'cause all three of them rode her in any case.

Well, he can't see how Treppie knows about him and his mother's business, 'cause he spends just about the whole day at the Chinese, week in and week out. He says he does odd jobs. But he can swear Treppie's got a thing going there. He always flattens his hair with Brylcreem before he goes to work, the whole car stinks of Brylcreem when they take him to the bus stop. And Pop sleeps day in and day out, so he knows nothing . . . and in any case, that just makes two, that is, if Pop still can, which he doubts . . . for the rest, Treppie and his mother are brother and sister, so they can't.

But: 'Three in one!' Treppie said, talking at the top of his voice. 'Services them all! Father, Son and Holy Ghost, into their glory!'

'Three in one,' his mother said.

Well, that garage man's laugh dried up right there, and when he looks back at it now, that must have been what Treppie wanted with all his dirty talk. 'Cause in the middle of all his sales talk, that dealer had a fat we-love-Jesus grin on his mug, and he'd stuck fishes on to the bumpers of all the cars in his yard. Fishes, fishes, fishes wherever you looked, big fishes and small fishes, it looked like the blarry Sea of Galilee there under those awnings. That's what Treppie said and what his mother also said, afterwards. And before he and Pop went to pay the deposit, Treppie told that salesman, who was now looking down in the mouth, that if there's one thing that gave him a major pain in the arse, it was a second-hand car dealer who tried to tell him religion ran on ninety-three and fishes stepped out in Firestones.

'Firestones,' his mother said.

But all the time that Treppie and his 'echo machine' were busy working off that goody two-shoes' smile, Pop just stood there and stared out into the distance. Only Treppie was laughing, and then Lambert saw how Pop took his mother's hand and gave it a little squeeze, as if to say, don't worry, and he knew she was just playing along for the sake of peace.

Then Treppie came with a new angle. He started singing a classical kind of tune in another language, something '-line', something '-line' and something else '-line'; he still doesn't know what all those lines meant. And then the garage man asked Treppie what he was singing now, and Treppie said he thought he was singing a famous German SS hallelujah song, from something called '*Der Rosenkavalier*', and it meant blood was thicker than water. All the way down the line.

'*Rosenkavalier*,' his mother said, squeezing Pop's hand.

In any case, from then on the car's name was Molletjie. Sometimes, when the car won't start so nicely, then Treppie says, come now, little sister, or he sings her the hallelujah of the SS. He says he's just glad it's another Volla, the same model as Flossie, 'cause, unlike the saying, it's actually the familiar that makes the heart grow fonder.

Now Elvis takes over the reading. His hands look all white and smooth as he sits there, holding his Bible. The woman leans back into Pop's chair, and her petticoat pulls even tighter over her thighs. She follows Elvis's reading in her own Bible. His voice is smooth, like his face.

'"I was in the Spirit on the Lord's day, and heard behind me a great voice, as of a trumpet, saying: I am Alpha and Omega, the first and the last: and, What thou seest, write in a book, and send it unto the seven churches which are in Asia: unto Ephesus, and unto Smyrna, and unto Pergamos, and unto Thyatira, and unto Sardis, and unto Philadelphia, and unto Laodicea."'

Triomf. That's where they've always lived. At least that's how it feels to him, cause he was six or seven when they first moved here. It was a big event and he still remembers it well, with all the fridges in the trailer behind the old Austin lorry. He was born in Vrededorp, but he knows nothing about that. His mother pulls a face when she says the word 'delivered'. Apart from that, all he hears are stories about when he was young, and now he can't remember which are stories and which the things he actually remembers, 'cause in this house everyone tells such tall stories you'd swear their lives depended on it.

His mother too, when she talks about his birth. She says it was a 'rough' delivery. He was a 'whopper' who refused to budge. Then they brought the forceps and they pulled him out by his head. Yes, by his head. Then she 'tore open', she says. 'Never again.' That's what she's fuckenwell supposed to have said after he came out and the nurses carried him away, with his lopsided, dented head. 'From now on' she told 'those with ears to hear', they 'must stop eating the tart before they get to the jam'. He doesn't know who 'those' are and what tart she was talking about. All he knows is that whenever his mother talks about his birth, Treppie always sings 'Sow the seed, oh sow the seed', and then Pop looks the other way.

Lambert reckons his mother's not all there any more. She's lost some of her marbles.

Pop and them used to rent a house in Fietas; that was when his mother was still a garment worker at the factory in Fordsburg. But then the factory filled up with cheap Hotnot women. They were a lot cheaper than white women, so she had to leave. A little while later, they bulldozed the kaffir-nests here in Sophiatown. Pop and Treppie came to see for themselves, they say. Some houses were just pushed down with everything still inside, so all you heard was glass breaking and wood cracking. Then Community Development started building here, right on top of the kaffirs' rubbish. Decent houses for white people. Treppie used to work for the Railways in those days, and he asked for his pension money early so he could put it down for a deposit. Like this – 'ka-thwack' – he always demonstrates, in Pop's hand, 'tied with an elastic'.

Then they started from scratch again on the fridges. Washing machines and fridges, but mostly fridges. They went and fetched them with the old Austin, stood them up in the yard at the back here, fixed them up and then took them back to their owners. And his mother took up her roses again. One thing he still remembers from Vrededorp is that he grew up around fridges and plastic buckets full of roses in the little backyard. His mother used to leave him behind, with Treppie, so she could go out and work. She says she doesn't trust Treppie further than she can throw him, even though he is her brother, but what was she supposed to do? she always asks. She had to help bring in some money, especially when they first came to live in Triomf. Pop used to drive her up and down all night long in the Austin, to the grand hotels and bioscopes and restaurants and places. By the time they got home, it was late already, and by then Treppie was drunk as a lord. It was a real balls-up. He's still got the marks on his backside where they say Treppie burnt him with cigarettes. 'So he'd shuddup,' Treppie always says about those days. Treppie says he, Lambert, was full of shit when he was small. Then he grins spitefully at his mother and Pop, and he says he wonders who Lambert really takes after. Takes after or not, he knows his worth, and he proved it by helping them out with the fridges when he got older. By the time he reached standard seven, he was head and shoulders above Pop, and he'd developed a helluva strong pair of arms. 'Like tree trunks' Pop used to say. He could pick up a fridge and shift it on to the back of the Austin lorry all on his own. That Austin's long gone now. The fridges and washing machines too. That time with Guy Fawkes. The day before Guy Fawkes, when he couldn't find his spanners in the grass. Now it's just the old Fuchs and the old Tedelex out there in the back. Real old heavies. Treppie says they don't make them like that any more. You can stuff a whole cow into just one of those fridges. And the washing machine from the war. The Industrial Kneff. It's an antique, he says. When he gets pissed, he tells the story of how Hitler used to wash the Jews in the Kneffs before sending them to the camps. Whole laundries full of Kneffs, full of Jews. Clothes and all. They had to go through the whole cycle, from pre-wash to spin-dry. Treppie says Jews are dirty. Even a spotless Jew is good for one thing only, Treppie says, and that's the gas chamber.

He's never been able to figure out this business of the gas chamber. Must've been a helluva contraption.

When Treppie finishes the story, he lets out a little sigh and then he says: It's all in the mind. And sometimes he also says: We should've had Hitler here, he'd have known what to do with this lot. But he doesn't sound like he believes it himself, and then he strings together a whole lot of words that he, Lambert, can't make head or tail of. Holocaust, caustic soda, cream soda, Auschwitz.

Treppie's the only one who's still got a job. At least, that's what he says. Pop's been on pension for ages now, and he, Lambert, gets disability, over his fingers and everything.

Treppie goes out on jobs most of the week. His mother says what work, he just sits and boozes with the Chinese in Commissioner Street. Treppie says, bullshit, he won't touch that rotten Chinese wine. He says he's the only expert the Chinese can afford; they're not the richest of people, and their fridges are old. And he doesn't always get cash from them, either. They give him take-aways or some of their old stuff. Like the video machine, which he, Lambert, fixed from scratch. Never touched something like that in his life before, and then he actually went and fixed the damn thing. With his own two hands. He looks at his hands. Then he looks at Elvis.

Elvis is reading about the seven candlesticks. He takes out a white hanky and wipes his forehead.

That's Triomf for you. People sweat around here. The houses lie in a hollow between two ridges. On days like this it smells of tar. Tar and tyres. And if there's a breeze, then you also smell that curry smell coming from the Industria side. Pop says it's not curry, it's batteries. But it's not nearly as bad as on Bosmont ridge, where the Hotnots live. When he goes there on Saturdays, to scratch around on the rubbish dumps for wine boxes, there's a helluva stink. It smells of piss and rotten fish. Treppie says it's coloured pussy that smells like that. And when he, Lambert, then tells Treppie it's all in the mind, Treppie wants to kill himself laughing. Why, he doesn't know. Treppie's also got a big screw loose somewhere. But it's a different kind of screw to the one that's loose in his mother's head.

The chappy from the NP also wipes sweat from his forehead like that, with a neat little hanky he takes out of his blazer pocket. Five minutes of talk about the election, five minutes explaining the pamphlets and then he's in a sweat. Last time he was talking about the pamphlet with the NP's new flag on it. Treppie said it looked exactly like a lollipop in a coolie-shop. The sun shines on all God's children, the bloke said, and Treppie said, hell, after all this time, the NP still thought it was God, with the sun shining out of its backside. God or no God, Pop said, he was going to miss oranje-blanje-blou a lot. How was a person supposed to rhyme on the new flag? But the NP-man's girl, who always comes with him on his rounds, suddenly said, 'The more colours, the more brothers!', and then she quickly straightened the straps on her shoulders again. That silly little sun on the pamphlet, his mother said, looked more like the little suns on margarine and floor polish, if you ask her. Now she'd really hit the nail on the head, Treppie said. The little sun stood for *grease*, for *greasing*. The NP was full of tough cookies, and you had to grease a tough cookie well before you could stuff her, he said. And then he looked so hard at that girl's tits that she got up right there and then, and walked out, dragging the NP chappy behind her.

Treppie doesn't like visitors.

His mother even takes off her overall for them. Her housecoat. She's got a blue one and a pink one, and it doesn't matter which one it is, when the NPs come, she takes it off and hangs it up on the nail behind the kitchen door. And then she fidgets with her bun and all to make sure she still looks decent. He wishes the NPs would move in here with them, so his mother would never have to wear the overall again. She says she keeps it on so she won't mess up her clothes. That's what she said when he was little and she still says it now. 'Mess up,' she says, pulling a face. But he saw, long ago, when Pop still wanted to, how she used to take the housecoat off for him.

The only other time she takes it off is when she and Treppie go sit in the back room to talk about family matters. What family matters? he always wants to know, but Treppie just winks that devil's wink of his. 'Family secrets,' he says. And then he smacks her on the bum as they go in through the door.

Not that there's ever much discussion behind that door. But then family secrets aren't things you go around announcing from the rooftops. Like the fact that his mother doesn't wear panties. It's that kind of secret. Treppie told him that. He says it comes from when they were children and there wasn't enough money for women's panties. They've got dresses after all, and no one needs to know.

Lambert doesn't mind that either. It's that housecoat of hers that gets him down. It smells sour, like the dishrags in the kitchen.

Lambert gets up. He pulls his shorts up over his bum and then switches on the fan standing on top of the sideboard. It makes a soft zooming sound, but it doesn't budge. He looks back into the room first, and then he smacks the fan behind its head. The blade and the head immediately start turning, back and forth. Pop half wakes up, almost falling off his crate.

'Lambert,' he mumbles. Lambert shifts the fan so the Witness with the pink dress gets the most wind. Her hair begins to fly about and her dress blows against her body. She takes over the reading. Her voice is a little higher now and her shoulders lift as she breathes between sentences. She's drawing on her spirit.

Lambert touches the front of his pants. Christ, if this dick of his would only stop playing up like this. He bends over double and walks back past the Witness. Then he sits down and tries to concentrate on what she's reading, about the Son of Man in the midst of the seven candlesticks, clothed in a garment down to the foot, with a golden girdle around the chest. Funny place to wear a belt. Must be something like the president's oranje-blanje-blou sash that he wears across his chest. He wonders how they're going to get all the new flag's colours on to the president's sash. They'll just have to make it broader, or the stripes thinner. Treppie will say it's all in the mind. That's just about the only thing he says nowadays, no matter what you talk about.

The fan's another thing Treppie got from the Chinese. Its head was jammed with rust and the wires were burnt into each other. But he fixed it. Now all it needs is a little smack and then it works. He, Lambert, knows what he's talking about when it comes to machines and gadgets and stuff. He knows how to make them work. A thing that won't work gets his goat. A thing that won't work is almost as bad as a thing that gets lost, something you can't find no matter how hard you look.

It does him the hell in. He fixes things. Or he searches till he finds them, even if he has to turn the whole house upside down or break things. Pop says it's the cross he has to bear in life, the fact that broken things get on his tits: fans, tape recorders, video machines, the lot. That's why he makes sure the lawn-mower is always tuned, and the grass is kept short, and that Molletjie's timing is set and her oil gets changed. That other Volla standing on blocks here in the back is his fucken end, but one day he's still going to kick it until it's fixed, kick it right into its glory. And he struggles like hell with the Fuchs and the Tedelex. The Kneff is completely seized up, but he'll still get the whole lot of them fixed and working again. Before his birthday. Before the election. And even if the election gets postponed for ten years, like some people say, he won't let it stop him. 'Cause his birthday can't be postponed.

The same goes for his birthday present.

Pop and Treppie will park around the corner and then bring her in quietly around the back so his mother won't see. His mother's the one who says he wasn't born to mess with women, he must 'make peace with his lot in life'. Who the hell does she think she is? Raquel Welch or something? He'll show her. He'll fucken 'make peace' with nothing. And he'll mess around as much as he likes.

Then they'll knock softly on the back door of his den and say: 'Lambert, she's here.' And when he opens the door, she'll be standing right there. With blonde curls all the way down to her shoulders and a pink petticoat and make-up and high-heels and the works. It will be the end of April, so maybe she'll be wearing a coat over her shoulders. Then he'll stand aside. And as she walks past, he'll say, 'Allow me.' He'll take off her coat and hang it up behind the door. His red light will be on. And he'll say: 'Take a seat. Would you like something to drink?'

Just like that. He'll take the ice out of the Tedelex's ice-box, and the nice cold Coke out of the inside door of the Fuchs, and he'll open and close the doors slowly so she can see. Yes, *see*. 'Cause even their inside lights will be working. She'll see how those fridges are stacked full of Castles and polonies. And the Spar's fancy dips, fish dip and cheese dip, and maybe even a box of wine. Enough for a week. He'll have his Simba boerewors chips and his Willards cheese-and-onion crinkle cut ready. And lemons for the Coke. Right there on his work bench. And peanuts, too!

Later, when things are going dandy, he'll switch on the Kneff for her, with nothing in it but water and washing powder, just for the hell of it. And then he'll tell her about Hitler's dirty Jews, and they'll stand on a beer crate and look down at the foam it makes, that Industrial Kneff from the war. And they'll put their hands on the Kneff and feel how nicely she runs, 'wish-wash-wish-wash', non-stop, without a hitch.

Lambert stares at the Witness in the pink dress. She's also got curly hair. But her curls are brown, not blonde. Now if her hair was blonde, she'd be dead right. All she needs is a little more make-up. He feels himself getting hot and cold, but he holds on. He tries to look at something else. He looks down. A mouse runs across the floor.

Mouse, his mother points. Her mouth opens wide, but she doesn't make a sound.

Just the Witness's mouth makes sounds. 'White like wool', 'as a flame of fire', 'unto fine brass', 'as the sound of many waters', 'the Son of Man'.

Elvis's lips move as Pink Dress reads, but you can't hear him. His eyes are on the mouth of the Witness who's reading. He rubs his hands softly over his legs.

Suddenly Lambert clicks. These two Witnesses are fucking each other. That's it. When they finish reading here, they go fuck their heads off. That's what they do. Fuck. She doesn't even take off her clothes. She just pulls up that pink dress of hers, with the petticoat and everything still on. Him too, he doesn't take anything off, he just unzips and pulls out his dong. Sticks it in. Nice and deep until she screams like a pig. That's the way they scream. On the videos as well. His mother too, but she screams too hard, and then he has to close her mouth with his hand.

Just look how Toby's hair is standing up. Toby's lips pull away from his teeth. When people get horny, Toby's hair stands on end. Come to think of it, Toby's hair stands up even more when those two from the NP are here. The chappy with the blazer and the girl with her straps. From the Rand Afrikaans University, just up the road. She says she's studying 'law', and he's just finished studying 'law'. What 'law', what 'studying'? They just fuck all the time, that's what. A person doesn't have to study 'law' to know what's what about fucking.

Gerty's coughing, too. She's coughing 'cause the Jehovahs are getting hot for sex. It makes Gerty feel like she's suffocating. Him too. It fucken makes him feel like he wants to pop. He's not stupid, and the dogs are also not stupid. They know when people are horny and they know when they're kaffirs. Gerty and Toby get just as worked up when they're around kaffirs, like that old woman with her cart: 'Potatoes, potatoes, missus, potatoes and pumpkin', up and down in the street here in front. Treppie says that old woman used to live here a long time ago, and now she's just checking to see if they're still looking after her place nicely.

Treppie can talk so much shit. But he always stops Toby and Gerty when they try to bite the kaffirs. No matter how full of shit they get.

Like that Nelson-kaffir with his brooms and dusters. Green brooms and pink dusters. He pumps them up and down in the air like he's cleaning walls that only he can see are dirty. 'Brooms, madam, brooms! Sweep your yard and dust your walls and prick up your ears when Nelson calls.'

Then Treppie says to his mother she'd better buy a broom, 'cause this is the New South Africa. But they never buy. They just go out and look when that kaffir starts shouting and whistling in the street. Then everyone comes out to look and all the dogs start barking and there's just brooms all over the place.

Pains shoot through his tail-end. He shifts on his crate. The grid cuts into his backside. He clears his throat. The air's thick. The fan blows the thick air around the room. Suddenly a bee flies in through the window. Must have lost its way from that nest under the house. The fan's air confuses the bee. When it gets caught inside the stream, it suddenly starts flying all over the show. But the Witnesses don't even notice. They're getting more and more worked up. The pink petticoat shows dark spots under the Witness's arms. She wipes her upper lip with her hand. Elvis passes her his hanky. He holds her hand for a while. She's getting hot. Too hot for any fucken fan or hanky. She holds her right hand up in the air with the hanky in it.

'"And he had in his right hand seven stars",' she reads.

Her eyelids flicker. She looks like someone who should be bathed in red light. For seeing things, for wanting to fuck, for feeling pressed, for wanting to make or break, wanting out, anywhere.

When Lambert starts painting, he puts his red bulb in. Not straight away, but after he's made a start, when he gets into it with his spray-cans. Into the never-ending painting. Then the red bulb has to go in. And when he digs his pit under the den to store petrol, he keeps the red light on, day and night, all the time, as that heap of kaffir rubbish gets higher and higher: bricks, bottles, window frames, drainpipes. The stuff even shines in the red light.

He feels the pain behind his eyeballs. It's coming. He knows it's coming.

He tries to stop it. He focuses on the floor behind Treppie. On the line of ants. Some of them march this way, others that way. But they stay in one line, except the ones who smell rain.

The Witness is reading about a sharp two-edged sword that comes out of His mouth. About His countenance that was as the sun shineth in His strength.

Poor Son of Man.

Sounds more like a fuck-up to him.

Toby begins to growl softly. He stands up between Pop's feet. His eyebrows twitch as he checks what's happening. Lambert feels the sweat in the palms of his hands. His mother just keeps looking at him. The scar where he stabbed her with a knife when she threw his spanner in the grass has gone white. She's got that funny look on her face, like she thinks he's a fucken devil from hell. He's not holding it together any more. He begins to shudder, down there in his tail-end where it always starts.

'Fuck!' says Treppie. He stands up quickly and walks straight out the front door. Treppie also knows when it's coming. First Toby and then Treppie. Treppie walks to the carport and rips open Molletjie's door. Then he starts her up and revs her until she screams like a pig. Lambert sees all this as the foam in his mouth goes hot and cold. He tries to hold it back. He feels his back arching into a hollow, and then he slides slowly off his seat. There's a burn-out in his head.

It's the beginning of October on the calendar. In less than six months he'll be forty, at the end of April. On the calendar. And then it's the election, the very next day. On the calendar. 'A test for Triomf,' as the girly from RAU says. When the sun's going to shine on everyone, like time, like a flame of fire, like the sound of many waters. As he sinks to the floor, he sees Treppie reversing Molletjie into the gate. The postbox falls down. He hears it roll over once, twice, into the street. But he can't see too well, the fan's blowing the ends of the curtain up and down in front of his eyes. It looks like the curtains are growing out of the Witnesses' backs, and the pelmet out of the curtains, the ceiling out of the pelmet, and the spot on the ceiling where the overflow leaks. The whole lounge looks like things running into each other, like each other's insides, the insides of the Witnesses, the china cat with a rose for a head, the Chinese's fan, the wall with Toby and Gerty's rub-marks at knee-height, the sideboard, the floor-blocks that keep lifting up, the front door with the hole that he kicked in last week, the lawn cut to the quick, the little carport roof, the gate, the gate-pole with the postbox lying on its side in the road. Pop and his mother slowly rising from their seats. Treppie standing outside and looking at Molletjie's dented backside. Everything a slow mashing of insides. The insides of the Witnesses running out of their spines and rising up like the ashes of paper above a fire. The insides of Triomf. Pink insides. His eyeballs are burning inside.

'Happy birthday, honey,' he hears her voice, on a megaphone, and it echoes away. 'Happy birthday, honey, honey, honey.'

The floor's hard under his head. He sees the Witness from underneath. Her shoulders are high. Her mouth's the wrong way around. Her lips open and shut as she reads: '"the first and the last he that liveth".' Like a horse drinking water. She stretches her one hand out over him, as though she wants to pull something up from out of him: his insides, his brain. She hangs from wings in the warm air. She flies without moving, like a vampire. But he's gone, disconnected. She speeds away into space, floundering among stars, a little Satan-bitch in *Star Wars*. The darkness rips open, white noise rushes into his ears, seven stars in his hand.

3

~

KNITTING

Mol sits on her chair in the lounge. The house is quiet – Pop and Treppie have gone to town and Lambert's sleeping. He sleeps like this when he's had a fit, for days on end. She's doing the stitches for the back of Gerty's new jersey. That's the easiest part. She always has to reduce the stitches on the tummy, so it'll fit tight, even when it stretches. Otherwise it drags on the floor. Gerty gets a new jersey every winter. She's hard on jerseys, but that's not her fault. It's Toby. He gets jealous and then he chews up her jersey. By the end of winter it's chewed to pieces. Then it hangs in tatters.

The truth is she knits so she can think. This is the earliest she's ever begun knitting Gerty's jersey, but it doesn't matter. She needs to think.

The most difficult thing about thinking is where to start.

When she knits she can start over and over again – too many times to count. Not while she's doing stitches, though; then she has to concentrate. But once the stitches are done and she gets going, she starts thinking so much that she can't keep up with herself any more. Then she knits like someone possessed, trying to catch up with her thoughts all the time. She goes so fast the stitches fall in bunches, and before she realises it she sees she's gone and made a couple of bad ladders.

Then she stops for a while to fix up the mess. But that's also okay, 'cause a person can't think so fast all the time without stopping.

Now she must do the ribbing. It's green. From last year's left-over wool.

42

Then the jersey was green and the ribbing pink – from the year before's jersey, when the jersey was pink and the ribbing blue. She always uses the same cheap balls of wool, which she buys at the wool shop in Main Road, Fordsburg. The coolie-women at the shop know her quite well by now. They keep all their left-overs for her, which is quite nice of them, seeing that they don't have to. But they like Gerty. She always takes Gerty along when she goes to buy wool there. Pop says she must watch it, just now Gerty pees on the wool, but Gerty never pees in public. It's only Toby who does that. He's a male dog, and males are the ones who do that kind of thing.

This winter, Gerty's going to get a yellow jersey with green ribbing. Just now, when she took out the wool, just before Pop and them left, Treppie said she must watch out, if she dressed Gerty in ANC colours the Zulus would beat that dog of hers silly the moment they got their hands on her. Then they'd want to know who knitted the jersey, and they'd stuff her up half-dead too, 'cause she was the only one in the house who knew how to knit. As if they don't already stuff each other enough. Knitting or no knitting, they're stuffing the shit out of each other around here nowadays.

It starts when the Jehovahs come to visit, but at least then she can prepare herself. On Saturday nights she puts a washing peg into her housecoat pocket so she won't forget. 'Cause Lambert always starts his nonsense before they even finish the reading. You'd think he'd learn, but no. It's that one with the pink dress. She's always asking for trouble. And Lambert doesn't let people get away with that.

The trouble also comes every few weeks or so when the NPs land up here with their pamphlets and all their high-falutin' new words. It starts even before they come, on Tuesday night. Wednesdays – that's their day.

On Fridays and Saturdays, most of the trouble is with next door. Next door on the left, or next door on the right. Or with the people behind. Lambert keeps bugging the people next door, on and on in bladdy circles, until the shit starts flying and then they all want to start knocking him around again. Then he goes and phones the police from across the road but across the road wants to do him in too 'cause he phones there so much. And then the police come and stop all the fighting, and if Lambert still has any stuffing left in him after that, he comes and stuffs her.

When he starts off like this, she always prays he'll stuff himself up completely before he gets to her, otherwise she gets what's left of him.

And God knows, the last bit of stuffing is always the bitterest.

What's more, the shit flies 'cause his thing is so hard these days, 'cause he's almost forty and he still hasn't got a woman. Never had one either. But what's she supposed to do about it? He is what he is. And he's no good for marriage, 'cause of the fits and everything. There's a reason for it, of course. That's something they all know. Except him. God help them the day he finds out.

She and Pop just try to stay on his good side. They do what they can. She does even more than she can. She feels she owes it to him.

Treppie's the one who looks for shit with Lambert all the time. Treppie's a devil. He digs up shit and then, when he finds it, he sees how much more he can dig up. Treppie says he doesn't want people here. She and Pop feel the same. Not the Jehovahs, not the NPs, not the police. Nobody. It's better like that. They're better off on their own. They are what they are. That's what she said to the welfare, and now they've stopped coming too, thank God.

But there's still Lambert. He wants company. He says how can he just stare into their faces all day long. He needs people to talk to. So he invites them in.

He actually stands out there on the pavement in the stinking heat and whistles to the Jehovahs to come inside.

She remembers when he started doing it. It was just before he left school. He was sixteen. That was when the Jehovahs came in for the first time. And once they're in, they're in for good. If one of them dies, they send new girls with pink dresses to come and sit here in their chairs on Sunday mornings, smelling of lavender.

The pile of *Watchtowers* in Lambert's den is now almost as high as the ceiling. That's in one corner. The NP's new pamphlets are in the other corner, on top of the box of pamphlets from the last time they voted. That was when the NP came to fetch them in a grey van and they voted

'Yes'. In their own backyard they do as they like, but to the outside world they always say 'Yes'. United they stand. Treppie too. It's best that way.

And then there's the heap of *Western Telegraph*s. And *Scope*s. And *See*s. Lambert reads the lot. Short stuff that you can read quickly – he says it's to keep his brain awake. Just not books. He says books put him to sleep. But that's what he gets from Treppie. Lambert repeats everything Treppie says. Treppie used to read lots of books when he was still young. But then one day he stopped, just like that, and even today he'll tell you the same story. He says he figures that if you've read ten Afrikaans books you've read them all, and in any case, the best stories are in the papers. He'd rather watch videos with Lambert, but then he sits and sleeps. Lambert too, sometimes.

She wishes Lambert would always sleep, like he's doing now. He's far too wide awake inside his head, and everywhere else, too. What he doesn't paint on those walls of his. Dicks. And moles, with things stuck up you know where. Roads for Africa. Cars and the insides of fridges. The insides of people, all on top of each other. And he keeps painting more, on top of everything else. Most of the time she can't make out what it is. Him neither, 'cause he writes names next to the drawings: star, cloud, bee, exhaust pipe, crack, fuck, cunt, pump, heart, rust, rose, evaporator.

He's always been too wide awake. That's what she said to Pop when he told her the child was backward. There was nothing backward about him, she said. He gets fits 'cause he's too clever, 'cause his brain's too busy.

And once he starts working himself up, it's a struggle to calm him down again. God knows, it's hard. There's only one thing that helps. She found this out when he was still very small. Just three years old. One day in the old house in Vrededorp, when he was squealing like a pig, she rubbed his little thingy for him. Then he suddenly became all meek and mild, smiling at her with his big blue eyes.

In later years, when Lambert began to swear and get wild, breaking all their stuff so that Treppie would drag Pop out from behind the bathroom door where he was hiding and say to him, come, let's pack our stuff so we can get out of this bladdy madhouse for once and for all, then she would say to Lambert he must come and lie down with her in the back room so he could find some peace for his soul.

She would rub his thing until he was finished and then everything would be fine again. But after a while that wasn't good enough any more. He wanted to put it in. He wanted to do it himself. What could she do? She lay down for him. She went and lay herself down. Housecoat and all.

This was the way she'd kept them all together, Pop and Treppie and Lambert and herself.

'Cause they can't do without each other. What would happen if something made them split up and they lost each other? They'd fall to pieces, the whole lot of them, like kaffirdogs on rubbish heaps.

So she'd lain herself down for them. For Pop, but he was good to her. He was gentle. Always has been.

And for Treppie, the devil, who's been stuffing her all his life. From the front, and later, God help her, from the back too. He says it's 'cause she's stretched beyond repair.

It's a little more than a month since he last wanted it. That business of Peace Day must be working on his conscience. If he has such a thing. She just hopes it lasts. He can write his little verses, anything. But he must just cut her out.

Mol looks up at Treppie's poem on the wall where she pasted it, along with all the other things.

'"And, not least, at last there is peace",' she reads. It's the last part of the poem.

Hmph, she's never believed Treppie would change his ways.

'But never say never, hey, old Gerty,' she says to the dog at her feet. 'That's what Treppie always says.'

And then there's Lambert. Lambert, who'll still be the end of her. The bloody end.

Lambert doesn't know when to stop. No, nowadays he wants stories too. Stories she doesn't know, about spy women with guns in their suspenders, in trains, in tunnels, under mountains in other countries, overseas. And stories about cowboy women.

At least she knows these stories a bit better. Poor cowboy women with long dresses who live alone on farms and shoot Indians with long rifles through the kitchen window. Lambert watches too many videos. And now she has to watch, too, so she knows what stories to tell.

'Cause otherwise, if it doesn't work, it's all her fault. Bitter, bitter is her lot in this house.

So, when the time for drinking comes, she joins them for a shot. Klipdrift and Coke. And then they say, 'Hey, old Molletjie, you jolly old thing!' and they smack her on the bum. 'Tell us a story, girl!'

Then it's different. Then it's the really old stories they want to hear.

She tells them about the roses. They know the story but she tells it anyway, it's her best story. It was the best time of their lives. Just after they moved into this house, and out of Old Pop's house in Fietas. Triomf was full of new people. They didn't know anyone and no one knew them, but that was okay. Everyone was young and they all wanted to make a fresh start in this new place. It was nice and jolly. The location was bulldozed and the kaffirs were gone. In those days kaffirs still knew their place. The National Party used to do the things they said they were doing. Not like now, when they say one thing but do another thing and she doesn't know what's what any more. But she couldn't really be bothered. The National Party has never been able to stop three men from getting the better of her in one morning. If they really want to help, the National Party must provide some prostitutes. Well-paid, plump, fancy broads to save women like her from their lot in life. If they have enough money to pay state murderers, as Treppie says, then why can't they also pay state whores? At least it won't kill anyone. It will just stop women like her from getting stabbed with knives and shut up in fridges with Peking Ducks. Maybe if she's had enough Klipdrift to drink one day, she'll say it to those two chickens from the NP who come here to do their canvassing. Those two are asking for it anyway. Maybe then she can have some fun too. It's not just Treppie and Lambert who can bugger around with people. Or make speeches. Maybe they need to see her in action for a change. Maybe then they'll have some respect for her. She'll stand up and make a speech, and she'll say: 'If you want to win the election for the New South Africa, then you must build a brothel here in Triomf. Painted on the outside and tiled on the inside, like a bathroom. With a nice garden in front, and pot plants in the reception with big shiny leaves. The HF Verwoerd Whorehouse. A brothel that does its business in the clear light of day, where no one will need to feel ashamed. Then all the buggering around in South Africa will come to a stop.' *Ik heb gezegd*, as Old Mol always used to say.

Shame, she can just see that little girly with the bare shoulders staring at her in shock. Knows nothing about life. As it is, her eyes look like saucers when she walks in here with her pamphlets. Then it'll be her turn to laugh. Then everyone, including the NP, will see what a jolly old girl she really is.

She's always been jolly. She's always been game for some fun. It was big fun to go with Pop to the market early on Wednesday mornings in the old Austin lorry. That was after she lost her job in Fordsburg, after they got the idea about roses. Those days it was still Hybrid Teas, Old Hybrid Teas, as she remembers it. Lady Sylvia, Madam Butterfly, Ophelia. And then there were the Prima Ballerinas and the Whisky Macs. Old-fashioned roses with a beautiful scent. She and Pop used to walk around for a long time, sniffing the different roses before they decided. Just for the joy of it. 'Like peaches,' Pop said about some. 'Like vanilla,' she'd say. They could spend hours like that, telling each other what the roses smelt like. A nice scent was important, and so was a long, sturdy stem, with a bud that was just beginning to open. The market was a lovely place. All those people, and the flowers, and all the mixed-up smells of vegetables and fruit and roses under that high roof. And so cheap. In those days you paid two shillings for a bunch of thirty Red Alecs. Red was everyone's favourite. Not hers, she went for yellow, but her customers wanted the reds, the ones she sold for a sixpence each to people in restaurants, or on the steps of the city hall after concerts, or late at night when the bioscope came out.

They'd buy three bunches, and sometimes Pop said, 'Don't tell Treppie, but aren't you also a little thirsty?' Then they'd go and sit in the café with the roses on their laps and order cream-soda floats.

And then they'd go home. She'd take Lambert from Treppie and put him in his walking ring, and she'd sit on the little step outside the kitchen, making up the roses, each with its own Cellophane and a ribbon around the stalk. Pop and Treppie helped. Treppie used to cut the Cellophane into strips and Pop pulled the ribbons over the scissors so they curled up. As soon as there were enough ribbons curling like that, Pop would go fetch his mouth organ so he could play them 'The Yellow Rose of Texas'. He played it nice and fast so Lambert could jump up and down in his walking ring. And then he'd play sadly and slowly and sway from side to side, and Treppie would get fidgety and leave everything just like that, saying this was no job for a man, that he and Pop should go fetch fridges now.

Treppie's the one who started with the fridges. He brought them along, to Triomf. If she could carry on selling roses, he said, then he could go on fixing fridges. Forget the fact that Triomf was supposed to be a more decent place than Vrededorp. Those days he still thought he was going to get rich.

And just look at him now. He sits and boozes with the Chinese all day long. She still doesn't believe he does a stitch of work there, no matter what he says. Gambling, yes. Horses, yes. But why should he need the Chinese for that kind of thing? Other people are a mystery.

She's always said to Pop she doesn't want to be rich. Pop says him neither, all his life he's just wanted to help Treppie, and now her. He says as long as he can keep himself busy and have enough to eat, he couldn't care about money. Not that he needed to care all that much. The fridge business was a helluva flop.

The roses were also not such a great success. All in all, they just managed to break even, once you counted the little Austin's petrol and the Cellophane and the ribbons and everything. But at least it was fun and it kept them jolly.

She used to leave Lambert with Treppie at night and then Pop would drive her around. First they looked in the paper to see what was on that night and then she used to put on her smart yellow linen dress, the one with the black piping, which she used for selling roses. After she put on some rouge and stepped into her high-heels, she'd put on her housecoat over her nice clothes so they wouldn't get wet when she and Pop loaded the buckets of flowers into the Austin. That housecoat only came off when they were right in front of the city hall.

She'd put fifteen Red Alecs and five yellows and five pinks into the cane basket and she'd say to Pop: 'How do I look, Pop?' And he'd say: 'Like the yellow rose of Texas, Molletjie.' Then she was ready.

Pop used to park the Austin around the corner so it wouldn't chase away their business there in the middle of all the smart cars, and she'd go stand in front of the city hall's great wooden doors, about five minutes before all the people came out, so she could first get herself ready.

She used to sing 'The Yellow Rose of Texas', to clear her head. Clear out the yard with all its broken fridges and the child who was so difficult.

She sang so she could forget how she closed her eyes and opened them and closed them again when she saw the deep, red burns on his little legs.

She sang so she could forget Treppie's high voice when he made all his excuses. 'No man, I was busy welding in the back and the next thing he was holding a red-hot piece of metal here against his leg.'

She sang so she could forget how Treppie began stuffing her the moment Pop turned his back, and how he fucked her while Lambert screamed his head off in his walking ring in the backyard.

She sang two or three verses of 'The Yellow Rose of Texas', until she began to feel better, until she herself began to feel like a rose, a yellow one, just beginning to open, so you could see it was almost orange on the inside. A beautifully scented rose on a long stem, wrapped up in shiny Cellophane, giving off little sparks in the stoep-lights of the city hall. Then she was ready. Then, when she offered someone a yellow rose – which didn't happen a lot, 'cause most of the time they wanted the red ones – it was almost as if she was offering herself, her best self to the gentlemen in their white collars and the fancy women on their arms. The self she could look upon and say: It's okay! It's okay! It's okay! So loud that she wouldn't hear that other voice, the one she hears most of the time when things start getting so rough. The voice of Old Mol: Bad! Bad! You lot are bad! And you're getting worse by the day!

But she doesn't tell the other three this part of the story. She just stops at the part where Pop drives the Austin round the block; where she stands, with her basket, in front of the great wooden doors. She just keeps quiet, swallowing down her Klipdrift and Coke.

She picks up the story again where the people came pouring out of those doors, and she had to talk English, 'cause not many Afrikaners could afford roses in those days. Ja, she leaves out that part about her becoming a rose. Drink that part down, 'cause it would just start trouble again. For bladdy sure. She's almost forgotten it in any case, that business about feeling like a rose and everything.

'And so, what did you say to those people, Molletjie,' Pop always asks, to get her going again.

Then she says: 'Good evening, sir, would you like to buy a rose for the charming lady at your side?'

At that, Lambert almost falls off his chair from laughing, and then he repeats, 'The charming lady at your side', and Pop smiles, too.

'We have here a Red Alec, a pink Prima Ballerina and a yellow Whisky Mac,' she says next.

'We,' Treppie says. 'We! What rubbish.' And he storms off to go drink outside on the grass.

Treppie always says he's got enough misery as it is. Why bother with yesterday's misery? He says he wanted to get rich with the fridges, but how can anyone get rich on fucken anything in Vrededorp or Triomf when other people go spend your money on roses?

That's what he always used to say, in Vrededorp too. 'Mol, you're wasting our money. I work my fingers to the bone and what do you do? Spend it on rubbish. What do you actually bring in? Bugger all! Red Alec my foot! You're just wasting time. We need food and clothes and a car that works. Not roses. And now you've got this child as well. Madam Butterfly! Why don't you go char for the rich people in Parktown. Or let them teach you to sell stamps at the Post Office. Then at least you'll be doing something useful. We're working at home in any case. We'll look after Lambert for you. At least the little bugger listens to me.'

And Pop always says: 'Ag, Treppie, leave Mol alone. It's her only real pleasure in life.'

That's what Pop says still, to this day, when she tells her story.

'Leave Mol alone, Treppie, leave her alone, man, it's the only nice thing she's got left to remember.'

Then Treppie says: 'All right, all right,' and he looks as if butter wouldn't melt in his mouth. 'All right, old Mol, tell us again about when we became a republic, old girl.'

When we became a republic. That's another story. Too difficult to tell, actually. But Treppie wants what he wants, so she tells the story.

Pop said they should make a day out of it. 31 May 1961. It was just after they'd moved here, to Triomf. The grass hadn't even been planted yet. There was just dust everywhere. But there was no stopping Pop. Poor old Pop, he's always been a sucker for the big occasion.

And that was now a palaver for you. It wasn't just a picnic in Pretoria, it had to be business, too. That was also Pop's idea. At least to start with. She's sure Pop's got a much better eye for business than Treppie. He just lacks the will. But those were the days when Pop was still young. Lambert was just seven. And Pop said Lambert could stay out of school for two days to help them get ready. At school they'd just be waving a lot of flags around anyway. In the end all hell broke loose 'cause Lambert didn't get his Republic Day medal at school that day. Gold medals with Dr Verwoerd's face on. Pop had to go ask Lambert's teacher afterwards to please order an extra one. Anyway, Pop's plan was to sell roses on Republic Day. Not reds. No, they went to the market the day before and bought orange roses. Four gross. Forty bunches. Las Vegas Supreme, that was their name. She'll never forget that. A fancy orange rose with no scent at all. But the colour made up for it. It was bright, like an orange sucker. They bought ten bunches of Baby's Breath, and ten bushes of display fern, a whole spool of blue ribbon and a spool of white. So they could make oranje-blanje-blou corsages. They bought small golden pins and a roll of green florist's tape. And rolls of cotton wool to moisten and then pack the flowers in so they'd stay fresh. In flat peach trays.

All Pop's idea, and a bladdy good one too. They worked right through the night. After a few hours she was squinting from all the work. She'd take an orange rose, cut the stem, add a spray of Baby's Breath, a twig of fern and a piece of green tape to keep it all together. Then a piece of white ribbon and a piece of blue ribbon, right around, push the pin through and it was done. Put to one side. They sat outside in the backyard in a circle, on crates, under a light on an extension that Treppie hooked on to the gutter.

'Check the Benades' assembly line!' he said.

'We're assembling the new republic,' Pop said. He was very excited about his idea.

'We're assembling it and it's going to pay! What will we charge apiece?' That was Treppie, of course. Then he held up one of the completed corsages, stood up and pinned it to his shirt, pushing out his chest and prancing around like a child of the devil.

'We mustn't charge too much,' Pop said. 'It's for a cause, remember.'

At that point, Treppie told her it was time to fetch the brandy and Coke, with glasses and ice, 'cause now they needed to talk about this 'cause'. Every cause had its price, he said.

Even today, if they talk about money, he wants to drink.

'Now, let's see. How much did you spend, you two? Spending's what you're both so good at, isn't it?' Treppie was looking for trouble. She could see it coming.

'Twenty-five rand,' Pop said, but it was actually thirty-five rand with all the extras. They were still thinking in pounds and pennies and shillings those days, anyhow.

'Hmmm,' said Treppie, 'and what per cent profit would you say a person should make out of a new-born republic?'

'Well, um, surely not more than about five per cent,' said Pop. 'Like I said, it's for a cause.'

'Are you crazy! I'd say one hundred or two hundred per cent! Or double that. Four hundred per cent. I'll tell you what,' said Treppie, in that high, devil's voice of his, 'we'll lie to those buggers. Let's tell them it's for a hospital. The HF Verwoerd Hospital. We'll take clean paper and write neatly on top: Republic Flower Fund. The HF Verwoerd, er, Institute, that's grander, for the Mentally Retarded.' Then Treppie smoothed down his voice and talked like the man who reads the news on the radio: 'With a column for your signature, sir, and a column for your donation, madam.

We'll tell them the price is forty-four cents. Then you'll see how we milk their sympathies. They'll search their pockets for change and hand over the first half-crown they can find. But who, on a day like that, will sign next to a donation of only six cents? So they'll fumble for more change and pull out a shilling or two, or three. Or more, much more! On a day like that people will want to show off. They'll dig deep into their back pockets. On a day like that they'll want to sign for a cause, in hard cash!'

She and Pop just sat there, stunned. Treppie's eyes were glittering. It was just too bladdy far-fetched for words. They just sat there with their mouths hanging open.

'And the cherry on the cake,' Treppie said, putting on that high little voice of his, 'the cherry on the cake is our mascot.' Then he turned his head slowly and looked at Lambert. Like the devil himself, he looked Lambert up and down. Christ, she thought, I can see trouble coming.

'Lambert,' said Treppie, 'come here to your, er, uncle.' Lambert went over to him and Treppie began telling him what to do. 'Lambert, let your mouth hang open,' he said. 'No, not like that, pull your bottom lip this way. Yes, like that. Now, turn your eyes to the inside, towards each other, and now up, yes, like that, but not too much, just about half-mast. That's it. Now, stare out in front of you, about two yards, at knee-height. That's it, yes. That's perfect, just perfect. And now watch carefully what your uncle Treppie's going to do.'

Then Treppie walked back a few steps into the dark, out of the light, and he waited for a while, and they also waited, her and Pop, and Lambert too, with his open mouth and his crooked eyes, like he'd been hypnotised or something, and then Treppie came out from the dark. Hell, he looked just like that Gadarene madman. He waggled into the light, with one leg dragging in the dust behind him, and one arm flopping from a twitching shoulder, slobbering from the mouth.

And those eyes! That was the worst. She'll never forget his eyes. Turned up so all you could see was the whites, his eyelids flickering like an old bulb about to blow.

'Come on, Lambert, my boy,' Treppie said with a thick tongue. 'Come on, come let your uncle show you how we're going to win over those mothers of the nation tomorrow. Every now and again you must smile through the spit, and then shake your head a little, like this. Don't worry, it's crooked enough as it is.'

And there they went, walking round in circles in the dust of the yard as Treppie showed Lambert how to act crazy. It was very queer, but they couldn't help laughing. Pop too. When Treppie and Lambert came and stood in front of him, swaying on their legs, with drool running down their chins, and Treppie sang, 'Ringing out from our blue heavens, from our deep seas breaking round', Pop just couldn't help laughing. Then Pop also made a funny face, rolling his eyes and acting crazy. After a while they were all pretending to be mad; even she kicked one leg out in front of her, slobbering with her tongue. Pop pushed his bum out and pulled his body into a hump, just like a hen. They had a lot of fun that night, there in that bare backyard.

'Ne'er would your children, who are free, have to ask,' Treppie shouted, spraying spit all over the place.

'Granpa rode a big fat porker in the pouring rain,' said Pop.

'The rain in Spain,' said Lambert, 'so he fell off, bang! and then he climbed on to its back again.'

And she climbed on top of the washing machine and sang: 'Whiter than snow, yes whiter than snow, o wash me, and I shall be whiter than snow.'

Whenever she gets to this part of the story, they're all on the floor, laughing. Then she can't carry on. Which is maybe for the best, 'cause it began to get a bit rough that night, a bit too rough. Lambert says he doesn't know, he says it must be the drink Treppie threw down his throat, but he can't remember a thing about that night, or the next day.

For everyone's sake, she just tells the story of the next day, the day they went to Pretoria. In the little Austin, with all the corsages, and how they made so much money, she says. For everyone's sake, she tells the story, but especially for Lambert. She tells how they made bags of money at the Voortrekker monument. She can still see it before her eyes, she says; the people stood there with stiff eyes, listening to the speeches, and they pulled out paper money from their pockets to buy the little corsages.

Almost six hundred rand. Five hundred and forty nine rands and twenty-nine cents.

When she gets to this part, Pop drops his head, and Treppie says 'Fuck!' as he walks out the front door. And Lambert says, the rain in Spain, sitting there in the lounge with his brandy. When she tries to go to the kitchen, he stops her: 'Ma, tell us more, tell about the speeches, and how the people pulled ten-rand notes out of their pockets when they saw me.' Then she tells him the story. She tells him what he wants to hear. Poor Lambert. That poor cockeyed child of hers. And then Pop lifts up his head and he helps her. He recites bits of Verwoerd's speech for Lambert, just as if he'd been there himself.

'And I say to you today, my people, the Commonwealth of Nations will bring us no gain. Not a single cent. I say to you here today, we're better off on our own. No one has any business meddling in our affairs. No one needs to stick their noses into our affairs. We'll work out our own salvation here on the southern tip of Africa, by the light we have, and with the help of the Almighty.'

Then Treppie comes in with a fat grin on his face. Now *that* sounds just right, he says. That sounds like good business. No one must come here and mess with them. Not with the volk and not with their brothers in the volk either.

And then Pop always looks Treppie in the eye, and he says, 'Ja, now there was a first-class statesman for you.'

'Oh yes,' Treppie says next, 'oh yes, old brother.' Treppie's voice drips with honey when he says 'old brother', and then he laughs like the devil himself.

And Lambert says, 'Oh yes,' shaking his head and swilling the brandy round and round in his glass.

And then they sit there and they say nothing, and she stands in the doorway and looks at them there where they sit.

4

~

POLISHING THE BRASS

It's Wednesday morning and Lambert's been shouting and screaming ever since sunrise. He wants everything fixed, now, on the double. How can they let the house look like a pigsty when the NPs are coming, he shouts at them from the den at the back. What will the NPs think? What will they think of the curtain that's still hanging over the pelmet? And the postbox that Treppie went and fetched off the street and then just chucked back on to the lawn, still full of dents, with its silver paint coming off.

After he blacked out, he was flat on his back for a long time. On his mattress. That much he figured out. The whole of Sunday, and all of Monday too, 'cause it was Tuesday morning before he could sit up straight again. Then he wanted Coke. Clean Coke. Coke always brings him round after a fit. They say everything goes better with Coke, and that's what he says, too.

He told his mother to buy him a *See* and a *Scope* at the café in Thornton. They sell *See*s there. The shop at the bottom of Toby Street just sells kaffir rubbish. And then on Tuesday night he ate half a loaf of white bread with Sunshine D, golden syrup and polony. Treppie came into the den and said he shouldn't eat so much white bread, 'cause he was still going to have to fit into his leathers before his birthday, wink-wink.

*   *   *

57

He knows Treppie's taught him a lot, and he owes him, but he can't fucken take it when Treppie winks at him like that.

He got up earlier this morning to see if his mother was hanging up the curtain by those hooks that go into the rings on the railing, but then his ears started zinging, so he came and lay down on his bed again. When he's had a fit, Coke helps for his stomach, but it doesn't stop the zinging in his ears.

Here comes Treppie now, walking down the passage. He knows it's Treppie 'cause Treppie doesn't drag his feet like his mother, and his one foot doesn't sound louder than the other, like Pop's. Treppie walks like a cat. You could even say Treppie creeps up on you. Don't creep up on me like that, he always says, 'cause it feels like Treppie's peeping into his head when he stands so close to him, peeping at everything he's fucken thinking, long before he even realises Treppie's there.

'What you reading there, old boy?' Treppie asks. He's leaning against the inside door of the den. He says 'old boy' with a twist in his voice, like what he really means is 'old dickface'.

Treppie says he, Lambert, has the longest, thickest dick he's seen in his entire life. He doesn't see how Treppie can know that, 'cause he's never been naked in front of him. But when he tells Treppie this, Treppie says he's so fucken far gone he doesn't even know when he's starkers and when he's wearing clothes. Treppie talks a lot of crap. If Treppie knows how big his dick is, it must be 'cause his pants fall down when he fits. His mother pushes washing pegs between his teeth to stop him from biting off his tongue. Sometimes when he wakes up his pants are gone. Then he sees them hanging up on the line outside. His mother says he pisses in his pants when he fits. How's he fucken supposed to help it? She can be glad he doesn't shit in his pants, too.

'I said, what you reading there, old boy?'

'Nothing.' He doesn't want to talk to Treppie. He can feel he's still not a hundred per cent, and when he's not a hundred per cent he can't handle trouble. If he goes off the rails when he's not a hundred per cent, then he really fucks out. Then he fucks out in a big way.

'Such bad manners! A person can't even ask what you're reading.' Treppie creeps up on him and snatches the pamphlet from his hands.

'So, let's have a look.' Treppie knows exactly what it is he's reading, but now he wants to put on a whole fucken show again.

'Jesus, this fancy print is so skew, not even a dog can read it. What? "The constitutional protection of minorities. Point one: language and culture". Hell, Lambert, but this is high falutin' stuff you're reading here, old boy. What "minorities" do they mean now?'

Treppie's acting stupid. Lambert knows this game; it's something Treppie does a lot, just to torment him. He knows he must just not say anything. If he does, then Treppie takes whatever he says and drop-kicks it up into the blue sky, to hell and back, and then he asks: Where was I now? Then he acts like he's also looking for the answer. There's just no end to him. His mother's right. Treppie's a fucken devil, but not a straight one; he's a devil with a twist, a twisted devil with a twitch in the shoulder. It's a nervous tick, as he himself says.

'Is that postbox fixed yet?' he asks Treppie. He knows he must try and get out of this thing now. He gets up on his elbow, but his ears are still zinging. When he closes his eyes, he sees green. His tongue still feels lame. Down in his back too. Lame.

'Hey? I asked if you fixed the postbox yet.'

'What for?' says Treppie.

'The NPs. They're coming today.' He knows what he just said must sound very dumb. Treppie always gives the NP hell when they come here. Why should he give a shit about the postbox?

'So what?' Treppie says.

'Pop!' he shouts. 'Pop!' Pop always helps him out with Treppie. But these days Pop's help isn't worth much. He's tired. So he, Lambert, has to fend for himself. Here comes Pop now, down the passage. First the hard foot, then the soft foot. 'Click-clack, click-clack' go the blocks as he walks.

'Pop, take Treppie with you to get the welder and the tools, and go fix up the postbox. That metal base is still okay.'

Pop doesn't say anything. He traipses around the room, looking for the welder.

'Hell, brother, you only let him order you around, hey!' says Treppie, twisting the words hard when he says 'brother'.

'Come now, Treppie,' says Pop. 'Cut it out, man.' He says it softly. He can't talk hard any more. He's holding Treppie by the sleeve, but Treppie jerks his arm loose.

'Listen to me, brother, don't come in here and push me around. I'm talking to old Lambert here. We're talking about "minorities" – ja, a minor past, a minor present and a very minor future. We're talking fucken deep stuff here, man. First the NP wastes time like it's for Africa, and now they're trying to make it a "minor" thing. Also for Africa. Beats me. Too fucken deep for me. But if you're as deep in the shit as old Lambert here,' says Treppie, kicking Lambert's scrap against the door, 'then a person has to think *very* deep . . .'

'Treppie,' Pop says, 'give it a break now, man.'

'Old Lambert, here,' Treppie says, like he's explaining something completely new to Pop, 'old Lambert's someone who always does his homework, you see. He's scared he'll have nothing to say the next time he sees that piece with the bare shoulders, that cute one from the varsity, the *Rôndse Ôfrikônse Univarsity*. So now he's swotting up these fancy pamphlets.'

Treppie, he thinks, is just like a dungfly buzzing bzzt, bzzt, against a window. But with a real fly, at least you can open a window and chase the bugger out. You don't even have to touch the blarry thing.

'Pop, tell Treppie he must fuck off from here, or there's going to be trouble.' Pop lifts up his hand, but then he drops it again. He opens his mouth, but then he closes it again.

'Ai,' he says. 'Ai, God help us.'

'Don't worry, Pop,' Treppie says. 'Everything's okay. I'm just having a bit of fun with old Lambert. Come,' he says, 'be a sport. Come and join us.'

He grabs Pop by the shirt and quickly pulls him in through the den's door. But Pop's foot catches and he stumbles. Treppie grabs him from behind, by his belt, and quickly pulls him up again.

'Oh boy,' Treppie says. 'Not so steady any more, or what am I saying, hey, Pop?'

When Treppie gets like this, it's like he's changing gear. All you hear are the revs, getting higher and higher by the second.

Treppie pulls up two crates. They're both full of empty one-litre Coke bottles. Then he turns the crates over with one hand, crashing the bottles on to the den's cement floor. Lambert can't see how many bottles are broken.

'Those are my Coke bottles, Treppie. Ninety-one cents each,' he says, but not too loud.

He pushes himself up straight, sitting against the wall. He checks to see where his shoes are, in case he has to make a run for it over the broken glass.

'So, Lambert,' Treppie says, seating himself on one of the crates. He pulls Pop by his sleeve. Pop sinks slowly on to the other crate, wiping his nose with his sleeve as he sits down.

'So, what are the issues supposed to be now, old boy? What's this election all about, anyway? Come, explain to us a little now.'

'Ag no, man,' Lambert says. He says it carefully and softly. He still doesn't feel right. He's just going to have to kick Treppie's questions right out of touch. Carefully he says: 'Here. Read for yourself.' He passes Treppie a bunch of pamphlets. Treppie knocks them out of his hand. They fall on to the floor.

'Ag, sorry about that, man, didn't mean it,' Treppie says. 'Just a little accident.' He kicks the pamphlets away with his feet. Pop bends over and picks them up. Then he puts them down on the bottom end of Lambert's mattress, where Treppie can't reach.

'Come, what can you tell us, Lambert? Things are looking a bit mixed up, aren't they?'

Treppie looks around the den, first at the floor, which is full of Flossie's engine parts – loose spanners, hubcaps, pieces of old silencer and rusted exhaust pipe. Then he looks up at the things hanging from the ceiling. 'One, two, three, four, five, six,' he counts, looking at the strips of flypaper. 'Such a bother, these flies, hey,' he says. 'Looks like they just love messy places like this.'

Now he's looking at the roll of second-hand razor-wire. 'It will stop the burglar, but it won't keep the fits out,' he says.

And then he says, 'Tsk-tsk-tsk, shame,' as he sees the old Austin's radiator-grid. The one Pop gave Lambert to hang up in his den, for old time's sake.

Treppie's full of sights. Now he's looking at the Tuxedo Tyres calendars, the ones they go fetch every year on Ontdekkers. For the pin-ups. They're lined up next to each other on the walls of the den, just under the ceiling, so that he, Lambert, can pick and choose when he's lying down on the bed. They're all there, from 1971 onwards.

But Treppie doesn't want to pick and choose, he wants to fuck around. He stiffens his neck and he turns his head, inch by inch, making little click-sounds, just like the fan's head when it gets stuck. 'Click-click,' he says, as he looks at the calendars, one by one.

All the calendars are the same. There's a fat lorry tyre on top of each of them, with TUXEDO stencilled on its grip. A girl in a bikini sits under all the tyres. The only part of her body you can see is from her head to her stomach, straight from the front, against a bright blue background. The girls all look the same, except for the hair and the colour of their bikinis.

'Tits and tyres, tits and tyres, the chickens are back in the coop and they're all a bunch of liars,' Treppie says, shaking loose his neck.

Pop wants to stand up, but Treppie stops him with a hand on his shoulder. Pop says nothing. He stays on his seat. There's that drop hanging from the tip of his nose again.

Treppie looks at the Fuchs and the Tedelex standing open at the back of the room. Boxes and magazines are stacked on top of them, right up to the roof. They're full of black fingermarks on the inside, and their seals are rotten. Lambert's half-loaf of white and a tub of margarine lie at the bottom of the one, and there's a half-full bottle of Coke in the other one's door.

Treppie shifts his crate and leans forward. He's looking at the paintings on the wall. Lambert follows Treppie's eyes, looking everywhere he looks. When Treppie looks at his den like this, it feels like a strange place. Treppie must stop this now.

But Treppie looks like he's seeing everything for the first time. South Africa's outline, almost completely faded by now. Koki's fade like that. Their house, with the postbox in front, the carport with the Volksie underneath; the dotted line going upwards; all the things on the lawn and in the sky. Treppie frowns, shaking his head.

'Fucken mix-up! What's that?' He points to the wall. It's a drawing with writing and arrows.

'It's been there for a long time,' Lambert says. 'It's how a fridge works.' He clears his throat. It's hurting from trying to keep his voice even. 'You drew it there yourself, when we started working here in the yard.'

'So you know how a fridge works, hey, Lambert?' says Treppie. 'Then you should also know how the NP works. Compressor: warm. Evaporator: cold. Thick gas, thin gas, round and round: prrrr, choory-choory-chip: off.' He smacks both his hands on his legs, looking serious now.

'Come now, Lambert, we don't have all morning. What are the vital issues in this election?'

'Well,' Lambert says, 'it's the constitution, it's the people who're going to write the new constitution. We have to vote for them.'

'And?' Treppie's eyes are glittering.

'Well, um,' Lambert looks at Pop. Pop must help him now. 'We've always stuck with the NP—'

'Oh yes?' Treppie says quickly. He waves at the flies. 'We've also stuck with Sunlight. That's how you keep the flies out, you wash yourself with Sunlight soap. Your arse and your head and your floor and your bed, the whole lot, whiter than snow.'

Lambert tries to straighten up. This is going too far now. If Treppie wants him, then he's going to get him. But his head's zinging. Pop signals: stop it now. He says please. Lambert shuts his eyes. Maybe that'll help his head a bit. Pop's voice is so soft, all Lambert hears is 'ease'. Then it's Treppie again. He's talking to Pop. Treppie sounds like a preacher.

'If you ask me, Pop, the National Party are a filthy lot. What's more, they're also confused and they're getting more confused by the day. One great fucken scrapyard, if you ask me. Now they say they're going to get their house in order, again. How, I ask you? How? Where will they begin? They must first get their fingers out of their backsides. That's what, and then wash them with Sunlight. That's all I can say, Pop. That's the hard reality. Old Lambert here, he knows very well what

I'm talking about. He reads those pamphlets. And he's not stupid, not by a long shot.'

Lambert opens his eyes. The only thing you can do here is play along. 'At least they've stuck to one thing from beginning to end. It's like a golden thread,' he says.

'Oh yes?' Treppie says. 'Now that sounds better. What golden thread?'

Lambert leans forward so he can get his pamphlets. Pop helps him, pushing them closer.

'Wait, let me read it.' He looks through the pamphlets till he finds the right one. Then he looks up. Pop stares down at the floor. Treppie looks him straight in the face. He reads.

'"The National Party of today is no longer the National Party of yester-day, but—"'

'Fuck but!' Treppie says, shooting up like a jack-in-the-box and grabbing the pamphlet out of his hands. 'It's not even the same party you voted Yes for that last time. Remember, when you could still fit into your smart clothes, your black charcoal pants with the shiny leather belt, and those boots with no laces. What did it say again on the label of those pants? Smart pants, those!'

Treppie gets up and walks carefully over the broken glass to the steel cabinet against the wall. He tries to shake open the doors, but they're locked. 'Quickly, give me the keys so I can see what that label says.'

'Boom!' Treppie slams his hand against the steel door. Pop jumps.

'Man About Town! That's it. Now I remember. Man About Town! That's what it says on the label. I still remember. The coolie at the Plaza showed us the label, at the back, on the inside.'

'Can I carry on now?' Lambert asks. Talking politics is bad, but not as bad as talking about his pants. It's not his fault he got so fat. It's the pills.

'"But . . ."' Lambert reads, '"there's a golden thread that runs from the early years of the National Party right through until today."'

'Stuff and nonsense!' Treppie says. He sits on his crate again.

'"Our first priority remains our own, our own minority, our own language and culture, and our own Christian faith."' He reads in stops and starts, the words swimming in front of his eyes.

'And our own postbox!' Treppie shouts.

Lambert raises his hand for silence. He reads: '"That's what we call the protection of minority rights. All minorities. So that there can be no domination by a black majority . . ."'

'So, do you buy that story, Lambert?' Treppie asks.

'Well, um, to an extent,' Lambert says.

'To an extent! You sound just like that pamphlet, old boy.'

'Well, if things don't work out then we've at least got a plan!' Lambert says. 'Remember what you said, then we take Molletjie and we load the petrol into the front, and on the roof-rack, and in the dicky, and then we go, due north. All of us, even Gerty and Toby. To Zimbabwe or Kenya. Where you can still live like a white man. With lots of kaffirboys and -girls to order around, just as we please! They're cheaper there!'

Treppie looks at him. He looks at Treppie. Why's Treppie looking at him like this now?

Treppie was after all the one who thought up the plan, one day when he, Lambert, was lying here at the back, when he couldn't pull himself together after a fit, and all he could do was pull his wire, but even that didn't want to work any more. When his mother was sick in the hospital. From asthma. At least that's what he thought. But then Treppie said it was a nervous breakdown 'cause he had fits all the time, 'cause there was nothing for him to do and he was wearing his mother out. And then Treppie came and sat here on a crate and said he'd found just the thing to keep him busy: the Great North Plan for when the emergency came. Yes, they must start storing up petrol, Treppie said, 'cause you never knew. He, Lambert, must dig a cellar under his den to store up petrol, 'cause petrol couldn't be stored above ground, at least not here at the Benades'; there were too many sparks flying around when they started welding. Treppie said the silver bags inside wine boxes were the best for storing petrol. They took up the least space, and you could fold them up when you were finished, and then fill them up again later. He remembers thinking it was a real stroke of genius. Treppie's got a lot of plans. But that's not all he's got a lot of and he mustn't come and be a nuisance now. He, Lambert, didn't go scratching around rubbish dumps just for nothing. On Monday nights, when people put out their rubbish, he walked up and down the streets so he could check those rubbish bags for wine boxes. Then he'd pull out the silver bags and throw back the boxes. By the time he got home he was stinking of wine and old rubbish. Sometimes people heard the scratching at their gates, and a few times they even came out with their sjamboks and their catties, 'cause they thought it was dogs eating their rubbish. Then they'd start shooting without even taking a good look to see who it was. One night a man with a pellet gun hit him a shot in the backside as he stood there scratching around. He hadn't even seen the man. And he didn't go looking for him, either, 'cause then he'd have to please explain what he was doing there in the rubbish. He couldn't very well go and tell other people about their plan, 'cause then they'd also start doing it, and then the petrol would run out too quickly. It's true what Treppie says, when there's trouble in the country it's always petrol that runs out first. Treppie said he, Lambert, could learn from the NP government – every time they got the country into trouble, they just stashed away more petrol. Treppie's like that when he talks politics. Actually when he talks anything. You never know if he means something's good or bad. And if you ask him, he says he's not interested in those two words, things are what they are and that's all there is to it.

Treppie wasn't even sorry for him when he got that pellet in his backside. He just stood there and laughed, holding the torch so his mother and Pop could get the little bullet out with a tweezer and a needle. Fuck, that was sore! He must have drunk a whole bottle of Klipdrift, lying there in the lounge on the loose blocks, with his backside up in the air.

'Lambert,' says Treppie, shifting a little closer. 'What if she wants to come with us . . .'

'Who you talking about?' Lambert asks. Pop looks down at the floor. Like he knows what's coming. Well, Lambert thinks, then Pop must know more than he does.

'Your girl, of course. The one we've ordered for your birthday.'

'You must be joking,' Lambert says, but he actually likes the idea. The thought never crossed his mind that she might want to come too.

'Yes, man, maybe she'll like you so much she'll want to come with us. Just after the election, when the shit starts flying.'

'But, um, Molletjie . . . there won't be enough space.'

'She can sit on your lap, man. And when you get tired . . .' wink-wink, 'then she can sit in front for a while, then we put Pop on her lap. Look at him, he's like a feather, man, he's ready for take-off.' Treppie lifts one of Pop's thin little arms and then drops it again.

'Hell's bells, that'll be something, hey,' Lambert says. He sits a little more upright on his mattress.

'Yes, man, it'll be fun. Just there after Beit Bridge, after we cross the border, we can buy a Coke and chuck some Klipdrift in and chill out a bit. Then you and her can go take a walk in the bushes.' Wink-wink.

Pop shakes his head. 'Treppie,' he says. 'Treppie.'

'Ja, Pop, man, I think she will. What do you think? You also saw her, man!' He pumps Pop in the ribs. 'Come, Pop, let's show Lambert how that girl danced in the disco there in Smit Street. You see, Lambert, it's like a display cabinet where all the girls stand and do their thing on a little dance floor, with a strobe-light and nice sexy music.'

Treppie gets up. He pulls Pop up too. He pushes out his hips and wiggles his shoulders.

'Come now, Pop, dance a little so Lambert can get the idea!'

Pop sways, first this way, then that. As if he wants to turn away from something. He stares at Lambert with a dull look. Like he's trying to look in somewhere where it's closed and dark.

'You see, we went to check them out a bit. You could say we went window shopping, me and Pop, when we went to look for her. Hey, Pop? So she can prepare herself for you!'

Treppie nudges Pop and winks at Lambert. 'Cleopatra's Queens. Cater for everything. Do anything you ask. For anyone. Discretion guaranteed. House-calls included. Cheapest rate is at the customer's house. Otherwise you have to rent a room, and pay for room service, towels, sheets, pillows. That kind of thing.'

Treppie lights up a cigarette and blows out smoke. He looks at Lambert through squinted eyes.

'It wasn't exactly easy to choose. Me and Pop stood there, trying to pick one out. Then I saw a tall one, a blonde, and I thought, that's her! That's Lambert's girl! But Pop said no, Lambert doesn't like long and thin, he likes short and fat. Then Pop pointed, there, look at that nice round one, on that side. Not so, Pop? And then I said, don't point, Pop, it's bad manners.'

Treppie laughs, slapping Pop so hard he almost falls off his crate.

Pop says nothing.

Treppie clears his throat. 'Well now, the one we chose for you in the end . . . should we tell him, Pop? Come on, Pop, be a sport, man . . .'

'Pop?' says Lambert.

'Ag, you know him. He's too old. He just wants to sleep. He's too old for this kind of thing. Farmed out, dried up. A dead shoot. Forget him, man. Now where was I . . .'

Pop stands up. He shuffles towards the door. Then he stops and shuffles around in a half-circle facing them again. He looks at Treppie and Lambert sitting with their heads together. Lambert's swung his legs off the mattress and he's smoking one of Treppie's cigarettes. He can see Pop wants to say something, but then he says nothing. He just turns around and shuffles out of the room. 'Click-clack' he goes over the loose blocks, down the passage.

'So, how'll you like it if she comes with us, hey, Lambert?'

'Well, it depends if she wants to. If she's game.'

'I promise you, she's game for *any*thing.'

'But if she comes with us she won't have a job any more.'

'No, but then she'll have *you*, don't you see?' says Treppie, laughing out of the back of his throat. Suddenly he stops laughing and looks dead serious again. His eyes are shining.

'But, Lambert, old boy, I need to talk to you seriously now. You've got to do something about your fat stomach,' he says, prodding at Lambert's belly. 'And your bum too,' he says, reaching for Lambert's backside.

Lambert pushes away his hand.

'Oh my,' says Treppie, looking at Lambert's crotch. 'Looks like you really want that floozy, my friend, like you really want her bad. Look at your dick standing to attention, just from a little talk. So, you want her to leave her job and come with us, right?'

Treppie gets up from the crate. Now he's all businesslike.

'Come, let's look at your clothes, then, old boy. Look, you've got those boxer shorts and another pair, and three T-shirts. That's all I ever see you wearing. A man can't go to the North looking like that. Especially not with a woman at his side. You're going to have to get back into your smart clothes. Your Man About Towns.' Treppie sways his hips.

'Look, you're welcome to borrow a shirt from me, but you see how thin I am. Like a plank.' He slaps his stomach. 'And then there's the mock leather jacket you got for your twenty-first. Come open here, man!' Treppie pulls at the doors of the steel cabinet. 'Come, come open up a bit here!'

'Just leave me alone!' says Lambert.

'Well, Lambert, please yourself, but if you ask me what's the most important issue in this election, then I'd say it's the fact that your birthday is the day before we vote. And that you're turning forty. And that we've been saving up out of Pop's pension and my salary for a whole year to pay for a girl. Just for you, alone, for a whole night. So we can get some peace and quiet in this house. Especially your mother. She's getting old. She's taking strain. It's your only chance, man. And now you want to go and fuck it up with white bread and polony. And Coke. It's a bladdy shame, if you ask me. Come now, come open this cabinet for me.'

'Just leave me alone!' Lambert says. He swings his legs back on to the bed and gathers up his pamphlets. Treppie mustn't start about his mother now. What does he know, in any case?

'That stuff you're reading there. Pure rubbish. You're still going to see all that talk explode in your face.'

'Yes, but we've still got a plan! We're going to bugger off from here!' Lambert says.

Treppie turns around slowly, away from the cabinet. He walks towards Lambert. Then he stands in front of him, hands at his sides, staring.

'Stupid fucken fit-catcher,' he says. 'You really do believe all that shit, don't you?'

Lambert looks up quickly. More because of the way Treppie says it than because of what he says.

'Huh,' he says. 'Huh,' and he feels his jaw dropping.

'It's a lot of shit, that,' Treppie says. 'It's just a lot of shit that I told you. Do you really think a Volksie with a rusted chassis, with no shocks to speak of, a clutch as thin as tin-foil, gears that keep popping out when you ride from here to Ponta do Sol . . . do you really think she'll take the four of us, let alone the tons of crap in your head about women, more than two blocks out of Triomf? You really think that? You're fucken mad, man!'

'But you said, you said so yourself . . .' Lambert wants to kick himself. Treppie's got him by the balls again.

'Yes,' says Treppie. His eyes are shooting sparks now. 'I know I thought that plan up. You want to know why? You really want to know why? It was to get you out of the way. To get you out from under our feet, out of the house so we could get some peace and quiet in this place. That's why. So you could bladdy shuddup and dig a hole, a nice hard hole full of pipes and bricks from the kaffirs. So you'd be so tired at night that you'd just fall on to your arse on your mattress and stay there, so you wouldn't bother anyone. So you'd stop giving us a hard time. So you could spend your days on rubbish heaps and scratch around like a bladdy mad thing. So I can get some rest for my soul. Rest, I say. Mol and Pop too. If we ever vote for a party, it will be for one that locks up your sort in a madhouse, a party that chains you to a hard little bed with iron wheels and then plugs up your mouth.'

Treppie flicks his cigarette butt on to the floor and steps on it with a hard twist of his shoe. His shoulder twitches wildly, once.

'And when they unstrap your hands, once a month, you'll be allowed to colour in those pictures of peace doves, the ones Mol and Pop bring, tiptoeing into your room 'cause they're scared you'll murder them if you wake up.'

'Treppie, that's my mother and father you're talking about. You just keep your mouth shut about them.'

'Oh yes, right, your mother and father, naturally it's your mother and father. It's 'cause of them that we're in our glory here with you. You think they're better than me, hey? Well, let me tell you something, my boy. They also lie to you, just like me. They lie to you to give you a better opinion of yourself. They talk the biggest lot of fucken shit, the poor fuckers.'

'Like what, Treppie? What do they lie about?'

'You'd love to know, wouldn't you? Okay, here goes.'

He looks at Treppie. There's a whole floor full of broken Coke bottles between them. He sees Treppie looking at the bottles. Treppie's got a disgusted look on his face. More than disgusted. He looks like he's got a rotten smell up his nose. Now he smells it too. A smell like piss. And the smell of his come, which he always wipes off on an old T-shirt. Iron and oil, he smells iron and oil. He feels like he's too much for himself. He swallows on something hot that's starting to rise in his throat. Spots in front of his eyes. He can hear what Treppie's saying, but it's zinging inside his ears.

'That story about when we became a republic, about the corsages and all that stuff your mother talks about when she's pissed, it's all a lot of lies, that. The part about making the corsages is true, we did that, but that was the night you went and threw your first fit. Just when things were starting to get going here. We were still having a big party and then your eyes did a somersault for real and you rolled right over into the trays of flowers and you shat and pissed and vomited all at the same time, right on top of the whole business. And then you lay there and took one fit after another till your back was as bent as a bucket-handle. Then me and Pop grabbed hold of you and strapped your arms and legs tight with our belts and took you to the hospital. They looked us up and down there and stuck up their noses and said you'd drunk too much brandy; epileptics shouldn't drink alcohol, didn't we know that? But if you fitted again, they said, with or without brandy, we must take an ice-cream stick and shove it into your mouth so you don't bite off your tongue.'

Treppie lights another cigarette. He pulls hard and blows out clouds of smoke.

'And from that day on you've spoilt every fucken party we've ever had here. You break every fucken thing in the house and you make shit as far as you go.

'Ja,' says Treppie. He kills the flame that's been burning in his hand all this time. Blue sulphur-smoke hangs in the air. 'And as far as Republic Day's concerned – no one went to Pretoria that day, and no one made six hundred rand, and you didn't charm anyone out of their paper money there by acting crazy with your donation list. 'Cause you weren't even there. That's what. Pop took those trays full of corsages, full of your vomit and your shit, and he buried them just like that, right here in the backyard. Ribbons and all. All the trouble, all the money – our money from the fridge business – into its glory, 'cause Baby Benade, the lamb of our loins, 'cause Lambertus the third – surprise, surprise! – turned out to be a genetic cul-de-sac. But that's too difficult for you, so just think of a bulldozer in a sinkhole instead.'

Treppie dusts off his hands, as if he's got dirt or fluff on them. 'Food for thought, hey?' he says, and he winks at Lambert as he starts walking back into the house.

'Hey,' says Lambert. He has to clear his throat. His voice won't come out so nicely. 'Hey,' he begins again, 'what about my girl, for my birthday . . .'

'We'll have to see, old buddy, we'll just have to wait and see,' Treppie says, and then he winks one last time.

In that moment, just as Treppie tries to walk here, right past his face, back into the house, Lambert takes one step forward, on to a piece of glass. But he doesn't feel anything.

He takes Treppie from behind, by the neck. Such a thin little neck. He gets a nice grip, on Treppie's throat. Then he drags him inside, kicking and squirming through the kitchen, where Treppie kicks over the Primus, spilling its cold Jungle Oats all over the lino. He drags him all the way down the passage. As they go, the loose blocks on the floor jump up. He drags him past the bathroom, past Pop and his mother's room, right into the lounge, where his mother's standing on a beer crate, trying to get the curtain rings back on to the railing and the railing back in under the pelmet. Gerty's with her. He hears Gerty bark a scared little bark. He sees his mother turn around. Her mouth is open. She swings the railing with her as she turns, she gets such a fright.

'Hey! You two!' she shouts. Treppie gets the railing full in the face. Mol swings again. She mustn't go swinging railings now. He feels the railing slide off his shoulder. He throws Treppie against the wall.

'Hic' goes Treppie as he hits the wall, sliding down on to his backside.

'You just stay there for a while,' he says to Treppie. He takes one big step towards his mother and rips the railing out of her hands. Gerty jumps up against him. He kicks her, and she lets out a yelp as she flies through the air. Toby comes to look as well. He thinks it's a game. He starts barking and gets two kicks. 'Ow-whoo, ow-whoo!' he cries.

'You people think you can lie to me, hey?' he says, bending the railing over his knee, curtain and all. It feels like a piece of tin. 'People mustn't lie to me!' he says. He takes a jump and grabs hold of the pelmet. One end comes clean out of the wall. That'll show them.

'Go get yourself ready, Ma, I want to see you in the back room as soon as I'm finished here.'

He grabs Gerty's green ribbing and the half-done yellow back part in one swipe, breaking the pins and pulling out the stitches on both sides. Fucken rubbish! Then he walks out the front door to the postbox on the lawn and kicks it with his bare foot so hard it smashes into the prefab wall.

He feels no pain. He feels fucken nothing. He picks up the postbox and throws it on to the neighbours' roof. As it hits the corrugated iron it goes 'boom!', and then 'doof-doof-doof' as it rolls down. It hits the gutter, tips over and falls on to the ground with a thud. He hears someone swearing next door. Let them fucken swear!

Then he goes back into the house. Past Treppie, who's still sitting against the wall in the passage. He leaves a trail of blood as far as he goes. He heads for the back room.

He sees Pop giving way in front of him. Good for him. Pop always goes and hides in the bathroom behind the door. Let him. He wants to go and tell lies. His mother's already in the back room. She knows her place. Now he'll first have to throw out that stinking dog of hers, 'cause she always sits there and looks. He doesn't like dogs looking at him when he's busy. And his mother had better keep her mouth shut. Nowadays she screams like someone's slitting her throat or something. Well, she'd better watch out or he'll squash her fucken voicebox to a pulp. They mustn't come here and treat him like he's a fucken idiot.

For a long time, Pop sat there with his fingers in his ears and his head against the cold middle hinge of the bathroom door. When he took his fingers out, Mol was quiet again. All he heard from the back room was sniffing. But now there were other noises too. People talking. Lambert talking to other people. Pop sat there for a long time, looking at himself in the piece of mirror in the bathroom cabinet. He looked blue and white, like stones. Then he went to the front to see who was talking, but by then they'd left already. It was the NPs. They'd dropped off their pamphlets and then got the hell out. And no wonder – the lounge looked like a hurricane had hit it. Lambert had a rag around his foot, with blood seeping through in a bright red stain. Treppie was holding a hand to a deep cut over his eye. And then Mol came out from the back, Gerty in her arms. Slowly and carefully she went and sat in her chair, Gerty still in her arms. Very slowly and carefully, like she was sore.

Later, when Pop saw Treppie locking the front gate with the chain for the night, he went out to have a word with him.

'Treppie, man, listen to me, you can't carry on like this with old Lambert. We'd better make a plan and find him a girl. Really. Otherwise he's going to kill the lot of us here in this house before long.'

Then Pop picked up the dented postbox from where next door had thrown it back on to the grass, and he carried it through to the back, even though it was getting heavier and heavier in his hands. He put it down at the foot of Lambert's bed.

'Here's your postbox, my boy. Tomorrow we fix it. First thing in the morning. I'll help you, me and Treppie.'

Pop didn't say anything to Mol. She was already sleeping, lying on her side in her housecoat, on the far side of their worn-out double mattress. She lay there with Gerty in her arms, the light from the naked bulb burning brightly above her head.

5

~

SWEET IS THE DAY

When Pop woke up and couldn't pick up the smell of battery acid from Industria, he knew it was going to be a good day. And when he hooked his braces over his shoulders, in front of Mol's three-piece dressing table – he was standing before the middle panel, the only one still there – he did it carefully, out of respect for the feeling he'd just had. Carefully, 'cause these days he feels to himself like a place he doesn't know, a place full of strange noises coming at him through a thick mist. Carefully, he blew the dust from the yellow plastic roses. Dust motes flew around his head, but he didn't move. He waited, bent over, for the dust to settle. You have to be careful on days like this.

And when he got to the kitchen, Lambert was already there. 'Pop, do you want a polony sandwich too?' he asked.

He said okay and then Lambert said he must come join them, they were sitting out in the yard.

And when he came round the corner, there they all were, sitting with their bodies in the shade and their feet in the sun. On Coke crates, with their backs against the den. Treppie pulled something out of the den for him to sit on, and Lambert brought him some coffee and a polony sandwich. 'Strue's God. Who would have believed it?

Now they're sitting peacefully there in the shade. Treppie's trimming his nails and Mol's feeding Gerty little bits of her sandwich. Flossie's hubcaps are lined up in a row in front of Lambert. The other day he knocked the dents out, and now he's using a fine little brush to paint the really bad spots with silver paint.

'How'd you sleep, Pop?' Lambert asks.

This can't be true.

'Huh?'

'I said, did Pop sleep all right?'

Can you believe it? Someone's asking him if he slept all right.

'Yes, thanks,' he says, 'I slept nicely.'

As Mol feeds Gerty, Pop sees her head jerk forwards, and then backwards again. No, jerk's the wrong word. It wasn't a jerk and it wasn't a shake; not a nod, either. It was like a little tremor. But she doesn't look up.

'Nicely,' Pop says, and his voice sounds like it's blowing from far away, through thin clouds. 'Nicely, thanks, my boy,' he says again.

Treppie gives a little cough. Then everyone's quiet for a while.

All you hear is Lambert's brush. 'Swish-swish' it goes over the hubcaps; Treppie's pocket-knife nail clipper goes 'clip-clip'; and Gerty's breath comes and goes heavily inbetween the bites of sandwich Mol's feeding her.

Around them, far and near, they hear the rush of cars, from Ontdekkers on one side to Victoria on the other, from Thornton's uphill stretch, where the cars go into lower gear, to the last bit of Empire, where they always dice to the robots.

'Look,' says Mol, and everyone looks where she's pointing. Someone's let his homers out for the morning. A whole flock of them, flying first bright side up, then dark side up as they turn around. 'Sweereereep', they come flying overhead, and when they come past again, they're even lower, 'wheedy-wheedy-wheedy'.

'When they're full of sights like this, it means the rains are coming,' says Treppie, clicking his knife closed.

'Right,' he says. 'Duty calls.'

'I'll give you a lift,' says Pop, pushing himself up on Lambert's shoulder.

'I'm staying so I can finish this,' says Lambert.

'No, fine,' Pop says. 'Then I'll see you all later.'

He taps Mol on the shoulder as he passes. She clears her throat. 'Bread and milk,' she says.

Pop pulls the car out from under the carport. He takes Treppie to the Chinese in Commissioner Street, just as he often does, but today he feels different.

As he drives home across the bridge, back over the railway tracks, he gets a sudden feeling that something's about to happen.

Once across the bridge, he switches lanes and drives towards Braamfontein. The taxis hoot, but he keeps to his course. He parks next to a meter in Jorissen Street.

He doesn't know what he's looking for. He's not looking for anything. He just wants to feel the rush of people around his shoulders; he wants to look at their faces.

He puts twenty cents in the meter. Then he takes one, two, three steps along the pavement. And then he stops, just looking.

People open up in front of him and then close up again behind him as he stands there on the pavement. He feels them brushing against him as they pass. So many strange, busy people.

Someone rattles a tin in his face. Pop throws twenty cents into the tin. He gets a sticker from the Association for the Blind on the front of his shirt.

People are selling vegetables and things on the pavement. Pop sees mangos, and he suddenly craves one. His mouth starts watering. Quickly he walks away. Then he turns around and walks back. He pays fifty cents for a mango and lifts it to his nose. The smell comes back to him from very far away. Fresh sheets, that's what the smell of a mango's peel always made him remember. Fresh sheets hanging up in the sun on the farm, before ironing.

He moves towards the edge of the pavement. Then he leans slightly forward, over the kerb, biting into the mango. He uses his teeth to pull back the skin, so he can get to the flesh.

Why don't they ever buy mangos at the end of the month?

He works out the lie of the mango's flesh, strangely crosswise on the flat side of the core. The fibres catch in his teeth and people bump into him as he stands there, eating. Piece by piece he spits the peel out on to the street in front of him, until he can put one end of the core right into his mouth and suck the soft mango sap out of the fibres.

Now all he's got left in his hand is the core. He looks for a place to chuck it. He sees a blue wire-bin on a pole. He smiles. That was really delicious. He throws away the core.

He wipes his mouth with the sleeve of his shirt and rubs his hands over the back of his pants. Then he hooks his thumbs into his braces, pulling them nicely over his shoulders again. He's got that feeling again, the one he had this morning in front of the mirror. It's sitting nice and deep now. He stands for a while with his thumbs hooked into his braces. He knows the feeling. It's as if two warm, open hands are holding him in front, against his chest, and from behind, between his shoulders. Under his skin and inside his flesh. Right up against his bones. He stands like that for a long time, feeling how it feels and smiling to himself. Until someone says to him, here at his feet: 'Please, boss. *Asseblief, baas*!'

Pop sees a black man with only one leg. The useless trouser leg is folded above the knee and turned back almost all the way to his bum.

Pop takes out twenty cents and throws it into the man's cap.

'God bless you, sir,' says the beggar.

'You too,' says Pop.

When he looks up again, he sees the Ithuba stall. Lambert's always reading from the papers how much money people win – widows, Post Office clerks, even tramps.

He feels in his pocket for the five-rand note. Mol said bread and milk. It's already become an expensive morning. What the hell, he thinks. He buys a ticket and puts it down on the counter so he can scratch. The black woman first has to explain to him where to scratch. She smiles a big smile at him. Never in Triomf has he seen a black woman smile at him like this. She smiles a lovely smile and then she says: 'It's all right, dearie, just go right ahead.' And: 'Maybe it's your lucky day today.' And: 'Don't worry, the others must wait their turn.'

All those behind him in the queue are black men in suits. And would you believe it, he gets three fives! He buys another ticket. Three twenties!

'Watch this old bugger, he's on a roll,' someone behind him says. As the woman counts out his money, he hooks his thumbs under his braces. 'Come on, be a devil,' she says to him. He wishes Treppie were here. Or Lambert. 'Come on, one more time, you can't lose now,' she says. He buys one more ticket. My word, three fifties! 'Now you must buy twenty-five tickets and carry on,' someone in the queue says. But he's finished. That was good enough. Three times lucky. He waits while the woman counts out his money, and then he adds it to the rest in his pocket. He's not sure how much he's got by now. 'Have a nice day, sir,' the woman says. And as he turns, a big black man takes him solidly by the shoulder and says: 'Hey, well done, old man, now wish me luck.'

'I wish you luck,' Pop says, smiling at the man, and now the feeling in his flesh runs like warm syrup through his bones and into his marrow, right down to his feet.

At first, he can't get Molletjie started. His hand's trembling, but then she takes, and he's off, with all that noise around his ears. From close up it's a lot of hooting and noise. He drives round the block, into Smit Street, and then under the bridge. He goes along Caroline Street until he hits Ontdekkers, towards the house.

He won't say anything. He'll show them later. Tonight. You should never announce good luck. He'll still think of something. Maybe the drive-in, or a decent bottle of brandy. Or maybe not. Don't be in a hurry. It'll come, like all things on a good day.

He drives past Ponta do Sol and stops at Shoprite for bread and milk. As he walks up and down the shelves, everything feels different. He can buy anything he wants. He takes out the money and counts it. Seventy-four rand and a few cents. He puts it back in his pocket in a little roll and then closes his hand around the roll.

A tin of ham? A few tins of bully beef? Sardines? He's really very tired of polony and golden syrup. Or he can go next door to Roodt Brothers Forty Years Meat Tradition and buy biltong and dry wors.

Pop smiles. No, he'll just buy bread and milk.

What he does with the money has to be more of a thing. He feels a thought coming from far off. It bothers him for a while before he works out what it is. Oh yes, Lambert. Lambert's birthday. New pants for Lambert.

No. Then it benefits only one of them. It must be something for everyone, all of them together. And it must be more than something you just buy, full-stop. It must be something that happens.

At the house he sees Mol looking at him all the time. In earlier years she would have said: So, Pop, what's with you, why you smiling so much?

He just smiles straight back at her, right into her puzzled face.

Just you wait and see, Mol, before this day's out you'll be smiling too.

Pop walks round the back to fetch Lambert. His four hubcaps are lined up neatly in the sun, drying.

Flossie stands here in the backyard, on bricks. When Pop finds Lambert, he's taping up Flossie's back window for spray-painting. Every day Lambert does some more taping. Pop's always telling him to get finished and spray her so the job can come out nice and even, but Lambert says it works on his nerves; he needs time to think, inbetween.

Lambert's got big plans for Flossie. She must be their 'long-distance vehicle', he says, so Treppie can use Molletjie to drive himself up and down to the Chinese.

Flossie's seats, he says, must be covered in light blue mock leather, to go with the midnight blue he's still going to spray-paint her. But now he's busy on the undercoat, which is yellow. Very yellow. How it's ever going to get blue, Pop doesn't know. But he doesn't say anything, even though he feels they should use Flossie for Molletjie's spare parts. Lambert must just stay busy. As long as he's busy, he's okay.

'Come,' says Pop, 'let's first fix that postbox of yours.'

'Right,' says Lambert. 'I've drawn up a plan.' He pulls a piece of paper out of his back pocket. It's a drawing, a thing that looks like a tent with ropes above and below the ground, and around as well. As if a big storm's coming, above and below the ground.

Lambert explains. They must weld the plate solidly on to the pipe. Then they take little arms of scrap iron, cut them at an angle on both sides, and weld them on to the pole on the one end, and on to the underside of the plate on the other. Then they can weld the postbox on to the top of the plate, also with arms.

'We'll show them what real welding looks like . . .' says Pop. He doesn't say anything else. It's Lambert's idea and when Lambert's got an idea you don't mess around with him. He'll help with the welding. On a good day he'll help with welding, any time.

All afternoon long they work. They find enough arms among the scrap in Lambert's den for struts, cutting them to length with a little metal saw. On one end they make a downward angle, with an upward angle at the other, to make the welding easier.

Then they go outside. Pop with a pair of welding goggles and Lambert with his big welding helmet and the welding box. They put the little struts down in a heap next to the gate.

There's a storm building, a thundercloud in one corner of the sky with a white head that looks like it's boiling over in big white clouds of steam.

'Watch us beat that cloud,' Lambert says, pointing up with his thumb. Then he sits down on his crate, with his back to the cloud.

'Right, let's go,' he says, and Pop hands him the first strut, for under-neath. They shift it around until it fits.

Each time Pop bends down to pick up another strut from the little heap, he can feel the big cloud above him. Like when someone stands next to you and you can't see him but you can feel his size and his warmth.

That cloud's tanking up, Pop thinks. He smiles.

He looks at Lambert's gloved hands. Sparks shoot in an arc around the gate. Everything in front of him looks dark blue, with bright points of light and glowing white smoke. It feels like being underwater, like the Blue Grotto of Capri they once saw on television.

Without taking off the welding goggles, Pop turns around and looks at the cloud behind his back. Short, white lines flash from the cloud's belly.

It's welding, he thinks. He smiles.

Mol walks out the front door. The tips of her housecoat flap in the wind like fins. She comes and stands next to them, nodding her head slightly. The plate's already fixed to the lower arms.

Would they like some Coke? she asks.

That'll be nice. Pop smiles at Mol from behind his goggles.

The goggles make him feel stronger. When he's wearing them, he feels he can smile more broadly. He can see Mol looking at him. She knows something's going on. Pop can see the sparks reflecting in her eyes. He wants to say something more, but he doesn't know what.

She goes inside and comes back with three glasses and a litre of Coke on the half-tray.

Lambert drops his helmet and Pop shifts the goggles back on to his head. Everything's clear again. They take big sips of Coke.

'The rain's coming,' Mol says, fastening her middle button. It's the only one left. She takes the glasses back inside.

'We'll be finished before the rain comes,' says Lambert, lifting the helmet to his face again.

Everything's working out, Pop thinks. Today everything's working out just fine. The welding head isn't clogging, the box hasn't blown, they've got a plan and the plan's working. Lambert's okay and Mol's recovered a bit from yesterday. And any minute now Treppie will come home too.

Then they'll take the dogs to the open ground behind the Spar in Thornton.

And then he, Pop, is going to treat them. Yes, that's what he'll do. He still doesn't know how. But he'll know when the time comes.

'Hey!' says Treppie, suddenly right here next to him. 'What's that spider you're welding there?'

'Good afternoon!' says Pop. 'It's Lambert's idea. Bladdy good idea, if you ask me.'

'Looks more like a spider doing push-ups on a mirror,' says Treppie.

'Just you shuddup and hang on to this for me,' says Lambert, giving Treppie the welding head.

Treppie pushes the button and watches the welding flame against the dark sky. 'Big storm on the way,' he says.

'We'll be finished in a minute,' says Pop. 'Then we'll go out with the dogs. You coming?'

'No, I'm tired. You go,' says Treppie.

'Ag no, man, it's no fun without you,' says Pop, smiling broadly from behind his goggles. Treppie's so surprised, he first looks this way, then that way, before looking back at Pop.

What's going on? he asks with his eyes and shoulders.

Pop signals with his eyes that 'something' is going on, but he doesn't say anything. All he says is: 'Go tell Mol to get ready so we can go.'

Treppie plays along. He's curious, thinks Pop. Toby and Gerty come running out too. They know it's time to go now.

Lambert finishes welding the last of his little arms.

'Right,' he says, 'now she's sitting nice and tight. Now it can rain or blow. She'll stay up. Even if you knock this pole out of the ground, the postbox will sit tight.'

Lambert gives the postbox a shove.

'Careful,' says Pop. 'Let the welding settle first.' Lambert bends over and picks up the tools. The flat spanner lies in a spot of long grass next to the fence. He almost doesn't see it. He kicks the spanner out of the patch of grass. 'Grass needs cutting,' he says.

'Let the rain come first,' says Pop. 'Then we cut.'

'Okay,' says Lambert, 'when the grass has dried off from the rain. Not a minute later.'

'Right,' says Pop, 'it's a deal. Take Molletjie out then.' He gives Lambert the car keys. Then he walks to the front door to put away the tools.

'Cause of his fits, taking the car out of the carport is all Lambert's allowed to do. He won't ever get a licence. He's not allowed to drive, even if he does remember to take his pills, and even if they do help. Pop knows Lambert drives around at night sometimes, but he says nothing. Lambert steals the keys from his pockets when he's sleeping. Treppie encourages him, but Pop says nothing. He's learnt his lesson.

Then they're on their way. The sky's dark already, but Pop smiles as he drives up Martha, across Victoria and right into Thornton. Lambert feels good – his postbox is sitting pretty again. He reads everything aloud along the way. He sees a small, black notice on a wire fence in front of the Congregation of Christ church: ALL RUBBISH AND JUNK REMOVED FROM YOUR PROPERTY R42 A BAKKIE LOAD. PHONE SMITTIE 684473.

'That's it, old Smittie,' says Lambert. 'Rubbish is rubbish.'

Then he reads the Congregation's text for the week, on a big, red board mounted on poles. THE GREAT DAY OF THE LORD IS NEAR, IT IS NEAR, AND HASTETH GREATLY. THE MIGHTY MAN SHALL CRY THERE BITTERLY.

Lambert cries like the mighty man. Toby barks.

Treppie sniggers.

'Lambert,' says Mol, 'control yourself.'

Lambert reads the list of continuous light blue writing on the gable of TRG Engineers. The place has been standing empty for more than a year now, but they still work in the yard at the back.

CRANKSHAFT GRINDING CYLINDER HEAD RECONDITIONING CONROD RESIZING MOTOR OVERHAULS STRIPPING SPRAYING UPHOLSTERING, he reads.

'What do they know,' he says, snorting.

When they pass Ponta do Sol, the dogs push their noses out of the windows. The smell of food and oil reaches right into the street.

'I'm hungry,' says Lambert. 'Nice and hungry.'

Before they can turn in at the Spar, they have to wait for a long line of cars to pass along Thornton. All the cars have their lights on.

'There's a helluva storm coming,' says Treppie.

The dogs jump out of the windows and run to the open veld before they even come to a stop.

Treppie finds the pink Day-Glo tennis ball in the back of the car. Then they all get out, except Pop, who stays in his seat. He says all the standing today has worn him out. He rubs his eyes. It's from looking at the welding.

When he opens his eyes again, he sees his family out there in the distance. They're standing in a loose triangle in the middle of the veld. Lambert, Treppie and Mol. They look small as they throw the pink tennis ball to each other. Treppie to Lambert, Lambert to Mol, Mol to Treppie. The dogs chase the ball like mad as it flies from the one to the other. Lambert keeps throwing the ball too high and too hard for Mol. She misses it. Miss, miss, miss. Then the dogs chase after the ball. If it's Gerty, she brings it back to Mol. Mol smiles each time she bends over to take the ball from Gerty.

She can't help smiling, Pop thinks. He said she was going to smile today. And she doesn't know how much more she's still going to smile. He feels in his pocket to make sure the money's still there.

Suddenly, lightning flashes in three different places at the same time – long white arteries with side-branches shooting all over the sky. Thunder breaks through the sky so hard that Pop hears the Spar's roof go 'kaboof!'

Mol gives a funny little jump, smothering a scream. Then she breaks into a run, making for the car with the dogs hard on her heels. Treppie and Lambert laugh so hard they slap their legs with their hands. They light up cigarettes and then stroll back to the car.

When everyone's back inside – when the dogs with their wet tongues have come to rest on the back seat, and the Volksie's tipping over to one side from Lambert's weight, and the first big drops of rain go 'plock, plock' on the roof – Pop asks: 'So who feels like fish and chips, or Russians, or hamburgers? How'd you like some take-aways, with tomato sauce and Coke?'

No, he doesn't ask. He says: 'So, who's hungry!'

'And what do we eat at the end of the month?' asks Mol.

'This is extra money I've got, old girl. Extra. Don't worry.'

'Extra what?' asks Lambert.

'Money,' says Pop.

'That you got where?' asks Treppie.

'Let's go and get some food. I'll explain on the way,' says Pop. He turns Molletjie's nose carefully back on to Thornton, towards Ponta do Sol.

'How does a person get extra?' asks Lambert.

'Yes, how?' asks Mol.

'Must be charity,' says Treppie.

'Yes,' says Pop, 'pure charity, just like that. First I ate this mango . . .'

'Then you bit into gold, right?' says Treppie.

'No, man, listen now. Just after I dropped you off this morning. I went to Braamfontein. Then I ate a mango.'

'A mango?' asks Mol. 'Mangos are messy.'

'Ja, but I wiped my hands on my pants and then someone wanted money for the blind. In a tin.'

'And then?' asks Lambert.

'Then I gave him some money.'

'How much?' asks Treppie.

'Twenty cents.'

'Jeez!' says Lambert, 'I bet he gave you his whole tin, right?'

'No, then a one-legged kaffir asked me for money. In his cap.'

'And then?' asks Mol.

'Then I gave him some.'

'How much?' asks Treppie.

'Also twenty cents. "God bless your soul, sir," the kaffir said to me.'

'Sir, I say,' says Treppie.

'Then you grabbed his tin?' asks Lambert.

'No, then I said: "And yours too!"'

'What?' asks Mol.

'"Bless your soul too," I said to the kaffir.'

'Pop, now you're having us on,' says Lambert.

'No, I swear, it's true,' says Pop, pulling up outside Ponta do Sol.

Everyone's looking at him. He smiles back at them, one by one. At Lambert, with his thin beard growing in patches under his chin. Lambert's eyes are wide open. Light blue, like the rest of theirs. At Mol, who's playing with her false tooth in her mouth. Every now and again she pushes the tooth right out. She always does that when she's thinking hard. And then Pop looks at Treppie. There's an Elastoplast on his forehead and stubble all over his hollow cheeks. You can never make out his expression, he's so full of wrinkles.

Pop sticks his hand in his pocket and takes out all the money. 'Seventy-four rand!' he says.

'Jeez,' says Lambert.

'Good Lord,' says Treppie.

'Hmph,' says Mol.

'Yes,' says Pop. 'It was my lucky day: a mango, a blind man, and a one-legged kaffir. And then I played scratch-cards and I won. Seventy-four rand.'

Pop opens his door. 'So, what'll it be, my friends? Lambert?' he asks.

'No, hell, Pop. Wait, we're coming with,' says Lambert.

They all pour out of the Volksie and run to the other side of the road with their heads down, out of the rain and into the warm, oily air of the shop. They stand there, trying to make up their minds. What'll it be?

'Four packets of chips, for a start,' says Lambert.

'Three's enough,' says Mol.

'No, four, five, even six if you want,' says Pop.

'And a piece of fish for me,' says Lambert.

'Me too,' says Mol.

'Steak roll,' says Treppie.

'And a boerewors roll for me,' says Pop.

Pop smiles at the black woman behind the glass counter. She must fix up their food nicely.

While they wait, they look around Ponta do Sol as if for the first time.

Lambert picks up a *See*, puts it down again and then picks up a *Getaway*. He pages through the magazine, showing Treppie a 'full frontal of a bushveld baboon'. The baboon's yawning.

'Look at his teeth,' Treppie says to Mol.

'Look at his you-know-what,' says Mol.

When their food's ready, Pop stands at the counter to pay. Lambert brings four Cokes.

'What about cigarettes?' asks Pop. He doesn't wait for an answer, but buys everyone a pack of twenties. John Rolfes for Treppie and Paul Revere for Lambert and Satin Leaf for Mol. He's been telling her for a long time now Lucky Strikes are too strong. For himself he buys Consulates, in a tin, instead of his usual Van Rhijn. And why not? He feels like a new person. They all feel new. Good evening, they nod at other people, and then they smile when the people nod back.

Halfway out of the shop Lambert turns back. 'More salt!' he says as he catches up with them again, holding up a bulging serviette. 'They always put too little on the chips.'

Pop takes a different route through the rain, over the Westdene Dam and towards the city.

'Where you going now?' asks Mol.

'Wait and see,' says Pop.

He turns right into Kingsway, past the SABC and then up the steep hill.

'Just look how they've gone and built here,' says Treppie. There's a big white building on top of the koppie, with its bottom sitting in a dam full of fountains.

'Ja,' says Pop, 'there used to be nothing but koppie here. But you can still see the view from the top.'

He parks the car in the small open space across the road from the tower, with its nose pointing north so they can see the whole city – from Northcliff on the left, across Emmarentia, right up to the other tower in Hillbrow. Big bolts of lightning flash across the sky.

'So,' says Pop, 'now we can see nicely.'

'Just like bioscope,' says Mol.

'Silent movies,' says Treppie. 'We have to say what's happening.'

'Psssht' goes Lambert's Coke as he opens it. 'How's that for sound-effects?'

'Sweet heavenly Co-o-ke!' Treppie sings.

'Right,' says Pop, 'get that food out. I'm feeling peckish now.'

Mol hands out the packets. She feels each one to find out which is which.

'Don't squeeze my fish like that,' says Lambert.

'It's not your fish, it's Pop's boerewors,' says Treppie, laughing. 'What will become of the Benades if they can't squeeze each other a bit,' he says.

'Go squeeze yourself, man!' says Lambert.

'Hey!' says Pop. 'Give it a rest.'

They eat in silence.

Lambert takes out his salt serviette and offers it around.

'How's that taste?' asks Pop after the first few bites. The car reeks of take-away.

'Tastes good,' says Mol.

'Nice, nice,' say Lambert and Treppie.

'You smiling yet?' Pop asks Mol, looking her way. He's feeling happy. She doesn't say anything.

'She's smiling, she's smiling,' says Treppie.

'Now, Pop, tell us more about those scratch-cards, man. You ate the mango; twice you gave twenty cents for charity; then what?'

'Well, then it was my turn.'

'What gave you the idea?'

'Just a feeling. Just a feeling like it was going to be a good day. Suddenly the booth was right in front of me and I thought, what the hell, let's see what kind of luck Pop Benade's got today. And then I won. Three times in a row.'

'You don't say,' says Lambert. 'And I've been buying them for two years at the Post Office without ever winning a cent.'

'You just have to choose the right day, that's all,' says Pop. 'You get good days and you get bad days.'

'What's a good day feel like? When is it ever the right day? What cock and bull story are you cooking up again?' says Treppie, his mouth full of steak roll.

'You feel it in your shoulders when you wake up in the morning and put your braces on,' says Pop. He's talking softly. He doesn't want to wake sleeping dogs.

'Ag bullshit,' says Lambert. 'And if you don't wear braces? Then I suppose you can't ever have a good day, or what?'

'You just feel it in your shoulders, that's all,' says Pop. He should never have opened his mouth.

'How?' asks Treppie.

'Treppie,' says Mol, 'eat your chips.' Gerty sits at her feet. Mol feeds her little pieces of fish and chips. The dog is all attention – her ears stand up and her eyes are big and shiny.

'Hell, it's only pouring now, hey,' says Lambert.

The rain's coming down harder all the time. Pop switches on the wipers. Lightning flashes all around them, breaking in strips and spots and glows. And there's no end to the thunder – quick, close slashes, and then hard, tearing sounds.

'Flash!' says Lambert.

'Well, naturally,' says Treppie.

'No, man, I meant it looked just like Flash Gordon was here.'

'Take your pick,' says Treppie. 'It looks more like the Lost City to me. Opening night.'

'Guy Fawkes,' says Mol. 'Fireworks.

'Peking Ducks,' she says, raising her voice on purpose.

'Is Ma going to start with all that again?' asks Lambert.

'Never mind,' says Pop. He points to Hillbrow. 'On this side it looks like a creeper with shoots. Shoots of morning glory or something. Every time it flashes you see more flowers on the shoots, blue ones with white in the middle.'

'No, fuck, Pop,' says Lambert, 'your food's nice, but when you talk shit you talk shit!' He slurps down his Coke and then he burps. He's having a good time. 'If you ask me, it looks more like a couple of okes sitting behind a dirty window, welding a helluva long silencer on to a Mobil lorry or something,' he says.

'Wait, wait, wait,' says Mol, 'have another look . . . there it is!'

'Morning glory, that's what it is,' says Pop. 'Grandfather's Hat, as the old people used to say.'

'Take your pick,' says Treppie, 'it's all in the mind. Welding flames, morning glories, grandfather's glory, it's all in the mind.'

'Pop's mind is a bit soft today,' says Lambert.

'Well,' says Pop.

'Pop's fine,' says Mol, 'leave him alone.' They've all finished eating now and they're folding up their greasy papers. Mol gathers the left-overs together. For Toby, when they get home. Only Gerty's allowed to eat in the car. She doesn't mess. She's a dainty little dog.

They all open their new cigarettes and light up. The smoke makes Mol cough. 'Open the windows a bit, it's stuffy in here.'

The side windows at the front and back are opened just a little. 'Don't let it rain into the car,' says Pop.

Mol draws deeply on her cigarette. She's feeling strong again. 'Now let me tell you what I see,' she says.

When Mol starts like this, it's always about the old days. Peking Ducks in the old days. Pop puts his hand on her leg, to remind her she must go easy, this is dangerous territory; and to comfort her, 'cause it's in the past. The lightning flashes deep yellow tufts in the sky in front of them, lighting up the inside of the car. Pop sees the faces of his people in the strange light. They look yellowish, but they're happy. Especially Mol. She smiles an ancient little smile.

'Here, right in front of us, I can see roses. Big bunches with lots of roses, or a single open rose with thick petals; it just depends how you look.'

'Take your pick,' says Treppie.

'Whisky Macs. Whisky Macs in full bloom. Almost ready to throw away.'

'Fuck, Mol, are you sure you didn't add something to your Coke there in front?' says Treppie. 'It's not nice to drink on your own, you know.'

Pop signals with his head for Treppie to shuddup.

'Just watch,' says Mol, and everyone waits, watching for the next flash. Then it comes. A big, round ball of yellow light, with darker, orange circles arranged more densely towards the middle. The lightning flashes from inside a cloud. Its edges and layers bubble outwards, and the whole thing really does look like a rose.

'Whisky Mac!' says Mol, slapping her legs with both her hands. Then her voice disappears in a tremendous smack of thunder.

'I see it too, Ma,' says Lambert, suddenly all polite.

'Oh my goodness,' says Treppie. 'When it comes again, you lot must watch carefully. It looks like a rotten old arsehole, man.'

'Treppie,' says Mol, 'you see arseholes wherever you look,' and then, on a sudden impulse, she adds: 'It's 'cause you give everyone such a huge pain in the arse!'

'Jeez, Ma!' laughs Lambert, like he can't believe what he just heard.

Pop also laughs a little.

'Well now, Mol, Klipdrift or not, from where I sit you're on top form tonight,' Treppie says, laughing a crooked little laugh.

'Our old Molletjie,' Pop says softly.

'Now, if you look this side,' says Mol, pointing to Northcliff, 'then you'll see something else: closed ones, closed buds. On their stems.'

Pop looks. Good for you, old Molletjie, now you're back with us. Everyone waits and watches. The rain has quietened down a bit, falling softly on to the car's roof. The city's lights seem small and remote to Pop after the spectacles of light in the sky they just saw. His heart feels warm. The day's holding out. His hip hurts a little from the weather, as always, but that's nothing. Then, just above Northcliff, lighting up the whole ridge, they see it, one, two, three, a whole row of flashes, each one with a pinkish, closed bud on its tip. On the stem they see flat, silver leaves trembling as if in a stream of warm air.

'There they are!' shouts Mol. 'Prima Ballerinas, all in a row, on their toes, with pretty little ballet dresses!'

Pop claps his hands. The dogs start barking.

'Let's go now,' says Treppie.

'That was very nice,' says Lambert.

Pop starts the car. The wipers go slowly back and forth, back and forth.

'Who's for pudding?' asks Pop.

'The last of the big spenders,' says Treppie.

'Me,' says Mol, throwing her cigarette butt out the little side window. The roses were there for everyone to see – now no one can tell her she's talking rubbish.

'Me too,' says Lambert.

'As long as it's not take-aways. I don't eat take-away pudding,' says Treppie. 'It melts and drips all over the place.'

'No,' says Pop, 'we're going to the Spur.'

Everyone's quiet.

'Which Spur?' asks Lambert.

'Wait and see,' says Pop. He coaxes Molletjie down the steep hill, past the SABC. At the bottom he turns left into Empire and then right again into Melville's main street. He stops in front of the new Spur. They wait for a CitiGolf to pull out and then park in the same spot. Between a Honda Ballade and a Ford Capri.

92

'Comanche Spur, I say,' says Lambert.

'Look, it's their birthday. Look at the banners,' says Treppie, pointing.

Pop sees a banner on top of the building: ONE YEAR COMANCHE SPUR. COME AND JOIN OUR BIRTHDAY CELEBRATIONS.

'You got enough money?' asks Mol. She sounds nervous.

'About fifty rand,' says Pop. 'Is that enough?' he says, looking at everyone with a big smile on his face. Then he switches off the car.

They go in at the bottom. A few young men who look like students brush past them in the doorway. They stare at Lambert, who stands there in his bare feet.

'You could at least have put some shoes on,' says Treppie.

'Fuck shoes,' says Lambert.

'Or your smart pants,' says Treppie.

'Fuck pants and fuck you too. Look at you, you haven't even shaved, and you've still got Elastoplast on your head!' says Lambert.

'Treppie!' says Pop. Treppie mustn't start now.

'Hey! Behave yourselves,' says Mol.

Pop looks at his people. They don't look so good under the Spur's stairway lights. He wonders how he and Mol look. Ag, what the hell. They are what they are. He looks up at the steps. Can't see where they end. He hadn't thought of steps.

'You two carry on,' he says to Lambert and Treppie. 'Go ahead and get us a table. I'll be there in a minute. My leg's sore.'

'Let me help,' says Mol, taking him under the arm. 'One at a time,' she says, 'then we'll be up in a jiffy.'

It hurts, but Pop climbs. One at a time. First the good leg, then he stands on his toes a bit and pulls the bad leg up behind him. After every few steps, they rest. They struggle like this all the way up the first lot of stairs.

'If people come walking past now,' says Pop, 'then we must stand to one side.'

'They can wait,' says Mol, 'we're also people.'

Wooden eagles and big Indian heads look down on them from the stairwell walls.

'What are these?' asks Mol, touching a green plant in a pot against the wall.

'Cactuses. Be careful, they've got thorns,' says Pop.

'They haven't. Feel,' says Mol.

'They're not real.'

'Cactuses,' says Mol, 'hmph!'

Now they're on the landing. One more set of steps.

'Come, let's first sit for a while,' says Mol. 'First rest a bit. Does it hurt?' she asks.

Pop nods. They go sit on the landing's little bench. More people come walking up. Out of the corner of his eye Pop sees Mol ironing down the flaps of her housecoat to make sure they cover her legs and knees. She puts her feet together neatly and folds her hands on her lap. The people stare at them as they pass by. Pop covers Mol's hands with his own and gives her a little squeeze. He winks at her. She touches her hair at the back.

'Come,' she says when the people have passed. She takes him by the hand and leads him slowly up to the top. It's almost dark upstairs.

'Can I help you,' a man asks.

'Yes,' says Mol.

'Yes, our people are here already,' says Pop.

'Oh, yes,' the young man says slowly, 'I think I know where they're sitting.' He leads them down a passageway. Mol's so nervous she starts giggling.

'Here you are,' he says.

Lambert and Treppie sit with their chins in their hands, listening to a waitress telling them the specials, all in a row: '. . . and our other special is the Spur Birthday Hamburger, which is two hundred and forty gram pure beef patties with the sauce of your choice in a bun sliced three ways. Then there's the Special Spur Birthday Spare Ribs, which are—'

'No thank you,' says Pop.

'Just pudding,' says Mol.

'Sweets,' says Pop.

'Suit yourself,' says the girl, giving them a funny look.

'It's okay just to eat just pudding, isn't it?' asks Mol.

94

'Of course,' says Pop.

'Then why's she looking at us like that?'

'Her arse,' says Lambert, pulling the plastic card with pudding pictures out of its plastic holder.

'Why did you let her start with her long story, then?' asks Mol.

''Cause Lambert's never heard it before,' says Treppie.

'We never get to hear it,' says Lambert. He's too busy looking at the pictures to see Treppie's making fun of him. 'And it sounds good: two hundred and forty gram pure beef patties with the sauce of your choice . . .'

'That's fuck-all too,' says Treppie, showing with his hands how big the patties are. 'These places are a rip-off.'

'Are you two going to order?' asks Pop. He motions to the waitress to come over. The night's getting too long now. His hip's hurting from the long climb up the stairs.

'Apple pie with ice cream,' Treppie says to the waitress.

'A waffle with syrup and cream,' says Lambert.

'You should have ice cream, it's not real cream,' says Treppie.

'With ice cream and lots of syrup,' says Lambert, leering at the waitress. She pretends not to hear him.

'And some syrup for you too,' he says. 'You look to me a bit sour.' Lambert's smile gets even bigger.

'Lambert!' says Mol, kicking him under the table. She smiles at the waitress.

'A cream-soda float for me,' she says.

'Sorry, ma'am, we don't serve floats, ma'am.'

'Ma'am,' Treppie mimics her.

'Just bring her a vanilla ice cream and a cream soda in a tin,' says Pop. 'And a glass and a spoon and a straw. And for me an Irish coffee,' he adds. Maybe it'll kill the pain a bit.

'Make it two,' says Lambert.

'Greedy,' Mol says to Lambert when the waitress goes. 'You mustn't start looking for shit here.'

'Well, this place is also shit,' says Lambert. 'This lot here think they're the who's who. Just look at them checking us out. Fucken common rubbish!'

Treppie laughs.

'Come now, my boy,' says Pop.

When their order arrives, they eat quickly. Pop makes a float for Mol, but the cream soda and ice cream won't all fit into Mol's glass.

'First finish this one, then we'll make another,' says Pop. 'Then we get two for the price of one.'

Lambert finishes his waffle in four bites. He sucks at the Irish coffee.

'A whisky mosquito pissed in here,' he says. 'We should've said double. Two mosquitoes. Pssst, pssst.' He pretends he's pressing two mosquitoes into the glass with his thumb and index finger.

Mol laughs.

'Hell,' says Treppie, 'the Benades are really on top form tonight.'

A man in a suit comes walking up to them with a big smile on his face.

'Just watch how they throw us out now, floats and all,' says Treppie under his breath. Lambert growls, getting ready. He knows his rights. He hasn't done anything wrong. They mustn't come looking for trouble with him now.

'Good evening, people,' says the man, smiling from ear to ear.

'Good evening,' Lambert and Treppie mumble. They haven't done anything wrong, but they look guilty. Still, no one must come and bug them now. They stare back at the man. All the people around them turn to look as well.

'Who's the host tonight?' asks the man.

'The what?' asks Lambert.

'Who's paying?' he asks.

'Me,' says Pop, 'I'm paying.'

'Well, sir . . .'

That's the third time in one day somebody's called him 'sir'.

'I have good news for you!' the man says, smiling at the other people too.

'It is my pleasure to announce that you are sitting at the lucky table tonight, the Spur's lucky birthday table. Your bill is on the house tonight and here in this envelope I have six free meal-tickets worth fifty rand each for you and your family, accepted at any Spur restaurant right through the country and valid for the next six months. Give them a hand!'

He hands Pop an envelope.

And there the whole Spur starts clapping. The man winks at three waiters, who bring three huge bottles of champagne to the table. Corks pop, glasses are brought and the Benades get served before anyone else. Then all the other people also get some of the champagne. A girl in a tiny pair of hot-pants and Indian feathers on her head comes disco-dancing right here in front of them. She goes and sits on Lambert's lap, proposing a toast to the Benades.

'Hi, honey,' she says.

'I like your feathers,' says Lambert. He touches the feather-stuff in the girl's hair. 'But your legs are cold!'

'Check Lambert out, he thinks he's in a movie,' says Treppie, laughing.

'In a *See*,' says Mol. She takes a big sip of champagne.

'Cut it out,' says Pop. 'Drink up, Lambert, we must go home now.'

'With an Indian on his lap! I'm still going to wet myself here tonight,' says Mol. 'What shallow little glasses! Let's use my float glass instead, it's better.' Mol grabs the champagne bottle and fills up the float glass. She takes a few more sips.

'Mol, it's not a cold drink,' says Treppie, trying to stop her. But it's too late.

The champagne's doing its job. Pop can see her coming loose at the seams, from the champagne, from today and from all the days that came before. 'I can float to England on this stuff,' she says. She laughs loudly, wiping tears from her eyes.

'Come,' Treppie says to Pop, 'let's fuck off now, before Mol starts seeing more roses.'

'Yes, that's enough of a good thing,' says Pop. 'My leg's hurting.'

Lambert's rubbing his own legs. The girl's gone. All you see of her are some feathers in the opposite corner, among a bunch of men.

'Lambert,' says Treppie, 'you help Pop. Come, Mol!' he says, pulling Mol out of the seat. She wipes her eyes with a serviette.

Pop struggles to get up. He limps all the way to the counter. Treppie goes with Mol to the car. Pop leans heavily on the counter. The noise of the cash register sounds like it's coming through a thick cloud. That's where Lambert finds him.

'Hey, Pop, we don't have to pay tonight, remember. Give me those other tickets so I can keep them for you.'

Pop just nods. He limps behind Lambert, who's pulling him to the exit by his shirtsleeves. At the stairs, Lambert goes two steps down, pulls Pop closer, and then lifts him on to his back. Pop doesn't resist. He feels like he's rocking in a thick fog. He sags forward, right up against Lambert's back. It's a wide, fat back and it smells slightly sour. He feels how Lambert's large, warm hands slide in under his bum to hold him up. He suddenly has no strength left, not even enough to hold on to Lambert.

'Hell, Pop,' says Lambert, 'you feel like you're nothing but air.'

The stairwell lights and the Indian heads pass by Pop's head at strange angles. He closes his eyes. His ankles knock first against this side of the wall, then that side of the wall as Lambert carries him down the stairs. It feels like he's going faster than he really is.

Pop pushes his head down a bit, into the space between Lambert's shoulders. He feels like he's slowly melting back into the place he came from, a place he doesn't know any more.

Where does he end and Lambert begin? He doesn't know. This morning's feeling is back again. But not just in his shoulders. He can feel it everywhere. Outside, on the pavement, he feels it in the air too. Pure honey syrup. Sweet, sweet, sweet. Without stopping and without end.

6

OH, IT'S A SATURDAY NIGHT

Lambert stands on the front stoep, looking at the moon. It's a golden-yellow ball floating just above the houses. He can smell braaivleis everywhere. People laugh and talk in their backyards and the air's thick with smoke. It's hot. Children play outside in the streets. It's almost dark but the children carry on playing with their balls. Some of them have skateboards. The only time they ever give way is when a hot rod comes past. It's policemen who dice like that; they think they're big shots around here. As they come past you can hear the thump-thump of disco music, and when they turn the corner they leave a smell of hot rubber behind them. He can swear the inside of those cars reek of aftershave. He knows, he sees them on weekends at Ponta do Sol, all washed clean and shaved for their night out.

Here comes another one. Lambert checks out the policeman. His shiny hair hangs down in thin, curly little points on his forehead. He drives fast but he's not even looking at the road. He's looking out from under his hair, checking out the houses, left-right-left-right, with a kind of a fuck-you-fuck-me look on his face. His elbow sticks out of the window and he works the gears with his other hand. Big shot!

Lambert knows what he's looking at. He knows what you see through bedroom windows on Saturday nights. Girls. Putting on make-up in front of their three-panel dressing tables from Morkels. They pout their mouths to put on lipstick and then they bend over with their bums up in the air, resting their feet on little dressing table chairs so they can paint their toenails. That's before they slip into their flimsy little white sandals. They've all got dates.

Sometimes Treppie comes and stands next to him, so he can also check things out here from the stoep. But Treppie doesn't look at the girls in their rooms. He looks at the wallpaper. At least that's what he says. Lambert doesn't know how he can see so far, but Treppie says all he sees are trees and dams and bridges, bunnies jumping on green grass and ducks and things. And blue hills in the distance. That's now supposed to be all on the wallpaper.

For fucking crying in a bucket, Treppie says, how can people lie to themselves like that, with walls full of mock paradise? But that's what happens, he says, when you take a place like this, full of prefab wagon-wheels and aloes, rotten with rubble, and then give it a name like Triomf. Then people think they've got a licence to bullshit. But that's a lot of crap, Treppie says, 'cause the only licence that counts is poetic licence.

He's already asked Treppie what poetic licence means. Treppie says it's the liberties poets take with life to make some things rhyme with other things. But, he says, those same poets have to live with poetic justice, 'cause words can boomerang badly, especially when they rhyme. He says there's fuckenwell nothing in the world or the stars that actually rhymes. So, you have to watch your step and tread carefully if you want to play around with rhymes.

So why rhyme, he asks Treppie, if it's such a lot of trouble?

But Treppie doesn't answer. Sometimes he just shrugs and says it keeps him on the go. Other times he winks that devil's wink of his and says it's a family secret.

Another hot rod comes past. A blue one with its arse up in the air and loud music blaring from the windows. Lambert feels the bass from the disco-beat vibrate low down in his back. All day he's been walking around with a hard-on from looking at the *Scope* centrefold – a blonde girl with big cans that she pushes out. They don't even put stars on the nipples any more. Funny, he actually used to like those stars. Nipple caps. He burps. His throat burns. Heartburn. From polony and white bread.

He wishes his mother would cook something so he can eat properly for a change. Potatoes and meat and sweet pumpkin. But she's gone bad. Doesn't give a shit any more. Just look at her kitchen. The other day he stuck some pictures of pretty kitchens on to the fridge. He took them from the *Homemaker* magazine that he finds in his postbox. But Pop took them off before his mother could see them.

He looks at the moon. It's light yellow and a bit higher in the sky now. That fucken moon works on his tits. And just listen to the flying squad and the ambulances. Sirens all over the place, in and out of the Saturday night traffic.

Next door they're playing Cat Stevens. They've been playing it the whole night. 'Oh, it's a Saturday night and I ain't got nobody.' Loud. They think they're the only ones in the street, as if Martha Street belongs to them.

When he walked through the house from the back just now, he looked at his people sitting there in the house. They act like nothing's wrong. His mother's in the back, knitting Gerty's jersey. Treppie's in his room reading the *Saturday Star* classifieds. What Treppie thinks he'll find in the classifieds Lambert still doesn't know. Pop's fast asleep in his chair in front of the TV, in the lounge. The TV's playing loud.

He feels pushed. Pushed from fucken underneath and from fucken above. He goes back in through the front. Then he looks around Treppie's door.

'So, what's new,' he says. He lights up. Maybe Treppie's got a story to tell. Or a plan.

'So, what does that Jew-newspaper say tonight?' he tries again.

Treppie looks him straight in the face. Here comes shit.

'Just look at you again. Sis, yuk, go pull your wire so you can get some rest!'

'Your arse, man!' he says. What else can he say? He wishes he had something else to say. Something that Treppie's never heard in his whole fucken life. Something that'll make him sit up and be cool on a Saturday night. Something that fucken rhymes. How's he supposed to help it if he gets a hard-on? He burps. Fucken hell! What now?

He looks into the lounge and sees Pop sleeping in his chair. A drop of snot hangs from his nose and there's slobber running down his chin. It drops from his chin on to his chest. Toby lies under the TV table. His eyebrows and ears twitch when he sees Lambert look at him. Pop shifts around in his sleep.

He'll still be sitting like that when he kicks the bucket one day, Lambert thinks. No, he doesn't want to think about that. Fuck that. 'Click-click' goes the floor as he walks with bare feet to the back, to his mother. That's another place. He knows when it's okay to go in there. Now's not really the time. It's his mother's room. Hers and his father's, but more hers. He sticks his head around the door.

'Nearly finished?' he asks. 'Can I see?'

She ignores him. Like she's been doing ever since the last time. That was bad. He could feel things breaking inside her. If she looks for trouble, she'll get it. But now he's looking for company.

'Has she tried it on yet?' he asks. She doesn't look up. He takes a step into the room.

'Gerty,' he says to the dog, who's sitting stiffly against his mother on the mattress, 'Gerty, have you tried on your new jersey yet, hey, old dog?'

His mother shifts away slightly. That means he must just not start looking for trouble again. Tonight it's peace and quiet. He draws deep on his cigarette. It's more than just trouble he's got in his body.

'What does the old dog say about her missus, hey? Also lost her voice, huh? Bad fucken company on a Saturday night, or what am I saying?'

Mol lets her knitting fall on to her lap. She looks at Lambert.

'So?' he asks. She says nothing. She picks up her knitting and carries on.

He takes a step closer. She shifts away some more. He squats next to the bed and pats Gerty on the head. Gerty looks up at Mol, making a little crying noise.

'What does your old cunt of a missus say tonight, hey? What does she say, the cuntface with no teeth, hey?' He's whispering very softly to Gerty and scratching her between the ears.

Mol suddenly gets up. She walks across the mattress and out of the door. Gerty follows. He stays right there, hunched on his heels. He hears her go into the lounge. He hears Pop wake up and say: 'What now? What's it, Mol?' His voice is thin. It's all that slime in his throat.

She stays quiet, and then she says: 'Lambert.' Just 'Lambert'. That's all. Her fucken arse too.

He scratches his head with both hands and then he scratches his arse. His arse itches. Everything about him fucken itches. He gets up. He's more than just 'Lambert', that's for fucken sure. He walks out, into the passage and through the doorway to his den. There's his bed. The thing's legs are standing skew. The mattress lies at an angle on the bed. Its stuffing sticks out on the one side. Slept to death. He, Lambert, doesn't even have a decent bed to sleep in. Fuck that. He grabs the mattress and throws it, with the *Scope* and pillows and blankets all still on it, against the open Tedelex. The empty Coke bottle on top of the Tedelex falls and smashes all over the floor. Fuck that too. He smacks the cabinet a shot with his flat hand. He can also make a fucken noise if he wants to! All night he's been listening to other people's noise. 'Oh it's a Saturday night and I ain't got nobody' over and fucken over in his ears. No, shit! He kicks an empty Coke crate with his bare foot. It flies into the scrap iron behind the door. A long piece of pipe comes loose, falling slowly across the room. It scrapes his painting on the wall before falling on to the floor. Silver paint comes off his mermaid's tail. This Saturday night doesn't want to work. This Saturday night is a fuck-up.

He walks out through the den's back door. He wants to see what those fuckheads next door are doing. He stands in the long grass and peeps over the prefab wall, into next door's backyard. The moon's sitting higher now. It shines light blue all around him. Wherever you look next door it's just yellow and red party lights, hanging from a wire between the gutter and the loquat tree. They're fucken braaiing again. Them and their fucken meat.

It's chops. No, it's not chops, it's T-bones. He counts eight of them. They cover the whole grill. The grill rests on a half-drum with four legs. There's another grill as well, also a half-drum with legs. This one's full of rolled-up boerewors. The wors sizzles and drips fat over the coals. Every now and again the flames flare up. Then someone has to douse them again.

He can't see who's killing the flames. All he can see is a hairy paunch and a hand going up and down. He can't see so well 'cause he has to look over the prefab wall, and then over next door's fast-food stands. That's what they are, fast-food sellers. All of them. They sell hot dogs and hamburgers from their stands. He's peeping underneath the flap of a plastic canvas sail and the stands below. All he can see is a strip of yellow light, some braaivleis and people's bellies. Every now and again a hand with a can of beer goes up, and then drops down again to a hanging position next to a body. He can see seven bodies: men's bodies and women's bodies, thin ones and fat ones. Two women are wearing bikinis, a pink one and a blue one. They're not so bad, even though they don't look as smooth and as tanned as the Tuxedo Tyres girls. These ones have lots of dimples on the backs of their thighs. Pink Bikini stands with her arm around a man in blue jeans. The jeans are tight and there's a bulge in front. Blue Bikini stands with her arm around Speedo. It's a black Speedo with an even bigger bulge. His bulge stands at an angle, pointing to one side. Speedo's got a big pair of thighs and a body-builder's stomach. Hairy Paunch's doing the meat. Lambert can see grey hair on his stomach. He's wearing a towel that keeps slipping down. Then there's another paunch, this one a little smaller, in khaki shorts. And there's a thin little thing with knobbly shins in a cotton dress full of little flowers. She's sitting on a plastic chair. Here comes another one, with big flowers on her dress. She comes and stands next to the fire.

'Johnny, don't burn those steaks now, you hear me, don't burn them like you did last time.'

'No ways,' says Hairy Paunch, 'these coals are just right now, just right.' He takes a long sip from his beer. All Lambert can see is his elbow lifting up, but it doesn't come down again. Big Flowers walks away.

'Mom, go see if Ansie's remembered the potato salad,' Hairy Paunch says to Little Flowers.

'Ai, Johnny, and I was just settling down nicely here,' Little Flowers says, but she gets up anyway. She grips the arm of the plastic chair to push herself up.

Nice and pissed too, he sees. He knows it's the old lady from Fort Knox.

She's the one who said they should take him, Lambert, and put him into a reformatory, that time he stabbed his mother in the cheek with a knife. In a reformatory or a madhouse, she said. Fucken old cunt.

It's Treppie who came up with the name Fort Knox. He says it looks like they're living on a heap of gold, like it's America or something, the way they put up burglar bars and gates in front, and Spanish burglar-proofing over all the windows, and spikes everywhere. There's a safe full of gold under the ground at the real Fort Knox. Fucken joke, that. As far as he can see, all they've got here is three fast-food stands and eight T-bones. And wallpaper.

'This meat's ready now,' Johnny Hairy Paunch shouts at the women in the kitchen. 'Bring the dishes. Where's the pap and stuff?'

Here comes Big Flowers now. She's got two bellies. One above the middle, then a deep fold, then another under the middle. Her dress creases into the fold. She's carrying a big black pot full of pap. On top of the pap she balances a bowl of tomato and onion sauce.

'Kiepie,' she says to Khaki Shorts, 'go fetch the dishes for Johnny. They're on the table in the kitchen. The shallow one for the meat and the deep one for the wors.'

Kiepie Khaki Shorts puts down his beer, walks off and returns with the dishes, the shallow one and the deep one.

Blue Bikini and Speedo come over to the food. Speedo's hand drops to her bum. They're standing next to Johnny, who's busy taking the T-bones off the fire. Kiepie's holding the shallow dish for Johnny.

'This here's a proper piece of meat,' Speedo says, bunching Blue Bikini's bum into his hand and squeezing it.

'Oh yes,' says Johnny, feeling the meat with his fork. 'Bought it at Roodt Brothers this afternoon. They know their meat there.'

'Forty Years Meat Tradition,' says Kiepie, 'the best in Triomf.'

'The best,' says Johnny. 'These were on special.'

'Special, hey?' says Speedo, moving his hand over to the other side of Blue Bikini's bum. Lambert watches as he gathers the soft meat of her bum into his large hand.

'*Very* special,' says Speedo, slipping his hand under the bikini's elastic, moving it lower and lower until he's right in there, between the split, right down at the bottom.

'Well,' says Blue Bikini, trying to move the hand away, 'if you ask me, it's that wors that looks nice.'

Pink Bikini giggles.

'Good Lord,' says Big Flowers, coming out the kitchen with bowls of salad, 'can't you two control yourselves?'

'Leave the children alone, Ansie,' says Little Flowers, 'horny is horny. Nothing to be done about it.'

'He can at least go and put some decent clothes on,' says Big Flowers.

'Auntie, Auntie,' says Speedo, 'it's like this, Auntie, I'm feeling too hot to get dressed. This way I can at least cool down a bit.'

Everyone laughs.

'Come, let's get the eating done now,' says Little Flowers, 'look how late it's getting. Otherwise that meat sits too heavy on my stomach and then I can't sleep.'

'Okay, Mom, we're just waiting for the pap and sauce to warm up a little here,' says Johnny. 'Make sure it doesn't burn,' he says to Kiepie, 'I'm going back to get some more beers.'

'Check if the baby's still sleeping,' Pink Bikini tells him. Blue Jeans rubs her on the shoulder.

This is how Lambert peeps at the people in Fort Knox. He listens to them as the moon shines blue light across his back. He watches how they take their seats on plastic chairs. He sees Big Flowers dishing up everyone's plates to the brim, there at the stoep-table. He can see three bowls of salad, one with bananas in yellow sauce, one with tomatoes and lettuce and one with potato salad. There's a T-bone and a piece of wors on everyone's plate. And a heap of pap with sauce on top. They have to push their food back on the plates; there's so much, it wants to fall off.

'Now, let's first drink to Fanus and Yvette,' says Hairy Paunch.

'Happy first anniversary,' says Little Flowers. Blue Jeans' and Pink Bikini's faces turn towards each other across the plates of food on their laps.

Lambert hears them kiss.

Now that they're sitting, all he can see is the top half of their bodies and the bottom part of their faces. Large bites disappear into half-mouths.

'Well now,' says Big Flowers. She holds her plate in both hands on her lap. 'You wouldn't say we're in a recession now, would you?'

'Eat your food, Ansie,' says Little Flowers.

'Don't worry, be happy,' says Speedo.

'So, Kiepie,' says Johnny, half laughing, 'you figure the kaffirs are going to come and take their houses back, here in Triomf?'

'Ag no, man,' says Pink Bikini, 'don't start with that again, you know how upset Ma gets.'

'Yes, don't upset me,' says Big Flowers, taking a large mouthful of pap and then a bite of wors.

Upset, Lambert thinks, upset! They reckon they know what upsets them. Let them just sit there nicely and eat their fucken T-bones. 'Cause right now his mother's going to cut the grass. She doesn't know it yet, but that's what she's going to do. Then they'll see what upset means. The kaffirs wanting their places back is nothing, completely fuck-all. He's going to set the blades so the revs run nice and high. And he'll put too much oil in so the machine comes out smoking blue. He'll see to it that the whole lawn gets cut, front and back, in the bright light of the moon. He'll upset the whole of Triomf. It's not just other people who can make a noise around here.

He walks with long strides back to his den, in through the back door and over the crates and pipes to the inside door.

'Ma!' he shouts down the passage before turning back to get the lawn-mower from his room. Then again: 'Ma!' he shouts over his shoulder as he pulls the lawn-mower out from under the blankets in the room. And once more: 'Ma!' as he drags the lawn-mower, 'rickatick-rickatick', over the loose blocks into the lounge.

And then, again, as he walks in through the lounge door, he shouts so loud that the windows rattle: 'Hey, Ma! Get yourself ready to cut. The grass is long!'

He pulls the machine into the middle of the lounge. Then he bends over, shoves open Pop's knees, and drags out his toolbox from under Pop's chair. He wants to set the petrol to 'open', but the lever's broken, so now he needs long-nosed pliers to shift the broken piece of stub. But he can't find the pliers. The fucken thing isn't in his toolbox. With one flick of his arm he turns the whole box upside down on to the lounge floor. 'Kabam!' Pop rises slowly from his chair. He's reaching out in the air for Mol. She's been up a while already.

'Where's the oil? Where's the petrol?' he shouts at them. 'Come, come, you're all half-dead in this house. Move! It's Saturday night!'

Treppie comes in, leaning against the lounge door. He says nothing. He squints at Lambert.

'Hey, what you looking at, Treppie? What you looking at?' Lambert shouts as he scratches among the heap of tools on the floor.

'Me,' says Treppie, 'I'm looking at a mad fucker with a big dick, scratching around for small pliers on a Saturday night.'

'Viewmaster,' says Mol, lighting up a smoke. It looks like she's surrendered. She'll go through with it. Whatever.

Lambert's up in a flash. He takes one stride towards Treppie and then lifts him up into the air by his shirt. Treppie has to stand on his toes. He shouts into Treppie's face. Treppie turns his face to avoid the spray.

'Now let me tell you what it is you see, you fucken bastard. You see a plastic pipe behind the bathroom door, and you see a fucken funnel in the den under the bed. You see an empty Coke bottle in the same place. You see how you siphon petrol until that bottle's full and then you fucken see how you bring that bottle here. That's what you see! Don't look for shit with me now. Move it! Go siphon some petrol!' He lets go of Treppie in mid-air.

Treppie finds his footing again, ironing out his clothes with quick, sharp little plucks at the edges.

'Go siphon your own petrol, you mad fucken arsehole,' he says, turning back to his room.

'Hey,' says Lambert, starting after him.

'Hold it, hold it,' says Pop. 'Leave Treppie alone, I'll get the petrol.'

'Okay,' says Lambert, 'but let me tell you one thing tonight . . .' And he turns around to face Pop and his mother, to tell them something as they stand there, next to each other, with their careful faces. ' . . . and I'm going to say it just once.' He wants to say it just once to his mother, who's standing there and fingering her bun. And he wants to say it just once to Pop, who's standing there half-asleep, pulling his braces over his shoulders with his thumbs. He wants to tell them, the two of them standing there like they're going down an escalator into a big dark hole – he wants to say it to them, but then he says nothing. He's forgotten what he wanted to say. It was too much to say. His eyes burn and his throat feels tight.

'The GTX,' he says instead. 'The GTX. It's under my bed. Don't open the full can,' he says, swallowing down the burning feeling and blinking. 'There's a can that's half-full. Bring it here.'

He looks down. The long-nosed pliers. It's fucken lying right in front of his fucken feet. He picks it up and goes down on his knees next to the mower. He sets it to 'open'.

Mol fetches the oil while Pop siphons some petrol. Treppie's swearing in rhymes in the passage: 'Dammit, fukkit, dogshit!'

That's better. He feels much better now. At least now there's some action. A person can't sit around like this and do nothing on a Saturday night.

'Sow the seed, oh sow the seed of the watermelon,' he sings as he sets the blades higher.

'Shuddup!' Treppie screams, but Lambert just sings louder.

'We must get a better siphon,' he tells Pop after they fill up the mower. 'This one messes too much.' He's talking loudly.

Pools of oil and petrol spread over the parquet floor. Mol goes to the kitchen to fetch a rag.

Lambert wants to start the lawn-mower, but the cord's slack. 'Grrr!' He pulls. 'Grrr, grrr!' Once more: 'Grrr!' 'Fuck,' he says. 'Fuck this piece of rubbish!' He kicks the lawn-mower.

Treppie walks past in the passage, looking into the lounge.

'I told you, you should pull your wire rather than pull that silly little string – then at least you'll have something to pull.'

Lambert picks up a spanner and throws it in Treppie's direction. Treppie ducks. The spanner hits the wall and falls on to the blocks. One of the blocks goes 'click' as the spanner bounces it loose. A big, thick piece of plaster goes 'poff' as it falls on to the floor and shatters into small pieces. Now there's a big hole in the wall, with hairline cracks all around it. Lambert looks at the hole. He can see powdery red brick where the plaster came loose. Big cracks running in all directions.

He bends over and rips the cord. 'Puff-ta-puff-ta-puff-ta-puff-ta-puff' goes the engine, and then it takes. He sets the petrol further open. There's a lot of oil in the petrol. Spot-on. The lounge fills up with blue smoke.

'Ma!' he shouts after Mol, who's gone back to the kitchen with the dirty rag. 'Come!' he shouts. 'Come, come, come!'

He pushes the lawn-mower towards the front door. Clouds of blue smoke rise from the machine and start pouring out of the door. He works the mower down the two steps. There's a sharp noise as the blades catch the edge of the stoep. Sparks fly. Mol follows him.

'It's night, Lambert. I can't see anything,' she shouts above the noise of the machine.

He lets go of the mower. Then he turns his mother so she faces the moon.

'There!' he shouts, pointing up. 'There! Can you see it? There's your light, Ma! It's a fucken heavenly spotlight! What more do you want? You start this side and then you go right around, hey.' He pushes the mower to the strip between the house and the prefab wall, where the grass has grown long.

Pop comes out the front door. 'Hey, Lambert,' he shouts, but the noise is so loud he can't hear himself speaking. He taps on his wrist where his watch used to be. It's a long time since he had a watch.

He motions with his arms to the moon. It's late, he shows with large movements. People are sleeping, he signals, folding up his arms next to his head.

Lambert signals back to Pop he must shuddup. He, Lambert, finishes what he starts. Everything's going nicely now. He pushes past Pop, who's standing there in the front door. Then he sits down in front of the TV, lighting up a cigarette.

Pop walks up and down between the front door and the lounge. He'd better just sit down now and stop walking in and out, in and out like a dog looking for a bone. He must close the front door now. Lambert hears his mother pushing the lawn-mower through the long grass on the side. 'Choof-choof-choof-choof' goes the mower's engine as it slowly runs down. Then it cuts out. Dead. Now he'll have to drag himself all the way back outside to his mother, 'cause the dumb cunt won't be able to get the thing going again.

He's up like lightning and out of the door before Mol even makes a move.

'Ja!' he shouts at her. 'What's your problem, hey?'

She points to the dead mower. God in heaven, surely he can see what's wrong?

'So, you let the thing die, did you?' he shouts. 'What you do that for, hey, what you do that for, hey? Hey?'

He bumps her out of the way, bends over and grabs the cord's handle. His shorts are almost right off his backside, but he doesn't pull them up. Let her look if she wants to. When he was a baby, his nappy also used to slip down like that. It's 'cause his bum is too high. That's what she always says. Stuff her. He can't help it if his bum is so high.

He pulls the cord so hard the mower lifts right off the ground.

'Put your foot on it so I can pull!' he shouts. Mol walks round to the front side so she can do what he says. The engine takes after the third yank.

'Right!' Lambert shouts. 'When she slacks off, you lift the nose up into the air, like this, and then you move the machine back, just a bit. Then you let it down again. Come, let's get going. Move, move, move!'

He watches her as she pushes the mower back up the strip next to the house, where the grass is longest. 'Choof!' The machine chokes again. He waits for her at the stoep as she drags it back. He's not going to let her off, no way.

'Can't you get it into your head, Ma, that you have to press the fucken thing down on your side so the fucken nose lifts into the air, so it can get some fucken air, so it can fucken run again, hey? Hey!'

He rips the mower out of her hands, steps on it himself, and starts it up again with one mighty heave. He shoves the machine back in his mother's direction. Then he points at her. Stupid fucken old woman. How could she let it die a second time? Pop's standing in the doorway, waving his arms like he's trying to kill flies. Lambert pushes him out of his way.

'Go sit!' he says to Pop. 'Go sit down so you can stop walking up and down all the time.'

Pop lights up a cigarette. He says nothing. They listen as Mol finishes cutting on the side, and they hear how she keeps saving the machine from dying at the last moment. She lifts the machine up on number ninety-nine, gets it up to speed again, and then brings it down for more cutting.

Treppie walks into the lounge with a bottle of Klipdrift and a litre of Coke under one arm, and three glasses in the fingers of the other hand. Then he steadies the glasses on to the sideboard.

'So!' he says. 'Busy, busy tonight at the Benades, hey, Lambert. Sow the seed, oh sow the seed!

'Sow the seed of the watermelon,' sings Treppie. He does a few dance steps, holding the bottle above his head.

'His mommy's arse's in the grass, his dad is dinkum telly-mad, his uncle's dandy with the brandy, so let's sow the watermelon!'

Treppie switches off the TV. Pop's holding his head at an angle so he can hear how Mol's doing outside. She's almost finished on the one side. Now she must do the back, where the grass is also long.

'A double for me,' says Lambert.

'But of course, Bertie old boy. Always double for the single man!' says Treppie, first pouring the Klipdrift and then the Coke, 'ghloob-ghloob-ghloob'.

'Doubles are forever, doubles are for always, doubles to clink on, for double fuck's sake, oh for double fuck's sake,' he sings to the tune of 'He's A Jolly Good Fellow'.

'Doesn't Mol get any?' asks Pop.

'Leave her be so she can cut the grass once and for all,' says Lambert. He takes his glass.

'The shit's still going to fly here tonight. Here's your drink, Pop,' says Treppie, handing Pop his glass. 'Drink up before it happens, 'cause when it does it's really going to fly in a big way.'

They drink in silence. Behind the house they hear Mol lift the mower again. But she doesn't put it down. The engine starts running fast and loud.

'What the fuck!' says Lambert. But he doesn't get up. He waits. He knows what he's waiting for. Then he hears the noise coming from next door. Two men start shouting over the Fort Knox wall.

'Shuddup with that noise! Shuddup! It's fuckenwell eleven o'clock at night! What the hell do you people think you're doing!'

'That's it,' says Lambert. He slams his hands down on his legs as he gets up. 'They're looking for trouble again. Think they're big shots. Think they can stick their noses in our business. Stuff them too!'

He hears his mother let the machine down again. 'Choof! Choof!' It cuts out. Here she comes now, round the other side. She doesn't want trouble with the neighbours. She parks the mower in front and stamps her feet to get the grass off. Then she fingers the bun at the back of her head. 'Enough,' she says. She pushes past him.

'Finished?' says Lambert.

'Next door's complaining,' she says. She points to the sideboard. 'Where's mine?'

'You'll get yours when you fucken finish cutting the grass. That's when you'll get yours. You hear! Do you hear me!'

'Next door,' she says.

'Fuck next door!' says Lambert. He pushes his mother on the chest.

'Sow the seed, oh sow the seed,' Treppie sings from where he sits. He smiles an old smile. His eyes are shining. When Treppie looks like this, then he's into the game, then he wants to play along, then things start cooking. Fine, maybe something will cook up here tonight.

'Mol,' says Treppie. 'Mol, you know what happens when the fucken grass is long. You know very well what happens. Then the shit starts flying. You remember what happens, don't you?'

'First rest,' she says. 'First sit.' She goes and fetches herself a glass in the kitchen. When she comes in again, she pours herself a drink. She sits down heavily, flinging her legs wide open.

'Close your legs, Ma, close your legs!' says Lambert.

Pop lets his head drop into his hands. 'Lambert,' he mumbles.

Lambert shoots a look at Pop. If Pop has something to say then let's hear it, he says. Didn't Pop hear what Treppie just said about the grass? Or has Pop suddenly gone deaf? And can't he even feel that long drop of snot hanging from his nose? Must he, Lambert, wipe it off for him?

Pop wipes the drop off with his sleeve.

'Still is the night,' Treppie starts singing.

'Pop,' says Treppie, 'Pop, where's your mouth organ? Hey, Pop, don't go to sleep now, man. The night's still young. Where's your mouth organ?'

'Leave him,' says Mol.

'You leave your glass, Ma,' says Lambert. 'That's what you must leave, now, right this second! Go cut the grass, so we can get some peace around here!'

'Sweet the moments, rich in blessing,' Treppie sings. 'Hell, but I feel like singing tonight.' He gets up and pours himself another drink. 'I feel like singing, singing and dancing. Waltzing. I feel like waltzing. And you, Mol, you also feel like waltzing?

'Waltzing Mathilda, waltzing Mathilda,' sings Treppie. He does a few steps with his arms held out. 'Click-click' go the blocks on the floor.

'Outside! Get outside and finish the grass! Now!' Lambert shouts. He plucks his mother up and pushes her out the front door, slamming it behind her. This is no time for dancing.

He watches her through the window. She stands on the stoep with her hands against her sides. Her one side is yellow from the stoep-light. Her other side is blue from the moon. Slowly she moves towards the moon's side. Where the fuck does she think she's going now? The mower's right in front of the stoep. What's wrong with the old bitch tonight? She must work the machine. She must make a noise. She mustn't go wandering around now. It's now or never. He goes out the front and starts the engine. His mother wants to get away from him. She grabs the mower and quickly pushes it away. 'That's more like it!' he shouts after her. Then he goes inside and watches her through the side window in the lounge as she cuts the grass on the moon's side. The lawn's looking nice and even. Except for the patch where the grass grows long, near his scrapheap. All Flossie's old parts. Pieces of the old Austin for just in case. He always keeps things for just in case. Then he knows he can look for things in the scrapheap. But he doesn't always find what he's looking for 'cause the grass grows too long around his stuff. Then he burns the grass. When he does that, everything else burns as well. All the metal stuff, till everything's pitch black. But the grass has to be short, otherwise things get lost.

There she starts on the patches of grass around the scrapheap. Yes, he's been waiting for it – right over a piece of iron. The engine dies. Sounds like a blade has gone too. Here she comes now, pulling that thing behind her again. He walks to the front window to watch her. She's standing on the stoep. She's sniffing, but she doesn't come inside. She turns around. Then her eyes open wide. She didn't think he'd stand here at the window and watch her! The old cunt looks scared out of her mind. He must go fix her up.

'Nearly finished, nearly finished,' she says as he comes out.

'This is the last time, you hear me! The last time! You're looking for me, Ma, and if you look for me you're going to get me! You're going to get me!'

'Okay, okay, Lambert. Just start it for me. Quickly.'

Her hands show he mustn't hit her, she'll cut, she'll cut till she falls over, but she'll cut. She's nicely broken in. That's the way it should be. At least there's one person in this house who does what he says.

It's long after twelve. Lambert's peeping over the prefab wall. He's wearing nothing but his shorts. The moonlight's bright now, but it's still hot. His mother gave him no more trouble. She cut the grass obediently, but nothing further happened, and he began to get sick of starting up the engine all the time. So when Pop said it was time to go to bed he was actually glad. His mother was ready to fall over in any case. And Treppie was so drunk, he'd started shoving handfuls of grass into his mouth, 'mooing' like a cow on the front lawn. He had to help Pop carry

Treppie inside, the mad wanker. They're all sleeping now. The house is dark. Now he can peep over the wall in peace. Why Fort Knox stopped complaining he still doesn't know. Must've had too much beer.

It smells of cut grass where he's standing. They're playing light music next door. He stretches his neck.

First he sees nothing. Then Blue Bikini and Speedo come shuffling past. Speedo's got both his hands on her bum. Lambert can see he's working her bum again. They're dancing so close you can't see Speedo's bulge any more.

The faces aren't visible but he can hear them kissing – it's a sucking and spitting sound, like eating a mushy guava, as Treppie always says. Mushy guava and cucumber power.

Pink Bikini and Blue Jeans lie on a blanket. They're kissing. All he can see is their legs, as far as their backsides. The flap of the canvas sail over the fast-food stand blocks his view. He can see legs folding over each other and feet clawing and curling into each other. The Cotton Prints and the Paunches are nowhere to be seen. Must be sleeping by now. Jesus, he wishes he could see a bit better. If he could just get a bit higher he'd be able to see over the top of the sail. But then he'd have to stand on the prefab wall and he wouldn't have anything to hold on to.

He goes to his den and fetches some beer crates. He stacks six of them on top of each other, against the wall. Like this he'll be able to hold on to the gutter with his one hand. But how's he going to get up the crates? He fetches another three crates to use as a step.

He lifts himself on to the stack of crates by climbing on to the lower lot first. Now he'll be able to see what's what in Fort Knox! He'll be two crates higher than the prefab wall.

As he finds his footing on the topmost crate something starts to wobble underneath him. He grabs the gutter and holds on, but he's falling. He sees the wall and the middle food stand coming towards his face. It's the hamburger stand. More than half his body's already over the wall. He makes a grab for the canvas sail. 'Crack!' goes the frame. 'Grrrts' goes the flap as it tears in his hands. First he falls a dent into the hamburger stand, then he thuds down on to next door's cement floor.

The next thing he hears are the screams of the bikini girls.

'Kiepie, Johnny! Come quickly, it's that piece of shit from next door again,' shouts Speedo.

Oh fuck me, Jesus, what now? He's jammed between the hamburger stand and next door's wall. His one side's on the cement, and now he can't move. He'd better get a move on, fast! Now he's really gone and made big shit. And now their fucken dog's gunning for him too, biting and barking from under the hamburger stand.

'*Voetsek! Voetsek!*' Lambert shouts. He flexes his body and kicks wildly at the dog, making more dents in the stand. Speedo and Blue Jeans are worming their way between the wall and the stands from both sides to get at him. He lunges for the top of the wall. It's easily two heads higher than on the Benades' side. He heaves himself up, gets his feet on to the stall, and pushes himself right over the wall. But before he can clear it, someone gets hold of one of his feet. He gives a hard kick backwards and feels his foot sink into someone's warm, wet mouth.

'My tooth, my tooth, my fucken tooth!' one of them shouts, letting go of Lambert's foot.

He falls head first between the two heaps of crates. The skin on his skull splits open and warm blood runs down his face. His foot throbs from the kick. What the hell's he going to do now? His head feels dizzy. Speedo and Blue Jeans are screaming at him over the wall. He sees their arms waving in the air. Then he sees Treppie's light coming on. Within seconds Treppie's outside.

'What the hell's going on now?' he shouts in a voice that sounds like it's breaking.

'I fell!' says Lambert.

Blue Bikini's head pops up over the wall. She's as blonde as a Barbie doll.

'Fell? The hell with fell! He was peeping at us! The fucken pig was peeping, that's what he was doing!'

Five heads pop up over the wall – Speedo, Blue Jeans, Pink Bikini, Kiepie and Johnny. There's blood running from Speedo's mouth and nose and he's spitting out red gobs. The Fort Knox people are on top of the food stands, shouting and pointing at Lambert, who's still on the ground, holding his head with one hand and his foot with the other.

'He fell straight into his glory!' says Little Flowers, whose head also pops up now.

'He fell smack on his backside, that'll teach him!' says Big Flowers, joining the Fort Knox party. Little Flowers and Big Flowers are both in their nighties.

Speedo's been back inside to change his shirt and put on a pair of jeans. He looks a sight. The whole of one side of his face is swollen. He grabs the prefab wall and climbs to the top.

Through the blood running down his face, Lambert sees him grab on to the gutter. Just two big movements and Speedo's on top of the Benades' roof.

'Come,' he says to Blue Jeans. 'Come up here with me. Give me your hand, I'll pull you up. Then we'll see what happens to people who peep, to fuckers who peep at other people when they're braaiing.'

'Ja!' says Kiepie.

'Ja!' says Johnny. 'Let's show them what happens.'

'Just look at our sail!' says Big Flowers, standing there in her flimsy yellow nightie.

'Just look at our stand,' says Little Flowers in her green nightie.

Pink Bikini, who still hasn't said anything, comes storming out with a glass vase and throws it, 'bam! ting-a-ling', right through the den's side window, glass flying everywhere.

'Take that, you filthy rubbish!' she shouts. 'It's 'cause you fucked up our whole night!'

Pop comes out the back door. His mouth hangs open. He's in his shirt and socks.

Then Mol pushes past Pop. She holds the flaps of her housecoat together.

'Lambert,' she says. 'Lambert, get up.'

'Ja,' shouts Speedo from the roof. 'Get up, you fucken freak, so you can see what we do to people who break our things!'

'And to people who peep at us when we braai!' screams Pink Bikini.

'Here we go!' shouts Speedo.

'Hoooo-haaa!' shouts Blue Jeans. They run around on the roof.

'Crack!' they break off the TV aerial.

'Crack!' they flatten the overflow.

'Crack! Crack! Crack!' they rip the gutters out of their brackets and throw them, 'bam! bam! bam!', on to the ground.

'Come!' says Pop, pulling Mol by the sleeve.

'Come!' he says to Treppie, pulling him by the sleeve as well.

'Come, we're going inside. Lambert, come now!' Pop says. But Lambert doesn't want to go inside. He's limping along the side of the house to see what they're doing on the roof, in front. He knows his rights. What they're doing now is not an accident, it's malicious damage to property. That's how Treppie explained it to him last time. This bunch from Fort Knox are breaking their house down, deliberately. With intent.

Lambert runs out the front gate to go phone the police. The women across the road must just let him phone now. But they say no, they'll phone themselves. It's 'cause they don't want him in their house. He knows, he's seen how they spray stuff to get rid of his smell when he leaves. 'Jesus, but he honks,' he even heard one of them say.

'Ag, thank you very much,' he says to the short thick-set one who comes to open the door. 'Thank you, man, but they must come quick. We're under siege here!'

The tall one dials one-one-one-one-one-one on the phone in the passage. He hears her say something about a 'domestic disturbance across the street here'.

'What!' he shouts. 'It's a fucken war, man!' He shouts at the top of his voice so the police can hear. Domestic disturbance, my fucken foot!

He runs outside again. Speedo and them are back on the ground and they're busy in front now. They're actually breaking his postbox. 'Zack! Zack! Zack!' go the little iron struts as Speedo breaks them off, one by one. Then he stands back a bit, dances towards the postbox at an angle and gives it a big Kung Fu kick. Lambert watches as the postbox and the platform fall right off the pole and on to the grass. One shot.

He stays where he is in the garden across the road, just behind the gate. But they've seen him.

'Come here, you fucken fat pig, so we can smash you up a bit,' shouts Blue Jeans.

'Yes, come here, you waste of a white skin who peeps at us when we braai!' shouts Speedo.

Waste yourself. He's not going to move an inch.

Here come the police now. They come from all sides, in yellow vans and yellow-and-blue Flying Squad Golfs. Looks like a bunch of Coloured cops again. No, there're two whites among them.

'Evening, evening,' say the men from the different cars. They know 127 Martha Street very well. But they never do anything. No one ever wants to lay a charge or make a case. It costs too much money. So they come and calm things down a bit, see that no one gets hurt too badly.

The whole lot from Fort Knox are in the street now. They're waiting for him, Lambert, to come out. He knows the two from across the road are watching him as he stands here behind their front gate. Pop and Mol and Treppie are also outside. They stand on the front stoep, holding on to each other's sleeves. They're also waiting to see if he'll come out.

Well, then, in that case he might as well do it. And let's see if Johnny has the nerve to grab him by the throat, here in front of the police. The police won't let them punch him around. They look cool, those police. They stand around with cigarettes, calming people down with their hands.

Toby and Gerty run up and down the lawn, barking.

Little Flowers looks like she's flipped completely. She walks in circles around the Fort Knox bunch, who are now closing in on him. 'Slip-slop' go her slippers on the tar. They grab him and start pushing him around.

'Knock him for a six, Johnny, knock him! Knock his fucken block off!'

Pink Bikini's hair looks wild. She's explaining to the constables. What does she know, anyway?

'And it was my anniversary, my party for my first anniversary. And then he started peeping at us.'

'Ja,' says Johnny, 'he peeps at us every time we braai, for years and years now, the fucken rubbish.'

'They broke our window, on purpose,' says Lambert. He knows that doing things on purpose makes a difference.

'That was my fucken vase, my vase that I got for my anniversary!' screams Pink Bikini. 'What were we supposed to do? He came over our wall and jumped on the hamburger stand. So I threw him with the vase!'

'Self-defence!' says Johnny.

'They broke our pipe, on purpose,' says Lambert, pointing to the roof so the policemen can see.

'Fuck your pipe, man,' says Johnny, 'and fuck you too, with or without a pipe!'

'My mom and them are old, and now the TV's broken and there's no overflow on the geyser any more,' says Lambert.

'Ag, man, your mother's cunt!' shouts Speedo. 'Your mother's hairy arse!'

Lambert sees people coming out of their houses all the way up and down Martha Street. Dogs are barking for blocks around. Couples coming home late from their Saturday night dates stop their cars to look. They switch off the car radios so they can listen.

He breaks loose. His mother and them must come now. Why should he take the shouting all on his own? They're also in this. But they don't want to come out. They just move a little closer to the wire fence.

'Just check, old Lambert,' shouts Treppie. 'People think we're famous. Check all the people, Lambert. The fucken Benades' fucken late night show! Scenes from forthcoming attractions. Bladdy movie stars, that's what we are!'

Fuck Treppie. He's fucken drunk and now he's shooting his mouth off too.

'What about our sail, hey? What about our stand, hey? Hey?' says Johnny Paunch, pushing Lambert around. The constables hold Johnny back.

'Come, Johnny, it's enough now,' says Kiepie.

'Yes, enough,' says Big Flowers. 'The police also have to sleep.' She smiles at the constable. Who does she think she is?

'It was a plain accident,' says Lambert. 'There was no intention.'

'No intention's backside, you hear me, it's backside! You, you peep at us when we braai!' It's Blue Bikini shouting at him now. She's wearing a man's shirt over her bikini.

'Hit him, hit him, Johnny. Knock the daylights out of him,' shouts Little Flowers. She still hasn't stopped walking around in circles in the street.

'Tell Lambert he must come inside now,' he hears his mother say. 'Come, Pop, tell him to come inside now.' His people move a little closer.

Pop's mouth hangs open.

'Button up your pants and go and tell him now,' says Treppie.

Pop walks up to the gate. He holds on to the fence with one hand and buttons up his pants with the other. He nudges the postbox with his foot, pushing it out of his way. It lies on the grass, its little arms sticking out in all directions.

'Peeep' goes the front gate as Pop carefully pushes it open. Lambert sees Pop coming. Pop works his way through the people, through big shoulders in uniforms. He pushes his way through, so he can get to Lambert in the middle. Then he finds Lambert's elbow.

'Come now, my boy,' he says. 'Come inside now. Everything's over. It's okay now. Just come inside.'

Pop pulls him out, backwards, backwards, away from the mob of people standing there. Some of them follow him, trying to block his way.

'Just you peep at us once more when we braai, you fucken rubbish!' says Johnny, who keeps following them as Pop pulls him further away.

'Next time we'll break your fucken overflow right off for you,' says Blue Jeans.

'We'll pull your wire right out next time! Out, once and for all, you hear me!' Speedo shouts into his face.

'So you can stop peeping at us when we braai,' say the two Bikinis, together.

'Hey, you lot,' says Big Flowers, 'leave the poor bastard now. Leave him. That's enough now. Come inside.'

Two policemen get into their car and drive off. Two other pairs stand around for a while. They look as cool as cucumbers.

'Just look at the house,' says the one. Lambert sees how they look the house up and down, with their hands on their sides.

'Looks like it's falling to pieces,' says the other one.

'Just look at all the rubbish under that roof,' says the first one.

'Bad,' says the white constable. 'Bad to the bone.'

'Ag, Jesus, shame,' says the Coloured constable.

'At least the lawn is nice and neat,' says another Coloured constable.

The radios in the police cars crackle and make 'peep-peep' noises. The cars are full of voices. Pop has pulled Lambert almost all the way to the stoep, backwards, backwards, backwards. His mother holds the door open. Treppie walks round the house. He chucks the broken pieces of pipe and gutter on to a heap. 'Sow the seed, oh sow the seed,' he sings at the top of his voice. Then he goes inside.

The front door closes.

The stoep-light switches off.

Lambert's mother pours him a drink. They all stand around looking at him. He's sitting in Pop's chair.

'Your foot,' says his mother.

His foot's swollen blue and purple.

'I kicked him slap-bang in the mouth,' he says.

'Black belt,' says Treppie.

'Your head,' says his mother. The blood has dried in long strips down his forehead. Where's the hole?

'Let's see,' she says.

'Don't touch!' he says, jerking his head away.

'Tough,' says Treppie. 'Tough like Stallone.'

'Bedtime,' says Pop. 'Come, let's go to bed.'

They all leave. In the passage, his mother picks up the piece of plaster that fell off the wall. She looks at the wall.

'Cracks,' she says. 'Just look at the cracks.' She wipes her hand over the wall, once, as if she wants to wipe away the cracks.

He remains seated for a long time in Pop's chair. He looks at the hole in the wall where the plaster fell off, at the cracks all around it. One by one he looks at the cracks, how they run up the wall, until he can't see them any more, until they disappear into the high-gloss paint.

But he knows, under the paint they go on and on, invisible to the eye. Once it gets going, a crack in plaster is something that keeps running. Once it starts, you can never stop it.

7

~

RUNNING REPAIRS

It's Monday morning. Treppie's standing on the front lawn, checking out Saturday night's damage.

Last night, Sunday night, he also came outside to look around. The only time he usually stands out here is when he gets home on the bus from the Chinese, 'cause Pop doesn't always come and fetch him. Then, in the last red glow of the sunset, he screws up his eyes until he lines up the evening star with the top of the overflow pipe's U-bend. He squints until he has the U-bend's upright aligned with the foot of the aerial. Then it looks like a weird little tree or something.

It's something he likes doing after the walk home from the bus stop in Thornton. It's his own time, after work, before he goes back into the house again. It's time that he uses to tune himself in, to organise the space in his head. He's noticed that when he doesn't first tune himself in, he's off-centre for the rest of the night.

But last night wasn't a work night and there was also nothing on the roof. Fuck-all he could use to get himself aligned with the evening star, and God knows, he needed it.

There goes my Christmas tree too, he said, speaking aloud to himself. But Mol had poked her head under the sun-filter curtains that he'd put up with nails, staring at him through the window. Then she came out and stood next to him, still holding the loose pelmet in her hands.

'What Christmas tree you talking about?' she asked.

Now how do you explain a thing like that to Mol? It would take a fucken year. So he just showed her the evening star.

Mol was quiet for a while and then she said: 'Little star.'

Lambert came out to look as well. Pop too. It was the first time since Saturday night that all of them were outside again. They'd spent Sunday indoors after the fuck-around on Saturday night. The whole of Sunday, Fort Knox played its music full blast. Looking for trouble again. Everyone looks for fucken shit in this place. And that's just about all you'll ever get around here, too. He once told them Triomf's name was all wrong, by a long shot. It should have been Shitfontein or Crapville. When he said that, Lambert asked him if he knew that there was a business called Triomf and that it made fertiliser. Lambert's not stupid.

Then Pop said they should count their blessings. They mustn't start looking for shit now.

Pop's fuses are blown. 'What blessings?' he asked him.

'Well,' Pop said, 'at least we still have each other, and a roof over our heads.'

That's what Old Pop always used to say, too, way back in the thirties when they kept fucking up so badly in Vrededorp. Time and time again.

So when Pop came out last night and asked, 'What you all looking at?', he took the gap and said to him, very nicely: 'We're looking at each other, Pop, and the roof over our heads, 'cause that's all we've still got left to look at.'

Then Mol said: 'We're looking at the little star on the Christmas tree!'

Suddenly Mol looked like she wanted to cry.

'What shit you talking now again, hey, Ma?' Lambert shouted.

Lambert always shouts when Mol looks like she wants to start crying.

In the end they all stood there like fucken zombies looking at the evening star, 'cause the overflow pipe and the TV aerial were lying on a heap next to the house where Treppie had chucked them, together with pieces of broken gutter.

After a while, Pop said: 'Stars are very old.'

Lambert said Pop was talking rubbish, stars were fucken dead.

'Dead from what?' Mol asked.

Lambert told her they were dead from time. Can you believe it, he actually said that.

When they go to the Newlands library to get books for Mol, Lambert reads all kinds of things in the *Encyclopaedia Britannica*. Then he repeats everything he's read to Mol, but he adds his own little bits to the stories he tells. It's easy to carry on like that with Mol. She swallows just about anything you say. Lambert learnt it by watching him, Treppie. He does it a lot with Mol, although he's really doing it for himself. But his own stories never come from the *Encyclopaedia Britannica*. They come from newspapers, about things that happen to people. Lambert's stories are about insects and engines and stars and things, about how everything works. His stories are about things that *don't* work. Not because they're broken, but because they are the way they are. Lambert tells Mol things 'cause he thinks it impresses him, Treppie. Lambert wants to show him he can also talk a hole into Mol's head. But he's not impressed. There's just a hole where Mol's head is supposed to be anyway.

When he, Treppie, tells Mol things, it's not to see if she can still think, but to see if she can still feel. He finds it hard to believe Mol can still feel anything. So he tries her out, every day. It's a fucken miracle. He can't figure out if he wants her to feel things or not to feel anything at all. That's 'cause what's better for Mol will be worse for him. Basically, he has to make sure Mol and Pop and Lambert still feel things, otherwise he, Treppie, will go to glory. It's just that he has to dig deeper and deeper nowadays to find Mol's feelings. First you get blood and shit and gore. Then only feelings. But it's Lambert's job, that. He doesn't even have to open his mouth. All he does is wind Lambert up a bit and give him the tools. Then he runs on automatic. Lambert digs, and when the arteries are open nice and wide, then he, Treppie, can go and do some inspection, to see if there's any gold-dust left in the dead mines. Pearls before swine. Who else can see them for what they are?

Sometimes Lambert says things that make Treppie think he's got a clue. Last night he went and said stars die from time. Mol just stood there and gaped at him. Lambert said yes, the stars died a long time ago. What you saw now was their light, still travelling after so many years.

'How far is it from here to there?' asked Mol.

'Light years, Ma. Light years,' said Lambert.

'What's a light year?' she asked.

Mol always asks more and more questions, until Lambert doesn't know what to say any more. That's what he, Treppie, likes, 'cause then he can spice up the story with lots of bullshit. That's the real surprise package. Lambert thinks he's fucken cute when he talks shit into Mol's head. But this time, just when he wanted to start improvising, those two wankers from Fort Knox stuck their heads over the wall.

'Just look how hard they're looking,' said the one.

'They're looking at their roof,' said the other.

'I suppose they're going to fix it now,' said the one.

'They must think they can see in the dark like vampires.'

Then they all quickly went inside again.

It's Monday today. A bright day, with no stars in the sky, dead or alive. The scum from Fort Knox left early to go and put up their take-away stands on street corners.

He knows he'll have to lead the way here today. Repair the damage. Pop's as good as dead and Lambert's half-dead from all his stuffing around. God alone knows how much more trouble he'll make if the television isn't working by tonight. Next thing he'll smash the TV to pieces as well. And then the whole lot of them will go to glory, 'cause TV's the one thing that keeps Lambert quiet. He sits and watches everything. He watches so hard he even forgets his Klipdrift. He watches *Thought for the Day* and the flag blowing as they sing the anthem, right to the very end. And then, when the test pattern comes back on, he watches the rubbish that he hires from Ponta do Sol. Lambert should get a TV implanted in his brain. Then he'll be fine. Then he can go lie down with a permanent car chase between his ears.

He told Mol and Pop, all those years ago: poke that child out with knitting needles, and then rinse yourself inside with Sunlight soap and Epsom salts. Before it got too big. But of course they didn't want to listen. He told Mol there's a fucken dinosaur coming out of her. At four months her stomach was already stretched to hell and gone. But they were nice and soft in their heads. Pop said: 'Ag, Treppie, it's someone who can look after us one day when we're old.'

Stupid fucken fools! And look what they've got now! A fucken freak show. And who has to do the looking after? Them! And it's not just a question of care, it's *cares*. Worries.

He's already warned them, one day the TV people are going to come and make a movie about them. He's not sure what kind of a movie, a horror or a sitcom or a documentary. He thinks they're too soft for horror and too sad for a sitcom, so maybe they're just right for a documentary. Documentaries are about weird things like force-feeding parrots for export. He told Lambert he'd better behave himself, otherwise they'd come and ask him to make a special appearance on *Wildlife Today*. Lambert said only threatened species got shown on that programme. The poor fucker kids himself.

Now the front door opens. It's Mol. Gone with the wind.

'What you looking at now?' she asks.

'I'm looking at the damage.'

'Damage,' she says. 'Terrible damage.'

'So, are you going to help me this morning, Mol?'

'Who, me?'

'Yes, Mol, me and you. We're going to play *Helpmekaar* and *Reddings-daadbond*.'

'Huh?'

'Never mind, Mol, just help a little here, 'cause you're the only who's up and about this morning. Or would you like me to go wake King Kong and Rip van Winkle?'

'Who? No, leave them,' Mol says quickly. 'I'll help you. Leave them so they can get some rest.'

'Fine,' he says. 'It's nice that you want to help; just a pity it's a bit late.'

'Late?'

'Yes, Mol, late, like a dead star. You should've helped when it could still have made a difference.'

'Difference?'

'Yes, it would have made a big difference if you'd brought him down.'
'Who?'

'Lambert, when he was still inside you. He's caused us nothing but misery, right from the start. Look at the roof. Look at you. We're all in our glory just 'cause you and Pop wanted to play housy-housy. Man and wife. Big happy family, I say. Next time Fort Knox will rip the whole roof down. And after that the walls. It's just a matter of time.'

Mol looks at the heap on the grass. Gutters, the overflow, the TV aerial.

'The poor bastard belongs in a madhouse,' he says, shoving the gutters around with his foot. Most of the pieces are rusted through. 'He should be strapped into a fucken jacket and put on to a steel trolley. Then the nurses can hose porridge down his throat with an enema pump.'

'Sis, man, Treppie!' says Mol. 'Sis!'

'Don't come and sis me,' he says. He can feel he's got her going now.

'You're a devil, Treppie,' says Mol, drawing in more breath for the next sentence. 'And he takes after you, Treppie, that's what! It's the truth. Look at Pop. He's soft. Look at me, I'm also soft. You're the one with the attitude. Stubborn! Devil's blood!'

'He's not my fucken child,' Treppie shouts. 'I always pulled out. Aimed high, to the side, 'cause I know what comes from that kind of thing! So don't come and talk shit here on a Monday morning!'

'Evil seed can fly,' says Mol.

'What? What you say there?'

'I said the devil's seed can fly through the air. Devils can't be put off. Once they've got their sights on you, it's tickets!'

'What rubbish you talking now?'

'Lambert says it's in the *Britannica*!'

'Let me tell you something, Mol. It's not in the *Britannica*, it's in Lambert's sick head. Together with all the other shit-stories he sells you.'

'Well, if it's shit, then he gets half of it from you, Treppie!'

He can see she thinks she's got him in a corner now.

'Ag really, Mol, like what?'

'Like that you and Pop are going to get him a whore for his birthday.'

'I see, and who told you that?'

'Pop said—'

'Trust him.'

'I said to Pop he must tell you, you mustn't do this kind of thing to Lambert. If you promised him, you'd better do it, otherwise . . .'

'Otherwise what, Mol?'

'You know bladdy well what, Treppie. In the end I'll go lie down and die in a heap somewhere. I'm completely buggered down under. I can't any more.'

'Don't come and moan at me, sister. I told you and that stupid fool of a Pop, long time ago, you must be careful. But the two of you thought you were playing leading roles in *Genesis*. Just like that first fucken batch – Adam and Eve, Cain and Abel – all in the same family, and Lot with his randy daughters, and Noah, whose own sons buggered him. No wonder the whole lot of them drowned in the end. They say inbreeding makes people's bones so heavy they can't even tread water.'

'Really, Treppie? Where did you hear that?'

'In the *Britannica*, Molletjie, in the *Britannica*,' Treppie says, cackling.

Mol picks up one of the postbox's broken struts and throws it at him.

'Devil!' she screams. 'Satan's child!' The strut flies through the air in an arc. Treppie has plenty of time to duck.

He laughs at her. 'You must aim for the middle wicket, old girl, the middle wicket.'

'No manners,' says Mol.

'You'd better get your aim right if you want to help this morning, old girl! Go fetch the ladder behind the den's wall so I can get up on the roof. Then drag the toolbox on to the stoep so you can pass me things I need. And when you've done that, go look on the scrapheap for a piece of pipe, about two fingers thick. Ask Lambert where he keeps his glue. And while you're there, you may as well bring out the welding box and the helmet as well.'

'Huh?'

'Ja, Mol. Running repairs.'

Treppie looks at her, standing there with dazed eyes. He first saw that look on her face when he found her sitting in the fridge after she lost Lambert's spanner in the long grass. The day everything burnt down. Ever since then, she shuts up like a clam the moment anyone asks her about tools.

'Huh?' Treppie mimics her. 'Huh? Huh? Huh?

'Come,' he says. 'Shake your head a little first, Mol, like this,' and he shakes his head.

Mol shakes her head. Then she stops. 'Why?'

'Just shake a little more,' he says, and he bends his head closer to her, as if he wants to listen.

'What?' asks Mol.

'Don't you hear anything?'

'What am I supposed to hear?'

'The loose screws in your head, sister, a whole assortment of nuts and bolts, all of them odd pairs – pop rivets, fissure plugs, wing-nuts, you name it!'

'Wing-nut,' says Mol.

'Nice and scrambled, hey,' Treppie says. 'It's hereditary.'

'Scrambled what?'

'Scrambled eggs, Mol, scrambled stories, scrambled genes, scrambled rails, we're one big pot of scrambled Benades.'

'One big pot,' says Mol.

'Yes, Mol, and they can put us inside a centrifuge and spin us till we burst, but we won't unscramble.'

'Centrifuge,' says Mol.

'Ja, old sister, we're twisted into each other like the innards of a fridge; remember, like those fucked-up fridges we sometimes used to get for repairs, when their motors seized up from the wrong voltage.'

'Voltage,' says Mol.

'Ja, from too little voltage. The motor gets too hot, and then it seizes. It's from too few volts that they do that.'

'Volts,' says Mol. 'We've got too few volts.'

'Now you're talking, sister. Now you're talking.'

Mol goes and sits on the edge of the stoep. She takes the cigarettes out of her housecoat pocket and lights up. 'First sit a little,' she says, blowing out smoke.

Treppie looks at Mol, who first wants to sit. The sky above Triomf is blowtorch blue. He looks at the half-cut grass. Then he kicks at a fresh molehill, and remembers how, all those years ago, they came to the city as children with Old Pop and Old Mol. All the way from Bloemhof, on a Railways bus. He was very small then, five or six. All their possessions were squeezed into trunks behind them, on the lorry's trailer.

He was still on Old Mol's hip the day she let the screen door slam closed for the last time. She closed the outside latch and said: 'Farewell, Klipfontein.'

Klipfontein was his grandma and grandpa's farm in the Western Transvaal. The depression stripped them bare. There was no water, any-way. Just stones. That's how his father explained things to him.

Then his father decided to write a letter to the Railways. He'd never been a Hertzog man, but he always said Hertzog's Railways plan for poor whites was the best thing an Afrikaner had ever thought up.

He can still see his father sitting at the scrubbed kitchen table, chewing the top end of his pencil. Labouring over that letter. His mother rewrote it carefully in ink when it was finally done. A fucken movie, then already.

After a month they got word: they must come, the Railways were only too happy to help their people.

His mother caught all forty of her geese. She stripped them bare so she could sell the feathers and the down to the Jew trader. Then she slaughtered the raw and featherless pink geese, together with the chickens and the turkeys. She cleaned them and then she took them to town for selling. The cows and sheep and their few pigs had long since been auctioned off.

Those days he still cried for the poultry. He remembers the scene with his turkey, a big old bugger who could go 'bifff! bifff!' with puffed-out wings and shake his red wattles, making a 'cooloo-cooloo-cooloo!' sound when he felt horny. He watched through the kitchen window as his mother cut off the turkey's head. It slipped off the block and out of his mother's hands. Then, with blood spewing from its neck, it began to throw high jinks in the dust, right under his nose. He couldn't eat for four days after that, not until they were in the city and their father bought them doughnuts at a coolie-shop. Grandpa put the turnploughs, forks and spades together in bundles, and a man from town came to write it all up. Then he loaded the equipment on to his co-operative van and took it away. The house's movable goods were also on the van. Spot and Buster had to go live with Grandpa and Grandma on another farm in the district, with one of Grandpa's brothers. Then, already, an inbred lot. He remembers how his Ouma, the first Mol, walked in slow circles around the house with a long-nosed watering can that she'd kept behind. She was spraying the last water from the rain-tank onto her stinkafrikaners. Her African marigolds. 'Shame, she's becoming a child again, leave her alone,' his mother said, and his father wiped his eyes with his arm. 'So, now the old people are becoming bywoners. Labourers on other people's land. And the new generation are trekking to Gomorrah,' he said.

That night, their last on the farm, they all sat around the oil-lamp on the wooden planks of the kitchen floor. By then the chairs were gone, too. In the middle, on a plank, stood a little bucket of milk porridge with cinnamon, and a pot-bread sent over by the woman on the next farm.

Treppie starts. What's that noise across the road now? It's that dyke-mobile with its loose bearings. When those two moved in here, the neighbours also came over bearing trays full of 'tuisgebak' for them. A Boer will be a Boer, dyke or no dyke. The more things change, the more they stay the same.

His father said he, Treppie, could have his mouth organ, only if he'd eat some of the milk porridge. But he didn't want to. Later he got the mouth organ in any case. Actually, he inherited it after his father's death. But he swore he'd never play it. It's bad luck to play on the instrument of a suicide case. That's what he said to Old Mol when she kept on so about it.

He actually meant murderer, 'cause Old Pop had beat the life right out of him, to say nothing of the little music that was left in him. So then he said Little Pop could have the mouth organ. Little Pop was musical, he had a good ear and he had the beat. But even though Little Pop learnt fast, playing the songs of old Hendrik Susan's band, and the Briels and Chris Blignaut and all of them, and even though he once did a solo at the Garment Workers' Union, he never played anywhere near as well as Old Pop.

Old Pop was a genius on the mouth organ. He remembers how Old Pop could keep a whole farmhouse hop-dancing with nothing but his mouth organ. Later, in Fordsburg, they didn't have a farmhouse any more and there weren't any people who wanted to dance with them anyway. But every now and again Old Pop still played. Most of the time he played sad songs or Salvation Army tunes. He used to play Old Mol into tears.

Old Pop played full-mouthed notes, with all kinds of trills and frills inbetween: majors on the out-breaths and minors on the in-breaths, the long notes stretched out on trills and then half smothered as he made a bowl-shape with his two hands, vibrating them on either side of the mouth organ.

Old Pop played all the way to Jo'burg. He played jolly songs. To give them courage for the City of Gold, he said. But Old Mol was already crying. A long day's journey into night, if you ask him.

The bus took them to the Railways boarding house in Vrededorp, for poor white arrivals. And there they stood, with all their trunks and things, on the front stoep. Before Old Pop could even knock, a fat woman with a cigarette in her mouth opened the door.

'You must be Mister Benade,' she said in English, without taking the cigarette out of her mouth. She ignored Old Pop's outstretched hand. She looked them up and down as they stood there and then she said: 'Ah, thank God, no small babies. We have enough of them here.'

She took a little bottle from her apron pocket and held it out to Old Mol. 'Before you do anything else, I want you to take a bath. Use five drops of this,' she said, pushing the little bottle into Old Mol's face. 'I don't want any vermin in my lodgings.'

Old Pop then said to the woman: 'We may be poor, but at least we are clean, madam.' But she said to him: 'Do as you're told. Beggars can't be choosers.'

They did as they were told. First Old Pop and Old Mol shared the bath water, the three children going next. Old Pop was grinding his teeth so hard his cheeks began puffing up. When he put the three of them into the bath, he said: 'Now we're being dipped like raw kaffirs.'

They stuck out the boarding house for just three days. Screaming babies kept Pop out of sleep, and the stench of old floor polish and cooked cabbage made Treppie and Mol and Pop so sick they couldn't eat.

After his third day of looking for a house, Old Pop came home with bright eyes. Oh yes, he'd found them a semi. The people who lived there were moving out in a week's time 'cause the old woman, a garment worker, was blind, and the man had lost a leg on the Railways. They couldn't afford the rent any more. The Benades could come straight away and help with the last week's rent – they could certainly do with a bit of help.

'What's a semi?' Old Mol asked, and his father said it was half a house. Then his mother asked, wouldn't there be too many of them, living with other people in half a house? But his father said it was temporary – after a week they'd have the whole semi to themselves. Two bedrooms, a kitchen and a bathroom.

'Are you sure?' Old Mol still asked. She didn't trust this business at all.

In the end they spent more than three full years sharing half a house with the Beyleveldts. And it wasn't even a proper half-house. There was a passage linking it to the other half, where three more families lived. All with strapping big children who were so famished they stripped the Benades' food cupboard bare. So in the end everyone was hungry, and they all stole each other's food.

Old Pop worked long hours. He was a stoker on the Railways. Mrs Beyleveldt took Old Mol to the clothing factory and presented her there as a replacement for herself. So at least there was some money in the house, even if it was altogether too little to plug the gaps. Old Mol had to take on piece-work: shirts that she repaired until late at night on Mrs Beyleveldt's old Singer.

They all lived in one room. The children saw everything the grown-ups did. And they heard every word the grown-ups said.

Old Pop and Old Mol fought bitterly. Mostly they fought over the Beyleveldts. Old Mol used to say the offer of the half-house had just been a trick to pick them clean.

They had to pay all the rent on their own, buy all the food and do all the housework, 'cause the blind woman and the one-legged man were incapable of doing anything for themselves. And Old Mol wasn't allowed to use the sewing machine 'for nothing', she had to 'hire' it at a 'per-day tariff', even though she could use it only at night.

'Now you listen to me, Martinus Lambertus Benade,' his mother always said. 'I didn't come to Johannesburg to be a charity worker. In Klipfontein I could at least spend some time in my own house, with my own family. I could slaughter a decent chicken for the pot and keep us alive by selling down and soap.'

Then Old Pop used to slam down his lunch-tin and tell her she must stop complaining. She still had both her eyes. He still had both his legs. They should count their blessings. They had each other. They had a roof over their heads. Ja, the story of their lives. Then his mother would ask his father to name all the things they were supposed to have. All she could name were the things they no longer had. Many times she complained how she'd baked two loaves of bread and cooked a big pot of soup, just yesterday. Enough for the whole family as well as the Beyleveldts. Soup that she made from the cheapest soup bones and barley, and from vegetables she found in the dustbins. It took her hours to sort the vegetables and cut out the good pieces. She'd worked until late at night with her own two hands, which were full of holes from the Singer's needles. And then, when she went to the kitchen the next morning, the pot was empty and both loaves of bread were gone.

Those days Old Mol used to knead the bread. For the first rise, she covered it with an old greycoat that someone on the Railways had given Old Pop.

But no one could live on bread alone, she used to say. When she started like this, nothing could stop her. She used to name all the things they would soon be needing but didn't have. New shoes. Warm clothes for winter. A pair of glasses for her 'cause her eyes couldn't take the poor light at the factory, and the light in their room, which was even worse. Doctors' fees and medicine for Little Mol and Little Pop. Their chests were closing up again. How was she supposed to know what was wrong with them?

Then his father would tell her to shut her mouth this very second, he couldn't bear it any longer. Wasn't he, a white man, doing work that no white man should ever have to do? But his mother wouldn't shut up. She said she wished they were kaffirs. Then at least she'd be able to give them porridge every day, with no salt or milk or sugar. Then they could dress in rags and no one would even know the difference.

At this point, Old Pop would thump her on the chest and tell her in that case she should go find herself a kaffir husband. So she could bring forth bastards, if that's how little she felt for her volk.

His mother always said: 'Not in front of the children, Lambertus.'

Later, Old Mol took to making their food on a Primus in the room. She locked the bread in a shoe cupboard. And she put up a sheet between the children and the grown-ups. But they still saw and heard everything. They watched the shadows on the sheet when Old Pop climbed on top of Old Mol and began riding her wildly, until she started crying and calling out the Lord's name.

When their mother and father were out working, the children stayed behind on their own until he, Treppie, was old enough to go to school. In the beginning, they all used to get up together, dress for school, and then eat the bread and jam their mother had made for them. Then his father used to say to his brother: 'Look after your sister nicely, Little Pop.' And his mother used to say to his sister: 'Look after Treppie nicely, Molletjie, remember he's the smallest.'

'All we have in the world is each other. Us Benades must stand together,' his father sometimes said with a crack in his voice. When his father said that, his mother's head jerked slightly, just like it jerked when old One-Leg Beyleveldt used to say to them: You must do this, or, You must do that. Then Old Pop asked Mr Beyleveldt how many Us there were in his alphabet. They were trying to look after their own. He must please just leave them in peace.

Old Mol was also getting nice and mixed up. She knew 'each other' was too little to live by, but what else could they do? Everything was starting to fuck out, even then.

And so that's how they learnt to look after 'each other'. How he and Little Mol and Little Pop learnt to take care of 'each other'.

'Look after' was supposed to mean they were valuable. More valuable than other people. Most other people couldn't look after themselves properly. That was Old Mol's opinion in those days. She clung to that belief, even though she knew there was something wrong with it. What's more, it also meant that if they wanted to fight or look for trouble, they had to do it with each other and not with other people. A 'well-looked-after' person was someone who stayed the way he was, a person who kept to himself, to his own kind.

His father always used to say: 'That which belongs together, must remain together.' That's why he voted for Malan's National Party in the 1948 election. Out of family instinct more than anything else. There was no other choice.

And that's why Mol still nods her head up and down so hard when those two snotnoses from the NP come and tell them how 'valuable' they are to the Party, how they belong heart and soul to the big National Family, whose members are now looking after each other 'across the boundaries of race, language and culture'. Mol doesn't hear the last part. All she hears are Old Mol and Old Pop's words.

To him, those two sound more like far-fetched versions of Hertzog or Smuts, like margarine that has everything to make it spread but still isn't butter. It's a long time since he's seen any butter. And he doesn't feel at all looked after by the NP and their so-called canvassers. He feels they want to use him like they've always used people. He knows they talk behind his back. Fuck knows what gets pumped into *their* heads at headquarters. He just wishes Lambert would corner that girl with the airs and give her some of his treatment, so she can also learn what 'belongs to' and 'look after' mean.

In later years, the three of them often stayed in bed together after the grown-ups had left the house. School was shit – they were made to swallow spoonfuls of cod-liver oil, so they stayed in bed instead. Little

Pop's dick could already stand up nicely by then. He showed Treppie and Mol how to rub it. They killed time on those mornings by rubbing Little Pop's dick. It took away the hunger. They were allowed to have their morning bread only once Pop had come three times; otherwise they'd get hungry for their afternoon bread too soon. And if that got eaten, they stayed hungry all day, until their mother came home from the factory at night.

Hungry time, time that you feel in your stomach, is a terrible thing. But what's worse is how time feels when you see the same things happening over and over again. Like things that get broken and then get fixed again. Over and over again, fucken broken and fixed again. And nothing ever gets fixed properly.

Treppie suddenly sees Mol coming round the corner. She's dragging the ladder behind her.

'Pick the damn thing up, woman,' he shouts. His voice sounds too high. He mustn't think about these things. It makes him shaky. It causes accidents.

'It's heavy, Treppie,' says Mol.

'Yes, Mol, that's what you call the effect of gravity.'

'Gravity,' says Mol.

'Yes,' says Treppie, 'that's the force that holds us down here in Triomf, in Martha Street, on our feet, in our skins, together, with a roof over our heads. Otherwise we'd all have floated away by now, one by one, and fallen to fucken pieces.'

Then, for the first time, he sees Lambert. He's standing on the stoep with no shirt. He's got that mad look in his eyes that he gets when he's been lying on his bed for too long.

'Ja,' says Lambert. 'That's why stars pass out sometimes, pfft! Not enough gravity there where they are. A star,' he says, 'dissolves in time. In light years. In space, like an Aspro in a glass of water.'

And as he says this, he looks like someone with a sledgehammer who wants to beat something to a pulp.

8

~

PEST CONTROL

Dear Lord, just look at her from all the stings. But now Pop's rubbing Prep on her sore places, and that's nice and cool. Mol's sitting in her chair with her legs spread out in front of her. She's holding Gerty on her lap. Gerty breathes heavily. The poor thing had the whole swarm on top of her and now her eyes have closed up from all the swelling. Mol can't bear even to look at Gerty. Instead, she looks down at her legs where Pop's busy rubbing on the Prep. Her legs got the worst of it. Her arms too, plus a few stings on her neck and two on her head, right on top. Right through her hair. Pop's already done her head and her neck. He started on top, working his way down, but now she stinks of the stuff. Pop said he would first rub Lambert, 'cause Lambert got the worst of it, then her, and then Treppie last of all. But Lambert didn't want any of it. And Treppie said no ointment in the world could make the Benades look or feel any better.

Treppie's acting nasty 'cause Pop's the only one who didn't get stung. Pop was inside, and Treppie sprained his foot. That's why he's feeling so sorry for himself.

Pop must get a move on with his rubbing. Any minute now the pest-control people will be here. It's Wednesday already, which means those two from the NP will also be coming. She's really not in the mood for them today.

Even before Pop took them all to the hospital for injections, on Monday, he phoned the municipality. Since then, they've all just been sitting around in the house, looking at the bees outside.

It was a hellishly hot day, and Treppie spent too long working on the roof. That's why it happened. Monday he decides today's the day he's going to fix everything Fort Knox broke on the roof. Just like Treppie to choose the hottest day for something like that. Then she had to run up and down fetching tools for him. And each time she walked to the den at the back, she saw the bees swarming around the vent, there near the foundation. But she didn't say anything. She was too busy trying to keep her head straight so she could remember what Treppie was asking her to bring.

It took hours. First Treppie cut the broken overflow pipe straight with a hacksaw and then he fixed it on to another pipe with glue, taping the whole thing up as well. He splinted the TV-aerial with a piece of iron and knocked it back into the roof. And all this time she had to pass all kinds of things to him up there on the roof. She had to climb halfway up the ladder each time. Up and down, up and down. After a while it felt like she was going to pass out, she was so tired. Lambert didn't even lift a finger. He just stood there on the stoep, screwing up his eyes. He felt dizzy, he said. But he wasn't too dizzy to chip in all the time.

Those joints Treppie was making, he shouted from the stoep, wouldn't stand the first strong wind. In that case, Treppie shouted back, Lambert would have to fix them, 'cause there was practically nothing those two hands of his couldn't do, or was he imagining things again? And then he winked at Lambert.

Treppie drives Lambert mad just by the way he says things. All Monday morning, up there on the roof, Treppie peppered him. Lambert, he said, was standing there on the stoep just like a shift boss. So now, he said, what did the Inspector of Works think about this or that? And if Lambert wanted to peep at the people next door, he shouted, then he should get on to the roof right from the start. With his welding helmet on so he could look through the sparks, 'cause from where Treppie was standing he could see right into Fort Knox's main bedroom. No one was there now, but he could see more than enough evidence of 'burning passion'. That was when Treppie began to play the fool, hugging himself up there in the hot sun. He was grabbing and touching himself something terrible. All you saw were those claws of his, groping himself around the shoulders. He began to sing 'Oh oh oh what a night!' Loudly, up into the sky. For all the world to see.

At first, Lambert didn't catch on it was Treppie who was working on his nerves so much. He thought the bees must be making him feel so mad. By then the bees had come out of their hole. They were flying round the house like bomber planes. Must've been worked up from all the commotion and the welding's white light.

Fucken bee, Lambert kept saying. He picked up the steel Treppie was clearing off the roof, and then he chucked it down again. Lambert was still slapping at the bees when he suddenly dropped everything. He grabbed the yellow bucket she was using to clean scrap iron for Treppie, and then he took it with him to the tap. 'Fucken bastards! Now I'm going to drown the whole fucken lot of you. Buzzing round my blarry head all the time!'

He limped off with his sore foot to go fill the bucket with water.

'Ag, don't be so spiteful, man,' Treppie shouted. 'They must think you're God's own double sunflower, with those crooked saucer-eyes of yours.'

But Lambert was already on the other side of the house. He was making for the air-vent in the foundation. The next thing she and Treppie saw him sprinting round the side of the house, with Gerty on his heels, his mouth opening and closing. The bees were clogged in a black swarm around his head. His face was white and he was running hell for leather with that big lumbering body of his, sore foot and all.

Treppie, meanwhile, was running in circles on the roof, trying to keep track of Lambert as he ran around the house. Then she also took off after him. As she ran, she pulled off her pink housecoat and dragged it under the tap, which Lambert had left running, so she could throw it over Lambert's head. But Lambert was shouting and swinging his arms like a windmill. And each time she and Gerty passed a window on their way round the house, she saw Pop's face trying to keep up with the goings-on outside.

'Stay inside, Pop!' she shouted. 'Keep Toby in!'

'Don't come out, Pop!' Treppie shouted, but he was laughing so much he could hardly talk. 'It looks like Kyalami out here. Old Lambert's doing laps! Bzzz! Bzzz!'

The more she shouted that Treppie must get off the roof to come and help her, the less he seemed to hear.

All she could see in front of her was Lambert's back, twisting and turning as he ran with the bees, who were bunched in swarms around his shoulders. Every now and again he managed to get a sound out, a kind of low growl she'd never heard coming out of his mouth before.

'Ow-whoo, ow-whoo!' Gerty cried as the bees stung her.

'Oo-ooo! Hee-hee-hee-hee,' Treppie laughed from the roof. 'Lambert, it's not a merry-go-round, man, change direction. Other side! Hee-hee! I'm going to piss myself here!'

Treppie was still laughing like that when his foot slipped and he began to slide down the roof on his backside. He turned on to his stomach as he tried to find something to grab on to. He wanted to break the fall by wedging his foot in the gutter, but the gutter wasn't there any more, and he fell, 'boof!' right on to the ground. He landed in the molehills, thumping red dust up into the air.

And there he sat, clutching his foot, unable to get up again. 'My fucken foot's broken!' he said.

It was actually his ankle. Sprained.

At that moment, Lambert came running another lap around the corner. He knocked himself silly over Treppie, who was still sitting there. Then she came up behind Lambert and fell over the two of them. And there they lay in a heap. And the bees came straight for the heap.

She was wiping bunches of those bees off Lambert's back with her bare hands. She took him by the scruff of the neck and pulled him up. Then she grabbed Treppie and pulled him closer too. And she dragged Gerty by her neck into the middle of the heap. She waved the wet housecoat around in the air to open it up, throwing it over the lot of them with one swoop. As they sat there, they could feel the bees walking over their heads on top of her housecoat. Every now and again a bee would sting right through the material. Lambert was moaning and groaning. Treppie kept saying: 'My foot, my poor fucken foot!'

144

She told them they must sit very still now, 'cause she remembered what Lambert had read in *Beeld* about the mad bees in Pretoria. Nowadays Lambert also wants to read newspapers like Treppie, but he says he doesn't read old news or Jew's news. There in Pretoria, he read, the bees swarmed under the foundations at the Union Buildings. The only time they came out was to sting people. Lambert said those bees could kill you with their stings. After fifty stings, your throat began to close. After seventy your heart went lame. And if you got two hundred stings, you were brain-dead. Nothing to be done about it but be a vegetable for the rest of your life. The whole Union Buildings were apparently full of brain-dead people. On every floor. Ministers, deputy ministers, typists, tea boys, the lot. Treppie said *Beeld* was talking crap. Lambert liked reading *Beeld* but Treppie said *Beeld* was a fucken joke. Still, the next day Treppie read them the same story in the *Star*. Only this time the ministers didn't go brain-dead when they were stung, they got like that the day they were sworn in. Yes, said Treppie, that wasn't such a bad insight for a paper like the *Star*. Just look at how Pik Botha's head was sunk into his shoulders. That's 'cause his brain was dead. A dead brain, said Treppie, was heavy. Like a ball of lead. That's why Pik Botha's head looked the way it did. The same went for old Magnus Mauser. His lower jaw bulged out so much 'cause his brain had collapsed, pressing everything else down as well. No wonder he became minister of bushes. And now he was minister of nothing.

Pop told Treppie he had no respect for the government, no matter whether they were dead or alive or brain-dead.

But now she realised they must make smoke under the bees. Lambert had read something about smoking out bees. They'd called the fire brigade to come make smoke at the Union Buildings. Smoke calms bees down.

She took Treppie's John Rolfes and his matches out from under the little flap of his pocket, sticking three cigarettes into her mouth. Then she lit them with one match and handed them out.

And there they sat, smoking like crazy under her housecoat.

That's why FW de Klerk smoked like a chimney, she said, trying to calm them down. Also John Rolfes. It kept the bees in the Union Buildings away from his bald head. Treppie and Lambert were sitting still, but they screamed like pigs every time a bee stung them. She was the only strong one. She must say, she really had the whip-hand that day. Thank God she remembered everything Lambert had read from the paper. About FW who smoked so much and his wife's face-lift, to take away the frown between her eyes.

Marike was the one who said, at the garden tea-party after her operation, that no woman could be a campaigner for peace with a frown on her face. Lambert showed her the pictures of Marike. She couldn't see any scars. There was a big water fountain in the middle of the garden with pink ice-cubes and watermelon slices. In trays that looked like shells.

The Jehovahs say it too. They say the end is near and we should approach it with the name of God sealed in our foreheads. Then there's no space left for a frown.

Sitting still and smoking like that made the bees nice and calm again.

Then she said they must get up slowly with the housecoat still over their heads, walk carefully up to the front door, and shout to Pop that he must have the Doom ready.

But Pop opened the door even before they began to shout. He sprayed Doom straight at their heads, especially Gerty, who was crawling with bees.

Mol looks at Gerty on her lap. Shame, the poor thing. It's a wonder the stings didn't kill her. Can't see a thing. And breathing so heavily. Mol can't bear to look at her. She looks out of the window instead.

Two bakkies from the municipality and a white lorry stop outside the house. She points. Everyone comes to look. They watch as the pest-removers unload their equipment. They've got silver rods with funnels in front. It's a smoke machine, says Pop. He says they should take their drinks and go see what the people are doing outside. But she says the rest of them should go, she's not feeling so well. She's had quite enough of bees, thank you. First go lie down a little. With Gerty.

Mol wakes up. There's a knocking noise against the wall, right next to her head. She gets up with Gerty in her arms to look out the window. No wonder. They're busy knocking a hole in the foundation. As soon as they finish knocking a little, they stand back, pick up the shiny thing with the funnel and stick it into the hole. The air's full of foul smoke. She closes the window. No wait, she may as well go look outside. She sees Pop and them through the smoke. Pop's looking tired. Treppie's standing on one leg. He's leaning on Pop's shoulder. Lord, just look at that Lambert. His face is so swollen he can hardly see out of his eyes. But he's talking and making big waving movements with his hands. Lambert loves gadgets and things, and he fancies the people who work with them too. He also likes drinking Klipdrift with everyone. The three of them stand there with glasses in their hands. She sees the half-tray with the bottle and the Coke on the grass. Not such a bad idea.

She walks towards the lounge. She's almost at the end of the passage when the sound of people talking stops her in her tracks. Just in time, too. Who's this inside their house now? She steals a look around the corner. One is sitting in her chair, and the other's in Pop's chair. They're shuffling their papers. Piles of pamphlets lie on the floor in front of them. It's the NPs.

'How much longer must we sit and wait here like this, Jannie?' It's the girly. She's wearing one of her dresses again, but this time there aren't any straps. The dress is cut low in front. It looks like it's about to fall off her shoulders. Why're they sitting there now? And how's she supposed to get past them? Those two make her feel funny.

The man looks at his watch. 'They said they were coming just now. Give them ten minutes or so,' he says.

'The people in this house are scum. They make me sick in my stomach,' she says.

Maybe she should go out through the kitchen. But what was that about sick in the stomach? She goes back. She knows you shouldn't listen to other people's conversations. But she didn't invite these two into her house. And what right do they have to sit in her and Pop's chairs, saying things about them?

'Where do you think the old bag is today, Jannie?' the girl asks.

'God only knows, Annemarie. Must be lying in the back here somewhere. Befucked. Bee-fucked!' He laughs.

'Sis, Jannie! You shouldn't make fun of illness.'

She slaps him playfully on the knee. He catches her hand and pulls her towards him. They kiss. Can you believe it? The girl pulls away.

'Hey, behave yourself, man! This place gives me the creeps.' She pulls her dress straight, looking around her with a fed-up expression.

Mol leans back against the passage wall. She feels funny. She wishes she had something to throw. Sit and smooch here in their lounge! Let her just get out of here and tell Treppie what they've been saying. Scum! Hmph. He'll fix them up. In no time at all. She can't believe it, but the thought of Treppie gives her courage. She must listen carefully what these two buggers say about them. Nobody can insult people better than Treppie. And this time she'll help him. 'Strue's God. Old bag, hmph! Befucked! Their bladdy arses!

'I don't know why we still canvass this lot. They're rotten, worse than . . .'

The man holds up his finger. 'Hang on, Doll, count your words. These people are the voting public. Every NP vote is worth its weight in gold.'

'Yes, but not the votes of backvelders like this lot. What are they good for, anyway?'

'You must try to think strategically, my angel. We don't have time for emotions or for whims and fancies. The main issue is to keep having a say in what happens, and if we can do that with the votes of this lot, then it's a say no less. You heard what the chief whip said. The issue is language and culture. No more and no less.'

'Ja, but what kind of culture will you find on this property? All I see here is brandy and Coke and crock cars.'

'Ag no, come now, Doll, try to think less emotionally. Think *laterally*, as Prof. Joubert says. What will become of us if there's no longer an Afrikaans-medium university in this country? You and I want to become academics one day, right? So we can fight for Afrikaans in the courts and everything. This is one of the few chances we still have left.'

'Yes, but . . .'

'No more buts, you must keep a sense of perspective here. These people are our foot-soldiers in the election. They're right at the bottom of the ladder and they feel threatened. They'll buy anything we tell them.'

'Yes, but they're the kind who'll vote for the far right. That's if they bother to vote at all. That idiot with the high backside, you want to tell me he can read and write?'

'You'll be surprised. Don't judge a book by its cover,' the chappy says. Mol smiles. They'll be very surprised, both of them will be very, very surprised.

'And the far right's looking for militants. They can't afford a bunch of inbred drunks. They want war. And we want peace, don't we, peace and a say in how we're governed?'

'It doesn't sound right to me, Jannie. It's not honest, man. Let's rather leave them alone. Let them work out their own destiny.'

'Ag no, Annemarietjie, what's wrong with you now? You heard what FW said. Election politics is not for sissies. Get a grip on yourself. There's always a light at the end of the wagon-trek, remember.'

The man doesn't really look like he's ready for wagons. He looks like he wants to fuck. He pouts at the girl. They start smooching again.

There's a knock at the front door. Slowly, someone pushes open the door. The NPs are so busy kissing they don't even see. Only she sees.

She sees an astronaut in a white costume with a high, white screen on his head. He's wearing thick gloves and white rubber boots with thick soles. The astronaut comes towards her with wide-open legs. There's too much stuffing in his pants. 'Rickatick' go the blocks under his feet.

'Dear Lord!' She almost drops Gerty.

The astronaut signals to her she mustn't be afraid. He talks in a dull voice behind his helmet. He says his name is Van Zyl. He's come to fetch the bees and he needs a bucket. Maybe there's honey. He relocates bees, he says. He lives just around the corner, in Meyer Street. Works with Pest Control. But, he says, for him bees are not pests, they're a source of extra income. He says he's sorry if he's inconveniencing her. He calls her madam. Does she have a plastic bucket or something like that for him? Then he says good evening to the NPs in the lounge. They're standing around now, looking all embarrassed. 'Good evening, madam,' they say to her.

149

'Good evening, yourself,' she says. To the bee-catcher, she says, no, fine, she'll go fetch a bucket. She addresses him as sir, but she looks down her nose at the NPs.

Mol fetches a bucket in the kitchen. She takes it round the back for Van Zyl. 'Thank you very much,' he says. There's a big, white hive next to the hole in the wall. She puts Gerty down at her feet. Then she takes Pop's glass out of his hand and swallows it in one gulp. He must fill the glass again, she says. Pop gives her a funny look. Fill up, she says. She's on the warpath. The NPs have come round the front.

She looks hard at the NP chappy. She looks at him so hard he starts talking about the weather.

'Not a cloud in the sky,' he says, looking up. Little twat thinks he can act like an angel here in front of her. But Treppie's there, in a flash. She doesn't even have to say anything.

'Good weather for bees,' says Treppie. 'You must watch out, those are New South Africa bees in that hole.'

'Foot-soldiers,' says Mol. She sees the girly shoot a look at the man. Ja, a bit of their own medicine.

The man keeps a straight face. 'Interesting,' he says. 'Do you know much about the, er, social habits of bees?'

Treppie laughs. 'Well, they don't have a president.'

'Yes,' she says, 'they get quite dizzy from the smoke, the scum, then they relax completely and pull in their stings. Like aerials, bzzt, just from a little smoke.'

'Hear, hear!' says Treppie. He puts his arm around her. 'My sister is the queen bee around here. She should know, she thinks FW smokes too much. Ask my nephew, and his mother, both of them are bee specialists.'

'Befucked,' she says, 'but not brain-dead. We can still read and write and all.'

Lambert laughs.

'Mol!' says Pop. He takes back his glass. He signals her to go slowly now. She signals back he must leave her alone. She knows what she's doing here. 'Just the little dog, she's suffering the most, but it's from the Doom.'

'Doom?' The girly looks frightened.

Treppie rubs it in. 'Yes, Miss. Doomsday blues. We've all got it, but the dog's got it the worst. Coughs terribly all night.'

She holds Gerty up so everyone can see. 'Yes, shame. Yes, this is my poor little dog, and I say to you, the great day of the Lord is near, and hasteth greatly. The mighty man shall cry there bitterly. Definitely not for sissies.'

'Jeez, Ma. Are you drunk or something?' Lambert can't believe his ears. Pop looks the other way. Treppie wants to kill himself laughing. He's playing along nicely now. He takes Pop's glass and pours her another shot.

Ja, he says, he doesn't know about the NP, but the Benades will enter the portals of heaven with the name of God written on their foreheads. Sorry, he means spray-painted, it's more resistant to the thin air in heaven.

'And without any frowns,' she says, 'just like FW's wife, she's the one who says you can't fight for peace with a frown on your face.'

'That's it, Mol, give it to them. Give it to them!'

Right. Then she'll let them have it.

'Otherwise we won't be suitable for the New South Africa, or for heaven. No culture on this property, just waste material.'

She draws deeply on her cigarette. She feels full of words. Full of mischief. 'We just want peace, peace and quiet and a say in what happens in the country. And free smoke.' She blows a mouthful of smoke right into the chappy's face. He takes a step back. He looks at the girly.

Now Lambert also smells blood. Let him. These two want to go and say ugly things about him.

'You two,' Lambert says, 'are you two also easy targets? For the bees, um, and the birds?' He winks.

'Lambert!' says Pop.

'Never mind, Pop,' she says. 'He means are they going to target the Union Buildings in a hurry, or the university. Those kind of people know lots about the birds and the bees, but after two hundred stings their brains sink like balls of lead. Then they think they can talk any old shit and people will buy anything they say.'

'Come now, you lot!' Pop nudges them. He says they must all go inside and pour another drink, so they can hear what the NPs have to say. The NPs also have a job to do, and it's getting late now.

'Why's that Van Zyl lying there so quietly?' She wants to know. She doesn't want Van Zyl to get hurt here in their yard. He looks like a decent man to her.

'Don't worry, Mol, he's talking to the bees. You have to negotiate with bees before they let you touch them.' It's Treppie. He slaps the NP chappy so hard on his blazer that he hiccups as they walk in through the front door.

'Look,' says Blazer once they're back inside and the drinks have been poured and they're all sitting down, 'for us this election is about spiritual matters, about the higher things.'

'Higher honey,' says Treppie.

'Higher than what?' she asks. Tonight she's not taking off her housecoat. Not for them. Not a damn. She puts Gerty on her lap. And she won't close her legs for them, either. Their backsides.

'Higher than the basics,' says Treppie.

'Exactly,' says the chappy. 'The higher things. Preserving the higher things, and having a say over them. Our language and our culture, for our children and for their children. It's one of the most important minority rights.'

'Why *minor*?' she asks.

'Minor as opposed to *major*, like in *majority*,' says the girly.

'Who's the majority then?' she asks.

'Well, madam, er, our, er, other countrymen, who're in the majority.'

'Other? What do you mean other?'

Lambert steps in.

'Ma, they're talking about the bantus. The natives, the plurals, the kaffirs. The darkies. The munts.'

'Like Nelson Mandela, Mol,' says Treppie.

'Ohh!' Now she catches on. 'That old tatta who wears such nice shirts and a cap? He looks quite jolly to me. And Tutu! Jaaa! Now that one's really jolly.'

She throws her arms up into the air, the way Tutu did it once, from a pulpit on a soccer field. 'We shall be *free*, all of us, *together*!' she shouts.

'Yes, madam, that might be what they say, but the blacks are fighting for basics. For food and houses and work and schools.'

'Mol,' says Treppie, 'let's rather put it this way.' He puts on his preacher's voice. 'Us whites, we must vote for roses. We already have a house, and wheels, and bread.'

'And polony.'

'That's right, madam,' says the girly, '*and* polony, but we must insist on the right to have roses too.'

'Constitutionally guaranteed under a new government,' says Blazer.

'Our right to the finer things in life,' says Annemarie.

'In other words, the right to our culture,' says Jannie. He brings his fingertips together and rubs them softly against each other, as if he's touching something soft.

'Culture for the backvelders – Klipdrift and Coke and crock cars.'

'Ja, that's it, Mol,' says Treppie. He laughs and winks at her. Now she's really on a roll. 'But you two are supposed to be educated, so tell us a little what culture really means.'

'Well,' Little Blazer says, looking at Girly, 'how did Prof. van Rensburg put it, culture is the, er, complex product of a creative, er, socially determined grasp of nature, er, such as historically determined by a language and a religious community.'

'Jeeesus!' says Treppie. 'Just watch how I determine this Coke by grasping the Klipdrift, old buddy!' He pours from both bottles into Blazer's glass at the same time.

'What?' says Mol, sitting upright.

Close your legs, Lambert signals to her.

'Let me put it this way, ma'am,' says Girly, looking at Jannie with big eyes. 'All he means is this: culture is looking after your own garden, yourself.'

'Your rose garden,' says Treppie quickly, 'your right to culture is the right to make your own rose garden. Yes, that's it, to make your own corsage just the way you want to.'

'You *and* your own cultural group.' Blazer's pointing his finger at Treppie. He'd better take that finger away, quickly. But it's too late.

'Puke!' says Treppie.

'Excuse me?' says Girly.

'I said puke-group, you and your own puke-group.' Treppie's eyes are glittering. He's talking softly.

'Treppie, I'm going to smack you,' says Lambert.

'Just you shuddup for now, old nephew!' says Treppie, shaking a long finger in front of Lambert's nose like he's a naughty dog or something. Treppie turns back towards the two NPs.

'It was about a month before we became a republic. Two little NP men came to visit here one day. Remember, Mol, you were visiting the school principal about Lambert's bad schoolwork. We received a letter about the matter.'

Treppie pretends he's taking a letter out of an envelope. He unfolds it.

She remembers. It was in terribly learned Afrikaans, and when they read it, Treppie had to explain almost every word. About how she must please come for an 'audience' with the principal, 'cause Lambert didn't want to do his work. And how he smelt bad, and how he was 'indecent' with little schoolgirls. And how important every single child was, and how the principal felt he could make a diamond from even this piece of coal. Then Treppie said Triomf should have been named after that principal, 'cause anyone who thought a school was like a mine must also think bulldozing kaffir rubbish was some kind of great victory.

Treppie pretends he's at the end of the letter. He signs the school principal's name with large, frilly letters in the air. 'Doctor Hans van den Berg,' he says slowly, as he signs. 'Bee-Ay-Em-Ed-Pee-Aitch-Dee,' he reads.

Treppie indicates that he wants the NPs to clap hands for the principal's letter. They must cheer, he signals. He waits. No one claps. The NP chappy just smiles, shaking his head.

Only Lambert gets up. He looks like he wants to start smashing people around. Treppie must block him, otherwise there's going to be trouble here again.

'But he turned out fine, old Lambert. Just look at him. All ship-shape.' Treppie sniffs in Lambert's direction. 'Always clean-shaven. Hair always neatly combed. Poor but clean, as befits an Afrikaner. And he never swears. Terribly civil to his uncle and his father, and especially to his mother. When the need becomes too much to bear – Lambert here's a bachelor, remember – then he does push-ups on the lawn. Push-ups! Forty at a time. Does he ever touch himself? Never. That Dr Hans fixed him up very nicely.'

Treppie slowly pushes Lambert back on to his crate. 'Come, Lambert, sit down so I can finish my story. I take it you still want to hear the story?' He looks at the visitors. Cutesy-Collarbones nods her head half-heartedly. She looks like she's scared of Treppie. Blazer's perched on the edge of Pop's chair. Pop's sitting on a crate with his head in his hands. Mol rubs Gerty between the ears. Let Treppie stir the pot here. He's the best one to do it.

'So, then those two snotnoses came here that afternoon. They were about as old as you two. Nice and wet behind the ears. Nats! Two little chappies in suits and waistcoats. The one had a little Hitler-moustache. They came round the back, where we were fixing fridges. And guess what they saw first? They saw the roses that Mol was going to sell that night. And guess what they said? They said how nice it was that the finer things in life were also getting some attention, here among the Afrikaans working classes.'

Treppie looks hard at the NPs.

'Ja, they said, didn't we want to make a contribution to Republic Day. Something like corsages, they thought. For wearing at the Republic Day festival at the Voortrekker Monument. That, they said, would be a cultural act of great distinction. I had to stop myself from kicking those two bullshitters right off the property. Those two schemers knew nothing about fucken anything.'

'That's it, Treppie, let them have it!'

'They knew fuck-all about fuck-all, but they wanted to come and tell us about the finer things. Us with our hands full of rose thorns and fridge oil. With our grandfather who lost his land in the depression and our mother who coughed herself to death from TB. And our father who

155

hanged himself by the neck in a Railways truck. They knew nothing at all about the meaning of misery.'

'Hey, Treppie.' Pop lifts his head. 'Leave it now. Just leave it right there, man.'

'Leave it? Just fucken leave it? Not a damn, Pop! When I do something, I do it properly.'

'Chief whip!'

'That's it, Mol, tell them. If they can't see it for themselves, tell them Treppie's the chief whip here at the Benades'!'

The girly looks at the chappy. Then Treppie goes 'ka-thack' in the air as if he's cracking a whip. The girly's head jerks, she gets such a fright.

'So, we learnt to know your sort very well.' He points at the NPs. 'We were still young then, but we remember.'

'There's always a light at the end of the wagon-trek!'

'That's it, Mol,' says Treppie. 'That's it,' he says, winking at her.

'It was the same bladdy story in '38, and again in '48.' He puts on his speech voice. 'There's always a light at the end of the wagon-trek. They never said there's a gun or bread or a factory or a trading licence there at the front of the wagon. No, always a fucken light, a column of fire, a Spirit, a Higher Idea, an Ideal of fucken Unity or something. And that's 'cause we're all supposed to be from the same culture. What kind of a fucken thing is that, I ask you, with tears in my light blue, poor-white eyes?'

'Wait, wait a minute now, Mister Benade!' The girly looks like she wants to stop Treppie with her hands. But there's no stopping Treppie.

'Don't come and Mister Benade me! If you think you can come here and sell us a wagonload of shit . . .'

'Well, then, in that case we'll be on our way . . .' and the girly half gets up.

'Oh no,' says Treppie. He gets up quickly, closing the front door. 'You're here now. And you'll stay to the very end. Here with us, with our roof above our heads and the bees under our backsides!' He turns the key in the door's lock. Then he puts the key in his pocket.

Dear God, now he's going too far. Now there's going to be trouble again. Let her rather go outside. Around the back.

Treppie's eyes are shining. 'No, Mol, wait now. Don't be such poor company. Who wants another shot?' He pours for everyone. For her too. Ja well, matters will just have to take their own course. The NPs shake their heads and cover their glasses with their hands. No thank you, they say. They're actually not allowed to drink on the job. Treppie fills Lambert's glass to the brim.

'Come, Lambert. Why don't you and your mother tell the story of how we became a republic. About how many hundreds of rand we made, in straight profit, just from an idea.' Treppie dances a few steps. 'Just look how jolly we are tonight! If Pop still had some breath left, we could have some music too. What you say, Pop? Where's your mouth organ?' Treppie slaps Pop hard on his back.

'Leave Pop alone. Just leave him alone.'

'It's you who should have left him alone, Mol. Look what we've got now from not leaving him alone. One fucked-up Fuchs and one total write-off of a Tedelex. And a pot of burnt-out Benades!'

'It's from not having enough volts!' says Mol. Yes, that's what they want to hear, so let them.

The NPs laugh nervously. Lambert also laughs a half-laugh. Pop lifts his head and smiles a little smile. Did Mol really say something funny?

'Hey!' says Treppie to the NPs, pretending to be serious. 'There's nothing funny about it. You can't help it if your lantern's a bit weak. Then all you're good for is to be a mascot. Come, Mol, tell them a bit about me and Lambert. How we walked around at the monument with white eyes, foaming at the mouth, like this!'

Treppie shows them exactly how, in the middle of the room.

'Come, Lambert, come stand here next to me, then we'll show our guests how we did it. They've fuckenwell seen nothing yet. Come, come, man,' he says to Lambert, pulling him up. 'Don't be so upstairs. Show them!'

Lambert gets up slowly and stands next to Treppie. Treppie pulls at Lambert's face until he looks mad enough.

'The HF Verwoerd Institute for the Mentally Retarded.' Mol says. She gets up. Right. Now she's going to play along too.

Treppie writes the words on his chest, fast and wild, with his index finger.

She picks up the half-tray, pulling the plastic rose from the cat's neck. Treppie and Lambert start shouting: 'Corsages, corsages for the baby republic!' They walk over to Pop's side, pulling her after them.

'Mister,' says Treppie, with a thick tongue. He lets the spit run from the corners of his mouth. 'Mister, check here quickly.'

'National colours!' Lambert shouts in Pop's ear.

'Mother, sister and brothers!' Treppie shouts in Pop's other ear, rolling his eyes to heaven.

Pop sits dead still with his head in his hands. He doesn't look up. She wants to keep them away from Pop. Can't they see he doesn't want to play? 'Hey, come here, you two. That customer's deaf,' she says, 'come let's try these two.'

'Just check these larnies, I say.' It's Lambert. He lets his mouth slop open. Slaver runs down his chin. 'They must have a lot of fucken money.'

'No,' says Treppie through the spit, 'money doesn't count here. Not if you're a Nationalist to the quick, with your heart in the right place and your hand ready for the golden handshake, give or take.'

'Now listen here,' says Blazer, 'we won't allow ourselves to be pushed around.'

'So fussy!' she says, pulling her nose up.

Treppie pats her on the back. 'Yes, spoilsports,' he says with his mad face.

'Come, Jannie. Come, let's go now.' The girly sounds like she's choking.

'First buy a rose, missie, it's only plastic but it'll last forever 'cause it stands for an Idea!'

'Hey, Treppie.' Lambert comes waggling up to him. 'Where will she pin it up? She's half-naked anyway.' Then Lambert pretends he's trying to find somewhere on her shoulder to pin the flower.

'Don't you dare lay a hand on her,' says Jannie. They're both standing now. Jannie puts his arm around Cutesy-Collarbones.

'But she must first buy our rose,' Mol says, shoving the plastic rose into

Blazer's face. 'It's a yellow rose, but it's better than nothing. The new flag's got at least one yellow stripe in it.'

'No, dammit,' says Jannie. 'I've had enough now.' He opens his leather wallet. He presses a fifty-rand note into her palm.

'Gee, sorry, sir, but now I don't have any change on me,' she says, pretending to feel for change in her housecoat pocket.

'Yippeeee!' shouts Treppie. He grabs the fifty-rand note and jumps up and down with Lambert on the blocks. 'Click-click!' they go.

'Afrikaners like parties, no doubt about that,' they sing, with mad faces.

Treppie suddenly comes to a dead-stop. He pulls his clothes straight with furious little plucks. All of a sudden he's dead serious.

'Fix your face,' he says to Lambert. Lambert does as he's told. Treppie shoves the money into Lambert's shirt-pocket. He slaps the pocket.

'See how easy it is?' he says. 'That's how a person makes money from talking a lot of crap.'

'We made hundreds of rand profit that night,' says Lambert.

'Inbetween the speeches. It was lots of fun. Very jolly!' Mol nods her head up and down.

'And if you want to see some more sports, then you must come again some other night. But you've seen enough for one day, not so?' says Treppie. He unlocks the door.

'Treppie, give them back their money.' It's Pop. Treppie pretends he didn't hear.

He opens the door. He makes a deep bow. Then he waves them out as if they're bits of fluff. Strangely enough, Van Zyl is standing out there on the little stoep, still in his helmet. There're a few bees on the net over his face.

Dammit, there she's gone and let this man give her a fright again. Where's Gerty?

'Not to worry,' says the bee-catcher, 'they're nice and tame from the smoke, madam. We've got the queen. Now we're taking the swarm away. You must just close up that hole, otherwise they'll come back. There was lots of honey.'

He hands over the yellow bucket. 'I washed it out nicely at the tap first,' he says. 'I'll say goodbye then. All the best, folks,' he says, waving a white glove behind him.

When he goes, they all look into the yellow bucket under the stoep-light. It's half-full of wax-pieces. A few larvae stir in the honey.

'I'm not eating any of that,' says Lambert.

'Let them take it,' says Treppie, 'then at least they'll have something for all their trouble.'

'And their fifty rand!' says Lambert, laughing.

'Thanks very much, but no thanks,' says the girly.

'Sights. They're full of sights!'

The girly looks at her with big eyes. Good, good. She's the one who wanted to come here and say nasty things about them in their own house. She pulls Blazer by his sleeve to the front gate. He still wants to turn around and say goodbye.

'Come, missie, don't be so high and mighty. There's strength in the sweetness. You might still need it!' Treppie shouts at their backs, but they're already in their car. It's pasted full of *I love FW* bumper stickers. Then they step on the gas, down Martha Street.

'The last of the great pretenders,' says Treppie. Pop says they must bring the bucket into the kitchen. He wants to work the honey. He tells her she must collect some bottles from under the sink. From those days when Lambert wouldn't eat anything but pickled onions.

They work until late. Pop piles up the pieces of wax on a tin inside the bucket, so the honey can run out nicely. Meanwhile, she washes the bottles in boiling water to get rid of the onion taste.

She washes those bottles over and over. Pop smells every bottle carefully before filling them with honey. After a while they've got twelve bottles. Enough for a whole year, says Pop. He's so tired of golden syrup.

At eleven they're finished. She cuts two pieces of bread for everyone and spreads them nice and thick with Sunshine D and honey. Then she makes coffee.

It tastes good.

'Mmm,' says Lambert. 'Tastes a bit wild.'

Ja, says Pop, it does. He just wonders what could be so wild, here in Triomf. Tastes almost like khaki-bush, or no, like flowers, the kind that grow on the island in the road, there next to Shoprite.

'Afrikaners,' says Treppie. 'Stinkafrikaners.'

9

~

COUGHING

Gerty's coughing so much Mol can't sleep. The poor little thing stands next to her side of the bed, staring at her. Every now and again she makes a noise that sounds like something between a cough and a long, drawn-out clearing of the throat. It's like the noise Treppie makes in the bathroom in the mornings, only worse. But Gerty doesn't spit. If she could just gob out that thick slime, like Treppie does, it might help.

Instead, she stands there and lets her head sag, as if she's lost heart. Her tongue hangs out. Thick, sticky tears drip from her eyes.

Mol lies on her side. She's looking at Gerty. All she can see is Gerty's face in the light of the streetlamp. She gets up on to her elbow and turns round to look at Pop. He's lying with his back to her. She can see the sharp points of his shoulders inside his shirt. His breath whistles. She keeps telling him he mustn't smoke so much, he must eat more, but he just shakes his head. He eats nothing and he says nothing. When he's not holding his head in his hands, he's lifting it up to light a cigarette. Poor Pop. Poor Gerty. She holds out her arm and Gerty takes two steps closer. The little dog lifts her snout. It feels warm and dry on Mol's hand. Then she hears the sound of Gerty's breath between the coughs. It's worse than the coughing. It sounds like it's more than just a dog's breath. It feels like the room itself is breathing, like a big in-breath that sucks all the air from the corners and the cupboards and from behind the dressing table, holding it all in.

Mol lies back on the cushion with Gerty's snout still in her hands. Suddenly she can hear everything, all the noises, inside and outside. The sound of the mattress as she and Pop breathe, the 'tick-tick' of a beetle on the ceiling, and above the ceiling the 'krr-krr' of the mice. Treppie says they're rats, but Treppie smells rats everywhere. The tap goes 'psheee' as it leaks in the bathroom and the overflow makes a 'tip-tip' noise on the roof. Then there's the sound of running water from next door. She's told Lambert it sounds like next door's running bathwater all night long, but he says she's imagining things. He's one to talk! And the fridge rattling in the kitchen. First softly and then louder and louder until it switches off, 'cheeree-cheeree-cheeree-kaplock'. It gets the shakes so bad from switching off that the Coke bottles inside the door start rattling.

She hears Toby wake up in the lounge and scratch himself. 'Click-click' go the loose blocks of the parquet floor as he comes walking down the passage to the back of the house. He always knows when she's awake. Gerty coughs some more and takes two steps back, as if she wants to step right out of the cough. Then she lets her head drop.

Toby comes to look at her with pricked ears. He moves his head closer, sniffing Gerty around the mouth and ears. Toby's been sniffing Gerty like this ever since she started coughing. In the old days he used to sniff her backside. Now Mol uses her elbows to push herself up. Both dogs look at her. The streetlight from outside shines right though their eyes, which suddenly look just like marbles. The sight almost takes her breath away. A big lorry changes gears in Ontdekkers, blowing 'phff-phff!' out of a hole in its guts.

Mol sits up straight. Dear Lord, what's got into her now? She folds the flaps of her housecoat over one another and feels for her slippers, here next to the mattress. Now she's in a hurry.

'Come,' she whispers. 'Come, let's go for a little walk.' She picks up Gerty and walks through the dark, to the bathroom. She can feel Toby's cold nose against her heels. Why can't Gerty's nose feel like that?

She puts on the light and tears off a piece of toilet paper so she can wipe Gerty's eyes. But before she does it, she sees a great brown moth on the floor of the bath. As big as her hand. Dead still the moth sits there, as if it has every reason to do so, looking at her from two deep-purple eyes on its back. Like a hand that can fly, with eyes. What does it see? Mol wonders. How much can a moth see? And why's it looking at her like that? What is she, to a moth? Under the light of the bare bulb she looks for her face in the last little piece of mirror. More pieces keep chipping out. She's told them, one day someone's going to look for his face in the mirror and then there'll be nothing. Just a piece of hardboard. But they won't listen to her.

All she sees is the area around her mouth. It looks like someone else's mouth. Skew. It moves in a funny way, like it's chewing something. She wipes her mouth with her hand. She's trying to wipe it away. She bends over to look for her eyes, but she can't find them. She must tell Pop he must get Lambert to fix the mirror. She wipes Gerty's face and turns off the light. Then she turns it back on again. That moth mustn't sit there and stare at her in the dark.

She walks to the kitchen. As she enters, cockroaches scuttle under the fridge. She opens the fridge door. It smells sour. She's told Lambert it's the fridge's oils and stuff that makes it smell so bad, but he says the fridge is just dirty. She takes out the milk and pours some into Gerty's bowl. Toby's bowl too, otherwise he just drinks Gerty's. Toby drinks his milk. Gerty stands in front of her bowl. Her mouth hangs open. 'Aaraagh! Aaraagh!' she coughs. Oh, dear God in heaven. What can she do? She picks up Gerty, but Gerty doesn't want to be picked up.

Mol walks back into the room and turns on the light. Pop's still in the same position. She crouches at Pop's side of the bed. Gerty and Toby sit on either side of her. They look where she looks. They're all checking if Pop's still alive. A little thread of spit dangles from his mouth. She turns her head to hear if he's breathing. She has to listen for a long time, above the noise of Gerty's breath and all the other sounds, before she can hear Pop's breathing. It's very shallow. She feels it more than she hears it. She feels it on her forehead. It's faint. Lukewarm. Lambert says a person's lungs work like a fridge's evaporator, cooling down your blood so you can live longer. That's why the out-breaths are warm. It's the warmth of your blood coming out. Blood must never be too warm.

Pop's blood isn't warm at all. The point of his nose always looks white, with that drop hanging there, and his lips are so cold they look slightly blue. His hands and feet too. Often, when they go to bed, he asks her to rub them a bit. Summer or winter, just his hands and his feet. Good old Pop. That's the only part of him she has to rub nowadays. His little old willy looks like a raisin, wrinkled and pulled back into a little ball. Pop says he's dried up now, thank God. Thank God? she asks. Then Pop says he gives thanks to God that he can't cause any more trouble. 'It's not so bad, Pop, we struggle, but we still have each other.' Then he says 'each other', blowing out his breath. It's not a sigh. It's more like he wants to blow out all his breath. Pop says he doesn't want to carry on. But she says he must want to carry on, otherwise what will become of her? Then he says that's exactly what Old Mol used to say, and look at Old Pop, he also carried on right to the bitter end. But he, Pop, doesn't have enough strength even to do what Old Pop did. In any case, where would he find a train? Old Pop wanted a train, Old Mol said, 'cause he was hoping the train would ride to hell and off into the Karoo after he hanged himself from his belt. So his loved ones would be spared the sight. To him, that still sounds like a good idea, Pop says. Spare your loved ones the sight. And the smell. And the expense. Anyone who's been swinging on a belt for that long in a railway truck in the Karoo is going to end up as dry as biltong. Light as a stick. Then all they have to do is dump you on the other side of De Aar. Matter closed, fixed up. Neat and tidy. No hole, no coffin and no headstone. Nothing, not even birds of prey, 'cause they don't eat biltong.

But she says that story's a lie, and then Pop says, no, that's what Old Mol said she was told by Old Pop, before he did it. Mol says it sounds to her more like the kind of thing Treppie would say, and then Pop says, mind you, he did actually hear it from Treppie. Old Mol told Treppie 'cause she thought he was the one with the most insight and understanding, and he also took after Old Pop more than anyone else. That's what Treppie says. Then she says to Pop, yes, but he's also Old

Pop's child and he doesn't take after Old Pop or Treppie, so what's the big deal? At that, Pop just blows out his breath and says, well, that's the way the cookie crumbles.

When Pop gets his breath back, he says Lambert doesn't take after him either. She, on the other hand, is unlike both him and Treppie. When Pop finishes saying this, he goes funny and quiet and then she knows he's wondering whose child Lambert really is.

When they were small, Treppie used to give her sweets, in exchange. Sweets that he stole from the café. Then, one day, Old Mol caught them. 'Why? Why? Why?' she wailed, beating her head against the wall with each 'why'. 'Why, why do you do it?' And then they both said, for sweets. Treppie told Old Mol he'd give her sweets as well if she'd just stop beating her head against the wall like that. Treppie took out his whole supply of sweets, a shoebox full, which he dragged out from under the bed. He told Old Mol she could have any sweets she wanted. But Old Mol knocked the box down on to the floor and began beating her head against the table. Then Treppie pulled down his pants and bent over. He said she should beat him rather than bang her head so hard against the table. Old Mol said she never laid a hand on anyone, but Old Pop would see him right. When Old Pop got home that night, he was already drunk. He dragged Treppie out from under the bed and took him all the way to the shunting yard, so no one in the house would hear. He said he was going to give Treppie the kind of hiding he wouldn't forget for the rest of his living days. When Old Pop got back that night, Treppie wasn't with him any more.

Old Mol began crying all over again. She asked Old Pop to fetch Treppie, but he told her she could go fetch that 'piece of shame she brought forth' herself if she wanted to. Then Old Pop turned to her, Mol, and gave her a look like he wanted to start hitting her too – she was very sickly those days and her chest was weak – but Old Mol jumped between them and said, 'No! No! No! Hit me instead!', and Old Pop slapped Old Mol so hard she fell right on top of Mol. They must make their own plan now, he said, 'cause he was buggering off. So she comforted Little Pop and Old Mol and they all went looking for Treppie, up and down between the railway lines, behind the warehouses and under the coal-wagons. After searching for a long time, they heard a little cry in an empty goods train, and there they found him, sitting in the straw. He was covered in blood. They had to half-carry, half-piggyback him all the way home. Old Mol laid him down on the kitchen table and began to clean him up with a towel. His face and body were badly cut up. Some of his teeth were missing and his eyes were so swollen he couldn't see a thing. His nose was completely broken. It remains skew to this day. His backside was covered with puffed-up, purple-blue welts from Old Pop's belt. And one of his ribs was cracked.

'God help us,' Old Mol kept saying, crying softly as she wiped the blood from Treppie's face and body.

She and Little Pop felt bad, especially Little Pop, 'cause he'd also done it, and now Treppie had been forced to take the punishment. Her too; she'd allowed it long after it stopped being a game. But if she hadn't, she'd never have seen a sweet in her life again and they'd never have taken her anywhere with them. Like the circus or the bioscope in the afternoons after school, or the horse races, where you could stand around the stables till someone asked you for something and then you said yes, but that will cost two bob, hey.

'This child must see a doctor,' Old Mol said to Old Pop the next day, but Old Pop said over his dead body, then the Welfare would be on to them again, and once the Welfare started with you, you had nothing but misery for the rest of your days. But they already had so much misery, Old Mol said. People who wanted to help couldn't be all that bad. But Old Pop answered her with his fists. He hit her so hard that both her eyes closed up.

For two days, Old Mol stayed at home to look after Treppie. Her plan was to keep the three of them inside until Treppie looked better. She told everyone he had mumps, so they wouldn't visit.

But everyone knew exactly what was going on. The children lay behind the closed curtain in the room, listening to everything the Beyleveldts said.

'A very weak kind of Afrikaner,' said Mrs Beyleveldt.

'Weak? They're worse than kaffirs, if you ask me,' said Mr Beyleveldt.

'It's easy for them to talk,' Old Mol said when they told her what the Beyleveldts were saying. 'They're only two in their half. People go rotten from living on a heap like this.'

'What makes people go rotten is loneliness,' Old Pop said. By then he was drinking heavily.

'People get lonely when they think they're better than other people,' Old Mol said.

She was right. Old Pop drank on his own. He didn't mix with the people at work. He also refused to go with Old Mol to the garment workers' concerts.

'All the other husbands go with their wives,' Old Mol used to say, begging him to come with her. But Old Pop just said no. He said he was too good for the city and its people. He was a man of the soil. He read to them out of newspapers about the government's plans to put the poor whites back on their farms. She'd still see what happened to white women who fell in with the Communists and the trade unions. Communists loved kaffirs and there were lots of kaffirs, he said. Lambertus Benade was a Nationalist and the kaffirs must know their place. That was the way Old Pop used to talk.

Mol's feet feel like they're going to sleep from all the crouching in front of Pop. Gerty starts coughing again. Mol rubs her little back. Pop opens his eyes. He moves his mouth as if to say: What you doing, Mol? But nothing comes out. He tries again.

'What you doing, Mol?' He reaches out to her with his hand, taking hers. His hand feels cold.

Mol wants to say: I'm looking to see if you're still alive, Pop. But she doesn't. She can see on his face he knows what she wants to say. She just says: 'Gerty's coughing.'

'Gerty's old,' says Pop. He closes his eyes again. 'Mol, it's the middle of the night,' he says, turning over.

'I'm coming now,' she says. 'I'm just taking her outside to pee.'

But halfway out of the house Mol forgets what she wanted to do. She's thinking about the look in Pop's eyes as he lay there, looking at her. It was almost as if he was looking at her from a far place, and he could see more than just what he was looking at. Like a circus elephant. The older Pop gets, the more that look in his eyes reminds her of an elephant. Heartsore eyes, as though he's looking through a peephole. If she remembers right, Pop's eyes began to look like that when he was still very young.

She remembers the day Pop came back from the shunting yard, after they called him to go see about Old Pop in the train. Then his eyes had such a faraway look that Mrs Beyleveldt made him drink sugar water before he left for the factory, to fetch Old Mol. Treppie kept dead quiet all day long. He'd never spoken another word to Old Pop after that beating in any case. If he was naughty before the hiding, he became even more hard-boiled afterwards. That's when he developed the twitch in his shoulder. Old Beyleveldt used to say he looked like a donkey with an itch. Treppie didn't shed a single tear at the funeral. And afterwards he began to act like he was boss of the house. It was also then that Treppie started running her into the ground. She tried to complain to Old Mol, but by then Old Mol was a broken woman.

'Your brother was terribly hurt, my child,' she said. 'There's nothing more I can do now. The three of you will have to sort out your own lives.'

By that time, Old Mol was very ill herself. She coughed terribly. And Treppie drank all her medicine, for the alcohol. He used to get completely knocked out from Old Mol's cough medicine.

Maybe if she gives Gerty some Klipdrift, it'll help. But the Klipdrift's in the sideboard and the keys are in Treppie's pocket. He's the one who always buys the brandy. He says he doesn't buy it for Lambert to throw it back in a single day. Not that it makes much difference. If Lambert wants to drink he just turns Treppie upside down and shakes him out like a pillowcase till those keys fall out. The only thing that keeps him away from the bottle is when she lies down for him in the back room. Or when Treppie says he's going to have Lambert 'certified', so they can tie him up on a trolley and force-feed him till his liver's big enough for export to Uganda. The kaffirs in that place are still nice and wild, Treppie says, they love eating white man's liver. Treppie says they call white man's liver 'patydefwagras' in Uganda. When Treppie says this, Lambert goes white in the face. And then Treppie says, yes, go catch a fit now too, then we can take you with your convulsions and all to the halfway house, so they can see with their own eyes what kind of lunatic we've got on our hands here in Triomf. Then Lambert goes back to his den and starts breaking things till he cools down. Or he makes a fire in the yard, throwing anything he can lay his hands on into the flames. She's lost three housecoats like that. Or he goes and paints on his wall for three days running. That's the best. Then he bothers nobody. Or he goes and looks for wine boxes. After that he's so tired he lies down on his bed and sleeps all day.

Mol pushes open Treppie's door. She stands in the dark for a while to see if she can spot where he threw his pants down. He and Pop both sleep in their shirts and underpants for a week before going to the laundromat in Thornton. Treppie says he can hardly believe it, they used to have a whole yard full of twin-tubs and now there's not even a single washing machine for their own clothes.

She can't see a thing. Treppie's put those sheets up against the window again. He specially went and bought himself sheets to hang up there. He says people who live in glass houses shouldn't take chances. When she asks what he means by 'glass houses', he says their house sits on a bare piece of lawn like a monument to fuck-all. All it needs is a pedestal. He says he wonders what people think they're actually exhibiting here. Then he says he wants to plant a hedge in front of the house so everyone will stop looking at them. But Lambert says he wants no more plant-rubbish near the house. His spanners just get lost in the plants.

Mol turns on Treppie's light. He's lying with his face to the wall. He snores, 'krr-phooo, krr-phooo'. And he's still wearing his pants, but it doesn't matter, 'cause the half-full bottle of Klipdrift is standing right here in front of her, next to the bed.

A line of ants makes its way towards the bottle. Where do they come from? Mol wonders. She looks down at her feet. The ants are coming from the lounge. She switches on the passage and lounge lights. She bends over to look. Some of the ants are walking this way, some the other way. But they stick to the same line, knocking heads before carrying on again. Mol walks carefully into the room. She takes the bottle and wipes off a few ants. Ever since the day he fell off the roof, Treppie's been drinking like this. He says his foot still hurts. The smell of Treppie's rotten brandy breath fills the room. He's lying with his head on a dirty white cushion.

No, he always says, you dare not use a pillow-slip in this house, they're just nests for earwigs. Ever since Treppie told Lambert earwigs make holes in epileptics' eardrums and eat out their brains, Lambert's been scared to death of the things. One day, soon after Treppie told him about the earwigs, Lambert took all the pillow-slips and burnt them up on a heap of grass. Just in case, he said. Now they all sleep on dirty cushions.

Mol walks quietly out of the room and switches off the lights. As she opens the front door, moist air hits her in the face. Mist. A rare sight in Triomf, but she likes the feel of it. Nice and cool to breathe. Good for the blood.

She sits herself down on the edge of the stoep, with Gerty here next to her. What's good for her must be good for Gerty too – thick mist and Klipdrift. Now she also feels like having a shot. She unscrews the cap and takes a sip. Her body shivers all the way down from her throat. Then she quickly takes another sip. The more you sip, the less you shiver. She prefers her brandy with Coke, but she's not going to search for Coke and a glass at this hour. The house is making her ears zing tonight.

'Come, my little doggie,' she says to Gerty, 'come take a sip here.' She pulls Gerty's head under her arm, and then with the same hand presses the corners of Gerty's mouth to force it open. Gerty's got no spirit left. She just opens her mouth. Mol lifts the bottle and slowly lets some brandy run down. 'Swallow,' she says, 'swallow nicely now.' She rubs Gerty's throat. Gerty swallows. Then she coughs and coughs and coughs. Mol holds on to her tightly. Her eyes sting.

That's also the way she held Old Mol at the end. Old Mol would never go and see a doctor. She was scared the doctor would see the black marks where Old Pop used to hit her. She also didn't want to ask for more time off work. It was bad enough that she had to send one of them to say she was sick every other day when she wasn't sick at all, just bruised from Old Pop's fists. Old Pop always used to hit her in the face.

'Hit me anywhere you want,' she used to say. 'I can put on long-sleeve overalls, but please, not my face.'

'Shuddup! Shuddup! Shuddup!' Old Pop shouted back. 'Or I'll give that jaw of yours some more panelbeating.'

To avoid bothering Old Pop in the middle of the night, Old Mol used to go cough in the bathroom. She coughed up blood, bending over the bath. Then she, Little Mol, went and held her tight. Sometimes Little Pop also did it, but not Treppie. Never. After Treppie got that hiding, he acted like he was deaf to the world. And after Old Pop died, Treppie got even worse.

'That's TB your mother's got,' Mrs Beyleveldt told Treppie. 'You must do something about it.'

Mrs Beyleveldt also thought Treppie was the most intelligent of the children. He was at home a lot 'cause he was the youngest, which meant he took a lot of stick about the Benades from Mrs Beyleveldt and her cripple husband.

By then she, Little Mol, was going to the factory with her mother every day. She started when she was fifteen, working next to Old Mol and doing two people's work. Old Mol was always behind with her shirts. She went too slowly through the thick parts, and then her needles would break. Then Old Mol would just pass it all over to her, and many were the days when she had to do Old Mol's work as well as her own. But at least they brought some money home. Little Pop began to earn a bit too, although all he could do was piece-work. He was slow, and weak, and he looked blue around the mouth all the time.

After Old Pop died, they gave Pop a soft job on the Railways, out of pity. A waiter or something on the Karoo train, but Pop did only one trip. He kept dropping things. After that he preferred to stay at home. Much later, he became a lift operator in a high building in Jo'burg.

That was okay, but it gave him even more of a faraway look, like an elephant.

Mol sits on the edge of the stoep, in the cool night air. She can feel their smell coming out of the house. The warm smell of people, slightly sweet. Sweat and drink and tobacco and something sour that she can't put her finger on. A sour smell that's very close to her.

She doesn't bath a lot, and the rest of them tell her she stinks. Not a damn. She washes herself. But now that moth's sitting in the bath and she wonders how long it's going to stay there. If she goes into the bathroom now it'll stare at her, and then she'll start thinking things again. Like the night Old Mol coughed herself to death. She hadn't woken up when Old Mol started coughing. It was a night when she'd fallen into a dead sleep after doing double work all day long. Then, early in the morning, she went to the toilet in the dark. And there she found Old Mol, bent over the edge of the tub. Two identical spots of blood lay in the bath, the way it looks when a blot of ink seeps through a piece of folded paper.

'It's the TB butterfly,' Mrs Beyleveldt said when she came to look. 'One wing of blood from each lung. And then away she flies.' Mol will never forget that. The crimson TB butterfly.

'Shut your fucken mouth, old woman,' Treppie shouted. 'I thought you were supposed to be blind.' Mrs Beyleveldt held her hands over her mouth. She never thought Treppie would shout at her like that.

After Old Mol died, Treppie got worse than ever. Only the big fire, when all the fridges were destroyed, calmed him down a bit, and that was many years later. Now, ever since Peace Day, he's become quite tame. How long it will last she doesn't know.

Pop says Treppie took a bad knock when the fridges burnt like that. She took a knock too. More than a knock. Something inside her head cracked that day, like when eggs break and the stuff runs out.

It all started when Lambert couldn't find his spanner in the long grass. The day before Guy Fawkes. By then, Lambert had been out of school for two years. He was so impossible at school that they eventually kicked him out. Then he spent all day and night at home and they were the ones who had to put up with him, non-stop. He was supposed to be helping Pop and Treppie with the fridges, but he broke more than he fixed.

In those days, it was just fridges wherever you looked. The ones that wouldn't fit into the den had to stand outside. Lambert's den was the workshop. And the fridges standing outside, the ones that were switched off, had to have their doors open so they wouldn't go rotten. Quite a few of them were running on extensions.

The grass grew long between the fridges, especially in the yard where they kept old ones for spare parts, like vegetable trays or racks or other parts from the insides.

One day, when Lambert was taking the insides out of an old fridge, she put one of his small spanners down in the long grass. Then, later, she couldn't find it again. Those days Lambert was even more impatient than he is now. She used to spend most of her time at his beck and call. Taking orders. Pass this. Pass that. Take this. Pliers and hammers and screwdrivers with different heads. She even knew their names.

Treppie and Pop were out on a job somewhere. They'd asked Lambert to take spare parts out of an old fridge for one that had to be ready that night. It was late. Lambert had already started looking for trouble earlier that afternoon, long before the spanner got lost. First he said her housecoat was ugly and why didn't she wear panties. Did she want the whole of Triomf to see her thing? Except he didn't say thing, he said something much worse. And how did she think he was going to entertain customers at his Guy Fawkes party the next day if she wasn't even wearing panties? How was she going to light the rockets if she had to bend over all the time with no panties?

He's mad, Treppie said earlier, nobody would come. But no one tells Lambert he's mad. For months already, he'd been putting invitations into every ice-box leaving the yard, with details about the party.

Don't mis it. Fireworks in the backjaart./ Moet nie dit mis nie. Vuur werke in die agter plaas. Kom maak a dop virniet op Gaai Foks. Come in for a free drink for Gaai Foks. Support your local electric appliance Repair Services. Ondersteun u plaaslike herstel diens vir elektriese toe stelle. RSVP.

One of those invitations is still pasted up behind the kitchen door. She sees it every time she hangs her housecoat up on the nail.

Lambert was ready for the party long before it was supposed to start.

He spent all his savings on fireworks, boxes of the stuff that he got from the Chinese. They were called 'Peking Ducks'. Treppie stood there, checking out those boxes. He said he couldn't wait to see if it was true they went off 'rack-a-tack-tack-tack' in the sky with subtitles in Chinese.

By then the whole den was full of the boxes. On top of the fridges, inside the fridges, stacked up to the ceiling. There were boxes of fireworks everywhere.

Lambert said if you wanted to do something you had to do it properly. He also bought six bottles of brandy, a crate of Coke and lots of plastic cups. Now only the people still had to come.

Treppie told Lambert if he wanted his party to look like an 'evening cocktail' he'd better cut the grass. He didn't want Parktown Prawns crawling up his customers' legs, did he? But Lambert hadn't gotten that far. In those days they had a manual lawn-mower with blades that jammed all the time. And Lambert wasn't so worried about the state of the lawn in those days.

So the grass was long that day before Guy Fawkes. Lambert was in a hurry to get the fridge finished and he shouted at her to bring his small spanner. Trying to find a little spanner in the long grass was just too much for her. So she gave him one that she thought would fit the tiny nuts he was trying to loosen. But it was the wrong spanner and he threw that one into the grass as well. It wasn't long before he took all the tools from the box and hurled them by the fistful into the long grass.

'This fridge must get finished! Now!' he shouted. 'Bring me my Phillips screwdriver.'

Now, finding a Phillips screwdriver in long grass is no joke. Each time she thought she saw it and bent over, he shouted: Ma, I can see your twat! Stand up! And when she stood up again, he shouted: Find my goddamn this! Or, bring my fucken that! After a while she was so confused that when he asked for pliers she grabbed the first thing she could lay her hands on and passed it to him, even if it was a hammer, or a nail, or a screw.

That's how she lost her bearings with the names of tools and things. After a while she was crawling on all fours in the grass, crying. It was dark and Lambert had put on the extension light. He said he was finished with things that didn't work, things that didn't run, things that didn't wear panties and things that got lost in the grass. And he was finished with fancy larnies who didn't RSVP to say they were coming to his party. Finished. Then he lost his head completely. He said if Triomf hadn't seen a Big Bang before, today was the day. And if people thought they made history in this place by bulldozing kaffir-houses, then they were in for a big surprise. Now they'd see what real history looked like. It wasn't bulldozing that made history, it was fire. Guy Fawkes. He took the spare can of petrol from the Austin and threw it all over the grass where the fridges stood. He told her to bring the boxes out of the den and pack them on top of the fridges. And then he poured petrol over the fridges, too.

She began to scream, but he said that if she didn't shuddup at once he'd see to it that she made such a big noise she wouldn't say another full sentence all the days of her life. He dragged her into the den and stuffed the pockets of her housecoat with Peking Ducks, shoving some into the front of her dress as well. He said it was a pity she wasn't wearing panties, 'cause then he could've shoved them in there too. It was actually under her backside that he wanted to make a fire, and her cunt that he wanted to shoot into its glory. Disgusting mouth he's got. He shoved her arms and her legs and her feet into the old fridge, and he slammed the door closed, knocking her knees silly.

That fridge was still running when the door closed. The light went off right there next to her head. It was cold. She remembers thinking this must be what hell feels like – sitting with squashed knees in a place that's so cold it makes your teeth rattle. And then, moments later, you take off like a rocket into the sky. 'Rack-a-tack-tack-tack!' Into the outermost darkness, with subtitles.

Other than that, she remembers nothing. Pop says Treppie found her inside the fridge, knocked out cold.

When Pop and Treppie got home that night, the whole street was outside, watching the fireworks. By then, the den was burning brightly, but the fire brigade came and killed the flames. Lambert was completely stuffed up. Lying in the grass, filthy dirty from soiling himself as he gave in. He'd bitten himself and his mouth was full of blood. Both of them had to be taken to hospital in an ambulance. She was given oxygen. Afterwards, she coughed non-stop for almost a year. The doctor said her lungs had been injured by the fridge-gas leaking into her blood.

Treppie took it badly. Pop too. He began to stare out of his eyes with an extra faraway look, like he was riding up and down in a lift all day long. Only Lambert still had some kick left in him when he came back from hospital. His mouth was so sore he couldn't manage anything but milkshake for a whole month. They had to spend their days making sure he was busy.

She told Pop they must give him things to fix, things that work in the end. If things don't work, Lambert gets a fit or he begins to smash everything to pieces. Or he makes fires.

That's how the postbox got there. But since the day Lambert first put up his postbox, it hasn't stayed on its pole for more than a month at a time.

Mol looks at the gate. It looks faint in the mist. Gerty shivers softly in her arms. When Gerty coughs, it feels like she's the one who's actually coughing. If only something would come out. But it sounds like it'd be too much if it did come out.

It sounds like Gerty wants to cough her heart right out. Mol wonders what Gerty's heart would look like if she coughed it out. Would it hang from her mouth by threads, or fall on to the bare cement and lie there, quivering?

She shuts her eyes tight.

'Ughrr-ughrr,' she helps Gerty cough.

'Hrrraagh-hrrraagh!' Gerty coughs.

'Ughrr-ughrr, hrrraagh-hrrraagh!' They sit there, coughing together on the stoep. Then Mol hears something else: 'Who-Whoo!'

She looks up. Can you believe it? On top of the lamp-pole, etched against the mist, an owl perches. It's got little ears. Must've gotten lost. The mist must be too thick for owls tonight.

'Ughrr-ughrr, hrrraagh-hrrraagh, who-whoo!' it goes in the front yard.

We're singing in turns, Mol thinks, like Friar Jacob. 'Ughrr-ughrr, hrrraagh-hrrraagh, who-whoo.'

10

~

THE NEVER-ENDING PAINTING

L ambert stands in front of the den's inside wall with a can of spray-paint in his hand. He's looking at his painting. The painting rises from behind his bed, filling up the whole wall.

Most of the time he sees nothing when he starts. It's weird, seeing nothing where there's so much.

But he knows he just has to be patient. If it takes too long, he can spray a spot or a line anywhere. After that he can always paint a tail on to the spot or a head on to the line. Then at least it looks like something.

'Cause not to know where to start, that's the worst.

Then there's just time and nothing.

Like when he left school. He was bored to death, especially between twelve and two in the afternoons. Time and nothing, like a draught down his neck. Without being able to close a door somewhere.

Then one day he began to draw South Africa with koki pens on the wall, copying from his history book.

The outer lines are green. They're almost completely faded out now. Koki pens are like that. The little red peaks for the Cape mountains and the Drakensberg are bigger and you can see them better. Molehills, molehills, molehills. And the Orange River and the Vaal River and the Fish River and all the other big rivers are there too, in blue. The best was when he drew big thick arrows in black to show how the kaffirs swooped down on the country from above. And he drew big yellow arrows for the Voortrekkers, who occupied the country outwards from the Cape.

When he began to draw that day, it was just after twelve. Like now. Just after he got up. By the time he was finished it was pitch dark outside. That's how the time flew.

The more things you've already painted, the easier it is to carry on. Until you've got too many beginnings. Then it gets hard again. Much harder than it was when there was still nothing. When he had nothing but the outline, it was easy to carry on. And he had to carry on, too, 'cause South Africa alone was too boring and empty. At first he couldn't think beyond rivers and mountains. He just painted more rivers, more mountains.

Then one day he decided to paint the house. On top of everything. And across the whole of South Africa. That was a brainwave. And when the moles began to push up their little hills on the lawn that night, the Drakensberg mountains were already there. Molehills, molehills, molehills. Things like that happen sometimes. It's just luck. But the black and yellow arrows didn't want to work for the lawn.

'What's this?' Treppie asked when he saw the painting.

'That's our house, 127 Martha Street,' he said, scratching 127 on the postbox in the painting with a black ball-point, just to make sure.

But that's not what Treppie wanted to know. He wanted to know what those arrows were. And when he told Treppie they were the kaffirs and the Afrikaners and history, Treppie said it looked more like piss-pipes and shit-pipes under the ground. Shit from this side and piss from that side. Then Treppie said same difference. Where you get people you get shit and crap going down the pipes, and he wished he was a dog, 'cause dogs were the only ones who got any love at 127 Martha Street.

Treppie's plans for when the shit starts flying are also in the painting.

Just under Molletjie's belly there's a thick, red, broken line, with a figure eight going out of the driveway to show how she turns into the street. She goes right over the lawn, the shit-pipes and the piss-pipes, heading north. But the further north she goes, the more of Africa he has to add to the drawing. He made South Africa too big to start with, so there was only a small space left for the rest of Africa. Then he had to start drawing everything smaller and smaller to make it fit on the wall.

When Treppie saw this, he said Lambert shouldn't make matters so difficult for himself, couldn't he see he had the whole fucken ceiling for Africa? But by then it was too late, all the countries in Africa had already been squashed flat to fit under the ceiling. There was still enough space on both sides for the horn and the shoulder of Africa, except they were too big for the body. And when his mother came to see she said it didn't look anything like Africa. Nothing he painted ever looked like anything, she said. Then he said, okay, in that case he was going to add titles, in capital letters. TENNIS BALL, CLOUD, HOUSE, DOG, MOLEHILL, SHIT-PIPE, PUMP, ROSE, DICK, CUNT, BEE NEST, HOUSECOAT, PLASTER CRACK, RUST, EVAPORATOR. Now all she needed to do was open her eyes and read what it said there.

Lambert looks at his painting. It's 'cause things kept happening and he started painting new stuff over the old stuff. Once he gets going he hasn't got the time for blanking things out. And now his mother's standing there with a pink Day-Glo tennis ball in her mouth. He couldn't help it. She was already there when he wanted to paint a ball for the DOG.

Gerty looks like she's been tied to the lawn-mower, 'cause two black shit-pipes run between her and the mower like reins. The mower itself has WINGS, 'cause the WITNESS is just behind it. All you can see are her shoulders with the wings, and then her legs. The lawn-mower runs over her belly. She's got JEHOVA on her forehead but it doesn't all fit. The JE and VA fall down on both sides. They make her look like she's wearing earphones. The EVENING STAR is in the sky above the house, its five points painted in silver hubcap-paint. HEAVEN begins just above the CAPRIVI STRIP. In that case, says Treppie, the Evening Star should be in Angola, not in Heaven, but then he says it doesn't make any difference, 'cause for that matter 127 Martha Street could be hell itself, down here at the bottom of Africa. That's Treppie for you. Everything has to be double upside-down before he's happy.

The sun's in Zaire. It first had rays, but now it's got little red points like the National Party's new sun. He's written SUNSHINE D inside the sun.

His mother's housecoat hangs from the horn of Africa, on the one side. It doesn't look like a housecoat. It looks more like a piece of slaughtered human skin. That's why he wrote HOUSECOAT there. Then, in brackets, he added (MOLE-SKIN).

CAPE POINT can still be seen at the bottom of the driveway. Then there's TABLE MOUNTAIN as well. The postbox is planted on top of it. On the one side of the postbox, next to Table Mountain, he's written HARRY THE STRANDLOPER. That's also from his history book. On the other side of Table Mountain you can see JAN VAN RIEBEECK with a ribbon across his chest that says MAN ABOUT TOWN. He's holding a bottle of KLIPDRIFT in his hand. Harry the Strandloper holds a bottle of COKE.

Jan van Riebeeck's got a pink feather in his hat. Same as the tennis ball. That was a nice pink. He can't find it in the hardware shops any more. It was Flossie's first undercoat. He had just enough left over to paint a pink DICK and a pink CUNT and to colour in the Witness's petticoat.

The last bit of pink was for Tsafendas's WORM. But the pink ran out halfway down the worm. Now the worm's half-pink, half-green. He cut out the picture of Tsafendas from *Your Family and You*. Still in jail over Verwoerd. Very old now, but he's still got the worm. He hung his Republic Day medal on Tsafendas's chest, on to a nail going right through his HEART. He'd drawn the heart on to the picture himself. Treppie came and asked if that was the Lord Jesus there with his bleeding heart. Then he asked Treppie if he was mad or something, Jesus didn't have a worm. 'Cause the worm starts in the heart and goes all the way to the guts, until you can't make out any more what's guts and what's worm. He painted the guts at the bottom of the picture too. Tsafendas is pasted up against the prefab wall, a little man with a gold medal and lots of guts that are full of worm.

You can also see Treppie's guts.

Treppie's lying cut open across the shoulder of Africa, but he doesn't know it's him. His insides are hanging out. To the one side, in the little waves of the ATLANTIC OCEAN, there's a huge, naked kaffir with a whopper of a black cock reaching right down into the water. He's eating Treppie's liver. 'PATYDEFWAGRAS,' the kaffir says. He's got a silver bangle around his cock.

Pop's head only just sticks out above a cloud, over the same ocean. POP'S HEAD ON THUNDER CLOUD is what he wrote there, 'cause you can't see very much of Pop. He first started to draw Pop rising up to heaven but then he painted the clouds over Pop, 'cause Pop suddenly began to look so lonely up there in the sky. You can at least see Pop's feet. They've been burnt to little pitch-black sticks, 'cause Pop's standing on a white flash of lightning that strikes from under the cloud's belly.

He, LAMBERT, sits in the VOLKSWAGEN under the CARPORT. He's smiling out the window. The roof-rack's full of silver bags, and there, on top of the silver bags, is his GIRL. A naked blonde. It looks like she's sitting on a silver waterbed. He used the silver hubcap-paint for that. It doesn't take so nicely on PVA, and every now and again he has to touch up the waterbed. He has to touch up his girl's silver fin as well, 'cause she's a mermaid with scales on her tail. She's got silver stars on her nipples. NIPPLE CAPS. On top of her head you can see the Volksie's aerial. There's a flag hanging from the aerial with DIAMOND LADY written on it. That's what he saw on Ponta do Sol's pinball.

If she comes back of her own accord and for free after the first night, then he'll drive her to Ponta do Sol for take-aways. They can play a quick game of pinball while they wait for their food. And when they come back they can eat here in his den. Then she can play pinball on *him*.

Lambert gets his angle right. He wants to paint a white, spouting fountain from the dick, but he's too worked up. He drops his hand into the front of his pants. Stabs of pain shoot through his tail-end. He closes his eyes and sits on the bed, feeling behind the bed for the T-shirt with which he always wipes himself. When he opens his eyes again, he sees his feet. They're dirty. He always walks around in bare feet 'cause he doesn't go anywhere in any case. The nails on his big toes are long and dirty. One is growing in. His other toenails are thick and skew from all the knocks. Dog-toenails, Treppie says. Why are his feet so big and his ankles so thick and knobbly? The skin around his shins looks thin. He can see dents there. His throat feels tight. He sees big, fat tears falling on to his feet. He's crying. What's he crying for? Fuck that. But the crying won't stop. He wipes off the tears with the T-shirt, first from his face and then from his feet. Then he wipes off the rest.

He gets up so it can pass. His back feels lame. He must just start painting now, then it'll pass. Suddenly he sees Gerty. She's sitting there without a jersey. He sprays on a yellow jersey for her. The green ribbing will just have to wait. He hasn't got any green now. He's got yellow and brown and black and white. He sprays Gerty's yellow jersey over and over, until Gerty's almost covered in it. Well, she's almost over the hill in any case. When she dies, all he'll have to do is blank out her head and her paws. She hasn't got a tail in the painting.

What else is yellow? He touches up his mermaid's yellow hair. Now it looks like she's got too much hair. This mermaid of his just doesn't want to work so nicely. Her tail's chipping off badly and now there's no more silver.

Lambert stands back to look at his painting. He thought he had a start with the yellow. But all he's got are dead-ends. The painting doesn't want to work today. He can't get the thing going.

Clouds work, stars work, the sun works. You don't have to make them work. They all just work on their own. Moles, bees, termites, ants. They all work. And mice and earwigs and cockroaches. They're pests but they do what they're supposed to do. They don't sit staring at their feet.

They don't get stuck. They don't wear out. They don't use oil like pumps and cars and lawn-mowers. They don't jam. They don't seize up and their timing doesn't go out like the timing of washing machines and fridges. And when they die, they die softly. They don't first start backfiring or missing. And they don't hum and rattle and click on and off in the night. They're cool. They don't just fade without a good reason. They don't need captions. And you don't have to struggle to get them started, 'cause when you find them they're on the go already.

Suddenly Lambert knows what to do. Where to begin. He smiles. He feels time slacken all around him. His dick hangs happily between his legs. He's got a plan. He drags a chair closer and puts a Coke crate on top of it so he can get to the spot. He starts taking down the Tuxedo Tyres calendars. Pink Bikini. Yellow Bikini. Blue Bikini. Off with you! Halfway round the den, when he gets to 1980s calendars, he sees a little photograph of the manager of Tuxedo Tyres and his wife. It's a round picture inside a tyre. *Gavin and Cindy Viljoen,* it says in small letters underneath. That's why those damn pin-ups all look the same! It's her, the manager's wife, she's just wearing a different colour bikini every time, and a different wig. Blarry rip-off! Think they can fool him! He steps from the crate on to the Kneff, pulling down four of the calendars in one swipe. And from there he steps on to the Fuchs and the Tedelex, and then on to the top of his cabinet. Off with the rubbish! Now for some things that work! Now for some bees and ants and moles!

He lets himself down from the steel cabinet. He pulls the chair and the crate back towards him so he can get to the last of the calendars, there in the corner. Funny how patient he gets when he knows he's got a plan. Now he takes his time. He takes more than his time. He knows it's a sure thing. It won't go away now. He can linger longer. He can postpone it, it just gets better and better, 'cause it gets clearer by the minute. Or no, it's not clear. It's a plan without a plan. How can he say it – he knows it'll work but he doesn't altogether know how. It's like coming in a dream, without those stabs of pain. And he smiles when he gets up. He doesn't cry and his feet don't bother him.

Now he starts getting his paints and things ready. The yellow spray-can. A few loose, wax crayons. And some half-finished kokis – a red, a blue and a purple. A tin of black high-gloss and two brushes, a wide one and a little thin one. And the white PVA that Treppie bought a year ago to paint the house. It didn't get used in the end and now it's half finished anyway. It takes nicely on the plaster. And then there's the brown government paint. Treppie got that from the Chinese, who got it from the police at John Vorster Square. Treppie says the police there spend the whole day painting the walls brown 'cause they're not allowed to manhandle the kaffirs any more. He says the police have become interior designers now. They have to sign three pieces of paper every time they want a baton. And ten pieces of paper for a gun. The batons and the guns have all been locked up in safes. He thinks Treppie tells stories the way he, Lambert, paints pictures. Most of the time it's all mixed up and you can't make head or tail out of it, but you can see a mile off when he's got a good one. He likes it when Treppie gets like that. It's just that Treppie never knows when to round off his stories. Most of the time he stops before the end and then he says it's all in the mind anyway.

He thinks Treppie just says that when a story doesn't work out so nicely. Nowadays Treppie ends before he even begins. He ends without an ending. He says it's all in the mind and people must just figure out for themselves what happened in the meantime. Stories give you a headache sometimes. His mother's stories never want to work so nicely, but he's not going to think about her now. He's putting her out of his mind. And the only way to get her out of his mind is to paint.

Lambert stands back and looks at the row of open squares where the calendars used to be. They're much cleaner than the rest of the wall. Such neat, pale, white squares. He smiles at his luck. Now he's got frames into the bargain as well. Now he can paint nicely inside the frames. And all the things that work will be the same size.

What first? No, where first? In the middle, the middle block in the back wall. Then he can paint backwards to the end on the one wall, and forwards on the other wall to the beginning. But the middle is actually the beginning. Maybe he should paint one block that way and one block this way, starting from the middle. Then everything will fill up evenly. Not like a line that you draw, but like a scale with arms that you load evenly so it balances out. Suddenly he's got a huge thirst from all the excitement. He grabs the half-full bottle of Coke in the open fridge without even looking, swigging a few big sips. He doesn't once take his eyes off the wall. He can fucken see it! A whole gallery full of things that work. Pests! Moles! Ants! Creepies!

Now, what first? In the middle frame? A bee, he thinks.

How does a bee look again? He must know, there were so many dead bees after the fuck-up when he threw water into the hive.

A bee's got two pieces. A head-piece and a tail-piece.

He gets on to the Tedelex with the narrow brush and the tin of black paint. He gets his angle right. First he paints the outline of the head, and then, a little bigger, the outline of the body. The outline comes out nice and smooth and shiny. But the bee's too small. It doesn't fill the frame so nicely. What now? He adds another piece of tail to the bee. And now? Now the head's too small. Wait, he knows. This bee is going to become Superbee. It's going to get two more heads, one on either side of the middle one. That's easy. Lambert gets down from the Tedelex and looks up at his Superbee. It's becoming a bee to beat all bees! He smiles. The more heads, the more legs and the more wings, the better this bee's going to work.

The bee's got seven legs on either side. Lambert draws a narrow seam for the head. He makes connecting threads between the head and the body, and between the head and the other body. Each head gets two blobs where the eyes are. The middle head's got the biggest eyes. Now for the wings. Four on either side. They're the most difficult, with all those little veins. He finds a match. He chews the back end of the match until it's soft, and then he pulls out a few threads until he's got a point. He draws the veins on to each wing, showing how they get thinner and thinner. The veins hold the wing up. What's a vein like that made of? Not bone, not wood. Maybe blood that's gotten hard. Do bees have blood? Is it sweet? Does it run in veins? Do bees have hearts?

Lambert stands back a little from Superbee. His head feels like a joystick. He wants to fly.

It's always like this when he paints. The smaller and flimsier it gets, and the more he has to screw up his eyes and hold his hand steady, the better it feels. It's only when he tries to fix small things in fucked-up gadgets and stuff that he loses his cool so badly. In his paintings he can do what he likes with the flimsy little things.

Now, how's he going to get the bee's wings to shimmer with colour, but in such a way that you can still half see the world through them?

In that case, first the world. He takes his wax crayons and adds in daintily, between the bee's legs and his wings, and between the veins in the wings, careful not to smudge the outlines – a blue mountain, a green aloe with three red aloe flowers, and a light yellow patch of grass.

But now the wings look completely see-through. He puts some spit on a clean match and works the colours of the world a little more densely between the veins – green and blue and light yellow and red.

Now for the final touches. That bee must gain some weight so it can stay put in the world. The three heads must shine pitch black and look solid. He leaves some white spots on the eyes so they can shine. Do bees' eyes shine?

The two bodies get fat stripes: yellow-black, yellow-black, yellow-black. Golden yellow and pitch black.

He climbs down to look at the bee. It looks sharp. A black-yellow, black-yellow Superbee with veins on his wings that you can only just see through. But something's missing. His bee's got an earth, but there's no heaven. Halfway up from the mountain, he makes a light yellow sun and slightly higher, a white cloud, with small pieces of light blue heaven inbetween.

He gets down to look again. How can it already be getting dark outside? He puts on the lights, the one next to his bed and the other on the ceiling, but the ceiling's light doesn't want to work. The bulb's blown. Lambert smiles. He unlocks his steel cabinet and takes it out. Of course! The time has come for his red light.

His bee looks magic in the red light. What kind of honey will a bee with three heads and two bodies make? Mega-honey!

He holds his head at an angle. There's only one problem with his bee: it looks a little stiff. Heaven and earth too, a little flat and a little stiff. Something jolly's missing somewhere. The sting! Where does a bee's sting sit? Well, this bee's going to have more than one of them.

Coming out the left side of the middle head, he paints a thin, black sting, with a curl that goes around the aloe-flower. And out of the right side of the tail, a sting that splits three ways around the cloud, with arrows at the ends.

Now that bee looks wired! He looks like he fucken wants to spark right off the wall!

To frame the bee, Lambert paints fine black lines around the edges, where the calendar used to be. He paints ER underneath, in the middle, so he can paint SUP and BEE on either side, without going wider than the painting. Then he goes and lies down on his bed with a Paul Revere to look at his SUPERBEE. He leaves it to the darkness to quietly fill up the world outside. While the light in his room turns an ever brighter scarlet.

11

~

THE SAVING PERSPECTIVE

MEAT ~

I t's a Monday night. The Benades sit in the lounge in front of the TV. It's tuned to TV1 but they're not really watching. Everyone's there except Lambert, who left just after five. Monday night is rubbish night, and Lambert's gone to search in the rubbish bags for wine boxes. He promised he'd put *Raiders of the Lost Ark* into the video machine for them when he got back. Only Lambert's allowed to touch the machine, so now they just have to sit and wait.

Mol's knitting Gerty's belly piece from scratch. When she let Gerty try it on this morning, it was miles too big. So then she had to pull the whole thing apart again. Gerty needs about twenty stitches fewer than she did last year. And now she'll have to make Gerty try it on again when she gets to the middle piece. She hasn't got a clue how much smaller to make it. Poor Gerty. She won't eat on her own any more. She only eats when Mol feeds her little pieces of food from her hand, begging her to take a few morsels. And she coughs so bad she can hardly breathe.

'Put her down. Put her down, so this misery can come to an end,' says Treppie, but Treppie's got no heart. Pop says he's got a heart, but she thinks if he's got one it must be a very strange kind of heart.

Treppie's sitting here now on his crate, reading a *Star*. One that he took from across the road's pile this morning before the lorry came to pick them up. First he read the classifieds and now he's reading the main news right from the beginning. Every now and again his lips move as he reads something but she can't make out what he's saying. The TV's too loud. She sees him lose his temper about something that he reads there. His shoulder twitches and he pages wildly without finishing anything he starts. Then he shakes out the folds violently like he wants to hit something right out of the paper, knocking the page in front of him with the back of his hand. Like he wants to smack the news back into shape. Treppie never gets like this with the classifieds. Then he reads all afternoon long, turning the pages nice and softly. And he chuckles all the time when he reads them. She wonders what's so funny about the classifieds. Funny or almost funny, 'cause Treppie laughs a little half-laugh through that twisted mouth of his. Sometimes she asks: 'What are you laughing at, Treppie?', and then he reads her an advert about something, or someone. Like the last time, about someone called Alex, who had just died. It was something like 'we all loved Alex as he was', and that he also 'loved everyone'. He loved all his neighbours and his friends and fish pies too. Her favourite part was when it said: 'Let God be with him and bear with us through our never-ending troubles, happiness and sadness.'

'That message is from Maggie Rip,' Treppie said, laughing his little half-laugh. So she asked Treppie who Alex and Maggie Rip were. Did he know them? She thought maybe they were connections of the Chinese. No, Treppie said, he didn't know them, but he could guess. Guess what? she asked. Then he said he could guess Alex was probably just another lost case, and Maggie was worn-out from letting rip so much. Treppie's full of nonsense. She still doesn't know what's supposed to be so funny about that. And then there was the time Treppie almost laughed himself to death over Frieda's wedding dress. This Frieda was also someone he didn't know.

'Hell, just look at all these wedding dresses for sale,' Treppie said, reading up and down about the dresses with a bigger and bigger smile on his face, until he burst out laughing: '"Wedding dress off-white. Very large. Veil and train. Satin shoes size 11. Instep supported. Brand new. Personal tragedy. Contact Frieda or leave message."' Poor Frieda, whoever she is, she thought, but Treppie walked up and down the house and pissed himself. Pop said Treppie had delicate nerves. That may be so, she said, but he wasn't delicate with her. Then Pop said she should just be thankful she wasn't Frieda, who didn't have anyone in the whole world. At least they still had each other. Treppie heard what Pop said, 'cause he'd stopped laughing now, and then he told her she must listen to Pop. Pop had a sense of perspective.

Well, whether Pop's got one or not, that's one of Treppie's favourite words. Perspective. It's the one word she remembers Treppie using over and over when they worked out the story for Lambert – that's now the story of their family set-up and about where Lambert actually comes from. It was all Treppie's idea. He said they should tell Lambert a story that would give him a perspective on the matter, one that both he and the rest of them could live with. And that's how they came upon the distant-family story. That Pop was a distant Benade from the Cape. A Benade who stole her heart at a garment workers' dance when he played a solo on his mouth organ, the only thing he still had left from his late father. And how they were married in community of property by a magistrate, 'cause that was the quickest and cheapest way to do it, even though they had far more in common than just property. And how afterwards there was a dinner and dance in the backyard at the Vrededorp house. And how Treppie was the master of ceremonies, making an unforgettable speech. About 'the holiness of marriage' and 'the godliness of the generations'. 'Cause he had to play minister as well. The magistrate seals the community of property, not the joining of souls.

Treppie practised that speech over and over again. That was the meat of the perspective, he said. Mind you, they all practised like mad on that perspective. Treppie said it had to be drilled into them so hard they'd also start thinking it was true after a while. He said a person needed that kind of perspective in life. No, he said, it was more. It kept you alive. Otherwise you wouldn't have a hope in hell. Actually, he said, the whole world and the whole business we called life and everything that went with it was just one big war of perspectives. One big circus – it just depended on how you looked at it. It was all in the mind, anyway. The point was you had to have one. A perspective, so you could fight. Or a different one, so you could laugh. Treppie says most people's perspectives are just bubbles to keep their heads above water. That's what you call a 'saving perspective'.

Well, it's not like they're exactly on top of things. They just muddle along through the rubble. But that perspective of Treppie's saved their backsides on many occasions. When Lambert started getting old enough to ask questions, they could tell him all about that heart-stealing dance and the Vrededorp wedding. About the people who came, what they were wearing and what they had to eat. Doughnuts and peanuts and Swiss roll. And everything Treppie had to say, as brother of the bride and master of ceremonies. The family as the cornerstone of the volk, and the near and distant family as the stronghold of something else. A lot of rubbish, she sees now, but when children began pestering Lambert at school with all kinds of gossip about the Benades, they could at least tell him what to say.

Then they'd dish up that old story of theirs again. Just like they practised it all those years ago, when Treppie made her wear Old Mol's marriage dress and Pop had to put on his black jacket with the black trousers. Not a suit, but at least both pieces were black. She used to wish Treppie would practise his speech and get done with it, 'cause that wedding dress was much too tight for her. She was already seven months pregnant with Lambert and he was a huge bastard. Treppie allowed them to practise the rest, about the distant family, in ordinary clothes, but for his speech he said they must dress up like a bride and groom. So they'd get a good grip on the perspective. It was like kissing someone with measles, he said. You had to expose yourself if you wanted to be immune.

Then Treppie would get up on a chair and hold up his hand for silence. Her and Pop had to shout 'Speech! Speech!' in their wedding clothes. And Pop had to whistle like lots of people, 'cause the way the story went there were almost a hundred people at the wedding. All of them garment workers and their fiancés.

Then Treppie would start: 'Ladies and gentlemen, my dear sister Mol and my brother-in-law from the old colony – distant family, but still a shoot from the same tree . . .' Sometimes he would say 'pip from the same watermelon'.

And then they had to shout 'Hear! Hear!' and sing 'For he's a jolly good fellow' all at the same time, the way lots of tipsy people do at a party.

When the applause was loud enough Treppie would raise his hand and carry on again. He always started with 'Every family has its secrets', or 'Every family has its fuck-ups.' The second sentence was: 'But all that counts is that we have each other and a roof over our heads.' His third sentence was addressed to them. He pointed his finger at her. At her belly. And at Pop in his suit, and then he said: 'Go out and multiply and fill the earth, or, as we say in good Afrikaans, sow the seed – sow the seed, oh sow the seed of the watermelon.'

After every sentence they had to cheer. And after the last sentence he made them sing 'How the hell can we believe him'.

Treppie told Lambert this was just the intro, nice and jolly, to make the wedding guests feel comfortable. The first duty of a master of ceremonies, he said, was to sweeten the audience so they could swallow the bitter pill.

The bitter pill was the serious part in the middle.

About how it was inevitable and predestined that these two people should come together, and how they had to stand by each other, come hell or high water. How they had to seek out their own destiny, live with what they had, and carry their own cross, the cross being the burden of the secrets and the weight of the fuck-ups that always came afterwards. And how they had to keep looking north. Look north, fuck forth! How the home was the cornerstone and the family the stronghold.

And how Pop had to understand he was now head of the house, and how, by the sweat of his brow, he'd have to reap what he sowed in the flush of his youth.

At this point in the practice Pop would pluck off his jacket and walk over to Treppie, who was still standing on a chair. Pop would tell him he'd better get off his pulpit now, 'cause he, Treppie, had played an equal part in the whole business, and who was he all of a sudden to make out he was so high and mighty?

Then Treppie told Pop he shouldn't be such a spoilsport. Had he forgotten? It was just a perspective they were trying to stamp on to

194

the fruit of their loins here. For their own survival. Fruit of their loins, yes, well.

Mol stretches the piece of knitting to see if it'll fit. Maybe she should knit Pop a cap or something for winter. He says nowadays the part of his head that sticks out when he sits in his chair, right on top in the middle, gets the coldest. Ice-cold, as if there's a draught on top of his head. Poor old Pop. He has to put up with so much. And when he's done complaining about his head, Treppie says, jeez, he always thought death rose from the feet.

THIS ONE'S FOR YOU ⌒

Pop's sleeping again. When he comes to sit here in front of the TV he falls asleep almost straight away, no matter what they're watching. Now and then she wakes him up so he can watch his favourite adverts. Both she and Pop have their favourites. What she likes about adverts is that they're short, and then you can play them over and over again in your head. Like the one about the three beds. Big double beds with a woman sleeping alone and waking up quietly, on three different mornings. In three different places.

She would also feel nice if she could wake up like that, all on her own. And so peacefully. Alone on a beach with dolphins jumping out of the waves in front of her. In a field of flowers full of cooing doves. Next to a waterfall with ferns and rabbits. On such a nice big bed, with such soft, warm bedding. In three different nighties, too. Sometimes, when Lambert gets so wild with her, she closes her eyes and goes to sleep on those beds, one by one. On the beach. In the veld. Next to the waterfall. Over and over again. She sees the dolphins. She catches the doves. And she stares into the face of a rabbit, with his soft, shiny eyes, until Lambert's finished. That helps.

But it doesn't work when he also wants to hear stories. Then it has to be stories from his videos. Then she has to concentrate on the story, which

195

means she can't think about her advert, about all those mattresses with springs. Their own mattresses are sponge. Her and Pop's mattress lies on the floor. Lambert took the base for himself. He says he refuses to sleep on the floor like a kaffir. She doesn't know where he gets his information about the way kaffirs sleep. She's told him, he must look at the way they drink beer in the adverts – in suits, together with white people. If you ask her, they look like they all sleep in nice soft beds with legs. And would you believe it, the other day she saw her favourite advert again, but this time a brand-new kaffir was sleeping in one of the beds. Never saw him before. Must be a New South Africa kaffir, that one.

Pop's favourite is the squirrel who wants to save his acorn at the bank. He says he likes to see the way every animal has its own little place. The round-eyed owl has a crack in the rocks. The ringed cobra's got a hole. The jackal with his pointy nose has a hollow. That's where they belong and everyone knows it, and they keep out of each other's way. When the squirrel gives his acorn to the Trust Bank man, Pop whistles the song again, and then he says: 'Go back to your tree, old curlytail! Trust Bank's just for your acorn, not for you!'

Treppie says she and Pop are suckers for adverts. He says he doesn't like adverts himself, but if he must choose, then the one he fancies is the elephant taking a crap on a shining white lavatory. He says he wishes he could also make a noise like that when he's done. That sounds like a really good statement, he says. When she asked him one day what he meant by a really good statement, he put his hands behind his ears and flapped them like an elephant's. Then he held his hands in front of his mouth, like an elephant's trunk, and he shouted so loud, right into her ears, that her heart almost stopped: 'I, Martinus Benade, have just shat out, at half past nine, what I ate at seven o'clock, and from now on for the rest of my days I'm going to eat, shit, eat, shit, over and over again, until one fine day I fall down and die. Praise the Lord with joyful fumes for all eternity. Amen!'

Treppie has a terrible time trying to shit. He spends hours on the toilet. Sometimes he sits there so long he reads a whole pile of newspapers, from top to bottom, all afternoon long. That must be what he does, 'cause he tells so many stories from newspapers, word for word, she can swear he learns them off by heart when he's on the toilet. Treppie's too clever for his own good.

Mind you, she also thinks he makes up some of the stories he says he reads in the papers. He thinks them up on days when he has to crap and there aren't any papers to read. She knows. She wasn't born yesterday.

Like the story about the mortuary assistant who screwed the dead woman. She'd been stone dead for three days, says Treppie. It was in Yugoslavia. She'd even begun to stink a little, 'cause they haven't got fridges for corpses there in Yugoslavia. But she was unbelievably beautiful. Just a little blue around the lips. Treppie says that's 'cause she died from blood that was too cold for one so young. Her heart stopped.

When that assistant sponged her down, there on the cold cement block, and he began drying her off, he suddenly got a big hard-on. From drying her long legs and her breasts that were lovely like marble, with dark, pink nipples. He got so horny he no longer smelt anything bad. But he held back and he held back, 'cause Yugoslavia's a Catholic country and Catholics have to hold back until they meet the woman of their dreams. That mortuary assistant had already been married for thirty years. He'd fathered seven children. And then the poor man had to make her up for the funeral as well. When he put the red lipstick on to her lovely mouth, and the rouge on her pale cheeks, he just couldn't take it any longer. So he ran off and locked the door of the mortuary, 'cause in Yugoslavia they cut your dick off right there and then, balls and all, if they catch you screwing a corpse. He climbed on to that corpse, there on the cold cement slab, and he rubbed some balm on, out of respect for the dead, and he made love to it, softly and carefully, with the fear of God so heavy in his heart that the tears were streaming down his face. Afterwards, he was so overcome he lay on top of her for a while, and then he kissed her mouth. 'Smothered her with kisses,' is how Treppie put it. 'He smothered her fair countenance with kisses.' Will you ever!

Treppie sometimes comes out with this kind of language. Then she knows he didn't read it in any newspaper.

That man was still lying there, feeling his chest getting colder and colder from the corpse. Then it suddenly began to feel warmer, lower down. So he decided he'd better pull out now. He didn't want to cause his soul any more damage. But when he pulled out, still on his knees there between her legs, she opened those made-up blue eyes of hers and she sat bolt upright. Right there on that block of cement. Like Sleeping Beauty, said Treppie, except he didn't think it was the kisses that did the trick.

Then there was a major run-around, one thing upon the next. The doctor who wrote the death certificate in the first place came to examine the woman. When he found fresh blood on the mortuary slab, he immediately smelt a rat. He examined her carefully down there, and he saw that the young woman's virgin had only just been broken.

Yes, said the woman's mother, when she died she was still pure. Untouched. Let me just get my hands on the fucker who raped my daughter, the father said, laying a charge of rape against the assistant before he did anything else. By then, that poor tormented man had been with the priest for days already, crossing himself over and over out of sheer panic. It was the priest who eventually saw the point, 'cause for Catholics there's always a point, Treppie says. The priest said the father and mother and daughter should actually praise the Lord for letting that God-fearing assistant get such a good hard-on. If he hadn't broken the young woman's virgin, then she'd still be a dead, cold corpse. Six feet under, where the worms would have violated her soft places anyway. Was life not more valuable, he asked, than a virginal membrane and a teaspoonful of blood?

So the father withdrew the case against the mortuary assistant. And that same man is still washing corpses, in that same mortuary, to this day.

Except that no one in Yugoslavia wants to marry the resurrected woman. Even though she's not dead any more, she's also not a virgin for the man of her dreams.

Can you believe it, Pop says when Treppie tells stories like this. Pray, can you believe it. Or: Who would've thought it possible.

But Pop has also learnt by now that you don't talk about believing things in front of Treppie. Or about praying, for that matter. So when Treppie reads something from the papers, like the Inkatha woman who put a tyre round an ANC woman's neck and set her alight, and then put another tyre around her waist because she didn't want to burn so nicely, then Pop just says: Really. And when Treppie says it looks like the necklace is out, but the hula-hoop's coming back in, then Pop just says: Really, hey!

One Sunday, Treppie gave the Jehovahs such a ticking off she thought they'd never come back again.

It was worse than Lambert's fits. When the Jehovahs took out their Bibles that day, he went and fetched a pile of old newspapers from his room. He threw the papers down in the middle of the lounge and said *that* was where the afflictions of suffering mankind were reported. They mustn't come and talk shit here about walls of jasper and streets of gold. He stood there, telling the Jehovahs he believed what he read in the papers and he hoped it would all come to an end as soon as possible. He said he didn't pray for God's intervention, he prayed for the End itself, without any mediation. And when they came and told him the End had hair like wool and a voice like many waters, then all he could say was, no, the End had eyes that were white with fright and it was running down a dirt road with a panga through its back, or it was jumping into the air with a bullet in its head, and pots of ferns and palms in its hands. 'Cause it was a gardener.

And then his voice went all strange and sharp, and he said he'd learnt to know the End when he was still young. It was hanging in a stoker's overall from a belt in a Railways truck, with a tongue sticking through its teeth. Completely humiliated in the struggle with death. Then he said he just wished he could understand how it all *began*. How, and why.

'Why? Why? Why?' he shouted, and the dogs began to bark. He shook the two Witnesses by the shoulders, first the one and then the other, so hard that their heads bounced on their necks. And then he let them go, suddenly quite calm again. 'Never mind,' he said. 'It's all in the mind. Just go and find yourselves a better story. I'm going to buy myself a paper now.' And then he winked at them and drove off to the café in Molletjie.

TETHER 〜

Pop says Treppie's come to the end of his tether. In that case, Lambert must be close to his breaking point too, 'cause he also shakes her by the shoulders like that when he doesn't like the stories she tells. He shakes her till her head bounces on her neck.

She does her best. She starts at the beginning. About the cowboy-girl standing on the stoep with her frills, waiting for the cowboy to arrive out of the distance. Hat over his eyes. She tells it all, just like in the cowboy movies. And if Lambert wants to hear them, she embroiders the parts she doesn't see in the movies. In English, too. 'Honey' this and 'darling' that, so he can just get on with it and be done. So she doesn't have to take too much punishment.

But she should never have let Lambert start saying things inbetween, 'cause now he's really full of nonsense. Now he keeps telling her what to say in the middle of everything, and then she loses her thread.

After a while, the cowboy who kept coming over the veld wasn't good enough any more. Then it was the Indian who had to come from behind. Through the kitchen window.

Lambert thought it up and then she had to play along. She simply had to learn the story and tell it like he wanted, otherwise he wants to tell it all on his own. What does she know about Indians, anyway? She told him it was against the Immorality Act in any case, but he said no, it wasn't. Indians were yellow, not black. Then she said she thought they were red, but Lambert said it cuts no ice, red wasn't black, so it was okay for the Indian to fuck the cowboy-girl. In any case, Indians did it from behind. Like dogs.

Like Treppie, she thought, but didn't say, 'cause that would've been like a red rag to a bull. Lambert wants to do everything Treppie does.

And she wouldn't be able to take that. It's bad enough as it is. Treppie says it's 'cause she closes up like a clam. He says stupid people clam up like that for fear of clever people. Then she asked him if he thought his intelligence was lodged in his thing, and hers in her backside. He laughed and said he was glad to see she wasn't really as stupid as he'd thought she was. He says he loses his bearings when he thinks too much with his head. So he rather keeps it under the belt. Those kind of thoughts are 'easily digestible'. Everyone can understand them, it's the 'basics'. Everything else is 'fancy footwork'. Well, Treppie must be using his head a lot nowadays, 'cause he's been losing his bearings in a big way recently. And he's been trying it less and less with her. Since Peace Day, not at all. He says she's worn out on all sides. But those are just excuses. He can't get it up any more. That's why he winds up Lambert against her. It's about all he can get up these days.

Mol smiles at her little joke. She must remember it, so she has something to say when he starts niggling her again. Whether he likes it or not. But it's not just with them that he's so touchy. He also lets strangers have it when they rub him up the wrong way.

Like the other day when they went to the Newlands library. Most of the time she and Pop go there alone. Pop only goes 'cause she wants to take out books but she can't drive. Nice books, like *Roses for Alice* and now, the last time, *The Raven-Haired Girl from Hope Springs*. Books about nice girls and their new boyfriends who're better than their old boyfriends. Boyfriends who come visiting and look at the girls with 'dark, brooding eyes'. Then they take them away to nice places, for picnics, with champagne in baskets. All just wallpaper, Treppie says when he sees her books. But sometimes when he's got nothing to do he goes with them, and then of course Lambert also wants to go. She asks what for, people stare at her enough as it is when she goes there, and if Lambert comes they'll stare even more. Then Treppie says, no, Lambert's his 'apprentice'. Where he goes Lambert must also go. Treppie does it just to make trouble. Him and Lambert stand around in the library and page through books, mostly the ones 'just for adults'. You have to sign for them in a black book. The books go missing otherwise, 'cause they're full of stuff about sex and naked people. They're just randy, she tells them, there's enough of that kind of thing in the cafés. That's if they really want to look. They don't even have to read anything. It's just pictures. But Treppie says he can't concentrate in cafés, there's too much noise, and in any case there aren't any *Britannica*s in the cafés. He doesn't just want to see pictures all the time, he also wants to learn. The same goes for Lambert. Lambert can't live from bread alone, and doesn't she, as his mother, also want him to broaden his horizons? Then she says Lambert's broad enough as it is, and Treppie mustn't start niggling her now. But Pop says it doesn't matter, let them come along. What harm can it do, after all?

Pop's always trying to keep the peace. But too much peace can also land you in trouble. Like the other day, when Treppie and Lambert stood there in the library, signing their names with red pens and asking the librarian to get them the most juicy books 'just for adults'. The woman asked them what they meant by most juicy? Treppie said they meant the books with grubby pages from all the fingering. Those were the best, 'cause dirty was nice, he told her, winking. Then that woman raised her eyes and said, ai, a librarian also had a dog's life in a place like Newlands, with this class of people. Well, Treppie lost it right there and then. But he didn't swear. He began with those sharp little remarks of his. Yes, he said, he did come from Triomf, which used to be Sophiatown. He knew it was kaffirs who lived there, but in the early days Newlands was also full of kaffirs. That's where the washerwomen came from. At least the kaffirs in Sophiatown used to play music on penny-whistles. Penny-whistles and trumpets. Altogether a better class of kaffir. And did she know, she, a librarian, who Satchmo was? No, said the woman, she didn't. Oh, said Treppie, then she had a terrible hole in her education. Shame, said Treppie, and he made it sound like she had a terrible hole somewhere else. That poor woman didn't know where to look any more. People who aren't used to Treppie never know which side he's going to come from next. Well, then he started singing a song at the top of his voice. 'Hello Dolly', in a gravelly voice. And he winked at her, playing trumpet with his fingers. Did she know whose song that was? No, said the woman, she didn't. Good God, said Treppie, she must be analphabetic, and he raised his eyes the way she had earlier, the way she was still looking as he spoke. He told her a long story about Satchmo, whose real name was Louis Armstrong, a highly talented kaffir who came from America. One day, this kaffir came to visit Sophiatown, and he gave his golden trumpet to a boy called Hugh Masekela. Just like that, for keeps. Hugh Masekela was eight years old then. Did she know who Masekela was? No, said the woman. Treppie shook his head: 'Tsk-tsk-tsk.' She would have to get her house in order before the election, 'cause that same Hugh Masekela was now the best trumpet player in the country. And his sister, Treppie said, making big eyes at the librarian, Masekela's sister was going to become the minister of libraries. Her name was Barbara, and Barbara didn't take crap, not to mention ignorance, from librarians.

Treppie cornered that woman till she no longer knew whether she was coming or going. He asked her if she remembered how jolly it was in Sophiatown's kaffir-shebeens. But no, she must've been too high class to go there. Which was a pity, 'cause the way she was looking now, it would've done her a lot of good to learn the foxtrot from a kaffir. That's where he'd learnt ballroom, Treppie said. From the kaffirs in Sophiatown, and for someone of his class it was an education all on its own. To tell the truth, in those days he went there just to find a drink on weekends, when the bottle stores were all closed. And did she know that Triomf didn't even have an off-licence any more, let alone a ballroom?

'Cause where the off-licence should be, in Sophiatown, there across the road from Shoprite, was exactly where the NG church stood now. And the NG's church bazaars were so spiritless it was no wonder there were so many cracks in their edifice, and they had so few members. And what little devil was telling him now, the way she stood there in her floral print dress and her string of fresh-water pearls, that she, too, belonged to the NG church, and that she, too, thought dancing was a sin?

By now the woman was completely red in the face, all the way from the neck up. All she could manage to do was point to the sign saying QUIET PLEASE, with a cigarette and a red line running through it. But then Treppie took out his cigarettes and slapped them down, 'ka-thwack!' on to the counter. What was her problem? he asked. If she wanted a smoke all she had to do was ask, and now would she please just give him the most juicy book 'just for adults', like he asked. Then he winked at her.

Hell, she thought she was going to fall right through the floor that day, 'cause by then everyone in the library had gathered round Treppie to listen, and when he finally got his dirty books, he sang quietly to himself,

> 'This is the way the boere ride
> the boere ride, the boere ride
> bold upright and legs astride
> booted, spurred and hat-brim wide
> this is way the boere ride, hooray!'

Everyone laughed. Why, she still doesn't understand, 'cause she didn't think it was funny, and neither did Pop. Lambert was so embarrassed he walked off to the *Britannica* cabinet on the other side, pretending he didn't know them.

Oh yes, that was one day she was very happy to sign her books out and go home. Except they still had to listen to Treppie's nonsense all the way back. He carried on like a pumped-up church organ, he was so worked up. About everything he'd read in that book 'just for adults'. One of those books was full of 'private parts', he said, but only in Latin 'cause the book was about professors and students and so on. They didn't say 'arseholes' in books like that, he said, it was 'anuses', and all the other parts were also named by their correct terms. Meanwhile, the ins and outs of those parts were described so well you'd swear the writer had looked from above and from below, through a magnifying glass, as the apostle says.

Pop said Treppie should go and read his Bible again. It said 'through a glass darkly'. He shouldn't twist the words of the apostle like that.

Ja, ja, said Treppie, maybe that was what the apostle said, but for him there wasn't anything dark about private parts described from so close that you lost your perspective on the bigger picture. Maybe that learned oke who wrote the book should rather have taken pictures for *Scope*. In *Scope* there were at least bodies with faces, so a person could see what was what and who was who. Pop said the way Treppie was carrying on, you'd swear he was starved for sex or something.

Then suddenly everyone went quiet, and they rode like that almost the whole way home on Ontdekkers. She couldn't find the courage to tell him her joke about all he could still get up, 'cause Treppie's face suddenly began to look strange. It was only when they turned into Triomf again that Lambert said he'd read interesting stuff about clouds in the *Britannica*. Did they know clouds had names?

Yes, said Treppie, Cloud Nine was where he'd always wanted to spend his life, but he knows better now.

Knows what? she asked. Then he said he'd learnt it was all in the mind, the ins and outs of things. It just depended on what names you gave them.

No, said Lambert, he was talking science now, about the proper names for clouds. They came in classes, like people. High clouds and low clouds and middle clouds. The high ones made haloes around the sun and the low ones were thunderclouds, with heads like anvils.

Yes, said Treppie, and what was the academic term for that low kind of thundercloud?

Then Lambert said, um-um-er.

Treppie said it was okay if Lambert couldn't remember the right name, he should just think up a name that wasn't too academic. That would be better than nothing and he, Treppie, would certainly not hold it against Lambert.

So Lambert said in that case, the low clouds with heads like anvils were Columbus Pilatus. The right name sounded something like that, but next time he'd copy it down from the *Britannica*, if Treppie really wanted to know.

Treppie said, no, thanks, Lambert could save himself the trouble, that was enough for him. 'Cause if the low classes could discover new worlds and then wash their hands in innocence, he was quite satisfied. And he reckoned it was more than the high classes could say for themselves, sitting in universities and churches with haloes round their heads like the sun shone out of their backsides, just 'cause they'd given ordinary stuff grand names, like 'anus' for 'arsehole' and 'culture' for 'fuck-all' and 'a man of sorrows' for . . . for . . .

Treppie couldn't get any further, so she thought she'd help him along a bit. His face was looking funnier and funnier. Then, without knowing how she got on to it, she mentioned Frieda Personal Tragedy who had to sell her outsize wedding dress in the classifieds.

'That's a woman, Ma, not a man,' said Lambert.

But Treppie said Lambert should listen to his mother, 'cause for a change she was right. 'Strue's God, that's what he said. She, Mol, was right. Women could also have sorrows. Naturally.

She said, yes, Lambert should catch up. Sorrows were sorrows, whether it was man, woman or child, and in her opinion, everyone – the mortuary assistant in Yugoslavia, not to mention that poor stuffed corpse, and those women who struggled so with the tyres, the one who got burnt and the one who made the fire – all of them were made out of sorrows. The one no less than the other.

Now there's a life-jacket for you, said Treppie.

'What life-jacket you talking about now?' she asked, and Treppie said it was one that would keep her on the go all the way to the North Pole, without food or clothes.

She told him she didn't want to go to the North Pole, it was too cold there. She was very happy where she was, thank you, right here in Triomf. And then of course Treppie almost killed himself laughing.

FRUIT SALAD ⌒

They hear the front gate creak outside. Here comes Lambert. Treppie looks at his watch.

'Half past ten,' he says. 'Fasten your seatbelts.'

Mol shakes Pop by the shoulder. He must wake up now, so he's awake when Lambert comes in, otherwise he gets such a fright. Lambert usually comes home earlier on Mondays, after leaving early in the evening to look for rubbish.

The door opens. He stands there with a big smile on his face.

'Christ,' says Treppie, 'are you the cat who got the cream or the dog with a bone?'

'Cream,' says Lambert. 'Cream and sex and strawberries, I say.'

'Come again?' says Treppie.

'I say, take your pick, Uncle, it's all in the mind.'

'Where're your silver bags?' she says. 'I thought you went to look for wine boxes.'

'Yes,' he says, 'but you don't always find what you look for, right?'

'OK,' says Treppie. 'Obviously you found something else. Tell us now and get it over with so we can see the movie. It's late.'

'That movie,' says Lambert, 'is fuck-all. It's fuck-all compared to what I just saw. Truly fuck-all, I say.'

'On the big screen between your ears, you mean,' says Treppie.

'No, in a bedroom, through the gaps in the blinds.'

'Must've been wallpaper,' says Treppie.

'Lambert, you mustn't peep at people,' says Pop.

'Yes,' says Mol, 'just now there's trouble again. Just now you fall on to someone's carport or their car or something, and then they break our whole roof down in front of us.'

'Were they braaiing?' asks Treppie, winking at Lambert.

'No, they must be vegetarians. They were eating fancy cheese from a little box and biscuits. On a breadboard. And lots of nice fruit salad in black bowl, with a *leaf* in the middle.' Lambert laughs a naughty laugh.

'Who you talking about?' asks Pop.

'Across the road,' Lambert shows, pointing his thumb behind his back. He sits down, smiling his smile.

'Yes?' says Pop. She can see Pop doesn't believe him. Neither does she. There's nothing but flowers to peep at across the road. Every winter the little round one sows pretty flowers in front of the wooden fence. Sweetpeas, says Treppie. And then she sows dark, pink ones, for summer. Treppie says it's cosmos. He says he's never seen such healthy sweetpeas or such colourful cosmos anywhere in Triomf. Those two look like the type with money to spend on fertiliser. He wonders what they think they're doing here in Triomf, and why they've got so much time for gardening. If you ask him, they don't exactly look unfit for employment.

She and Pop have told Lambert to leave them alone, there across the road. They're not his class of people. But every time trouble breaks out he goes there and phones. Until the last time, when they told him their lives were private and they didn't want him to use their phone any more. There was a pay-phone at the Westhoven Post Office, they said.

Lambert says the one's Afrikaans and the other's English. The Afrikaans one plants the sweetpeas. The English one drives the blue Cortina with those flat shocks. The one that never wants to start. Lambert always wants to go and help them, but Pop says no. A Ford isn't a Volkswagen, and a Volkswagen mechanic like Lambert must stick to his own line. He mustn't mess with other cars. That's how Pop tries to console Lambert so they can keep the peace, at least with the people across the road, 'cause with the people next door, on both sides, it's just one big crisis after the other.

But now the problem is the Afrikaans one drives a Volksie and Lambert's dying to grind her points. Even she, Mol, can hear the Volksie across the road sounds rough. When Lambert goes and offers his help they always say no thanks, they've got their own mechanic. Can't be a very good one, he says, but what can you do?

He always comes back with some story or another. He says they give their garden-kaffir a knife and fork to eat his bread and wors with. Then they all sit together on chairs around a plastic table in the back garden. He says after a while that poor kaffir doesn't know where to look any more, what to stick his fork into, or what to cut with his knife. Yes, Treppie says, it comes from not being properly connected with the world. They think they can make their own connections, but all they've got is a silly mixed-up business. He says he thinks they must be Communists or something. Then she gets a fright, and she tells Lambert he mustn't get mixed up with Communists. They've got enough trouble as it is. She bumps Pop. He must tell him.

'Lambert,' says Pop, 'you must leave them alone there across the road. They're Communists.'

'Well, maybe they're Communists, but that's not all they are.'

'Hey, Lambert,' says Treppie, 'have you got a story or haven't you got a story? If you have, let's hear it, 'cause you're extremely boring with that knowing smile on your face.'

Ja, well, she's tired now. She wants to go bath. She takes a clean lid from her pocket. It's from the dog food.

'No, wait, Ma, this one's for you,' says Lambert.

'Well, then, tell and get it over with!'

'Those two across the road. They fuck each other!' Lambert says.

'So what's new?' says Treppie.

Pop shakes his head at her. God knows what Lambert will come up with next.

'How?' asks Treppie.

'With candles and things!'

'And what if they see you,' says Pop.

'I was hiding behind the bushes. Those two have planted bushes all over the place, Pop.'

'Ja,' says Pop, 'bushes and sweetpeas!'

'They play classics and then they fuck each other. Check this tune, Pop!' Lambert puts on his classical music face and then he whistles the Trust Bank tune. 'And it's just candles, candles, all over the place!'

'Can you believe it,' says Pop.

Treppie smiles. 'And then?'

'Squirrel.' It's her, Mol, who says that.

'Mol,' says Treppie, 'that's just the point. They don't have one of those, neither of them. That's why I want to know. How?'

'How what?' She presses her thumbs into the tin plate. It's not completely flat. When they get like that, they don't keep the water in.

'How do they do it, Ma. That's what Treppie wants to know. Well, let me tell you something here tonight. They do it with fruit salad!' He sits down. 'Ice cream and fruit salad!' he shouts, slapping his hands on his legs as he laughs.

Now she also wants to know how.

'They stick it in, Ma. Don't act like you don't understand.'

'Stick what in, where?' She looks at Pop to see if he knows, but he just sits there with a silly smile on his face.

'Christ, Mol, you weren't born yesterday,' says Treppie. 'They stick it in the sweet spot, of course!'

'Front or back?'

Lambert laughs. 'Well, Ma, let me tell you, those two stuff it with fruit salad wherever they can find a hole. Nose, mouth, ears, backside and frontside. And wherever they can find a split, they stick it in. In the bum, between the fingers, the toes. Behind the ears, you name it. After a while there's so much juice on them they both look like tropical forests. Then they put the music louder.'

Lambert whistles the Trust Bank tune again, harder and quicker. Pop shakes his head.

Treppie pants with mock excitement. 'The Amazons in Triumph, Part Two: The Revenge of the Fruit Salad!' He rubs his palms together so hard they make sucking noises. No decency. Never in his life has he had any manners. 'And then . . . and then . . . oh, what happens then?' he asks.

'Well, then they work each other up with their hands and they say Ooh! and Ahh! and they take all the fruit salad out again – banana, paw-paw, strawberries, the lot. They kiss each other with ice cream in their mouths. And then they lie down next to each other, with their eyes closed, and they sigh.'

'Shit, Lambert,' says Treppie, 'now you're lying. How could you have seen all that? Didn't they maybe invite you inside, the Benade with the golden banana!'

'What do they say to each other?' she wants to know. If you ask her, fruit salad should come with stories.

No, he couldn't hear so nicely. The music was playing too loud. And when the music stopped, they were already finished. Then they put new sheets on the bed 'cause the old ones were full of fruit salad, and he heard the one say to the other she thinks she'll be able to fall asleep now.

'"Are you sure?" the other one asked. And then the little round one moaned about the city grinding her points or something.'

'Fuck, no, Lambert!' says Treppie. 'You must've been lying under the bed to hear all that. Which one did you want to do first, the little melon or the English rose? I must say, I admire your restraint, old boy.'

'Treppie, I'll smack you! I swear, man, the window was open. I was standing right in front of the window, in the bushes. I heard everything. You could almost say I heard it in stereo.'

'What else did they say?' She wants to know.

'Well, then the one said something about being grateful, at least they still had a secret garden. And the other one said, yes, thanks a lot, the whole world's a secret. Then the other one said or a bubble or something. We'll never know.'

'So much for the voice-overs,' says Treppie. 'What about the lighting? I thought you said they did it with candles.'

'Oooh! Ouch!' Don't they burn themselves? she wonders.

'Now that's what I call burning desire!' says Treppie.

'No, man, Treppie,' says Lambert. 'They blow the candles out. It's one of those affairs with seven candles on a holder.'

'Seven?' It sounds rather a lot to her.

'Ag, come now, Mol,' Treppie says. 'There's nothing that can still surprise you.'

'Lambert means candlelight, Mol,' Pop explains. 'They do their thing by the light of seven candles. Then they blow them out. Then they go to sleep.'

'Now how's that for you, I say,' says Lambert, lighting up.

'Soft focus,' says Treppie. 'What do they know, anyway?'

Then everyone's quiet for a long time. But she thinks what she thinks.

'Well, it sounds nice and soft to me.' The words come out before she can stop herself.

'Oh my goodness,' says Treppie. 'Now Mol wants to become a lesbian *as well*. What do you say to that, old Gerty?'

'Leave Mol alone,' says Pop.

She wants to make her point here tonight. She doesn't always get the chance.

'No, I was just thinking,' she says. 'I wouldn't mind if it was only strawberries that got stuck into me. With ice cream in my mouth. Then you must feel like an ice-cream float, with strawberry juice.'

'But strawberry juice doesn't have any fizz, Mol,' says Treppie. 'For a real float you need fizz.' He laughs.

'Red Hubbly Bubbly, then.'

But Treppie's not listening to her. He just shakes his head. 'A bubble,' he says. 'A fucken bubble.'

'Well,' says Pop, switching off the TV, 'it's bedtime now. Too late now for *Raiders of the Lost Ark*. Tomorrow's another day.

'Mol,' he says as he walks down the passage, with his back to them, 'you can bath tomorrow. Otherwise the overflow drips all night. Lambert, go get some rest now,' he says as he enters into the bedroom.

She puts the lid from the dog food tin back into her housecoat pocket. She looks at her thumb where the lid cut her. Try as she might in this house, no one listens to her. She's a woman alone here, that's for sure. She'll just have to accept it. Stuffing it with fruit salad. She smiles.

Treppie locks the Klipdrift in the sideboard. He takes the glasses into the kitchen.

'Stuffing it with salad, oh stuffing it with salad,' she hears him sing, to the tune of 'Sow the seed, oh sow the seed'.

Lambert's gone out the front door again. He's got a big grin on his face. She watches him through the window. He stands in front, at the fence, looking across the road. She looks where he looks. It's pitch dark over there. Just night and bushes, she sees, and lots of small, white flowers. The secret garden. Ja, well, secrets remain secrets, with or without sweetpeas.

12

~

DOG'S HEAVEN

Mol stirs in her bed, half awake. She can hear the big lorries taking to the roads outside. It's pitch dark and something's not right. She tries to prick her ears, but she's still too groggy. And she can't move her limbs, either. This is her usual waking up time – about two hours before dawn, when the big lorries set out for the day, with their large, flat snouts, their swivelling heads, and their thick, double wheels. Some mornings she tries to count them on both sides of Ontdekkers. The first stretch to Roodepoort is downhill. Then they change gears, roaring and snorting. She lies in bed and thinks about all the drivers who have to get up so early, each one in the dark in his big lorry, alone.

Inbetween, she hears the softer noises of the first cars. The cars get more and more. They zoom. After a while she can't pick out the lorries any more. It's just one big noise. The noise fills up the whole city as far as she can hear. It fills the air above and it runs into the hollows below.

When the noise is loudest, the sun comes up. Then it feels like her whole body starts droning softly, along with the city. That's her sign to get up, otherwise she begins to feel sick in her stomach. She likes getting up first, so she can wake up alone and get herself ready. In this house you have to be ready for when the others wake up. Otherwise you see your arse. Especially her.

But it's much too early to get up now, and something's not right. It feels like something she won't be able to do anything about, a wrong thing that wants to do something to *her*.

She listens as the hollows under the city begin to rumble. She feels it before she hears it, in the pit of her stomach. Like the earth tremors. She feels them in her stomach too, long before the windows start rattling.

Jo'burg's like that. It's hollow on the inside. Not just one big hollow like a shell, but lots of dead mines with empty passageways and old tunnels. Treppie says that's why it's become so expensive to get buried in Jo'burg. There just isn't enough solid ground left for graves. And even if you do get a grave, he says, you still can't be so sure, 'cause most of the corpses fall through after a while. Coffins and all. And the headstones sink at a funny angle into the ground. Or they fall right through, on to the coffins. Getting buried in Jo'burg is a waste of time and money, Treppie says. After you've lived in this place there's not much left of you in any case.

Sometimes whole houses fall into the ground. Roads too. Those are sinkholes.

No wonder she feels so sick in her stomach. Whenever the tremors begin she sees a coffin fall through its hole. Further and further down it falls, head first. Then the stone falls on to the coffin and everything breaks, the wood and the stone. And then she sees that poor corpse, with its rigid eyes and broken bones, falling down the tunnels.

Or she sees a house with everything still inside and the people hanging upside down from the windows as it falls. And then the house smashes into the bottom of the earth.

She wants to be cremated. Ash is light. It stays above ground. If you're ash you get blown away with the first wind. You won't sink into the depths.

She turns towards Pop. She can move her limbs now. The lame feeling has gone. Some light comes into the room, but it's still grey outside. Pop lies on his back with his mouth slightly open. His nose is very sharp and white, and his eyelids are flickering. His hands make little shivering movements on his chest. He's dreaming. She watches Pop as he dreams. She can see he's watching his dream from the way his eyeballs move to and fro under his eyelids. She'd love to be able to peep through a hole in the back of Pop's head so she could watch with him. He smiles a little smile. Must be a nice dream. She's glad, 'cause sometimes Pop wakes up looking like he's seen a ghost. That's when he has a white nightmare. It's the same dream, he says. Over and over again. In the dream, he's surrounded by white. White in front and white all around him. It's so bad he can't see anything but white. It makes him feel suffocated. When he's inside the white he can still hear, but he can't see anything and he can't get out again. And when he tries to break out, all he sees is more white. White what? she asks, but he doesn't know. Wool? Clouds? Sand? Soap-suds? Teeth? Walls? Milk? He must know what it is, if it's so white. But he doesn't know. It's just white, he says. White nothing. Pop says the dream makes him feel scared and lonely. He says he wouldn't mind any other colour, even black. Or red-green-yellow-blue. Just not white. On days when Pop dreams white he's even quieter than usual. Then he just sits and looks at the world. But right now she can see he's not dreaming white. 'Oooh,' he says in his sleep, like someone getting a big surprise.

Surprises come in colours. Yellow roses. Yellow dresses.

Yellow's her favourite colour. She wouldn't mind dreaming about yellow every night of her life. But not yellow nothing – she wants to dream about yellow things. Roses and dresses and things that move, things that smell nice. All in yellow. When Pop dreams white, she's sure he doesn't move like he's moving now. Then he lies dead still. But in that case, how will she know he's dreaming?

Gerty also seems to be dreaming white nowadays. She doesn't move when she sleeps. In the old days she used to dream she was chasing cats and playing ball. Then her ears, eyebrows and feet used to twitch, and she used to growl and carry on in her sleep. But not any more.

Mol suddenly sits bolt upright. It's Gerty! That's what feels wrong. Where's Gerty? She wants to get up, she wants to go look. Now, immediately. She begins to move, but she feels completely paralysed. She's been awake for a long while now, so this is a different kind of heaviness from that other feeling. Now she's sitting upright, wide awake – and lame.

No, not Gerty! She hears 'click-click'. It's Toby. Toby never comes to her before she's properly awake. But Gerty's always with her, even before she starts waking up. At the foot of the bed, next to the mattress, or somewhere else in the room. Here comes Toby now. But he's not coming from Pop's chair in front, where he usually sleeps. And he's not walking his usual path, either. He's coming from the bathroom. He takes just two little steps into the room and then he stands at the door with his ears pricked. He looks at her and wags his tail once or twice. Then he looks back to the bathroom and back to her again as she sits there, upright, unable to move. 'Ee-ee-ee,' he says softly. He remains standing, right there, and she sits as though she's stuck to the bed. No, God, please, no.

'Aaah-aaah,' Pop yawns, here next to her. 'Aaah-aaah,' he yawns again. 'Such a nice dream, Mol, so nice. What you looking at like that?' Pop lifts himself up on to his elbows and looks where she's looking.

'Morning, old Toby,' he says.

Toby waves his tail once, and then again, looking over his shoulder to the bathroom. 'Ee-ee,' he says.

'Ee-ee-ee yourself,' says Pop, yawning again. He lies down on his back, puts his hands behind his head, and smiles. To think that Pop should smile on a morning like this. It's not something she sees very often. Most of the time he just swings his legs off the mattress. Then he sits there resting his head on his knees. For a long time he sits like that. After a while it looks like he doesn't ever want to let himself go again. She always has to say to him: come now, Pop, stand up, put some clothes on so we can go to Shoprite, or something like that. Pop says he's got no strength left for anything any more. But now he's lying there with his hands behind his head and he's smiling. And she doesn't know how to say it to him.

'Toby,' she says. Her voice feels like it's coming from a strange place. She tries to clear her throat, but it sounds funny.

'Maybe he just wants to pee,' says Pop. 'I'll do it now-now. Just listen to my dream first. Ai, ai, ai, such a nice dream, Mol. If only I could dream like that every night.

'I was dreaming,' says Pop, 'that we were all in heaven. Me and you and Treppie and Lambert. But we were dogs. Dogs with wings. We weren't walking, we were flying, and we could talk. Dog-angels, that's what we were. And the people-angels looked after us, but we didn't eat dog food

216

from tins, we ate at the Spur. Every day. We ate T-bones with knives and forks and we all wore the jerseys you knitted for us, Molletjie, just nicer, jerseys like rainbows, and that's why we had serviettes stuck into them, so we didn't mess on the nice jerseys. Every now and again the people-angels came to ask if there wasn't anything we wanted, and you said you didn't want a T-bone, Mol, you wanted honey on toast with white bread and lots of butter, and then you began to break off small pieces and you fed them to me, but my mouth was full of T-bone, and you said it didn't matter, sweet is nice. Do you have any idea how delicious T-bone and honey-bread taste, Mol? Mol, are you listening to me? Isn't it wonderful? I really tasted it in my dream, honey and T-bone and toast. And I could taste much better than usual. I wonder if dogs really taste everything so nicely. That dream has made me hungry, man.'

'Pop, Toby . . .' she says.

Pop waves his arm. It's nothing. 'Hey, Mol, wasn't that a lovely dream? And it's not all, you know. When we finished eating at the Spur, we flew out the windows – forget walking up and down stairs! We didn't have to pay a cent in that Spur in heaven. The people-angels flew with us and then we played magic balls in heaven. They throw the balls and we fly after them, high, high above heaven's green lawns, right to the sun and the moon, and then we fly and catch the balls in our mouths and bring them back for the angels, and we put them down at their feet. Magic balls that look like little suns and moons. They make little sparks in your mouth like that sherbet stuff Lambert used to like so much when he was small. What was that stuff called again? Spacedust! Then we went to bed. We all slept in hammocks strung up from the stars. And all you could see were our ears and our tails as we lay there in our hammocks among the stars. The stars all have points in a circle, but actually they're postboxes with a mouth so you can post letters to your loved ones on earth. In fact, they're two-way postboxes with doors at the back that you can open, and every day you get mail from your people on earth. Every day we get letters from people we don't know, but they say they're family of ours. Then we read them to each other. Dogs can read too in heaven, you know. The letters are full of nice news from the world below.'

217

Pop rubs his eyes.

'Then Lambert tipped the big Coke bottle for us. A giant Coke bottle on a hinge that pours out into a dam, "ghloob-ghloob-ghloob", a dam with ducks like the Westdene Dam, and we drank Coke from the dam with our little pink tongues. But it tasted different. Nicer than ordinary Coke – like champagne-Coke. And the ducks were talking to us. Everything in heaven talks to everything else, duck language, dog language, people language, and everyone understands everyone else in their own language. The ducks are also angels – duck-angels. They've got their usual wings but they've also got two extra rainbow-wings above their backs that vibrate, like butterfly wings. But we don't ever chase them 'cause they're our friends. Everyone's friendly with us in heaven. We're not alone. Everyone's happy and our hearts feel light and the air we breathe tastes sweet. So sweet.

'Treppie's also a dog, but he's musical. He plays on Old Pop's mouth organ. The mouth organ's in two pieces. Treppie's got the low notes and I've got the high notes, and then we play all those old songs from Vrededorp and we keep in tune without missing a single note. And everyone dances round the dam and up in the air and the ants also dance. Even the moles come out into the sun and they dance with their eyes open.

'Ai, Mol, I wish I could dream like that all day long. What you think, Mol? I forgot, there's a wool shop in heaven, like the one where you always buy wool for Gerty's jerseys, but there's more wool there, it looks like a whole shed full of wool, with coolie-angels flying all over the place, carrying balls of wool in their arms, and—'

'Stop it! Stop it! Stop it!' she shouts. Suddenly her voice is back, but it sounds hoarse.

'What's with you all of a sudden? It was just a dream, man,' Pop says, laughing.

'It's not!' she says. 'It's not!'

'It's not what?'

'It's not just a dream. It's Gerty.'

'No, wait a minute, Mol,' says Pop.

'I'm telling you,' she says, standing up. 'Come.'

'Ee-ee-ee-ee!' says Toby. Toby runs around in a circle, right there where he's standing.

'Toby wants to pee,' says Pop. 'I'm coming now. Put him out so long.'

'Are you coming?' she asks.

'My pants,' says Pop. He reaches for his pants next to the bed.

'Leave your pants. Just come!'

'Hell, Molletjie, what's eating you this morning, hey?' Pop stands up in his shirt.

'Eating.' Her voice cracks. 'Pop,' she says, 'Gerty.'

Pop comes round the bed to her side. Can't he see something's wrong? She's got the shivers.

'Are you cold, Mol? What's going on, hey?'

She takes him by the arm. Why's he so slow today? She points to Toby. She pulls Pop so he's in front of her. Then she pushes him from behind, into the bathroom. Toby runs between their legs. Pop looks into the bathroom. What does he see there? She looks past his shoulder. She was right. And Pop was right too. In his dream.

There lies Gerty, in front of the bath. On the worn old mat made of woven tyre, with a patch of blood in front of her mouth. Sticky threads of spit hang down from her mouth, into the blood. Her lips are raised and you can see her teeth. Her feet are pulled up towards her body, lying at an angle. Her eyes are closed, with white drops in the corners. Her face looks small and her ears are flat. Behind her tail there's another patch. Blood. Or something darker.

'Ee-ee-ee,' says Toby.

'*See*?' she says.

'Ag no. Ag no,' says Pop. 'Please God, no!'

She feels like a big wave wanting to break in a closed place. She feels like the wave and she feels like the closed place, but she can't break. The thing struggling to break hurts her chest. She bares her teeth like Gerty.

'Come away there, Toby,' says Pop. He pulls Toby by his neck, away from Gerty.

'Take Toby, Mol. Put him out the back. You can go sit in the back, too. Leave this to me.'

'No,' she says. She rubs her eyes.

'She was very old, Mol. And sick. It's better this way.'

'It's not,' she says.

'Go fetch a bag,' says Pop. 'Two of the white ones. Those municipality bags.'

'No,' she says. 'Not a bag.'

She goes back to the room. Their bed's in front of her. There she lay, just a minute ago, and she knew it, without knowing she knew it. Pop too. He also knew it, without knowing he knew it. She throws off the blanket. Worn old blanket with a hole in it. It still feels warm to her hands. The sheet too. Still warm from their bodies. She gathers up the sheet, as if she wants to gather together the warmth in there. She holds it in a bundle to her breast and walks back to the bathroom. Her feet feel high and low, all at the same time.

Pop sits hunched in his shirt in front of Gerty. His knees stick out. His back is bent and knobby.

'Here,' she says, 'take the sheet.'

Pop just looks at her as she stands there. She can see he doesn't know what to say.

'She's completely stiff,' he says. 'And cold. It must've happened early in the night.'

'I heard nothing,' she says. 'I always hear.'

'It's better you heard nothing,' says Pop. 'She must've struggled terribly.' He points to the blood. 'It's better you slept. There was nothing you could do for her.'

'It was very painful,' she says.

'She must've started coughing again,' Pop says.

'Coughed herself to death,' she says. 'Like Old Mol, in the bathroom.'

She looks at the bathroom. There's a brown mark where the tap always drips. Then she looks at the cabinet above the basin. The little door's open. There's one small piece of mirror left in the bottom corner. But what's that strange, dark shape showing in the piece of mirror?

She looks at the white wall behind Pop's back. And there she sees the big moth. Its red-brown wings are spread open on the wall. Dead still.

She shows Pop. He turns around.

'The TB butterfly,' she says, losing her voice.

Pop gets up, with the sheet still in his arms. He stands in front of her in his shirt, and then he puts his arms around her. She presses her face into the sheet. She smells all their smells. Gerty too. Gerty was with her when she fell asleep last night. She held her until she began to breathe more calmly. Gerty smelt strange. And bad. Now that smell's in there. In the sheet. Poor Gerty.

Suddenly her ears feel deaf.

'Don't worry,' she hears Pop say. He presses her, and the sheet, against his chest. She feels small in his arms. 'Poor Mol,' he says. Yes, poor her. Gerty never left her alone, never ever. Everyone else always leaves her alone when they're finished with her. Pop too. Lots of times, although his strength's going now. But Gerty was always there. Gerty was her dog, and she was Gerty's person. She thinks about Pop's dream. They were each other's angels, she and Gerty. Now she feels Pop drop his head on to her shoulder. He also wants to cry. He shakes his head slowly on her shoulder. Lightly, he rocks the two of them. She feels herself give a little. Let them just rock a little here on their feet today. Pop lets out a big sob into her shoulder. She knows what he's thinking, and she's thinking the same. No sun or moon making little sparks in their mouths today. Just the salt taste of tears.

'Oh my God, and what do we have here!' It's Treppie. He's coming down the passage in nothing but his shirt.

'Isn't it a little early for this kind of thing? I say, poochy-smoochy! Let me pass, I have to pee!'

Treppie pushes past them into the bathroom. 'Shorrrr', he pees into the open toilet. As he pees, he looks down to his left, at Gerty.

'Seized up!' he says. 'Total systems failure! Complete black-out! So, aren't you two even going to clean up this mess? Why you standing there like that? Mol, you should've put this stinking dog of yours out of her misery a long time ago. Now look what you got.'

Treppie pushes lightly with his toe against Gerty.

'Sis, yuk, fuck!' he says, pinching his nostrils with his thumb and forefinger.

'Please, Treppie,' says Pop. She sees how Pop motions to Treppie with his eyes, he must stop it now. So now she knows it's actually her who must please stop crying. She wipes her nose with her hand. Her housecoat that she slept in hangs open in front. Pop reaches out to close it for her. She takes hold of the flaps herself. Now the last button's also off.

Treppie makes a face, as if he suddenly understands. He pushes past them again on his way out.

As he walks away down the passage, he lowers his voice to a deep bass, and then he sings like Jim Reeves:

> 'Across the bridge there's no more sorrow.
> Across the bridge there's no more pain.'

Pop's taking the lead this morning. First he sat her down on a beer crate next to the fridge and now he's fixing bread for all of them. The water's boiling on the Primus. Here comes Lambert.

'Bread with honey,' says Pop. 'You want some?'

'Huh? Yes, fine. What's up?' says Lambert, dragging a crate closer and checking them all out. 'Huh, what's going on here this morning?' he says. 'You two look like the dogs took your food or something.'

'Gerty's dead. Here's some bread for you. Your coffee's on the table,' says Pop, sitting down next to her on a crate.

'I see,' says Lambert. 'So, what now?'

'Now nothing,' says Pop. 'Eat your bread.'

'One man's bread's another man's honey!' It's Treppie, standing in the kitchen doorway. 'Don't I get any?'

'Make your own,' says Pop. 'There's the honey, there's the knife and there, on your sides, are two arms. You're man enough and you've still got many years left in you.'

'Take that!' says Lambert, slapping his leg with a flat hand.

'Well, smack me with a wet fish!' says Treppie. He lifts up his hands, looks at them, and then drops them again. 'I must be dreaming,' he says.

'Come again?' He cups his hands behind his ears and makes a face like he doesn't believe what he just heard.

Everyone ignores him. It's dead quiet in the kitchen. All you hear is Lambert's chewing and swallowing. Pop drinks little sips from his cup. Her bread and coffee stand on the floor in front of her. She's not hungry. Toby sits next to her with his ears pricked. He looks from face to face to see what the people will do next.

Treppie comes and crouches in front of her, holding his hands against his head, like dog-ears.

'How much is that doggy in the window? Whoof whoof!
The one with the waggily tail,'

he sings in her face. Then he puts his hand on her knee, pretending to comfort her. She pushes it away.

'Sister dear,' he says, 'what's in a dog? I mean, in the grand design of things, your life, my life, dog's doily, cat's backside! It's all the same, not so, in Triomf or Parktown North, Honolulu or Siam!'

Treppie wants to get up, but before he can steady himself Pop stretches out a long arm, grabs him by the shirt-front and pulls him up towards his face. Treppie half falls over her food. He knocks over the enamel mug. She leans back a bit. She wants to think about Pop's dream now, but she can't get up to speed. The picture of Gerty lying like that in the bathroom keeps coming back into her head.

And now Gerty's in the sheet. Here at the back, in the shadow between the prefab wall and the house. Pop wiped everything nice and clean again. And he held her tight. Pop understands. But he mustn't over-exert himself now.

'Treppie,' he says, 'have you no respect? Are you the very Satan himself, straight from hell? You stop now, you hear me? If you want to go looking for trouble, go find it with one of your own kind. Go look till you find someone like yourself, that's if you'll ever find another one like you. Just leave us alone here today. We've got business to see to.'

Pop pushes Treppie against his chest so hard that he ends up on his backside in the middle of the coffee.

223

'Whoof!' says Toby.

'Lambert,' says Pop, 'take Treppie to his room and make sure he stays there.'

'Right,' says Lambert. He likes what he's seeing here, she can see that. He didn't know Pop could still cut Treppie short like this.

'Wha-wha!' shouts Treppie. Now he's acting like he's three years old. 'I doan wannoo an' I'm not gonnoo!' he screams with his thumb in his mouth. Lambert's got him by the collar. He drags him down the passage, into his room, with his feet still half off the ground. They hear Lambert locking him into the room. Lambert brings Pop the key and Pop puts it in his pocket.

'Wha-wha!' Treppie shouts again from behind the closed door. Then he's quiet. After a little while there's a muffled 'whoof-whoof', then nothing.

'So much for that,' says Pop, standing up. He puts the cup down on the sink. Then he takes a rag and wipes up the coffee.

Pop's a different person in the presence of death, she thinks to herself.

'It says in the *Western Telegraph*,' says Lambert, 'that they cremate dogs for free at the SPCA. In Booysens. No charge. They've got a crematorium for animals there.'

'Ja, ash is nice and light.'

'Ja,' says Pop, 'ash . . .' He thinks a little. 'I'm just thinking. Then we'll have to sign all kinds of papers again.' He thinks a little more. 'How about here at the back, in the yard. Then it stays our business. Then she's still here with us. What you say, Mol?'

'The earth is hollow.'

'Come again?' says Pop.

'Just now she falls through. Down. Through a sinkhole.'

Lambert catches on quickly. 'That story was just a lie, Ma. It's all right. I promise. The earth is still very hard here in Triomf. Packed hard. It's all just bricks and cement from the kaffir-houses. She won't just fall through. I promise.'

'But we must wait till dark,' says Pop. 'Otherwise everyone stares at us. Or next door complains. And we don't want the police here again, hey, Mol?'

Mol shakes the tin of yellow spray-paint. It doesn't want to come out so nicely. She can't see what's going on, either. It's getting too dark. But she told them they must have the funeral and get done with it. She doesn't want to spend the whole night lying awake, trying to think of something nice to write on Gerty's grave.

Lambert's gone to see if he can find another tin of spray-paint and Pop's fetching Treppie. He must've cooled down by now, says Pop. And shame, he also knew Gerty. What's more, Treppie's a man with a text for every occasion. Pop must've noticed – she doesn't know what to say or write.

Now the paint's coming out better. 'So, Toby, what should the missus write here on the wall, hey?' Toby stands next to her. He knows very well what's going on. When they marked out the little grave with stones and tins in the late afternoon, Toby stood and watched them with his ears pricked. It was only when they started digging that he got some life back into him. The digging was a struggle. The earth was full of rubble, and they had to use a pick to wrench loose and lift out some of the big blocks of cement. They got only three feet deep when Pop said enough. He was tired and Gerty didn't have to go six feet under, she was only a dog, after all.

But Mol climbed into the hole herself and stamped her feet to test how strong the earth was. She was listening for hollow spots. She even lay down to see if the lie was right, with her cheek on those pieces of raw brick. It was an eerie feeling, but she had to know. Toby also jumped into the hole out of sheer panic. He was trying to pull her out by the flaps of her housecoat.

Then she went and fetched Gerty's half-finished jersey and put it in the grave with her. She also fetched what was left of the ball of yellow wool. It won't be needed next year for ribbing. And then it was time to close up the grave.

Suddenly, Toby began to bark terribly. Pop had to give him bread so he'd shuddup. They were scared next door would come out and see what they were doing. It was against the law, Pop said.

She doesn't mind. She's glad they didn't hand Gerty over to strange people.

She gets her angle right. Then she aims for a spot between the two upright poles of the prefab wall. The ground on the grave is soft under her feet and the light spilling over from the streetlamp is very faint.

Here lies Gerty Benade, she writes. The paint sprays on to her fingers. She stands back. The writing runs skew down the wall, but you can still read it. Now for the next line:

Mother of Toby Benade
and sweetheart dog of Mol ditto.

'What about the date?' Lambert suddenly says, behind her. He passes her another tin. She sprays into the air. It sprays much better.

Here come Pop and Treppie now. Treppie's got a torch. She asks him to shine it so she can see. What else?

'Rip,' says Pop.

No, she's got an idea.

Now she's in dog's heaven, she writes underneath. Yes, that sounds good.

'The date,' says Lambert.

'No, wait, Mol. Wait.' It's Treppie. She turns round. She can't see what's going on 'cause the torch is shining in her face. Treppie's voice sounds different.

'Wait for what?'

'That's very nice, Mol, about dog's heaven. I like it. But it's not finished. Write this underneath: "where the dogs are seven eleven".'

Treppie sounds like he wants to cry. Did he really have a soft spot for Gerty all this time? She looks at Pop.

'Write!' says Pop.

She has to bend down low. There isn't much space left.

. . . *where the dogs are seven eleven*, she writes, smaller and smaller, 'cause the ground runs upward to the one side. She remembers seven eleven, the lucky numbers in dice, from the stories Treppie told them about gambling with the Chinese.

She stands back. Treppie shines the torch on the words. He reads everything from the beginning. Pop puts his hand on her shoulder.

'That's better,' says Treppie. 'Death deserves an ending that rhymes well, even if it isn't the truth.'

She looks up, at Pop. Is Treppie mocking her again or what? But Pop's face is dead serious.

'Much better,' he says. 'How about a nice stiff brandy?'

Treppie says, yes, he agrees. Four fingers for each of them, 'cause that's what you deserve if you bury a dog with so much love and respect.

She can't believe her ears, but he really isn't playing the fool with her. She takes the torch and shines it into his face. Treppie's eyes are shining and there's moisture in the hollows around his mouth.

'What you looking at, hey? Switch that light off,' is all he says. And then he bends over and rubs Toby's head, hard.

13

~

LUCKY FINDS

I t's the Wednesday before Guy Fawkes. Things here at the Benades
are going to have to be shipshape for when that girl of his comes.
Everyone will just have to put their best foot forward. Treppie will
have to behave himself and watch that dirty mouth of his. And his mother
must learn to keep her legs together and leave that tooth of hers where
it belongs. And Pop, Pop must just stay cool. He must lift his head off
his knees and wipe his nose and make some conversation. Then he,
Lambert, will be satisfied. As for himself . . . Well, that's something he'd
like to fix up: his hair, his fat belly, his backside. He needs some clothes,
and some underpants so his dick won't hang out of his shorts all the
time. Women don't like it. That's what his mother says, but what does
she know? Bugger her anyway.

If only things would work. Cars, fridges, the lawn-mower. If everything
was nice and tidy; if all the rubbish got cleared up; then, he reckons, maybe
his girl will want to come back again.

He's just going to have to make a start, today. Things must start getting
fixed-up around here, so it'll be a helluva pleasure to visit their house.
It must be so shipshape around here that his girl will stay longer and
longer, until she doesn't want to go back to her own place any more,
until she just wants to stay on and on, maybe forever. And if the shit
really starts flying after the election, then he'll tell her she must come

with, to the North, 'cause it'll be her only chance. She might even say yes. Maybe.

His head starts zinging. He sits down on his bed. Just the thought that his girl will stay forever, or go with them to the North, makes him feel dizzy.

And if the shit doesn't fly, he'll take her for a spin in Flossie every night when it's late. On those new light blue seats with romantic, late-nite music from Radio Orion in their ears. Flossie will get a sound system second to none. Not even a policeman in a hot-rod will have a better one.

Right. Now he must start thinking nicely about what needs to be done. So he can begin, now, at the beginning.

The most important is that they must be ready when the shit starts flying. They must have enough petrol. Enough to get to the border. He figures one full tank, plus another one-and-a-half, maybe two, in bags. That should be enough. Those bags take five litres each, so he'll need about sixteen to eighteen of them. He's already got about eleven, but when he filled one with water, it started leaking. This stuff mustn't start leaking on him now. So, he must take all the bags he's already got, fill them up with water and then pack them into the hole under the den. On top of each other. That's the way they'll get stacked on the roof-rack. And then, after a day or two, he must check them all for leaks. That means he still needs about seven bags, make it ten for the ones that leak. That hole under his den will have to get a bit bigger. The bags can't just lie here all over his room. The day before his birthday he'll go fill them up with petrol. Then they'll be ready.

So, that's number one. Petrol. No, number one is Flossie. He must get Flossie going again. Pop says all she's good for is spares, but he'll show Pop a thing or two.

Of course, if Pop's right, there's always Molletjie to fall back on. So, petrol's still number one. Let the cars sort themselves out. Cars are like that. Take what you can from them and forget the rest. Cars won't let you push them around.

But lawn-mowers are a different story. All he has to do is weld a new lever where the old one broke off. Then he can clean the carburettor and check the petrol pipe for dirt. He thinks the petrol's not coming through so nicely. That's why it cuts out all the time. So, that's number two, the lawn-mower, 'cause the grass will have to be cut to a T, in beautiful straight lines, one way up, one way down. Not the way his mother does it, in crooked strips, skipping patches and ripping out big chunks of grass.

And then number three is definitely the postbox. He's just going to have to put it up again.

Not to mention the gutters those bastards next door broke off, 'cause when it rains nowadays there's a big 'shorrr' noise all over the place, like they're living in a rain forest or something. It leaks inside, too, but fixing a roof is another story. It must please just not rain that night. And the whole house needs a coat of paint, too. A long time ago the house used to be yellow, Pop says, but now it's just dirty. It needs a coat of pure, beautiful white.

To him, a house without gutters and paint looks like a cake with no icing. Come to think of it, when his birthday comes, and his girl pitches up here, a cake with icing will be just the thing. It's a long time since he saw cake, never mind icing.

He must remember that! Something sweet for the occasion. He's been thinking of salty things 'cause they go with sundowners and nightcaps. But where there's salt, there also has to be sweet. Something sweet is nice for breakfast. Maybe she'll stay for breakfast. Surely that's not asking too much?

And what else? A lot!

He's going to have to fix the spot on the lounge wall where the plaster came off. With Polyfilla, and then paint over it, in fact the whole wall, 'cause it's so dirty from the dogs. And those naked bulbs everywhere. They must get shades, even if it's just cheapskate enamel ones. And the floor-blocks in the lounge – fasten them down and varnish them. The passage too. And he mustn't forget the pelmet he ripped off last time when he got so pissed off with Treppie's nonsense.

What's more, he's sick and tired of his mother's headless cat. Either he must chuck it away or he must get a new one from Shoprite. One with a head.

And the hole in the front door. A thin piece of plywood should do the job.

What else? Christ, there's a lot! He's not going to do a fucken thing to Treppie's room, that's for sure. The only thing you can do there is close the door. Pop and Mol's room too. But something will have to be done about the bathroom and the kitchen. They say in the adverts women like their bathrooms 'flawless'. They like them to smell 'fragrant'. And they also fancy those American kitchens with breakfast counters, but that's aiming a bit high. To start with, maybe just scrub the lino. Clean the fridge.

And then there's that blocked drain in his mother's kitchen. From the washing basin. Blocked to the nines with about three months' worth of muck in there. He'll have to get some Drain Buster, the one in the black bottle. He remembers seeing it in the hardware shop. Maybe then they won't have to chuck the dishwater out the kitchen door any more. That's what his mother does, anyway. If she wants to clean something, she pours a cup of water into it and stirs it with her finger. That's what she calls cleaning. This kind of thing's going to have to stop. They must start washing up properly in this house, with green Sunlight from a bottle that makes foam. A whole mealtime's dishes and glasses and pudding bowls and dishing-up spoons, with just one teaspoon. Shining bright. Never mind the fact that they haven't got all those dishes and glasses and things.

And the toilet. That's another fucken story. It's got a crack in it, so it leaks on to the floor all the time. And Treppie never flushes. His pee stinks like horsepiss. Everyone's going to have to learn to flush on the spot, so at least the water on the floor won't be piss. 'Cause a new toilet will cost more than a hundred bucks. And a plastic seat with a lid will cost almost the same. Hell, if he can just get a seat . . . that china under an oke's backside is fucken freezing, man, not to mention a woman's backside.

And then there's the bathroom mirror that his mother complains about so much. Jesus, that's also another story.

Now his head's really spinning.

Where's he going to get all the money from?

Treppie says he and Pop are putting away all their extra money for the girl. Quality girls cost a lot of money nowadays. That's what Treppie says. Somebody told him. He, Lambert, has almost no money of his own. Cigarettes, sweets, videos and beers. That's about all he can afford at the end of the month. Plus maybe some duco for Flossie, and GTX for Molletjie and the lawn-mower. Then he's really had it. Treppie buys the booze and most of their food, 'cause Pop says he can only afford the basics. Bread, Sunshine D, polony, milk, coffee, Coke, dog food in tins. Pop says only two tins of wet food a week, and for the rest Toby must eat dry food. Treppie buys those Dogmor chunks in big tins from the Chinese. They get it wholesale. Treppie says the Chinese eat those Dogmor-dogs. Chopped up into the sweet and sour. He says they call it chop suey.

At least now there's one dog less in the house. Not even a Chinese would have eaten her.

If they want meat and jam and peaches in a tin, Pop says, then Treppie must buy it. And Klipdrift too, so they can keep up with themselves.

Pop says he's also saving up for coffins and things for him and Mol one day. And it's going to cost even more if she wants to be cremated like she's been saying lately. Pop says he's going to have to make a plan, somehow.

Where was he now?

Suddenly he can't remember a thing on his list. The stuff's flying through his head and he can't get a good grip on it. He knows only broken things fly through his head like this. There're too many broken things to fix up. Too little time. And fuck-all money.

Hell, he must just keep track here. He'll make a list, that's what he'll do. He'll start again from the beginning and write everything down on his list, then he can tick them off one by one as he finishes each thing. Then he'll know what's what. Then he can work out a time-table. One thing at a time. Each thing must have its own time and its own day, from now on, up to and including the big day. And when he's finished, he can draw a line through each thing. Then he can see at any time how far he's already got and how much he still has to do.

Right, let's make a list, then. There on the back wall, where he can see it all the time. But where on the wall? It's so full. He looks around his room.

It's all going to happen right here, in this room. But he must first get rid of the rubbish. All these boxes and things. And that heap of *Watchtowers*.

He grabs a handful from the stack in the back corner. But then the whole pile starts tilting over and it comes crashing down all over the place. Fuck! He grabs bunches and bungs them into empty crates. Now he's got six crates full of *Watchtowers*. Just going to have to burn them. Later. Let him first find a space on the wall to write down his list. He sees half a painting sticking out where the *Watchtowers* used to be. What was that painting, again? He's forgotten all about it. He pushes the Fuchs to one side so he can move the Tedelex and look at the painting. Bottles and boxes come crashing down around his ears and on to his feet. When he gets everything out of the way, he sees two paintings, both badly faded. The one's called THE JEW IN THE WASHING MACHINE. The other is THE MOLE IN THE FRIDGE. The Jew's for real. You can see his glasses and his nose and his little hat behind the washing machine's glass. The machine's running and the Jew's spinning. He's singing 'Fare thee well, my own true darling' upside down as he spins. It's a jolly painting.

As for THE MOLE IN THE FRIDGE, that's another story. It doesn't look like his mother, but it's her. Her body fills up the whole fridge. Her head's stuffed into the ice-box. There's a gap for her neck to go through. Her head's blue from being frozen so hard and her two front teeth stick out of her mouth. She doesn't have a chin, and her belly's fat and pink. She looks like she's been slaughtered. There's a Peking Duck inside her, at the bottom, with a fuse sticking out and flames shooting sparks at the tip. On top of the painting it says: BIG BANG 1970.

He remembers. He painted it that time when he came out of hospital, after the fire. His mouth was bitten to bits, and he had to lie around at the back here for weeks on end. He wasn't allowed anything except soft things like milk and stuff. It was all his mother's fucken fault. His mother, who let his spanners get lost in the long grass. She fucks everything up. But he's not going to think about her now. He wants to write his list. He's going to write it on top of the Jew. He shifts the Tedelex in front of THE MOLE IN THE FRIDGE. Pop will complain if he sees it, and his mother will tell him he's got no decency. Right now he doesn't want any more trouble with anyone. He just wants to keep things going, so everyone will stay cool.

He takes his ball-point and goes to the wall. He starts high up, so he'll have enough space. He knows that lists can go on and on forever, like that time he made a list for the Guy Fawkes party, and the list of everything he needs to do on Flossie.

When he's finished, his list looks like this:

1. *Bags (20) check for leaks*
2. *Lawn-mower weld clean blades (time will tell)*
3. *Put postbox up*
4. *Gutters on*
5. *house white*
6. *Fill holes lounge (1 box Polyfilla, 2 litre high-gloss)*
7. *lampshades (4)*
8. *pelmet panelbeat*
9. *glue all blocks (31 new ones) or more – check*
10. *new cat (Shoprite) chuck old one away*
11. *patch hole front door (12" x 12" plywood single)*
12. *scrub linolium kitchen clean (Ma)*
13. *drain (Buster)*
14. *flush horsepis. always/immediately (gentle reminder!)*
15. *Toilet seat (Spur?)*
16. *Mirror bathroom (measure) bath plug*
17. *den (sweep burn wash)*
18. *everything must work fridges (Kneff too)*
19. *Change mattress? bedding? (Treppie window sheets!)*
NB 20. Lambert: toenails push ups
underpants . . . ???
20. *burn Ma's housecoats*
21. *zips for Pop's pants (Ma)*
22. *Money. (6 Spur tickets?)*

(R50 NP?) fuck them!
Take empties back
23. *dip Toby.*

He takes a step back and looks at his list. He rubs his eyes. Fuck. It's a lot. But now at least he knows what he has to do. Now things are properly lined up. Now it's first things first. One thing at a time. Every day a few.

He walks out the door to the tap in the backyard. He washes his feet. Then he tiptoes back over his dirty floor. He takes the T-shirt from behind his bed and dries his feet. He almost puts the T-shirt back in its old place, but then he stops and stares at it. Fucken piece of rubbish! Out with it! From now on, it's out with everything that's rubbish around him. He chucks the T-shirt into a crate next to the *Watchtowers*. He's going to have to stop pulling his wire so much. Fuck that. He'll wait. Save himself up. If it gets too much for him, he'll just do some push-ups. Or paint. Or make a fire with all the rubbish. Just watch him. He wasn't born yesterday.

He puts on his lace-ups. It's his only pair. He bought them 'cause Pop said that's what he needed for his weak ankles. But they look funny when he wears them with shorts. What he really needs is a decent pair of takkies. North Stars with soft soles. But if he's going to walk to the rubbish dumps now to look for bags, then he must walk, whether he looks funny or not. He usually walks barefoot around the streets near their house, but the dumps are too far for bare feet. He looks at the list. It's great. He salutes his list. Then he remembers something. Under 23. *dip Toby* he writes: 24. *paint the gallery! Ant termite wasp, Mole II, bat, etc.*

That's to entertain his girl. If all else fails, he can say to her: look at my painting on the wall, the one in the middle. Look at those stings, curling round the cloud in three different directions. That's the many-headed Superbee. And then he'll say: you want to know why that Mole there is called Mole the Second? Well, come, let me show you Mole the First. Just don't get a fright, hey!

'Cause what happens if she's very nice and everything, but she doesn't say a word? Like Pop. What'll he do then?

He must just not make a fool of himself. Then all the trouble and everything will be for nothing.

He gets up. He doesn't even want to think about that. That it could all be for nothing. He walks through the den's inside door and into the house. He fetches a municipal rubbish bag in the kitchen, folding it carefully into a nice little square. He feels around on top of the dresser for the Spur tickets, where Pop said he must leave them. He's not sure why he wants the tickets. He just feels he has to be ready for anything. Then he walks down the passage, 'click-click-click', over the loose blocks – the whole fucken floor's full of loose or missing blocks. He counts twenty-three loose blocks by the time he gets to the end of the passage. He must check again. Maybe they need more than thirty-one.

Treppie's out, at the Chinese. Pop's sitting in his chair, looking through one of those *Homemaker*s they keep throwing over the fence. His mother sits and looks where Pop's looking. Or she looks like she's looking. Since Gerty died, Mol keeps looking where everyone else looks, but she sees nothing. She's fucken blown away, that's for sure. Pop says his mother lived for that dog. Well, she must wait, she'll still see what to live for. With those fused-out eyes of hers. She'll see how he fixes this place up. How he scores a proper woman. No one fuckenwell tells him he's a miscarriage. No one tells him his brain is fucked. No one tells him he's got a dick like a dinosaur, so why doesn't he go fuck dinosaurs. There's nothing these two hands of his can't do. He just gets fits, and sometimes he misses out on chances – that's all. It could happen to anyone. Who does his mother think she is? What makes her think she's better than him? Her fucken arse, man!

'Right, I'm going now,' he tells them.

'Where to?' It's his mother. She looks, but she doesn't see him.

'Where to? Where to?' he mocks her. 'Why don't you fix Pop's zips, Ma, then you'll be doing something useful. And, Pop, measure the space for the mirror in the bathroom, so we can get one cut the next time we go to Newlands. At the mirror shop. I can't see my face any more when I shave.'

'Okay,' says Pop. 'I'll do it.'

'Where you going, hey, Lambert?' It's his mother again.

'That's my business, Ma.' He squeezes between them and the sideboard so he can get the NPs' fifty-rand note out of the headless cat, where Treppie stuffed it that night, right next to the plastic rose. Pop said they must put it there so they could give it back to the NP, just in case the NP wanted to take them to court or something. He pulls out the rose.

'Keep your hands off!' says his mother.

Pop doesn't notice. He's staring at a picture in the *Homemaker*. It's a wooden house that looks like a king-sized dog kennel.

'Off what?' he says. She must shuddup. He shakes his finger at her, stuffing the money into his back pocket.

It's hot outside. The sun's sitting right on top of the sky. He stands under the little carport, next to Molletjie, with his hands at his sides. A cloud's building up on the one side. Which way? He wanted to go to the dumps in Bosmont, but that's too far in this heat. And the fucken Hotnots always stare at him, like he's a fucken kaffir or something. Hotnots don't like kaffirs, that's something he knows for a fact. Still, he doesn't know what their case is, and why they shout at him like that: What you looking for over here, hey, whitey? Not that they can talk. One Saturday he was in Bosmont's Main Street, on his way home with his wine bags, when he suddenly saw these bouncy bunches of Hotnot-majorettes come marching past him, "boompity-boompity-boom". They were jamming the whole street with their bands and everything, young Coloured girls, all of them in shiny dresses. Some of them were real white, a proper inside-bum white, but they're still Coloured, you can see it. You can see it by their hair and those missing front teeth. He couldn't get across the street, so then he had to stand there and watch the parade with all those Hotnots. They were jostling him from all sides, and then one of them said: 'Ooh, watch out, this hillbilly's getting a hard-on for our girls here!'

At the time, he pretended he didn't hear, but afterwards he asked Treppie what a hillbilly was. Treppie said it was English for Ampie, and then he asked Treppie who Ampie was. Treppie said Ampie was a dirty oke with a rag-hat, stretched braces, rawhide shoes and khaki pants that were too short for him. He was a bit slow in his top-storey and he spent his time sitting in a ditch, eating a tin of sardines and a tin of condensed milk while conversing with a donkey. And somehow, this oke was still a big hero.

Sometimes Treppie can talk the biggest lot of crap. He told Treppie, rubbish, man. He, Lambert, didn't eat bread with sardines or condensed milk, so how could *he* be like Ampie or a hillbilly? Sis, how was that supposed to taste anyway! But Treppie said bread with polony and golden syrup would qualify just fine. In the nineties, he said, an outsize dick hanging from fucked-up boxer shorts were the same as stretched braces and khaki pants that were too short. And what's more, Treppie said, he should figure out for himself what he thought of an oke who looked for empty wine boxes on rubbish dumps, an oke who screwed his own mother till she hopped instead of talking to donkeys, and, to top it all, who lived in a place called Triomf with a big smile on his dial. Treppie was drunk as a lord when he said that, otherwise he would've finally smashed him to a pulp. Who the fuck does Treppie actually think he is? What makes him think he can talk, anyway? He also lives in Triomf. He boozes with the Chinese, and they're not even white. As for the Hotnots, it's true they're getting whiter by the day, but they must just understand, once a Hotnot, always a Hotnot. They must keep their mouths shut about him and his private life. He has his pride. He knows his rights, even if he is a minority. He'll vote for his own protection. And they will look after him, 'cause he's not the only one.

He decides not to go to Bosmont. He'll just go here, at the back, to the Martindale dump. The one behind the old jail in Long Street. They turned the jail into flats, but he reckons that anyone who lives there now must feel like a jailbird behind those tiny windows. All they did was take away the bars. He'll go see what's inside those containers today. Maybe his luck's in. Sometimes the wine boxes get mixed up with plastic in the recycling bin.

He walks up Martha Street, across Victoria and into Thornton. Then he turns left and walks past Triomf Garage. Volkswagen experts. But the Benades prefer getting their parts from the Chop Shop in Ontdekkers. It's cheaper that way. Anyway, they don't need experts – he's already one, for Molletjie and Flossie. There's nothing anyone can tell him about those cars that he doesn't already know. If only those two dykes across the road knew how completely daft they are for not letting him look at their Volla. But they'll be sorry, they must just wait. They're still going to be very sorry.

He walks past the entrance to Triomf Shopping Centre. On a blackboard next to the entrance he reads the advert for Roodt Brothers Forty Years Meat Tradition: YOUNG OX: R9 A KILO STEWING MEAT.

Sis, ox-meat for stewing. Sounds a bit off to him. Beef-braaivleis, now that's what he wants. A nice thick T-bone or two, like next door had the last time. Haven't had another braai since then. Maybe ice-cream sellers can't afford braaivleis every other day.

He's almost beyond the parking area when he hears someone calling out to him.

'Hey, excuse me! Hey, sir!' He feels wind blowing on to his face from all the shiny cars as they rush past him. They must wait, they're all still going to run out of petrol when the shit starts flying in this place. Pride comes before a fall, he remembers from his schoolbooks.

He turns to see who's 'sir-ing' him now. He's not just anyone's 'sir'. People must be very careful before they start calling him things like that. Maybe it's not even for him.

Across the road, two men stand next to a caravan. They're wearing khaki pants and maroon berets. Must be selling hot dogs. But no, there's a little table with papers, under a red and white umbrella. And a bottle of Oros with glasses and a jug of water. Must be traffic cops. He wants to carry on walking. He hasn't done anything wrong. He's not even driving and he wants nothing to do with papers. But the men call after him again: 'Hey, sir!' and then they smile big friendly smiles at him. Smiles like he's never seen on the faces of traffic cops or policemen. Maybe it's hot dogs after all. Surplus army hot dogs or something. But there aren't any other people in the area. So what's their case?

'Hey, good morning, I mean good afternoon, sir. Come see here please, maybe you're interested,' the one shouts, and the other motions with his arm: Come! The sun's burning his head. It's fucken hot. The whole street smells of tar and tyres. He's not used to walking like this. And his one ankle's starting to hurt already.

He looks up and down the road, left-right-left, before crossing over. Let him go and have a look, then. But he sees quickly it's not him who's doing the looking. It's them. They're looking at him. They look him up and down.

'Howzit, China,' the one says.

Now he's a Chinaman. First he was 'sir' and now suddenly he's a fucken Chinaman. These okes must watch out, he's not feeling so cool today. Pop always tells him he mustn't talk to strangers and he mustn't trust them, 'cause they just use you for their own purposes. But he wasn't born yesterday, he won't let anyone just use him. And he'll first ask them what they want. Both of them carry guns in holsters.

'Good morning, gentlemen,' he says. 'How can I help you? Lambert Benade.' He offers the one man his hand.

'Du Pisanie,' the man says.

'A pleasure,' he says. The man laughs and signals to his friend he must also shake Lambert's hand. The other one's smoking. He puts his cigarette in his mouth and sticks out his hand.

'Van der Walt,' he says, squinting. He shakes Lambert's hand just very briefly and then takes the cigarette out of his mouth again.

'Glad to meet you,' says Van der Walt, blowing out smoke. The men look at each other and smile. He wonders what they think is so funny. Didn't they specially call him over? Why are they smiling so much, in that case?

'Gentlemen, may I ask what you wish to achieve by talking to me?' he asks.

Du Pisanie goes and sits at the table. He sticks his head into the papers. Van der Walt suddenly starts coughing from his cigarette. He turns round and finishes his coughing. Then he turns back again. His eyes are full of tears from all the coughing.

'Mr Benade,' says Van der Walt, 'can you shoot?' He taps with a flat hand on the gun in his hip-holster.

Du Pisanie looks up from his papers. 'Mr Benade, the real question is, do you *want* to shoot?' He pulls his gun out of the holster and puts it down, 'ka-thwack', on top of the papers.

Lambert shuffles in his lace-ups. Now they're asking him a question. What's he supposed to say now?

'Shoot,' he says. He feels just as stupid as his mother.

'A glass of Oros for you?' Van der Walt asks.

'Yes, please,' he says. 'Nice and hot today.'

'Yes, hot,' says Du Pisanie.

Van der Walt pours three glasses of Oros with water. They drink.

'Aaah,' says Du Pisanie, putting down his glass.

'Aaah,' says Van der Walt, putting down his glass.

'Was nice,' he says, putting down his glass.

Now what? First shoot, then Oros. What's their case? He looks at them. But they're looking at each other. They look a bit funny, if you ask him. He thinks he should rather get away from here now.

'Well, then, gentlemen, I'll be on my way. Goodbye, then,' he says.

'No, wait,' says Du Pisanie.

'We're recruiting,' says Van der Walt. 'For the AWB's task force on the Rand.'

Du Pisanie pats his sleeve. Only now does Lambert see the AWB badge. Red and white, with things that look like little black hooks.

'Soldiers, chefs, cleaners, anything . . . medical, technical, telecommunications. Were you in the army, Lambert?'

Suddenly Du Pisanie sounds soft and friendly.

Now suddenly he's 'you' and 'Lambert'. These people want to use him, not for shooting, but for 'anything'. No thanks, he's no one's skivvy. And he wasn't in the army, either, 'cause of the fits. But that's none of their business.

'Sorry, gentlemen, I'm NP.'

'Oh, my God,' says Van der Walt, smacking himself on the forehead with a flat hand.

'What you think the NP's going to do for your kind, Lambert? Tell me, what?' asks Du Pisanie.

'They're going to protect me, 'cause I'm a minority,' he says.

Why do they say 'for your kind'? What's wrong with him? He is who he is, full-stop.

'Some more Oros?' offers Van der Walt.

'No thank you.'

They're not laughing any more.

Du Pisanie shakes his head. 'It just goes to show,' he says to Van der Walt. Then he turns back to Lambert. 'We want to help you to protect yourself, Lambert. We want our people to be independent. And to look after themselves. We want our people to stand on their own two feet, in peace as much as in war.'

Now Van der Walt's very serious. He taps the table as he stands there next to Du Pisanie. 'Independent', tap, 'look after themselves', tap, 'stand on their own two feet', tap.

'Listen nicely now, Lambert,' says Du Pisanie, 'can you peel potatoes?' He sounds like he means even if Lambert can do nothing but peel potatoes, he's made for life.

'Or wash dishes, or scrub floors?' says Van der Walt. Van der Walt sounds like he means if Lambert can do nothing but wash dishes or scrub floors, the world is his oyster.

'Listen to me,' he says to Du Pisanie, 'I'm not your kaffirgirl.' He takes a step back. 'I'm not your kaffir that you can order around. Peel here, scrub there!'

'It's for the task force, man!' says Van der Walt. 'Not everyone can do the shooting.'

'Says who?' he asks.

'Lambert, listen to us now, man.' It's Du Pisanie. Now he sounds like he's begging. He winks at Van der Walt. Van der Walt must play along nicely now. 'Can you fix things, things that are broken, machines and things?'

'Volkswagens,' he answers.

'And what else?' asks Van der Walt.

'Lawn-mowers, fridges, washing machines, video machines, fans, you name it,' he says.

'Excellent!' says Du Pisanie.

'There's nothing that these two hands can't do,' he says. He shows them his hands. Van der Walt and Du Pisanie look at them – Lambert's big hands with their funny, bent fingers, some of them too short, with knobs on the wrong places. Then they look at each other.

'But we can certainly use you, old friend!' says Van der Walt. Du Pisanie looks quickly at Van der Walt, shaking his head hard, just once.

'He means you'll be an asset to the AWB's task force, sir,' says Du Pisanie.

But no one's going to 'old friend' him and then 'sir' him in the same breath – he heard what he heard.

'No one uses me. I'm my own blarry boss. I don't do kaffirwork. Take your fucken AWB and stick it up your backsides, man!' He takes a few steps back.

'Hey!' says Van der Walt, taking a step closer. 'What did you say there, hey? Come again, let's hear you say that again, hey . . .'

'Leave the rubbish alone, man,' says Du Pisanie. 'We're wasting our time with him, he's just a piece of rubbish, man.'

'He's worse than a kaffir, the fucker. Just look at him!' says Van der Walt.

'Jesus,' he hears one of them say behind his back as he walks away, 'I really didn't know you still got people like that around here.'

Lambert walks away, fast. He's limping. His ankle got sore from standing so long there under that big umbrella. He's so spitting mad he could scream. He could chew up a car he's so pissed off. Give him a car and he'll bite right through the bumper! Fuck! His throat burns. Their fucken arses! Their fucken mothers' arses too! Them with their fucken Oros! To hell with their fucken task force! They can peel their own fucken potatoes. They can go down on their own fucken knees and scrub their own fucken floors. What fucken floors, in any case? They're the kind of people who piss on carpets. That's what Treppie read in the papers. The AWBs pissed on the carpets at the negotiations. Just like Toby. If he sees a carpet, he pisses on it. That's why they chucked all the carpets out at home. They stank too much from Toby's piss. Fucken dogs! As if he's going to wipe up their stink piss. He's not their blarry servant-girl! And he's not rubbish either, he's no one's rubbish. Just fuck them, man. Fuck them to hell and back.

And so Lambert talks to himself as he walks in the hot sun, towards the dumps. He talks out aloud. As he walks, he drags one hand along the prefab wagon-wheels on the prefab walls. He keeps his head down and looks at his feet. People mustn't waste his fucken time like that. He's got his own plans. He's got a whole fucken list of things to do. And not enough time to do them in. Today it's first things first. To the dumps. Get wine boxes. Take out the bags, so he can put petrol in when the shit hits the fan.

Treppie says petrol's always the first thing that dries up when the shit starts flying.

He wonders what's all this shit that's going to fly so much.

When he asks Treppie what kind of shit he means, Treppie says shit is shit. You don't specify shit, you duck for shit. And even when you've looked for it yourself, you still duck. You don't just stand there. You've got a pair of eyes in your head, after all.

Treppie says that's why there's so much shit in the country. It's 'cause everyone who looks for shit, stands for shit too. They think if they keep standing for shit, they'll be heroes. But actually they're just shits. After a while they're so full of shit they can't duck any more, even if they wanted to. And so everything becomes an even bigger load of shit. That's why he thinks the Benades should just fuck off, 'cause he's not going to stand for the shit that other people look for, and keep looking for. And it's coming, he says, the shit's coming, for absolutely sure it's coming. It's coming like lava from two sides.

When Treppie's finished with the shit-story, he sings: 'Tides of benediction!'

He can't understand how shit coming from two sides like lava can be tides of benediction, but that's Treppie for you.

And that's how he knows Treppie. He wishes Treppie could've been with him today. He would have fixed those two fucken 'task forces', that's for sure. Treppie doesn't have to lay a finger on a person to fix him. He just does it through the air. He can make people feel so small it's like they aren't wearing pants any more, otherwise they lose their cool so badly they walk around for days in a sweat.

He turns right at the T-junction, to the dumps. It's a Wednesday morning, so there won't be so many people dumping today. But there're a lot of kaffirs sitting and waiting for work. Loose kaffirs. You always find bunches of them sitting there. They sit in the shade across the road, against the rocks, and when a car comes, they all stick their fingers into the air. It means: 'Take me, I'm a loose kaffir and I want piece-work'. The kaffirs inside the dump are fixed kaffirs – they work for the municipality. They wear overalls and they've got big, thick gloves. When people bring their rubbish, they throw it into big containers. They've got containers for bricks and containers for stones and others for grass and leaves and so on. They've also got containers for household rubbish. That's now the rubbish that's too much or too late for Tuesday. And that's exactly where he wants to be. The kaffirs who work with those containers always open up the bags to see what's inside. Sometimes they find old food. Then they eat that rotten food right there without even taking off their gloves. But it's not just rotten food you find there, it's all kinds of stuff. Radios, shoes, hairdryers, old clothes. He's even seen whole fridges there. He once told Treppie he must come see the fridges, but Treppie says he doesn't want to see another fucked-out fridge for the rest of his living days, let alone touch one. He says he's done his bit for fridges. From now on he only wants to read about them in the classifieds. He doesn't want to own them. He says it gives him great pleasure to see how far they travel, second-hand, third-hand, fourth-hand. But once they're beyond redemption he doesn't want to see them any more. He's had his fair share of lost fridges. That day in the yard when everything burnt down. He says there was so much fireworks going off into the sky he felt like he was in *The Towering Inferno*. It was bad, but it was also high drama. And a rubbish dump, he says, is not the final movie he wants in his head one day when he pops off, with fridges in the main roles, thank you very much. Treppie can talk a lot of shit. But at least he always has something to say.

He wants to go in at the gate, but first he has to wait for two container lorries to pass. One's coming in and the other's going out. They're making a hell of a racket. It looks like they're too high on their wheels. Pitch-black smoke pours out from the exhausts under their bellies. The smoke blows full into his face. He turns away his face and puts his hand in front of his mouth. The lorries are loaded to the brim with red-brick rubble and bits of plaster. The containers bump and grate against their frames. The lorries roar and blow. They brake and scrape their gears – the one to make its turn down the hill, and the other to get up the hill so it can turn into the road. The municipal kaffirs on top of the lorries shout and whistle and scream here above his head. The drivers sweat and swear. Their muscles flex as they turn the big steering wheels. Yellow-red sand sifts through the rims as the lorries turn, and the big wheels spin on all the loose gravel. Stones shoot from under the tyres.

Christ almighty! Suddenly it looks like the lorries want to open up their jaws here in front, at the grids. Like they want to bite him with teeth of yellow, dusty iron. He feels pain shoot into his tail-end. No, not that! God in heaven, please, help! Not here. Just keep a hold, now. Fucken lorries. They're all over him in his fucken head. He can feel himself going white in the face. Foamy spit bubbles up inside his cheeks. And now his mother's not here with her washing pegs, either. He wipes sweat off his upper lip. Down, down, he wants to fall down, to the ground.

'Hold on, Benade! Hold on!' he says to himself.

Then everything feels like it's on top of him. He goes down on one knee. The lorries roar, now this way, now that way, like demons straight from hell. They look like they're floating on air, with flames under their wheels. Then he feels someone grab him by his arm. He looks up but he can't see properly. Sparks blow up in front of his eyes. The man pulls him up and away, across the road. Away.

'Sit, sit down, man!' says the man. He sits. He can't see where he's sitting.

'Here, my man, drink some Coke, man!'

He gropes for the bottle in front of him. He swallows, but his throat feels tight. He takes another sip. Open up, throat, open, please! His eyes feel stiff. He rolls them around. His tongue is lame. He licks his lips. Jesus, fuck, that was close. That was close, fucken close! Thank you, God, Jesus thanks!

He opens his eyes. In front of him, sitting on his heels, he sees a kaffir. The kaffir's got a faded, sloppy hat on his head. And he's wearing reflector shades. There's a cut on his cheek. His face is sharp and yellow. He looks rough, like he's a rough, loose kaffir or something. But Lambert's not sure. The kaffir's wearing a faded denim shirt with holes where the sleeves used to be. Dirty threads of denim hang down on to his arms. There's a green band around his wrist and a copper bangle around the other arm, high up, just above the elbow. Long, thin arms hang like sticks from his shirt. His pants are too short and the skin sticking out underneath is rough. As far as Lambert can make out, the man's legs are like broomsticks, with a string of beads round one ankle. Red and green and yellow. Almost ANC, he thinks. Almost Inkatha. But not quite. He wonders what this yellow kaffir's case is. He's a different kind, this one. He looks clever, and it looks like something's tickling him. God knows what's tickling him so much. He looks at the kaffir's takkies. No socks, no laces. This is not even a loose kaffir.

This, he thinks, is a tsotsi-kaffir. As thin as a wild dog. What does he want with me?

Lambert wants to get up, but his back feels lame. He can't get up nicely. The kaffir presses him softly against his chest, back down again.

'It's okay, my bra. I'm just checking for you here. Wait, sit, it's okay. Are you feeling better now? You faint or what? Those lorries nearly got you, man. You were nearly squeezed flat, my man, flat like a pancake. But I watch out for you, my man. I pick you up, I bring you here. I give you Coke. I'm your friend, man. Don't panic.'

'I'm not your friend,' he says. 'I want to go home now.' But he can't get up.

The kaffir stands up. He takes a big step backwards. He motions with his hands. This kaffir's full of sights.

'Okay! Okay! Okay! You're not my friend, hey, you are my boss, right? Big boss, *ja baas*. I'm just a kaffir at the dumps, boss, okay? I catch whiteys who faint here. That's my job, yes? Here a whitey, there a whitey, faint. Faint left, faint right, faint centre, all day long. I'm the fainting boy, right?'

The kaffir turns his back to him. From behind it looks like he's laughing. Then he turns around again.

'Okay? Relax, my bra, just relax. Boss, king, president, chief, caesar. Whatever. God in heaven, anything you want, I say. Any way you want it. At you service. Excuse me boss, please boss, thank you boss, *ja baas, no baas*, sorry boss that I live boss!' The kaffir turns away again. His hands are at his sides. He drops his head and makes little shaking movements.

'I did not mean that so, man. Thanks for your help, man, many thanks. I just must go home now, that's all. I'm not feeling right, you see.'

But he sags back against the rock. He sees now he's going to have to wait. He can still feel the little stabs in his tail-end. Better to let it pass, otherwise it might come back again. Otherwise maybe it'll happen in front of Shoprite, next to the stewing-meat sign. That'll be fucken bad, even worse than here in front of the gates at the rubbish dumps. He sees the kaffirs sitting and looking at him across the road. But they're sitting with their fingers up in the air. They want a job, that's all they want. They couldn't give a shit about him lying here on the other side of the road with a back that feels lame. Why should they? Well, he figures, he's had some luck with this tsotsi-kaffir. If the kaffir hadn't helped him, he'd be lying there right now having a fit in the dust. Pissing in his pants, with all the lorries and cars full of people waiting in a queue for him to get finished.

'Hey,' he calls out to the kaffir, who's still standing with his back turned. 'I mean it, you! You saved my life there, man! Thank you, man. Thanks again very much.' And then as an afterthought: 'I owe you one.'

The kaffir turns around.

'Okay, okay, that's enough,' he says. Now he looks the hell in. He sits down next to Lambert. He takes a packet of tobacco out of his back pocket and rolls a cigarette. Then he shakes a few green crumbs from a matchbox into the tobacco.

Dagga, Lambert thinks. This kaffir actually thinks he can sit here and smoke a joint in front of him, a white man!

The kaffir makes the joint with his long, thin fingers. He licks the paper. He's concentrating hard. You can see he's been rolling joints for a long time. He folds the paper into a cigarette shape, twisting one end closed.

Then he smooths the joint nicely with his fingers, pressing them together like a nozzle. He's got two long nails on one hand. The kaffir lights up and takes a deep pull. He offers Lambert the joint. Lambert shakes his head. No thanks. The kaffir shrugs and looks the other way.

He stares at the kaffir who's looking the other way. This is one cheeky fucken kaffir, he thinks. How does he know Lambert won't go and report him to the police? How does he know he isn't a policeman himself? He thinks about this. No, he reckons he doesn't look like a policeman. He checks out the kaffir again. The kaffir looks like he's forgotten about him. He's looking into the street, now this way, now that way. He's looking at what's coming. He smokes his joint so hard the smoke floats around his head in clouds. He wishes the kaffir would take off those sunglasses, 'cause he doesn't know where to look when he looks at him. All he sees there is his own reflection. He feels the kaffir can see him better than he can see the kaffir. This is not a scared kaffir, he decides. This kaffir isn't afraid of anything. He's an okay kaffir, this.

'I'll take a pull now, thank you,' he says. Why not? He's sitting here on his backside, anyway, at the entrance to the rubbish dumps.

'Sure, man, sure,' the kaffir says. He passes him the stub.

Lambert takes a pull. He just hopes this kaffir hasn't got germs. But so what, anyway. He, Lambert, is not always so clean himself. The joint makes him cough.

'Easy,' the kaffir says to him. 'Easy now, my bra,' he says, and Lambert feels how he smiles, right through the dagga smoke, back at the kaffir, as they sit there, across the road, in front of the gates of the rubbish dump. And he sees how the kaffir smiles back at him. And he, Lambert, smiles even more. And the kaffir too, all you see are teeth. Then the kaffir starts laughing. He takes the joint that Lambert's handing back to him and he laughs and coughs and he smacks Lambert on the back so hard that he starts hiccuping. And then Lambert laughs and pushes the kaffir who's laughing at him with his shoulder, and the kaffir loses his balance. He falls over on to the grass, on his elbow.

'Hey, man!' says the kaffir as he props himself up again.

'I say, man!' he says. 'Ha-ha-ha-ha-ha-ha!'

'Ha-ha-ha-ha-ha-ha!' he and the kaffir laugh, there under the trees, next to the rocks, in front of the gates of the rubbish dump. They laugh so much they start crying. And when they've almost finished laughing, he says: 'So now, what's your name, hey?'

'Ooooh!' says the kaffir. 'I've got many, many names. One for every occasion. But to you, my friend, I'm Sonnyboy, just Sonnyboy, plain and simple. And what's your name?'

'Lambert,' he says, 'Lambertus Benade.'

And then he feels himself offering the kaffir his hand. Ja, can you believe it? And the kaffir smiles at him from behind his reflectors, and Lambert sees in the reflectors how he smiles back at the kaffir. And then the kaffir takes his hand. He shakes Lambert's big, knobbly hand. He half lets go of Lambert's hand and then he swivels his own hand, grabbing hold of Lambert's thick thumb. Lambert gropes to get hold of the kaffir's thumb, and when he does get a grip on it, a thin little thumb, the kaffir suddenly lets go and turns his hand straight again. Lambert gropes for the kaffir's hand until he gets hold of it again. And then he gives it a good shake.

Now they really start laughing. They sit there and clutch their stomachs, they're laughing so much. They smack their legs to help them get all the laughter out. They make grabbing movements in the air to show how they missed each other's hands, and then they laugh so much they fall to the ground. There by the rocks, under the trees, across the road from the Martindale rubbish dumps.

'So now, where do you live, man?' the kaffir asks when the laughing dies down a bit.

'Just there, the other side, in Triomf,' he shows with his hand.

'Triomf,' says the kaffir.

'Yes, Triumph,' he translates for the kaffir.

'Triumph, I see,' says the kaffir, and he gives a little laugh.

'And you,' he says, 'where do you live?'

'Me? Ho, ho, here, there, everywhere. Sonnyboy pola everywhere,' says the kaffir.

'I see,' he says. And then, after a while: 'A rambling rose.'

Then they laugh some more.

'I mean, where do you come from?' he asks next.

'What do you reckon, my mate?' says the kaffir, smiling.

'Well, um, it's hard to say,' he says.

'How come, hey?' says the kaffir. 'You're supposed to be able to tell just by looking at me, hey, boss?'

'Um, it's not so easy,' he says.

'No, now you must please explain, my man, 'cause I'm just a damn kaffir.'

He knows he's being teased. But he doesn't mind. This kaffir's his pal. He likes him.

'Well, you're too yellow,' he says, 'and you don't talk like a kaffir. Maybe you're just a Hotnot.'

'Hear, hear!' says Sonnyboy. 'This whitey can't classify me!' He leans over to Lambert as if he wants to tell him a secret.

'Look, that's how the dice fell for me here in Jo'burg. I'm a Xhosa, I come from the Transkei, and some of us are yellow.' He touches his face. 'That's why the bladdy Bushmen thought I was one of them, so I got a room in Bosmont right in among them. And they began talking real Coloured Afrikaans to me. So I got the hang of it on the sly, and I didn't say nothing, 'cause the less a Bushman knows about you, the better. It's a bad scene, the Bushman scene. They drink themselves stupid and then they rob and stab you and leave you for dead . . .' Suddenly Sonnyboy sounds different. He shifts even closer to Lambert.

'Now listen to me, brother.' From behind the rocks he pulls out a pink bag with a zip and handles. 'Don't you want to buy something from a rambling rose? I need the money, man. I haven't got a job. I live by my wits, you could say. I'm hungry, man. I haven't eaten fucken nothing for three days, man.'

'Shame,' Lambert says. 'That's bad.'

'Bad, man, big bad,' says Sonnyboy.

He looks round to see if anyone's coming. Then he unzips the bag and feels around among papers and rags. He holds open the bag for Lambert to look.

'Fuck!' Lambert says.

In the bag, on top of dirty rags and newspaper, lie a revolver and a pair of binoculars.

'Jesus fuck!' he says. 'Where you get that kind of stuff, man?' He puts his hand into the bag, but Sonnyboy grabs his wrist hard and takes out the hand again. He zips the bag closed.

'Right,' Sonnyboy says. 'You think about it. Think, man, it wasn't easy, I tell you.'

'That's too expensive for me, man. Just look at me!' And he points to his clothes, his perished boxer shorts. He lifts up his arms so the kaffir can see the holes in his green T-shirt. 'I'm also poor, you know!' he says.

'But you're not hungry, man. You are not hungry like I am,' says Sonnyboy, rubbing his stomach.

'Well,' Lambert says, and he doesn't know what gets into him, but he says to Sonnyboy, right there under those scrappy trees, among the rocks, across the road from the dumps: 'I'm hungry for love, man; now that's a really bad thing, man.'

Sonnyboy looks at him. 'Hey?' he says, and he looks away. Then he looks back at him. 'Shame,' he says. 'That's bad, man.'

'But I'm getting a girl, you know.'

'Yes?' says Sonnyboy, looking like he doesn't believe him.

'Yes, my father's getting a girl for me on my birthday, for a whole night. I want to make everything nice, so maybe she stays with us forever.'

''Strue?' Sonnyboy smiles a little smile, but Lambert can't work out what that smile means. 'Cause of the shades. This yellow kaffir from the Transkei mustn't come and laugh at him now. He must know his place, yellow or not. He must know what he is and who he is. To hell with Hotnot tricks.

'Where you got those things in any case?' he asks, putting a bit of attitude into his voice.

'Oooh,' says Sonnyboy, 'here, there, everywhere, boss!'

'I see.' He nods slowly at Sonnyboy.

Sonnyboy nods slowly back.

'How much?' he asks.

'Hundred,' says Sonnyboy.

'Too much,' he says.

'Eighty,' says Sonnyboy. 'Have a heart, man.'

'I haven't got eighty,' he says.

'What have you got then, man?' Sonnyboy sounds impatient. 'Take it out, let's see,' he says. Suddenly it looks like he wants to get up and walk off.

He knows he must play his cards carefully now. He wants that gun, that's for sure. He's not so sure about the binoculars, but he knows they'll come in handy, sooner or later.

'I've got fifty,' he says, feeling in his back pocket for the NPs' fifty-rand note.

'Ag no man!' Sonnyboy protests. 'What do you take me for? This stuff here's worth a few thousand!' He reaches out for Lambert's fifty.

'Tough!' Lambert says, pushing the note back into his pocket.

'But a hungry man is a hungry man,' says Sonnyboy.

'You said it,' says Lambert, 'and beggars can't be choosers.'

'Don't come and look for shit with me!' says Sonnyboy.

'I'm not looking for anything,' he says. 'I've got something. Six free meals, fifty bucks each.'

'That's nothing!' says Sonnyboy.

'No, 'strue's Bob. For the Spur, six tickets. I was lucky. The Spur had a birthday. I won them.'

'Spur, hey,' says Sonnyboy, 'birthday, hey?'

'Yes, man, the eatplace, Spur. Spur Comanche, Spur Blazing Saddles, any Spur. You can go too. In town. Blacks and Coloureds can go too, now. This is the New South Africa, remember. In Melville too, I swear.'

'Hmmm,' says Sonnyboy. 'How many did you say?'

Lambert feels in his back pocket. He feels past the fifty-rand note until he finds the tickets. Then he unfolds them. Pop's luck is still rolling here today.

'Tear on the dotted line,' he says to Sonnyboy, counting them out. 'Six, there's six here. Here, take a look, man. Fifty rands' food on each ticket. You can eat for a week, every day a T-bone.'

T-bone, Lambert thinks. And what will Pop say when he hears about this deal of his? 'Cause it was Pop's luck that day with the pudding at Spur, not his. He never has any luck with this kind of thing. But today he's getting some luck. He must just play his cards right here. He folds the tickets up and puts them back into his pocket.

'I give you four tickets. Fifty rands and four tickets,' he says. 'And I'll keep two tickets for myself. I also fancy a T-bone some time. My girl too. I'll take her for a T-bone, if she wants to stay. 'Cause the first night we'll just eat snacks in my room. I thought of everything. I've got a list. Cheese dips, fish dips, crinkle cuts, salt and vinegar chips, the works.'

Sonnnyboy laughs.

'What are you laughing at, hey? Hey?' He also laughs a little.

Then they both sit and stare out at the world in front of them. Lambert thinks about his deal. The shadows are getting long. Almost all the loose kaffirs at the gate have gone home for the day. The fixed kaffirs inside the gate are taking off their gloves. Any minute now they'll close the gates. A wind starts up, blowing plastic bags and loose dirt across the dumps. The bags blow up against the wire fence. Some of them get stuck under the fence. Others snag on the razor-wire on top of the fence. The late-afternoon sun shines gold on the rusted containers inside the dumps.

'Do they work proper, those things you've got there?' he asks after a while.

'Sure, man, sure!' says Sonnyboy. 'I'll give you a demo.' He unzips his bag.

Then he pushes out the revolver's round magazine. 'Click,' and he clicks it back into the middle. He spins it, 'rrrrt', with his finger. 'Click-click-click' he shoots, inside the pink bag.

'Satisfied?' asks Sonnyboy.

'Now the binoculars,' he says.

Sonnyboy takes out the binoculars and sets them. He looks through them for a long time. Then he passes them to Lambert, laughing a funny little laugh. He points to the dumps.

'You see that container there, hey? The one, two, three, four, fifth one from this side. Now look there, on its side, number five, what can you make out there?'

Lambert lifts the binoculars to his eyes. The wire and the plastic bags rise up into his vision. Then he finds his bearings. He sees the light of the sun shining on things. It looks gold. Then the first container, the second, the third, the fourth. Through the binoculars, their sides look like aerial photos of the land taken from very high up. Lines and cracks and bare patches. Plains and dams and bushes, other countries, all spray-painted in gold. Then he gets to the fifth one. It looks like mine dumps and koppies, with thick rows of shapes and blocks, some in crowded rows on top of each other, and others in loose, mixed-up strands. It looks like the aerial photo of Jo'burg on the Chinese calendar in their lounge.

'Read,' says Sonnyboy. 'Read to me what you see there.'

Lambert looks on the side of the container. He reads out aloud. 'CTR 517. Municipality of Johannesburg TPA.' The letters are stencilled on to the container in white.

'Right,' says Sonnyboy. 'Now go down to the right. Just a bit. Now what do you see there? It's small. Do you see it? Then read, brother, read that line for me.'

'One settler, one bullet,' Lambert reads. The letters have been scratched with a nail on to the rusted side of the container. He lowers the binoculars. This yellow kaffir's jiving him in a big way now. That's what he's doing. He's a cheeky mixed-up fucken kaffir, and now he's screwing me in the ears, Lambert thinks.

'I'll knock the shit out of you, kaffir,' he says to Sonnyboy.

'Sorry, boss, but why?' Sonnyboy laughs. 'I didn't write that shit there, man! Just relax, my bra! Sonnyboy's not into politics, man, I do the dumps, in my own way. That crap's all over the place, man. Kill this, kill that, one this, one that, viva this, viva that, long live this, that and the other. I love the NP, I love Mandela, I love Biko, I love Amy. So much love in this place, it sounds like fucken paradise! I love all that stuff. I can't be bothered with all that shit, my man. I just want to show you. This thing here works.'

Sonnyboy takes back his binoculars. He puts them in the bag and zips it closed.

Both of them stay quiet for a long time.

'I don't know,' Lambert says. 'What can I do with them, the binoculars? I'm not a spy!'

'Well,' says Sonnnyboy, 'you can show your girl the city. From high places.'

'Hmmm,' he says, 'and what do I do with the gun? I haven't got a licence.'

'What you need a licence for, man? Protect your girl with it. Jo'burg's a dangerous place, right? She'll feel safe and sound with you, man.'

Lambert sees the sun's already down. Around the closed gates of the dumps the light's looking grey, and here under the trees it's already dark. He and Sonnyboy go round in circles, with long quiet periods inbetween, as they work out their deal. Then they've got it. Lambert pays the price: fifty rand, plus all six Spur tickets. He puts the gun into the binoculars' plastic bag. He also gets a plastic bag full of cartridges. Sixty of them, says Sonnyboy. For the hot shot of Triumph Town.

What's Sonnyboy feeling for now in his pink bag? He takes out something.

'Free bonus,' he says, and he ping-pings on the thing's iron teeth.

'What's that?' Lambert asks, taking the short piece of wood with its strips of iron from Sonnyboy.

'You make music on it,' says Sonnyboy. 'You Boers call it a kaffir-harp. It's like a Jew's harp a little bit. You know?' And Sonnyboy demonstrates with his mouth.

'I see,' Lambert says.

'We call it a mbira,' says Sonnyboy.

'Umbiera,' he says, 'I'll remember.'

'You remember,' says Sonnyboy. 'If you practise you'll get a tune out of it some day.'

'Okay,' he says. 'I'll practise.'

'Okay,' says Sonnyboy.

They both hold out their hands, and this time they shake all three grips smoothly, in time with each other.

'Now we're tuned,' he says.

'Greased and oiled!' says Sonnyboy.

'So long,' he says, 'and thanks again for saving my life, hey!'

'Thanks for saving mine!' says Sonnyboy.

What does he mean? Lambert thinks. But he's already turned to go home. Sonnyboy too. He goes right, and this sharp, yellow kaffir goes left. There in front of the closed gates at the Martindale dumps. It's almost completely dark now. Lambert turns round one last time to look. He sees from behind how Sonnyboy takes off the glasses. He won't know him without those sunglasses, he thinks. But that's okay, it's against the law to buy stolen stuff and anyway it's not good for a person to know a kaffir-thief too well.

When he walks past Triomf's shopping centre on the way home, the AWBs and their red caravan are gone. He's almost glad, 'cause he knows he would've been tempted to shove his new gun under their noses. Just to prove a point. But that would have caused big trouble again and now he's in a hurry to get home.

At the house, he climbs softly over the fence so no one will hear the gate and come and ask where he's been all day. He hasn't worked out a story yet. He sneaks round the back to his den and puts on the light. Then he takes all the stuff out of his bag and arranges it on his bed. Before he sits down, he locks the inside door. Then he sits for a long time and looks at his lucky finds. Eventually, he leans backwards against his cushion, propped up against the wall. 'Ping, ping, ping,' he plays on the stiff teeth of his umbiera.

In front of him, he sees his list from this morning.

He smiles at his list and gets up. Underneath the last number he writes another three numbers: *25, 26* and *27*. And next to them he writes: *gun, binoculars, umbiera (Kaffir-harp)*. He makes little ticks next to each one. With a red ball-point.

14

~

FIFTH OF NOVEMBER

FROM DREAM TO DREAM ~

op half wakes up. He smells fire. He can't work out if he's awake or asleep. In his dream everything was also full of white smoke. Now he keeps his eyes closed. He stays where he is. He's trying to work out what's burning and where. His skin feels dry and there's a rustling noise in his ears. It feels like he's lying inside a dry pod. He feels light, as if he's tumbling about inside a shell as dry as the wind, a great big droning wind full of white smoke. He can't tell what's above and what's below. His head spins. It's as if many different hands are swinging him by his feet, letting him go and grabbing him again. As if each hand doesn't know what the others are doing.

Pop struggles to get out of the dream, but just as he begins to get out, he lands up in another dream. His eyes burn when he tries to open them, and there's a noise in his ears like the sound of crashing. He can hear voices shouting, louder and then softer, in a rush of sounds that blow over him in waves.

BLOW HIGH THE FLAME ~

Pop sits up on the mattress. The room's full of smoke. He turns towards the window and pulls the curtains away so he can see outside. But he sees nothing outside, no grass and no wall. Just thick, white smoke. He hears big things falling, doors slamming, and the walls shaking.

It's Lambert. Screaming. A terrible bellowing. The other voices are those of Mol and Treppie. Mol's voice is low. It sounds like something simmering, like Jungle Oats cooking on a stove. Treppie's voice is high. Pop also wants to scream, but he can't get a sound out of his mouth. His throat has closed up from all the smoke.

Have they really forgotten about him here in the room as the world consumes itself outside? Did they think he should rather just fall asleep, finally, without his even realising he was crossing over? Maybe they thought it would be more merciful like this. And maybe they were right, too. But now he's awake and he must get out of here, 'cause he can't breathe. Pop gets up, still in his shirt. He feels for his pants, but his eyes burn when he opens them. He can't find his pants. He's looking for the door. He walks into the dressing table, catching sight of his face in the cracked, middle mirror. All he sees there are dark holes where his eyes should be, and the white point of his nose. His mouth and chin and cheeks are blotted out in the semi-dark of the room. He rubs his hand over the bottom half of his face. The stubble makes a scraping noise. So, at least his face is still there.

It feels to him like time's dying, like the end of time itself is approaching. The last judgement, the judgement of fire, when the clock-faces melt in the towers and the seconds burn into the wrists one by one.

Pop turns away from the mirror. If the mirror's here, then the door must be there. He takes a few steps across the floor. Behind him the window slips off its catch and blows open. He turns around. The curtain flaps up high and a wave of warm smoke-wind catches him full in the face. He loses his breath, stumbling backwards into a doorframe. Now he's in the passage. There, far away in front of him, he sees a light. It must be the front door. But the back door's closer. He hears sounds like shots. Things are exploding out there in the backyard. He feels hot and cold in his shirt. The smoke swirls more and more densely round his head.

Pop feels like he's in the belly of something that's been set on fire and stoked up, something you can't stop until it all burns up. Like a furnace. Or an oven where bricks are being fired.

He stands in the back door. Through the waves of smoke he sees Lambert swinging a big metal plate over the fire. Flames shoot up from under the plate. Lambert roars. It looks like his feet are in the coals. He's taking high steps and his legs look like they're burnt black, all the way up to his knees.

Slowly, Pop registers what he's seeing. Flossie's not on her blocks any more. She's not even on her chassis. She's right off her undercarriage, like something fleeing its own skin. What's more, it looks like someone's taken a sledgehammer and smashed the dislocated Flossie even further into her glory. Bits of her lie scattered all over the place. All that remains on her chassis are the seats, the engine and the steering wheel. It's almost like a king-sized dog with jaws of iron decided to tear her to bits. And her shell, standing to one side with its doors thrown open, looks like something that wants to fly, a thing with broken wings and no face, 'cause the front window's been smashed in as well. The doors have been pushed almost right out of their hinges, and the nose of the bonnet's been twisted upwards, out of shape. The engine cover too. God in heaven, how could he have slept through all this? Maybe he's still sleeping. Maybe he'll wake up in a minute or two and find it's just an ordinary day.

Slowly, Pop moves his sore hip down the kitchen steps. Still in his shirt and socks, he takes a few steps through the wreckage. A blowtorch lies in the grass. He sees the big monkey-wrench and the electric saw for cutting iron. Pieces of iron piping and bricks lie scattered everywhere. He wants to get to Lambert, over there, standing in the flames. He must stop Lambert. He must try to stop him before he goes too far. He must say something, before Lambert takes to the streets and breaks down the whole of Triomf. But the smoke and the heat stop Pop in his tracks. He can't go any further, the wind's blowing everything into his face. There's soot in his eyes and he can smell rubber.

Suddenly he sees Treppie and Mol running towards him, through the smoke. Mol's coughing. Her hair stands up wildly. Treppie's waving his arms.

'Back! Back!' he shouts.

'Around the front!' Mol shouts.

'Here!' Treppie rips the steering wheel out of its rod and pushes it into Pop's hands.

'Take this!' he shouts at Mol. He rips something loose. It's a piece of the back seat.

Treppie grabs one more time. He tears off one of Flossie's loose mudguards at the back. 'Come!' he shouts.

Pop finds himself in the middle of a procession. Back through the kitchen door, down the passage, up towards the front door. With Treppie in the lead.

'He's gone berserk!' shouts Mol.

'He's flipped,' shouts Treppie.

'Everything must burn!' shouts Mol.

'We must go round the front!' shouts Treppie. 'The wind's too strong, we must throw the stuff into the fire from the front.' The wind blows the warm smoke full into their faces. From the back, they can't even get close to the fire.

'He wants to see fire,' shouts Mol.

'Quick,' shouts Treppie.

Pop wants to say 'police', he wants to say 'fire brigade', he wants to say 'neighbours', he wants to say 'Lord God, please help', but he can't get a word out. He slips on the floor as he shuffles down the passage with the procession, steering wheel in hand. Then they're out through the front door. Ahead of him, Pop sees Treppie starting to run. Flossie's mudguard scrapes a long, white mark against the front door. From behind, Mol pushes Flossie's seat into his back. 'Hurry, Pop. Run!'

Toby squeezes past their legs. He barks in a high voice and tries to jump up against them. They're out in front now, running around the corner. Vaguely, Pop sees a bunch of people watching them from the street, but he can't make out who it is. Mol's hurrying him up all the time.

'Fetch!' Lambert shouts from behind the fire. Pop can't make Lambert out. All he hears is Lambert's voice, which sounds different. Like it's coming through a loudspeaker, or the mouth of a bugle.

'Hurry up, you fucken dung-beetles . . . rotten bastards! I haven't got the whole fucken day!'

261

Then they're at the fire.

'Throw it in! Throw it in! In the middle, so it burns. I want nothing to do with rubbish. Rubbish must burn! Time is short!'

Lambert stands behind the fire. With his long arms he throws boxes, papers and rags into the fire. The smoke's so thick, all you can see is his outline. The old Kneff's also in the fire, Pop sees. It looks like a big, burning white ship. How the hell did Lambert get that heavy thing outside?

Treppie takes Flossie's seat from Mol and throws it on to the heap. It gives off a cloud of thick, black smoke. It stinks. Then the insides of the seat catch fire.

'Hooooo-haaa!' Lambert shouts.

The fire shoots up high.

'Hooooo-haaa!' he shouts. 'More! More! Come, come, come! What you all standing there for? Never seen a fire before, hey? Never seen how rubbish burns? Fucken rubbish must fucken burn. It must burn!'

They scuttle back round the corner of the house. Treppie gets to the remains of Flossie first. He rips and pulls at her shell.

Treppie gives Pop a door. Pop looks through the broken window and sees heads from next door looking over the prefab wall. Mol gets the wipers and a piece of floor mat and some plastic from Flossie's insides. Treppie rips a chunk out of the back seat. Fluffy stuff, brown woolly bits and coir bulge out of it. They go back in through the kitchen door. Toby barks. All the way along the passage he pulls things out of Mol's hands. She tries to pick the stuff up, but when she does, Toby bites her.

'Voetsek!' Mol shouts, but she's almost lost her voice. Pop's behind her. He tries to kick Toby with his socked foot, but all he manages to do is kick Toby's tail as it waves around in the air. Toby's wild. He thinks it's a party. He runs round them in circles with his ears flat against his head. He dances on his hind legs and the blocks on the floor dance up and down with him. Then they're out again, through the front door. They go round the corner, towards the back, until they get to the fire. They throw their things on the fire. Then back through the smoke to Flossie and back in through the kitchen with more pieces. Round and round they go. Pop's short of breath. He can't any more. He falls over his own two feet. He stays down, lying there with Flossie's dashboard in his hands, still quite a way short of the fire. He's looking at the world from underneath, from an angle. Toby's face is in front of him. His tongue hangs out. Pop pushes Toby away. Here come Treppie's shoes. The heels have been worn down at one side at the back. Now he sees Mol's legs. She's full of bruises and grazes and her brown socks have sagged down to her ankles. Pop looks up Mol's legs. The hollows of her knees are full of knobbly, purple veins. Above the hollows, the skin puffs up in bulges and, further up, it hangs in folds. Pop's looking up into Mol's depths. He lets his head drop again.

'Up! Up!' he hears Lambert screaming. 'Don't go lie down now, there's still lots more that must burn!'

Toby gets hold of Pop's shirt-sleeve. He pulls at it. Pop gets halfway up. He's on his knees, looking round him on all fours. Toby stands next to him, at the same height, looking into his face with pricked ears. Toby's waiting to see Pop's next move. But Pop doesn't move. He watches as Lambert drags Flossie's entire shell on to the fire, swinging and plucking wildly. Isn't Lambert also burning? The flames shoot up all around him. Now Lambert's doing funny things with his head. It's pulled down deeply into his shoulders. He looks like he's biting at something in the air. Pop crawls nearer on his hands and knees, alongside Toby, who still thinks it's a game. Then he kneels on his shirt; a piece rips loose from the collar.

As Pop and Toby reach Treppie's and Mol's legs, they stop to look at Lambert. It looks like the warm, smoky wind is about to blow Lambert away. Mol's legs give way slightly, as if she wants to sit down, but she stays up. Treppie bends over and puts his hands on his knees. He hangs his head. It looks like Treppie's crying. His face is all screwed up. Treppie turns his upside-down face towards Pop and Toby. Upside down, it looks even more like he's crying.

Are you crying? Pop wants to ask. It's a long time since he last saw Treppie cry. It was that time when there was a similar fire in the yard, when all the fridges burnt up.

263

Are you crying? Pop wants to ask, but all he does is open and close his mouth a few times. Are you crying, are you crying, are you crying? But he's got no moisture or sound to talk with.

Treppie's upside-down mouth makes a strange shape. He's saying something. Toby barks at Treppie. Pop can't hear what Treppie's saying, and he can't read Treppie's lips, 'cause they're upside down. All he sees is a row of teeth wedged against Treppie's lip. Then Treppie's face is gone. From his position on all fours, Pop looks to Mol's side. Toby also looks up. They see Treppie's hand go down into Mol's housecoat and come out again with nothing in it. Now Pop looks up, higher. Mol's hand goes up and feels for her bun that's come loose. Then Pop and Toby look in front of them again.

Where's Lambert now? They can't see Lambert any more.

Pop tries to get up. He steps on his shirt again and it tears further. Mol puts her hand under his arm to help him up. Pop's back on his feet. He looks at Treppie. Now he can read Treppie's lips. Treppie's upper teeth are set tightly against his lower lip as he says: 'Fit'.

'Fit, he's having a fucken fit, that's what it is, another fit, from making fires,' Treppie says. 'Come!'

Through the smoke, around the back corner, they struggle. The smoke blows into their faces. Pop coughs. Treppie's the first one to get to Lambert.

Lambert's lying with his feet almost in the fire. They're black and grey from the ash and his skin looks like it's burnt all the way up to his knees.

His back is hollow and his head's thrown back. His arms look stiff, with the elbows twisted strangely outwards. His hands are open and his fingers look like they're clutching something, but there's nothing there to clutch on to.

Toby pulls at Lambert's T-shirt sleeve. Mol takes one of Lambert's arms and Treppie the other. It looks like the arms have turned inside out in their sockets. They pull him away from the fire, but he's heavy, and they struggle to drag him to a safe distance.

Foam bubbles from Lambert's mouth. As they drag him through the ashes, his shorts come off. His thing hangs across his thigh at an angle. It's thick and purple. Pee spurts out of it.

Pop puts his hand to his breast. It feels like there's a small fit happening in his heart. His eyes burn. Then he realises he's also crying. Just like the last time when he saw Lambert lying there in the long, green grass with blood on his lips. When Treppie also cried.

'Matches!' Mol says. 'Treppie, pass your matches!'

'What?' Treppie says, but Mol's already taken the box out of his shirt-pocket. She shakes the matches on to the grass and squeezes the box flat.

'Pull open his mouth!' she says to Pop. Pop looks at his hands. They're filthy. He wants to wipe them off on his backside, but he's not wearing pants. He wipes his hands on his chest. On his torn shirt and his vest.

Treppie's hands are also dirty, but he's too busy to start thinking about his hands right now. He pulls Lambert's lips apart. The teeth are clenched. No tongue sticking out, so at least he hasn't bitten off his tongue. That's the one possibility. The other is that he could swallow his tongue. That's what the doctor said, epileptics have a problem with their tongues when they fit, they bite them off or they swallow them.

Treppie sticks his two forefingers into one side of Lambert's mouth, where he can find a gap, where Lambert's wisdom and molar teeth were taken out. Slowly he prises the jaws away from each other. 'Hold open his mouth!' he shouts at Pop.

Pop works his fingers between Lambert's front teeth. He pulls up with one hand and down with the other. He can't get a good grip. Lambert's mouth is slippery from all the slime. As Pop gets the mouth open, Treppie takes his forefinger and hooks Lambert's tongue out from the back of his throat. He pulls it into the mouth and straightens it out.

'Almost swallowed it.' Now Mol's there with the flattened matchbox.

'Double,' says Treppie, 'fold it double.'

Mol folds, once, twice, three times over. Treppie holds the box between Lambert's front teeth. 'Right,' she says, 'let go.'

Pop lets go. Treppie keeps his fingers in until the last moment, so he can keep the tongue nice and flat at the bottom of Lambert's mouth.

Pop stands back. He wipes his hands off on his shirt again.

Treppie wipes his hands on the back of his pants. Mol's still bent over. She holds the folded matchbox ready. Toby's standing on the other side of Pop's head.

Toby takes a step closer and then back again. 'Ee-ee,' he says.

'Dear me,' says Pop. At least, that's what he tries to say. But there's still no sound in his throat.

'Fuck,' says Treppie. 'Jesus, no, fuck it.' He wipes his forehead with his arm.

Slowly, Lambert's jaws sag back into place again. His teeth fit back on top of one another, over the folded matchbox.

Mol pulls Lambert's lips back over his teeth. Then she also moves back.

Just the folded back end of the red lion sticks out of Lambert's mouth. Toby sniffs Lambert.

'*Voetsek!*' Mol shouts.

Pop rips the half-torn side of his shirt right off. Right off the collar and out of the sleeve. He spreads it over Lambert's lower half. Mol pulls down Lambert's wet shorts, over his feet. As she pulls, little pieces of black skin come off here and there. It looks pink under the skin.

'He got burnt,' she says. 'Some of his skin burnt right off.'

'You people must get an ambulance,' they hear someone say. They look up. It's someone from next door, one of the Fort Knox women, looking over the wall. Then a man's head also pops up. 'That fucker looks like he wants to cop it.'

'Mind your own business,' Treppie tells the man.

The man laughs. He lights a cigarette. 'Anyone for a smoke?' He holds his packet out, over the wall. 'After action, satisfaction.'

Treppie motions to the man he wants nothing to do with him.

But Mol's looking at the man, who's walking closer to them, along the wall.

'Mol,' Pop says, without a voice. Why does Mol want to go and bugger around with next door now?

But Mol wants a cigarette, one of those the man's offering over the

266

wall. She wants to see another person's face. She wants to touch another person's hand. If someone wants to give her a cigarette, who's she to say no? Some people still care when they see you're suffering. That's what Mol's thinking. Pop knows. Shame. Poor Mol.

Pop watches Mol take a cigarette. He sees the man from Fort Knox lean over and light it up for her. The man cups his hands round the lighter and holds them close to Mol's face. He sees how the Fort Knox women look over the wall at Mol from both sides of the Fort Knox man. They're looking at how she lights her cigarette, but they're also looking her up and down. Her body, and her legs. Their faces look like they want to say: Sis. But they're also curious. Like the faces of people looking at an old tortoise or reptile or something eating its food in the zoo. Eating food or shitting. Or shitting off. 'Cause now the Benades have taken another big blow and everyone's staring at them, as if they're the only people who have setbacks like this. Pop feels something like anger rising in his breast, but it's weak. Behind him something sizzles. Then, suddenly, there's white steam all around his head. He turns round. More people appear through the smoke. They're from next door, on the other side. The fish-breeder's people. They're using hosepipes to put out the fire. Big clouds of steam and smoke rise up into the air.

Mol comes back from the wall. They stand and look at the clouds of smoke.

The man from next door shouts at them. 'We're going to put the municipality on to you! Do you think you're the only people in this street, hey? Just look at the mess here again. Everything full of soot and smoke! My carp can't breathe in this air. They're still going to come and take you away from here, the whole lot of you and all your fucken rubbish. You're worse than kaffirs, you lot! Blarry filth. A plague. Sis! Sis! Don't you have any shame?'

Pop pulls Treppie by the sleeve. He takes Mol by the shoulder. Come, let's go inside, he wants to say, but now his voice is even further away than it was earlier.

He bends over and takes one of Lambert's arms. Treppie takes the other. Mol takes the head. She holds it straight so the tongue won't move. They drag Lambert back inside through the back door of his den. As she walks backwards, Mol kicks rubbish out of her way. They want to get Lambert on to his bed, but there's no more bed. The mattress has disappeared. And the bed's legs have folded inwards. Bits of spring stick out from under the frame.

'He burnt it,' says Mol.

'Now he can fuckenwell sleep on the floor,' says Treppie. 'He's the one who wants to go and burn his bed.'

'He'll catch a cold in his kidneys,' says Mol.

'So what,' says Treppie. 'I wish he'd catch something else in his kidneys. He's busy wiping us out here.'

'Wiping,' Pop wants to say, but just 'ing' comes out. He wants to clean his hand on his shirt. Lambert's arm was full of slime when Pop dragged him. But Pop's shirt isn't there any more. All he rubs are his ribs. It feels like he's got too many ribs. Can it be that he's gotten more ribs from all the misery?

Treppie mops his forehead with his arm. He looks spent. Utterly spent. 'I must get to the Chinese,' he says. 'I'm late.'

'Late,' Pop hears himself saying. His voice is back. But it doesn't sound like his own voice any more.

'Go,' says Mol. 'We'll manage.'

'It's okay, go,' Pop tells him.

But Treppie keeps looking around him, at the den's walls. He throws his arms up into the air. Like the Witnesses do at the end of their sessions, when they pray. But Treppie's not praying. He's looking. 'Look. Just look how mad the fucker is.'

They look where Treppie's looking. He's looking up at the wall, just below the ceiling. Where Lambert's calendars used to be.

'Creepies,' says Mol.

The animals in the depths. Pop doesn't know why he thinks this, it's not animals, it's creepies and pests. And they're not roaring in the depths, they're painted on the walls. The strangest things he's ever seen. All of them with too many wings and too many legs and heads. Snakes and mice and things, but they don't look right. They look deformed. You can tell what they are only from what Lambert wrote underneath. Some are still just names. Others have a bit of outline, or a piece of wing. It looks like Lambert wanted to paint everything at the same time.

TERMITE, EARWIG, COCKROACH, SNAIL, ANT, SUPERBEE, MOUSE, MOTH, RAT, WORM, BAT, SPIDER, WASP, MOLE II.

'Mole the Second,' says Pop.

'Second what?' asks Mol.

Pop shows her where on the wall.

'I only see one,' says Mol. 'Where's the second?'

'It's like the kings and queens of England,' says Treppie. 'Henry the Eighth, Elizabeth the Second.'

'I don't see any queen,' says Mol.

'Just shows you how mad he is. He thinks a mole is a member of the royal family. He must figure he's a prince or something himself. Prince Lambert the Executioner, known for his fires, his fucking with the neighbours and his painting on walls. The only son and heir of Queen Mother Mol. He'll be remembered for that.' Treppie's grinning. After everything that happened here this morning, he's getting his bearings back again.

Pop grins back. Just to feel if he still can. It's not that he thinks Treppie's funny. There's nothing funny going on here. He feels shaky. He's over-exerted himself. He needs to sit down. He finds a crate. 'What happened?' he asks.

'You were sleeping,' says Mol.

'I dreamt everything was white, meanwhile it was smoke all the time.'

'We left you to sleep,' says Mol.

'I must go now,' says Treppie.

'First tell us what happened,' says Pop. 'I'll take you to the bus stop in Melville.'

'He started last night. First he tried to get the Tedelex going, but it didn't want to work. Then he began fucking around with Flossie, but not a single part of Flossie wanted to co-operate. He said everything had to get fixed for his, er, birthday. Then, later, the noise woke me up. It sounded like a fucken canning factory in the back here. So I went out to look. I told him he shouldn't expect miracles, times were bad. He said to hell with bad times, he was only going to be forty once and he wanted to face the New South Africa like a decent man, with a good woman on his arm. Then he showed me his list.'

Treppie shows them the spot on the wall where the list is. They read it. Treppie picks up a pen from the floor and scratches out *(time will tell)*. He also draws a line through the words *everything must work,* as well as *change mattress.*

'How do you know?' Pop asks, pointing at number 18, the fridges.

'I know,' says Treppie, 'they've been standing here all seized up since before the fire, before the previous big fire.'

Treppie turns slowly from the wall. Then he smiles a disbelieving little smile. 'Come to think of it . . .' he says.

'What,' asks Mol.

'What's the date today?' Treppie asks.

'November,' says Mol.

'November the what?'

'Fourth. No, it's the fifth,' says Pop.

Treppie claps his hands. 'That's it!' he shouts.

'That's what?' asks Mol.

'Method in the madness! It was Guy Fawkes the last time too, remember. When he made that fire. Fifth of November. He wanted to have a party in the back here.'

'To advertise,' Mol says.

'Then his spanner fell in the grass, and then there was that big fuck-up.'

'So we fuck along, so we fuck along,' Treppie sings to the tune of 'Sow the seed, oh sow the seed'.

'Just look what's been ticked off here,' says Pop.

They read:

25. gun
26. binoculars
27. umbiera (Kaffir-harp)

'Which he gets where?' Mol asks.

'He's lying, man! Prince Lambert, the Prince of Lists, says he's got a gun!'

Treppie writes *28. list* underneath Lambert's list. And under that he writes: *29. fit (the prince is dead, long live the prince. Guy Fawkes 1993).*

'He's not dead,' says Mol. 'Leave his list alone.'

'And then?' asks Pop.

'And then what?'

'When Flossie didn't want to work, what happened then?'

'Then he started raising hell, all through the night. He didn't sleep a wink. Me neither. Then I thought, let me just watch, 'cause here comes big shit again.'

'It was *you*, Treppie,' Mol says. 'You went and stirred him up again! I know you. You torment him, just for the hell of it!'

'He doesn't need tormenting, Mol. He fucks out all on his own. Like a thread stripping on a jack. Strip! Slip! Kabam! If only he'd take his fucken pills.' Treppie shakes a plastic bottle full of pills that he finds in the Tedelex's door.

'"Epanutin. L. Benade. One tablet three times a day. With meals",' he reads.

'Meals,' says Mol.

'Yes, Mol, meals, like the food you cook in this house. Fit for a king, isn't it? Bacon and eggs for breakfast. Pill. Rice, meat and potatoes for lunch. Pill. Wors and baked beans for supper. Pill.' With each would-be meal Treppie throws his head back like he's swallowing a pill. He smiles a silly smile at Mol, knocking his knuckles against his head, as if the pills are making him feel better.

'Leave them alone!' says Pop.

'He says those pills make him feel dull,' says Mol.

'He can do with being a bit dull. The bright spark of the family,' says Treppie, laughing through the side of his mouth.

'Stop it,' says Pop. 'And then what?'

'Then he started smashing up everything and dragging things outside. By seven o'clock this morning he was ready for fireworks. He threw petrol over everything. You were still sleeping. And from then on, we've been feeding the fire. Shoes, mats, *Watchtowers*, you name it! Blow high the flame! Hoist the flag! Trumpets away! Brothers and sisters, now there goes a man. His name is Lambertus Benade!'

Suddenly Treppie's mouth is full of spit. He spits, 'plop!', and a mouthful of gob lands next to Lambert on the cement floor.

'Sis!' says Mol.

'I'm going now,' says Treppie. 'Otherwise tomorrow we won't eat again. Coke and bread and polony, polony and bread and Coke, bread and Coke and polony. For what we are about to receive, may we be thankful, Lord, praised be thy name, amen,' Treppie sings.

'Okay.' Pop's feeling sick. He looks at Lambert lying there without pants, and with arms that look like they've been turned inside out. With a flat box sticking out from between his teeth. He can feel Mol looking at him. He knows that she knows he's feeling sick. He feels white. Treppie's also looking at him. Treppie's talking so much 'cause he knows Pop saw him crying when he was upside down.

'Go fetch the cushions from the chairs in the lounge,' Mol tells them.

'Let's first straighten his arms out,' says Pop.

WATERMELON ~

Mol stands in the lounge doorway. Pop's sleeping in his chair. Mol's just been to the back to look at Lambert again. For the third time tonight. At least he moved. He turned his head this way and then that way, shifting on to his side, with his fat, white bum facing her. Then she went and fetched the bottle of Coke in the kitchen and put it down next to his head. And she went to check the washing line to see if his shorts were dry yet. But they weren't. What more can she do? She turns around and goes back to their room, where she fetches the faded old blanket, full of holes. Let her go put it over him, over his naked bum.

There's so much rubbish and scrap iron on the den's floor, she struggles to reach Lambert from the inside door. Enough for another three fires.

272

She looks up, at MOLE II, there on the wall. Where would MOLE I be, then? She looks at Lambert's list again. Number 12 reads: *scrub linolium kitchen clean (Ma)*.

Mol walks back to the kitchen. She sticks her head round the door and looks inside. The kitchen looks funny, but she can't figure out why it looks so odd. Then she sees the bits and pieces of Flossie that they carried through here this morning – half-melted, half-burnt plastic. And rubber. Like monsters' body parts, or something. Scales and tails. Let her just close this door, for now. If they get hungry, she can always fix their bread in the lounge. Later.

She finds herself standing in the lounge doorway again. The TV's on but there's no sound. A little while ago, when Pop fell asleep, she switched it on. The news. Shooting and talking. So she turned off the sound and watched the never-ending talking and shooting, and the corpses under blankets in the dust, and people pointing this way and then that way. It's always the same. Now she walks up to the TV and switches it right off. She's walking slowly. Her legs feel like they don't belong to her any more.

She walks round the back of Pop's chair to go look out the window. She doesn't see anything. Every now and again she hears people shooting off their Guy Fawkes crackers, far away. Usually the Benades have crackers too. Lambert's the one who shoots them off on the little stoep in front. Pink ones that whistle, or green ones that make a small fountain, or silver ones that go 'whoosh!' up into the sky, shooting sparks like rain. So pretty.

But tonight they've got nothing. Tonight they stay inside. Tired. It's been a long day.

Mol walks around Pop's chair, on the front side. She bends over to see if he's still breathing. She can't see anything, so she listens. She hears nothing, but his chest moves slightly, up and down, up and down. His eyelids look like two shells. He doesn't move. He must be having a white dream again.

She goes and sits down in her chair. Without cushions the chair's very hard. How can Pop just fall asleep? she wonders. And he's so thin, too.

273

But he hasn't moved an inch since he came to sit here this afternoon, after they got back.

Before they took Treppie to the bus stop, they all helped to make Lambert a bed with cushions from the chair. It was a helluva struggle to get him on to those cushions. He was like a dead-weight. In the end Treppie said for a job like this you need leverage. So he and Pop used iron pipes to work Lambert on to the cushions. Then Pop put his torn piece of shirt neatly over Lambert's bottom half again, and she took his shorts to rinse them under the outside tap, 'cause what she saw in there was more than just pee.

Did they think he'd come to again?

Give him a chance, Pop said.

'Maybe he'll become a vegetable,' Treppie said. 'A king-sized water-melon. Suits me fine if he dangles from a stem for the rest of his life. Under a leaf, nice and quiet, then all you have to do is water him every now and again.'

Sis, Treppie, she said to him. Treppie can be so cruel. But he can't help himself. That's what she wanted to say. Instead, she just kept quiet.

They put on some clean clothes and then they got into the car to take Treppie to the Melville bus stop. They all felt better after washing themselves.

All except Pop. Pop was white in the face. That's why, after they dropped off Treppie, she said to him they must first go to Shoprite and then take a little drive up Ontdekkers.

Pop wanted to know why.

Just to get out a little, she said. She took Pop by the arm, but then she let go again. She could see he was far away. Too far. She could feel it on his skin.

So it wasn't long before they were back home again.

At Shoprite they bought a tin of dog food for Toby. But not Butch, his usual. She said if Toby felt the way she did today, then he must also feel like he needs a holiday. And, as Treppie would say, a change is as good as a holiday, so they bought him some Husky instead.

When they got on to Ontdekkers, Pop remembered he still had the paper in his pocket with the measurements for the bathroom mirror. So they went to the Mirror Shop at the corner, 'cause they knew Lambert was dead serious about fixing that mirror. It was one of the things on his list.

They cut the mirror straight away. Sixteen by twenty-five. Ten rand fifty.

And then they just came back home again.

Poor Pop. She watched him from behind as he walked over the loose blocks to go pee, with the mirror in his arms. The house stank terribly of smoke. And there was soot all over the walls. It looked like there'd been a war. Pieces of burnt, black paper were flying about everywhere, inside and outside. Pop waved his arms, trying to catch the stuff. But when he did catch a piece, it was like catching nothing. When he opened his hand, there was no more than a black smear on his palm. He showed it to her, as if she knew the answer. But what could she say? All she could do was wipe his hand with her own, and then she got the soot on her hand too.

When he finished peeing, he pulled the last piece of mirror off the cabinet and began fitting the new one. But it was too big. A hair's breadth too big. Not even. So Pop put the little mirror down in the bath. He'd in any case forgotten to buy glue. He'd make a plan later. Or Lambert would.

So then they came out and sat down here in front. She tried to talk to Pop, to keep his mind occupied. About mattresses, how they should get a new one for Lambert, or pass theirs on to him and buy themselves a new one, 'cause they were two to a bed. And they were old. But Pop didn't want to talk. He looked like he didn't even want to live any more. His chin just kept sagging lower and lower on his chest. She was still talking when she saw he was fast asleep.

Now she looks at Pop, here next to her. He's kicked off his shoes in front of him. He's still wearing the same socks he had on this morning, when they were sliding and slipping around in the passage. It's his only pair. Worn right through at the heels. All his toes stick out in front. The toes look like fingers. Black from soot. Shame, poor Pop.

As he sits there, she stares at all the bits of his body. He looks like his joints are too thin, like all the places where his hands and feet and head should be fixed to his body are joined by nothing more than the power of mercy. Mercy. Suddenly she feels she dare not look away, 'cause if she does, the mercy won't hold any longer. And then Pop will break apart, right here next to her, all along his joints. And she would've been the only one who could've kept him together, just by looking. So she looks and looks. Her eyes get heavy. She must just not fall asleep now. Everything depends on her. The joints in Pop's body. And what would she amount to, without him?

Suddenly the front gate creaks. It's Treppie. Thank God, he's back from the Chinese. Now there'll be some life in this place. She fingers her bun at the back and pins the loose pieces back into place.

HAPPY GUY FAWKES ～

'Happy Guy Fawkes,' Treppie says loudly as he walks in through the front door. Mol indicates he must shush, Pop's sleeping.

'Happy fuck-up,' says Treppie, even louder. He pulls a handful of Tom Thumb crackers out of his trouser pocket. 'Here, Mol, I got these from the Chinese. I thought maybe you'd want to salute the day. Twenty-one shots into the sky. For the heroes who died. And for the one who had a fit.'

She takes the crackers from Treppie and puts them into her housecoat pocket.

'Has that fucker come to yet?'

She shakes her head.

'Maybe you should put the crackers into a golden syrup tin and throw some matches in as well. Right next to his head. Shock treatment. Maybe then he'll wake up. Off with a bang, on with a bang. Bang! Bang!' says Treppie, pretending to shoot a pistol into the sky.

'They say there's no harm in trying your best shot,' he says, 'or do you really want a little melon in the house? Sorry, kaffir-watermelon!'

Treppie sits down on a crate. He takes out his pocket-knife and slaps it, 'ka-thwack', on to the palm of his hand. He looks at the knife. Then he looks at Mol. Slowly, he pulls out the smallest blade.

'Frog-killer,' he says softly, 'a man's best friend. Frog-skins, mole-skins, mole-necks, mole-tails!'

He looks at Mol again.

Mol's looking hard at Pop. She wants him to wake up now. She leans forward, out of her chair, towards him. 'Pop, Pop, wake up. Treppie's here.'

'Here I am again, with a pocket-knife to your brain.' Treppie kicks Pop's feet.

Pop wakes up. 'Treppie.' He swallows hard.

'What you think, Pop? I was saying to Mol, she must stuff that, er, buster of yours full of crackers and bang him awake. Then she can get even with him for that time when he locked her into the fridge with the Peking Ducks. Then they'll be quits, after all these years. Then they can start with a clean slate, all over again.'

Treppie gets up quickly. He pulls Mol out of her chair, holding the knife against her throat. 'March!' he shouts into her face, turning her towards the passage.

'Come, Pop, it's time for fireworks!' Treppie laughs. Mol can't work out if he's serious or not. She tries to wriggle herself loose.

'Let her go!' Pop says.

But Treppie won't let go. He pushes her down the passage, holding the knife to her throat. She hears Pop coming after them. Is there no end to this day's evil?

Once in the den, Treppie pushes her backwards, against Pop. She and Pop almost fall over. But Pop holds steady. Mol pulls Pop so he's standing next to her. Treppie looks at Lambert. First look, then kick. One, two, three kicks. There goes the blanket. Lambert doesn't come to, he just groans. He looks like a sea-creature, floating belly-up. A white belly.

Treppie shifts the Tedelex. They must look, he says, he's going to show them MOLE II's younger sister. And then he shows them, piece by piece, what those scratches on the wall are. Terrible. Pop looks the other way. Treppie sings:

> 'Head in the ice-box
> Cracker in the twat
> Belly all pink
> Mole I can smell the rot . . .'

Sis.

'Enough!' says Pop. He pushes her towards the door. He wants her out of here. He looks like he wants to talk to Treppie, alone. But she stays right there, in the doorway. She watches Pop as he tries to get his sentences lined up, but his mouth just opens and closes. Treppie's one up on him again.

'Shut your mouth, Pop, or you'll start catching flies,' says Treppie.

Pop shuts his mouth.

'There's nothing you can say to me, brother,' Treppie shouts, ''cause I'm fully educated in suffering, so to speak. Let me tell you my latest insight. The worst two feelings you can have at the same time are to be hopping mad and to be bored out of your skull.' Treppie's shouting so hard into Pop's face that Pop takes a step backwards. He stumbles over the rubbish on the floor and almost falls over again. Mol pushes him up, from behind.

Has Pop heard of the word implode? Treppie asks. That's the way big buildings explode, from the inside, when they've got dynamite in their seams. And has Pop seen how those buildings collapse neatly in a heap. In a heap, ready for taking away. Without even disturbing the traffic.

Pop shakes his head. He can't say he's seen that.

No, he doesn't expect Pop will understand. So, instead he'll talk a language they both understand. As for her, she must stop hiding away there, behind Pop. She must come out from behind that door and open her eyes. It's meant for her too, this insight of his. 'Cause it's connected to a wish, and after all she's an expert in wishful thinking.

Pop holds her hand. Treppie's shoulders are twitching. 'I wish I could cut my own fucken neck off, but for that a person needs a chainsaw. One that cuts on its own. Then all you have to do is get the angle right. Hold it nice and tight until it gets a good grip on the meat of your throat.'

Treppie shows them how. He pretends he's got the saw in his hands. His whole body shudders, and when the shuddering stops, his shoulders twitch.

'Aaaah!' he screams. It's too terrible. Suddenly he stops. First he lifts up his head, then he lowers it again. He looks at them.

'But of course if you do that you leave a big mess for other people to clean up. And you might disturb more than just the traffic.'

They say nothing.

Treppie makes as though he's brushing away dust and ashes from his face. He pushes past them, going for the door. Pop follows him. They leave her standing there.

She pulls Lambert's blanket straight where Treppie kicked it off. Let her also go to the front, then. She's too tired tonight to get worked up over Treppie's horries. She walks back up the passage, with a new idea in her head.

She stops at the kitchen door. She can't remember why she came here. Maybe if she opens the door she'll remember. There's so much stuff lying around on the floor, the door won't open properly. She puts her hand round the doorframe and switches on the light. Then she steps over all the stuff, into the kitchen. Now she remembers. She goes to the dresser and fishes out a full box of matches from the top drawer. Very softly, she closes the door behind her, leaving the light on. That rubbish looks like it wants to multiply there in the dark. Mol rubs her eyes. Treppie switches his horries on and off like a TV set. But the horries that she sometimes gets are different, they buzz in her head like horseflies on a windowpane. A window with no handle so you can't open and close it. All she can do is hush the buzzing in her head. Knitting helps. But she hasn't got wool. And she also hasn't got a dog any more.

Now Treppie's door is shut tight. She puts her ear to the door and listens. 'Grrrt-grrrt,' she hears. She knows that sound. Treppie's tearing things out of the paper. He finds other horries in there, so he can cover up his own.

Pop's sitting in his chair in front. His eyes are glued to the TV. It's on so loud he doesn't even hear when she comes in. She looks to see what Pop's watching.

It's a game with a big wheel full of colourful lights around the edges. The wheel turns, then stops, then turns, then stops again. Screaming people try to guess the numbers. A man with rolled-up jacket sleeves tells everyone who's right and who's wrong, who wins fridges and washing machines, who gets nothing and who loses everything they've already won. There's a wild monster's head in the middle of the wheel. Some of the numbers make its mouth open up, and then a big, flat, red tongue comes out. Then the audience screams like it's going mad. And the man in the jacket pushes up his sleeves again and takes the microphone in the other hand and flicks back his hair.

She must come and sit next to him, Pop signals, so they can watch together what happens with the numbers and the monster and the turning wheel. But she doesn't want to. She wants out. Out! It's Guy Fawkes out there and now the TV's playing so loud she can't even hear the crackers any more. She wants to see and she wants to hear. She doesn't want to miss it.

It's just once a year that all the people in Martha Street come out of their houses and spend some time together. They watch the fireworks and they talk. It's the only time they're friendly with each other, the only time they're interested in each other's fireworks and things. Just once a year. People say hello, even if they don't know you. It's like a party. Not that she feels in the mood for a party tonight. She feels empty and tired. Her heart's beating too fast. What's more, there's another one of those flies buzzing up and down the little window at the back of her head. It's after eight now, and they've been there since this morning. It's useless trying to sleep in a state like this. She's all worked up from the goings on, and from Lambert lying at the back there under the worn old blanket. Lambert, who doesn't want to wake up.

She signals back to Pop that she's going out. What for? he asks with his hands.

It's Guy Fawkes outside, she says, but he can't hear. He points to his ears. She points to her head. Pop nods. Yes, it's okay, he knows. He motions to her she must turn down the TV, he wants to sleep now. That's okay. That's fine. It's the only thing that works for him.

Once outside, she walks up to the wire fence and looks up and down the street. Just children wherever you look. And grown-ups, standing together in groups.

'Careful! Watch out!' they say to the children. 'Don't let the crackers go off in your eyes!'

The fireworks shoot and whistle and bang in greens and reds and blues. Rainbows and stars with tails. This will fix you, get lost, you damn bug!

She feels Toby's wet nose against her leg. Ag shame, last year Gerty was here too, but Gerty was always so scared of the crackers. You had to pick her up, otherwise she'd run inside and hide under a chair in the lounge until it was all over. But not Toby. He thinks it's a game. Then again, he thinks everything's a game.

Mol walks back to the little stoep. She hasn't got the guts to go into the street alone, or to say hello to the people and look at their fireworks. In earlier years they'd all go outside together, with Lambert in front. He likes talking to people. Not that he has much of a story. He starts with a 'ja, well', a bit of story, and then another 'ja, well' at the end. Or you know, followed by you never know, without adding much of a story at all. People listen to him 'cause he looks the way he looks. They think he's funny. But then again, people think everything's funny.

Mol feels for the matches and the Tom Thumbs in her pocket. She's never set off a cracker on her own before. No, dear Jesus, she's scared she'll shoot out her eyes. She looks back into the street. Everyone's jolly. She stands on her toes to see what they're doing at Fort Knox. Maybe that man from this morning will give her another cigarette. But they're very busy next door. They stand in a bunch and then they shout: Sputnik! Hellfire! And then they all run for cover and a big, wild thing shoots up into the sky, making red arrows all over the place and a noise like an ambulance.

Mol turns back to the house. But she's still not ready to go inside. The house is dark and closed. She can see the cracks on their outside walls in the light of the streetlamps. The house is just a shell. But, she knows, the stuff inside that shell is thick. Thick and quiet from all the things that have happened. All that escapes from the thick stuff inside is the flickering blue light of the TV, playing without sound behind the curtains.

Mol calls Toby, but she doesn't know why. She doesn't want to go inside. She pushes herself, yet her feet won't move. Not into this house where things keep happening. Funny, you'd expect the house to be heavy from all the stuff that goes on. But the house is light. It looks like it wants to float up, like a little balloon. Maybe it's just her head: tight and loose, thick and thin, light and heavy.

Mol feels her heart. She feels her breath.

She thinks: God, just watch me. Tonight, I, Mol Benade, will shoot off a cracker. For my heart and for my breath, so they can run smoothly, and for the little thing buzzing inside my head, so it can settle down, and for the house, and the walls, so they can get some strength, and for the quiet, thick insides, to give them a little light. And for us, to pep us up a little. And for next door, this side and that side and across the road. For them, a gentle reminder, as Treppie would say, that we're still here. Before they start thinking we've all given up the ghost here behind the curtains. They're likely to go and put the welfare on to us again, or something like that. All that's needed is a bit of noise from our side. To show we're still kicking and we're not planning to throw in the towel yet. Not a damn. Come hell or high water.

Mol feels her strength returning. She feels her face twitch as she tries to smile. Right. Smile, cracker, matches. Ready, steady, go!

She strikes a match and feels in her pocket for a cracker, but their fuses are all knotted together. She pulls a whole bundle of them out at the same time. The match burns her hand. 'Ouch!' She throws down the match. Wait. First sit down. No, not sit, then she won't be able to get out of the way fast enough when the thing goes off. Hell, what now?

It takes a while before she finds her bearings with the crackers. She pulls them apart and puts them down in a row on the edge of the stoep. She tries to make one of them stand up so she can light the fuse, but it keeps falling over. Then she puts it down on its side and lights the fuse, but the thing goes out before reaching the cracker. How's she supposed to get this fuse working now? Mol looks at the crackers in her hand. Then she gets an idea. No, Jesus! Yes, what the hell! She'll take the damn thing in her fingers and shoot it off. In her bare hand. That's what she'll do. If she wants to make a mark for them here tonight, that's the only way to do it.

She smiles. To think she'd have so much courage here tonight! But she's got nothing to lose. There's very little in life that she hasn't yet seen. So what's a silly little cracker, then?

Pop wakes up. He feels something going on behind his head, here behind the window. What's Mol up to now, out there on the stoep? What's all that fiddling around? He gets out of his chair. He has to try three times before he manages to get up. The chair's too deep without its cushions. He peeps through the curtains. Goodness gracious! Mol's holding a flame to a cracker! She brings the flame to the fuse and holds it till it takes. Then she stretches her arm away from her body, turning to one side and looking away. On one leg. She's standing on one leg. It looks like she's trying to do a funny dance. Now she wriggles her fingertips, working the cracker further and further up till she's holding it just by the tip.

'Poof!' it goes off.

'Whoof!' barks Toby.

'Hoo-eee!' shouts Mol, shaking her hands next to her sides. Now she runs round the corner, with Toby on her heels. Who would ever have thought it possible?

Here she comes again. Toby's up on his hind legs, dancing in front of her.

Pop stands on his chair to look out the window. He pulls open the curtains a bit more. Mol's truly in top form here tonight. She's going from strength to strength. Pop feels his own strength coming back too. Little sparks in his insides, like a slow dynamo starting to run. On-off, on-off goes the light. Is it possible? This is a day that got him down so bad he thought he'd never be able to get up again. And now just look at Mol, the old diehard! She's getting braver with each cracker. Now she's holding three Tom Thumbs at the same time, right in front of her chest. She gets them lighted in no time at all.

'Poof! Poof! Poof!'

'Whoof! Whoof! Whoof!'

She throws them on to the grass. And then Toby goes looking for them, running up and down on the grass until she shoots some more.

'Poof! Poof! Poof!'

'Whoof! Whoof! Whoof!'

Quicker and quicker.

Goodness, Mol, where do you get the strength from, old girl?

He knows how scared she is of crackers.

All Pop can make out is Mol's outline against the dark night sky as she moves around. The stoep-light's off and so are the lights in the lounge. But each time the fireworks light up behind her in the street, he sees her more clearly. Once or twice, as she turns sideways on the stoep, he catches a glimpse of her face as she strikes a match and cups it with her hands till it takes nicely.

Mol's face flickers against the dark as the flame dances up and down. He sees the ruts and nicks and bags under her eyes. He sees how she sucks her lips as she concentrates. Mol looks different. It's 'cause she's not wearing her tooth. Nowadays she never keeps it in her mouth any more. She says the plate's too big.

They're shrinking, both of them. They're shrinking right out of their teeth. God in heaven, that people should start shrinking like this, gums first.

Pop goes out the front door. He pulls back his shoulders and straightens himself up. He clears his throat.

'And what have we here! Fireworks, hey?'

'This is fun. Look how jolly everyone is.' Mol points to the street. 'Come, Pop, you must also let one off. I've got two left here, one for you and one for me. Let's light them together. Here! Don't be scared, it's nothing. I'll light them for you.'

Mol's eyes are shining.

Toby stands in front of them with his ears pointing up and his forelegs spread out wide. He lowers his front and wags his tail.

'He's trying to catch them, like tennis balls,' says Mol. 'They go "poof! poof! poof!" and then they're empty, then there's nothing left. Poof! Finish! Just a shell, with nothing left inside.'

'Out of our shells. We're shooting out of our shells. Poof! Finished!'

But Mol doesn't want to hear. 'Are you ready?' she asks.

Pop holds up his cracker. Mol lights it and then quickly lights her own.

'Poof-oof!' they shoot, almost at the same time.

'Whoof-oof!' says Toby, running in a wild circle on the grass.

Pop sniffs the shell in his hand.

'Yuk, throw it away,' says Mol.

'A bit of powder, just one shot. A spark, and then we've had it.' Mol here next to him is pretending to be deaf. Shame.

'Hoo-eee! Look! Look!' she shouts. Suddenly, from behind the houses of Triomf, from Brixton's side, a huge, red rose rises up into the sky on a long, thin stem of light. Slowly, without sound, it folds open and then falls away into the black air, layer upon layer. Like the folds of a dress. Or like someone turning slowly in a dance.

'Red Alec!' shouts Mol.

And then a yellow one.

'Whisky Mac!' Pop feels the name in his mouth. It almost tastes like something. Like what?

'Beaautifull!' says Mol, clasping her chest.

'It must be at the showgrounds.' Pop swallows. The taste is gone.

Together with all the people in Martha Street, they watch and cheer the showgrounds' fireworks. It carries on for quite a while.

'It's a long time since we've had a Guy Fawkes like this, hey, Pop,' Mol says when it looks like the show's finally over.

'Long time.' He puts his arm around her and pulls her towards him. 'I smell rain.' He rubs her on the shoulder.

She looks up at him. He can see what she's thinking. She's thinking why's he so lovey-dovey all of a sudden? Yes, why? He also doesn't know why.

'Come, come let's go have a bath. It's been a hard day.' Let her think what she likes. He just needs to touch her.

OVERLOAD ⌒

Mol waits for Pop in the dark passage outside the bathroom door. When they came back into the house, he asked her not to put on the lights. They were too bright, he said. Now he's gone to the kitchen to fetch a candle. He's looking on top of the dresser where they always keep candles, with the little lids to stand them on. Why's he taking so long now? She hears things falling over. Pop bumbles around so much lately. Let her light a cigarette here in the meantime. Pop's got his reasons. Maybe he's getting a feeling in his bones that the lights will cut out again tonight. The electricity's always been bad here in Triomf. Ever since the day they moved in. An overload problem. That's what the municipality's workers say when they come and work on the boxes. Not that the working ever makes much of a difference.

Treppie says that's the way it goes in places like Triomf. He says it's a sub-economic disease. It's meant to remind you who you are and where you live. For that, Treppie says, nothing works better than cutting off people's electricity.

Then of course there's another never-ending argument, 'cause Pop says Treppie's talking the biggest load of rubbish under the sun. He says the people in Triomf are the state's own people. And the houses here were built by Community Development. For young civil servants, for policemen and Post Office workers, and for the people from Parks and Roads, Railways, Licences, Customs, Refuse and Gardening, and Pest Control. And don't forget the people from Water and Electricity. You name it, says Pop. If you want to find them, you needn't look any further than Triomf. You could almost say the whole municipality of Jo'burg lives here. And make no mistake, says Pop, these people understand the ins and outs of things, from top to bottom. They're the kind of people who know how to help themselves to state property. Not to mention state electricity.

And if Treppie bothers to open his eyes, Pop says, then he'll see how many people still paint their doors and their gutters with Public Works paint. Government brown. And how all the gardens behind the prefab walls are full of the Gardening Department's left-over aloes. And how bricks and cement still get offloaded here by the lorry-full, in front of private houses. In broad daylight. Everything from municipal lorries to municipal kaffirs. Plastic pipes too, and bathroom tiles and wire-netting and paving stones and steel plates and trees in plastic bags. From the state nursery. You name it.

Not that Triomf has many trees. The roots struggle to get a grip. They first have to grow all the way through Sophiatown's rubble. Pop says you have to dig six feet under Triomf's tar before you find the old topsoil. Inbetween there's just rubbish. It takes a tree three years to find the soil. And then it has to be a tough tree that kills everything in its path, like a black wattle or something meant for a state plantation. And even then, it's a struggle. The only reason the oak tree at the bottom of the street is so big is 'cause it was planted before Triomf's time.

That's why they never planted anything here on their own plot. Never mind Lambert and his spanners.

So, Pop tells Treppie, when the lights cut out all the time it's not a sub-economic disease, it's a stealing disease, plain and simple. And if there's any overload problem, it comes from the sins of bypassing. The municipality people connect their houses with wires that bypass the boxes. Then nothing shows on their meters and they pay bugger-all at the end of the month.

But it's the women who pay the price. The women have to pay twice over. With their lives. That's what comes from stealing, Pop says. He says Treppie must just open his eyes a bit – Pop used to backchat Treppie like this in the old days, when they still had a business in the yard – Treppie must just open his eyes a bit, Pop would say, and then he'll see how many times little children come running out of their houses, screaming that their mommies have shocked themselves blue on the washing machines. Or they're stuck on to the handles of the fridge. Burnt black. That's what comes from wrong bypass connections.

And he, Treppie, must count his blessings and thank Community Development for giving him an affordable roof over his head. And he doesn't need to join in the thievery just because he happens to be living among the publicans and sinners in Triomf.

Then Treppie says Pop might have his facts right, but he still draws cock-eyed conclusions. That's if he manages to draw any conclusions at all. It's not a matter of sins, he says. It's a matter of structures. From sub-economic structures you get sub-economic sins. That's how the thing works. Treppie says for him there's only one conclusion: Triomf is a place where the state's one hand washes the other, and then it says you mustn't come and point fingers, it's all in the family. All in the backyard. Community Development in the true sense of the word.

BATH ⌒

Mol closes the bathroom door behind them. She's glad Treppie's mouth is shut tonight. His door too. She's glad he's not standing around in the passage, at the end of this Guy Fawkes of a day, to see how she and Pop go into the bathroom together in a pitch-dark house. With a candle. And the lights haven't even been cut off.

She must say, she wishes she could pull the curtain on this candlelight business. But it looks to her like Pop can't be bothered any more with pulling of any kind, never mind curtains.

Treppie, on the other hand, would have pulled out all the stops on this little matter, that's for sure. He would've said things about overloads in their top storeys. Or about their nervous systems tripping, or their fuses blowing, and so on. She knows him. He pulls out monkeys from behind every bush.

Pop gives her the candle and takes the mirror out of the bath. He looks around him and carefully places it on top of the bathroom cabinet. Then he takes the candle from her and puts it down in front of the mirror.

'So,' he says, 'now there's a double light.'

He smiles a little smile at her and then takes something out of his pocket. What now? A bath plug! Wonders never cease.

'Where did you get that from?'

'Just got it somewhere.'

'How?'

'Picked it up.'

'But where?'

'Here. There.'

'My guess is as good as yours?'

'Correct.' They laugh a little.

Shush, Pop signals, they mustn't make a noise. Just in case Treppie wakes up.

'Yes, let sleeping dogs lie.' They giggle.

'Ee-ee,' says Toby, in the passage. He wants to come in too.

Pop opens the door for him.

Toby comes in. He sits himself down against the wall and pricks his ears. His eyes are shining – this is a day when the fun and games just won't stop.

She smiles at Pop. They both know what Toby's thinking.

'Right,' says Pop, 'now you can run the bath.'

Pop sits on the edge of the bath as it fills up. He starts taking off his clothes. She stands there, looking at him. Never before has she seen Pop undress like this, in front of her, from beginning to end.

'Aren't you going to bath?' he asks.

'You first.' Why's she feeling so shy all of a sudden?

'No, together,' says Pop. 'I wash your back, then you wash mine.'

First he gets lovey-dovey and now he wants to wash her back. *Aikona!*

'Come on,' says Pop, 'I don't bite.'

Oh well, it can't do any harm. She loosens the one button on her housecoat. It's a very long time since they last bathed together. Never in this house, except that time when she came out of hospital after Lambert stabbed her with a knife. She was lame for a while after that. Pop used to help her into the bath and wash her a bit, but he never got in with her. The last time he did that was in Vrededorp, in the old house. But then there were other reasons. And it was always her who said let's go bath. That's what she did when she wanted to go somewhere with Pop and Treppie, or if she wanted sweets or something. Bathing with Pop was the price she had to pay. But it was okay. Pop was soft with her. Most of the time she just rubbed him, or sucked him. And it didn't take long.

But now she's not so sure. Maybe today's been a bit too much for Pop. For all she knows, maybe he did hit overload and trip a fuse today. Maybe he's getting funny with her. She must try to get out of this thing.

'My washrag. I haven't got my washrag.'

'We'll make a plan,' says Pop, standing there in nothing but his vest. 'We can use this old shirt of mine.' He picks up a bundle lying against the wall. It's the shirt he took off this morning, before they gave Treppie a lift to the bus stop. The one with its front part torn out. Now Pop tears off the shirt's collar too. He pulls off the buttons and puts them down on the cistern.

'To keep,' he says. 'You never know when you might need a button.' Then he rips off the shirt's collar. 'See, now it's nice and soft.' He bunches it up in his hands. And now? Now she hasn't got any more excuses.

'A towel. There's no towel here.'

She wants out.

Pop's knees look like pointy things in flour sacks.

In the light of the candle, the bone in the middle of his chest sticks out. Under his throat, and on both sides of his neck, are deep hollows where it looks like there's not enough skin. Just a thin layer, like the wrinkled skin of boiled milk.

'Behind the door, in our room,' Pop says. 'My towel's hanging there. Go get it. No, wait. I'll do it.'

'No, I will!' Now she must be quick.

Pop looks at her. He sees right through her. She doesn't want to look him in the eye.

'What's wrong, Mol?'

'Nothing.'

But Pop keeps looking at her.

Then she says: 'You're a bit funny tonight.'

Pop lets his head drop.

Shame. Maybe he means nothing by wanting to bath with her. Maybe he's just tired. When he came stumbling out through the smoke this morning, still half asleep, she could see something was wrong. And then there was all that running, round and round the house. He didn't even get a chance to pull on his pants. And all the people laughing at him over the wall, pointing to his thin little legs sticking out under his vest. Maybe he wants to touch her so she'll touch him back. Let her just be straight with him.

'I'd rather not play around with you, Pop,' she says.

'I feel . . .' Pop says. He points to his whole body, with hands that open and then close again. He can't say what it is he's feeling. But she knows.

'Overload?'

'Overload.'

'Me too.'

'Fused,' says Pop.

'Tripped out.'

'That makes two of us,' says Pop.

'Poor us.'

'Never mind.' Pop stretches out his arms towards her. She takes a step closer to him. Then he puts his arms around her. He rests his head heavily against her body. She must be smelling sour and sweaty by now. It's from today's things, from the deadly panic.

'I stink.'

But Pop doesn't mind. 'At least we still have each other,' he says.

'And a roof over our heads.'

She pushes him away. 'I'll go fetch the towel. You get in in the meantime.'

'But you're coming back to bath with me, hey, Mol? Please?'

'Okay.'

'It'll do us good,' says Pop.

She goes and fetches the towel in the bedroom, feeling for it in the dark. She doesn't want to put on the light. Why, she can't understand. Maybe the dark's like warm water. And maybe that's also what Pop's thinking. Maybe he's thinking it'll make them feel better after this day. Each to his own. If she could have her own Guy Fawkes, then she supposes he can play with candles. Just like the dykes. She smiles at herself in the dark. Same difference, as Treppie would say. Every family has its own secrets. And no one's any better than the other. Her eyes are getting used to the dark now. The small light in the bathroom seems to be lighting up the whole house.

She closes the bathroom door behind her and takes off her clothes. Pop moves up so she can get in behind him. The bath's nice and hot. And full.

'Wash nicely now, Molletjie.' Pop passes her the shirt-washrag over his shoulder. She rubs soap on to it. Pop's back is right in front of her. Hard and white like the trunk of an old bluegum. There's more strength in there than she thought. A mystery like death. She shivers.

'This old back of yours,' she says, just so Pop won't start wondering why she's so quiet.

'Now you. Turn around!' says Pop.

Their bums get stuck. As they turn in the bath, their bodies make noises. Water spills over the edge. Toby wants a closer look. He wants to lick their wet arms with his long, red tongue.

'Hey, you!' Pop splashes Toby. 'You wanted to bath, didn't you, so there! Old Toby-dog. What do you know about life, anyway?' Pop rubs his wet hand between Toby's ears.

Now it's her turn. Pop squeezes hot water from the shirt on to her back. Ow, it burns. But she says nothing. He'll start thinking she's a ninny.

'Looks like you were in the wars, old girl. Full of bruises and scratches.'

It must be from this morning. She remembers bumping and scraping against things as she ran down the passage with that car seat. It was too wide. And her back was against the wall most of the time, first this side, then that side. It was more than the wars, it was hell! 'Hell.' She'd rather not think about this morning.

'Never mind,' says Pop, 'it's all over now.'

She wonders if Lambert's come to yet.

'When we finish washing, we can go see how things are looking at the back,' he says.

They wash in silence.

'Ja, well,' they say as they help each other out of the bath. Suddenly they face each other, stark naked. She gives Pop the towel. He must dry himself off, before something in his body snaps. But he takes it out of her hands. What now? Now he's starting to dry her off! She can do that herself! But Pop doesn't want to stop. She pushes him away, but he insists. He's on his knees in front of her, with the towel in his hands. It's as if he wants to give her something. She looks down, at where he's drying her off, at her old legs, her shins that are full of dents and cuts. Between her legs he dries, her worn old skin, her folds and her belly that sticks out. And her breasts that hang down over her stomach. One by one, softly, Pop lifts them up and dries underneath them.

'Turn around, Molletjie.'

She doesn't want to. In front is one thing, but behind is another story.

Pop doesn't want to listen. He wants to dry her off everywhere. He says he's counting his blessings.

He dries her sore back, dabbing softly with the towel. She must lift up her arms, he says. He wipes the drops from under her arms, and he dries her hollow, woolly armpits. Then he wipes the big, flat moles on her upper arms, carefully, as if they're sores. And her buttocks. She knows how they wobble when she walks. And inbetween too, in her crevice, which she feels is getting broader and flatter these days, as if her buttocks want to pull apart towards the bottom. And the back parts of her thighs, all puffy and full of blue veins – she knows, she's looked at them in the bedroom mirror. He doesn't miss a single spot, but he's like someone who's lost his way.

That's enough now, she motions with her body. But Pop keeps looking at her. God knows what's gotten into him.

'You know what I see, Mol. I see time passing. It passes, together with blessings. You count them like seconds. They don't stand still, they just pass.'

Suddenly Pop pushes his head into the hollow of her hip. A shudder passes through his body. Now Pop's crying. From bathing with candles. Oh yes, she saw it coming. But what's she supposed to say to him now?

All's well that ends well? That he can stop now, everything will be okay? But how can she say that to him, now? 'Cause she can see the row of knobbly bones running down the middle of his back, right here in front of her, and she knows he's crying about everything. About everything that's just more of the same in their lives. And in the end it's all nothing.

She'll put on a brave face. She'll say the best thing she can think of, under the circumstances.

'A person can cry, Pop, but actually you should laugh, man. It's like Guy Fawkes. A few little crackers and a rose or two up in the sky. Poof! Poof! Then it's over. In two ticks! Before you can say Tom Thumb!'

She takes Pop's head in her hands. She wants to look into his face so he can see her smile. When she smiles, he always smiles back at her. But Pop's neck is stiff. She can't turn it. All she can see is one side of his face, from an angle above him.

Elephant eye! Looking out from a hole, a faraway, dark place, with an old wrinkled eyelid that half covers the eye. And the wrinkles underneath, down and across, from so much looking out. And tears! But not elephant tears. Human tears! 'Plop-plop-plop!' they fall on to her feet. Thick, fat, lukewarm tears. Dear Lord, have mercy!

She feels her own breath coming quickly now, her own heart skipping a beat. She doesn't want to look at that eye of his any more. Not at his mouth either, Pop's mouth that's all in a pout with crying. Just like an elephant's. All he needs now is a long trunk reaching out blindly into the air. Reaching out for her! No! She mustn't start thinking about elephants now. Better not.

'Ag, Pop man, you're making me all dirty again with these tears. Watch or I'll have to take another bath.'

Pop knows all too well it's getting a bit much now. He tries to make a joke, sniffing inbetween the words.

'You should be glad, old Mol, at least there's still some moisture left in me!'

But the joke doesn't come off. And now he's really crying. Now she also can't take it any longer. Dear Lord, Jesus. She can't hold it back any more. She joins in, nothing to be done, she'll cry with him a little. She goes and sits flat on her backside, next to him, there on the cold cement floor. Weighed down by all the crying. Toby pushes himself between their legs. He licks their tears.

'Hell, old Toby, and we haven't even had a drop to drink!' says Pop.

Mind you, maybe that's just what they need right now. A stiff tot to fix them up a bit.

'All right,' says Pop, 'maybe that's just the thing.'

He blows his nose into the wet rag. Then he passes it to her so she can also blow her nose.

'Get dressed, Mol, I'm going to get the sideboard keys out of Treppie's pocket.'

He knows he's taking a chance. A naughty little look breaks through the misery on his face.

'Just watch me,' he says, worming his wet arms through his shirtsleeves. Then he's out of the door, in nothing but his shirt. In the candlelight, his thin, white calves look like little dry sticks.

MAN OF STARS 〜

They walk to the den, each with a glass in hand. She holds the candle on its little lid. Pop's got the Coke and the Klipdrift. He pulls up crates so they can sit on either side of Lambert. He puts down the candle next to Lambert's head. The flame throws funny, dark little patches over Lambert's face, and long, pointy shadows on his painting; the one of their house and the things in Africa. Toby sits near Lambert's feet.

They sit down. Washed clean and done now with their crying, they look at Lambert lying there on his back. Only his head sticks out from under the worn old blanket. Funny shadows play on his face. He snores quietly. Pop sits back a little.

She holds out her glass for Pop to pour. He pours for both of them.

'Well then, cheers,' he says, clinking his glass against hers, just above Lambert's chest. He does it very carefully.

She points. At least he's not blue in the face any more. She takes a sip.

'Strong as a horse,' says Pop. 'He's sleeping nicely now.'

She remembers that Lambert's shorts are still on the line. Pop waves it away, she mustn't worry, that's the least of their problems.

'Tomorrow's another day,' he says.

'Should we wake him up?' She looks at Lambert's fat cheeks going in and out as he snores.

'What for?' Pop looks scared.

'For a sip of Coke.'

'The game's not worth the candle. It's best to leave him.'

Mol suddenly feels silly. 'Not the candle, the Coke. And not the game, the watermelon! The watermelon's not worth the Coke.'

'Don't play games, Mol, God can hear you.'

Pop points a finger at her, but he can't help it, he also smiles a bit. 'Shsssh!'

Lambert stirs. His arm pushes off the blanket. Now his big fat forearm lies across his chest. It's full of scorch-marks. His mouth opens and closes. He's mumbling something. She signals to Pop he must come closer so he can also listen. They bend over to hear what he's saying.

'Light blue, my beloved, for ever and ever,' he says in his sleep. Back and forth he turns his head. His lips are pouting and his cheeks tremble. There's a deep hollow between his eyes. It looks like his face was assembled from many different pieces, as if it's not one face but many faces. Mol looks at Pop, as if to ask, will he ever be okay again? Pop looks like he wants to run away, like he wants to scream. He looks the way he looked that time when Lambert put on the video of Frankenstein's monster, when that terrible creature got up from its bed with its pasty face and then walked right through the door, killing live electric wires with its big paws. That was a horror. Pop doesn't like horrors.

Lambert's talking again.

'Orion washes my feet,' he says. Now it's his legs that tremble. His blanket slides off on one side. His stomach looks blown up. His thing moves a little. Then he lets out a big sigh.

'He's dreaming,' says Pop.

She motions to Pop, he must straighten the blanket.

'No, you,' says Pop.

Carefully, she pulls the blanket over him. She imagines he grabs her right now and strangles her to death, in his sleep. She's getting the creeps here!

She sits back. Lambert's quiet again. Pop pours another drink.

'Light blue, my beloved.' Does Pop know what it means? Yes? No?

'Orion washes my feet'? Pop shakes his head.

'Who's Orion again?'

'I've shown you before, Molletjie, it's the man in the stars, the one with three shining jewels in his belt.'

'Where is he?'

'In the sky at night. I'll show you. He's easy to make out among the others. You can recognise him by his belt.'

'I thought the stars were burnt out.'

Pop reaches out to her over Lambert's belly.

'Don't worry, Molletjie, if the light from their fires reaches us, you can be sure they're still full of life. Even though Orion is worlds away from us, his light will always reach Triomf. For ever and ever.' Pop squeezes her hand.

Poor Triomf. Endlessly far beneath the stars. A very sad business, if you ask her.

'You could say it's heaven's fireworks, Mol. Our Father in heaven's Guy Fawkes. And it carries on and on, across the generations.'

When Pop starts like this, then it's the Klipdrift talking. Then he tells her far-fetched stories about heaven. And it always makes her sad. She fights back her tears. Enough crying for one day. They must go sleep now.

Should they take their blanket? she wonders.

No, he says, he's got a plan. He finds the old greycoat in the trunk on top of their cupboard. The one Old Mol used to wrap the dough in after the first kneading, so it would rise in the night. They can sleep under it, says Pop. It's not so cold tonight, anyway.

TO SLEEP ⌒

When she blows out the candle, it's very dark in the room. She lies on her back with her eyes open, like Pop, lying here next to her. Now that her eyes are used to it, she can see a bit.

The wind starts blowing outside. She feels funny in her stomach. It must be hunger. They didn't eat a thing all day long.

'That's rain coming,' says Pop.

The loose panel in the dressing table suddenly shakes, 'cheeree-cheeree'. There's a rumbling noise somewhere deep under the ground. The house shudders.

What was that? She puts her hand on Pop, under the coat.

'Just a little mine tremor,' he says.

A sinkhole, more like it.

Then they lie and listen to the wind and the first thunder, rumbling in a different way now. They watch the flickering against the wall as the lightning gets closer and closer.

'Kabam!' it strikes, right above them, so hard that the windows rattle in their frames.

'Good God!' says Mol, almost jumping out of her skin.

'Never mind,' says Pop, 'we're lying on rubber. And the house is earthed.' He puts her hand back where it was.

Now the first loose drops of rain start falling, 'plop! plop! plop!', here and there on the corrugated-iron roof. The room is white from all the lightning. The sounds of the storm begin to fill up the whole world.

'There it is, now,' Pop says when the rain finally comes down.

'Shorrr' it runs off the gutterless roof.

'It's from all the trouble today,' Mol says, 'this rain.'

Pop gives the hand lying on top of him a little squeeze. Mol gives him one back. Then Pop's breath starts to come more evenly. He's almost asleep now. She hears the first drips all over the house. She forgot to put out bowls. Too bad.

Just before Mol falls asleep, she feels Pop's little thing moving slightly under her hand.

She smiles in the dark.

He rises in his sleep, she thinks, just like Old Mol's bread. The rain on the roof makes her sleepy. It feels like her eyes close all by themselves.

15

~

URBAN ANGEL

Lambert looks up at the helicopter. His mother and Pop and Treppie stand next to him. He went out early this evening, and when he got back from doing his rounds, the helicopter was there. Then he went inside and told his people they must come out on to the front lawn. So the neighbours and the people in the helicopter could see the Benades had nothing to hide.

Now the helicopter dips and turns, flying low over the houses of Triomf, block by block. Its blue searchlight shines into everyone's backyards. The whole street's full of people who want to know what's going on. They stretch their necks this way and that to see if they can catch a glimpse of someone running away or climbing over a prefab wall. Everyone leaves their front doors open. Some of the houses have little Christmas trees with lights that switch on and off all the time. It's two weeks into December already. He's told them he wouldn't mind a tree like that in their own lounge, with little lights and things. For putting on the sideboard. Treppie says it's kitsch, but then he says it actually depends on your class. What's kitsch in Houghton is art in Triomf, he says, but his heart bleeds for anyone, never mind his social standing, who spends so much money on material things. Whether it's kitsch or art, a tree like that costs a shithouse full of money. And the fuckers who get rich from selling those trees know all too well it's not an electrical trick their customers are looking for. What they want is Jesus on an automatic time switch. Jesus on, Jesus off. And it's been a bit rough on that poor Son of Man, Treppie says, inbetween all the onning and offing. For years on end. But no one seems to want to know anything about it. That's why angels are so blessed, he says. They're permanently switched on to 'Hosannah in the highest'. But not with electricity. With holy current. That must be quite something, he says, but he doesn't look like he believes what he's saying.

Now the helicopter's blue light shines right into their faces.

'Ow!' says his mother. She holds up her hand in front of her eyes. Pop looks the other way.

No, man, what are his people doing now, they must look straight into the light, with open eyes, so they can make themselves known to the protectors of the law. Let them shine their fucken light. If they want to interrogate him here in his own yard, then he'll say to them, look, if it wasn't for his regular patrols in the streets at night, which he does of his own free will, without expecting anything in return, then Triomf would be the same as all the other suburbs. Full of murder and robbery and killing. As things stand, Triomf is one of the safest areas in the whole of Jo'burg. You wouldn't say it, with all the riff-raff and scum just a stone's throw away, there on the other side of Ontdekkers. It's all thanks to one white oke who can be seen regularly on the streets at night. They know they can't just come and take chances here in Triomf.

That's why, when he's out at night and he walks past a munt, he shines his torch right into the munt's eyes and then he says: Watch your step, my mate, I'm checking you out.

And nowadays he also tap-taps on his gun. Which he wears in his belt. Then their eyes go big, like saucers.

He sticks the gun in the belt that he took off his Man About Towns. He made a new hole right at the end of the belt, and now he can only just get it on again, under his belly. The stretched elastic in his shorts won't hold the gun nice and tight. When he puts the gun into his belt, everyone can see it.

News travels. By this time, anyone who's up to funny business will know about him. Especially now that he's armed.

His family don't know about the gun yet, but they stare at him like they do. 'Specially his mother. He figures that maybe they saw his list. And he thinks his mother saw more than just the list. He swears she saw THE MOLE IN THE FRIDGE. All his stuff was shifted away from the wall when he came to. But maybe he did it himself, when he was burning the rubbish. Or maybe they scratched around in his things when he was lights-out.

No respect for his privacy. But what can he do? He can't remember so nicely any more. And when he woke up, he wasn't wearing his shorts.

Lately, Treppie's been holding his hands in front of his eyes like binoculars, and then he sings, in a deep voice:

'I see a bad moon rising
I see trouble on the way.'

Or he pretends he's pulling a gun out of a holster and then he does a crazy little dance with his mouth open and his tongue hanging out and his head pulled back into his shoulders. Then he pretends he's shooting up into the sky, 'crack!-crack!-crack!'.

And when he asks Treppie what now, then he says no, he's just playing Lambert, the Sundance Kid.

Treppie's arse. He doesn't need to know about the gun. Nobody needs to know. He's not going to start bothering about a licence now. In any case, nowadays it looks like every second kaffir's got a gun, especially when they march up and down the streets and shoot off their weapons into the sky. No one can come and tell him they've all got licences. He'd thought it was against the law, but the policemen don't do anything. They just lie on their tanks and watch. Treppie says that's the official standpoint of the Ministry of Law and Order. Dis-cre-tio-nary po-li-cing. He says it's just another word for shit-scared constables. But, he says, their shit comes in two different colours: one for when the Inkatha impis are on the march with their guns, and another when they think it's APLA. When they reckon it's APLA, they go on a raid across the border at night and shoot the APLAs full of holes in their beds. Never mind if they're just apprentice-APLAs who're still wet behind the ears. And with the ANC they don't even bother any more. Treppie says that's 'cause the ANC's the biggest cannon of them all.

Well, all he knows is that if trouble comes their way, he'll be on the right side. The police will still be grateful for people like him one day. People they can rely on. He stands for law and order here in Triomf. Like that little bloke in *Urban Angel*, who works for nothing and then gets a kick in the teeth for thanks. But in the end he's still everyone's hero.

So he doesn't mind. He's looking after Triomf, and he knows his day will come. Every dog has its day, no matter what Treppie says. Treppie says he mustn't walk around so much on his own at night, 'cause he hasn't got a groundswell behind him. He's an individual, and the police are hard on lost individuals.

Well, he reckons the police are far too busy with discretionary policing to worry about people like him, never mind patrol Triomf. The only time they come here is when there's trouble. And even then it's a struggle to make them believe you've got a case. That's if they ever get here. When they do come, it takes them hours to arrive.

Like when he phones about the people next door. If that bunch at Fort Knox isn't making trouble, then it's Fish-Eye and his lot on the other side. That Fish-Eye's beginning to look just like his blarry fish, with his one flat eye and his scrappy little moustache-beard. He says he eats those fish of his. Sis! Carp. He keeps them in a Penguin Pool, with a pump that goes through seven phases. Carp have got to have bubbles, he says, otherwise they die. The pump starts off low, then it gets higher and higher. 'Eeeeee!' At phase five it starts shaking. 'Drrr!' It gets so bad that he, Lambert, can't get to sleep in his own den from all the noise. Never mind the poor fucken carp. But he supposes carp don't ever sleep.

He's already told Fish-Eye, he knows all about machines. There's nothing that these two hands of his can't do. He'll tune that pump for him in two ticks so it runs as smooth as a sewing machine, 'zick-zick, zick-zick, zick-zick', all day long, through all its phases. But then Fish-Eye told him he must fuck off. Just like that. Uneducated bastard.

And then the shit started again, just the other day. It was a Saturday night. That machine was making such a noise his mother began to think the whole of Jo'burg, all the way from Sandton to Bosmont, was falling into one big sinkhole. She started running up and down with her

303

housecoat open and her stomach wobbling, screaming that she wasn't ready, the Lord must forgive her and protect her from the jaws of the animal in the depths.

Then he thought, no, enough is enough, now he's going to phone the emergency number. So he went across the road and asked the dykes very nicely. They were in a jolly mood, and they said okay, he must just stay there, they'd bring the phone to him. So they brought the phone to the lounge, with an extension.

'Disturbing the peace,' is how he began his story. Then he mentioned the carp and he explained about phase five.

But he was connected to the Flying Squad and they were using a radio telephone. Other people kept talking on the radio. The men from Murder and Robbery in Brixton were saying they'd run out of wet bags and wires, and where did you get wet bags after one in the morning in the New South Africa, and how did things look there at Johan Coetzee station, didn't they maybe have some bags and wires to send over? And while they were at it, they could also send their little red Hotnots along so they could clean out their gills for them. They were sitting around in Brixton with nothing to do. Every time Lambert got a word in, he had to start the whole story all over again, and each time the constable couldn't understand what carp and phase five had to do with disturbing the peace. Likely blarry story, if they knew what wet bags and little red Hotnots and boredom had to do with each other. But he supposes every oke has his own way of frying fish.

That's also what he said to the dykes, and then the tall one told the short one she would put this story of his before Lawyers for Human Rights, and the short one started laughing so much she had to go sit down and hold her head in her hands. He couldn't figure out what was so funny, but he kept quiet. It was then that he clicked why Treppie says they're so dilly. Treppie says you get two kinds of dykes, diesel dykes and dilly dykes, and these two across the road are definitely the dilly kind, if you ask him.

Anyhow, then the police came. They stood there next to the wall and they listened, but they said they could hear sweet blow-all, and he, Lambert, mustn't waste their time like this. They were the Flying Squad and all they really handled was serious crime.

By that time the pump, of course, was a long way past phase five. It was running softly on phase one and all you could hear was 'plop-plop' as the carp took bites out of their bubbles.

Meanwhile, Fish-Eye was standing there behind his aloes, smoking and listening to everything they said, acting like he knew nothing.

Lambert tried to explain what happened each time the pump got to phase five. And how many hours it took to go through the whole cycle. If the Flying Squad came back at about six in the morning, they'd see exactly what he meant.

Then the policemen said, with their hands on their hips, 'Mr Benade, do you or don't you want to lay a charge?'

So he said no, 'cause by then Pop and Treppie were outside, pointing angry fingers at him behind the policemen's backs. He said no, he just wanted them to put some pressure on Fish-Eye about his pumps that were making such a noise.

Then those policemen told him they weren't in the pressure business, they were in the shooting business. And if it's pressure he wanted, he should go to the World Trade Centre, where they were also into phases and stuff like that. Those politicians knew all about pressure, they said, laughing themselves to death there on the Benades' front lawn.

It wasn't just the dykes who were dilly, he thought to himself.

And the next morning, when Pop took the key out of the postbox, he found a letter there, from Fish-Eye. Treppie grabbed the letter and made a whole performance out of it, so Lambert still doesn't know if everything Treppie read was true or not. The long and the short of it was Fish-Eye saying his property was losing its value as a result of all their meddling, and he'd be much happier if a decent kaffir like Cyril Ramaphosa came to live next door to him one day. Ramaphosa might even plant something along the boundary wall, he said, 'cause he saw Ramaphosa was planting weeping boer-beans there at the World Trade Centre, in a suit too, which was more than he could say for the Benades, despite the fact that they were white. And then he made a long list of complaints about them disturbing the peace and using the Lord's name in vain. And about Pop's zips that always hung open, and his mother who walked around with no panties all day long. And that they must watch out before he mobilised the whole neighbourhood against them,'cause they were sticking out like a sore finger. And then, right at the end, the fucker actually wanted to know if they'd paid their dog taxes all these years, for their one departed and their one surviving dog. He was just asking, although he felt it was only fair to inform them that he himself was a police reservist, and that he had family who were high up in the municipality too. One word from him and the Benades would be in their glory, dogs and all. Thanking them in anticipation, J.J. Volschenk.

He swears Treppie sucked half that letter straight out of his thumb, but by then he had them all wound up anyway, which must have been what he wanted.

Treppie said the honourable Mister Jay Jay Volschenk doth protest too much. He schemed Jay Jay was himself so low down in the pecking order that he got a kick out of writing high-and-mighty letters to the untouchables.

Then Treppie had to explain to his mother what untouchables were.

Not that he, Lambert, knew so well what it meant himself.

Of course, Treppie went and said the worst thing he could think of, just to torment her. He said the untouchables wiped off their shit, er, er, pardon, he meant their excrement, with their hands, and then they used it to write messages on the walls, for aliens. 'Mene Mene Tekel.' Aliens were the only ones who were still interested in them. Hadn't his mother noticed how people were taking a wide berth around them nowadays?

Then she asked him, but what about the Witnesses? They still came to visit, out of their own free will. But Treppie said the Witnesses were interested only in their souls, not their excrement; although, come to think of it, their souls were probably lodged in their excrement, otherwise he also couldn't figure out what the Witnesses thought they were looking for here at the Benades. But, he said, one of these days the Witnesses would have to come visiting on stilts, 'cause they were already deeper than knee-deep, and they were sinking fast.

Pop asked Treppie if he didn't have a drop of self-respect left in him. But Treppie just acted like he hadn't heard. He pinched his nostrils and sang like the main coolie-singer on top of the mosque, the one they always hear from Bosmont when the wind blows in the right direction:

> 'Lemon tree very pretty
> And the lemon flower is sweet
> But the fruit of the poor lemon
> Is impossible to eat.'

So, that's why Pop's wearing blue shirt-buttons to close up his khaki-pants nowadays. His mother spent the whole day sewing them on, with pink cotton. It doesn't look right, she says, but at least Pop looks decent again. She also tried to fix Pop's zip-up pants, but he uses a safety pin to keep the fly closed. And Lambert thinks they must've bought his mother some panties too, 'cause every now and again he sees them hanging on the line.

He's got his own plans for Fish-Eye. When he goes out on his rounds, late at night, he takes a crate to stand on and then he pisses into Fish-Eye's postbox.

Fish-Eye thinks it's the kaffirs. Lambert's seen how he waits for them behind his wall on weekends, early in the evening. But Fish-Eye has to wait a long time. It's mostly just kaffirgirls who walk up and down Martha Street, and they wouldn't be able to piss into that postbox of his, even if they wanted to. Every now and again a few kaffirs come walking past and then Fish-Eye shits them out. He calls them hosepipe-dicks. And he asks them if they'd like to know what it feels like to get their king-sized dicks caught in a mouse trap. He'll give them something to write home about, he says. They mustn't think they're the only ones with cultural weapons around here.

Then, one day, a long stick of a kaffir came walking past with his hair all tied up in strings. He was wearing sunglasses, with a red, green and yellow cap. Lambert's mother thought he was a Zulu, so she hid behind the bathroom door. But Treppie said, no, Zulus had knobkieries. This was a Rasta-man, and they must check now how this Rasta-man was going to jive old Fish-Eye, who was shitting him out something terrible there in the street. That Rasta-man just stood there, cool as a cucumber, rolling a zol and checking Fish-Eye out as he screamed at him from behind his wall.

And then the Rasta-man actually had the guts to give Fish-Eye a talking to. 'Cool it, my man. Smile, God loves you,' he said. He even threw Fish-Eye a peace sign. Fish-Eye went completely purple in the face. He ran around like a madman. It was so bad they thought he was going to jump into the Penguin Pool to be with his carp. But he didn't. He went and set the little mousetrap in his postbox, and then it snapped on to his finger.

Lambert's clever. He first takes out the mousetrap. Then he pisses into the postbox. When he's finished pissing, he puts the trap back again. He doesn't let people fuck with him. Now Mister Reservist can read piss-letters until the day he dies. And he gets a lot of letters, too. From Absa and Sanlam and the Bible Society and the AA and Readers Digest. Serves him right. And the police must also watch out, discretion and all. Treppie read him a story the other day about two policemen from Triomf who raped a woman at Johan Coetzee police station. De Bruin and Visagie. Lambert still wants to find out where in Triomf De Bruin and Visagie live. And that clever-arse traffic cop at number 101, who races up and down Martha Street on his motorbike must watch out too. A person's life is in danger around here. The place is full of dogs and things. He can just see an accident happening.

When the police themselves become a danger to society, then you know something's wrong.

So he patrols. Somebody has to do it.

When he walks up and down the streets of Triomf at night, with his stick and his gun safely in his belt, he feels like he was born to patrol. He feels sharp. The kind of person other people can rely on. And he checks out everything, even the stuff that looks okay. It's when things don't look different that you drop your guard. So he checks, not only inside all the windows, to make sure that every mother and father, grandma and grandpa, child and grandchild, brother-in-law and step-sister, what have you, is sitting nicely at the TV and watching the news; and not only that all the front gates and the driveways and the car windows are closed, and that the number plates are still on. He also checks the things no one else ever looks at, the things that tell you straight away when something's wrong. Like the stop signs. He checks to see if they're the right colour and the right height, and if they're standing on the right side of the road; and he checks the streets' name-plates, to make sure they're the same as the names on the kerb, and that they point in the right direction; and the streetlights, to make sure they're all switched on; the telephone wires, to see that they're still nicely connected; and the manholes, whether their lids fit the holes nicely. Nowadays the kaffirs even steal manhole covers and sell them for scrap iron. Ten rand apiece. Treppie says it's to keep the balance in the New South Africa, 'cause for a long time now the antiquarians have been stealing pressed metal ceilings from old houses, to sell on the black market.

So he also tries to check if all the houses still have their ceilings, although Triomf's houses have only pressed cardboard. And he looks inside the rubbish bins, to make sure they've got the kind of rubbish they're supposed to have: old bread and newspapers and rotten vegetables and stuff, not heads or cats or babies. People throw away the funniest things nowadays.

He checks the green fuse boxes on the pavements to see if their little doors are closed, and to make sure no loose wires stick out or lie around. Treppie says people siphon off electricity illegally, but no one ever gets caught. Triomf's a closed shop, a law unto itself, he says. Not if he, Lambert, can help it. He's going to check out this closed shop very carefully to see what openings he can find.

And with his sharp eye he sometimes sees things he's sure no one else ever sees. Things on the ground and things in the air. On the ground, it's mostly bugs and funny little creatures that come out of their little holes. He once spent the whole night on the veld across the road from Shoprite, at that bus stop in front of the police flats, watching with his torch how termites come pouring out of their holes after the rain. They just kept coming, in a never-ending line, like someone was pulling them out from above on a string. Then they broke loose and swarmed up into the sky. Some of them fell down and died. Moles also do their pushing at night. Rats too. The rats are breeding like mad in the drains. That's where they live. They go 'trrrips!' one after another through the gaps in the pavement, down into their holes. Like someone's reeling them in by their noses, downwards.

He once saw a baboon-spider walking across the street. It was as big as his fist, with legs that moved on their own, as if they were tied to separate threads. That was at the end of Martha Street, on the koppie-side. You see some interesting things on that side. Rabbits with eyes like reflectors, who feed in the beds at the Centenary Old Age Resort. Once he even saw a little buck, and often he sees owls. That's when he realised there was more to Jo'burg than met the eye. And he's glad that he sees all these things. It feels like he's got secrets that are his only. But when he sometimes tells his folks a little something, they just laugh at him. Then they say he's having them on.

Treppie says if there were just one wild buck left in Jo'burg, it would be worth saving from fire and brimstone, but there obviously isn't. He says all he can hear in Jo'burg are sirens and gunshots. All he can see are things that burn. And all he can smell is blood and iron. He says Jo'burg's like a massive big iron dinosaur devouring itself, tail first, screws and brackets flying through the air.

Then his mother asks Treppie where he sees this ugly monster, and Treppie says if she'd just use her eyes like the good Lord Jesus intended her to, she wouldn't be able to miss it. And then his mother spends the whole day waiting for the dinosaur to pop out somewhere. Behind the Hillbrow tower; on the open ground behind the Spar; or behind Northcliff hill. She says she can't see any dinosaurs. All she sees are roads and cars and buildings and shops and people and things.

She's looking in the wrong places. Treppie too. It's just him, Lambert, who knows where to look. Only he sees everything there is to be seen. 'Cause he's a patrolman. It's in his blood. If you're a born patrolman, you see everything, near and far, big and small, and you look at things carefully. You check to see how they work and what their movements are, inside and out.

And you pick up vibes.

He feels bright and breezy when he's finished his patrolling for the day. He keeps on looking till he starts picking up vibes. Some nights there's nothing. He knows there're vibes, but he doesn't always get hold of them so nicely. Then it's just an ordinary night. Nothing special.

But other nights are different. Then he picks up the vibes on the ground and he follows them through the air. The vibes of things that fly, things that travel far. Stars with tails. He sees lots of stars falling. Stars dying. And he sees sputniks too. Bright side, dark side, bright side, dark side, as they dip through the night. That's when you know the little monkey can't settle down. Or the little dog.

Treppie says sputniks are full of over-excited monkeys and dogs. Some- times the sputniks are empty, just cameras and things taking pictures of the earth and the moon and the stars. But others have astronauts inside. Space travellers. They patrol the heavens. Treppie says those astronauts are even more fidgety than the dogs and the apes. They've got ants in their pants. That's why sputniks sometimes explode before they even take off, like the *Challenger*. Treppie says everyone's a challenger, but sometimes people take things too far, or they do nothing. If they do nothing, they open their eyes one day and they're knee-deep in something that someone else took too far. Then there's shit to play.

Treppie's a fine one to talk. He's always challenging him, Lambert, and he always takes things too far. A pity, 'cause Treppie's the only one among his family with anything between his ears.

Sometimes they have interesting conversations.

But as soon as it gets interesting, Treppie starts fucking around.

Lambert looks at Treppie next to him, here on the lawn. 'Wakey-wakey!' Treppie says. 'All is quiet on the white side of Ontdekkers.'

The helicopter turns to the Bosmont side.

Martha Street's residents go back into their houses. The moon's sitting high.

'They're looking for a Hotnot,' says Pop.

They stand and watch for a while as the helicopter searches, up and down, up and down, its red tail-light flashing. The searchlight cuts

Bosmont's dark streets like a thin, blue probe of glass. Sirens wail all over Jo'burg. Shots go off on Ontdekkers.

'Who's shooting?' his mother asks.

'Those are just the taxis that are missing, Ma.'

'It's Jo'burg that's missing,' Treppie says.

'Her points are dirty. Her timing's out. Who'll give Jo'burg a service?' he sings. Treppie started hitting the Klipdrift early tonight.

Lambert goes back to his den. There was nothing special on the go tonight. He went up and down Martha Street and then into Gerty and down Toby, to the bottom, where he always checks out the cars on the big advertising boards.

Those boards have long strips running downwards. First they turn one way, then the other, making a 'ting!' sound after each turn. And there's a different picture each time.

Tonight it was a car driving through a veld fire.

Metallic blue. 'Ting!' *It curves!*

'Ting!' *Opel Kadett 140.*

And then it starts all over again. The blue car with its wheels in the fire. No one inside.

'Ting! Ting! Ting!'

Over and over again.

Then the moon rose like a big, yellow ball above the advertising board.

And then he thought, no, now he'd better go home.

He goes round the back way to his den. Once inside, he feels for the key at the back of the Tedelex's ice-box. He unlocks the steel cabinet and takes out his binoculars. Should he strip them? He once opened a kaleidoscope that Treppie brought home from the Chinese, just to see how it worked, how it made the little patterns that were all the same but also all different. But the pieces of glass fell out and he couldn't get them to fit together again. Common piece of Chinese rubbish. Anyway, a Chinese is a sort of a Hotnot. The Japanese are the ones with real class, Treppie says. They're honorary whites. They can make motorbikes. Suzuki, Kawasaki. Sounds more like Zulu to him.

He lies back on his mattress. The mattress he inherited from Pop and his mother. They actually went and took the new one for themselves. They say if he wants to burn his own bed he mustn't complain about what they give him. Mind you, theirs is also not brand new, it's a second-hand mattress from the pawnshop in Brixton, with an inner-spring. Not bad. And they bought a base, too, a shaky one, but what the hell. Now at least there's one decent bed in the house. When his girl comes he'll swop the mattresses around. They mustn't try to stop him. You can't let a guest sleep on a fucked-up piece of old sponge on the floor.

He focuses his binoculars on SUPERBEE. He sees it from so close that all he can make out are some of its parts. It takes him a while before he realises he's looking at SUPERBEE's body. Then he clicks it's the middle sting, the one curling round the cloud. He can see on the black line how his hand was shaking when he got to the narrow part at the end. He looks down, at the wings, where the world shines through, softly blurred with spit between the veins. Yellow grass and red aloes. This bee's more than a Superbee. This bee's heavenly! It should actually be called ANGELBEE. Maybe he can still change it. Same number of letters. He'll first have to paint white over SUPER and then write on top of it again.

He looks at his painting. There's still a helluva lot to do. Lots that he has to fill in. Here and there he's drawn a piece of outline. Most of the squares only have names. He looks at the names. Actually, everything should get wings like Angelbee. Angelbee's got a vibe. None of them must lie thick or heavy or flat on the earth. They must fly. Things that can fly up into the air have vibes from other worlds.

Termite angel. Angel wasp. Heavenly rats and moths. Angels for Africa. Then the whole ceiling can get stars, so it looks like heaven.

He sees yellow spots on the ceiling. Must be the geyser leaking, or the overflow. And black specks, from the damp. Or maybe it's fly-shit.

In the one corner he suddenly sees an off-white clot of threads. Things that look like sticks.

What is it?

He sets the binoculars to see better, but it blurs on both sides. He turns and turns until he gets it into focus.

The ball-thing's moving. No, what the hell. What's this now?

Slowly the little ball begins to tear open on the one side. Something's moving around. Then three little folded-up things pop out. For a while they just hang there. Then they slowly open up.

Spiders.

Daddy-long-legs.

'I spy with my little eye,' says Treppie, suddenly here next to him.

Lambert jumps. He sits up quickly, trying to hide the binoculars behind his back. But Treppie doesn't want them. He's sitting on a crate, holding his hands like binoculars in front of his eyes. He looks up at the ceiling.

'The sky's the limit,' he says.

Then he takes away his hands.

'And the heavens declare!'

'Just don't start with me now.'

'I'm not starting with you.' Treppie winks. 'I've got a suggestion for you. Put on your shoes, and then bring those binoculars of yours. I've got the Klipdrift. We can tell Pop and them we're just going for a spin to Brixton. Then I'll take you on an outing. Then I'll really show you something.'

'Like what?'

'Shit with what. If you're scared, bring your gun.' Treppie winks a double-wink at him. First with one eye and then the other.

Okay, so he knows, the bastard. Nothing to be done about it. And with all that Klipdrift in him, he's capable of barging into places he doesn't belong. Well, okay then, for just in case.

Lambert takes his belt from the steel cabinet and fastens it under his belly. He loads the gun. One bullet for every hole. Six of them. Then he puts the gun into his belt on one side. His binoculars dangle from his neck.

Treppie stands at the door, looking at him. He rocks slowly on his feet.

'I'm ready if you're ready.'

Treppie salutes. It's weird, his fist makes a dull noise as he knocks it against his chest. With the other hand, he lifts the Klipdrift high into the air, and says:

> 'It's the knight of Triumph
> Look, look, look over here
> He can see around corners
> And his barrel is loaded
> But where, oh where is his Guinevere?'

Treppie mustn't go and fuck with him now. He wants to know who this Guinevere is, but he decides to leave it. One thing at a time. He's feeling a bit jittery about this outing.

Treppie doesn't drive to Brixton. He drives down Long Street, with a smile on his face, till he gets to the gates of the other big Jo'burg dump, the one between West Park cemetery and the police flats. That building's so high you can see it for miles around. It even flashes a red light on top to warn aeroplanes at night. From its windows you can see the dumps, the cemetery, and from Northcliff hill all the way to Florida, where the water-organ plays. On the other side it looks out over the northern suburbs, right up to the Sandton Sun, which shines like a bar of gold in the night, also with a light on top.

They climb over the high gate. Treppie walks in front between high piles of rubbish until they get to the back of the flats. The moon shines brightly all around them. A fucken weird place to visit at this time of night! He wonders what bee Treppie's got in his bonnet. They walk past an old kaffir sitting next to his konka. The poor bastard must live here.

'Evening, my masters,' says the kaffir, taking off his hat.

'Evening, chief,' they say to him.

It takes a long time before they get to where Treppie wants to be – a big heap of stones.

Up here, Treppie points. 'That's it,' he says when they get to the top.

Not rocks, Lambert sees, but stones. Smooth, shiny cut-offs from polished granite, the left-overs from West Park's headstones. Lambert looks at the big block of flats. Then he looks around him. A person can see far from here.

'Must be nice to live here, with a view like this. You can almost see the whole of Jo'burg.'

'Oh yes, as long and as wide as God's mercy.'

Lambert looks at Treppie. He's full of tricks again. He was hitting the Klipdrift early tonight, even before Lambert went on patrol.

'Yes,' says Treppie when they both find seats on flat pieces of stone, 'and if you ask me, they need it, too. Fucken heavenly garages full of mercy. With a view, for just in case. Not that it'll help. A policeman's eyes sit too closely together, like a baboon's. He just looks straight in front of him. Never sees what's under his nose.'

Treppie shows with his fingers and his nose how the baboon-policemen look out at the world. Then he takes a long sip from the Klipdrift bottle and passes it on.

They drink and then they look at the big block of flats in front of them, with all its little squares of light.

'These people don't even close their curtains.'

'Why should they?' says Treppie. 'On this side it's just dead bodies and the city's rubbish. But us, we're here now, we're alive and we've got a gun. And binoculars.'

Only now does he click Treppie's plan.

'And a snort,' Treppie says. He holds the bottle up high and says 'Cheers!' to the flats.

It's funny to be so close. Pop always says the flats look like a honeycomb from a distance. That's when they go for a drive and they come back on the Albertskroon side. Then Treppie always says: A honeycomb with no sweetness in it. It looks more like a mouth organ to him, Treppie says. Then everyone laughs and says, but it hasn't got any music either.

Those are their jokes about the big block of police flats. They're bored with it.

But this is a completely different story. Now the flats look like lots of little square movies, all running at the same time on a big screen.

'So now,' says Treppie, 'pass me that mean machine of yours so I can find us a nice one. Take your pick. Comedy, thriller, action, romance. The works. What you in the mood for tonight, hey, Lambert?'

Treppie's nice and greased, he thinks. He smiles. Never a dull moment when Treppie's in a jolly mood.

'Mmm,' says Treppie, looking through the binoculars. 'Just what I thought.'

He looks where Treppie's looking, up and down with the binoculars. They're in for fun and games, 'cause Treppie will make up all kinds of things about what he says he sees there. All you can really see are the insides of the bottom flats, and the ceilings and walls of the flats higher up. But let's give Treppie a chance here.

Treppie drops the binoculars. He keeps quiet and looks around. The broken pieces of headstone look eerie. He drinks from the bottle and holds it up against the moonlight to check the level. Then he starts singing:

> 'Oh sentinel on the ramparts
> How endless seems the night
> But now the dawn is blushing
> And soon the morning will be glad and bright.'

'Hey, come now, man!' He presses Treppie on the shoulder. He must be careful now. He knows Treppie well. If he stays jolly on the Klipdrift, then he'll go to bed in a jolly mood. But if he starts getting the blues now, he'll just get more and more miserable as the night goes on. And then he'll start spinning heavy shit about him, Lambert, and the rest of them. And then, later, everything will get completely out of control.

Lambert looks through the binoculars. Let him just find something to cheer Treppie up now, 'cause Treppie looks like he wants to start crying or something. He looks at the bottom windows. There's a row of candles in one window, a woman holding up a piece of meat in another, and then there's a dog with his feet up against the glass, trying to look out. No luck tonight. But Treppie's too drunk to care. He hands him the binoculars.

'Shame, the poor dogs!' Treppie suddenly sticks his nose up into the air and lets out a long dog-cry. 'Hoo-eee-a-a-hoo!'

317

His voice echoes against the high flats. A few dogs bark in the distance. Lambert feels a cold shiver run down his tail-end.

'No, shuddup now, Treppie, if they catch us here, what'll you say then?'

'Then I'll say you're my guardian angel! Or my guide dog!' Treppie laughs a drunk little laugh.

'Let's just go home now.'

'Okay, but let's just check first.' Treppie takes the binoculars.

'Check what?'

'The moon.' Treppie turns around in circles with his arms open. 'They say there's a man in the moon. But I've heard a different story.'

'Ag don't talk rubbish, Treppie!'

Now he's not sure any more which way Treppie's going. He's got that twisted smile on his face, only now it's even more twisted than usual from all the Klipdrift.

'I heard there's a cart up there, with two horses in front and two people in the carriage.'

'Rubbish, Treppie, you're fucken drunk, man!'

Lambert looks around to see if anyone's coming. He doesn't want any trouble now. Suddenly it feels like they're very far from home.

'You're pissed, man.'

'Not pissed, and not drunk, just tickled. That's what my grandma always used to tell us. Your prehistoric great grandmother, the one you never met. She said there was a cart on the moon, with a bride and a groom, and two bay horses pulling the cart. On honeymoon.'

'Bay horses, hmph!'

Treppie stands up straight. He shows Lambert he must get up too. He gets up. He and Treppie cast short little shadows on the stones. They look up into the sky. Thick balls of cloud glide through the open sky. The clouds are black underneath. Their heads look like white stones in the bluish light from above.

'Check!' says Treppie.

'Check what?'

'The bridal cart, man. Look if you can see the bridal carriage!'

Lambert lifts the binoculars to his eyes. Now he must just be cool here, that's the best. Maybe it'll pass.

'Got it yet?'

'I'm still looking!'

Lambert finds the moon between balls of cloud. He focuses nearer and further till he gets it nice and sharp. There's a pale circle around the moon. Pinkish on the inside.

'Now look,' says Treppie. 'That's Koos Krismis and Laventeltjie, his wife. They're on honeymoon, there above Klipfontein's stars.'

Lambert looks. All he sees is the rough surface of the moon.

'And there, next to the cart, is a wedding guest who wants a lift.'

Treppie's voice sounds funny. Lambert looks for the guest. All he sees are patches and grey specks. The moon looks grated and chipped.

'And the groom's got a knapsack with a guinea-fowl inside. It's for the pot, for tonight. The guinea-fowl's head and its blue wattles are hanging out, and there's blood dripping on to the dirt road.'

No, Jesus! He looks at Treppie. He wants to tell him he's talking crap again. It must fucken stop now. Wallpaper, he wants to say. But tears are running down Treppie's face, down into the wrinkles around his mouth. Strange birds call in the dark. High up in the flats, somewhere, doors slam and people shout.

'There's a dog running next to the front wheel, with his tongue hanging out.'

'You're drunk, man, that's your problem.' This is all he can think of saying. Now he just wants to get the fucken hell out of here.

'Horries,' he shouts. It makes him uncomfortable when Treppie cries like this, here among the old stones and stuff.

'She's wearing a little hat with lace netting, and behind the lace her eyes shine like dew on a spider's web.'

Treppie swallows a sob. Then he sings:

> 'Oh the dog is broken winded
> His tongue is hanging out
> Oh the dog is spent and footsore

319

From running at a trot,
From shadowing the bonny bride
From shadowing the groom
'Neath the waxing and the waning
Of the unrelenting moon.'

'Stop your rubbish now, Treppie, shit and rubbish! The moon's in the sky and it's full of holes. Let's just fuck off from here now.'

Lambert grabs Treppie, but Treppie resists. He steps backwards, letting his unsteady body lean even further back.

'Maybe it's rubbish, Lambert, but who's going to open your eyes for you? Fuck those binoculars of yours, man, fuck them! It's all in the mind. And what's in a name? The moon is a sickle, a coin or a pickle, teaching is cheating, God is a dog, just Eve is all side same side. Anything you say. Triomf or Doris Day, we're here to stay!'

And now, why's Treppie grabbing his balls? No decency. No, it's not his balls. Treppie wants his gun! He grabs the gun out of Lambert's belt and pushes him so hard on the chest that he almost falls into his glory down the pile of stones.

'Give my fucken gun back!'

Treppie motions from above, he mustn't worry, he's just looking at the gun here a bit. He puts the thing against his head, and then into his mouth. Oh shit, here comes trouble! Lambert scrambles back up the pile of stones.

'That fucken thing's loaded, man, don't start fooling around with it now!' He should have known. That business of taking the gun with them. Another one of Treppie's plans.

'Six of the best!' Treppie holds the gun up high, away from himself. Lambert can't get to it. Jesus, help! What if Treppie shoots himself here tonight? What'll he say to Pop? He lunges for Treppie's arm, but he misses. Suddenly Treppie turns towards the flats.

'And this one's for you!' he shouts. 'Boom!' He shoots.

Somewhere in the distance, glass breaks. Oh Christ! Now they're in big shit here.

'Boom!' Treppie shoots another shot at the flats. 'Zing!' the bullet comes back. Lambert ducks. No, fuck, how's he going to stop Treppie now? Without getting a bullet in the head first? Jesus, how could he have been so stupid? He grabs for the gun. He misses, again. Treppie just swings his gun-hand away from him all the time.

'One for the dog in the moon!' he shouts.

'Boom!' he shoots up at the moon. With his other hand he throws the empty Klipdrift bottle and it breaks into pieces on the rocks. Then the gun falls out of his hand, clanging down. Lambert sees it lying there.

Are you fucken mad or something? he wants to shout, but his throat's too dry. He hears the sound of people talking, windows opening and closing. Now they must get the hell out of here, fast. So-called fucken outing! He fetches his gun from between two stones. Then he slips his binoculars around his neck. He grabs Treppie and drags him down the heap. Treppie doesn't want to get up or walk on his own. He's lying on the ground with a big piece of white headstone in his arms. He wants to take it home for Gerty, he says. Lambert will have to drag him away on his backside, he says, with granite in his arms.

He kicks Treppie to make him get up. But Treppie won't get up. He falls flat on to his back again, with the slab of stone still in his arms.

'Chip off the old block, chip off the old moon,' he cries, with his face on the stone. Tears roll down his cheeks.

Lambert drags him, stone and all. He can't just leave him here like this. He'd never hear the end of it.

'Evening, my masters,' the old kaffir says as they pass. He lifts his hat.

Stupid fucken kaffir, why doesn't he come and help instead. Can't he see they're struggling here? The gun sticks into his belly and the binoculars swing on his neck. Treppie's so heavy he leaves a trail like a fat python in the rubbish. Only at the entrance does he let go of the stone. Lambert manages to get him over the gate. He's completely limp. There go his pants too. 'Grrrr!'

Lambert has to drive. Treppie keeps falling against him in the car. Oh shit, what's that blue light he can see now in the rear-view mirror? God, is it them they're after? He changes back to second to get some speed going. The Volksie makes a 'heeeee' sound as it goes into third. Now he must just turn into Gerty. Get the police off their back. He checks in the mirror. It's a van, driving like hell, but it carries on down Thornton. Right. Now Lambert feels sharp. He's Treppie's guardian angel. At the bottom of Gerty he takes the turn without even slacking down, and then he goes up into Martha. Here's their gate. The moon shines bright into their yard. He drags Treppie out of the car and around the back of the house.

What's that big tearing noise above their heads? It's a Jumbo, taking the whole fucken sky for itself.

'Jaws,' Treppie hiccups, 'snap!'

They watch the Jumbo.

A strong wind pushes the clouds across the sky. The Jumbo sails with its nose against the current. As it flies, clouds slide off its sides and moonlight covers its body, making the whole jet shine except for its belly. The Jumbo pushes its nose slowly into the sky as it flies away from them, towards the moon. Its dark shadow passes, and then the noise follows, louder and louder, until they can hear nothing but a terrible blowing sound.

Lambert sees Treppie's mouth open as he shouts something at the Jumbo, flying towards the moon. He shakes his fist at the sky.

'What?'

'Angel of Retribution!' Treppie shouts into his ear. The Klipdrift is heavy on his breath. 'Shadowing the bonny bride, shadowing the groom.'

'It's going to land at Jan Smuts. Let's go sleep now.'

He pushes Treppie from behind, into the passage. Then he helps him on to his bed.

He walks back to his den and switches off the passage light. As he passes, he stops at his mother and Pop's closed door, opening it slightly to listen. 'Ghrrr-ghrrr,' his mother snores. 'Phewww-phewww,' Pop snores. 'Swish-swish' goes Toby's tail. Must be on the bed again. Ever since Gerty died they've been letting him sleep on the bed. So they're okay.

322

So now, all in all, it wasn't such a bad night. He must say, he feels quite good. He's a patrolman with class. What did Treppie say again? The Knight of Triumph, who looks after his own people. 'Cause they can't always do it for themselves. That's for fucken sure.

16

~

THE QUEEN OF ENGLAND

Lord, have mercy, they're screaming and shooting again behind those rolls of razor-wire. It's been going on like this all night now – flashbacks of what happened during the year. The little man on TV says they're first having the flashbacks, and then, only later, the Queen. It's that time between Christmas and New Year again, when this is all you get to see on TV. Mol's tried the other stations too. Just speeches and marches and dead people under blankets wherever you look.

Every time Treppie pokes his head out of his room and sees more bodies under blankets, he says he'll bet his bottom dollar those are Operation Snowball's blankets. Charity's not what it used to be, he says.

Nothing to be done about it. She'll just have to wait for the Queen of England. At least it's something to look forward to.

The house is peaceful tonight. Pop's sleeping next to her, in his chair, and Toby's lying with his head on Pop's shoe. Treppie's reading newspapers in his room. Lambert's in his den. He says he's painting. When he's not painting, he's digging his hole: his storage cellar, he calls it. He says it's still not deep enough. Every day he picks something from his list to work on. Then, when he's finished, he comes and stands here in the middle of the lounge with his hands on his hips, and he says: three down, twenty-six to go, or, five down, thirty-two to go.

Treppie says they must get ready, 'cause they're well into the countdown now. Not to be launched, he says, but to implode.

As far as she can see, Lambert adds things to the bottom of his list faster than he ticks them off at the top. So, this is no count-down, it's a count-up. And she wouldn't be able to say what that means as far as blowing up or conking in or imploding's concerned. They'll just have to wait and see.

To top it all, Treppie's gone and talked a new fencing story into Lambert's head. Mister Cochrane's Security Fencing, with spikes. 'Neat and nasty security spikes from Stiletto's.' She has to listen to it almost every day now.

She's seen a lot of houses with those spikes, but they always put them on top of high walls. Their house hasn't got a high wall. But Treppie says it's not a problem. All they need to do is hammer a few spikes into the roof – around the overflow pipe, where the corrugated iron is coming loose. And then they can put Mister Cochrane's electrified razor-wire on top of their own wire fence in front, and on top of the prefab wall, too. That will make them the neatest and nastiest of them all, Treppie says. Then they'll be ready.

Ready for what? she asks. And he says, ready for any eventuality.

Treppie says Mister Cochrane is a man after his own heart. He's an oke who takes a gap when he sees it. And he doesn't just take the gap, he looks for it too, all over the world. If he doesn't find it, Treppie says, then he wouldn't be surprised if Mister Cochrane goes and makes his gap with the help of the state.

When she asks him what gap, Treppie says: Oh, it's like something that still hasn't been given its right name. Mister Cochrane trekked right through Africa following the gap, until he arrived here at the southern tip. Things only began to go well for him in Nyassaland, which is now Kenya. It was there that Mister Cochrane saw the Mau-Mau, and that was one of the gap's first names. So he made his fencing to close up the gap.

Mau-Mau.

Treppie says there's just one thing about this kind of gap: once you've closed it up with security fencing, it starts getting bigger and bigger again and you can never keep up. You think you're closing it but actually you're opening it. He says that's what you call a paradox, but security is full of paradoxes like that.

All she needs to do is use her own two eyes, he says, and then she'll see all of Jo'burg sparkling with Mister Cochrane's security fencing. Around the golf courses, the Vroue-Landbou-Unie's home for unmarried mothers in Brixton, around schools and factories and the JG Strydom Hospital, Shoprite's loading zone at the back, Triomf's NG church, the coolie-church in Bosmont, everywhere. It's been put up once around the botanical gardens and three times around John Vorster Square. Even the Chinese in Commissioner Street have fenced in their yards, except now they can't chase the rats out any more. So they add them to the sweet and sour, for bulk.

Bulk.

You can even see the fencing on the walls of the Rand Afrikaans University, as if that wall isn't bad enough as it is. Seven million rands' worth of wall, says Treppie. You'd swear RAU was a raptor or something, trying to break loose.

Raptor.

He says it won't be long before they surround the whole of Jo'burg with that fence. But Mister Cochrane still won't be finished, 'cause then he can make fences inbetween and more fences around and inbetween and around and inbetween until he's gone right around the world.

Security fencing has become South Africa's biggest single export product, Treppie says. Everyone wants it, all the way from the Sudan to the Kruger National Park and to Chile. Treppie says Mister Cochrane has been invited by the United Nations to go to Bosnia and Hertzego-whatsitsname to come make his fences, so the Moslems and Christians will stop wiping each other out over there. And during the Gulf War, just a few years ago, there was lots of interest in Iran and Iraq for Mister Cochrane's fencing. Which doesn't surprise him at all, says Treppie, 'cause South Africa sold cannons to Iraq for that war, and war of any kind always opens up gaps that have to be fenced in again. When those two countries were at war, the government exported security fencing to both of them. The more fighting, the more fencing. The more fencing, the more fighting. That was like killing two birds with one stone. Boom! Snap! says Treppie. Boom! Snap! Boom! Snap! Very profitable.

Nowadays, he says, it's not guns and roses any more. Now it's guns, gaps and fences. And the one hand doesn't wash the other, they're both equally dirty now. Both know what the other's doing. And they're both in it right up to the elbows.

It sounds mixed up to her, but Lambert keeps nodding his head as if he understands exactly what Treppie's saying. And now, on top of everything, Lambert says he wants to buy second-hand fencing from Mister Cochrane, so he can close up the gaps around their house. But the only second-hand security fencing you ever see is the kind that lies around in rusted heaps and spiked balls that can't ever be undone again. Those terrible blades hook into each other, and then they catch bits of grass and plastic and stray cats and things. She's seen those balls of wire, next to the roads and in the scrapyards.

Treppie says Lambert doesn't understand the first thing about security fencing. He just pretends he does. Second-hand security fencing, he says, is a contradiction in terms. Mister Cochrane sells only new fencing.

That might be, but new or old, she doesn't want to be the cat, not to mention the kaffir, who lands up inside that wire.

Treppie says 'put up' is the wrong way to describe what you do with a fence like that. What you actually do is roll it off and turn it out, 'cause it comes rolled up tightly on a big spool. Then you turn the spool with a handle so the wire can roll off, in stiff, stabbing circles. Treppie says it's South Africa's Olympic emblem. Never mind our flames.

If you try to cut that wire with pliers, then the two loose pieces shoot out around your hands and bite deep holes into your flesh. And the more you try to pull yourself out, the deeper it digs in.

They once saw a cat inside one of those balls of wire. It was second-hand fencing, which made it worse. The cat looked like someone had tried to make muti out of it. It was hacked into little squares, making it look twice its size, shame. Nowadays, apart from the blades that hook, the fence comes in a double layer, too, one outside and one inside. The inside layer shocks you. That's after you've already been cut into chunks and you're still trying to get in to wherever it is you want to get into. Then it shocks you as well.

Treppie cut out Mister Cochrane's advert and pasted it up underneath the old calendar with the aerial photo of Jo'burg. He says it's so we make no mistake about where it is we come from. He underlined the important words with a red ball-point:

Detect the Intruder
Stop the Intruder
Shock the Intruder
Low-Cost Aggressive Asset Protection

It's still two and a bit hours to wait for the Queen of England. First it's *Agenda*. Tonight's *Agenda* is about peace: they show the part where Chris Hani asks for peace and then it's the dove who fell down next to Hani's coffin. Must have been dizzy from all the people and the flowers and the shots into the sky and everything. Poor little dove.

But she saw this before, at Easter. They said they took the dove out before closing up that grave, although she saw people throwing handfuls of dirt and petals on to the dove. It kept blinking its little eyes all the time.

Now they're showing the faces of people they're scared will also get shot, just like Hani.

The first one is Terre'Blanche of the AWB. Treppie says that man will shoot himself in the foot before anyone gets a chance to shoot him anywhere else. And then, when someone does eventually kill him, he'll get a hero's funeral. That, says Treppie, is what happens when you shoot a cripple Boer.

Now they're showing how Terre'Blanche keeps falling off his horse. Three different horses, in three different places. Always under some flag or another. Treppie says they would do better to pull him around in a rickshaw.

The AWB boss is talking. He asks whether people want the plots being hatched in the cold cancer chambers of Communism to come to fruition in our beautiful country. No, they mustn't, she thinks, but then Terre'Blanche must also learn to ride a horse properly.

Now they're showing Winnie. They're scared people will shoot her from several different angles. Now that's a dizzy palooka for you, Treppie says.

He says it's from that headgear she wears. Anyone who wears a ball of green satin bigger than her own head, with points on top, is bound to start talking a lot of crap. 'We shall liberate this country with our matchboxes,' she says. Not enough blood to the brain, says Treppie.

Then they show Peter Mokaba. He's got no hat on his head. Yes and no, he says. No, they mustn't shoot the Boere, he says, but yes, they must. Treppie says Mokaba's going to become the Minister of Tourism in the new government, but he'll cool down quickly once he has to look after a herd of zebras.

Then they show Hernus Kriel's face. He looks like someone's just told him he's an arsehole. And Kobie Coetzee, with his pop-out eyes. Treppie says you see eyes like that on people who're about to get golden handshakes. Like the one Kobie's lined up for himself. And then it's Buthelezi. He's in skins and he's got his sticks with him. And the mayor of Jo'burg, with a grey dove on his head. Everyone wants to shoot him over the rates.

But if you ask her, not a single one of them jogs. Hani used to jog every day in his tracksuit. Jogging's good for you. The president of America jogs around the White House every morning with his bodyguards. But Buthelezi doesn't jog. And he's not wearing anything underneath those animal skins, either. That's what Treppie says. He says the skins are just for show, and someone who's on show must sit still with his legs together and his hands folded neatly in his lap. Roelf Meyer jogs. She saw one day on the cover of *Your Family and You* in the café. He runs in his jogging shorts with his dog, one of those bull terriers with piggy eyes and a tail like an aerial. But no one's worried about Roelf getting shot. He's for peace. Treppie says he's a poofter and a kaffirlover, but he looks quite okay to her. It's just that he's getting thinner by the day. His collars hang loose and his Adam's apple jumps up and down like an oil-pump every time he talks. It's from negotiating, Treppie says, from throwing all his weight into the negotiations. Then it's Pik Botha. Pik's talking so much the spit flies in all directions. He says they can try shooting him if they want, he'll just shoot back. Pik's a jolly bloke, even when everything's falling to pieces all around him. That's what she says. She hasn't once seen Pik really get rattled. He always has something to say for himself, or he's got a plan for other people. Pik reminds her a lot of Treppie. If he wants something, he just takes it. And when he's finished, he gives it back again. He starts a fight, and then when he's finished he makes peace again, right there and then. Without batting an eyelid, says Treppie.

Pik's nose is also red, just like Treppie's. Hee-hee, she must remember to mention that to him.

There's Constand now. He's the leader of the Freedom Front. His neck's stiff and when he pulls away his bottom lip, his teeth show. He gives talks to women with perms. He stands on a stage with a flag behind him and a flag in front of him. The women look grim.

Treppie says the general's a brilliant strategist. He means business. He says he read somewhere that the general's got a twin brother who looks just like him, but his brother's as meek as a lamb. Hell, if you ask her, to be attached to a brother like Constand must be the same as getting stuck inside Mister Cochrane's security fencing. It's just as well they're not Siamese twins. Treppie's nickname for the general is Salamiboy. He says he's got a picture of the general somewhere when he was still chief of the defence force. In the picture, he and his top brass hold up the biggest salami ever made in Africa. Salami and smiles for the boys on the border. Treppie says those boys on the border didn't get to see much meat at all, never mind salami.

Treppie's got a whole pile of newspaper clippings where important people hold funny things in their hands – pumpkins, sheep, sucking-pigs, sculptures of presidents' heads, mielies, the works. He says it's incredible what people in this country are prepared to pose with. The Benades have never posed for any newspaper and maybe they're a bunch of poor white has-beens, but as sure as God's in heaven, he doesn't see the slightest difference between them and the top brass.

Now they're showing FW. He's standing on a red carpet at an airport with his hand on his heart. It's in Chile. The Chileans march past with guns and helmets. Next to FW stands his wife, Marike. She's wearing a little hat with netting on, and she holds her handbag in both hands in front of her. They saw this piece on the news when it happened. She remembers feeling so sorry for that poor Marike. She looked so miserable standing there, with her eyebrows all screwed up and a deep furrow in the middle of her forehead. She looked like she wanted to cry, standing there on a mat at that windy airport in Chile, with the aeroplanes far away in the distance and her floppy blue dress flapping round her legs. If she went on like this, Mol said at the time, then that face-lift of hers would come right down again, within a year. That's 'cause a frown is something you have to unlearn. It doesn't help to cut it out, it'll just frown itself back on again. But how do you unlearn something like that, in times like these?

Then, to top it all, Treppie began mocking Marike. He went and stood in front of the TV with two little knocked-together ladies' knees, and he held his hands in front of his crotch, putting on a smile just like the one Gerty used to wear when she did a number two. To tell the truth, that was the closest thing she's ever seen to the expression on Marike's face that day in Chile.

Then Treppie sang in a high little voice:

> 'I wonder what's bothering mee-ee
> There's trouble in my heart
> A tim'rous little butterflee-ee
> Forever from the garden barred.'

Pop says Treppie missed his calling in life. He should've been an actor. He says it bothers him terribly that such a talent should be wasted, without anyone even lifting a finger to do anything about it. He'll go so far, he says, as to say Treppie deserves a subsidy.

SECOND OF SEPTEMBER ⌢

She must say, the Benades have their moments. Like the other day, just a few months ago. It was still spring, and then they walked smack-bang into peace.

Treppie saw an advert in the smalls for an office furniture sale in Braamfontein, so they decided to go. Treppie said you sometimes found a handy piece of plank or something at the most unlikely places, for next to nothing. The trip was actually for Lambert. He was struggling to get his work bench nice and smooth for his girl, and he was starting to look dangerous again. He said he wanted to mix the cocktails on his work bench. And he needed it to put out the peanuts and the dips and the chips. The bench had to be nice and neat and smooth. That rough old railway sleeper standing on prefab slabs wasn't good enough, he said.

Well, in the end they didn't get anywhere near that furniture sale, 'cause when they turned into Jorissen Street it was suddenly just kaffirs wherever you looked. White people too, but mostly kaffirs. They filled the whole street, holding hands and singing and dancing, and they pushed Molletjie all over the place, until she jammed against the kerb. And there they sat. All the other cars also sat like that, stuck in the crowds of people with their lights on.

'Here comes big shit!' said Treppie. They couldn't see what was going on. At first they thought Mandela was there, or Mandela was dead, or maybe FW. Another huge bladdy funeral party.

The kaffirs kept pointing to Molletjie's front and back number-plates. They slammed their hands on the roof, looking at their watches and telling the Benades that they must get out of the car now.

'MDM!' they shouted.

'MDM!' they carried on shouting, pointing and shouting with open mouths.

'Right, people,' Treppie said, 'what's happening here is what I predicted a long time ago with these number-plates of ours. It was a big mistake. Now all of you better just act like you're the Mass Democratic Movement!'

She remembers, they waited a terribly long time to get those number-plates after Pop lost the papers. And when they went to fetch them, Treppie said it was a chance in a million. Of all the cars in Jo'burg, theirs had to be the one with MDM on its number-plate. Treppie said he foresaw a problem of mistaken identity, 'cause MDM stood for Maximum Democratic Merrymakers. That was a nice little mistake, she said. She wouldn't complain about an identity like that. Treppie thought it was very funny, but he told her she shouldn't push her luck too far. Well, she didn't have to push anything, 'cause in the end that day turned out very nicely, even if it did feel like touch and go at the time.

Pop sat dead still. He pulled the keys very slowly out of the ignition and put them into his pocket. The next thing, people were pulling them right out of their seats.

Lambert's eyes went wild from not knowing what was going on, and he shouted: 'Stay together! Just stay together!' She remembers feeling in her housecoat pocket for a peg.

But they quickly got mixed up in the crowd. Treppie on this side, Pop on that side, Lambert on the far side, and her right on the other side. So many strange people around her. Then a black girl with a Chicken Licken cap on her head came over and said: 'Peace be with you, Ma,' and she smiled at Mol and pinned a light blue ribbon, with two doves on a bright blue pin, one white and the other light blue, on to her housecoat. Only then did she see what was going on – everyone was wearing ribbons and doves and holding hands. So that was the story! And all this time the young girl kept squeezing her hand and smiling at her with shining eyes. She smelt like Chicken Licken and her hand was a bit greasy, but then Mol squeezed the hand back, even though she'd never touched a black hand before, clean or dirty. On her other side was an old man with only one leg, leaning on crutches. He stuck one of his crutches under his arm and then he shook her hand. That hand was cold and the skin was loose. And the bones felt like they had come apart. But he held her hand nice and tight.

She saw the old man had no blue on, so she worked her hands loose to give him her own ribbon. He motioned to her: here, she must please put it on for him. And so she stuck it on for him, right there on his lapel where he showed her. That old man's jacket was completely worn through, but the blue pin made it look nice and new again. And then she smiled at him, and she saw the young girl smile as well, and then all three of them were smiling much better, and they all took each other's hands again.

She looked around and caught sight of Pop and Treppie and Lambert, all of them with ribbons on their shirts. All of them holding strangers' hands. But they weren't smiling. Only Pop had a slight smile on his face. He looked a bit panicky.

Suddenly everything went so quiet you could hear a pin drop. All around her people began to cry. The old man dropped his chin on to his chest and closed his eyes and then tears started rolling down his cheeks. Next to her, the black girl was sniffing. The next thing, that girl picked up her hand, with Mol's hand still in it, and she used it to wipe her nose. Mol thought, ja, it's hard to believe, but if that girl had rubbed her snot off on the back of Mol's own hand, she would really not have minded. There was such a nice feeling in the air that she almost started crying herself. But then the silence was over and all of a sudden it was just hooters and bells and singing and people in taxis throwing peace signs. A young man in a striped tie grabbed her and they did a little two-step like she last saw in the days of Fordsburg's garment workers' dances. Eventually, she pushed her way through to Pop and said to him, with a smile on her face, 'Peace to you, Pop,' but she saw Pop was crying, too. Ai, Pop, he's got such a soft heart, truly.

When it was all over and they got back into the car, Pop turned around and asked her if she'd ever in her life heard of a coincidence like this, but that old man with only one leg whose hand she was holding was the very same man he gave money to in his tin, the one who said to him: God bless you, sir. It just shows you.

Lambert was over his shock by then, thank God, and he said he didn't know what it showed, but he also felt it showed you something.

Treppie was completely speechless.

But completely.

It was like someone had cut out his tongue.

When they drove past the Spar in Thornton – no one was in the mood for office furniture any more – Treppie suddenly popped up with the strangest idea. She could hardly believe her ears; it's the kind of thing she'd expect Pop to say, but Treppie said it was such a nice spring day and it was almost one o'clock, and weren't they also hungry? Why didn't they go buy something tasty and have it for lunch at the Westdene Dam?

Oh yes, the Benades have their moments. Even if they first have to stumble into peace, in the full light of day. In streets full of pealing bells.

That day just got better. They bought fresh bread and Springbok viennas and oranges and a litre of Coke and a coconut macaroon for each of them. Treppie paid for the lot from his back pocket. Just like that. They went and parked at the gate in Seymour Street, but she felt something was missing. It was Gerty, of course. Gerty was still alive then. Old and sick, but still alive. Shame, she's been dead almost a month to this day. She misses Gerty all the time.

But on that spring day Pop drove patiently back to the house to fetch Gerty and Toby. He knew they didn't always get a chance to play at the dam. When they got back to the dam they parked at the same spot and the dogs began wagging their tails and it was all very jolly. They took their lunch and found a place to sit in the slight shade of the willow trees that had just begun sprouting, opposite the island, where there were some more willows and a hadida.

It was all quiet and calm. The only other people there were on the other side, having a braai.

'Must be policemen,' said Pop.

'Maybe they work night shift. Shame, they must also crave a bit of sun,' she said.

So they unpacked their food and ate in silence there on the grass. Every now and again someone said something. Like: Look at the ducks. Or: Look where Toby's running now. Or: I wonder what kind of bird that is?

Except for Treppie, who didn't say a word. He just sat there, writing on his cigarette box. He'd write something, scratch it out again and then write something on the other side. After a while he was even writing on the macaroons' paper bag.

'What you writing there, Treppie?' Lambert asked after a while, and then she and Pop also asked. But Treppie just bit the back of his ball-point pen and scratched his head. He didn't say a word.

Then, after a long time, when they were passing around the Coke bottle for last sips and smoking their second cigarette, Treppie asked if they were ready to pay attention now, 'cause he'd written something special, for a special day. It was called 'This is not wallpaper' and this was how it went.

He stood up and smoothed down his clothes, and then he recited his little verse. So all that time he was sitting there writing a little verse, on his John Rolfes box, and on the macaroons' paper bag.

He put on his stage voice, gestured across the water, and read from the paper. It's the same piece of paper she can see now, pasted under the aerial photo of Jo'burg:

2 September 1993
THIS IS NOT WALLPAPER

> *The African coot creases the water*
> *And the Egyptian geese shout wha! to the sky*
> *And the hadida, that old bachelor*
> *sits there on the fronds of a willow.*
> *He shakes his feathers and stretches his leathers*
> *and shouts ha! to his friends on the bridge,*
> *ja-ha! They must look,*
> *this is not wallpaper*
> *not this time, no, not this time,*
> *it's spring, yes it's spring*
> *at the old Westdene Dam—*
> *and, not least,*
> *at last there is peace.*

Treppie's little poem left them speechless. For a long while all you could hear were the birds. Toby began to cry, 'cause Treppie kept standing there in that funny way with his one hand up in the air and the other still holding the macaroons' paper bag. So Lambert started clapping and they all joined in. Pop put his fingers in his mouth like he used to when he was young and he whistled a whistle with a wild twist at the end. And then of course Toby started barking and jumping around in circles.

They all wanted to hear the verse over and over again. Treppie had to recite his poem four times, and each time it sounded better, and different.

'A poet and you don't know it, hey?' Lambert said to Treppie as they walked back to the car.

But Pop said: 'He knows it, all right, he knows it,' and he put his hand around Treppie's shoulder.

When Pop took the turn into Martha Street, past the prefab wagon-wheels, Lambert said: '"This is not wallpaper, not this time, no, not this time",' and when they got to the house and she climbed out to open the gate, Lambert shouted: '"And the Egyptian geese shout wha! to the sky".' And when they walked in through the front door, Pop said: '"And, not least, at last there is peace."'

That's when she said to Treppie he must give her that paper bag, she wanted to paste it up nicely on the wall under the aerial photo, next to Mister Cochrane's security fencing. He looked at her hard and then she smiled back at him. She couldn't stop herself. She said: 'So we make no mistake about where it is we come from.' Then he also smiled and winked at her, giving her a little hug around the shoulders. Ja, can you believe it, a decent, brotherly hug.

It just shows you.

What a day like this can do to a person.

Now she hears Lambert wants Treppie to write a rhyme for his girl, before even meeting her. In English, too. But she's not so sure about this business, 'cause by that time there won't be any peace left. Then it'll be elections.

CHRISTMAS ⌒

Hell, but it's a long wait for the Queen of England tonight. Still another quarter of an hour. It had better be worth the wait.

Maybe she should start throwing away the Christmas cards on the sideboard – if they're still there by New Year she can just see the trouble it'll cause again. Not that she meant anything by putting them there in the first place, one at a time, as she found them in the postbox. She stood them upright with their pictures showing to the outside, all of them with houses, houses, houses, except the one with a path to heaven and a little sun. She stood them there so Christmas would at least look like something, for a change. Most of the time their Christmases are just miserable bugger-ups.

But this year they were lucky. Christmas turned out much better than for a long time. They got together in threes and gave presents to the fourth one. Lambert carried on and on about wanting to have a braai with T-bones and watermelon, so they could all learn to be nice and sociable. He said that was something the rest of them were going to have to learn fast in the New Year, once he and his birthday-girl started going steady. They'd have to learn how to treat visitors nicely, and they'd have to start eating some decent food, too. They also needed to learn the meaning of hospitality. And no, she wasn't allowed to fry those T-bones in the pan, on top of the Primus. They had to be done on a proper wood fire, in the backyard. Lambert actually went and bought five silver balls at Shoprite, and then on Christmas Eve he hung them up on the fig tree in the yard. He told them they must all come outside now, he wanted to practise making a jolly fire. He said he knew how to make big fires, but a braaivleis fire was a different story altogether. For a braaivleis fire you needed an audience.

He bought three bags of firewood, one and a half for practising and one and a half for the real thing.

Then he wanted old newspapers to put under the wood, but Treppie said, uh-uh, he wasn't finished reading them yet and Lambert should've thought about this when he burnt all his old *Watchtower*s. The next thing, Lambert tells her she must go fetch those stupid Christmas cards from Seeff and Johan Bekker and Nico Niemand and De Huizemark and Aribal whatshisname so he can use them to make his fire. She said no way, Christmas wasn't over yet and his Christmas fire would die for sure if he went and sent the season's greetings up in flames. Then he said season's foot, they didn't mean it, it was just estate agents' sales gimmicks. Gimmick himself, she said. What about the NP's little Christmas card, did he want to burn that one too? No, he said, she must leave that one. The NPs had been in their house so many times they were almost family by now, and in any case the NP was safer than houses.

Then of course Treppie couldn't keep his mouth shut again. He told Lambert if he went into the election believing those two snotnoses from the NP were any better than estate agents looking for a commission, then he'd learnt nothing in all his forty years.

Treppie said Lambert must ask himself this: if the DP paid its workers one rand for every black vote they could get, and the ANC was willing to pay as much as fifteen thousand rand for just one bankrupt white cop with a drinking problem who'd seen the light, then how much more wouldn't the NP pay for all the Ampies of the nineties who still lived in Triomf? Hadn't he noticed the smart car that nosepicking Groenewald drove around in, and did he perhaps think the NP got money like that from selling doughnuts at church bazaars? He could assure Lambert now, without a doubt: money like that came from one place and one place only – the taxpayer's pocket. It was a fucken shame.

Treppie said he was even tempted to go and join the Inkathas – that was at least a kaffir party whose doors were wide open to white people. At least then you knew you were dealing with a kaffir who was sick to death of being used by the NP, someone who kept to his own path, even if he did still dress in skins sometimes. Served them right, Treppie said, he wished old Mangope and Oupa Whatshisname and that cocky little Bantu from the Transkei and all the others who sold out would also bite the NP's hand. Its backside too. Would the NP never learn?

Treppie was so worked up he started getting the shakes, and Lambert wanted to knock him sideways with a piece of firewood. On the very eve of the holy Christmas. But she told them that unless they calmed down she wouldn't 'marinade' their T-bones, not a damn. The closer Lambert gets to his birthday, the fancier his words get. She said if they didn't stop, she and Pop would go across the road and ask the police to take Lambert in a straitjacket to the nuthouse. Treppie too, 'cause she didn't want to sit through another Christmas with people who were full of the horries, never mind the election. That was if they ever made it to the election. Pop said he agreed. He begged them, didn't they want to try getting through just one Christmas without another big hullabaloo. Maybe this would be his last.

That shut them up nicely. It was the first time they'd heard Pop say anything like that.

So, she almost didn't stick around for Lambert's fire practice.

But it would've been a great pity to miss the giving of presents. And that business with the presents was a jolly affair, from start to finish.

They worked out that if they bought in groups of three for the fourth one, they'd save money and they could give each person a nice present. And they could also make sure everyone's present was worth the same money. In other years, someone always cheated, and someone else always felt done down, and that's where the Christmas trouble always started. The new plan was Pop's idea. Treppie said it sounded to him like a real New South Africa idea.

It worked like this: she and Pop and Treppie had to give Lambert something, and she and Lambert and Pop would give Treppie something, and then Lambert and Pop and Treppie had to give her something. Then she and Lambert and Treppie could buy something for Pop. And all of them gave Toby a packet of soup bones. Ag shame, why couldn't Gerty also be here this Christmas?

A proper negotiated settlement is what Treppie called it. That's now what he called transparency. And she said yes, transparent, that's the way she's always known Pop to be.

On the Thursday before Christmas they all went to Shoprite. They reckoned Friday would be too busy, but it was busy on Thursday too – so busy you could hardly swing a cat in there, never mind a trolley. So they took baskets instead.

The one whose present was being bought had to stand around at the magazine rack at the entrance with his back to the shelves, and the other three were given fifteen minutes to find something. Those three paid for it at the farthest till and took it back to the car. After that they could come back for the next round.

They worked out beforehand where each one's plastic bag would be kept to avoid a mix-up, 'cause all the bags looked the same. Pop's bag had to go in the bonnet, Lambert's in the dicky, hers behind Pop's seat and Treppie's in the front, at her feet.

Lambert was the youngest, so he had to wait first. She and Pop and Treppie bought him a new pair of shorts and a packet of Gillette blades for his razor. That's when she saw the passion meter. Treppie said it was rubbish, Made in Taiwan, but she said, no, this was really just the thing for Lambert, and in the end they all agreed. For Treppie, she and Pop and Lambert bought a short-sleeve shirt, a golf cap with Michael Jackson written on it and a packet of peppermint humbugs.

Lambert said the humbugs were for the smell, 'cause nowadays Treppie's Klipdrift breath was so bad it was enough to get the lawn-mower started.

For Pop, she and Treppie and Lambert bought a pack of four hankies. White ones with curly blue *P*s in the corners. They also bought him two pairs of socks and a new set of braces. His old ones were so stretched they couldn't hold anything up any more, neither his pants nor his bum, although his bum's been shrinking to nothing lately. And a big tin of Ovaltine, just for him, so he can build up his strength. For strength you need more than braces.

As for her, she knew there was at least one thing she'd find in her bag from Pop and Lambert and Treppie. And she was right, too. It made her happy to see Pop could still make his influence felt.

It was a new housecoat. The same kind Pop always gave her for Christmas. But this time it was a yellow one, golden yellow, her favourite colour. With two packets of cigarettes in one pocket and a surprise in the other – a new cat for the sideboard, to replace the one with no head, which has been like that for more than three years now.

Treppie and Pop and Lambert all stood there and smiled at her. She still doesn't know whose idea it was, but it was a good one.

The best present of the night, by far, was Lambert's passion meter. She wished she could've taken a picture of him as he stood there, reading what it said on the box. Something to do with demonstrating the 'principle' of being hot and how it relieved stress and boredom in just three seconds. 'The perfect gift'.

Lambert hardly had that glass ball with the red stuff in his hands before it began boiling all the way up the little neck, and of course Treppie couldn't keep his mouth shut again. He said, no, instead of messing around with his paintings all day, Lambert should spend his time sitting quietly in the Tedelex so he could cool down a bit before his girl came. Otherwise he was going to crack her radiator, for sure.

But Lambert was so happy about his temperature that he just laughed and forgot about Treppie.

The practice fire also worked out well in the end, and the next day's T-bones were almost okay – they had to be cooked one at a time on a loose piece of bathroom burglar-bar. When Lambert looked for the old Austin's grid to use for the braai, he remembered it was one of the things he'd burnt up in his Guy Fawkes fire.

They had some potatoes and baked beans to go with the meat. Treppie bought a two-litre box of wine for the occasion. Drostdy Hof Stein. They polished it off in two ticks. It made them all so mellow that in the end they didn't cut the watermelon. They went and lay down in the shadow of the fig tree instead, with those five silver balls glittering and twirling among the dark green leaves.

Now Mol finds herself standing in the kitchen. She can't remember why she went there. Oh yes, to throw away the Christmas cards. Ja-nee, things are on the move here in Triomf. She reads on the back of Aribal Catalao's season's greetings:

> It's true! A new force has erupted in the West. For an instant market evaluation or free advice on the sale of your property, phone 477-3029 (home) 837-9669 (bus).

The FOR SALE signs are going up all around them. But the sellers are struggling. The only people who've sold are those two across the road. Their sweetpeas are so pretty. Fort Knox's been on sale for months now. They painted their black iron gates and their other stuff light blue, with everything else in white. Treppie says they look like Triomf's Peace Secretariat now. But blue or not, they're not triumphing, not a damn, he says.

Treppie says if the prices go up after the election they can maybe think of selling, but they must first paint. Then she asked him: sell and go where? He said he felt like going to Ten-Elephants-in-a-Row-Ville. Where was that? she asked, and he said it was in the heart of the country, but she mustn't come and ask him exactly where, 'cause he didn't think he could find a place where elephants were so well behaved.

She said she'd rather stay right here where she was. The rest of them could go if they wanted.

But wait, she'd better go back now. It must be time for the Queen of England.

ALSO JUST HUMAN ⌒

It's a grey day and the Queen has to pose for a portrait. She's dressed up in tassels and fur and she's wearing her crown. She sits dead still. At first, the artist paints only her head. The Queen's favourite little doggy sits at her feet, his eyes shining and his ears pricked. He's looking to see what his lady's doing.

The camera shows the lobes of her ear, the pearls and the soft flesh on her neck, and then, one by one, the precious gems in her crown.

Mol sees her cheeks and her nose and the wrinkles under her eyes. The Queen is powdered and painted for her sitting, but Mol is not fooled by her tight little smile.

Now they're showing how much of her the artist has already painted. Her face and a trimming of white fur around her neck. The likeness is good and the fur also looks genuine.

But the Queen keeps turning the tassels around and around in her lap. And she's rubbing her thumb over the thick, bushy ends. They say she's sad about Windsor burning down. The damage was huge and now the treasures are fewer. They show a picture of the fire.

The Queen looks out of the window. It's raining outside. Further down, far away, the Royal Guard marches around the fountains. The soldiers are small and red, like ants, with stripes down their trousers. They stamp their feet and then they put down their guns. Each one's got a cord on his sleeve and a high, black cap, as if he's in mourning.

'It looks like a rainy day,' says the Queen, and: 'How did this session go?'

But the camera shows she's thinking about something else. About how she went and looked at Windsor, walking in the rain through the rubble. In a yellow plastic hat, black rubber boots and a thin old overcoat. A fireman with a helmet helped her step over the beams. Shame, she's also just human.

'Oh, what a shame. My, what a pity. Alas, history reduced to mere ashes.'

'And now, Molletjie, why you crying?'

It's Pop. He's just woken up.

'I'm crying about the Queen of England and her palace that burnt down.'

'Never mind,' says Pop, 'she's only a queen, and she's got many more.'

17

~

PEACE ON EARTH

To shit is a fine skill, that's for fucken sure. And, if anything, a turd is a work of art. So help him God. Some are water paintings of Sahara sunsets, and others are statues in the park. But a masterpiece of a crap is one that works its way down from your guts in one piece like a tapestry, evenly textured and solidly braided, not too light but also not too dark. With all the colours blending but not so much that it gets boring. Delicate, bright flowers shining against the grass and the white horse resting his horn meekly on the Madonna's lap.

Treppie sits and pages through an old calendar he found among the dykes' newspapers yesterday. There's a broken guitar painted by one Braque, and a rough-looking oke with a bandage around his head. It's a Van Gogh, by Van Gogh, who cut off his own ear, it says at the bottom.

Well bric-à-braque and all a-gogh. The stranger the name the stranger the dog.

He'll take the holy virgin, any time, with her poor old horse and its single horn. All of it in invisible stitching. At least it looks like something. And he doesn't mind the fact that they don't know so nicely any more exactly who made it. If you asked him, a whole swarm of nuns must've sat working on those little flowers till their tongues started hanging out from tiredness and they got completely cross-eyed from concentrating on all the tiny stitches. So that after a while they began to see visions, and that was when they started stitching in the Mother of God in her blue

345

dress, and her weird little horse, on top of the flowery lawn. Mystics can't be choosers. And neither can the constipated. It's a cross and it's a calling. To look at what doesn't exist, and to sit without results – both are ways of escaping the fine-grinder.

And it gives rise to shithouses full of art. God be his witness.

And the world is evidence thereof.

That's why he buggered off from the lounge to come sit here with his newspapers. He doesn't feel he's got the slightest chance of producing a turd today, never mind art, but what the hell. To sit quietly on the toilet is a million times better than listening to those horny Jehovahs preaching to that fucked-up family of his, who sit there like obedient little dogs.

It's not even March and the Jehovahs are into Exodus again. Every year they make the same mistake. They try to get through the whole Bible, piece by piece. But their timing's way out. They start too quickly, and then at the end of the year they have to read Revelation twice in a row, verse for verse, 'cause they hit the end too soon. Many's the time he's told them, spare us the Revelation, dears, we've heard it all before. But before you can say Jack Robinson, the sun's become black as sackcloth of hair and the moon's become as blood, for the umpteenth time.

What they're reading today he already knows off by heart. About how He led them from the land of the Egyptians and took them to a good, wide land, a country flowing with milk and honey, where the Canaanites and the Hittites and the Amorites lived. Then Mol goes 'ites-ites-ites' with that flabby mouth of hers as she tries to say all those names. She thinks it's funny, the old bitch.

The only thing that's different about this year's Exodus is the musical accompaniment. Lambert's sitting there on his crate and playing 'ting-tong, ting-tong' on that thumb-piano of his. As they get to the pests and the plagues, he plays it quicker and quicker. What works on Lambert's tits the most are the frogs that jump from the rivers into everyone's beds. And the tabernacle puts him clean on to a high, about Aaron's robe, with its bells of pure gold and pomegranates on the hem so he'll tinkle and stay alive when he goes before God. Lambert's got a horse-high hard-on for that woman again. Ja, shame, the poor bugger, he must be playing on that thing to stop himself from getting another fit. He looks quite worn out from all the fits he's been having lately. Fits for fuck-all nowadays. Three, four times in January alone. And he won't take his pills either; he says he needs to have all his wits about him so he can fix everything he's still got to fix. He's working himself into a bigger and bigger state as it gets closer to his birthday. But everything he touches, he breaks. This Benade is no Midas, that's for sure.

Like the other day, when he found out the bathroom mirror was too big. A ghost of a millimetre, but still too big. Then of course Lambert tried to cut the mirror himself. Broke the thing to pieces. He told Lambert those pieces were still quite okay for pasting on to the hardboard, but of course he went and lost it again. He took a hammer and smashed those pieces one by one until there was nothing left but grit. So now he sits there and plays a tune without end, for the sake of his fits, for the pillar of cloud and the Red Sea and the bitter waters of Marah. 'Pe-ting, pe-teng, pe-tong.'

So he can't bear the sight of Lambert either.

Not to mention Pop. He sits there with his fly gaping 'cause the buttons that Mol sewed on have all come off again and Pop keeps losing his safety pin. The trouble started early this morning when Pop was shoving his shirt and vest into his pants so he could cover his shame, as he puts it. Mol kept pointing there with her finger. Then he, Treppie, asked them if they thought they'd just been kicked out of paradise or something, and if they reckoned their shame sticking out all the time was likely to bother anyone.

He actually just said that to cheer them up a bit after last night. It was Saturday and the grass had to be cut in the middle of the night again, and there was almost another fuck-around with the people next door.

But then Pop suddenly decided to get difficult, and he let rip right there in the passageway.

Didn't he, Treppie, know that death was the biggest shame of all, and that nothing whatsoever could cover it up? Just look, he said, raising his eyes to the ceiling of the passageway, just look at the state in which he would have to meet his maker – with empty hands and not a single button on his fly. And surely it wasn't asking too much that your shirt at least cover your shame while you were still alive? That was the least a person could do, he said. And, he said, the ones who survived him had better make sure he got washed decently and laid out nicely for his final journey to the pearly gates.

Pop's been making these heavy speeches lately, at the funniest times and in the strangest places. Like this one, in the middle of the passageway, on an empty stomach. Or in Shoprite. Like when he started giving the baked beans in tomato sauce a sermon the other day.

He was looking everywhere for Pop and he couldn't understand where he'd got to – all they needed was dog food. He found him standing in front of the specials shelf. That day it was baked beans.

You beans, Pop said, you might fancy yourself in your tomato sauce. But I say unto you, let someone just add some pigfat and then you'll be worth bugger-all. 'Cause it's all just a matter of pigfat and pulses. Which means it's all about nothing. Poof! The next thing you know, someone farts, and then someone else says sis, what's that smell, and then that's it, you're finished. Nothing! Finished, out, gone! Pffft! No one, but no one can escape this trinity of beans, farts and death. Amen.

Not bad, not bad at all. He didn't catch everything Pop said, just a word here and there, but from what he could make out it sounded nice and sharp.

What he didn't like was Pop's face and Pop's voice. Pop didn't laugh and he didn't smile, and his voice sounded like something rattling in the wind. He sounded completely different from the way he, Treppie, would've sounded if he'd suddenly started giving the beans a talking to. And God knows, he preaches a lot, whether his audience is on special or not. But it's always a game. This speech of Pop's was different. It wasn't a game. 'Cause the next thing Pop went and swept those beans right off the specials shelf. First he swept them off the top two racks, with his right arm to the one side and his left arm to the other. Then he put his foot to the tins on the bottom rack. They went crashing far and wide. It was so bad he had to drag Pop to the car kicking and screaming. You would've sworn it was Lambert carrying on like that, not Pop. Or even him, Treppie, 'cause he gets unhinged pretty bad himself sometimes. But Pop's a softie, never allows an angry word to pass his lips. Yet here he was lecturing at the beans. Kicking tins around in Shoprite and swearing his head off. Not that he was completely sober, either. The two of them had thrown back a couple earlier that afternoon, but most of the time the Klipdrift just makes Pop sleepy. And wine makes him silly. He'd never seen Pop go off the rails like that before.

When they got home, he sat Pop down in his chair and switched on the TV full-blast, so Pop could fall asleep. Then he went and told Mol what happened.

It was Lambert, she said. Pop was worried about Lambert going backwards before he even started going forwards. And it broke his heart that things always seemed to go like this with the Benades. Generation upon generation. Lambert wouldn't even have a generation to come after him. What would happen to him one day when the rest of them kicked the bucket?

Well, yes, that's surely enough to make anyone want to preach to the beans.

He, for one, really doesn't want to be around the day Lambert finds himself all alone in the world, without any children he can call his own. The day he has to make a polony sandwich on his own. Or mow the lawn.

In January alone, that postbox came off three times. And every time it happened, the whole lot of them had to jump to attention, or else. Then Lambert lifted all the loose blocks from the parquet floor, even the ones that were just half-way or quarter-way loose. Dug them out with a screwdriver. He said he wanted to sand the things underneath so they'd stick properly the next time, once and for all, but then he made another fire and burnt the lot of them. Now the passage is full of potholes and everyone's feet keep catching. Now it's not just Lambert who suffers from the falling sickness here in Martha Street.

Take Mol. She tries to get into the kitchen with her Shoprite bags, but she's down before she can get past the kitchen door. Then it's just plastic bags all over the passage. Or Pop. He tries to switch off the TV after the peace song, but he trips over his own two feet and knocks his head against the sideboard. Then the sideboard falls off its brick. And the cat off the sideboard. Now they've got a headless cat again. Some things never change.

Flossie stands out here in the back like a beetle without its shell. At least her wheels are on again. Now Lambert's talking about using not one, but two cars when the shit starts flying. He reckons that he and his girl are going to ride in front, in Flossie, with no roof and no doors, hair blowing in the wind. He, Treppie, and Mol and Pop must follow, in Molletjie. Lambert says they've got more chance of getting to the border with two cars than with one. The one must be a travelling spare part for the other, in case of a breakdown. That's what he says.

Which one for which one, he can't say.

Sounds more like a travelling disaster, if you ask him. He's already told Lambert, travelling under any circumstances is really looking for shit, let alone in times like these with loose bullets and things flying all over the place. All you do is expose yourself. As if you're not exposed enough as it is, with your soft human skin and its holes for seeing and smelling and tasting and farting – that's if you're lucky enough still to do all those things. And with your two little legs and their forward-facing feet, and your hands each with their five little twigs. Always trying to grab on to things in the void here in front of you, never knowing what's coming next. Or what's likely to trip you up.

All the more reason for sitting quietly and waiting for the perfect shit. Reading helps. Not the world's headlines, and not the main cats' moves, either. That's fucken boring. What he looks for are all those odd little fuck-ups in the lives of the underdogs. If it proves one thing, it's that the Benades aren't alone in the world. They're not the only ones who've turned out funny.

Like the story about the spinster and her goldfish. It was winter in England and it was so cold those fish were about to freeze. So she put the goldfish bowl on top of the heater to warm them up, but then she went out and clean forgot about the fish. When she came back they were all over the floor. The bowl had burst. The biggest one, whose name was Jonah, was still moving around on the carpet. She gave him the kiss of life, blowing into his mouth and gills, but nothing could bring him back to life again. So she swallowed him whole, so she could share in her little fish for life ever after.

The only conclusion he can draw from this story is that small fry always land up in the bellies of bigger things. Makes no difference if it's people or fish.

Now that kind of story really gets his guts moving. Maybe something will still happen here today.

And what else? The story about two newly-weds who wanted to show some guests their engagement video. Made by the groom and his friend, the best man. That was in America. They were still standing there with their mouths full of wedding cake when the best man started screwing a pit bull terrier on the video. And the groom was holding the dog down by its head, 'cause a dog won't just stand still for something like that. Oops! Wrong video. The bride flipped so bad she's still in the loony-bin today. That accomplice and his best man are now smitten with remorse. They go to the loony-bin every day with a bunch of white roses for the flipped-out bride.

He doesn't even want to start drawing conclusions about that Dog-Day Wedding. Too many of them.

In Harare, he reads, the main telephone exchange is so full of cockroaches no one can get through any more. In India, Kentucky Fried Chicken's going bankrupt 'cause the coolies' chickens are so thin the Colonel's secret chicken batter won't take on those oriental budgies. Never mind the mudslide in the mining town of Harmony. This time he just hopes they'll give that place its rightful name – No-Leg-to-Stand-On or Slip-'n-'Slide or something like that.

So, all in all, the Benades haven't got too much to complain about. That's just the way things go in this world. In-out, on-off, here-there, dirty-clean, dog-dog. Two of each kind in the ark. One continuous two-stroke activity. And so everyone buggers along, living it up, killing time. From the days of the Israelites already.

Take the piece the Jehovah woman was reading just now about the tabernacle's candlestick. God knows, those desert wankers had lots of free time on their hands! That candlestick thing was so full of bowls and knobs and flowers, totally excessive if you remember a candlestick is actually meant for putting candles in, for light. Six arms, three on each side, and three bowls made like unto almonds on the one arm, plus a bud and a flower. And on the other arm three bowls, plus a bud and a flower. Etfuckencetera. And under each arm as well, and on the candlestick, four bowls made like unto almonds, with their knobs and their flowers. All of it one 'beaten work' of 'pure gold'. And then there were still all those curtains and things, too. Just loops and tassels wherever you look. It's as if the poor fuckers thought decorations and embroidery could save your soul.

He'll put his head on a block that redemption is granted to the idle. To those who do completely fuck-all, with an open mind about the comings and the goings. But that's high-powered stuff. You have to have your wits about you for that. Who's he anyway to try going big on bugger-all? So he chooses the lesser of the two evils, and that boils down to shit-stirring. Not that his little bit of shit amounts to 'beaten work' of 'pure gold', but it's better than nothing. Now and again it's Quality Street shit and that's the best he can hope for. For an oke like him, sitting in a place like Triomf, it's quite good enough. 'Cause to tell the honest truth, Triomf doesn't even have the redeeming features of a desert. It's just a dump. Like the rest of Jo'burg, mind you.

But it feels to him like he's the only one of them who actually clicks this little fact. One by one they trot like sheep after the fire in the cloud. And this fucken sheep-attitude comes a long way in his family.

Like that time all the wagons came through Fordsburg. That was in '38. His mother still made little bonnets for herself and Molletjie just for the occasion. Genuine Voortrekker bonnets with big flaps in front. Tight around the neck.

That Solly-Jew who did the organising for them at the clothing factories also told them they were mothers of the nation. He told them they were made of the same steel as their descendants who'd trekked over the Drakensberg on bare feet. Clever fucken Jew, that. But of course he had his own Communist plans for them. He just used the regular story that they all knew. Everyone always has plans for them, some or other story.

They've always been in some fucken person's plan or story or horizon or background or adventure. Without ever wanting to be in it, or at least without him ever wanting to be in it.

Pop, for example, was completely into that '38 story. But he was soft in the head even then. They recruited him in the yard at their house in Vrededorp. Made him buy a little waistcoat with a silly white scarf to put around his neck for when the wagons came by. And a hat with the brim turned up on one side. Old Mol still had to go and buy it from the coolies. Pop really fancied himself in those clothes. He spent hours posing in front of the mirror. After a while he even had chicken feathers in the hatband. But he, Treppie, wanted nothing to do with it, even though he was only ten. That was after Old Pop had beaten him to a pulp in the train that time and he didn't speak to anyone for years on end. Soon afterwards, Old Pop hanged himself. Then he started talking again, but he still didn't want to sing along when they sang 'God of Jacob' and 'Afrikaners, children of the soil', which they had to sing all the time in school in those days. Not his scene, that. If ever there was wallpaper, if ever you wanted interior decoration, that was it.

And there they walked down Fordsburg's Main Street, cracking their whips! Whips with leather knots on the ends that echoed 'ka-thack!' among the houses. For crying in a bucket! And the Afrikaner bulls were shitting non-stop – Fordsburg's Main Street was strewn with shit and the dogs were going berserk from all the strange smells and the commotion. One of those dogs got between the legs of the oxen. He was kicked to death on the spot. Not a good day for a dog. And no one even bothered to pick up the poor thing. He just lay there in the road. Everyone hypnotised by the wagons. High on the Great Trek.

The names of those wagons took the biscuit. Each one more 'symbolic' than the next. That was the day he learnt you can make any fucken thing you like 'symbolic', from a pisspot to a postbox. It just depends whether you've got enough power. Then you can even win an election with a symbolic pisspot. Or a hosepipe or a wheelbarrow or a monkey wrench. It's all in the mind, anyway.

One wagon was called The Concentration-Camp Nurse. It had a tent pitched on top with its flap thrown open so you could see inside, and there, in the tent, sat the nurse, wearing a black dress buttoned up to the neck, her hair pulled into a tight bun. Her face was powdered completely white, with black rings painted under her eyes and rows of wrinkles drawn on her forehead. On her lap lay a child pretending to be sick unto death. He was made up all purple and yellow so he'd look ghastly and mortally ill. Next to them was an enamel basin for the fake water, and every now and again, when people looked into the tent, the nurse would dip a rag into that fake water and wipe that child acting half-dead on his powdered forehead. Except she couldn't really wipe his forehead 'cause then she'd wipe off the make-up and the whole scene about the terrible suffering of women and children in the camps would go to glory. So she just dabbed at the air above the child's forehead.

Now if that's symbolic then it's really very silly. That's what he thought then, and that's what he still thinks now. People mustn't try pulling that kind of crap on him. About Jopie Fourie and Racheltjie de Beer and Johanna van der Merwe.

Johanna was also there, with her twenty-one assegai wounds, which you could count, one by one. Big red spots painted all over her body. All she needed next to those 'wounds' were some numbers, one to twenty-one in koki pen.

He remembers how that Johanna winked at Pop, with her twenty-one polka dots and all. She'd been placed on a bier, and she lay on her back, with her bonnet and her Voortrekker-dress lying under the wagon's hood. The flap was left open so you could see her nicely. The heroine, resting at peace after the battle.

And then, just as Pop ducked under the wagon to smear some grease on his scarf – that was the big thing for the little boys that day, getting fake Voortrekker grease on their clothes – just as he did that, she winked and asked him if he didn't want to take a ride to keep her company. It was so boring lying there on her back in state, under that canopy.

Pop told that story for years afterwards, over and over again. To this day he still tells it. He says he'll never forget how he rode with Johanna and her assegai wounds in the wagon. He didn't ask her what her real name was, but he rode along all the way to Braamfontein. When they saw people looking into the tent, Pop made as if he was a young Voortrekker grieving over his beloved, with his head on her chest. That was something he did with great pleasure, he said, 'cause she was 'a beautiful woman in the prime of her life'. That's how Pop always tells the story. And what a fluke shot it was that the kaffirs didn't stab her in her lovely face. That's also what Pop used to say.

If you ask him, Pop's a sucker for wallpaper. Nowadays it's on TV instead of wagons, but nothing has changed about the way Pop sees life. Or how he wants to see life. Ever since the day Pop gave the baked beans a talking to, he's been getting more and more difficult. The other day he even went and bought Mol a rose bush. Just imagine it – a rose bush with two yellow roses. He drove specially to the nursery just to get it, to the larnies' nursery in Jan Smuts Avenue. He saw they had cheap roses there on special. Keith Kirsten's nursery. Going to a place like that was quite a business, he said, but he didn't mind how far he had to drive as long as it made Mol happy.

He, Treppie, didn't go. He was at the Chinese. Pop took Lambert with him, and Lambert told them afterwards that people were staring at them so much there among the plants, like they were from Mars or something, that he just went and sat in the car. Pop stayed away for a long time. He was looking for a Whisky Mac. He said he wouldn't come back before he'd found one. When he did get back, he had a rose bush in his arms and he was smiling from ear to ear. Got that rose completely for nothing, he said. It wasn't a Whisky Mac. Keithy Boy had never in his life heard of such a thing. But it didn't matter. The colour was right.

The people at the nursery wanted him out of there, he said, so they said here, take it and leave. And then of course it was a whole palaver again, 'cause Mol started crying when she saw that rose bush. It was 17 January, her birthday. Pop had remembered it for the first time in ten years.

If you ask him, Mol will say any day in January is her birthday. Their IDs have been locked away in the sideboard for so long now that none of them remembers exactly when their birthday is. They know more or less.

Everyone except Lambert, who knows exactly. Twenty-sixth April. And that's something none of them must ever forget, otherwise there's shit to play. But they know their own birthdays only by month. His birthday is sometime in November, and Pop's is in May. It's a long time since they did anything about it.

Then of course that rose bush needed planting, but Pop was so tired he couldn't lift a finger. Lambert said when he dug holes it was for petrol, not flowers. So Mol got on to his case. He, Treppie, must plant the rose bush. Pop even had a list of instructions from Keith-Buy-Now-Flower-Later about how to make holes for rose bushes. This wide, this deep, then you mix this, that and the other into the ground, with so much water and with this spray for that insect and he didn't know what else. He told Mol this rose bush would bring her nothing but misery. And then she really started crying.

It's almost a month now, and that rose bush still hasn't been planted. He sees Mol watering it every morning in its black plastic. It's getting yellow underneath. Why she doesn't just dig the bladdy thing into the ground somewhere he doesn't know. She's got two hands of her own, after all. When she gets into the mood, she walks around the yard with that rose bush all day long, asking everyone where must she plant it, in heaven's name, where?

Pop says in front, next to the postbox. Lambert says no, at the back, next to the fig tree. That's the only other plant in the yard. He, Treppie, says nowhere. Toby pees all over the place and she should wait until Toby's also in heaven before she starts fiddling with roses.

Then Mol just wants to start crying all over again. The older she gets, the more she cries. It makes him feel like his guts are tied up in knots. Then he spins her a lot of crap about how roses never die in heaven, especially not from dog-piss, and how the heavenly roses have different colours and fragrances, all on the same bush. The more the divine dogs pee on them, the more colours and fragrances they get. He embroiders one never-ending story for her until she shuts up and gets that silly smile on her face again. Then she puts the rose down in the shadow of the kitchen door, still in its plastic.

And that's where it's still standing, today, among all the stuff Lambert carries in and out of the house all the time as he tries to get through his list. So much rubbish. Next to the rose bush on the one side lies the bathroom cabinet, the one Lambert ripped right off the wall the other day when the mirror didn't fit. And next to that, a few odd planks Lambert wants to use for a bigger and better bathroom cabinet. Always wants to be bigger and better, that's Lambert for you. On this side of the kitchen, three used-up Dogmor tins and a crate of empties. And on the other side, three old GTX tins and a box of empty Klipdrift bottles. Also very symbolic, if you ask him, of how they struggle by the sweat of their brows to dot the 'i's and cross the 't's and get the little mirror mirroring on the wall. Then there's Lambert's old bed, with its imploded legs and its exploded stuffing, pushed up against the other wall. He wants to fix it, he says. And the bathroom's burglar-bars, which didn't want to fit so nicely after they'd used them to braai their T-bones at Christmas. Lambert says they got twisted in the heat, so now he wants to bend them straight again. Just proves his point, it's never too late to build a tabernacle.

The latest is that he wants to paint the house. Now it looks like 127 Martha Street has to be painted snow white for the fucker's birthday. And as the devil would have it, they found a letter in the postbox about painting houses the other day, with a golden stamp in the middle and a number under the stamp. At the bottom of the letter they found a list of numbers, including their own, which meant they could have three thousand rand worth of free paint – a little present from Wonder Wall for the New Year. That's what Lambert read there. And then he started going on and on about the paint until Pop filled in their address and everything to say yes, please, they'd be happy to accept the free paint. Lambert posted it the same day, like the letter said he must. He, Treppie, didn't even get to see it. He was at the Chinese. They only told him about it later, and then he asked them if they'd read the fine print. This was going to cause shit. But they didn't even know what fine print meant. Fat lot they know! Then, just a few days later, the shit arrived in the form of a little man in a striped shirt and a tie full of flowers. He measured the house with a little wheel that he pushed around by a handle. The ceilings too. He asked for a ladder and he climbed on to the roof, measuring: 'katarra! katarra!' all over the corrugated sheets. Pop and Mol and Lambert were at Shoprite, and so there he sat, all alone. Him and the man and his little wheel with its little meter, measuring their house inside, outside and on top.

The man took out his Wonder Wall letter and showed him the signature on the dotted line. He asked if Treppie knew whose signature it was. That's when he should've said, no, he didn't. But the man looked him straight in the face and so he said, yes, it was his brother's signature. The man said, no well, fine. If it was a close relation, then he, Treppie, could sign these other papers while his brother was out. The man pulled out a long paper with three carbon copies, all of them so full of fine print it would've taken three days to read. Please just sign, here, here and here, he said. It was a mere formality, just to say yes, they confirmed they wanted free paint to the value of three thousand rand. He told the man he should leave one of those carbon copies behind so his brother could go through it, but the man was already halfway out the door and he said the carbon would come when they delivered the paint. It would take a month or two, 'cause they had so many pledges they couldn't keep up. Next thing, whoosh, he was gone in his Uno.

Pledges, he thought, but what had they actually pledged? They won some paint with the right number under the gold stamp. That was all. Why would you want to pledge anything if you'd won something? Unless it was your faith in Wonder Wall. He could swear there was a fucken snag of sorts somewhere.

To tell the truth, that wasn't the worst of it. What made him feel really sad were all those thousands of metres the man clocked up on his little wheel. All of it painted white, pure white, without a trace of their comings or goings.

He looks at the bathroom. The man measured in here too. It would make for a bit of an unsociable shit if paint was the only thing you could smell around here. He knows every little mark and crack in this room. In fact, if there's one room in this house he can call his own, it's the toilet. This is where he catches his breath, and this is where he figures out what's what and who's next. It's the place where he scratches the monkey for fleas, as Pop always says when he stays inside for so long. Well, whether or not it's fleas he doesn't know, all he knows is that it's a necessity.

Treppie looks around in the bathroom. There's the soft rubber tube they use for siphoning petrol on a nail behind the door. Their toothbrushes, warped and lopsided, in the little blue plastic glass on the shelf. His and Pop's and Lambert's razors, on the window ledge. And Mol's hairbrush, so full of caked, grey hair you almost can't see the brush any more. Three bent-open hairpins. Two buttons.

In the same way, you'll find their personal effects all over the house. Their spit and their blood and their breath. And paw marks, all over the walls.

Yellow afternoon light shines through the bathroom's frosted window, making a dull spot of light on the wall. Just there, someone's oily hand touched the wall. Must've been Lambert. King Kong was here.

What the hell, what will be, will be. From high-gloss to matt-finish in the space of a single lifetime. Maybe it's also not such a bad thing, after all. With every face-lift you lose something, but what have they got to lose in any case? Not exactly what you'd call museum pieces. Just the collected works of wear and tear. The little bits of baggage from the Benades' Great Trek, full of dirty marks. Burnt black, caked up, flopped out, moth-eaten, unstitched, sticky and rusted, with dog-hair on everything too.

Not quite wallpaper, this. And by no means a tabernacle. Just the blues of 127 Martha Street. The fine print of fuck-all. The dregs of Triomf!

Would you believe it! And he's sober as a judge. His guts must be full of gas. At least it's a case of self-generated intoxication. Not like the hot air and the fine-tuning that gives Pop his kicks.

Take for example how Pop and Mol fell, hook, line and sinker, for Malan's story in '48. Another Great Trek story. This time it was on the wireless. Old Mol was no longer with them. Just the three of them sitting around the kitchen table in Vrededorp. He still remembers saying blah-blah-blah when that flat-mouthed old toad in a hat began croaking about the election. About how his party, the 'Purified' National Party, was depending on everyone to bring the Great Trek to its logical 'conclusion'.

Pure, undiluted shit! How his party would lead them through this new Great Trek, through all its ditches and drifts and its risks and dangers. And how his party would fend off every threat, how it would destroy the enemies at the Blood River of the labour market, fighting to the bitter end. Because this time it wasn't a Great Trek upcountry to escape the English, he said, this time it was the rural Afrikaner's Great Trek to the cities, and for those who were already there, the poor and the reviled, it was the Great Trek to the higher professions and big capital.

Come again, he said. It was a Great Trek back under the English yoke. Only now the yoke had a drill-bit and its name was Anglo. But Pop and Mol told him he must shuddup, they wanted to listen.

How they listen, if anything gets said about the Great Trek, the Promised Land, Everyone-Together-Through-Thick-And-Thin. How they listen!

Whether that place is full of milk and honey or full of petrol and oil and bricks and mine dumps, it makes no difference. And if, on top of it all, the voice promising everything sounds like a preacher, then they're all ears. Fired up. Ready for take-off.

That's why Mol thinks that Niehaus chappy from the ANC with his bedroom eyes is such a together little boykie. She says he reminds her a lot of Malan. In that case, he tells her, she should vote for the ANC, but she says not a damn will she vote for the kaffirs. Then he asks her, but what about Niehaus, he's a white oke? In that case, she says, maybe she will vote for the ANC after all, 'cause Niehaus looks to her like the kind of leader you can follow with complete trust to the bitter end. What's more, he looks like a man who'd follow his own leaders to the bitter end, come hell or high water, and that's enough for her. Then it feels like the National Party.

Ja, the poor fools, it *feels* like. He wonders if the leaders of that party feel like anything to themselves, never mind National. When he tries to imagine what they feel like, he detects the stirrings of a bowel movement. And that's a fucken compliment, 'cause they're not even worth a good shit. Liars and thieves with their hands on their hearts. The plural lying party, here a coup, there a coup, meanwhile they're cooped up with their own kind all the time, grabbing each other's balls. State ball. A dance for this one and a dance for that one. Here a gun, there a prayer. Excuse me while I waltz all the way to the Nobel Prize.

Now it's supposed to be 'New' National Party. New be damned. Turning their own 'foreign' partners back into internal affairs, digging out the bombs they planted themselves, firing their own big shots, and then state enemy number one becomes the state's redeeming partner. Teach the Bushmen aerobics, give the Koevoets cabbages to plant. And they call it new! It's not new, it's the same old rubbish recycled under a new name. But the rubbish itself is a brandless substance. Nameless horror in sackcloth of hair, if you ask him.

That's why he egged Lambert on to start throwing stones at those two new NPs the other day. They thought they could come here again with their crap in the middle of the day. Lambert was digging his petrol cellar, so he had lots of ammunition to hand. Old Sof'town's bricks for stoning the new NPs. He hopes that was now a permanent removal. Those boy scouts couldn't get away from here fast enough, ducking all the way. It's a good thing they weren't NPs from the old school, 'cause they would've stood their ground and took it like men. Good old times. Now they duck for a living. He's seen on TV how things are going in the townships. That's where they've learnt to become such experts in the art of ducking. Think they can barge in wherever they like. And now they scheme they're suddenly good enough for the red-carpet treatment. Long live the Ducking Party. And so the pendulum swings. If FW learns the art of ducking in Meadowlands, then you can be sure old Meddlebones is coming back to Triomf to reminisce. It's taken a long time, but now he, Treppie, has finally clicked this mathematics of history.

So when Mol let out a yelp one day last November, and called them to come see, Mandela was driving down the road in an open car, but he'd turned white overnight and he was wearing a black dress, he, Treppie, knew exactly who it was. And there stood the old dog-collar, in a black limousine, with a whole bunch of other Roman doggos in red and purple dresses in the cars behind him. They were smiling so much you saw nothing but teeth. He recognised him by his hair, still shaved close like in the old days when he used to run around here trying to save what there was to be saved. But now he was very old. He looked like a little powdered peach and he was smiling all the way down memory lane. Pointing here, pointing there with his shaky little hand, like he was sprinkling holy water, with everyone looking where he was pointing. And right at the end of the procession, on an open lorry, rode His Holiness Huddlestone's private band. They were playing full tilt, jolly jiving music on saxophones and penny-whistles and things like that. The whole band was full of old-timers with hanging dewlaps from all the blowing, but they followed their lead player, who was blowing like mad on his little trumpet. AFRICAN JAZZ PIONEERS, it said in stencilled letters on the lorry. That lorry was swaying on its wheels from the way they were pulling and pushing those shiny, long arms on the trombones. 'Viva Kofifi!' one old bloke was shouting. 'You are the captain!' another one called. And then everyone sang a song for that papier mâché captain, standing there in front, pointing over the roofs of Triomf as if they were a tempest-tossed ocean. Was he imagining things, or did he even start liking him? He had the gift of the gab, and if there's one thing you need to survive with a dress and a collar round your neck in this country, then it's being able to talk yourself in or out of anything.

He's still got the man's speech from the newspaper. That was now truly a priceless piece. About the way Sophiatown used to look in the old days, how it was a place you could 'look up to', with its 'grey-blue haze' of fire smoke 'against a saffron sky'. And the little red-roofed houses on top of each other, how it always made him think of Italy, and the 'shapely blue gum trees' all over the place. There you have it! But the closing line was the best, about the Church of Christ the King on the hill, its steeple visible from afar, north-south-east-west, 'riding like a great ship'. Now there's a tapestry for you. Stitched together with lovely words.

That's his fucken end, this endless fucking with words. In this country everything's got a name which is actually something else's name. Pik Botha, Vleis Visagie, Slang van Zyl, Brood van Heerden. And just look at their own names. Pop's truly never had any pop in him. And Mol can try as much as she likes, she'll never push up a molehill. And if one considers that her real name is Martha, one could dub her Martha

Street's presently serving Martha. But that's an altogether different kind of service and a different kind of Martha from the story in the Bible that the Jehovahs always want to read. Of all of them, only Lambert's name sounds like something. Lambertus Benade. It sounds like an ambassador or someone like that, with a carnation in his buttonhole. But anyone can see that's more than a misnomer, it's a fucken miscarriage. His own name is a total fuck-up. Nothing left of Martinus, and according to Mol he should rather have been named Judas Iscariot. That's also okay. Where would her soul have been without Judas, he asks her.

That's not even to mention their dogs, who end up being named after streets. Toby and Gerty. He read somewhere that the streets here in Triomf were named after the children of the man who used to own the farm on which Sophiatown was built. Bertha and Toby and Gerty and Edith. And Sophia was supposed to have been the man's wife. Then, just for the hell of it, he checked in the *Britannica,* and it said something about Holy Sophia being the name of a church in Turkey with a dome that looked like heaven.

For shitting through an icing tube, where will it all end? The whole world is just names and nothing is what it is and everything's what it's not, it's all in the mind! And the mind's a bottomless pit.

Legion as the Gadarene swine are the names of things, and then they all fall down in droves into that steep place, one on top of the other. A loose scrum in the depths. Not worth the breath it takes to utter them, never mind the paper they're written on.

Treppie kicks the newspapers away. He throws them around a few at a time. Papers fly all over the bathroom. Fly away, Peter, fly away, Paul!

He's fed up with the whole business, fed up, sick and tired of it all. Words swim before his eyes. Names whirl around in his head.

He folds the newspapers double and throws them up against the ceiling. 'Kaboof! Kaboof!'

The Freedom Front's got lead in its head. Hells bells in the house of Shell. And Goldstone's teeth are but few. See how the train rides, how the train rides, all aboard the gravy train. Civil Co-operaton Chowder.

Consensus-Atlantis-hortus-conclusus. The apple of his father's eye, his mother's darling, Sophia-Maria-Maryna, pretty girls in a row.

Noises start coming from his body. Hark the mighty roars. They hold much promise.

He feels his guts moving. Swing low, sweet chariot. Blessed is the stool's motion, happy in its peals, its psalms to the end of all meals. He tears the newspaper into small pieces. He's making confetti. Triomf, Triomf, here comes the bride, big, fat and wide.

He wipes his arse. Truly, when this happens, it feels like the seventh day, the day of rest. Emptied and unburdened. Everything well. Peace on earth.

18

~

TRIOMF TRIALS

FAMILY BIBLE ~

Mol sits in her chair, sewing the middle button back on to her housecoat. The old button got lost, so she's using one of Pop's shirt-buttons that she found in the bathroom cabinet. It's smaller, which means she'll have to close up the buttonhole on the one side. But she doesn't mind, it keeps her busy. When she's not busy, she worries too much.

Lambert hasn't set foot out of his den for three days now. Only a few minutes ago she went and took a peek at him. They told her she mustn't bother him.

He's sitting there with clean hands in front of his work bench, on a straight-backed chair that he fixed himself. He's studying the refrigeration book. From first page to last. With a pencil in his hand and a Croxley exercise book. The two mugs of Frisco that Pop put down next to him look like they're cold, and the ants are eating his polony sandwich.

'He still hasn't eaten or drunk a thing,' says Pop, coming back from the den and sitting down in his chair next to her.

It's Treppie's book, which he lent Lambert after Pop begged him, on his hands and knees, in God's name, to please help out a bit with Lambert.

If Lambert didn't get those two fridges in his den up and running before his birthday, Pop said, then Treppie would still live to see the most terrible butchery with long knives ever seen in the long history of the Benades.

At first, Treppie was completely bloody minded.

Lambert would never use a sharp object, he said. Pop's knowledge of human nature was failing him. Lambert was the kind of person who would definitely use a blunt instrument.

And sometimes, he said, as in the case of seals who bred too much, maybe that was the best thing for an environment's balance.

How a thing like the environment could have trouble with its balance, like a tightrope walker, is beyond her. When she asked Treppie, he said balance wasn't just a circus trick, it was the trick of life itself, except the Benades had never yet got the hang of it. But it was never too late to learn.

In fact, he said, Lambert should consider a general culling of the Triomf population while he was at it with his blunt instrument. The blunter the better, he said, like a pestle in a mortar, to stamp some national blood into the soil. A little blood would do the soil in Triomf no end of good, 'cause nothing exhausted a place like old bricks.

Pop begged and pleaded. It was so bad he even called up the memory of Old Pop after a while. Right here in the lounge. Pop went down on his knees, spreading out his arms with a bottle of Klipdrift in one hand. Right in front of the TV, like he wanted to embrace the Big One.

Was it Old Pop's lost and homeless spirit tormenting them like this, year in and year out? he asked. Was it because Treppie had never forgiven Old Pop for that terrible hiding? Well, no one's ever told her how you're supposed to talk to a ghost, but Pop sounded like he knew how, 'cause he came out with some terribly high-flown language.

Oh troubled spirit, Pop said, his eyes rolling in his head, wilt thou not have mercy on us, thou who lurkest in the dark corners of empty coal trucks. And as thou holdest thy hand on thy neck, where death lashed thee, wilt thou not, we beseech thee, if a sacrifice is brought in the year of Our Lord, 1994, soften thy heart towards us? A sacrifice by the same child who since his eighth year hath refused to speak to thee and given thee no place in his heart whatsoever.

It was never too late, Pop said, for a living person to reconcile himself with a spirit who couldn't come to rest because he was upset about that person.

Well, after that Treppie's mouth dried up completely and he went and sat in his room behind a closed door for days on end.

Then it was suddenly so quiet in the lounge that she sat in her chair with nothing but fear in her heart. You could say she sat for days on end, 'cause the only time she ever got up was to give her rose some water, or to put her ear to Pop's mouth to see if he was still breathing. She'd once heard about people who sink into a state of near-death, and that's exactly what Pop looked like. It was from getting so worked up and tired and drinking three times more Klipdrift than he was used to. When she held that old piece of mirror to his mouth she could see only the merest wisp of breath. It was the last piece, the one she hid in her housecoat pocket when she saw Lambert was about to smash the new mirror to pieces.

Never before had there been such deathly quiet in the lounge. It felt eerie, sitting in silence like that.

It was also very quiet at the back, but that was a different kind of silence.

Every now and again terrible bangs or shots went off, with big chunks of quiet inbetween. Or things fell over so hard all the walls in the house started shaking.

It was almost like a big, wild thing was busy waking up in his cage after being shot with a dart, like those darts they shoot into the backsides of rhinoceroses when they're put to sleep.

The problem was, she knew Lambert didn't have a dart in his backside, and if something didn't happen fast he was going to break out of his cage and come get them all, one by one, tearing them up piece by piece until there was nothing left.

So, under the circumstances, it was like mercy from above when Treppie came out of his room with his thick refrigeration book in both hands, looking terribly formal and serious.

Treppie's treated that book like the holy scripture all his life. He bought it when they first moved to Triomf, when he still had plans to get rich from fridges.

No one was allowed to look in that book and no one except him could touch it. If Pop or Lambert or a customer wanted to know something about fridges, then Treppie would go into his room and, behind closed doors, look in his book. He'd come out a bit later and tell them exactly what the book said, on page this or page that, about this, that, or the other thing.

There Treppie stood, with that book in his hands. He said Pop must wake up now so he could go fetch Lambert. He wanted to say what he needed to say in front of witnesses.

It was for everyone's sake, Treppie said, and for the sake of the spirits too.

Pop rose out of his deathly sleep and shuffled like a sleepwalker with eyes that stood stock-still in their sockets, while sickening bangs and crashes came from Lambert's den.

She still thought, ja, there was Pop rising from one kind of death and walking with open eyes into the jaws of another.

Treppie held the book to his chest and stood there with his head cocked to one side so he could hear Pop walking down the passage.

Toby was also in a state. He went and sat in the lounge doorway with pricked ears, shifting his front paws excitedly. First he'd turn round to look at her, and then he'd look at Treppie again, his mouth opening and closing all the time. That Toby was so scared he almost began talking right here in the lounge that day.

Pop came back and sat down in his chair.

'He's coming. Get ready.'

She saw Treppie take the empty Klipdrift bottle by the neck. Pop felt under his chair for the small toolbox, pulling it out in front of his feet, and she took cover behind her chair, holding on to the back-rest. She told Toby he must come stand next to her. Toby came and sat down with his head turned up, as if to say, what now?

And then Lambert entered. He was black with oil and grease, and he had open wounds all over his body. It looked like something had burnt right through his T-shirt. His eyes were swollen and red. His one hand was trembling slightly and his feet looked like they'd been boiled. And he stank to high heaven. It was an odour like burnt hair and pee, along with that sharp, sour smell that floats over from the factories.

'Compressor burn-out,' said Treppie, walking slowly around Lambert with the bottle in one hand and the book held tightly to his chest. Shame, he looked that poor Lambert up and down the way someone would inspect a broken engine in a scrapyard.

'Sour oil,' he said, fanning his nose.

He plucked at the sleeves of Lambert's T-shirt. 'Blown-out windings,' he said.

Then he cupped his hand behind his ear and put his head to Lambert's stomach, as if he was listening to the sound of his insides. Lambert just stood there, dead still, with those mad eyes of his.

'Rattles and hums and harmonic vibrations,' Treppie said.

Then Treppie knocked himself a shot on the head with the bottle and rolled his eyes. He looked very strange, like he was on stage and he wanted to start crying or something.

'Not a muffler in sight,' he said. 'Not on the intake stroke, nor on the exhaust. No gas, no pressure, bugger-all.' And he looked at her and Pop as if they were mechanics who knew exactly what he was talking about.

'How do you save a fridge,' Treppie asked, 'with a condenser that won't condense and an ice-box without ice? God's own evaporator. One big heavenly leak.'

But, he said, there was always hope.

'There's still hope, Lambert, there's still hope,' he said, tapping his book with his fingers.

Lambert just stood there, saying nothing. He went completely dumb when he saw that book. He'd heard a lot about it, but he'd never been allowed anywhere near it.

He even stuck out his hand, the one that was shaking, as if he wanted to touch it.

But Treppie turned away, pressing the book even closer to his chest.

'Uh-uh,' he said, 'first wash handies. Handies and footies, and while you're about it you can wash the rest of you too. Then you must put on some clean clothes.'

Treppie stopped talking and looked around him to see if everyone was listening.

That's when she allowed herself to take another breath, 'cause she saw Treppie was about to make one of his speeches again. And when Treppie starts making speeches, you know he's okay.

'This here is the family Bible. This is where you'll find the writings of the prophets and the law, and everything else you need to inherit the earth, be blessed and live in eternal glory with your Fuchs and your Tedelex. But for that you must first do your catechism, my boy, before you can be accepted into the bosom of the congregation. The congregation of Triumph Electrical Appliances. Without the knowledge of pressure and gas, and without an insight into the temperatures of the high side and the low side, you're not worth a straw. The holy Electrolux be my witness!'

He held the book in front of his face and blew on to it, and then he put it down on the sideboard and wiped his hand over its hard, shiny cover.

He'd give Lambert a week, he said, after which he'd conduct an examination. If Lambert studied properly, to his satisfaction, he'd have a look at those two antiques of Lambert's. 'Then we'll fix them,' he said, 'you and me. So help me God!'

Ag shame, the next thing Lambert's mouth began twitching into a smile, right through those spots of oil, like he wanted to start crying or something. And that smile just got bigger and bigger. He smiled at her and Pop, and then they smiled much better back at him.

Only then did she come out from behind the chair. And Pop shifted the toolbox back under his seat.

'Go wash yourself now,' Pop said to Lambert.

Yes, go take a bath, she also said, not that it worried her whether Lambert bathed or not, but this was a different story.

Treppie suddenly got all concerned about Lambert. No, he said, they must immediately go buy some ointment for those burns of his. It was too late for Prep. They must tell the chemist it was burn-out oil from a fridge. He'd know what ointment to give them. And something for his eyes too, Treppie said. She thought, hell, this was too good to be true, Treppie must be joking. But he saw what she was thinking and he said: 'Honestly, it's no joke. It's chemistry, this.'

* * *

And that's how Lambert came to be treated for his sores. He even got dressings on the worst of the burns. She picked up his dirty clothes outside the bathroom and threw them on to the rubbish heap, just like that. Then she nagged Pop and Treppie until they went to Pep Stores in Ontdekkers to buy him a new T-shirt and a pair of shorts. The only pair they could find were Extra Large, with little black blocks on it.

'This is an expensive round,' Pop still said, 'it's no use buying him shorts if he won't wear them.'

'He will,' said Treppie, 'he'll even chew fucken ladybirds now if you ask him to.'

JESUS' BLOOD NEVER FAILED ME YET ~

In those days of Lambert's studying, Treppie had a funny look on his face. She couldn't make out if he was sad or what it was. It was like he knew what was coming, but he didn't know when. And he knew it was bad, but now it must just come and be done with.

He began to drink even more than usual and by early evening he'd already be singing such sad songs. Hallelujah songs like 'Pass me not, oh gentle Saviour' and others like 'Red River Valley'.

Until one night, when he went into his room and scratched around for the keys to the sideboard's top drawer. He opened the drawer, took out Pop's mouth organ and tried it out, with a hum on the high notes and a hum on the low notes. But the first hum sounded like a pain in the gut, and the second like a pain somewhere lower down. That's what she said to him, but he just gave her one of his looks. He passed the mouth organ over to Pop and asked him to play something. Play what? Pop said, but Treppie wiped his hand over his face and said, anything, anything would do, thanks.

How Pop got on to it was a mystery, but he chose an old tune that the Salvation Army used to play in the streets of Vrededorp. By the time Pop had played the tune three times over, each time more smoothly with more and more notes in their proper places, Treppie began to remember the words and started singing along:

> 'Jesus' blood never failed me yet
> never failed me yet.
> Jesus' blood never failed me yet
> there is one thing I know
> for He loves me so.'

They played that song and sang those words over and over again. The more Treppie remembered the tune and the words, the more trills Pop began coaxing out of the mouth organ. He played low notes like cellos and high notes like trumpets. After a while he played exactly like a harp in an orchestra. It was like the tune of a completely different psalm, but to the same words and the same song that Treppie stuck to. After a while it began to sound like some kind of a classic or something.

That Pop should have so much breath, and so much music left in him, and that Treppie should suddenly sing so much Jesus-stuff took them all by surprise, Pop too. What surprised them even more was that the music was so good, even though lots of Klipdrift had passed through their gills that night, and the mouth organ was so old, with missing notes here and there. After a while Pop and Treppie's eyes began twinkling from making so much music together. Each time the song swung to a new verse they'd look at each other and wink. And then Treppie would raise his part of the tune by half a note, and Pop would catch that half-note clean out of the air, and there they'd go again.

> 'Jesus' blood never failed me yet.'

The next verse they'd take in a minor, and the one after that in a major, and so on, with all kinds of trills and frills as they went along. They'd play the song like a waltz and then faster again, and then like chapel music, and then jolly again.

> '. . . there is one thing I know
> for He loves me so.'

372

They were playing Lambert through his catechism, she thought, they were playing sharp and clear air back into his head, so he could study well. For the fridges. They were singing and playing 'cause the family Bible had changed hands.

That was the fourth night of Lambert's studying.

TICKEY ∼

It's exactly a week tonight since Lambert began his studying. And here he comes now, out of his den and down the passage. All three of them have been waiting here in the lounge. She's told Pop three times already she wants to go sleep, but each time he says, no, she must wait, and Treppie also says she must wait, they're still going to make history here tonight. She doesn't want to miss out on history, so she thought she'd better sit and wait. She's making all her buttonholes smaller, even though there's only one button left. And here he is, at last, standing in the doorway with the fridge book under his arm. It doesn't look like history to her, it looks more like trouble. She gets up and puts on her housecoat.

'Now I'm fully swotted up,' says Lambert. His voice sounds like it's coming from a hole somewhere. He's standing there with his legs slightly apart, swaying a little, like he's leaning into a strong wind. He looks thin in the face and pale and wan, with dark rings under his eyes. She can see scabs and sores all over his body from the acid. He doesn't look so good. But he's acting tough and he's smiling. She smiles a little smile back at him.

'Hell, Lambert, if you'd studied like this at school you'd have gotten far by now, my boy!' Treppie says. Give with the one hand and take with the other.

But she can see nothing will put Lambert off tonight. He made a deal in front of witnesses, and now those witnesses had better stick up for him. She'll do her part, she'll bear witness. He doesn't have to remind her. She buttons up her housecoat in the middle with the new, small button.

'Stick to the point, Treppie,' Pop says in a straight voice here next to her.

373

'Ja, I agree,' she says. 'A promise is a promise, let him have his exam now and be done with it, so he can get his fridges fixed.'

'Fridges that work are another chapter altogether. You two mustn't expect miracles.'

Now Treppie's talking like a preacher. She can see he's about to take off again.

'The only thing I'm glad about,' he says, 'is that for once I'm seeing some real commitment from a Benade. 'Cause that's the one ingredient we've been missing all our lives.'

She nudges Pop. Pop must be strict with Treppie now, before he really gets going.

'Don't start talking rubbish,' Pop says. 'All our lives we've been doing our best with what we were given.' She hears him take a deep breath before carrying on.

'Or with what we think we've got,' he says, ''cause you don't always know what your own possibilities are, and your eyes are not always open to your own talents. Anyone can look right past that kind of thing. It's no one's fault. It's just the way things are.'

Pop looks Treppie up and down. She also looks at him. Up and down.

'And you, of all people, should know what I'm talking about.' Pop looks around to see if he's got everyone's attention.

Dear Lord, Pop mustn't go and overdo it now.

'You, for example, missed the fact that you should've been a clown. Yes, a clown at Boswell Wilkie circus.'

Pop holds up his finger to show he's not yet finished. He must be careful with that finger. He knows what comes of it.

'And don't get me wrong, I mean it as a compliment. I don't mean it in an ugly or funny way.'

Now she must help Pop a bit here. Now he's taking big chances.

'Tickey,' says Mol. 'Not Treppie, Tickey.' They always laugh when she says something. They think she doesn't know how to be funny. Well, she doesn't know much about history, but she knows how to play the fool.

'With a red nose,' says Lambert. His voice sounds a bit better now.

'Yes,' says Pop, 'a clown who laughs and cries at the same thing, so

374

people can never make up their minds. And that's a good thing, 'cause the last thing this world needs are people who keep making up their minds about bugger-all. You have to be patient and take each thing as it comes, good or bad. And, Treppie, my brother—'

She gives him a little kick under the chair. Pop's brain is soft. He does it more and more these days. He forgets his perspective. He mustn't go and lose his perspective now.

'And, Treppie, my man . . .' Pop says. He acts like it was nothing. But she saw Lambert's eyes shifting uneasily when Pop said 'my brother'. It's her end, the idea that Lambert still hasn't realised anything.

'. . . let me just tell you one thing, and this is a piece of wisdom I picked up from you. You taught me this, and it's not the kind of thing a person usually picks up from fridge mechanics.'

Pop's looking at Treppie so hard that Treppie doesn't say a word. There's a sort of shy smile on his face. If you want Treppie in your pocket, just praise him. Ai, old Pop, he's so smart tonight. In his own way.

'It's never too late,' Pop says, 'to recognise the talent you missed and to do something about it.'

Treppie gets up, with his shy smile and all. He tiptoes to his room, holding up his finger to show they must be quiet and wait a bit, he's coming now. As soon as he's closed his door, Pop tells Lambert to sit down. Now she can go and make him a nice mug of sweet coffee and a sandwich, 'cause a person can't do exams on an empty stomach. She says nothing. The air's full of surprises tonight, never mind history.

Mol sits on the stoep in front. She looks at the sparrows pecking the car's hubcaps. They think it's other sparrows, but it's just themselves they see there. They go on and on, peck, peck, peck. After a while they're just about falling over, but still they carry on. Then she says to Toby: 'Fetch!' and he chases the birds away. But they come back again.

There's peace and quiet in the house now that Treppie's helping Lambert with his fridges. It's been more than a week already, thank God. Even Pop's like a new man. He gets up with her in the mornings and they make sandwiches together in the kitchen. Pop takes Lambert and Treppie's sandwiches through to the den, and then he comes and sits quietly here on the stoep with her. They drink coffee and look at the sparrows. And then they laugh all over again about the exam that Treppie gave Lambert.

Not that it was all fun and games. There was almost trouble, quite a few times, but in the end it all went off very well. It's 'cause she and Pop kept their heads. Especially Pop. Pop was really on top form that night. Lambert too. Shame, she's never seen him try so hard.

Lambert had hardly finished his sandwich that evening when Treppie came out of the room in one of Pop's floppy old hats, striped pyjama pants, a vest full of cigarette holes, and red socks that were so old his toes and heels stuck out. He'd smeared his face white with Brylcreem, except for a wide space around his crooked mouth, which made it look much bigger than usual. On his nose was a plastic bubble they'd got for nothing at the Shell garage after Red Nose Day, when there were too many noses and not enough people with money for charity.

Treppie stood next to that box of red noses and said he wanted to take one for just in case, a person never knew. Charity was a house with many mansions.

He was right, too, 'cause here was that nose again, finding its day and its place. The place of Treppie's lost talents. And the moment of truth for poor old Lambert, if you ask her.

'Circus, circus!' she and Pop called when Treppie came out, walking like a clown and sticking out his neck like a rooster.

'No, no, no, there won't be any circus tricks around here,' he said, snorting through his nose.

'Examination. Fridge exam. Fridge trial. So that the knowledge of the fathers may be passed on to the children. Triomf trials. And such occasions, as my brother, er, excuse me, er, my brother-in-law rightly said, such occasions deserve a special kind of approach.' She looked at Pop, but Pop didn't look worried. Pop always knows when things are okay.

At the word 'approach', Treppie smacked Lambert a hard shot on the back as he sat there on his crate. Lambert flashed him an angry look, as if to ask if that was really blarrywell necessary. But Treppie hiccuped like it was him who'd gotten the blow and he fell over. And then he just lay there on his back in the passage.

That was when she saw Lambert click that his exam wouldn't be so bad after all.

Lambert was right. Everyone relaxed and they all felt relieved. She even took her hand out of her housecoat where she'd been feeling for a peg, 'cause in her mind's eye she'd seen Lambert having another one of his terrible fits. From doing exams at his age.

But he didn't look so old that night. You can't be old in a circus. All you can do is jolly it up and play along. Fall down and stand up, take smacks and dish them out again, roll your eyes and stick out your tongue. Get kicks in your backside and have your arm twisted. Let out farts and eat your hat. Until you're completely buggered.

That's exactly what Treppie did with Lambert. When he saw Lambert was losing heart or getting tired, he let him have the red nose for a while so he could also play the fool.

And that's how they got through the whole business. It was jolly and full of fun, and even she learnt something. She'd thought parables were only in the Bible, like the sower and the seed and the wasted talents, but then Treppie asked Lambert to tell everyone the parable of how fridges worked. It was a good story, too, about the canoe that leaked. And Lambert told it so nicely.

About how the heat inside a fridge was like water that kept leaking into a canoe, and how the heat was soaked up by the fridge's gas – just like you sucked up water from a leaking canoe into a sponge, and then squeezed it out over the side, back into the ocean. That's why a fridge was always warm at the back. It was where the heat came out, from the inside, allowing the fridge to stay cool. And that's why the sea was always full of water, Lambert suddenly said. It was from the leaking canoes that people were sponging dry all the time. Treppie said, no, that was enough now, he was taking the parable too far. He should remember a parable was a truth with a short shelf-life. There was nothing in the world that was exactly the same as anything else. Then Treppie said a funny thing. He said that's why he wouldn't mind if he didn't go to heaven one day, 'cause heaven was a place where everything was exactly the same as everything else, so they didn't need parables over there. It was just pure, undiluted, eternal truth, without words. That, he said, sounded terribly boring to him, in fact it sounded like hell itself.

Pop said Treppie mustn't start losing his thread, but Treppie said he'd already lost it, there was nothing to be done about it, and if heaven was like hell, then hell had to be like heaven, and he reckoned that was a place where everyone sat around and told weird parables all the time and no one ever ran out of things to say. It was a place where the truth kept flashing behind your eyeballs all the time, like multi-coloured fireworks on Guy Fawkes.

Horries, that's what she said, just horries.

Circus, Treppie said, just circus. And he took Lambert further through his exam. What did it mean if there was too much ice in the ice-box and the pump had stopped and the on-off-on-off cycle got mixed up? It all meant the fridge was too warm, Lambert said. Full marks! And why did a fridge get too warm? He must please list the reasons. Then Lambert listed them on the tips of his fingers: blocked condenser pipe, broken seals, too little gas, old oil, broken thermostat. Full marks again! She and Pop clapped.

Treppie asked him about materials, tools and troubles, a whole list of things a person must know when you service a fridge, and Lambert got through that list with flying colours. He even knew you had to insert a spring into soft copper tubing before bending it, otherwise the tubing would break or pinch closed. Treppie asked him how you work the valves on the manifold gauge to purge or to vacuum. Lambert knew it all, how you use a piercing valve to connect a service line to the system. If he was allowed to make a comment, Pop said, he just wished Lambert would learn the Afrikaans words for all these English terms, 'cause the English may have invented the fridge, but they didn't have copyright on fridge language. Then Treppie said Pop shouldn't get all puritan now, as long as a fridge worked he couldn't be bothered with language. Lambert said he agreed. All that mattered was that a thing worked.

Then Pop asked Treppie in what language he thought those sinners were telling their parables, the stories that exploded like fireworks behind their eyeballs in Treppie's heavenly hell. Treppie laughed so much that his nose fell right off, and then he bent down with his back to Pop and pushed his hand through his legs, shaking Pop's hand from upside down. Now that was a bladdy good point, he said. 'Cause as far as he knew, all you heard in hell was your mother tongue, and then he farted out aloud.

Boy, they laughed themselves sick that night.

And through it all, Lambert stuck to his guns. Most of the time he sounded like a real expert. Here and there he hit a blind spot, like what if a valve seat came loose in a pump and you didn't have a new one with you? Or what was a scotch yoke piston arrangement? Pop told Treppie he mustn't get too technical, those were the kind of things you learnt only in a workshop situation. She also said, yes, Treppie mustn't get too technical, and then Treppie answered the questions himself, giving Lambert a whole lesson. Lambert took notes until he said he now understood, and then he closed his notes and repeated the answer from memory, until Treppie was satisfied.

MULTIPLE CHOICE ⌒

The fun really began when Treppie gave Lambert a series of multiple-choice questions, from the chapter on safety measures and accidents.

Lambert had to choose the right answer. Like what should you do if you burn yourself with acid oil after a burn-out? Treppie gave a long list of multiple choices: smack the fridge, or your mother; swing the compressor by its oil line like a slingweight and let it fly when it's going really fast; eat polony; put ice on your wounds. And then he got rude as well: pull your wire; or take a bath in Coke. Really! And the last one was, phone the Flying Squad.

Lambert guessed the right answer straight away. Put ice on your wounds.

But the next question, also a multiple choice, was a different matter altogether.

For this one, Treppie pressed his nose more firmly on to his face, and then he went and stood in the lounge doorway like a clown who wanted to run a race. Just in case. Toby started barking 'cause he thought the game was for him, but she and Pop told Toby to shuddup. He went back to his spot under the TV and lay down with flat ears.

The question was this: what was the single worst thing that could happen to Lambert Benade as a top fridge specialist? Treppie began talking high falutin' language, like he was reading from a book, and he pulled his mouth this way and that.

Lambert had to pick the correct answer out of ten really bad things. And then Treppie started getting difficult again. It was so bad she can still remember all ten of those evils, even now. From his uncle moving to better pastures, to his long-nosed pliers getting lost. Or burning his 'fridge manual' by accident. Together with his *Watchtowers*. The fourth one was getting 'liquid cooling agent' on to his you know what. And then there was having a fit while doing a 'deep vacuum', or, even worse, while 'demonstrating a triple evacuation'. There were three more: forgetting to open the windows while the gas blew out, or forgetting to pull out the plug while welding the fridge's body.

What the next one had to do with the price of eggs she still doesn't know, but for number nine Treppie began talking about the NP 'unbundling' and the AWB 'mobilising' before the election, so that violence began rising to 'unacceptable levels' long before anyone had the chance to vote. For crying out aloud!

At that point, Lambert said Treppie must first stop, he wanted to write everything down. He couldn't make up his mind in mid-air about so many mishaps. He'd already heard nine options and all of them were in terribly difficult language.

Then Treppie repeated all nine in ordinary language, and after Lambert wrote them down, Treppie asked him if he was ready now, 'cause there was a last little thing in this multiple choice that could still complicate matters a bit. Lambert checked Treppie out and Treppie checked Lambert back. Then he straightened up out of his take-off position and said, no, he wasn't so sure any more.

But Pop wanted to know what he was supposed to be so unsure about.

Ja, she said, how couldn't he know any more? He was after all the one giving the exam.

Sure thing, Treppie said, they were right, he was giving the exam, but they must remember he was also the court jester, and the best test for anyone in life was the test they gave themselves. That's why he reckoned that Lambert himself should say what the last choice in his multiple choice should be. The one thing that would really complicate matters and which would be the worst thing that could hit a fridge specialist of his standing. The thing that would mean the end of this whole story. Choof! Off! One shot. And there he actually went and gave away the answer. The right answer was the last one, and now it was much easier. It was just right or wrong, no choice at all. 'Cause the end of the story was the end of the story, period.

What end of what story? Lambert wanted to know.

'Our whole story here together, between these walls full of plaster cracks, and our roof that leaks on to our heads, and our floor full of holes, and the moles who make molehills on the lawn, and . . .' As Treppie listed the things, 'and', 'and', 'and', all the sides of their story, its beginning and its middle and its end, which was now approaching, he pointed with stretched-out arms that looked like they were being pulled by strings, up and down, up and down, as he turned around in a circle, pointing closer when he meant 'now', and further when he meant 'then', and still further in another direction when he meant 'eventually' and 'at the very end'.

At that he shuffled around in a circle on flat feet as if he was standing on a turntable.

'You mean the kind of thing that means nothing will be left of us?' Lambert asked. He had a clue what Treppie meant, but he wasn't completely sure yet. His head couldn't get a good grip on it, 'cause it was still so full of fridge things, lists and lists of things he'd swotted up.

'Exactly,' said Treppie, 'the thing that means not even a single brick will be left standing in this place.'

'The thing that means everything will be for nothing?' Lambert was beginning to feel uncomfortable. She could see he knew more and more clearly what that thing was, but Treppie was putting him off with his straight, white face.

'Precisely,' said Treppie, 'the thing that means no one will be left to remember what happened, and no one will remain to hear the story, 'cause a story without anyone to hear it is no story at all.'

She quickly said that she knew the answer, just so something could be said, 'cause Treppie was standing there and tapping his foot on the floor as he waited for Lambert's answer.

Pop said he knew the answer too, just so Treppie would stop his tapping.

They must shuddup, Treppie said. This wasn't their exam.

Well, said Pop, in actual fact they were all together in this story after all, so why couldn't they also be together in the exam? And if the biggest test in anyone's life was the one they gave themselves, then they were all together in this thing with old Lambert, in sickness and in death, and surely they were allowed to help him a little in life.

Then she had an idea. Let them write down their answers, she said. People thought better when they wrote.

'Write what?' Lambert asked.

'Written examination,' she said.

'The answer,' said Pop.

'Repeat the question,' Lambert said, trying to win time. She could see things were going a bit too fast for him.

'Lambert, it's easy. The worst thing you can think of that could happen to you,' Pop said. 'You know very well what it is.' Pop wanted to help Lambert, but Treppie gave him a real dirty look.

'We know what it is,' she said, just to keep Lambert at ease, 'cause now he'd gotten up and he was starting to get restless.

'Yes, we know,' said Pop. 'Nothing to worry about.'

And what if the answer was wrong, Lambert wanted to know, but Pop said this wasn't a question of right or wrong, what counted here was consensus. Pop looked long and hard at Treppie to make him understand he had to go easy now. But Treppie acted like he hadn't seen.

'Consensus can be wrong,' he said, taking off his nose and paging through the fridge book. 'In any case who's to say if it's consensus or not?'

Go sit down, she told him then, 'cause it looked to her like he was finished with playing and now he was just looking for trouble.

Yes, sit down, said Pop, they weren't finished with the exam yet, but Treppie may as well close that book of his now. They didn't need it any more.

Lambert looked back and forth. He was confused, not about what he had to write, but what would happen when he handed in his answer.

Pop told Lambert to tear a page for each of them out of his exercise book, for Treppie too, so they could all write down what they thought was the worst thing that could happen to him, and what would mean the end of the world for all of them. When they were all finished they had to paste the answers up on the wall. Then they'd see who thought differently from the rest.

She said, yes, and that one was going to get a drubbing. Everyone stared at her 'cause she sounded so dead serious. And while everyone was looking at her like that, she took her chance and added, that person would plug the test!

Lambert just said, hell, Ma, laughing and shaking his head as he tore out the pages. He couldn't believe she would stand up for him like that. But she always stood up for him when she saw him taking strain. It was mostly Pop who took the pressure, but even more than Pop, it was her who took the strain in the end. Most of the time it was just the two of them, her and Pop, who stood up for each other against those two devils. But Lambert isn't as much of a devil as Treppie.

During the exam, she'd seen how Lambert's spirit rose every time he got full marks and she clapped hands for him, and how Treppie was beginning to look silly. She could see it wasn't just that red nose of his that looked silly. It was him too. He hadn't realised Lambert could still study a book like that so well.

Now Treppie was acting like he didn't know what a written exam was. Like he was completely stupid, scratching his head through that clown's hat of his.

But she and Pop carried on. Pop asked Lambert for his pencil and she asked Treppie for the red ball-point clipped on to the front of his vest.

'Clips!' Treppie pulled out his pen, turned it around and passed it over to her carefully, the way he'd normally pass a sharp knife. She couldn't see what it was he was thinking, but she could guess.

Pop leant on the chair's arm-rest to write.

She went and wrote at the sideboard. After a while her tongue was sticking out with the effort. She hadn't written anything in ages, let alone exams.

'Now the two of you must write,' Pop said when he was finished. She gave Treppie his pen back. Lambert took the pencil from Pop.

Treppie pretended he was struggling with his answer. He wrote something and then he scratched it out again, and then he'd peep at them from under his hat. After a while he even asked for more paper.

'Ja,' she said, 'not enough studying.'

'Ja, he hasn't learnt his lesson in life yet.' Pop sounded like he was pointing a finger at Treppie.

'Hmmm,' said Lambert, 'and what if his answer's just wallpaper?'

'It better not be,' she said, trying to sound like Pop.

'No,' said Pop, 'not wallpaper, it'd better be consensus.'

'And peace,' she said.

Ja, peace, said Pop. They really couldn't afford anything else.

They waited a long time for Treppie to finish.

Pop stood up and took everyone's papers. Treppie didn't want to hand over his. He kept holding it in front of him and looking at it through narrowed eyes. He was still thinking, he said.

He must think and get on with it, she said.

She went and fetched the tape out of the sideboard drawer, where Treppie had put it after sticking the cat's head back on.

She and Pop pasted theirs and Lambert's answers on to the wall, next to the picture of Jo'burg.

But Treppie still didn't want to hand in his paper. By then he'd been writing for longer than half an hour.

'Last-minute changes,' he said. He was still scratching things out.

Pop went ahead and read out Lambert's answer. She looked at the big, round letters as he read. Like the notices people put up at Shoprite, with big writing filling up the whole page.

The biggest Balls Up of all Balls Ups that is the Worst and the End of our Story, it said on top of his answer. And then underneath: *that certain people*, and then in brackets, *(with red noses)*, wouldn't give him his birthday present that they promised him. *To hell with them in advance*. And, right at the bottom: *that is my answer*.

Pop signalled that she must read out the next one, which was his. Pop's writing was shaky, but his shakes were from something other than not writing for a long time.

Pop had written on his paper that Treppie *mustn't raise Cain on Lambert's birthday*, and then there was just *and*, with a dash.

'And what?' Treppie asked. He looked at Pop. 'So, *and*, and what?'

'Too ghastly to contemplate,' Pop said. He, Treppie, wouldn't want to hear it. Then Pop read out her answer, in one breath.

The End, she'd written on top. And then: *that some people they know who they are break their promises that they know they made and they also know what the promise is. To Lambert. Then all hell will break loose and the graves will fall down into the holes holes holes.*

'You left out the commas and full-stops, Mol,' Treppie said, but he sounded like he was actually telling her she'd lost her marbles.

By then Lambert had lost his patience. She could see by the way he took one big step towards Treppie, holding out his hand.

Treppie picked his moment. When Treppie holds up his hand for attention, you know he's not about to miss a chance.

Before he went on to matters of life and death, he said, he first wanted to finalise the formal part of the examination by announcing that this nephew of his, boffin that he was, had passed his Big Fridge Exam with distinction here today, and that he'd held the name of the Benades up high in the process. And hopefully in the future he'd continue holding their name up high. High! Upright! Firm! Strong! Treppie said.

He made a rude, stiff-arm sign at the ceiling. She thought Treppie was going to ruin everything again, and Lambert thought so too, 'cause he grabbed Treppie from behind and lifted him right off the ground, so high that his toes only just touched the blocks.

'Read that answer!' Lambert shouted into his face.

She felt very sorry for Lambert. His voice stuck in his throat and he didn't look as strong as he usually was. But she could see Treppie was playing along. He stood on his toes and pretended he weighed almost nothing. He fumbled with the paper and then he dropped it again.

She thought, no, now she must lend a hand here, so she went and picked up that piece of paper herself. But she couldn't make out a word of Treppie's writing. Pure Greek. She gave it to Pop.

Pop brought the paper close to his face and then drew it away again. He said not even a dog could read this, whatever it was. Maybe it was mirror-writing.

In the end Treppie had to read it himself, 'cause Lambert also saw nothing but scribbles there. The reading was a whole new to-do. Treppie made them all stand against the wall, near the calendar. It felt just like posing for a family picture, with her and Pop in front and Lambert at the back, all of them with big smiles on their faces. Treppie was enjoying playing the fool, prodding them and moving them around until he felt satisfied. After a while she clicked, he was using her and Pop like sandbags. Sandbags that Lambert would first have to jump over before he could get to Treppie. But by then it was too late. Treppie was clearing his throat and starting to read his answer. It went like this. His answer had a name: 'A Prophecy', if you please:

> 'When Lambert got his service at forty
> He thought he was so naughty
> But try as he might, he couldn't drain his oil
> And to naught was all his great toil
> His pressure was low
> And his tubing had taken a blow
> Which is why at forty
> Lambert could no longer be naughty.'

Lambert grabbed Treppie so he could kick him up the backside, just as she'd thought. What did he mean, what the hell did he think he meant with that clever-arse answer of his? Lambert shouted. And Treppie, of course, pointed to his paper and said he meant exactly what was written there.

'But what's written there is fuck-all!' Lambert roared.

'Well, exactly,' Treppie said, 'that's exactly what I mean. Fuck-all!'

It was Pop who saved Treppie from getting a drubbing that day. He told Lambert it wouldn't be worth his trouble, 'cause Treppie's answer didn't qualify. It was a spoilt answer, Pop said. You could say it was like an illiterate person handing in a ballot paper with scratch-marks in all the squares.

A vote like that got counted as a spoilt paper, and all it showed, Pop said, was that there were lots of people who couldn't make up their minds, people who actually belonged in a circus.

Lambert was still angry. Hadn't Pop just said it was a good thing when people couldn't make up their minds? Hadn't he said it was a talent?

It was a wonder that Pop kept his head that day, every time, and that he said, yes, but if Lambert recalled correctly, he'd said people shouldn't just make up their minds about bugger-all. And it was as clear as night from day that this here wasn't bugger-all, this was something definite. Something important. And that Lambert shouldn't confuse clowning around in a circus with the real thing, with life as it was. After all, Treppie was allowed to say what he liked, if what he said was actually fuck-all, if all he was doing was playing Tickey. It was all a game and games were fuck-all.

Lambert stood there with a cock-eyed look from all Pop's talking. Treppie was laughing so much he was on the floor. After a while he rolled his 'answer' into a little ball and began chewing it like gum until it was small enough to swallow. He blew up his cheeks and used his finger to make a popping noise like a champagne cork. He went on like that for five minutes, popping champagne corks into Pop's face, to show him his mouth was empty and everything that happened that day was fuck-all, completely fuck-all.

She could see the whole business was making Treppie upset. He didn't have a good grip on himself. If you ask her, Treppie chewed and swallowed that silly answer of his 'cause he felt bad. He felt bad about poor old Lambert, with all his sores, studying so hard for his exam. Lambert was pale and sickly from trying so hard, from trying like that all his life long. And he felt bad about her and Pop, who praised Lambert so nicely and stood up for him when things got out of hand, 'cause most of the time they just tried to stay out of his way. She knows. Treppie's not the kind of person who can show he's sorry the way other people can. He's scared of feeling sorry. She remembers, at Old Mol's funeral, he didn't shed a single tear. And he didn't even try comforting her and Pop when they cried. But when the minister asked if anyone wanted to say a few words on behalf of the family, Treppie was quick to present himself. That was the first time he really put a few sentences together after Old Pop's death.

But actually they weren't just feeling bad and sorry for each other, that day of the exam. They were also scared. Scared about allowing Lambert to be the hero, and about the fridge book passing into his hands. That book that was now his, alone. It had been a family trophy and where the trophy used to be there was now just a big hole, a hole she knew none of them would ever be able to fill again. They were scared 'cause they knew this – and she could see Treppie and Pop knew it too – and 'cause they knew there were still lots of other things in that hole, and the whole caboodle was now making its way straight to Lambert. They wouldn't have a leg to stand on any more, never mind a perspective to live from.

Treppie was looking a bit shot after he washed his face and came back into the lounge in his old clothes. No more red nose. He poured himself a stiff drink and threw it back just like that, clean, standing there next to the sideboard. She and Pop gave each other one look, as if to say: Treppie took a big knock today.

And he knew that they knew, 'cause when he turned around again with his second tot in both his hands, as if he was looking for something to hold on to, he gave them a wink, not a devil's wink, but a half-mast wink, like he was half-sad. He cleared his throat and he put on a face and he said: 'Well now, people, fasten your seatbelts, the playing fields have been levelled for a miracle, whether you believe it or not.'

*   *   *

Early the next morning, just after she and Pop woke up, Treppie came in and hurried them up. They must come now, he said, this thing began with witnesses and it had to end with witnesses. They couldn't sleep at a time like this. When they got to the lounge, Lambert was already there, sitting and waiting in Pop's chair. Excuse me, he said, but Treppie had told him to stay put. Pop pulled Lambert's crate to the other side. Treppie sat in front of him.

Now, said Treppie, if Lambert thought the family Bible was something, then he had news for him, 'cause that was nothing. There were still the family jewels.

Treppie went into his room. He huffed and he puffed and then he brought out a great big trunk, dragging it right up to Lambert's feet in the middle of the lounge.

He went and dug around some more in his room and he came out with a long army bag that rattled with long-necked things.

He even brought out his black sling-bag, the one he took with him to the Chinese every day.

Treppie laid his long fingers on the lid of the trunk. His hands trembled and his shoulder twitched.

Theory, he said, was one thing. It was book-learning. A vexation to the spirit, as Ecclesiastes said.

Ecclesiastes, hmph, this Treppie can really lay it on thick.

But practice, he continued, was something quite different, full of its own pitfalls, which you never saw until you were up to your neck. But not without rewards, which you also didn't see until they hit you full in the face. Like a rainbow, one minute everything was grey, and the next there it was, filling up the whole sky.

'Ahem!' Pop cleared his throat. Treppie must please get to the point now.

But Treppie was already at the point. With Treppie, there's never just one, clear point. You first have to set the scene, as he always says. The setting itself is half the point.

It was dead quiet there in the lounge. She could almost hear her own heart beating. They all watched Treppie as he opened the trunk's lock.

Then, with a wide sweep, he lifted the lid and opened it out. It was a broad, deep lid. Took her breath clean away.

Neat little rows of tools were hanging there, each one sparkling in its own leather clasp. All the tools of refrigeration work. An expert's toolbox.

'Heaven,' said Treppie. 'This is heaven.'

Even Toby stuck his nose into the box to smell the strange new smells in there.

'Well, I never,' said Pop, lighting up a cigarette.

Lambert's eyes glittered. He rubbed his big hands round and round in the hollows of each palm. She'd never seen him look at anything in that way before.

Treppie's tools. His pride and joy. Ever since that terrible fire when the fridge business burnt down, he'd never used them in public again. Before the fire, when he did use them, he used to bring them out one at a time, and no one was allowed to touch them. Then at night he'd take them back into his room again. And she could see from the condition they were in that he'd been cleaning them all these years, shining them with a petrol rag every night, taking them out one by one and putting them back carefully in their places, in the trunk's lid.

'Now, take note: the first commandment of the practice,' Treppie told Lambert, and she saw he was keeping a straight face, but he was starting to play Tickey again. 'Order, hygiene, discipline. You can work with these tools, all of them, but if this trunk doesn't look like this every night when you're finished, then I'll take the whole lot back and keep it behind lock and key. Then I'll withdraw completely from you and your fridges and you can see how far you get on your own.'

When he's in a setting, he always comes up with grand words.

But when he began to tell Lambert all the names of the tools, and what each one was used for, he was back on solid ground again. Lambert played his part nicely. Every now and again he chipped in and told Treppie what that tool's name was, and what it did, 'cause he was 'theoretically qualified' now, as Treppie himself had said.

And each time they said a thing's name, she said it after them, so everyone could see her head was still firing nicely. When it comes to the names of things, she knows she'd better pay attention, otherwise she'll be gaga before her time.

They worked through all the spanners. From the nut spanner and the pipe spanner to the flarenut fittings and the other sockets and spanners, the six-point to the twelve-point box spanners. And then the punches, the centre punch and the starter punch, and the pliers, the cutting pliers and the squeezing pliers, the clipping pliers and the slipjoint pliers, and then of course the smallest and the finest, the needlenose pliers, which Lambert showed her with a little laugh. Pop squeezed her leg to tell her she must just smile now, 'cause this was a whole new beginning with pliers.

And the screwdrivers with their many different bits for different screws, the Keystone, the Cabinet, the Philips, the Frearson, the Clutchhead, the Allen and the Bristol. Treppie took them out, one by one, showing them to Lambert. And Lambert said their names, with her repeating them afterwards. It was like catechism, just nicer.

Then there was the iron saw, with a thin little packet full of brand-new shining blades. The flaring tool, the tube-cutter and the tube-clamp, the different hammers with thick and thin heads, and, right at the end, the mechanic's stethoscope, which you use to listen to the rattles and the hums of a fridge, as Treppie put it. What about the 'cheeree-cheeree' and the 'click-click'? she asked him, but Treppie said those were noises you could hear with a naked ear. If you wanted to hear the music of the spheres, you needed a stethoscope.

Treppie put the stethoscope's plugs in Lambert's ears and said he should hold the probe to Pop's chest so he could hear what music was playing in there.

Lambert listened and said: 'Silence is golden,' and he laughed 'ha! ha!' at his own joke. But there was nothing funny about that joke.

Pop said, no, maybe the little amplifier wasn't working.

Treppie said everything in his trunk worked. He switched on the amplifier so Lambert could listen again.

'Looba-doop-doop, looba-doop-doop, looba-doop-doop,' Lambert mimicked Pop's heart.

'That's a reggae beat you've got there, Pop!' Lambert said.

She wanted to know what reggae was. All they could come up with was an argument about kaffir music. Treppie said it was music from the kaffir-paradise north of the equator, but Lambert said it was what Lucky Dube played in Soweto and, as far as he knew, that was on the western side.

North or west, that toolbox session didn't pass before everyone listened to everyone else's heart, and they all laughed about the strange beats and the blowings and suckings of valves in each other's insides.

She was the only one who didn't think it was so funny, even though she pretended to laugh along for the occasion. After a while she told them a person would swear they were a bunch of fridges standing in a circle. They shouldn't make fun of sickness.

But who was so sick, then? Treppie wanted to know, and she said no one in particular, sickness was always looking for a place to slip in.

Treppie said she mustn't be silly, sickness wasn't something that floated around in the air, it was something that bred under people's skin and in their marrow. Only lunatic germs survived in pure air and came in through people's ears, like earwigs. Then Pop said everything was going so nicely this morning, Treppie shouldn't start multiplying germs now, and she shouldn't worry about what was in the air, or about his heart, and Lambert was hearing wrong, it wasn't a reggae beat, most of the time his heart beat like a hesitation waltz, otherwise it went like a slow foxtrot.

That sounded like a hectic medley, Treppie said, but fortunately he stopped poking fun at sickness.

When he was finished with the things in the trunk, all the regular joints and fittings, the gaskets, rolls of soldering wire, flux, files, iron brushes, gum in bottles, the aluminium that you melt to fix ice-boxes, and right at the bottom, a heavy, black thing, the high-vacuum pump, Treppie opened up his army bag.

He began to take out long-necked things on stands, with heads that made the lounge look like it was full of spacemen. Cylinders for fridge-gas and service cylinders, and the multiple gauge with its black pipes rolled up like centipedes. The hand pump and the special cylinders for welding, one with oxygen and the other for welding-gas.

'Oxy-a-ce-ty-lene,' Lambert said slowly, blowing 'tssss!' through his teeth and making slow figure eights in the air as if he were welding. Treppie passed him the goggles so he could see if the rubber band fitted his head.

'Watch out for that thing, hey,' he said.

'Yes,' Pop said, 'when you were small, you took that hot flame and pressed it to your flesh.'

'Never mind,' said Treppie, 'if he hadn't started welding himself so early he wouldn't have been Lambert the Iron Man today.'

The last thing Treppie took out of his bag was the volt-meter, which he showed Lambert how to work, as well as a set of thermometers with funny dials on curved stalks. That was for sticking into the places in a fridge where warm and cold need to be measured. Then Treppie wanted to stick one of those things into her, as if to take her temperature, and they all chased her around the house. Pop too, but she knew it was only a joke, and that all they meant by it was that she's the only woman in the house. Who else can they chase around? They were glad she was such a sport. He wouldn't try taking Lambert's temperature, Treppie said, 'cause he remembered how that Passion Meter had boiled in two ticks and he didn't have the money for new thermometers.

She and Pop helped to drag the trunk to the den, catching on loose blocks all the time. They felt it was enough of a business now. Things had to finish now.

Pop was very tired afterwards. He said the whole business of handing over the family treasures had exhausted him. But it was done now, and he felt light again, as if someone had taken a burden off his back. He said he felt reborn. Really. He even sings in the bathroom in the mornings. Not that she likes what he sings, 'Nearer my God to Thee', 'cause he actually feels further away from her than ever.

19

~

THE MIRACLE OF THE FRIDGES

THE FIRST MIRACLE: TINY BUBBLES ~

It's late. Lambert's lying on his back in bed so he can listen with both ears to the hum of his fridges. They sound as if nothing's ever been wrong with them. He smiles to himself in the dark.

They should start with the Fuchs, Treppie said, sniffing at the black shell of the Fuchs compressor on the workshop bench, 'cause if he remembered right, this wasn't a burn-out, it was just a leak or two. Or a thousand and one, for that matter. After '76 they sometimes took in fridges that leaked like they'd been in a riot. Birdshot, buckshot, that kind of thing. A fridge was a flimsy thing when it came to riots.

They put the compressor back into the engine and they bent the condenser tubes back into shape, the ones Lambert had ripped out. They welded the joints and cleaned everything up.

They also deep vacuumed the whole system, drained the oil and flushed the motor with R-11 before pumping new oil and gas back into the fridge.

When they started it up, Treppie showed him on the gauge how the pressure began falling to hell and was gone within an hour. The cycle ran all the time, without stopping inbetween, and the ice-box didn't want to ice up properly.

'This fridge is rotten with leaks. You must find them and mark them with a pencil on the joints and the tubing and the evaporator and everywhere else, the outside seals too. Then I'll help you fix them. Then we simply fix them one by one till they're all done.'

And he must remember, Treppie said, to open all the den's windows, otherwise he'd get stoned from the gas. People who got stoned from fridge gas didn't ever get liquid again. Their heads stayed solid until kingdom come.

He listened carefully to everything Treppie said, and he did everything Treppie said he must do. Working with Treppie was a big rave. They worked all February and March, and today's the 17th April already. For more than two months they worked, morning, noon and night. The only time they stopped was when Pop brought them sandwiches. When Treppie had to go to the Chinese for a day there was always enough work to keep him busy in the meantime. He could see Treppie was also enjoying it. He's been checking Treppie out. Ever since the fridges began working again he comes in here a lot, for this or that, he says, but he actually just wants to rest his hands on those two old fridges so he can feel how nice and steady they run.

Lambert feels for his cigarettes. He lights up and smokes in the dark, on his back. As he inhales he watches the little red coal glow. It's good to think about how those fridges got fixed again. It's so nice he just can't stop thinking about it.

The first thing he tried using on the Fuchs was Sunlight, but the leaks were too big and there were too many of them. The soapy liquid was so runny that he couldn't see very well what was going on.

Then he had a brainwave. He thought, let me send Pop to the big CNA in Melville to buy seven bottles of bubbles.

Late that night, after Treppie came and helped him pump more gas in for the test, he switched on his red light and asked the Good Lord and all the fridge fairies to please help him now, and he smeared every inch of that Fuchs with a thick layer of Fabulous Paradise Bubbles. Then he switched on the Fuchs at the wall.

The next thing there was a bubble bonanza like he's never seen in his life before. The whole den was full of them. Big ones and small ones blowing from the holes. And all the sides of the bubbles shone with square pictures that bulged out as they caught the den's reflections.

He must say, his jaw dropped when he saw that bubble bonus. He felt quite lame in the back as he stood there watching them. They just kept coming, one on top of the other, popping out of that Fuchs' thick white body, some of them stuck together in five-bubble bunches, and then they separated and floated out the door and through the open windows, into the night, suddenly accelerating as the wind caught them.

The mouth of the ice-box, in front, was one huge bubble. When it came loose it was as big as his head. It floated there, in front of his face, wobble-wobble, like a big, hollow ball of jelly.

'Strue's Bob, he walked right around that bubble. It just hung there. And with every step he saw a different angle of his room reflected on the bubble's surface.

Everything looked completely different.

His bed, with all its rubbish-blankets and dirty pillows, looked like a lovenest full of secrets. And the painting above his bed, which was also in the bubble, looked like a masterpiece on a flowerpot, something he could never have painted himself. The Fuchs blowing bubbles was also in the bubble, like a magic machine in a science-fiction movie. And all the pieces of scrap iron, the tools, his steel cabinet, the crates full of empties, his painting of things with wings, looked like Treasure Island. He was also in the bubble. He looked like something from outer space, with ears that faded away to the back. His mouth and nose, popping out in front, like a goldfish in a glass bowl.

After a while he couldn't take it any longer, but he also couldn't snap out of it. So he took a deep breath and blew hard into that bubble as it floated there in front of him, like something in a nice dream. Then everything fell apart. The bed split into two floppy pieces against the ceiling, the Fuchs floated upside down into his eyes, his nose disconnected from his face. And then he followed his nose out the back door, weightless like an astronaut, up and away into the dark sky among the stars.

The bubble burst with a soft, cool, wet 'plop' on his face, like he'd walked with open eyes into a wet spider's web.

Then he went and sat down on his bed, quite dizzy, and wiped his hand over his face. But there was nothing.

*   *   *

Lambert draws deep on his cigarette. That was really a special moment. From that moment on his den started feeling like a completely different place.

His mother said one minute she was standing in the front waiting for Toby to pee, and the next something suddenly began to bubble up from behind the house. She still thought, oh boy, here's another big fuck-up, so she called Treppie to come and look. Treppie told her he reckoned that he, Lambert, had finally exploded, and what she saw there was his soul bubbling up to the heavens.

The next thing, Pop and his mother came running in from outside, smacking the bubbles left, right and centre. And then Toby came, almost running them right off their feet. His jaws went 'clack-clack' as he tried to bite the bubbles. Treppie waltzed in through the inside door, singing: 'Tiny bubbles, in the air.'

Meanwhile, he was crawling around that Fuchs on all fours, with his pencil, quickly marking with circles the places where he saw bubbles popping out. There were so many of them that he couldn't keep up. After a while everyone began smearing bubble juice on to the Fuchs. And the next thing Pop was smearing Mol and Treppie was smearing Pop and everyone was smearing everyone else full of Fabulous Paradise. And so they ended up having a whale of a bubble party there in his den.

Treppie said it just showed you what fun you could have with crocked stuff. Come to think of it, he said, where was the fun in a fridge that worked? Just ice and cold polony.

THE SECOND MIRACLE: SHOCK TREATMENT ⁓

It took them three full days, testing with bubbles, pumping out the gas, cutting tubes, making new joints and filling up with gas again. Then they'd test with bubbles again and close up little pin-prick holes before filling up and testing the pressure yet again. Over and over until they had that Fuchs sort of sealed up.

But that was child's play compared with the Tedelex. The Tedelex was a burnt-out case that had stood for years here in his den, stinking through its open valves.

He filed open that compressor all along its join to see what was going on inside. He took one look at the suction and liquid line pipes, the ones that go in and out of the shell, and he ripped them out with his bare hands, the oil line too. That was when he burnt his skin so bad with acid-breakdown oil.

'Jeez!' said Treppie when he saw the inside of that compressor.

Treppie made him put on gloves, and he put gloves on too, plastic ones that they hurriedly went and bought at the Spar, 'cause Treppie said he didn't feel like being buried skinless one day. He didn't see why he should have to be a take-away for the worms.

The pump inside was completely eaten away by acid. The insulation was perished right through, the windings were in their glory and the coils were burnt pitch black. When they opened it up some more, they saw that the gaskets on the cylinder head and the valve seats were totally non-existent.

Treppie said he wasn't the god of fridges, so he couldn't fix this kind of fuck-up, but then he saw Treppie's eyes sparkle and he schemed that maybe he could push his luck a bit here.

He got Treppie to go as far as to order some of the most important parts for the Tedelex along with the orders he wrote out for the Chinese's fridges. He even bummed some spares from the workshops around Triomf, West End Electrics and Century Appliances.

They spent weeks reassembling that compressor. The whole den was full of cut-up Dogmor tins filled up with parts and oil.

Every now and again Pop looked in, and he'd whistle between his teeth and say, goodness, it looked to him like Triomf Appliances was back in business.

But the day they welded up the compressor shell, reconnected the wires and tubes and tried to start the Tedelex, that compressor just sat there, jammed. Completely seized up.

'Ag no, man,' Treppie said after they'd cleaned it up for the umpteenth time and gone over everything again and checked the volts. 'It's like trying to get blood from a stone.'

'What about a capacitor?' he asked. 'Then we can reverse the thing.' That's what the fridge book said you do with compressors when they get stuck. In *Modern Refrigeration and Airconditioning*, on page 355, middle of the page.

'Christ, no, I won't touch one of those things,' Treppie said. 'Once I saw a Chinese trying to reverse a compressor. He blew himself up, together with the compressor and the capacitor and everything else too. All that was left of him was a hole in the wall and a wet spot!'

'Yes, but that must have been a big pump, a commercial systems pump, for one of those helluva big walk-in coolers full of sweet and sour.'

He kept on nagging Treppie about the capacitor. He knew he'd give in eventually, even though Treppie stood there and looked at him in that funny way.

'Come now, Treppie, man, we can reverse it just a touch, and then a bit more. You must just organise a capacitor for us.'

He'd think about it, Treppie said, wiping off his hands with a ball of cotton waste and walking out of the den's back door.

But Treppie spent too much time thinking about it for his liking. And then, that same afternoon, he had a second brainwave. One that made his hair stand on end.

He pulled Flossie right up to the den with its battery side next to the outside door, and then he pushed the Tedelex close to the door as well.

At the very last minute he figured out that he'd better pull the Tedelex's plug out of the wall, otherwise he'd shock the whole of Triomf into a different blood group.

He took out the jumper cables and connected them to the running-winding and the starting-winding wires on top of the compressor shell. He tied the other ends of the cable to Flossie's battery.

And then he climbed into Flossie and started her up, putting his foot down.

That was how he jump-started the Tedelex, there and then, Model 104, burnt out for almost twenty years and reconditioned under doubtful circumstances, as Treppie said. Just like that. One shot, first try!

It was a miracle. Neither Treppie nor Pop nor Eddie at West End Electrics had ever in their lives heard of a thing like that. Lambert had to explain over and over how he did it, and Treppie just stood there, shaking his head. 'Cause a car battery gave a straight current, not one with waves like a fridge needed, he said. Treppie asked him again what he'd done before jump-starting the Tedelex, and he said he'd kicked the fridge five times up its backside until it shat itself, and then Treppie said, aha! Now a light went on in his head, but he never said what kind of light he meant.

Light or no light, just hear how they run, both of them, like the terrible twins there next to each other on the den's cement floor. He puts out his cigarette. Then he swings his legs off the bed and walks carefully through the dark, in bare feet, to his fridges. He opens both doors at the same time. Just check how bright those inside lights burn! He feels the ice-trays in the ice-boxes. Ice for Africa! He puts his head against the sides of the fridges, first one, then the other. Running as smoothly as a healthy heart, without a hitch. He feels behind for the condensers. Both are warm.

'My ma bakes roly-poly'

he sings as he climbs back into bed

'My daddy combs the goat
My brother rows the leaky boat
And I fix Frigidaires.'

He sings the last line of the song a few times until he gets it to fit nicely with the tune and the beat of 'Sow the Watermelon'. No one must ever come and tell him not to expect miracles. There it is, against all odds! 'Click' goes the Fuchs as he settles into bed. 'Clack' goes the Tedelex as he rolls on to his side.

20

~

SUNRISE, SUNSET

FINISHING TOUCHES ~

L ambert looks at the watch that Treppie got for him at the Chinese. It was to correct his sense of time, as Treppie put it, so his biological clock would stop running ahead of itself so dangerously.

A cheap piece of Chinese rubbish, but at least it shows the time and date. Five o'clock in the afternoon. Twenty-fifth April.

He's sitting on a Dogmor tin, surveying his handiwork.

Actually, he's looking at his hands.

They're full of cuts and bruises. There's still a plaster on the palm of one hand. It's one of the spots that wouldn't heal after the acid burnt him. Now the plaster's black and frayed around the edges. He must remember to put on a new one before tonight.

He turns his hands so his nails face upwards. His fingers are trembling and his back feels lame from all the running around. And God, how his feet ache. But he'd rather not start looking at his feet now.

It's Treppie who hurried him up so much. He thought he'd be getting his girl on the night of his birthday, which is the 26th. But then, yesterday, Treppie came with a new story, in front of his mother too, the bastard.

Actually, Treppie said, he was born just after midnight and it was 'therefore' already the 26th, and it was then that his birthday should begin, and 'therefore' his birthday present should be handed over to him on the night of the 25th. Handed over, he said, making curves in the air with his hands like a woman's body. Handed over in good time, he said, so Lambert would be ready for the hour of reckoning.

His mother said, hmph, what reckoning was this now, his birth was more like an hour of tribulation, God alone knew.

No, Treppie said, she had to be positive now. For Lambert it would be an hour of triumph, not despair. And, he said, when you have a birthday, you rejoice the loudest, all the days of your life, the exact minute when someone held you upside down and smacked you till you said: Eh!

And he, Lambert, had to be ready, and everything else had to be ready too, on that exact moment just after twelve, as the 26th got going, so he could perform at his very best.

It was nothing less, said Treppie, winking that devil's wink of his, than the bounden duty, nay, the heavenly command of a person who finally, on his fortieth birthday, gets to fuck someone who isn't his mother. Or, mind you, someone who isn't his father either, 'cause that possibility should also not be excluded – just look how the world was swarming with misfits who couldn't let go of the apron strings, or for that matter, the braces of their parents.

At that point, he, Lambert, decided he'd had enough of Treppie's rubbish, standing there in the kitchen door with that holier-than-thou look on his face. He took a king-size swing to smash in that foul mouth of his, but Treppie ducked and he knocked his fist right through the door of the kitchen dresser instead. His mother cracked up when she saw him punch his fist through the dresser, so he gave her a couple of good smacks too to make her shuddup, but she just sat down on her backside on the lino floor and pissed in her pants from all the laughing.

And then it was almost another big fuck-up here in Martha Street. But Pop quickly came and gave them all a shot of neat brandy. He can bet Pop doctored those shots with fit pills, 'cause once he'd swallowed his tot he suddenly began to feel calm again, and his mother's laughing came out slower and slower, like a wind-up toy running down, and Treppie brushed at his face weakly, as if he'd walked into a spider's web, or a thick mist.

Pop said they must wipe up the mess on the floor. Everything was okay, they must just wait calmly. He was going to take Treppie to his room quickly, he said, 'cause it looked like Treppie wanted to fall over.

When Pop came back he helped the old girl to her feet and stood her up against the wall. All this time she'd just been sitting there with her legs in that pool of pee in front of her, and all she could do was light up a cigarette.

Then Pop said he, Lambert, must apologise to his mother, and why in heaven's name was all that necessary? He told Pop how Treppie had talked a lot of rubbish into their heads and how he'd wanted to punch Treppie, but Treppie ducked. So it was the dresser that got punched instead and his mother started laughing when she saw him miss, as if it was a fucken joke or something.

She couldn't help it, she said, standing up against the door with her legs wide open, right there where Pop had stood her up, with a cigarette in one hand and that doctored brandy in the other. She couldn't help it, it was so funny, and then she started laughing all over again. She showed Pop in slow motion how he, Lambert, had thrown himself into that big punch. And then she ducked like Treppie, but in slow motion, putting her fist slowly through the hole in the dresser. 'Boom! Crash! Ting-a-ling!' she slurred, and God knows it looked so funny that he and Pop started laughing too, and then she laughed even more.

So he said sorry very nicely to her and told her he hadn't meant it. Then he began to feel sleepy again and Pop led him off to the den. When he woke up it was evening already, and it hit him like a bomb: if his girl was coming just after midnight tomorrow – that's now today, which at midnight becomes his birthday, the 26th – then he still had a helluva lot to do. And ever since then his hands have been shaking.

Come now, Lambert, Pop said, there was nothing to tremble about. They must just calmly see what they could still do with reasonable certainty and capable speed. It wouldn't help to try and move mountains in the space of twenty-four hours.

His mother made them all eggs on bread with tomato sauce, and then they sat down in the lounge with pen and paper and worked out what each of them could do to get things ready, even if it was just on the surface, 'cause it was appearances that counted.

His mother said if he got the lawn-mower running nicely for her, she'd cut the grass, right away. That's 'cause there was a full moon and next door wasn't allowed to start complaining before ten o'clock. Tomorrow, she promised, she'd tackle the kitchen.

Treppie said unfortunately he had to go work the next day, but he'd get some nice colourful Chinese lampshades, and then it would look like a jolly party. Pardon, he should say they would create a festive atmosphere, and he was sure he'd be able to get his hands on a plastic Chinese toilet seat as well.

Pop said he'd make a plan to find a mirror for the bathroom. There was still a whole panel of looking-glass left in the dressing table in their bedroom. He'd take it out of its frame and stand it up on top of the toilet. And then he'd put up the postbox, too, but this time, he said, it would be for good. For ever and ever, his mother said, and Treppie began singing: 'Sunrise, sunset, sunrise, sunset.'

And what about the gaps in the wall where the cement was gone and the red bricks showed through? Lambert asked. But Pop said if his girl said anything he could just show her the Wonder Wall papers. Painters always fix that kind of thing before they start painting. Then she'd know everything was okay.

Well, this morning he asked Pop for those papers and then he phoned the Wonder Wall people from across the road to ask when they were coming. The lady on the switchboard said, no, most certainly today, and if not today, then by the latest tomorrow, and thank you for your patience.

More than that he couldn't do. If they come tomorrow, on the day of his birthday, then maybe his girl will still be here and then at least there'll be something interesting on the go. Then she'll be able to see with her own two eyes that the Benades aren't just any old Tom, Dick and Harry from Triomf.

But what about the hole in the front door? he asked.

Treppie said that was easy, all they needed was to take a saw and widen that hole a bit. Then, abracadabra, he could say it was Toby's dog-door, so that Toby could go in and out during the night and then she'd think they were 'thoroughbred dog-lovers', and that their dog, despite his inferior origins, still had very good manners. It was manners that counted with dogs, Treppie said, not pedigree.

He began to think Treppie was making fun of him again, but his face was completely serious.

And what about stuff to eat and drink? He couldn't very well let his girl sit there dry-mouthed the whole night.

Treppie started to say that it shouldn't be her dry *mouth* he worried about, but then Pop waved his finger at Treppie and luckily he shut up.

No, Pop said, if Lambert made a nice list, he and Mol would go to Shoprite. But he said they must go to the Spar in Melville instead. The Shoprite in Triomf didn't stock those nice dips he wanted for his girl.

Treppie said he shouldn't overdo things, that girl they were getting for him was a saucy little dip herself. *She* was the one who was coming to get dipped. Lambert should remember that he had to do the dipping, and if he wanted to get his chip properly dipped, then he shouldn't be too stuffed with all kinds of snacks. But Treppie saw he was going too far again and he quickly tried to cover it up with all kinds of talk about dips and chips and chips and dips. He listed them, all the kinds of chips you get, from salt and vinegar to boerewors and barbecue, and all the dips he could think of, from garlic to angel-fish to avocado pear. All he was really trying to say, he said, was that Lambert should get on with it and make up his mind.

After that, they could all breathe more easily. Pop said Treppie might be an expert in dips and chips, but he'd better behave himself, or he'd give him another dose.

'If we only had love,' Treppie sang.

They carried on like this until very late last night. His mother mowed the lawn, with him supervising to make sure she kept in straight lines and cut evenly. Pop hammered the pelmet in the lounge straight and Treppie helped him put it up again. They even got the curtain hanging after a fashion. Treppie sawed the hole in the front door evenly, and then they swopped his mattress around with Pop and his mother's inner-spring mattress. He managed to get that buggered old bed of his back on to its legs again but the bed springs were sticking out all over the place, so he just snipped them off with wire-cutters. He didn't have time to mess around any more with that kind of thing. When they all went to bed last night, he wrote out his shopping list for Pop and his mother, and he made a list for himself, a short one from the long one, which was now longer than any list he'd ever made in his life before. It was so long it made him cross-eyed.

When he eventually got to bed, the sparrows were already singing.

It was the end of that long day. It was actually today already, the 25th, and he swears he slept only about four hours before he woke up again. And then it was still today.

And now, as he sits here, it's the night of today, but it already feels like tomorrow.

Except that tomorrow only begins after twelve tonight, and it feels like all the watch-hands and the church clocks are depending on him. It's like he has to extend himself to the utmost to make tomorrow come, his birthday. He has to make his own birthday happen. Then he'll be forty. That's if he can get it all together. But it's actually a misnomer, as Treppie says, 'cause after twelve he's already past his fortieth year. Then he's into his forty-first year. That's 'cause when you have a birthday, you don't count what it is now, you count what's already been, and then you're actually on the way to the future again. But you don't say it out loud, and you don't add it on when it's your birthday, which is actually a mistake, but you pretend for the sake of the party spirit. In the heat of things you just go ahead and say that, for the time being, you're so many years old, but actually you're always so many years old and a bit more. Forty point nought nought one into the next year. And if your watch is good enough, like an Olympic sprinter, you can even try keeping up with the facts of your lifetime, but it would be so fucken boring, keeping up like that. Tick-tick-tick-tick all day long, and between the ticks even more ticks, going even faster, and still more ticks and faster ones between those, until after a while time just zings by without even stopping for the ticks any more. Head first into your glory like a shooting star. Whoosh! Make way!

Lambert feels dizzy from thinking about time. He sits wide-eyed and stock-still, watching the things in his den. All the things stand there so quietly, you wouldn't say time was zinging to hell and back in their insides, in their guts and in their seams.

'Click' goes the Tedelex as it switches itself on.

'Clack' goes the Fuchs as it switches itself off.

Suddenly a terrible fear grips his body. It pushes up from his tail-end like a wall of water. He wants to hold on to the bed but all he gets is a fistful of sheet in each hand. There's a flashing behind his eyeballs. His head feels like a TV that's busy fucking out. Lines and snow. Crash! Bang! Christ!

No, it's not a fit, or anyway it's not him that's fitting. It's a general seizure. He's sitting wide awake right inside it and there's no black-out to take him away, no blowing of fuses so he won't know anything about anything. Everything is quiet and clear. The quiet convulsions of all the things in time. On and on it goes, forever. He feels like he's shrinking down to the size of a pin-point and, at the same time, swelling beyond the walls of his den, shot through and blasted by time zinging through him.

'And now? Why you sitting here like this with big eyes like you've just seen a ghost?' someone suddenly says here next to him.

It's Pop. He didn't hear him come in.

How can he explain all this to Pop now? If he does, Pop will go tell the others and then they'll all start saying something's wrong with him again. He rubs his eyes.

'Come see if you like what I did with the postbox.'

Lambert feels Pop's hand on his shoulder. Pop's voice is soft. He's not so bad, old Pop. He sees Pop looking at his chair, his and Mol's chairs that he dragged in here today. Pop didn't say a word, but he can see the old man doesn't really like it. He looks where Pop's looking. Yes, he has to admit the chairs do look a bit funny here, as if they've been shrunk or something. The light falls on them in a different kind of way. You can see the hollows in the cushions made by Pop and Mol's bodies. Those chairs have been sat to death, but they're better than nothing. After all, he can't very well let his girl sit on a crate. Where would she put her drink down? He looks at the chairs' arm-rests. They're full of coffee rings and black marks, from cigarettes. Tonight he'll put his red light on and then she won't notice a thing.

Pop sighs a deep sigh, here next to him.

'Just for tonight, Pop, then I'll take them back to the lounge.'

Pop shrugs. It's okay.

He points to Treppie's clock–radio next to the bed. Five past five, it says. Pop checks his watch to see if his time is right. Why's Pop so worried about time all of a sudden? They worked everything out nicely, after all. When Treppie comes home, it's just the finishing touches, then Pop and Treppie will go fetch the girl and drop her off here, and then, he told them, they must go out for a long drive with his mother. He doesn't want to feel like he's being spied on. He wants to be alone with his girl. That's the least a person can expect of his own family.

Pop prods him gently. He must come outside now. Pop walks in front, straight down the passage and out the front door. He points to the postbox. It's up, but Lambert must go look inside to see exactly how he did it. Lambert looks in through the little door. Fucken sharp!

Pop's made the mother of all plans. He drilled a little hole through the bottom of the postbox and then he stuck some fridge tubing into the hole, twisting it on the inside so it wouldn't slip out again. Then he stuck the other end of the tubing down the hollow gate-pole, till it almost reached the bottom.

'Now it's foolproof,' says Pop, standing next to him.

'Fucken sharp!' he says again. But it's not the engineering he's praising, it's the decoration. Light blue. Ja, just the thing. With its number painted pitch black in front: 127. 'Not bad, hey?'

'Ja, I saw there were some dirty old paint tins next door in the yard, from when they painted the roof. So I asked if I could have them. There was more than enough for a postbox.'

Now only does he notice Pop's got blue paint-spots all over his face. He looks like a bird's egg with a thin shell full of spots, standing there with a big smile on his face.

'Thanks, Pop, man! You're a champ.'

'Postbox for peace!' It's his mother. She's also come out on to the little stoep, standing there with her hands on her stomach, watching them. Here she comes now, walking over the lawn. When she gets to the gate, she looks up the street.

'Treppie,' she says.

Right at the top of their block, where Martha Street crosses Thornton, they see Treppie walking towards them. Apart from his black working bag, he's also carrying a big black rubbish bag full of stuff.

Must be the lampshades. He makes a tick next to lampshades on the list in his head.

Today he's flying through his list like the wind. He even saw to the moles. Last night he borrowed next door's hosepipe and then, first thing this morning, he connected the pipe to Flossie's exhaust and connected their own hosepipe to Molletjie, filling up those holes one by one with exhaust fumes. Now there's no danger that he and his girl will be eating breakfast here in the yard tomorrow morning and she suddenly spills her coffee 'cause a mole's pushing up a hill under her nose. Moles are ugly things with whiskers and two teeth in front. He's sure you don't get moles in Hillbrow. Cockroaches, yes, and termites. But he reckons those have also been seen to, with all the fumes on that side.

And talking about breakfast, the breakfast cake is also ready. It's a small Swiss roll, just enough for two people, in a closed white box in the fridge, together with all the other snacks for tonight. His stomach churns.

His mother was fine about everything. When they arrived back here this morning with all those chips and dips and things, she helped him pack everything into the back of the fridge. Then she said he must wait, she had a surprise for him – she didn't think he should display all those fancy eats in shop-packets and plastic bowls. So last night she asked Pop to get the key for the sideboard from Treppie, and she unpacked all the stuff that was inside there. Those things, she says, are all she's still got left from her mother, Old Mol – two thick wine glasses with patterns, two round-bellied brandy glasses, and lots of plates and bowls in old cream china, all of them with a red stag in the middle, jumping among pine trees across mountains white with snow.

And now everything's standing there neatly on his work bench, which he tidied up so nicely. His whole room's been swept clean and dusted down, with planks covering his petrol pit. They washed and ironed two of Treppie's window sheets and pulled them neatly over the bed. As Treppie said, a man couldn't ask for more. And his mother found two cushions and covered them with bright pieces of cloth, 'cause he'd burnt all the slips in that fire to kill the earwigs.

No, he must say, his mother co-operated very nicely. She even washed the kitchen floor twice. After she finished cleaning it the first time, the silly old cow went and threw a whole bottle of drain acid down the kitchen sink, just like that. It bubbled and bubbled and then it exploded, 'kaboof', shooting up from the bottom of the sink right across the lino floor, all the way to the other side of the room. Sis! Dirty brown goo.

But his mother just went down on her hands and knees and cleaned the whole floor all over again.

He had to use plastic tape to close up the pipe under the sink, 'cause that acid burnt a couple of holes right through the pipe. That drain stuff is almost as bad as fridge burn-out oil.

That was all this morning. He's just glad the smell has gone. It was a whopper of a pong. And he's also glad Treppie wasn't there when it happened, 'cause then of course he would've had lots to say.

Here he is now, at the front gate. He looks pissed.

'The burghers of Triomf!' he says. 'Why you all standing here like you're going to church? It looks like you want to get baptised or something.'

His mother points. The postbox.

'Light blue.'

'Yes, I see, it's breaking out like pork measles, the national peace epidemic, vote blue, vote pig, the Benades are going aboard the peace brig! Coor-doo, coor-doo!' sings Treppie, flapping his arms like a dove.

'Now the postbox is fixed for ever and ever.' Pop winks. He can see Pop's telling him he must just stay cool. He'll handle Treppie.

'Sure thing,' says Treppie, 'hope springs eternal. Go fetch the ladder so we can start. I've got lampshades for Africa here, and you can choose between a yellow or a blue toilet seat.'

410

'Blue,' says his mother. He agrees. Blue's better. Blue or pink, but not yellow. Yellow's too close to shit.

Treppie says he'll hang the yellow one behind the bathroom door as a spare. That's cool, he wants to say. If he, Lambert, spent as much time on the toilet seat as Treppie, then he'd also want a spare. But he doesn't say it. He holds back. He doesn't want to rub Treppie up the wrong way. Treppie's on his ear already.

And he's full of tricks, too. No, they can't touch his bag. He wants to unpack the stuff himself, inside, not here. They must come into the lounge. His mother closes the door behind them.

Lambert feels Pop pulling him by the sleeve. He must sit down on his crate so Treppie can start. Treppie's wired. He acts like that rubbish bag's a king-size lucky packet. He must just be cool tonight. The closer they get to the election, the more crazy Treppie gets. Like the other day, when they heard someone say the voting would now be over three days – the first day for special votes, and the next two for ordinary votes – Treppie started spouting rubbish again. Seeing that he, Lambert, was in the special class at school, Treppie said, he should by rights bring out a special vote on the 26th, which was also a special day for him – his birthday. But he needn't be afraid, Treppie said, he'd go with him, they didn't allow special cases to make their crosses without the guidance of an adult. He was just about to give Treppie another smack when Pop explained a special vote was something people made in 'exceptional circumstances', like drought or a plague, but then Treppie said, in that case the whole of South Africa should go vote with Lambert, so he wouldn't feel lonely. Then they could all make one helluva big cross with white stones on RAU's rugby field, right inside those new walls. Then maybe a few UFOs would come land there. Treppie says UFO stands for United Foreign Observers. Typical Treppie rubbish.

Here he comes now with the first shade. Just a yellow square, really. What kind of a shade is that? But now Treppie's unfolding it like a fan. It's a great big sun with a wide, red mouth that smiles.

'A sun! Good show!' says his mother. She holds out her hands.

'Don't touch!'

Treppie hotfoots it up the ladder. 'Hold tight,' he shouts.

Pop holds the ladder. Treppie works the shade around the bulb till it fits nicely.

'Ta-te-raa!' he says. 'Now it shines on everyone!'

The second one's a round blue light full of little silver stars.

'Ooh! Give here!' It's his mother again. She sucks her lip, in-out, in-out. Doesn't want to wear her false tooth. If his girl comes again, after tonight, he'd better nag Pop to find her a tooth that fits. She looks just like a worn-out old slut nowadays. And now she's falling in love with those little stars. She's getting soft in the head. Better just to leave her alone.

'Okay, Ma.' He tries to keep his voice even. She and Pop have helped him nicely today. They may as well have the stars for their room. He'll even hang the shade up for them. As he walks down the passage, he hears Treppie mumbling something to his mother. Must be talking about him again. Let them, they're still going to see a thing or two in this house.

He has to stand on the mattress to hang up the shade. He struggles with the strings around the hole where the bulb goes in. Fucken frills! He can hear them dragging the ladder around as they hang things up all over the house.

'Don't fall,' he hears his mother say. It sounds like she's talking through a rag. She even stinks from her mouth nowadays. After tonight he'll be finished with her. Then he'll do his own thing, in his own way. He must just have the right touch with his girl tonight. Then she'll come back again and, who knows, maybe this will become a decent house.

He can't get the bulb through the hole. It's too small. So he just pushes it, 'grrt!', right through the paper. He ties the strings on to the electric wire. Right, it's tight enough now.

He walks through the house. Shades hang from the ceiling everywhere. Full moons and crescent moons and pointy little stars and things like that. Some of the suns are even winking at him. No more naked bulbs. The left-over shades have been hung up by their strings from the ceiling. They've put up two shades in his den. He heard Treppie telling his mother and Pop about the red ones being the hot planets, and how they had to keep watch over tonight's other two stars. Treppie must watch his fucken jokes now. This is serious business!

'Yippeeee! Party!' Treppie shouts. He comes jumping up and down the passage, touching all the moons and stars and suns with his fingertips as he runs. They swing and turn on their strings. Toby 'whoof-whoofs' after him. He stands to one side. They must go slow, now! Slow!

'Lights!' Treppie shouts. 'Lights!' It's already quite dark in the house. Then Pop switches on all the lights. Suddenly he sees yellow and orange shadows everywhere as the shades light up the walls.

'Check it out,' says Treppie, 'the Orient is with us! Now all we need is some sweet and sour. Come, it's time for room inspection. Step up! Step up!'

Treppie pushes his mother and Pop down the passage, into the den. Lambert feels shy, he's pissed off. It's his stuff, this! Why must they do this, now? They just want to go and spoil everything again! He must act like it's nothing, just stand there with a straight face and push out his chest. No one's going to get him down now.

First they inspect the den's walls. The insect paintings are nearly finished. All of them got some new wings this morning.

'Good enough for an opening night,' says Treppie.

In the deep, red light, the insect-things look almost real. His mother gets the creeps. 'Yuk!' she says.

'Lost City,' says Treppie. 'It glows with eerie brilliance!' He flings out his arms and prances around the room like a master of ceremonies. 'Lost City or Cango Caves, and here comes the caveman, too!'

Treppie smacks him on the back. It burns, but he says nothing.

Then Treppie picks up the glasses one by one and makes as if he's wiping off dust. Full of shit again! He polished those glasses himself. There's no dirt on them.

'Look, all the little buck!' his mother says. She's looking at the bowls that he lined up in a row on his bench. He turned all the bowls so the stags' feet point to the bottom and their heads to the top. What's so funny about that? He wishes they'd just fuck off.

On the bed, on top of the white sheets, lie his clothes. A light blue shirt from Jet, and a dark blue, double-breasted blazer that Pop found on special at the Plaza. And a brand-new pair of white pants with funny pleats on both sides of the zip. Pop bought everything with his own money. He's already looped his belt, with its extra hole, into the pants. And there lies his new, blood-red Speedo, on top of the pants. His polished boots stand at the foot of the bed with a pair of Pop's socks in a ball on top.

They stare at his clothes. He feels naked.

'Phew!' Treppie whistles. He picks up the Speedo, stretching it open with his hands.

'Hey, Lambert, how you going to get your whole pedigree into this, old boy? Pit bull terriers! Njarrr! Looks a bit small for champion stock, don't you think?'

'Hands off!' says Pop, taking the Speedo away from Treppie. Pop puts it back on to the bed. He motions with his hand. He's trying to tell him he must just hang in there, it's almost over. They'll be out of here any second now. They fuckenwell better.

But now Treppie's trying a new angle, sticking his fingers into his shirt-pocket with only his pinky sticking out. Like a poofter. Sometimes he thinks Treppie should've been a poofter. It's only poofters on TV who throw scenes like he does. He's got a lot of fucken airs, this Treppie.

'I almost forgot!' Treppie looks round to see if everyone's eyes are fixed on that shirt-pocket of his. 'Rough Riders. Look, Lambert, a cowboy on a horse! We don't want you to go and get the load, hey.'

His mother grins.

He wants to tell Treppie he's a fucken poofter, but his voice gets stuck. He looks at Pop. Please, Pop, please. Pop takes Treppie and his mother by the arm.

'Right, Lambertus, get yourself ready. We're leaving any minute now.' Pop nods at him as if to say everything's okay, he needn't worry.

He watches them as they cram through the door. Fucken bunch of sheep. He looks at the alarm and then at his watch. Only quarter past seven. God, help!

He calls after his mother. She must come here, he wants her to tell him something. He hears her shuffling back.

'Yes?'

He points. 'Does everything look all right here?' He can hear his own voice. It sounds panicky. He doesn't want to sound panicky. What for?

He says it again: 'Everything's ready, right?'

'All ready,' his mother says, nodding her head up and down. 'Just perfect!'

She's also on her ear. He saw her pouring herself shots all afternoon long. She doesn't usually drink alone. Seems like she's also got the jitters. What for?

'What else do I need?' He points to the room.

'Beauty sleep. Hic!'

Hiccup or no hiccup, he wants to try this just one more time.

'Pleased to meet you.' He shakes his mother's hand.

'The pleasure, hic, is mine,' she says, just like he taught her.

But he can't sleep. He baths and shaves and puts on his new clothes. Then he puts out his dips and chips and lemons on the service counter. All in a row. Pop and Treppie have been away for more than an hour now. Wait, let him quickly go and see if everything's still okay in the house. His mother's fast asleep. Huddled on the bare mattress in her and Pop's room. Toby's lying behind her back. Now Toby lifts up his head and pricks his ears. 'Swish-swish' goes his tail on the mattress. The blue lampshade with its silver stars throws strange spots and shadows over his mother. And across the mattress and Toby and the floors and the walls. Weird.

Let him just leave her to sleep, even though he really wanted her to tell him a story, to get him right and ready. 'Cause he doesn't feel ready.

Maybe it's just as well. Now he can go pick the yellow bud on her rose bush without her seeing. It's the first bud. He's been eyeing it all week. That rose bush is still sitting there in its plastic bag.

It's for the little bottle next to his bed. 'Cause if you ask him, a real flower's the only thing he's short of.

SERMONS ON THE MOUNT ⌒

Mol wakes up. She's not altogether sure where she is. 'Tip-tip-tip', she hears. It's raining. Where's it raining now? She sits up. Here's Pop, next to her. There's Treppie, on the back seat. Pop and Treppie are both sleeping. Toby's awake. He looks at her with big shiny eyes from where he's sitting in the dicky at the back. All she can see through her window are drops of water. She winds down the window. It's the Zoo Lake parking lot. That's where they are.

First they were on the koppie. That's right, now she remembers. With sermons. And Klipdrift. She touches her head. It hurts. Too much Klipdrift today. The stuff just makes her feel sleepy, but what could she do, with all the nerves in the house about the girl who was supposed to be coming, and everything. So when they finished looking at Lambert's den, she helped herself to another shot. And then she went and lay down, 'cause Pop and Treppie just couldn't get themselves going. Before she knew it she was fast asleep. The next thing, Pop was shaking her. All she could see were little stars.

'Get up! Quick!' Pop said. He was standing in the door, looking down the passage towards the den and then back into the room. In and out, in and out he kept looking, completely white with nerves.

'She's here!' Pop said. 'Quick! We must go!'

So she dragged herself to the front, even though she wasn't properly awake yet. She only really came to when they got to the koppie. And not by herself. The sermons did it.

Pop stirs in his seat next to her. He looks all broken-jointed. His head lolls over the back-rest and his knees are jammed at an angle against the gear lever. Shame, he must also be tired after all the fuss. He was wiped out even before they left the house.

They had to stand on the pavement next to the car, waiting for Treppie. He'd taken the girl through to the back. Pop was pacing up and down, blowing out clouds of smoke. They told her later they'd looked high and low to find a girl, and in the end they decided to pick one up off the street. With a touch of the tar-brush, Pop said. Shame, a little touched. And Lambert himself is also a bit touched in the head. She wonders when they'll be able to go home again. What's the time? Probably early morning already. Lambert should surely be finished by now? Finished! God help her!

Pop said the girl cost a packet. He said Treppie tried to bargain with her, asking if they couldn't first pay her a deposit. Then that girl told Treppie she may be a rent-piece, but she wasn't yet a lay-by. Not slow on the uptake, Pop said. A real livewire. Well, so far, so good: that's what Lambert said he wanted. Now he'll see how things really work. Not everyone's just going to do what he says. She hopes the whole thing doesn't turn into a big fuck-up again. Pop said Treppie told the girl a lot of stuff and nonsense that she had to spin Lambert. That she was a high-class whore, a Cleopatra or something. And that she should keep a close watch, 'cause Lambert sometimes got wild. And if Lambert did get a bit wild she should pull his pants down over his feet and get the hell out of there. Pop said Treppie almost ruined the whole business with his horror stories. In the end they had to pay all the money in a lump sum, more than a hundred rand, just for an hour. Mol has her doubts. This woman is a stranger to Lambert. She'll have to know her stuff, 'cause sometimes Lambert takes a while to get going. It's a good thing they got out of the house. She told Pop, she really didn't want to be there if the whole thing blew up, 'cause then she'd be the one to fix what that whore went and stuffed up. She could just see it coming.

She's never before seen Pop in such a hurry. Treppie had hardly gotten into the car when Pop took off so fast that her head nearly jerked off her neck. They were thrown sideways, this way and that, as Pop wheeled around the corners. And when he skidded to a stop outside Ponta do Sol, she almost bumped her head in front. Pop was in a state all right. They bought Cokes and things and rushed back to the car. Then she asked him where was he taking them, but he just leant forward and stepped on the accelerator.

Treppie sang: 'Up, up and away-y-y in my beautiful balloon!'

417

By this time, he was in high spirits. Mission completed, he said, now they could relax with a drink and a wide-angle view. So that's where they were going – to the Brixton koppie.

Why did they have to go there again? she asked, but Treppie was running off at the mouth. He told her she should see it as a visit to the Mount of Olives. They would pour Klipdrift into their cans of Coke and drink them down to the very dregs! Yes, that's what he said!

Pop was dead serious. He said this wasn't the time and place for profanities. Didn't Treppie realise how much depended on tonight? They should all hope and pray that everything went off well.

In for a penny, in for a prayer, Treppie said. They didn't need to push him hard, 'cause when he had the city at his feet like this, he could pray a bird right out of a bush.

When they eventually settled down under the tower, she saw Pop would far rather drink than pray. 'Ka-pssshhhtt!' He ripped open the tab on his Coke tin, taking a big gulp – she saw his Adam's apple jump and fall – to make space for a decent shot from Treppie's bottle.

So there they sat, looking out at the view, the city's lights shivering as far as the eye could see. More like candles than electricity. Far out to one side, they could see the Florida Lake water-organ and its lit-up fountain. Must be a lovely organ, that. She's already told them she wants to go there and see it close-up, but they never get that far. Too many other things.

Then Treppie started up again.

> 'All people that on earth do dwell
> Sing to the Lord with cheerful voice'

he sang, just from seeing an organ in the distance. He's got a head like a see-saw, that's all she can say.

The next thing, Pop also started up, out of the blue: 'What if you know you're dying?' he said.

She got such a fright she almost fainted. Pop wiped his mouth with an angry swipe and passed her his chocolate.

No, God, she said, there, eat your own chocolate, Pop. But he took the chocolate, ripped off the paper and flipped it right over his shoulder for Toby at the back. A whole half a Snickers. And Pop so loves his chocolate.

She thinks Treppie got a fright, 'cause he started talking about Toby being so spoilt and how he must think he's part of a travelling church bazaar – if it wasn't Snickers, it was Smarties. Treppie didn't really want to change the subject. He made that speech of his about bazaars and things just to play for time. She could hear from his voice he was brimming with that topic of Pop's. Meanwhile, Pop sat and looked straight ahead of him. She could see he was gritting his teeth. It was a long while before he started talking again.

No, what he meant was this: say you were dead certain you were busy dying, quite fast. So fast you could more or less count the days still granted to you. Pop's voice was slow and dead even, like it always gets when he's telling you what he's saying isn't small-talk.

She wanted to change the subject, so she said in the end everyone had to go, anyway – what was bothering him so much all of a sudden?

But by then Treppie was up and away already, running with that ball.

Ja, he said, pointing past her and Pop in the front seat, they must look at all those lights. 'I say unto you, for every one of those lights, someone will either give up the ghost or give his first cry tonight.' When Treppie starts with 'I say unto you', then you know he's halfway up the pulpit already and you're not going to get him down again so easy. 'It's one and the same thing. Breathe in, breathe out, eat, shit, eat, shit, poof, gone! No one asked for it.'

But Pop said, no, that wasn't his point.

Well then, he'd better get to the point before the point got to him, Treppie said, and she said, yes, Pop should get to the point so he could get past it.

That's what she thought, then. But it was a helluva long point, that.

No, Pop said, what he meant was, what did you do if you knew your time was running out. What *should* you do if you knew?

Now it was getting a bit too much for her. She switched on the radio 'cause she didn't know what else to do, and the car suddenly filled up

419

with a love song, something about 'only a heartbeat away'. That turned out to be completely the wrong thing to do. Treppie stuck his arm past her and switched off the radio, shouting, 'Shuddup! Shuddup with that fucken rubbish!' right into her ear. Even Toby said 'ee-ee', he got such a fright. Then Treppie sat back heavily, his chest heaving. He tried to light a cigarette but he was striking the matches so hard they kept breaking. 'Fuck!' he said after each match broke.

It was Pop's *should* that threw Treppie so badly. If there's one word you must never say in front of Treppie, it's 'should'. It was like someone had poured turpentine on to his tail.

'Should,' he said. 'The fuck with should! When you die, you die, period, over and out. You don't owe anyone any *shoulds* 'cause you never ordered it. You never asked to be born, nor to live all the days of your life in this furnace pit.'

At first Pop said nothing. He just looked in front of him out of the window. Treppie blew smoke into Pop's neck as he talked. It looked like Treppie was about to start shooting fire from his nostrils, like that dragon on the video he brought from the Chinese one year for Guy Fawkes.

Then Pop said, 'Furnace pit', so softly you almost couldn't hear what he was saying.

So she asked, what was a furnace-pit.

'Yes, ask!' Treppie shouted. 'Ask!' It was a hole full of bricks, he said. A deep, burning hell-hole where you sat and baked bricks, all day, every day, and when you were not baking them they sat and looked at you, stacks and stacks of those rough, red things.

Pop turned his head a bit, like nothing at all was the matter, and he asked Treppie how it was that he came up with this kind of thing.

He came up with what he came up with, Treppie said, Pop didn't have to worry about coming up with anything whatsoever; all he had to do was look in a dictionary. There it stood, in letters as large as life, for anyone to read: furnace pit. And he was sure Pop knew all the other names for that pit. Arse-end, deep-end, furnace-hole, hell-hole, long-drop, Treppie said, hauling out all the names for holes that he knew, and he said the

Benades were sitting in the lot of them. That was the one thing. And the other thing was it wasn't their fault.

Her chocolate was sticking to the top of her mouth by now. She's never been able to chew when people fight. She felt quite paralysed. 'Cause if there's one word that she can't stand, then it's fault. Old Pop always used to say everything was *her* fault, and then Old Mol would jump in front of her when she saw a punch coming her way. Or she, Mol, would jump behind Old Mol. Then she felt it was all her fault, twice over, 'cause Old Mol was always looking black and blue from taking the blows meant for her.

Treppie must have seen her say the word fault, even with her mouth full of Snickers.

Yes, fault, Mol, fault, he shouted, making his mouth droop and saying fault in the same way she does when she doesn't have her tooth in her mouth and she says something. It was so bad she put her hands over her ears, and when she took her hands away again, Treppie was still saying it wasn't their fault, because of something.

Because of what? she asked. Now she was curious, but she had to ask Treppie three times before he gave her an answer. By then he was drinking the Klipdrift straight from the bottle, 'ghloob-ghloob-ghloob', as though it was water on a hot day.

No wonder he's now fast asleep at the back here with his mouth wide open. 'Gaaarrrgh-gaaarrrgh', he goes. She can smell it from where she's sitting. Lambert says Treppie's breath is enough to fire off a rocket. Lambert. How will he know what to do with that woman he doesn't know from a bar of soap? Maybe she should wake them up now so they can go and look. But then again, maybe not. Pop needs his rest. Let him sleep. And maybe Lambert's still awake. Maybe he's waiting up for them. In that case, she'd rather sit here until sunrise.

Pop also asked Treppie, because of what? It wasn't their fault they were in the furnace pit, because of what? Not that he knew, Pop said, what that had to do with knowing you were dying and what you should do in the circumstances. Can you believe it, there Pop went and said *should* again. She thought something must have come over Pop. Once was enough, and she could see Treppie wasn't even finished with the *first* should, not by a long shot. And here Pop came with another one. And it wasn't as if you could duck out of Treppie's way.

'Everything!' he shouted into their faces. It had everything to do with it, 'cause if *their* mother and father hadn't been so backward, and if *they* had been raised better, and Old Pop hadn't shouted at him, Treppie, so terribly before he even knew what went for what, and if Old Pop hadn't beaten him to a pulp when he did know what went for what, then everything would've been different.

Then what would have been different? Pop asked, and she thought to herself, now Pop was really asking for trouble, he should know he can't square up with Treppie. But she was wrong, 'cause Pop just pushed on. Then what would have been different? he asked again.

What would've been different, Treppie said, was that he might've had a choice. He might've been able to choose how to die and what to do if he knew he was dying. And with that he sat back, boomps, against his seat and said it may be that Pop had begun to die only recently but he, Treppie, had been dying ever since his eighth year, and it was the kind of dying you do twice over – in body and in soul. The ruination of his soul, and the blood of his limbs, he said, was on Old Pop's hands. May Old Pop hear him wherever he was and may Old Pop gnash his teeth in the outermost darkness for ever and ever.

At that point she wished she was a Catholic so she could've crossed herself against Treppie's terrible Satan words, 'cause Treppie began swearing hellishly terrible words inbetween every other word he said, above and below and on each side, so much so that she and Pop were wiping his spit from their necks after a while.

All Pop said then was, honour thy father and thy mother, and she recited the rest, 'cause that was all that came into her head: '"That thy days may be long upon the land which the Lord thy God giveth thee."'

That was the last straw.

'*Honour*, for what should I *honour* him – all that's left of me is a drop of blood, a wet spot with some skin around it struggling for breath. A lump of scar-tissue with a heart in the middle.'

Suddenly Treppie told them they must switch on the inside light. He plucked up his shirt and pushed his pants down over his hips so they could see his scar-tissue.

'Krrrt-krrrt!' she heard as Treppie scratched around here above her head to get the little light on, but it didn't want to work.

So they had to use their lighters to look. Toby jumped right over the back seat – he also wanted to look – but Treppie let fly and smacked him so hard he didn't even make a sound. His head just went 'doof' against the door. Shame, the poor dog.

'Hold closer!' Treppie yelled, and she and Pop turned around completely in their seats, lighting up his stomach.

Then she saw how terribly those blows had set into Treppie's skin. She hadn't known. She'd thought people outgrew things like that. Treppie's stomach and hips were covered with nicks and grooves, as if he'd been tied up with ropes and beaten over and over again.

Treppie must have seen on her face she couldn't believe what she was seeing. So he said she mustn't come and act holier-than-thou all of a sudden. Didn't she remember what he looked like that night when they dragged him out of the train? 'Marked for life!' he said, prodding his finger into the nicks and scars on his skin.

What could she say? So she lit up a cigarette – her lighter was burning anyway – and said: 'Shame.'

That was also not the right thing to say.

Fuck shame, Treppie said. That's all that she and her mother could ever say, shame this, shame that, and shame everything else. But they never stood up for him, not once, when Old Pop screamed at him so terribly and hit him for no reason at all. Not once did they take his side.

It was then that Pop said he could explain to Treppie why Old Pop used to beat him up so badly. It was something she and Pop had known when they were still small.

Treppie was a chip off the old block, Pop said. Of all of them, it was Treppie who took after Old Pop the most. Yes, he said, it was 'cause he had the same light blue eyes as Pop and the same stuff-you look in his eyes, too.

Then she felt Pop take her hand and let it go again and she knew they were both thinking of Old Pop. There they sat, looking at Treppie in the glow of their lighters, and it looked almost like Old Pop sitting there in front of them, just smaller.

The same short fuse, the same moods, the same delicate constitution, Pop said.

And then she remembered how Old Pop also used to struggle to shit, but she decided not to mention that 'cause Pop had already mentioned more than enough similarities. 'Chip or no chip off the old block,' Treppie shouted, 'it's no excuse for smashing up your own flesh and blood.'

He was one to talk, she thought, but she kept quiet. Treppie knew what she was thinking. He thumped her seat from behind.

'Tsk-tsk-tsk!' Pop said.

Then Treppie suddenly wanted out of the car. So bad that he didn't even wait for her to get out. He just shoved her forward in her seat, almost climbing right over her.

She and Pop also got out, and she suddenly felt a chill, not from the cold air but from the height. That tower reaches up very high into the sky and its little head on top looks like it wants to bend down and fall over. Toby also wanted out, but they made him stay in the car. They could hear him going 'ee-ee' from behind the window. Then it was quiet again for a long time. They just stood there, looking at the lights and passing around the Klipdrift.

And then Pop started again. She'd thought he was finished, but he actually went and started all over again. About the forgiveness that Treppie had to find in his heart and that he'd thought Treppie had already softened when he gave Lambert all his stuff and helped him so nicely with the fridges. That, Pop said, had looked to him like a kind of forgiveness, and forgiveness was infectious. If you forgave the small things the big ones followed. Or the other way around, forgive the big ones and then the little things would begin to look like small fry.

Pop tried so nicely to get through to Treppie there on the koppie. She took his hand again and said, yes, if Treppie could make a circus and play the fool like that, then he couldn't really still be so angry with Old Pop, then deep down everything was surely okay.

Treppie didn't have to chastise himself so, Pop said. She didn't have much time to wonder what chastise meant 'cause Treppie suddenly exploded. His eyes went white with anger, lighting up from the inside. He was so angry he got the shakes. Up and down he paced, poking the air with those little bird claws of his, as if he wanted to grab on to something and pull himself up into the air, right out of his skin.

Fucken shit, he said, they were talking the biggest lot of shit under the sun. What did they know, anyway, fuck forgiveness, fuck it right into its glory. Phew! Her ears are still burning.

Then she thought, no, God, now she must get away in a hurry before he goes and murders her and Pop right there on the koppie. She looked around and saw she could run this way or that way, but no matter which way she went there weren't any people, so what would it help, anyway. She looked in front of her and all she could see was the tower. It looked like it was growing out of the back of Treppie's head. Up, above her, and all around, she could see nothing but dull lightning going off inside the clouds, big black bunches of clouds that were blowing towards them. She looked down to the bottom of the koppie and there she saw ambulances racing past, going 'pee-poh-peeh-poh' with their red lights flashing. A horrible accident somewhere.

Even though it was so dreadful and scary up there on the koppie, the thought crossed her mind that it was just like being on a stage. And that Treppie would probably even want to breathe his last on a stage one day, with lights and curtain calls and people shouting, 'Encore!'

There he stood beating his breast like Charlton Heston in a Bible movie. He shouted, forgiveness be damned, no one was going to get forgiveness out of him. He was angry and he'd stay angry until his last breath and he was going to shove their noses in it so they would be forced to partake of his legacy of anger. And why, he shouted, should he be the only one who felt haunted? From now on he was going to do the haunting.

Pop still tried to stop him, but Treppie just went on and on. Forgiveness, he shouted, was just wallpaper. Like a drizzle after thirty years of drought. Who needed that? Then everyone posed for the *Farmer's Weekly* but the ground water was still rock-bottom. All this time Treppie was drinking non-stop from the bottle, but he was spitting out more than he swallowed. He said if Morkels could they'd sell forgiveness together with their five-piece bedroom suites. That was why the Day Spring Church was so full of policemen every Sunday. It was a branch of Morkels – forgiveness at a special price. Hallelujah, praise the Lord. One down payment with the collection every week.

Then she said amen, from pure panic. It was all she could think of saying. Pop moved closer to her and said she should not say anything now, but Treppie had already heard. Yes, she must shuddup, he said, 'cause if anyone should know all about suffering, it was her, but for some reason she refused to understand it. She thought to herself, yes, he was right, suffering existed. That was all there was to it. Why should you also tire yourself out by understanding it – it was there, deep in your bones. But she didn't even finish her thought before Treppie started shouting again. If he had to suffer in his heart and his head, he shouted, then they had to suffer too. That was his hand, he said. That was his trump card!

She heard Pop say softly, 'Joker,' and she didn't understand at all, 'cause the next thing Pop was standing up straight and grinning right into Treppie's face. Pop normally sits with his head in his hands when things go mad like this. Maybe these were the very dregs. Maybe Pop thought he had to take it like a man.

And she thought to herself, if Pop could do it then she could do it too. So she said: 'Sis man, Treppie,' as if he'd only farted. She thought if she acted like his whole dreadful sermon was no more than a smelly fart, he'd maybe shut up by himself.

'Sis man, Treppie, sis man, Treppie!' he mimicked her.

At that stage she already saw foam bubbling in the corners of his mouth. Pop still tried to put his hand on Treppie's shoulder, but he slapped that hand away like it had stung him. He grabbed Pop by his shirt and shook him so hard his head jerked to and fro. Toby was going crazy behind the closed windows of the car. He thought they were playing a game and he didn't want to miss out on the fun. Then she remembered how poor old Gerty always knew the difference between fun and fighting. But what would poor little Gerty have done on this koppie tonight? It was more than just an argument, it was like Jacob wrestling with the angel, if she remembers her Bible correctly. Treppie began pushing Pop further and further backwards over the patches of grass next to the road. She could see them getting knocked over if they didn't watch out. Careful, she tried to say, but there was no stopping Treppie.

'Brother Addlebrain!' he shouted. Shove. 'Brother Stickdick!' Shove. It was terrible. And then he wanted to know what Pop's dick was looking like nowadays 'cause he thought it must be looking like a five-day-old Russian behind the counter at Ponta do Sol. That dick of Pop's was the place where all the trouble started, he said. He had to suck Pop's dick like it was a lollipop, remember? And he hadn't understood anything, he was still too young, but when the lashes were dealt out he was always the only one who got them. And why had Pop always just stood there with big eyes while he got the hidings, while he got beaten to within an inch of his life? Would he just answer that one question for him? Would he, please?

Then, thank God, a car came driving up the hill, slowing down and shining its lights on Pop and Treppie. The car was full of people stretching their necks out the window to see what was going on. The three of them must've looked like wild buck or something with their eyes shining in the dark. It was a chance for her and Pop to stop Treppie's shoving. Pop said he was cold and if they all got back into the car, he'd tell them a story.

Treppie, she said, the people are staring at us. She knew Treppie hated people looking at him. He'd rather get back into the car than be looked at. But this time she was wrong. Treppie showed them the finger and then he walked quickly towards the car, which was now idling on the slope. 'Kaboof!' He slammed the roof with his hand, so hard that the driver clean forgot how to pull off. You just heard gears crunching. In the middle of the crunching she heard Treppie screaming at them. They could watch if they wanted to, there was a variety concert here under the Brixton tower tonight, and if they stayed a little longer they could hear a story too, a story by Old Sweet-Sucker over here. 'Cause very soon the Benades would be flying off into their glory, anyway, and then no one would've heard their story. They must be on the look-out, next time he'd send out complimentaries for the famous Benade roadshow, ta-te-raa, the tallest story in the western suburbs, better than any cowboy movie they'd ever seen. Good value for money. Then that driver finally got his bearings and pulled off up the koppie. 'Doof!' Treppie kicked the bumper as it took off. Only then was he ready to get back into the car, but Toby first wanted to take a little walk. So they all stood there and looked on while Toby found a pole to piss against and a patch of grass on which to do his business. He bent his back and stretched his neck and pushed out a long turd, followed by a few small ones, 'clip-clip-clip', and then he did a few little back-kicks, making the stones fly out behind him.

Aaah, said Treppie, lucky dog. At least one of them had found some relief here tonight. They might as well get back into the car and listen to Pop's story now. And it'd better be a good story, he was fed up with fucken fairy tales full of forgiveness, fed up with fucken ocean liners with forgiveness in champagne glasses on all three decks, allow me to top you up, sir.

See-saw. That's what she says.

So, that was the end of Treppie's sermon on the mount.

And only then was it Pop's turn to preach. They should be grateful she isn't one for sermons, 'cause then their bums would've all been worn down and they would've needed an interval, first. It makes her tired just thinking about everything that went on there tonight on top of that koppie.

Mol winds down the window. The rain has slowed down a bit. She feels in her housecoat pocket for her cigarettes. Only one left. She was smoking one after another there under the tower tonight, but she wasn't smoking any of them right down to the end. She kept throwing them away half finished, 'cause every five minutes there'd be a whole new flare-up all over again. Now she's struggling to get her lighter working. She has to turn it upside down before it takes. No wonder, after all that lighting up to look at Treppie's scars. Lighters weren't made for inspecting damage in the dark. She looks at Pop. The way he's sitting there now you wouldn't say he could string so many sentences together. His head is propped up against the window and by the light in the parking lot she can see the little hollow above his collarbone in front where his shirt hangs open. It looks like the skin on top of boiled milk when it goes cold – like fine little crinkles. She has to look long and hard before she sees the shadow of a pulse under his skin. When they all got back into the car on the koppie and Pop started talking, she prayed that he'd just keep going. He even held up his hand to show Treppie he didn't want to be interrupted. Clever old bugger. He started by buttering Treppie up. More than butter. Toffee! He said it was true, all of them would've come to nothing if it hadn't been for Treppie. As it was, they were little more than skin and bone, but without Treppie they wouldn't even have cast a shadow. Then Pop stopped talking 'cause he couldn't find the exact word to describe how important Treppie was in their lives. By now she'd caught on to Pop's plan and she thought, let me quickly chip in here. She had just the right word for him: 'Vital ingredient'. That was exactly the word, Pop said, winking at her to say thanks. Treppie was their vital ingredient, he said, and he wasn't really talking about Treppie's job at the Chinese either.

Of course not. Treppie says he does odd jobs for them, servicing their fridges and writing up their menus in English, but she thinks he just sits there and gambles. Gambles and plays the horses. Sometimes he's suddenly flush and then for weeks on end he's broke again. So she agreed with Pop, it wasn't really a matter of working at the Chinese. Pop said what he was really talking about was wiring. Treppie kept them wired up with his stories 'cause Treppie always had an angle on a thing. He always saw a corner or a twist or a side or a colour in a thing, no matter how flat and white and nothing that thing was.

Then she saw Pop's eyes starting to shine like in his younger days when he had a plan. She could see he was getting right into the heart of his sermon now. And so she also began to feel stronger.

But that was only one side of the matter, Pop said. Yes, she said, it was just the one side, and then she threw in one of Treppie's favourite sayings: 'It takes two to tango.' Spot on, she was spot on. Pop squeezed her hand a little so that Treppie wouldn't see and he said, spot on, now she was reading his thoughts. Spot on.

The point was, Pop said, and he turned around in his seat, pointing his finger to the back, but she quickly took that finger out of Treppie's face. She knew that was another thing Treppie couldn't stand. A finger pointing in his face.

The point was, Pop said, if Treppie hadn't been stuck with the rest of them, who were nobodies, and if he hadn't had their never-ending bullshit around him all the time, the pointless bullshit, the insignificant bullshit, if he, Treppie, hadn't had that, then he'd also have been nothing, 'cause that's what kept him going. It was he who stomped and kicked and lied and went wild in that bottomless pit, Pop said, until he began to see some sparks inside there. If Treppie didn't understand him, then he'd explain it to him in his own language. They were like a system with a dead earth. And if he got some spark out of them, then they got charged up like a turbine. Pumped up like a power plant. You could say, Pop said, that if you managed to connect them up properly you had power for Africa.

Pop isn't the only one who understands Treppie's language, so she slipped in her own word: 'Generator.' That's what Treppie was, she said. He was their generator.

Now she'd really hit the nail on the head, Pop said. Through thick and thin, in sunshine and in rain, until death do them part, high current, dead earth, hand-in-glove, the one couldn't do without the other.

Pop took a deep breath and she also took a few. The car was blue from all the smoke and they both turned around to take a good look at Treppie in the back seat. But he just sat there with his head down.

Now Pop came to his second point. If Old Pop hadn't beaten Treppie to a pulp, he said, then Treppie wouldn't have been the man he was today. Then he'd have been just like anyone else and he would have been at peace, not giving a damn. So, in fact, Treppie should be grateful to Old Pop, 'cause without him Treppie would have been nothing.

Treppie just sat there and mumbled, with his head hanging down like that, so you didn't know if he was saying yes or no. Pop lifted his finger again, and this time she left it, 'cause she saw this was his third point, and it wasn't just any old point. The only true peace Treppie would ever find, Pop said, was the peace he made with himself, 'cause peace wasn't something you just got for nothing. Pop said if Treppie made peace in his heart with Old Pop, he might stop shorting out all the time. If they didn't mind, Pop said, he wanted to use the language of electricity again. His theory was that Treppie was scared of making peace with himself 'cause if he did he might unplug himself and lose his spark completely.

Then Treppie mumbled something that she couldn't make out, and Pop said, excuse me, what was he saying, but she could see he wasn't finished yet.

Well, said Pop, he didn't care if Treppie thought he was talking Boere-electricity or Boere-psychology. It was worth the trouble to try making that peace. Just look at you, Pop said. Ja, just look, she said. Nothing but skin and bone, said Pop. Ja, skin and bone, she said. At this rate, Pop said, Treppie was going to fall down and die like a dog. Like a dog, she said. And dead is dead, and Klipdrift is Klipdrift, whether or not Old Pop ruined him and beat him to a pulp. What did he have to say to that? Was it maybe Treppie's way of paying them all back? Must they now feel bad for the rest of their lives, and must they feel even worse one day when Treppie died from the horries? If you asked him, Pop said, that was what the English called retribution from the grave, and that was indeed one way of doing things. But it was a very unfair and selfish way of dishing out punishment, to say the least of it. It was a terrible way to make sure people didn't ever forget you.

Stop now, or you'll make him cry, she said to Pop when she saw Treppie's head stay down. She couldn't stand the thought of anyone crying, especially Treppie. As far as she knew he'd never once cried properly in his entire life and she didn't want to be in his company when he did.

But by this time Pop was so into his sermon that he was ready for anything. No, he said, everyone needs to cry a little, from time to time, and the next thing he was wiping his own eyes with his Christmas hanky.

Then there was a long silence in the car again. All you heard was 'tiffa-tiffa' as Toby scratched for fleas and kicked the seat. Pop held out his hanky so Treppie could take it.

But Treppie didn't take it. He didn't even sniff. He just let out a little sigh, and when he opened his mouth again, his voice came out straight and cool, like Klipdrift on the rocks.

Thanks for the sermon, old boy, he said, but Pop should understand, it was too late.

'Too late for tears,' he said. 'But never too late for a laugh.'

Then he almost sounded like he was sad in an old-fashioned way, and when they turned around, he surprised them again. There he sat with a smile on his face. Such a mixed-up little smile, half-shy, half-soft, with a little gleam in his eye. Like he was saying to them, here's a smile for your trouble. Take it! Now what could they say after that?

So she said it was nice of him to smile for a change.

Ja, said Pop, he could go ahead and smile, it wouldn't kill him.

But then she looked at Pop and saw that he was looking straight ahead of him. He wasn't smiling at all. Suddenly he looked like the whole world was pressing down on his shoulders.

She had to nudge him three times and tell him it wouldn't kill him to smile either. And only then did he smile for her. He opened his eyes wide and gave her a look that said, everything's okay, she mustn't worry.

Well, by then they'd outstayed their welcome on that koppie. They'd had enough looking at lights and listening to sermons and drinking Klipdrift. And they were hungry. So they drove to the all-night café in Brixton and bought some take-aways. Nice sloppy hamburgers. Between the bites Treppie said he reckoned Lambert was doing an epileptic strip-tease for that floozy in his den right now. But neither she nor Pop thought it was funny and Treppie didn't say anything more on the subject.

Then they went for a joy-ride, all over the place. She thought now she was finally going to see the end of Jo'burg, but the lights just carried on and on, forever.

Where did they stop? she kept asking. Treppie said she should under-stand, a city like Jo'burg was like a human heart. It was boundless. There were as many lights in a city, he said, as there were hopes and plans in the human heart. Then Pop said, ai, that was now really nice and philosophical, Treppie should write it down sometime.

And then they were allowed to switch on the radio again. First it was speeches by that Eugene-man, explaining how Paardekraal was a beacon in the nation's history, and how the Waterberg was the place where the soldiers of Jesus were being trained to defend God's chosen people on earth against the black heathen hordes. It turned out to be Radio Pretoria, broadcasting from Blackangle. Another city.

Treppie said that lot were sitting in more dark corners than they realised. Then he started singing 'Jesus bids us shine with a pure, pure light' before switching to another station. Highveld Stereo. Just love songs, one after another. But Treppie was on form again, and he made them laugh by changing the words of all those love songs. Like the words for 'Distant Drums'. Treppie made up his own ballad to that tune, about Eugene Terre'Blanche and all the different colours of his underpants, with bits of speeches inbetween about how the mummies and the daddies and the grandmas and the grandpas and the dogs and the cats and everyone must learn to shoot with stolen guns, 'boom! boom! boom!' It was very funny.

And they even stopped to buy soft-serves before going to Zoo Lake. To rest a bit, Pop said, but they all fell asleep very quickly.

Mol turns around and makes big eyes at Toby. 'Whoof!' says Toby. Oh God, she didn't mean to make him bark now. Toby jumps out of the dicky, over Treppie and into the front. He's tired of sitting in a car. He wants out. Mol opens for Toby so he can go for a walk. Her too, she also wants to stretch her legs a bit. She walks around the back of the car. Raindrops glisten on the car's roof. She looks out, first to one side, then to the other. Her neck is stiff from sitting. She sees the sky's getting paler on the one side.

'Come, Mol, we're going now.' It's Pop, he's awake.

'Did you sleep all right?'

'Ja, fine,' says Pop. 'Just not enough.'

They drive home through the grey morning and smoke a last cigarette for the night. Treppie says right now a cup of coffee would hit the spot. She asks Pop if he thinks everything at the house is okay. Pop says he can feel in his bones everything's just fine.

'All quiet on the western front,' says Treppie. They take the top route, along Jan Smuts Avenue. The big lorries are on the road already, splashing water on to the Volksie's windscreen as they pass. Pop switches on the wipers. In Empire he turns down his window for some fresh air. Deep in the hearts of the trees, she hears the sparrows starting to chirp.

LAMBERTUS AND CLEOPATRA ⌒

It's a quarter past eleven.

There's a soft knock on Lambert's outside door. 'Rat-a-tat-tat-tat'. He knows that knock well. It's Treppie's 'look who's here' knock.

Take a deep breath. Stand up. Stomach in. Back straight. Now, slowly to the door, just like he practised it, with footsteps like those in the movies when you see someone's feet walking in the underground parking but you don't know who it is, and you figure it's the unknown hero.

Let him first check if everything's ready: rose, sheets, lounge chairs, fridges, service counter, all glowing in the red light. It looks full and empty at the same time. A carpet, he could at least have got a piece of carpet somewhere for the cement floor in front of the chairs. Or in front of the bed. There's a stabbing feeling in his tail-end.

The doorhandle feels cold in his hand.

'Ta-te-ra-a-a-a!'

It's Treppie. He's blowing through his fist like a trumpet. Pissed again.

'Triomf, Triomf, the time is ripe and here comes the stag over the hills!'

Treppie shows with his one hand how the stag approaches, but it looks like the stag's doing something else. Christ, can't he fucken behave himself just once? With his other hand Treppie pulls someone into the light.

'Straight from Cleopatra's Classy Creole Queens! Meet Mary, the Creolest of them all!'

Mary. She looks at him. She looks like she can't believe what she's seeing. Well, neither can he.

'Lambert,' he hears himself saying. 'Lambert Benade.' Now he must greet her nicely. A firm handshake, but not too firm, like Treppie said. The way he tried it out with his mother.

'Pleased to meet you,' he says, just the way he practised it, over and over again.

'Hi,' is all she says. 'Mary.' She doesn't take his hand. She looks over his shoulder, into the den. She's standing right here in front of him.

Her whole head's full of shiny little curls. Her face is thin. It looks tanned, with lots of make-up. And her mouth seems a bit too big. But her lips are shiny and she's not sucking them in like his mother does. Red, her lips are red. Her shoulders are high, like she's pulling them up to say she can't help it, or sorry, she doesn't know what to do. She needn't worry. He'll show her everything. He'll show her everything very nicely. A bag hangs from one shoulder on a long, thin strap. She's got tiny, shaky little hands and she's holding one hand inside the other, in front of her bust.

'Well, I leave him in your capable hands, Mary, my dear! I hope you have a Creole of a time!' Treppie squeezes Mary's shoulder as if he's known her for a long time. Is she maybe his piece or something? No, he doesn't even want to think about that. She doesn't look Chinese, anyway.

Treppie winks at him. For fuck's sake, this isn't the time for winking!

Now he must stand aside so she can come in. He wants to take her softly by the arm and welcome her into his den. Help her up the step. Show her that he knows his manners at all times and in all places, whether she's Chinese or Creole or whatever.

But his hand comes up too fast and he grabs her too high. She feels soft and slippery. He can see she's upset about his hand touching her like that. Maybe she noticed his buggered fingertips. But that's nothing. Apart from his fingers he's okay. She'll still see. Completely okay.

'Steady, old boy,' he hears Treppie say. 'Don't grab, it's bad manners.'

Treppie must shut his mouth now. Fast. Couldn't he see it was an accident, that high tackle?

'Don't worry, Mary, old Lambert here is fully domesticated. Our local hero with a heart of gold. Meek as a lamb!'

He must close this door, now! In Treppie's face, so he can fuck off here from his door. He mustn't come and make big eyes at him now. Treppie looks like he wants to say something with those big eyes of his, like sorry, she's all they could find and he must just make the best of it. That's not what he needs now. Right now he's ready to make a whole new start. That's what he wants!

He turns around. He feels funny, like he's too heavy or his feet are sticking to the ground or something. Now Mary's standing in the middle of the room. She's looking at the painting above his bed.

'Holy Jesus!' she says. She walks closer to the wall, bends down and looks at the postbox, where South Africa begins.

'Who's this supposed to be?' She points to both sides of the postbox.

He moves closer. Just stay nice and calm now. His voice jams. First clear the throat a bit. Yes, like that.

'This here is Jan van Riebeeck, and that's Harry.'

'Harry who?'

'Harry the Strandloper.'

'The what?'

'Harry the Hottentot, man!'

What's this peeling off here now? Let him scratch it off quickly, then it'll be okay again. Harry's got three coats of paint on his body.

'Government brown. It peels.'

'I see,' says Mary, in a shriller voice. 'Is that how the cookie crumbles around here?'

What fucken cookie's she talking about now?

He stands away from the bed with his hands on his hips. He feels her eyes moving over him. And now? What's so funny now all of a sudden? He must have checked in his mother's mirror at least six times. His back feels strange from walking so upright all the time. Did he say something wrong now, or what?

He hears people talking outside. Pop says: 'Quick!' Then the front gate squeaks and the Volla takes off. It's Molletjie. She roars through first, second and third, and then she's gone. Now it's just him here at home. Now he must smile. The time has come to say: We're on our own now, just me and you. But his mouth opens and closes and he can't get a word out.

Mary's voice sounds like it's coming from a far place. Mister, she says, if you want me to go, I don't mind. Her voice fades. He tries to cock his ears so he can hear what she's saying. How do you cock your ears? he wonders. It's like focusing your eyes, but different.

'I really don't mind leaving, you know. In fact, I don't give a shit! Not this much!'

She clicks her fingers in the air. She doesn't care *shit*. No, wait. No, fuck, just hold on a minute now! He sticks out his arms to stop her. No, that's not what he means, not at all. His feet move towards her. She moves out of his way. She keeps dodging him. Why? He's not a leper or something, is he?

'No, no please! I haven't got the plague, man, please don't go. That's just old personal stuff. It's my hobby. Painting. Wall painting. Yesterday I put the wings on. Finishing touches, like my uncle says. They did it in the churches, overseas, way back, everything had wings on, he says, even the donkeys. My uncle's a very clever oke, you know, he runs the show here, he's a very educated man, self-educated and all, he's a, how do you say it, auto-addict, he remembers everything. Got a photographic memory.'

What else does she want to hear? She just says, 'Hmm.' She must still be feeling a bit strange here in his den.

'Well, and I've burnt the *Watchtowers*, the whole lot of them, and I jump-started the Tedelex, for you, from a car battery, even. Hey, can you believe it? That was nearly a big fuck-up. But it was a miracle, afterwards. And over here's chips and dips and peanuts. You like peanuts, Mary? Like I said, everything I've got. Even a Swiss roll for breakfast. And I have a party trick as well, you look like you will make him cook, I say, but that's for later.'

She pulls a face. But she needn't worry. When he puts his hand over hers that thing will really start boiling.

'And I got music too, specially for us tonight. Listen.' He points with his finger, but his finger feels funny. He takes it away again.

Now he must get to the music, quick, but his body doesn't want to move. He mustn't start tripping over things now. He turns the little dial.

He tuned the radio already, earlier this afternoon, setting it to FM, 94, 95, where Radio Orion used to be, and where Highveld Stereo is now. Christ. Now it's too loud. Turn it down! Quick! Keep smiling, like Treppie says. It keeps your customers happy.

'Did you get a fright? Nice little radio, hey?'

He knows she's just standing there looking at him. She's still not in the mood for smiling. He turns the dial, first this way and then that, playing for time. Just a little time. What do you say to a girl who just stands there and looks at you like you crawled out of a fucken hole or something?

'Nice romantic background music.' He tries a wink, but both eyes close at the same time. Now he can't even wink here tonight! But it doesn't matter, she's turned around again. Now she's standing there with folded arms. She's checking his service counter. Eat, that's what, eat something nice. He must get in front of her so he can be next to the snacks and offer her some.

'Like I say, anything you need, anything you want, you name it, I've got it. Late-night snacks. Dip a chip, Mary, man. Here you are.'

Which one? Make it two. A dip and a chip. Avo and a crinkle cut. He holds them out for her.

She shakes her head. No thanks. But he stands firm. She shakes her head even harder. Now it's more than just no thanks. He puts down the bowls. Maybe she's not hungry. Maybe she's thirsty.

'What about a drink, hey? I got everything.' Let him open the Fuchs a bit so she can see.

'Everything to please a queen!' He points to the things in the fridge. He packed and repacked those drinks so you could see them all at a single glance. His beers and his Cokes, all in tins so they won't go flat like in the bottles. His Drostdy Hof Blush, right through to the orange juice, for just in case.

'You see, enough for a week.'

No see? Okay. Later. Why's she saying fuck-all now? All she does is put down her handbag and take off her black jacket. She hangs the jacket over his mother's chair.

'Well, maybe enough for two days, hey? What do you say? Then we can go get some more!'

Now he sticks to his spot, here next to his fridge. His hands are opening and closing from not knowing what to do next. Things must start clicking here. Fuck! This night must get a move on!

'For the rest, everything's right. You missed the bubbles man, Mary, just bubbles, bubbles, bubbles. Everywhere. But now this old thing even makes ice, hey, I swear. I couldn't believe it. Check here, man, just check this!'

He takes out the ice-trays. Now look, woman! Fucken rock-hard ice! No dice. Put it back again. Maybe she's a bit raw. Not used to things. If your audience is asleep, Treppie always says, try another angle.

'And the postbox is fixed. Did you see it? I made him myself, quite a tricky one, that one, kept falling off. Can't tell you what trouble I had with that piece of shit. But now it's even painted the colour of peace, thanks to my old man, he's got a knack for the finishing touches, for sure! And tomorrow they come to paint this whole house, white as snow, good as new, you won't recognise it. And when they paint, we go, you and me, to get the petrol. I checked all the bags for leaks, two times. And I've got a hole!'

Now he'll show her something! She needn't keep her face so straight. There's only one hole like this in the whole of Jo'burg, that's for sure!

Lift up the plank. Shift it away nicely, so she can look inside. Come now, woman!

'Come, come here, Mary, come look! Now this was the biggest job of all, hey, nearly broke my back here, just rubble, rubble, rubble. There was another town here, a black one, just bricks, bricks, bricks, kaffirs didn't live under plastic and cardboard in those days, hey! But now it's big enough for the petrol, for an emergency, you know. You never know, that's what I say. And my uncle agrees. A person must be ready, hey? What do you say? For when the shit hits the fan. You know what I mean, hey? Then we hit the great road to the North. I checked on the map. In the CNA. Will take a day or so. Then we're over the border. First we make a picnic and then we make a new beginning.'

She doesn't look like she's making the connections. His hole is open, his fridge is open and he's wide open. All his stuff is lying here, open. But she's not looking. Maybe she wants to look at the painting again, at his map.

'Check, here's our route, in red, here, here, here.'

Christ, she must be able to see a dotted line! The line's in red, too. It goes over the lawn, the molehills, the black arrows, the yellow arrows, his mother's body and the tennis ball in her mouth. He points it out to her.

'Tennis ball in the mouth. Didn't have enough space here. Dog's games, you know? But it's my mother, this one. Nice lady, full of sports!'

He feels too big, standing here next to his painting. His body doesn't want to shrink. He tries to grin but his mouth doesn't want to. Grin! That's his mother, she's enough to make anyone laugh. Fuck! Let's try the mermaid. Maybe she'll think it's cute. That mermaid is actually her!

'And this is you on the car here, Mary. I dreamt of you, long before you even knew me.'

Maybe she doesn't like laughing at herself. Well then, let her laugh at him then, him with his big ears and his sideburns, sitting in the driver's seat.

'And that's me, ready to take you wherever you want to go, to the wild open spaces . . .'

At last! A smile! About fucken time too. Just a half-smile. But that's all he needs. Take the gap, Lambertus, take it!

'. . . to the sleepy villages, where the lion roars tonight! Hawhimbawe! Hawhimbawe!'

His mother always laughs when he sings that song. Ever since he was small. But now the smile's gone again. Maybe she thinks his plan isn't good enough. Maybe she doesn't like the sound of his lions.

He points, north, north, *north*, he points where he wrote in the names this afternoon. Those are not petrol stops. The petrol's been sorted out. They're just piss-stops. Pretoria, Nylstroom, Naboomspruit, Messina. He wrote Messina in big letters. Across the border. His plan is fine. There's nothing wrong with his plan.

'And she'll make it, Mary, don't you worry, she'll make it. I tuned her, I checked her points, I tapped off her oil. And in any case, we'll take Flossie with us, the beach buggy, for spares, for in case. As we say in Afrikaans, there's always a light at the end of the wagon-trek. Hey, old Mary, man, even if it's a long way to Tipperary, hey? You know that song?'

Fuck, he's really doing his very best here. Maybe he should sing instead, he's in any case singing for his smiles tonight. It's a long way to Tip-per-rar-reee! She'd better open that red mouth of hers for a change. He can't do all the fucken talking all fucken night long!

'Listen, my china.' Here she comes now, but she's coming too slowly. Oh, shit, what now? Now she's swaying her backside at him. She's even turned around so he can see her backside.

'I haven't got no time to waste, hey. I'm a busy lady!'

Fuck! Let him get out of the way here. She mustn't come and act all high and mighty and start swinging her backside around. He's also been fucken busy!

Jesus. Now she's on the bed, legs and all. Loosening buttons. Yes, that's what she's doing, she's unbuttoning her blouse. Lots of buttons. What's that underneath? A bow, a fucken little red bow. In the middle. Between the tits. The tits are in a see-through bra. Black net-stuff with holes in it. Sit, she motions to him, he must come and sit here next to her on the bed. Please, God! Those long red nails!

'Hey, hey, wait now, Mary, man, let's not rush things now, man. Come, there's nice chairs here, man, look, specially for you!' Pop's chair. His mother's chair. Next to each other. 'Nice chairs, I promise, family chairs, they come a long way, they can tell stories, these chairs, man, like you won't believe, stories for Africa.'

It's the truth. He's not talking nonsense now. Right. That's better. She's buttoning up again. Yes, better.

'As you wish. I hope you know what you're doing. Time is money, you know that?'

Of course he knows. What's the time there on Treppie's clock–radio? Only twenty to twelve. He checks his watch. That's fine. The night's still young, as Treppie always says. What's she getting so worried about, anyway? There she sits in his mother's chair now. It looks funny, but at least she sits nicely, with her legs closed.

'Don't worry, just relax, Mary, I'll get you a drink. What do you like? I also got brandy and Coke. Come on, what do you say?'

'I don't drink on the job, Cleopatra's house rules.'

Why's she grinning again? It's the oldest trade in the world, after all. Her kind fancies a snort. She mustn't think she can come and spin him a lot of crap here.

'Cleopatra's foot in a fish tin, man!'

'Just Coke, I mean it.'

'Suit yourself, lady.' If he can just get a snort or two into her. But he must tune her nicely now. Don't rush a woman. That's what Treppie always says when his mother takes so long to do things. When a woman's revs finally get going, they really run high. Then you struggle to bring them down again. He says he's seen it time and time again.

'I have lemons, I have ice, might I make you a Lee Martin, just like in the Spur? You know what a Lee Martin is? No? Crushed ice and lemon and things?'

She shakes her head. No.

Looks like she doesn't know bugger-all. Fucken weird, that's all he can say. Maybe the Cleopatras don't go to Spur.

'Never too late to learn.' Take a deep breath. 'Never too late, my baby.'

Mary just sits there, looking at her nails. She says fuck-all. It looks like that 'baby' went straight over her head, like she didn't even feel it. Maybe he said it too early or something. Fucken worse than a jammed compressor! And he can't very well go and kick her, but he's tempted, hell, a nice kick under the backside is exactly what she needs. There go his knees now, jerking up and down under the skin. It must be 'cause he's thinking about kicking her. He mustn't kick her. She'd fall to pieces, first shot. No, he won't kick her. He'll just stand here next to his work bench. Stay nice and cool. He grabs the edge of the work bench, his service counter that he prepared so neatly, with so many nice things on it. Ai, fuck. He hears her lighting up, here right behind his back. That's what he needs too, a good old cigarette. Sit for a while, in Pop's deep chair, with his legs stretched out in front of him so his knees can stop jerking. Yes, a cigarette.

A thought begins to form in his head, but he can't get hold of it properly. Come now, Lambert! Got it! It's the thought of an ashtray, and an ashtray is the other thing he forgot. A carpet and an ashtray. Can you believe it? Most of the time he tips his ash on to the floor and he stubs his cigarettes against the wall, just anywhere. He had to sweep so many cigarette butts out of here . . . never mind, she won't know the difference. He picks up one of the bowls with painted stags and passes it over to her.

'Ashtray.'

'Thanks,' she says.

'Some ashtray, hey.' Mary looks at the ashtray. Then she turns it round and looks at the back.

'I inherited it from my grandmother. Grand old lady. They did it in style in those days.'

'Hmm,' is all she says. 'How's the Coke coming along?'

'Won't be a minute.' But before the words are out of his mouth he realises he's got a new problem. How's he going to give her crushed ice without making a mess? If it was just him alone it would be a simple matter – he'd take a hammer and smash the ice-blocks to pieces on the work bench. Not that he needs crushed ice every day. Ice-blocks are good enough and even those came into his life only after the fridges were fixed. He's seen in the movies how they put ice in a dishcloth or something, in those fancy American kitchens where everyone stands around with drinks in their hands, then they knock the ice against a wall with neat little thuds, like it's something they do every other day. But now he hasn't got a dishrag. And it's not something he does every other day. When he does knock things in kitchens he makes holes in the doors of dressers. Fuck! As far as he knows, the only dishrag in the house got used up today, to clean all that drain-goo on the floor. And he's not going to open up his steel cabinet to look for anything 'cause then all those pipes and dirty clothes and GTX tins that he stashed in there will come piling out.

Maybe he should go fetch something in the house. Look in his mother's room. Suddenly he sees himself crushing ice on the den's wall with his mother's dirty housecoat. Crush, crush, crush. No!

He'll just tell her the ice-crusher's broken. Out of order. He's never seen one, but he's sure you can buy them.

'So, have we suddenly gone as quiet as a mouse, big boy?'

Is she really smiling at him here behind his back? Yes, she is, with a pouting mouth too. Well, well, what have we here? Wait, let him first get this ice out of the tray. Fucken ice-tray. Hit the blarry thing, that's the only way. 'Thock! Thock!' he slams the tray against the edge of the work bench.

'I've just got a problem' – 'Thock!' – 'with my ice-crusher. Looks like it's out of order.'

'Well, I'm getting mighty thirsty here, ice or no ice.' Now she doesn't sound like she's smiling. She switches that smile of hers on and off, on and off, faster even than Treppie. Get that smile going again, lady! If I can, you can! Keep smiling, girl!

'Thirsty, hey, and we haven't even started yet!' Shit, that one just slipped out before he could stop it.

'Well, at this rate . . .' Mary says, but that's not what he wants to hear. He pours himself a stiff brandy and Coke. One glass in each hand. Steady, now. He's standing in front of Mary. He's standing wrong. He can feel it. He mustn't stand still, he must move, keep moving. Make a noise.

'Listen. Nice song they're playing there.'

The Highveld Stereo woman is talking. She says it's Leo Sayer. She says he's always so spot on about the eternal questions of love.

> *When I need you*
> *I just close my eyes and I'm with you*
> *And all that I so wanna give you*
> *Is only a heartbeat away*

Mary takes her Coke. Right. Now sit down a little. With a cigarette. It's in his jacket pocket. But where's his fucken matches now? He checked a hundred times to make sure they were in his pocket. You don't want to get stuck looking for matches in the heat of the moment. Just shuddup a second, there, Leo. Fucken close my eyes and find my fucken matches, now! He can feel Mary looking at him as he digs in his pocket.

Here she comes with her lighter. Come closer, she motions. He doesn't trust this.

'I don't bite, honey. Come, let me light your fire.'

There's that half-grin again. That tongue, licking her lips.

Grin back at her, Lambert. Now you're even her honey! But it doesn't sound right to him, this 'honey'. And what's this about a fire? He still doesn't feel warm. He feels strange and cold. The insides of his hands are sweating.

He leans over. No one has ever lit up for him like this, let alone a woman.

'Chick!' goes her lighter as she flicks it on. 'Sssss!' goes the little flame, here next to his face. Those longs nails right here next to his cheek. Christ! Now he's gone and breathed too hard. Out goes the lighter. God in heaven!

'Easy, boy!' She flicks it back on again.

Now he gets it right. He leans back in his chair. Man, this cigarette's going down well. He takes deep pulls. Nothing helps like a nice deep pull. He feels a slight shudder down his tail-end.

From where he sits he has a full-frontal view of his fridges. The cigarette's helping, but it's not helping enough. And his fridges can't tell him fuck-all, either. They look fucked. Small and dirty and fucked out.

He steals a glance at Mary. She also says nothing. She's smoking with her eyes screwed up, drinking her Coke in small sips. She doesn't take her glass away from her mouth.

Now their conversation mustn't go and dry up. If push comes to shove he can always go and fetch the TV from the lounge. Maybe there's a scary movie on Bop, or fast American news, there-then-here-now. If only Treppie was at home. He would have known what to do. But maybe not. Treppie would've stuck around too long, until it was too late for him to make his birthday happen.

He sees her looking at her watch. She looked just a minute ago. Ten to twelve. Time to try another angle.

'So what do you think's going to happen on the twenty-seventh?'

'Why?'

Why? Why? He's not fucken asking her which side the sun rises every day.

'Well, uh, it's a turning-point in the history of our country!'

She gets up quickly.

'Jesus Christ! You need to find your own bladdy turning-point. Come *on*, now!'

What's that she's taking out of her bag? She throws it down on the bed. Fucken FL's! Right, if she can push, he can also push.

'Are you challenging me, lady? I've got my own, you know. Rough Riders. Very nice. So get ready for a bumpy ride!' He gives her a fat wink. Now he must move!

'Shall we dance first?' Turn up that radio. For Christ's sake, let's have a good song now! 'Just right for a cheek-to-cheek, hey. Nice song. Jim Reeves. Golden Oldie. Big fan of Jim Reeves. Do you know him?'

'Lord, have mercy!'

Just look how she flicks away that stub with her fingers! Not bad! Stamp on it, girly, stamp on it with that dainty little shoe of yours. That's more like it. A bit of a temper is better than nothing. Here she comes, on her high horse.

'That's what I like in a woman! She must be game for everything!'

Now he must hold her tight. Like the heroes in the movies who dance close with their girls. Soft guava! That's what Treppie always says when those scenes come up. Soft guava and cucumber power!

Here she is, now. Right up against him. With that shiny hair of hers right under his nose.

'So, what are you waiting for, Prince Charming?'

She smells sweet. Too sweet.

His hands feel her hands taking hold of them. She puts his hands on to her hips.

'Come on, Lambert, we haven't got all night.'

446

Now she's swaying her body into his, but the beat isn't actually right for a slow dance. She pulls him so he can start moving. No one has ever pulled him like this before. His hands slide further and further down her dress. Smooth, no funny bumps. No, hell, wait. He moves his hands up again. Rather listen to Jim Reeves.

> *Mary marry me*
> *Let's not wait*
> *The time we have*
> *Is all there is*
> *And then it might be too late.*

'Do you hear that?' She's pulling him by the jacket now. 'The time we have is all there is.'

But now she's starting her shit again. Here comes more loosening of buttons. This time it's *his* buttons. Three, four, five, look how quickly she works those thin, brown hands of hers. Christ, those red nails here high up against his white skin! Well, at least it's just here around the top. Don't lose it now.

'You know what we call this type of dance, Mary?'

She shakes her head so hard the curls whip into his nose.

'Soft guava, we call it the soft guava.'

'*Papkoejawel!* You think I don't know that word?' Mary laughs.

He doesn't like that laugh. Is she trying to play the fool with him or something? Let him rather laugh along. Ha-ha-ha! Then he can button up his shirt again, pour himself another drink. If she wants to laugh she can sit down and laugh till she's finished.

'So, you can speak a bit of Afrikaans?'

Now she's suddenly packing her cigarettes back into her bag. Where does she think she's going? Maybe she thought he was talking about *her* guava.

'Look here, man, what do you take me for? The man in the moon? Of course I can speak Afrikaans.'

'I thought you were a Creole, from Creolia or someplace!'

'Creolia? Ha-ha-ha! Very funny. A Creole, *lat ek vir djou sê*, Mister

Ballroom Champ, is ma' just a lekker coffee-colour dolly what can mix her languages. So if that's your problem, if that's what's putting you off, I'll just leave sommer right now. I've got my money. I've got nothing to lose. Time's nearly up anyways.'

24:00, it says on Treppie's clock–radio. Forty!

'Please, please don't go. I don't mind. Really, I don't.'

A darky. So, that's what Treppie was making big eyes about. Well, he's not bothered by a piece of coffee-skirt, if that's what Treppie's idea was. A bit of the dark stuff is no problem for him!

A neat brandy. Without Coke. Then he'll be ready. 'It's all right, man, anyway, you are so nice and smart with your make-up and everything, I bet you can actually pass for white any time, Mary, hey? You get my drift? I mean, it can't be too difficult for you. What about another Coke, hey? With half a tot? What do you say?'

Dead silence here behind him. What's it this time? He turns round. Mary's looking at him with wide eyes that shine like daggers.

'You bastard! Look at you! Look at this place! Who the hell do you think you are, hey? You're not even white, man, you're a fucken backward piece of low-class shit, that's what you are. Useless fucken white trash!'

'Excuse me? What did you say there? Is there something wrong with my ears or is somebody calling me a piece of shit in my own house?'

Now all hell is loose. But no one can teach him anything about talking shit or making shit. If this off-white number doesn't watch out he'll knock her and all her shit as flat as a pancake! Yes, retreat, retreat, you'd better, you toffee-cunt. Let her, she can't get further than that inside door. He sees her feeling for the inside door's handle.

'You're too late, Mary, too fucken late! Rather give that hand of yours here.' He locked that door before she came, early tonight, to keep out his mother. And Treppie. They said they were going out but you never know with them. Fuck, if only they were here now, then he could go and call them to come help a bit. Then they could all help him to put this cheeky slut in her place, for once and for all.

'I said, let go of that door!'

Her breath's on his face now. Her mouth is thin. She's got lines round the outside of her mouth. 'Zing!' goes his head. Through the zing he picks up a song playing on the radio.

You are the sun
I am the moon
You are the words
I am the tune
Play me!

Forty years and a few seconds old! Fuck! She turns her face away. Red stuff on that Coloured cheek of hers.

'Do you hear that, Mary? You must be nice to me now, hey. You'd better behave yourself now, hey! I don't like spoilsports, that's one thing I don't, um, tolerate.'

Nice that he remembered that word.

'Let go, you're hurting me!'

She doesn't sound very hurt to him. She sounds more like a coon-girl with designs in her head.

'Don't be a sissy, man. Your sort have seen it all. As long as you play nicely, you won't get hurt. Got it?'

Another cigarette, that's what he needs now. Matches. Where? In his shirt pocket, top pocket. He sees his shoes. They look too big. He sees them 'cause he's not standing upright. He's bent over forwards. His arms are hanging out. He must get back into his gentleman's pose. He's got half a hard-on after that bit of action, but it drops quickly again. This business must get back into swing. Christ, this is worse than fucken fridge repairs.

He tells her she must look on the crate, there next to the bed. In the Coke bottle.

'Look, I even got you a rose, man, want to smell it? My mother is into roses, you know. Her whole life long. This one here is a Whisky Mac. But there are lots more. Prima Ballerina, Red Alec, Las Vegas Supreme. That last one is an orange one. Hell, I must tell you that story! You won't believe it. We were in the HF Verwoerd Institute for the Mentally Retarded that day, me and my uncle, he put me up to it, when we became a republic, you know, at the Voortrekker monument.'

Must he go and take it out for her or what? There, let her take the fucken rose. Can't she see he's okay again?

'Go on, smell it!'

Move it, slut! He waits for her to smell. Christ, no, he must get another drink. And this time he'll stay right here in front of his counter. She mustn't start getting scared of him now. That business a second ago was nothing.

'So what's your favourite colour, Mary? Come, sit down again, come, sit here by me, in my mother's chair. Let's make friends again, hey? Let's talk nicely now, like civilised people, hey?'

'Civilised! Hmph!!'

To hell with hmph! Now it looks like she doesn't even want the rose. She's singing something.

> 'The night was heavy
> And the air was alive
> But she couldn't push through.'

'What was that, may I ask?'

Fucken full of shit, that's what. And she mustn't look up at the ceiling, she must look at him!

'Just a song. You know Highveld Stereo, like all the songs they play, say just the things you want to say?'

Fucken chancer! What's that she's looking at now?

'So tell me, Michelangelo, what's all this here supposed to be?'

'You can read, man, just read it.'

At least she wants him to tell her something. Stand up straight. Tummy in. Let him show her. Michelangelo. Who's that?

'It's my gallery of foolproofs. Much better than that stupid Cindy Viljoen from Tuxedo Tyres. Blue bikini, pink bikini, they think they can fool me!'

'Cindy Viljoen?'

'Yes, man, old Cindy on the calendars, I had them all, from '76, all round here, to keep track of the time, you know, but then I discovered it's the same Cindy in the tyre, just with different hair and things. It was all the same. People are not stupid, you know. On last year's calendar she had so much make-up on, even on her neck and all, past redemption, not even worth a retread. But these things here, they'll last forever. I finished it yesterday, just for you. They can all fly now, you see? They don't wear and tear like lawn-mowers, or cars or fridges. They work, like, like, um, like paradise!'

'Huh?'

'You still don't get it? Look, they all got wings on. It's like heaven. Everything can be an angel in heaven. Rats, cockroaches, everything. There's even a mole, MOLE II. It's my mother, you see, even she has wings there. Not in MOLE I, there she's in a fridge, frozen mole, ready to be fired off, but that's another story. I gassed all the moles this morning, Mary, so you don't have to look at them pushing heaps with a mouthful of Swiss roll.'

He can hear his voice going quicker and quicker. It feels like when you try to weld leaks. You can't keep up with yourself. She looks like she thinks he's got the horries or something. Stupid fucken floozy, that's what she is.

'So on the ceiling I will go on with heaven, all the stars and things, some dead, some alive, the black holes and the time warps and the sundogs and the rim of the dark moon that one can see in the earthshine, 'cause the earth shines too, did you know that? And old Gerty, shame, she'll also be there, we buried her, jersey and all, in the back here, with a poem on the prefab wall. My uncle is a poet, you know, but he doesn't know it, not always. He rhymes like shit, I mean, he can make a poem out of nothing. And a speech, without thinking. He made an unforgettable speech at my mother's wedding, master of ceremonies. He's quite a devil, you see – just needs horns. Even he liked Gerty, but not as much as my mother, my mother liked Gerty more than soft-serve, but Gerty coughed so much, she died of TB in the bathroom, just like my grandmother.'

'Allah preserve me!' Mary puts her hand in front of her mouth.

'It's just a dog, man. Toby's mother – he's also a dog. Gerty's son, like our streets here, Gerty Street, Toby Street. But he's still alive.'

He can't very well tell lies about the streets. Maybe he should take her for a walk so she can see with her own two eyes.

'I dipped him this morning, that Toby, so that the fleas won't bite you. Very much alive that dog. He pisses on carpets. It's like the AWB. Do you know them? They also piss on carpets. Like at the World Trade Centre, that time. All the policemen took off their caps after the pissing and prayed with the pissboys, they pissed inside and prayed outside!'

'Have mercy!'

She's looking up at the ceiling again. Wait till she hears his next story.

'You know, they even wanted to recruit me, the AWB, just up the road here, opposite the stewing meat, with Oros, 'strue's Bob, for their task force, they wanted a mechanic.'

'Not surprising.'

'Not at all, hey? But they can forget it, there's more to me than nuts and bolts, I say!'

'More nuts.' She laughs loudly.

See, it just takes a little time. Wait, let him get some peanuts for them. From his counter.

'I've got a gun, you know.'

Nice, these peanuts. Now she must watch carefully. Let him just finish chewing this mouthful, then he's going to get the gun out of his cabinet. Why's the door jammed like this? Come, bastard! Boom! It's open. The stuff starts falling on to his feet: scrap iron, pipes, spanners, tins.

'Holy shit!'

'Sorry about that, odds and ends, you know.'

No, Lambert! You knew you shouldn't have opened the cabinet!

'Sorry if I gave you a fright, man.'

Where's that gun now? Here at the bottom, under the rags. Now he's going to impress this Cleopatra big time.

'Don't come near me with that thing.'

'Don't worry, man, it's not loaded. I've got bullets, but it's not loaded.

I load it only when I go on patrol. This thing was a real bargain, man, I tell you. You don't know how lucky a person can get on a dump. I got binoculars too, but that's for sightseeing – the moon and the stars and the belly of the Jumbo. Big sports. But this is serious business, this is for protection.'

First just move away this rubbish a bit. Under the bed with this lot! He sees her putting her hands over her ears. Bit of a nervous girl, this one. But she'll still learn, they make a lot of noise around here sometimes.

'So you, er, patrol?'

'I patrol, man, I patrol. These days you can't leave anything to the police, you know, they've got their hands full, man, they don't have time for open manholes and that class of thing. In any case they're a noisy lot, they drive like maniacs.'

'But I mean do you patrol for a living, like, I mean for Springbok Patrols or such?'

'Over my dead body, I'm my own boss. I patrol as a, um, concerned citizen. Free and for nothing. I service the whole of Triomf. But mostly Gerty and Toby.'

'So, er, what do you do for a living, like?'

It's high time. Now she's nice and mellow. Looks like she's going to dip herself a chip at the counter.

'Well, um, we've got a little fridge business. Triumph Appliances. But these two here I fixed on my own, just for you. Shit, you should have seen the bubbles, man. Just so big as my head, hey. My whole room was in it, heaven and Africa and everything. Looked like magic, I must say. Not like I painted it myself, I mean like a masterpiece it looked. Like the Lost City. My uncle is not from this world, hey, he gave me an exam with Brylcreem on his face. Multiple choice with a red nose. It was very funny. My uncle's an operator, you know. He sings when the Ding-Dong passes. And he taught me to make the dogs go funny, I'll show you one day. But I passed with distinction that time. Do you want to hear the dogs go funny?'

Is she getting cold or something now? It's a nice little coat that. There's more to life than a housecoat, if you ask him. But what's she doing now with that bag of hers? Over her head, around her neck goes the strap. And then under the one arm!

'Ag no, man, Mary. Where are you going now? Everything is going so nice now, man. Let me show you my penny-whistle. It's from the kaffir hole. It has ar-chae-lo-gi-cal value, my uncle said.'

'Penny-whistle, my foot!'

What's she pointing to now, here under his belt? She's pointing this way but she's walking that way. Christ, has his zip been open all this time! No, it's closed. What was that pointing all about then? No manners.

'I figure you got a French horn or something in there. Out of tune. From playing solos all the time!'

'French horn, ha-ha! But you're full of sports, girly!'

'Time's up, mister! You've had your chance. A woman must eat, you know.'

Shit, where does she want to go and eat now? What's she doing at the outside door with her hand on the handle? And it's not locked!

'There's all this food to eat here, man. I spent all my money, every fucken last cent, chips, dips, drink, everything. Why don't you stay, man, my family's not so bad, man! My old man can play the mouth organ like you won't believe. I swopped the beds, I took the sheets from the windows, we washed them. And there's a mirror in the bathroom and a toilet seat, light blue, for a shit in peace, and lampshades from China. It was a lot of trouble, man, the pelmet is panelbeaten straight as hell, and there is a hole in the front door but it's for Toby, he's really a decent dog, I promise. Pedigree don't count, that's what I say, just decency. Decency, do you know that word? Decent? I've got a passion meter too, you want to see it? Educational value, relieves stress and boredom. Give me your hand!'

'I'm leaving, Rambo, you sit here nicely and relieve yourself like a good boy. I'm getting out of this fucken madhouse, before it's too late!'

Let her just fucken try. Now she's twisting her hands, trying to slip them out of his! Quite strong, for a Coloured chicky like this.

'Listen to that nice song they're playing, man. Let's have a shuffle, what do you say? Come, wrap your arms round me, like just now. Let's sing along, come on!'

> *Rock me gently, rock me slow*
> *Take it easy, don't you know*
> *That I have never been*
> *Loved like this before*

'Jesus, Lambert, what have you done to your hand, man?'

His hand? Okay. If she wants to know. His tongue feels like it's moving in slow motion as he tells her. About time that zings, about how all your birthdays tick past, about how Treppie told him you can make that tick go tick once more, about how he wanted to show Treppie a thing or two, but his hand went right through the dresser, and what a big joke that was, a big hole, and his mother pissed herself from all the laughing and everything.

'But what's a little hole, after all? Now things can breathe a little.'

'And that other hand, Lambert, what happened there?'

The plaster-hand? That plaster still looks fine to him.

Christ! How did she get his belt loose and his zip open so quickly?

'Ooh, Big Boy, and all in red, too!'

'You mean my fingertips? That's nothing, man. My uncle pushed me, by accident of course, got stuck in an escalator.'

'No, I mean that plaster, man.'

She must go nice and easy with his plaster-hand, but she grips it too hard. Ouch, fuck! What does she know, anyway? Does she really want to know? Okay, let him tell her then. Does she have any idea how hard it is to file open a compressor, does she know how poisonous the oil is, would she know what to do if she got it on to her hand one day? He knows, he's an old hand with fridges. But that still doesn't mean you won't get hurt if people grab too hard. Not that that's the point, the point is there's nothing these two hands of his can't do. Look! She must look at his hands!

'Maybe you're handy with fridges, honey, but your hands are a bit too rough for women. Have you ever had one at all, hey?'

'Of course! Plenty! There's this girl from the Jehovahs. She gets the hots from Exodus, from the frogs that jump, in the lounge here, and the pillar of fire, that kind of thing. She fancies me, that one, and I give her quite a go, but she isn't my type, she's too, um, how shall I say?'

Too what? Where's the word he's looking for? Just in front of him in the air here.

Fuck! Here go his pants now. Speedo and all! Down, over his knees!

'Your uncle's advice if it gets too hot. Sorry, man, but you're also not exactly my type!'

All he sees is patent leather. Flash! Out! Hey!

Tackle her! But his feet stick to the ground. Just a bush of shiny hair in his hands. Without a head. Fuck! Trying to run away, hey! Just wait!

Ouch! He feels blood. He's flat on his backside. Ow, Jesus!

'Fucken whore! Fucken rotcunt. Fucken cheapskate! Stupid Swiss roll of a slut!'

He feels his nose. It's still bleeding. He wipes the blood on to his naked leg. Flossie doesn't want to go any further. Nor does he. He can't. He's fucked out of his mind. Klipdrift and beers and Blush. Out of the bottle, out of the cans, out of the box.

He took the stags and smashed them, mountains and all, one by one against the ceiling. He stashed the Fuchs full of sheets and papers and then he set the whole lot on fire. He stoked the fire in the fridge till it made a soft 'boof!' sound. And then he sat for a long time, watching the long, thin lines of blue smoke coming out of the seals. 'Tip-tip-tip', he heard as something dripped out of the condenser pipes at the back. One down, one to go. He must still sort out the Tedelex.

But he didn't forget the postbox. He ripped it out of the pole and swung it round and round, like a slingweight, until it was going nice and fast. Then he lobbed it, one shot, through the lounge window. Ting-a-ling! Boom! Crash! Sail on, silverbird.

He rattled those loose slabs on their walls till all the dogs in Triomf were barking. Till they were going strong. And he started crying, and after a while the dogs were also howling much better.

Then he thought, wait, let him get into his dream car. He started her up, 'cause he wanted to drive off somewhere, to get lost good and proper, God alone knows where, with all those dogs running after him. Like he was in a circus or something.

But now it's raining. Thunder and flashes of lightning crash into his ears. And now he just sits.

He looks up into the sky. He's sopping wet. Hot and cold on his face. Blood and tears and rain. Where's Mary motherfucker's curls, let him wipe his face.

He rubs his dick. For what, anyway? For fuck-all. It feels like it's getting smaller and smaller. But he rubs, anyway, harder and harder. It's all he can think of doing.

REPORTBACK ⌒

It's almost one o'clock in the afternoon, 26 April.

Mol stands in the passage, behind Treppie. They're in front of Lambert's inside door. She's holding on to Pop's sleeve, here behind her. At first she and Pop didn't want to come, but Treppie said no, this was their baby too, they couldn't start ducking out now. It was time for Lambert's reportback.

You wouldn't guess Treppie was given a talking to just a few hours ago. He's so full of the devil it looks like he's ready to start hopping. When they got home this morning he just smashed his way through the hole in the lounge window. Glass breaking everywhere. No, he said, now he was entering a war zone. Doors and thresholds were for civilians, and if they wanted to play doorsy-doorsy under such circumstances they were free to do so, they must just remember FW said war wasn't for sissies. Then she said as far as she could remember FW said nothing about doors and thresholds, he said elections weren't for sissies. Treppie said, no, now she was really falling behind, hadn't she realised they were holding their own fucken election here in this house and they were allowed as much foul play as they liked, 'cause the playing fields under their feet were never, ever going to get level.

Then she gave Pop one look and they both knew they were just going to have to shuddup, 'cause Treppie's head was like a merry-go-round. Even after three mugs of coffee.

So, here she stands behind him now. His one shoulder's twitching again, like a broken jack-in-the-box. He signals to them they must get ready, he's about to start knocking on the door. Not with his knuckles, she sees, but with a shoe that hasn't got a heel. He found the shoe near the front gate. A small, black shoe made of patent leather. When he saw that shoe he said it looked like someone had popped Mary Poppins right out of her shoes, and he just hoped, for their sake and for the whole of Triomf's sake, that the rest of her was unscathed. And intact.

Intact.

'Rat-a-tat-tat-tat', Treppie knocks. No answer. There's a funny smell coming from the den. Treppie raises his eyebrows. What should he do now? Lambert's coffee's getting cold here in his other hand. How's she supposed to know? He won't listen to her in any case. Pop pulls at her from behind. He doesn't want to go any further. He wants to go sleep, she knows. Where he got the strength from, she doesn't know, but this morning he still wanted to patch up the front window with the plastic cover Lambert uses to cover Flossie when it rains.

'Leave a shooting-hole,' Treppie said, but it wasn't necessary 'cause that plastic was no longer covering Flossie. It was under Flossie. And it was rotten with holes. Flossie was sopping wet. She stood there like a little bulldozer, her bumper pushed up against the prefab wall. She looked properly pooped.

Now Treppie pushes open the door. He has to shove with his shoulder, there's so much stuff in front of the door. He makes high-stepping motions like the kaffirs when they march. The coffee goes 'plops-plops' over his hand. Come help, he signals to her with the shoe.

'Viva Lambert, *viva!*' he shouts as the door gives way.

'Whoof!' says Toby, pushing past everyone's legs to get through.

Not her, God no, she's staying right here where she is. All she can see now is Treppie and Toby and how they're staring at Lambert. She can't see Lambert. He must be sleeping.

Earlier, Treppie picked up a whole bag of beer tins and a Klipdrift bottle outside the den. Judging by the damage, he says now, it looks like more than just a hangover that Lambert's sleeping off here. It looks like Lambert's sleeping from pure despair, the kind of despair that comes from one thing and one thing only: not enough blood to the balls.

Couldn't get it up.

Well, then, maybe that Mary was very lucky here last night, and, if you ask her, that kind of luck is worth the price of a shoe.

It's them who'll have to pay the price. The first thing they found was the postbox on the lounge floor. Shame, and Pop fixed it up so nicely for Lambert, painting it and everything. The paint must've still been wet 'cause there's a blue smudge right in the middle of Jo'burg. What's more, the whole house had been turned upside down.

That pelmet was so bent and twisted, Treppie said even the devil in hell wouldn't be able to panelbeat it again. And her mirror, the one Pop specially put up in the bathroom yesterday afternoon, was in a thousand pieces all over the bath. And there were loose blocks everywhere, from the passage. It looked like they'd been dug out in big patches with a spade.

Pop pushes her from behind. They must either go in or go out, he motions, but he's not planning to spend the whole day standing here in the doorway. Let them see what's what and be done with it. He's tired.

Just one step, so Pop can also see. Glass wherever you put your foot down. And a thick line of vomit on the floor. 'Sis!' Toby sniffs it. 'Yuk!'

Pop must go fetch some newspapers in his room, Treppie says. Then they can use dry vomit to cover up the wet vomit.

'God help us,' Pop says. She watches him as he walks down the passage. It'll be a miracle if Pop survives this day. Well, she's stronger, let her take the lead here instead.

Treppie spins the little shoe on his finger like he's doing a circus trick, spinning a plate on a stick. Just look what they found on the front lawn, he says. If they look long enough for her other parts they might even be able to reassemble the Creole Queen before the end of the day – is that what Lambert understands by value for money.

Lambert doesn't hear a thing. He's lying on his stomach in his shirt and his red underpants. The underpants reach only halfway up his backside.

Come, sing along, Treppie says.

'Wake up, wake up, it's a lovely day!' Treppie sings. 'Oh please, get up and come and play!' Let him sing if he wants, she'll just pick up the broken glass. Before there's another accident.

What's this flying through the air now? A shoe. Treppie's thrown the shoe at Lambert.

'Huh-uh,' is all Lambert says. He rolls on to his other side. His shirt is full of vomit.

'Time for reportback!'

How does Pop always put it? Treppie will drill into a dead hole until he finds a spark somewhere. Well, he can try, but this time she's not so sure. Lambert looks like he's lost to the world. His mouth hangs open.

Treppie mustn't come and shove things in front of her nose now, it's not her who has to do the reportback.

'Hey, old Mol, check, he even stole your rose for the occasion!'

A rose is a rose is a rose, he always tells her, but she better not throw it back at him now, 'cause today she's sure a rose will be something different.

Here's Pop with the newspapers, but he won't give them to her. He throws them down on top of the vomit himself. Looks like he's throwing big, thin leaves into a hole. So carefully, like he's at a funeral or something.

'Did he fit?' Pop asks.

Treppie bends over Lambert. He pinches his nose closed, holding his pinky up in the air.

'His tongue's still here!'

Treppie takes Lambert by the shoulders and shakes him hard. He must be careful, or he'll set off more than a spark in there.

'Fuck off!' is all Lambert says.

They must get him awake and moving again. That's what she thinks.

'Bring some water,' says Pop.

Treppie bows. 'Allow me,' he says. He winks at them and goes out the door. He's capable of bringing in the hosepipe. She looks at Pop. What does

460

he think? But no, it's Toby's red bowl full of water that Treppie carries back with him into the den. He holds it up solemnly over Lambert's body.

'Let oh Lord thy countless blessings rain down upon thy servant here,' he says, his head tilted up. Treppie pours the water from high up in a thin little trickle, first on to Lambert's crotch, then over his stomach and chest, and then, suddenly, he chucks the rest straight into his face.

'I told you to fuck off!'

This is what she's been afraid of. More than just a spark. Let her just get out of the way here, quickly. The outside door is open, thank God.

Lambert sits up straight. His eyes are wild. She can see he's looking this way and that, but he can't find his focus. Water drips from his face.

Pop stands in the one corner, Treppie in the other. She's in the outside doorway.

Now it's very quiet. Something goes 'tick-tick-tick', but it's not her. It's coming from the Fuchs, burnt black on the sides. Brown stuff runs out of it.

Lambert sits on the bed with his legs spread out wide in front of him. His shirt's too tight. He tries to use his arms to stop himself from falling over.

He wants to know what they're all looking at. What's so funny and who do they think they're looking at? She uses her hands to cover her ears. He roars like a lion, this Lambert. Now his arms give backwards and he falls over. His thing is hanging out from his underpants.

'Pit bull terrier!'

Oh heavens! What's she gone and said now? Pop looks at her. She covers her mouth with her hand.

But here comes a thing now flying towards her through the air. 'Whirrr!' Lambert's thrown something right into her face. What is it? Oh God, no, it's all hair and it smells like a person and now it's stuck on her face like a thing with claws and it won't come off!

What's Treppie singing there now? A 'disjointed' piece of what? No, he's singing about a 'Creole tarantula'. What can that be? She can't see

461

anything. She throws the thing down. Oh God, it's a head full of hair. But where's the head, then?

Pop takes her hand. She mustn't worry, it's okay. 'Wig,' he shows with his mouth. It's just a wig.

'Get out, get out of here!' Lambert shouts, but he can't pull himself up.

He must rest, Pop says, they've just come to see how things are going with him.

'My boy.' That's what Pop says to him.

'Ja, old boy,' Treppie says. Lambert must just calm down, they only came to say happy birthday and good morning and viva Lambert and he must look, there's some coffee on the table for him, he can't say his uncle doesn't have his best interests at heart.

Pop picks up Lambert's boxer shorts in front of the cabinet. Here, he says, put on some decent clothes. Pop picks up things lying around and then lets go of them again. He picks up the fallen-over chairs. Their chairs. Hers still looks okay, but Pop's chair looks like someone broke its back. Its one arm is loose. Pop pushes the little peg under the arm-rest back into its hole. Poor old chair!

Now Lambert's got his shorts on, but he can't get his balance. Her too, she also feels paralysed.

She must come and sit, says Treppie. He pulls up her chair. He even makes as if he's dusting off the cushions, just for her. Full of tricks. Never before has Treppie pulled up a chair for her. She'll only sit when and if she herself decides to. She'll first stand here for a bit, although that tarantula made her legs feel like jelly. Now Lambert's drinking his coffee. He goes 'shlurrrp!' as he drinks. Now she'll sit. But just on the edge.

'We thought we'd leave straight away last night, so you could have some privacy,' Pop says, trying to soft-soap Lambert, but Lambert just says 'Uh!' like an ape.

Let her look at this hair again. Lots of curls that jump back quickly when you pull them out and then let go again. What's this sticky stuff here? Sis!

Now Toby's on the bed too, lock, stock and barrel. He wants to say, hullo, Lambert, but all he gets is a kick. He's sniffing in the wrong place. Come, Toby, come sit here with your missus.

Lambert holds his head. He wipes the drops off his face, then he holds his head again.

She must go look in the kitchen dresser, Pop says. There's some Panado there. And while she's in the house she can bring a towel so Lambert can dry himself off.

Maybe Pop wants to talk to Lambert on his own. He tells Treppie to take Molletjie and go and buy a Coke at Ponta do Sol. Lambert's Cokes are finished. But Treppie doesn't want to. He wants to be here so he can hear the father-to-son talk. Her too, she also wants to hear it. She stands behind the door and peeps through the chink. But Pop says nothing. He says if Treppie's got something to say, then he must say it now. All he wants to say is that he's here to support Lambert.

Lambert needs more than fucken support, Treppie says. All the Panados in the world won't take Lambert's headache away. And all the Cokes under the sun won't change the facts. And he, Treppie, thinks that what Lambert needs after a night like last night is a beer. He's sure he can find a beer in one of these two fridges.

Facts, yes, she also wants to hear about those facts, but all she hears is 'eeny-meeny-miny-mo'. It's Treppie. She stretches her neck. He's standing in front of the fridges, pointing to each one in turn as he says his rhyme to determine which one to open. It's the Fuchs, the one that's been burnt black all down the sides.

'Lambert,' he says. 'This thing's leaking again, isn't it?'

Treppie tries to open the fridge. She can't see him, but she can hear him pushing and pulling the fridge. Then there's a 'boom!' Treppie almost falls right on to his backside. He's pulled the door clean out of the fridge. Its rubbers hang down from the sides, burnt to cinders. 'Kaboof,' goes the door as Treppie throws it on to the floor. Now he must be looking into the open fridge 'cause he's brushing soot and stuff from his face.

'Jesus,' says Treppie. 'I thought I knew what a burn-out looked like, but this looks more like the eye of Etna!'

Who's poor old Etna now? And why's her eye burnt out? It doesn't sound like a fact, it sounds more like a fairytale to her.

Did he stick his immersion heater into the Fuchs or something, Treppie asks Lambert. Or his dipstick? In that case he must have been overheating something terrible – no decency, as usual.

'Or,' says Treppie, 'maybe it couldn't take a service. Probably too old for servicing. And to think of all those leaks we had to weld! But some things are simply beyond redemption. Those kind of things just fuck out, anyway. Boom! But, well, we did our best, didn't we, Lambert? And this kind of mistake happens in the best of families. Or what am I saying, hey, Pop?'

Let her go fetch the Panado. All this talking is just a lot of rubbish. She wants it to be tomorrow so they can go vote and get it over and done with. And if the house has to get painted, then let it get painted and be finished. Maybe they'll all feel better and a bit stronger then. Hope springs eternal, Treppie always says, and as far as she can see, she's the only one with any hope left, although she's not sure she wants to put much hope on a white house. It's really just the roof that matters. The rest is the rest. She almost feels like this year should start all over again. It's been one long struggle to get everything fixed and ready. First this, then that, then the other thing. And for what? Sweet blow all! And there was nearly another disaster to top it all 'cause right at the last minute they went and shifted the election date all over the place as though it was a Shoprite trolley. First to the one side, then the other, and then the far side as well. Now there are no fewer than three days for the voting. Today, tomorrow, and the next day. And all of a sudden tomorrow's a holiday, too. Wonder Wall sent them a letter saying they don't work on holidays, so Treppie phoned them up – she was with him, at the Westdene public phone – and told them they must understand, nicely now, that this was an ad-hoc holiday, and a contract was a contract. They must watch their step, otherwise he'd take them to the small claims court. So they said, no, fine, sorry, they'd come.

Let her first go and see if it's safe in the den. She can see neither Treppie nor Lambert. Just Pop, looking down at the floor. He's puffing out clouds of smoke.

Now Treppie appears in the gap between the door and the frame. He's taken a beer out of the Fuchs. Why does that beer can look like it's got a bulge on one side? Treppie takes the beer to Lambert, going round the other side of the bed. 'Down a Lion!' is all she hears.

Right. If Lambert's drinking beer, then he must be feeling better. She pushes open the door.

'Watch out, Mol!' It's Pop. Now what? Why must she watch out all of a sudden? 'Ka-pssshhhht!' Treppie's spraying Lambert full in the face with the beer, a long white jet, and she's getting some of it too.

'Oh, sis, God in heaven!'

Her front is full of foam and little white crumbs.

Lambert looks like he wants to murder Treppie, but he half falls over instead. That's also why Treppie keeps standing there – he knows Lambert's useless. Chuck that towel this side, he motions to her. Sis, now she smells of beer.

So sorry, Treppie says, passing Lambert the towel. Here, wipe off your face.

Ja, always so sorry, this Treppie. And what about her housecoat? Lambert sits up on the bed with his face in the towel. He doesn't wipe off anything. He just sits there. But she can see his cheeks, they're bulging, just like that beer can. Let her quickly put these Panados down where he can reach them, before he explodes like that beer. Once was enough, thank you.

Pop gets up. 'Come,' he says. 'Let's leave Lambert for a while so he can wake up in peace.'

'Ag never! He's as strong as a horse, man.'

Treppie makes rude movements to show how strong Lambert is.

'And horses like him usually have wonderful horsey-stories to tell, especially when they've had a birthday as good as old Lambert here's just had.'

Pop must look, and she must look, Treppie says, Lambert's having a big birthday, it's a birthday for Africa. They must sit, here's a chair, and here's another, and there's even a crate for him, 'cause now they're going to visit nicely here with Lambert in his den, on his birthday.

She doesn't visit where there's vomit, she wants to say, but she says nothing. She can see he's the one who wants to tell all the stories, not Lambert, even though he's on a crate and not a pulpit. And when Treppie wants to tell stories, then you'd better just sit and listen, otherwise you don't hear the end of it, especially when it's a bullshit-story. Just listen how he's lying to Lambert now about how the girl they found for him wasn't just first choice. About how she was such a livewire, you could just see it immediately there in the showcase at Cleopatra's Creole Queens. That's what makes Treppie's bullshit-stories so terrible. They're not outright lies, they're semi-lies he builds on to. And it's not like he first tells the truth and then adds on at the end. He lies all the way through the story, as far as he goes, and after a while you don't know what's what any more. Now he's saying she was a livewire in a showcase, a dynamo and a back-kicker and a high-powered escort and a Voortrekker of a woman – with enough volts to set Lambert's compass permanently due north.

And all Pop said about her was that she was a livewire on a street corner. Period.

So what was the truth about her, then?

Cinderella, says Treppie. A Cinderella who wanted to cross the Drakensberg mountains on bare feet, together with Prince Lambertus the Third. And does Lambert perhaps know where her other shoe is? Or maybe they can find this one's heel and give it back to her tonight. Once she's had a chance to catch her breath, that is.

See? How does Treppie know she's out of breath? She can see that's what Lambert's thinking, too. He takes the towel away from his face to ask Treppie how, but Treppie's looking up at the ceiling as if it's the first time he's ever seen it. He blows smoke rings and looks up through the rings.

'Look, Pop, look, Mol, look, Toby, see how the stars shine in the firmament,' Treppie says.

All she sees are blobs. Pale blobs. Some are pale green and others are pale red.

'What do you see, Pop?'

'I can't see that far, Mol!'

'Ja, old dog,' says Treppie. 'It's a pity they sit so high, hey, all the Great Dippers, fish dip, avo dip, garlic dip!'

Toby licks his lips. He looks at Treppie and then at the blobs, up and down, up and down.

'Also curious, hey, even if you're just a dog,' Treppie says. 'You'd also like to know how the young master created that universe, hey? Maybe she said to him the sky's the limit and started throwing the fish around. And then maybe he asked her whether she fancied a pie in that sky and threw up the garlic and avo on high!'

'Hee-hee.' Quite funny.

She can see Pop's also got a smile on his face now.

Toby too. 'Tiffa-tiffa-tiffa' goes his tail against Treppie's crate. His red tongue hangs from his open mouth.

'Garlic yourself!' is all Lambert says. He's drinking down the Panados with rose-water. Sis, he just chucks that rose on to the floor and then he empties the whole bottle, 'ghloob-ghloob-ghloob'.

'Hell, but you're thirsty, hey?'

Oh shit! Duck! Here it comes, but it's not coming at her, it's sailing towards Treppie, not straight but in a slow arc. Treppie's got lots of time to duck. He ducks in slow motion and then watches the bottle as it falls. He whistles, 'pheeeeeeww!' like a slow-motion bomb. 'Boof!' it goes against against the wall. Treppie wipes off his shoulders with finicky little fingers, like he's flicking off little flakes of dust.

'This Mary, could she at least duck?' he asks Lambert.

Pop points his finger at Treppie. He must go easy, now. No, Treppie signals back at Pop, it's okay, he just wants to get Lambert going again, just like she, Mol, said he must.

Poor Lambert. He really looks like he's had it. But she says nothing. If he has to suffer, then so be it. Just look at the house! And she's the one who'll have to do most of the cleaning up, as usual, even with three men in the house, or maybe one should say two, 'cause Pop can't do anything any more. She's got to cut the grass and she's got to wash the car. And when Lambert goes wild, she has to pick up the pieces.

Like Treppie's saying now, it looks like they were doing a bit of kick-boxing here in the den, fridge-kicking and chair-kicking. He says it depends on your taste, but some people get turned on by the strangest things – Chippendales, crinkle cuts, fruit salad, fridges, frescoes, kick-boxing, you name it.

She pushes Pop. 'Frisco, not fresco, Frisco. Tell him.'

'No, Mol,' Treppie says, 'fresco, it's not instant coffee, it's paintings that they do on wet cement, on the walls of churches, about the so-called beginning and the so-called end.'

She catches Pop's eye. Here we go again.

'Pay attention, Mol, otherwise you won't ever learn anything. You remember that story about the sixth day, when God felt a little lonely up there among his carp and his cactuses and things, and he made people so they could keep him company?'

No, she doesn't remember God feeling like that. He's God, after all. He always feels good.

'Always is a very long time, Mol. And don't forget, even God has a prob-lem 'cause it's the devil who finds work for the hands of the bored.'

'The hands of the idle, Treppie, not boredom, idleness.' It's Pop. He must be so tired of correcting Treppie. He's been doing it all his life.

'Same thing,' says Treppie. 'Now watch nicely.'

What's he doing now? He's shaking and jerking Lambert's mattress.

'Hey, Lambert, you want to see some fireworks, my man? You can't sleep now, life's too short, too valuable!'

Treppie holds his two forefingers together, the one pointing and the other limp.

'And so the Great Idler, sitting around during his Sunday rest, schemes up a little ploy to amuse himself. Suddenly he's the Great Electrician in the sky. Bzzzt! He jump-starts little Adam right out of the earth!'

Open, closed, open, closed, the limp hand responds to the charging finger. Then suddenly he meshes the fingers of both hands so hard that the joints crack.

Hey! It looks sore.

Pop just shakes his head here next to her.

'Founding the nation!' says Treppie. 'Refreshment station. Off you go, now you can paint him on your wall, your Adam. Fit for small talk till the end of his days, dust to dust, tall stories, world without end!'

No, hell, man, now she doesn't understand so well here. Pop looks like he understands some of it but not everything. He tells Treppie God will punish him but he doesn't say what for.

Treppie pretends he doesn't hear a thing Pop says.

'I wouldn't like to guess what he's feeling now,' Treppie says.

Who's feeling what now? Adam?

'Never mind, Mol,' says Treppie. 'Feeling is feeling. Whether it's the Creator or Adam's sister's wife or the painter or the poet's distant hell-bent family it cuts no ice, 'cause it all started at the same point and it all boils down to the same beginning in the end – the smoke that thunders!'

What's Treppie on about now? Pop just sits and smokes here next to her. He's dead-quiet.

'Waterfall,' says Pop.

'That's it! Ai, Pop, I'm so glad there's at least one person who understands me here today. We are the waterfall, hey, and if a person looks carefully you'll see it's a never-ending story of evaporation and condensation. Liquids, gases and solids, an automatic cycle and a closed circuit. Perpetual motion!'

'Well, I think I'm going now,' says Pop. Yes, her too, if Treppie wants to sit here and tell stories to prolong the agony then he can do so on his own. Life must go on and you dare not slow down if you don't want to be left on the shelf. That's what Old Mol always used to say. Shame, Old Mol had such high hopes for her. She said men would be men and in the end it was the women who took most of the strain, no matter what the men said, and never mind if they did have the whiphand, pretending they were experts on everything. That's what Old Mol always used to say when Old Pop started drinking and talking politics at night while she had to sit there and stitch the shirts, patch their clothes, cook the food and pack Old Pop's lunch-tin, all at the same time. At nights, long after they went to bed, she would hear Old Mol say, from behind that sheet: 'Oh hunted hart with trembling haunches who from the huntsman did escape.'

Shame, Old Mol would turn in her grave if she had to see how things were going with her now – not on the shelf but underneath it. And that's where she's remained, even though she kept on trying. As for the hunt, she's never gotten away.

Just listen to Treppie now. No, he says, they mustn't go, it's still going to get jolly here in this den of iniquity today. Lambert's going to tell them a story or two. They must just give him a chance. It will be a story, he says, to comfort and to edify them and to make them long for the days of their unprofaned youth.

Unprofaned.

Ai! God help us!

Look how Lambert's sitting there and looking at them, his head moving left-right, left-right. He supports himself against the pillows, arms on either side. She can see he doesn't know which way to go 'cause the whole lounge is inside his den now, chairs and all. Everyone's got him in their sights. And she can see he hasn't even got a plan, never mind a story. He can't even focus properly. And now Treppie's on to him like a swarm of mosquitoes. Bite here, sting there. Won't let go until he's finished, she can see that. Treppie's smelt blood and, if you ask her, he smelt it back there on the koppie already. Now he's followed it all the way here to the den. He looks like he knows the death blow is close, but whose death it is, she doesn't know.

'She was nice,' says Lambert. 'A nice piece.'

'Aha!' says Treppie. 'At last. Pop, come, come sit up nice and straight now, here comes Lambert's story, at last. Right, you old tomcat, you, everything from the beginning, hey!'

'We talked. We talked a lot!' Lambert doesn't sound like he's so sure of his case.

'Ja-a-a-a,' says Treppie.

'That was just the beginning, the talking.'

Treppie's waiting to hear if there's any more. But there isn't. Lambert slumps on to the cushions. He looks sick.

'Shot!' says Treppie. 'Glad to hear it. You hear that, Pop? And remember we agreed that if we brought Lambert a girl she'd have to be a talker, a real companion, one made from the rib. A girl who can guess the word that's on the tip of your tongue. Ja, someone who can pick up your broadcasting, wireless, or who you can wire into if you need to get totally enmeshed!'

Cochrane's wire.

'Pof!' Treppie slaps Pop on the back. 'Come on, Pop, don't you want to know what the kids were talking about all night long?'

'What were you talking about?' Pop asks. She can see Pop's only saying it 'cause Treppie's pushing him. And Pop can't push back.

'What about what?' Lambert doesn't know his arse from his elbow. He looks at her, as if she should know, but how's she supposed to know?

'The topic, Lambert. What you talked about, you know, the subject of your discourse!'

'Well, um,' says Lambert. He tries to straighten himself against the wall. It looks funny. It looks like his head's in the postbox and Van Riebeeck's talking into his one ear with Klipdrift, while Harry's talking into the other with Coke.

'And, um, she asked what I thought would happen on the twenty-seventh.'

'I say! And then?'

'Then I asked her, why?'

Treppie nudges her. And he nudges Pop.

'Hey, you two, bladdy good question that, don't you think? Why indeed?'

Treppie leans forward on his crate. He wants to hear some more.

'And then?' he asks Lambert.

Lambert rubs his eyes as though he's got dust in them. Must be those little white crumbs from the burnt-out beer.

'Then she said how can I ask why, it's a turning-point in our history!' Lambert's face looks funny. It looks like he first has to think who said what.

Treppie cups his hand behind his ear, as if to say, come again?

All you hear is 'tiffa-tiffa-tiffa' as Toby scratches his ribs. Lambert looks at Toby like Toby must please tell him what to say next. No, hell, let her light a cigarette here. This isn't funny. And Lambert mustn't start picking on her now, either. She's not a dog. Why's he looking at her like that? She hasn't done anything.

'Close your legs, Ma,' he says. 'And wipe that stupid grin off your face. Now!'

As she says, she never escapes.

'Yes, Mol, wipe that grin off your face. There's nothing to grin about.' It's Treppie.

What her legs and her grin have got to do with the price of eggs, she doesn't know. She looks at Pop but Pop doesn't look back. He just takes her hand and then lets go of it again. That means she must accept her lot. She knows this from the way he takes her hand. Sometimes it means 'never mind, it'll pass', and other times it means 'don't worry, it's not your fault'. But this time she must accept her lot. Heavens above!

'Turning-point. How come?' It's Treppie. He's trying to get Lambert back on track now, 'cause Lambert's clearly lost it again.

'Then I told her, that may be the case, turning-point and everything, but it's fuck-all compared to the way I can turn on a point. I'm the turning-point of Triumph, I told her, just watch how nicely I can turn! Corkscrew!'

Corkscrew. What's so funny about that now? But Lambert thinks it's very funny. 'Ha-ha-ha!' he laughs at his own joke. Treppie laughs with him. 'Hee-hee-hee-ha-ha-ha!' Treppie shows with his hands how Lambert turns on a point. 'On a pin,' he says, 'neat as a pin in Triomf!'

'And then she wanted to dance as well.'

As well. Hmph! Lambert's telling lies here, she can see it on his face. He thinks he can lie to Treppie. Treppie looks like he can see the dancing before his very eyes. He's putting on a helluva big show again.

'Classy girl, hey, and then you two rock'n'rolled until the legs fell off these chairs, hey?'

Treppie's up in a flash. He sings:

'When I was a little bitty baby
My mamma would rock me in the cradle'

Out comes his foot now. He pretends he's dancing, but he's not dancing, he's kicking. He kicks the bed's leg, 'crack!' It sags slowly on to its one side.

'Whoof!' says Toby.

'Oh, shit, sorry, old Lambert. Just a little accident,' he says. Just look how sorry he looks.

First he sprayed beer and now he's kicked the bed, but it's all just a little accident. As if there isn't enough of a mess in this place already.

Lambert mustn't worry, says Treppie, if he just gets off the bed for a second he'll shift a crate underneath. Then everything will be fine again. There, see? No problem at all. And if it wasn't rock'n'roll, then what kind of dance was it?

'It was a slow dance,' says Lambert. Mol can see he's holding himself back. She saw how long it took him to weld that leg back on to the bed. He doesn't sit down again. He props himself up against the wall.

'It was a shuffle,' he says. 'On Highveld Stereo.'

That's just what Treppie wants to hear, 'cause now he's standing at the ready with the radio that he just picked up from the floor. The radio's in its glory. Its insides are hanging out on the one side.

'I see,' he says. 'Cheerio, Highveld Stereo!' he says, throwing the radio down on to the floor with a 'crack!' and then kicking it under the bed. Toby thinks it's for him to go fetch. All you see is his tail wagging as he dives under the bed, chasing after the radio.

Does Lambert remember what song it was? Treppie wants to know. The song they were shuffling to.

No, says Lambert, he can't remember so clearly now, but it was a Jim

Reeves song. A Golden Oldie. Oh yes, she can see a thing coming now, now Treppie's head's working like a clock.

'Soft guava!' he shouts. Doesn't she and Pop also think this calls for a demonstration? There he goes again. No stopping him. Pop sinks deeper into his chair here next to her.

'Mary, marry me,' Treppie sings. He makes his voice deep and smooth, like Jim Reeves. Too many voices in there for one voice box, she always says.

Now Lambert is moving. He unsticks himself from the wall, bends down and grabs that broken leg, swinging it at Treppie.

'How do you know it was that song? You fucken bastard! How do you know? Did you fucken stand outside and listen?'

Treppie stumbles backwards over the newspapers. 'Hold it, hold it!' he says. It's all just a coincidence. They all heard the song on the car radio, and if Lambert really wants to know, he should ask his mother, she's the one who wanted to listen to the radio. She wanted to be with him in spirit, she said, and there was nothing like love songs, she said, to transport her spirit.

'She said!' Sis, Treppie! It's not her who's been looking for trouble here. Why's he doing this to her now?

'Not so, Mol?' Treppie asks. Now he stands there looking all innocent. But he doesn't really want her to say if it's true or not. He wants to sing. He's holding that little heel-less shoe tightly, with both hands, in front of his heart, and he puts on a face of love and yearning. He sways on his feet, like a little tree in the wind.

> 'I hear the sound
> Of bugles blown.
> Far away, far away.

'Tate-raaaa-tate-raaa!' he blows on his trumpet inbetween the singing.

'Lambert,' Treppie calls between his singing. 'Come show us quickly how you shuffled, man, or we'll start thinking you're telling lies again!'

'I'm not lying!' Lambert shouts. 'We danced the whole fucken place to a standstill, man!'

Well, then there's no need to be so modest, says Treppie, then he must come here and show them. God, what now? Now Treppie's got Lambert round the neck and he's making rude movements. He's pushing his hips between Lambert's legs.

'Where's the guava, where's the guava? Oh shit! No guava and no cucumber either!'

Sis, Treppie, sis!

Toby jumps up against them. This looks like a nice game. If she'd been a dog she'd have thought so too. But she isn't a dog.

Lambert shoves Treppie so hard that he almost lands with his backside in the fridge.

'My goodness, Lambert, are you trying to send me to the cooler, old boy?' says Treppie, as if honey's dripping from his tongue, but he's up on his feet again, ready for more. If only Pop would do something.

Well, says Treppie, if he's not good enough, then Lambert must try his mother. 'Nothing like a mother's touch!' he says. Treppie plucks her clean out of her chair. Now he's putting that wig on her head! Here she stands, and no one's even helping her! Pop just looks at her with those dead eyes of his.

'Woman, behold thy son,' Treppie shouts.

He shoves Lambert right into her. She feels Lambert's arms going around her. He squeezes her so hard her voice goes 'eep!'

'La-la-la-eep!' Treppie sings.

'Shuddup! Shuddup!' Lambert shouts.

Lambert's pushing her across the floor like a wheelbarrow. Newspaper and glass under her feet. Lambert's barefoot. Doesn't he feel anything?

'Shuffle, Ma, shuffle!' Lambert shouts.

Pop's holding his head in his hands.

Toby barks.

Treppie sings his song.

'Just you shuddup!' Lambert shouts at Treppie. He'll sing his own song, he says, and she must keep her feet together, she must keep them flat on the ground so he can demonstrate, Lambert shouts. From the one side of the room all the way to the other side. All you hear are feet. Now Lambert starts singing.

'Rock me gently
Rock me slow'

he sings, but his voice is low and tuneless. She can feel his voice trembling against her body.

'Yippeee!' shouts Treppie. He claps his hands and whistles. 'Just check, Pop, just check how our old sis here can still soft-guava with this boy-child of ours. A person would swear they're sweethearts. Our own sleep-in Cleopatra, queen of the hive. We needn't have spent so much money at all 'cause what more does a person want now, hey?

'Take it easy, don't you know
That I have never been
Loved like this before.'

She squirms but Lambert's holding her so tight she can't even breathe. He shuffles her right up to her chair and then shoves her so hard she sits down with a 'hic'.

'Ai, ai, ai,' says Pop. His eyes are wet.

'So, are you lot satisfied now?' Lambert asks. 'I shuffled that darky until she couldn't any more, 'cause that's what she wanted. After a while she didn't even know where she was.'

Darky? Why's he calling her a darky now? Does Pop know?

'Ja, Ma,' says Lambert. 'He knows, him and Treppie. They think they can bring me a Coloured floozy for my birthday.'

'And then he kissed her!' Treppie sings.

'Fuck you, you motherfucking bastard!' says Lambert to Treppie.

She'd better make herself scarce here.

'There's your mother, son, fuck her!' Treppie points to her.

'What do you say, brother?' he asks Pop. 'There's a mother and there's a son, even if the fathers were poorly shuffled.'

Treppie shakes Pop by the shoulder. Pop sits with his head hanging down.

So, has this been Treppie's plan all along? Does he want to go and bugger up the whole perspective now? After all that practising? He's still not 'immune'. All for nothing!

Suddenly Treppie looks like he's a video on fast-forward. He ducks to one side and quickly picks up something from the floor. It's the little packet with the cowboy on top. He shakes it under Lambert's nose.

They must just check, he says. Lambert took her with his bare hands. 'Boom, boom,' he shouts, pretending to shoot into the air.

'As long as Lambertussie can shoot his load, hooray for the scent of a kill!'

Treppie quickly bends over again and picks up something on the other side. What's that, now? Christ! A gun! It goes 'pof!' as Treppie throws it down on to the bed. It's pitch black, with a curved handle. Where did that come from?

'Oh, trusted steed, don't fail me in my greatest need!'

Please, Pop, help! But Pop's already seen it. Where's the head that belongs to the hair? There's a corpse here in the den! Lambert stuffed a corpse! No, God help us, was there really a murder here last night? While they were sitting so blissfully there on the koppie?

'Grandpa rode a porker!' shouts Treppie. 'And then he went and pumped his floozy into her triumph and glory!'

Ja, Treppie, now all hell is loose, just like you wanted. She looks at him standing there and rubbing his hands, like he's making a fire with sticks. The fire's nice and wild now. Now things are going to start flying.

Just as she thought. Lambert grabs a long piece of iron from under his bed and swings it like a golf club, but he doesn't hit a ball, he hits an empty GTX tin.

'Hole in one!' shouts Treppie as he catches the tin in mid-air. Softly, softly Treppie puts the tin back on the ground. He gives it a little tap on the lid, as if to tell it to sit there nicely now, 'cause there's a lot of hustling going on and they must all sit dead still. That's also the way she's sitting, here in her corner. Dead still.

Doesn't Lambert want a cigarette? Treppie asks.

Lambert doesn't hear.

'She brought her own fucken FL's!' he roars.

No, that's fine, says Treppie, he was just teasing. You're forty only once in your life, and it's fine to have the night of your life with someone, just once in a lifetime.

Treppie's breathing fast. It looks like his sentences are coming too quickly.

'And then you took her for a proper spin, didn't you, old boy? I see you parked Flossie in front, so she's ready for us when we take back your girl's wig and her shoe, later tonight.'

Lambert says nothing. He's still holding on to his golf club. Treppie's smoking hard.

'And did Flossie at least behave herself, Lambert? She's not really used to, er, joy-rides, you know!'

Lambert throws down the piece of iron. He turns around. All you see is his fat back. His lifts up his head and looks at his paintings, like he wants to start praying or something.

But here comes Treppie, the mosquito-man.

'Er, tell us a little, old boy, was the joy-ride before or after?'

He doesn't say what came inbetween, but she can imagine.

'I mean, did you take her home, old boy? Did you put her back nicely in her show-case, like the little doll that she is, end of story? Hey, Lambert? Tell us, man, or where did you go driving around?'

Lambert's in a corner now, she can see. They all know he's not allowed to drive, 'cause of the fits, and he hasn't got a licence. They'd catch him very quickly among the grand cars in that crock of his without its shell.

Treppie acts like he knows what Lambert's busy thinking, and that those thoughts are very impressive. Very quick on the ball. He does it with all of them. He gives them 'perspectives' and things so-called to save their backsides, but then he cancels them again, laughing at the lot of them for even falling for any of it in the first place.

'Aha, you naughty boy!' says Treppie. 'So then you took your girl for a ride around the block for a smoke break, 'cause that barrel of yours was hot, hey! Martha, Toby, Gerty, and then, when you'd finished the holy trinity, you came back for more, right?'

Wink, wink at Lambert, wink at her, wink at Pop.

Lambert tries to wink back, but his eyes are too wide open. All he does is shut them.

'Yes, first we went and patrolled around Triomf a bit, but then she wanted to see my paintings again. She said she's seen lots of paintings in her life, but not, um, as you say, frescoes like these.'

She must remember to go look inside that Frisco coffee tin in the kitchen. Doesn't taste like paint to her, but then again her sense of taste isn't so good any more. The other day she poured Vim scrubbing powder over the eggs and everyone except her tasted the difference. Treppie asked her if she was playing Daisy de Melker. He wouldn't hold it against her, he said, but she'd have to increase the dosage. Then, luckily, she found the salt under the sink. No need to swing by the neck for nothing.

'Where did you get that thing?'

It's Pop who's suddenly talking now, here next to her. He sounds like he's trying to scold Lambert, with his last breath.

He points to the gun on the bed. Look how his hand's shaking! Let her take his hand and put it back on his lap. It makes her feel eerie, hands shaking like that.

'I bought it from a kaffir at the dumps for fifty rand. Pop. It's for our protection, for when the shit hits the fan.'

Pop looks at Treppie as if to say, look where all your talking's got us now! But Treppie pretends he doesn't see Pop.

'Yes and no,' says Treppie. 'It's for the shit when the shit hits the fan, but it's actually for shooting the fan when the fan doesn't work.' He sticks his index finger in his mouth and pretends he's pulling a trigger. 'Boom!'

'Give it here!' It's Pop again, with that shaking hand of his.

'Not a damn will I give it to you,' says Lambert. 'It's my gun and only I can touch it!'

'Give it to Pop, he just wants to look at it. It's true, isn't it, Pop, you just want to look, don't you?'

She wishes Pop would say 'just want to look', but he says nothing. He keeps that trembling hand of his held out. It's shaking all the way up to where the arm connects with the body.

'I said, give it here!'

'Not a fuck am I going to give you my gun, Pop!' says Lambert. 'The AWB has already recruited me to help shoot when the, um, when the . . .'

'When the what?' asks Treppie. He looks like he's conducting exams again.

'When the fan breaks. Fuck!' Lambert looks like he wants to cry.

Treppie claps his hands. Now, he says, Lambert has demonstrated an insight into a particular mentality. And Pop must leave him alone, too. One thing at a time. Treppie says, he first wants to test that insight a little.

Whoosh! Treppie grabs the gun out of Lambert's hand.

He walks up and down with his hand under his chin. He pretends he's thinking so hard that he's kicking little stones, but he's actually kicking tins and newspapers and the insides of radios. Then, suddenly, he gets a brainwave. He goes 'snap!' with his fingers in the air.

Jeez, he says, he hadn't thought of it before, but maybe Lambert will land up on Robben Island. He mustn't worry, though, they'll send him polony so he won't have to eat that watery porridge they give people there. And then, he says, Lambert can write a nice letter to Mandela, asking him if he can paint on the walls, but he'll have to promise nothing but the New South Africa – just doves and AKs, doves and AKs, from the Cape right up to the North, on top.

Should she go make some tea? she wonders, to bring some relief here.

'Detention without trial!' says Treppie. 'Article Twenty-nine! Mind you, there's a new rumour doing the rounds. Want to hear?'

Yes, they want to hear, Pop nods.

'They say Robben Island's not going to be a prison any more in the New South Africa. It's going to be a museum. But that makes no difference. They'll still need Lambert there. He'll be indispensable. Behind glass. Instead of Bushmen and Hottentots. Then he'll be able to demonstrate nicely, hey?'

'Give back my fucken gun!'

'Aren't you tired of your own voice yet, Treppie?' asks Pop. 'Don't you think you've showed off enough for one day?'

'Yes, ask the fucker, ask him!' says Lambert. He lunges for his gun, but it's not necessary. Treppie gives it to him nice and neatly, with the grip facing forward. Lambert puts the gun under his pillow. Then he sits down on top of the pillow, on top of the gun.

No, Pop needn't worry, says Treppie. Everything's okay. He's finished playing games. Now he's coming to the serious business.

What serious business? In that case, she'd rather play games.

'You want to know what it is, hey, Mol?' Treppie says.

Treppie can see right into her head, that's for sure. Never mind, he says, she must strap on her life-jacket, so long, and Pop must throw the goat overboard and then comb the horizon, 'cause this leaky boat of theirs is heading for the rocks, fast.

She sees Pop looking at Treppie and wondering, what now? She also wonders, but Treppie's on the move again.

'Now, where were we?' he asks Lambert.

'Oh, yes, you came back from Triumph by night and you looked at all the paintings, from Genesis right through to Revelation. But wasn't your time up by then, Lambert? Hell, man, we had to drive a hard bargain for that slut, my man. And in the end she wanted two hundred rand just for one hour. Look, you have to realise, she wasn't exactly on a special offer, unless she was on top of *you*, old boy.'

'She didn't say anything about time,' Lambert mumbles. He doesn't look Treppie in the eye. He's looking at the wall.

'She visited nicely here with me, and I'd watch out if I were you, 'cause she said she's coming again next week. I told her she's welcome, we've got plans for when the shit starts flying.'

Treppie holds up his hand. What did Lambert say, there?

'For when the shit starts flying, Treppie, and you can take that stupid joke of yours about the broken fan and shove it right up your arse!'

'In it goes!' says Treppie, pretending to stick something up.

'I hope it does something for my constipation. Then at least there'll be one thing left in working condition in Triomf after the election, even if it's only a working stomach!'

481

'Shuddup, you!' Lambert shouts at Treppie. Now he's talking to her and Pop. It sounds like he's begging.

'There's no more apartheid, so she could easily come with us and everything. I told her we don't mind smart Coloureds like her.'

'Try for white, I see!' says Treppie. 'And then I suppose she went and powdered her nose?'

Now he makes as if he's in the bathroom, pretending to powder his nose.

> 'Mary, Mary on the wall
> Who is the fairest of them all?'

he asks a make-believe mirror here in front of him.

'And then she saw, oh Lord, but I'm not a blonde mermaid on the roof-rack of a Volkswagen. And then that mirror cracked into little pieces, all over the bath!'

Or can Lambert tell them how the mirror got into the bath? Did they do it on top of the mirror, inside the bath, under the water? Hell, that takes his mind very far back, he says. Can she, Mol, still remember those naughty days?

No, Treppie. She shakes her head. He must really stop now.

'Well,' Treppie says to Lambert, 'maybe I'm the only one, but I remember well, your mother was still very young, and she used to take her older brother in hand too, in the bath. Those days her little brother was still very small, smaller than her, but when his sister got tired, then kid brother just had to take over. And you wouldn't say it today about your mother's older brother, would you, but in his young days he just couldn't get enough. There was no satisfying him!'

She can feel Pop looking at her, but she'd rather not look back right now. She looks at Lambert. Thank God in heaven, it doesn't look like he's clicking. He just looks upset. Thank God he's got other things eating him today – a broken shoe and a headful of hair. A hangover on top of a night that went soft on him. He won't be making any missing connections today.

'Ag, you're just talking shit, Treppie. Just shuddup!' he says.

'Yes, Lambert, he's just talking shit!' Her voice comes out louder than she means it to.

'Now listen to me carefully, both of you. It's not a shit-story, it's the story about how everything began. And if there's one thing about a good story it's that it has to have a beginning. The second thing that makes a story good is that it must be true. Now this story is a true story, as true as true can be. And the third thing about a good story is that no one must ever have heard it before. Okay, granted, the only one here who hasn't heard it is Lambert, but where will you find a better audience than Lambert? Like a lamb to the slaughter. Innocent! Those who don't know won't be punished. So it is written. And I, for my part, don't take punishment for other people. So Lambert must hear the story. He's grown up now. He can hold his own. We know that. He can fix fridges, he can drive a car, he can shoot, he's been recruited and he's just been serviced, so why can't he know where he comes from? It's his right, isn't it? Or what do you two say?'

Treppie looks at them and then he looks at Lambert. Treppie's face looks like he's making ordinary conversation on an ordinary day. He takes out his pocket-knife and begins to clean his nails with long, fancy strokes. 'Grrtt-grrtt!' goes the knife under his nails. He holds them out for inspection. He's not happy with them.

He's talking to Lambert, glancing at him sideways as he scrapes.

'You're a person who knows your rights, hey. You must stand up for your rights. That's what I say. And this right is a basic one. It's your birthright, and that's a human right. To know about your, er, origins.'

Treppie stops talking. He holds both hands out in front of him. Now he's satisfied. 'Click' goes the pocket-knife as he closes it again. He puts it back into his pocket.

'Anyhow,' he says, 'everything in good time, right? Where were we now? Oh yes, the mirror in the bath. And what else? The postbox. Just imagine. After all this time, that postbox is still an invariable in this story of ours. You weld it, you paint it, but when you look again, it's fucked up and it's lying in a whole new place. But this time, Lambert, the angle of displacement is a little too wide. On the lounge floor! Via the window! A spot of wet peace in the heart of Jo'burg.'

Via.

'Ja, Mol, via, Via Dolorosa. But let me finish questioning Lambert here. Come, Lambert, explain a little now. When you and Mary came back from wherever, you were so, er, hard-up, that you rather went for the postbox instead, hey? But that hole in the front is too small, if you ask me. And its sides, wow man, they're a bit on the sharp side, not exactly what I'd call, er, nesting material, er, for a pecker, er, I mean, even if it was a Sacred Ibis or, er, a pelican or something like that! But that's the only way I can figure out how it came flying through the front window. Some or other monster of a pecker. Shot clean off its pole. Maybe it was a freedom dove!'

Lambert's sitting with his head down. He's twirling his thumbs around each other. His whole body heaves as he breathes.

'Now, Lambert, I don't know how things are on your side of the Speedo, but that postbox, er, saw its arse. And notwithstanding that . . .'

Why's he stopped talking now? He looks at her, then he shuts his eyes tight as if she's about to throw something at him.

'Notwithstanding,' she says.

Treppie jerks his head as if something just hit him.

'Right!' he says. 'Now we can carry on. Thank you, Little Miss Echo! And notwithstanding that, the postbox now has a whole new look about it. It's back on the gate, I put it back, but it's taken quite a blow. Now it's a postbox with an attitude. And I'd say it's rather an artistic attitude, an attitude that holds promise and one that, er, radiates expectation. Now it looks like it's stretching its neck to look up Martha Street. To see which way Mary's coming. Oh, dear little Mary with her one shoe!'

Treppie's got that little shoe in his hands again. He throws it into her lap.

'Try it on quickly, dear sister, maybe the two of you wear the same size. Wonders never cease!'

Now Treppie's on fast-forward again. He's at the Tedelex. Open goes the door. Out comes the little white box.

'So, my old hotshot,' he says to Lambert, 'do you also feel like a piece of birthday cake, old boy? People who swing from pelmets like Tarzan the apeman also need something sweet in their lives, don't they? Me Tarzan, you Mary, low white, high brown!'

'Chomp!' goes Treppie as he bites into the side of the Swiss roll. He passes it on to Lambert in the same way he passed Lambert the gun – with the thick side to the front.

'Hmmm, hmmm,' he goes, his cheeks full. Now he's a monkey, scratching the underside of his armpit with his loose hand.

Lambert's white in the face. Out, she signals to Pop. When Lambert looks like this, there's a fit coming. She feels in her housecoat's pocket. No peg.

Lambert takes the Swiss roll, but he doesn't eat. He just puts it down on the bed without taking his eyes off Treppie. Jam drips from the one side of the Swiss roll. Toby's wondering who the Swiss roll belongs to. He puts his front paws on to the bed and takes a bite.

Stupid dog. Sis! Off!

'Yes, off!' says Treppie. 'That's not your cake.'

Treppie waves at them, as if he's enjoyed his visit and he'll come and see them again some time.

'Well, then, cheers, I'm going now. All's well that ends well, as they say in the classics, or, further west down the road of suffering, as ye sow, so shall ye reap, even when the harvest is in Martha Street.'

'Biff!' he hits Lambert on the back. Thanks for that nice piece of cake. Lambert must eat it now before it gets stale. Lambert says nothing. He's looking straight in front of him.

But Treppie's forgotten something. Oh yes, Lambert must please let him know when he's finished with the sheets. No rush, mind you, Lambert must take his time, 'cause life only begins at forty.

At the door, Treppie turns around one last time. He looks at her and Pop, and then he shows them they must smile. What the hell, it's all over now.

Toby goes with Treppie.

'Whoof! Whoof!' says Toby as Treppie kicks blocks for him all the way down the passage.

Let her also go now. She looks at Pop. Then she looks at the Swiss roll. Two bites. A human bite and a dog bite. On any other day she would've taken a bite too, from the clean side, but today she feels sick to her stomach. Any moment the ants will be there too. She points, but Lambert's not looking. He's just sits there on his bed. She really hopes he won't have a fit now, too.

Pop gets up. He looks like he wants to say something. He looks like he wants to say Lambert mustn't worry, everything will be okay and next year they can try again. But he can't say it out aloud. She takes him by his sleeve so he can come. He doesn't want to. Come now, Pop. As they shuffle out, Pop wants to touch Lambert's shoulder, but Lambert sees Pop's hand coming. He turns away. She really hopes he's not going to have a fit now. 'Cause his lips are trembling.

Lambert takes the gun and shoots his list right off the wall.

Items one to ten are hard to shoot, but the further down he goes the easier it gets, 'cause the plaster's soft from a damp spot in the wall. After every shot big pieces fall out of the wall.

He counts his bullets. He works it out. He's got three for each of his gallery paintings, and then there's still one left.

First the wings. One bullet on this side and one bullet on the other side of SUPERBEE. Sorry, SUPERBEE, but I'm going to have to shoot you from close up. He puts on his welding helmet in case the bullets bounce back. Right, straight into the wall and out the other side again. Small holes. Cheap bricks!

Now for the welding torch. He burns SUPERBEE's wings with the flame till you can't see any more of him, and also nothing around him, neither his heaven nor his earth.

He keeps the last bullet for his mermaid, but as he points the gun, first at her silver fin, where the paint's peeling off, and then at her yellow hair, which is too long and too much, he starts shaking so much that he shoots himself instead. A direct shot, right in the head. There's just a black hole between the two ears in front of Molletjie's steering wheel.

His head's zinging from all the shooting. And his tail-end's jerking hard. Let him put this gun away nicely now. In the steel cabinet. Let him go lie on his bed. Let him sleep.

21

~

NORTH NO MORE

PARALLEL PARKING ~

T
hat was morning and now it is evening. Treppie stands on the little front stoep with a glass in his hand. With his other hand he clutches his shoulder. It's jerking like mad, as if someone's throwing a switch on and off inside his body, somewhere near his navel. But the current has nowhere to go, so it slams into his skull and shoots back down into his shoulder. He feels wired, from head to toe. Vibrating, all the way down to his guts. It must be that bite he took from Lambert's cold Swiss roll this morning. Fucken cardboard roll from Spar. Smeared full of slimy jam, although that might also help a bit. Unfathomable are the ways of digestion. If the Holy Spirit ever descends upon him, he reckons, it will be in the form of gippo guts. Then he'll be truly blessed. He should actually try going to the toilet now, try to tune it in for a symphony, but this business here in the yard is something he wouldn't miss for all the money in the world – not even for a turd in the toilet.

It all started this afternoon, when Pop woke up in his chair after sleeping like a dead thing right through all that shooting in the back. He'd hardly opened his eyes when he said, right, now Mol must come, he'd had a 'visitation'. If there was one last task awaiting him before he was taken up into the house of the Father, it was to teach Mol to drive. Lambert wasn't allowed to drive, and what would happen if there was suddenly a crisis and Treppie was 'incapacitated'? he asked. Then Mol would be stranded. Believe it or not, that's what he said, as if they were all quite happily on their way to paradise in the *Drommedaris*. And yes, he said, no matter how exhausted he was, the final driving lesson would have to start immediately. He just wanted to check, first, how things were going with Lambert there at the back. They said nothing about the shooting. He and Mol just sat there rolling their eyes at each other as Pop shuffled down the passage towards the den.

After the first shot, Mol had started screaming. She wanted to go to the back to stop Lambert. But he sat her down on her chair and explained to her nicely that she'd just have to leave it now. History had to take its course and none of them could do anything more about it. By the thirteenth shot, when Mol began shivering and shaking, he told her it sounded like Lambert was shooting at a tin in preparation for tomorrow's election. No need to worry, he said. But he didn't tell her about the visions he'd been having of the whole of Fort Knox lying in a bloody heap in the backyard.

So, he and Mol were both relieved when Pop came back and said everything was okay. Lambert was still sleeping. He said he couldn't figure it out, but Lambert's paintings were full of holes and there were chunks of plaster all over the floor.

The bastard should fuckenwell have shot himself in the head, and the rest of them too, one after the other. Then all of their problems would've been solved for good. And then this whole blasted story could have ended in blood and guts and a smoking barrel. The perfect South African family murder. Then everyone would've been happy – common rubbish living their common lives, making the rest of the fucken scum feel good about themselves. He can just see the headlines: BLOODBATH IN TRIOMF, THE LAST OF THE POOR WHITES IN OLD SOPHIATOWN, MASSACRE OF THE INNOCENTS. Take your pick. Better than any Western. Then, after their death, they'd maybe even become the flavour of the month with all the fools who think they're bigger and better than everyone else. Well, no one's going to get rid of them quite so easily. In any case, he's far from ready. And what's more, he won't just lie down for any old trick. He has his pride, for fuck's sake. And just let anyone – let alone that wretched Lambert – try to run them down like they're the Big Five (the fifth being the Klipdrift bottle). For that arsehole he'll set a booby trap in which the bastard will get stuck for the rest of his goddamn life, right here among them. Under their roof. Then the sod can run up against the walls, trying to escape, north-south-east-west, until kingdom come. Like an ant in a saucer.

And as a consolation prize he'll see one hell of a performance every now and again. Like Pop in front here, for example. He's busy putting up candles on a row of Dogmor tins, all along the prefab wall. He told Pop it looked more like a landing strip for a Dogmor-angel than a parking lot for Mol.

This is now going to be a lesson in the dark. 'Cause this afternoon it was party-time in the street again. He'd half hoped they'd forget about the driving lesson. It felt to him like they'd all been in a long nightmare for weeks now, with Lambert's birthday and everything. Like they can't wake up, no matter how hard they try, and it's just night all the time. And now, on top of everything, there's one bomb after another.

First, this afternoon, he felt the ground rumble under his feet and he thought, this had to be the bomb for Jo'burg-West. Then Mol called him from his room. He must please come, there was a roof-removing machine outside in the street. Poor Mol, all she can worry about is whether they'll still have a roof over their heads. The fact that it's been leaking like a fucken sieve for years doesn't seem to worry her at all. She spent half the past summer walking up and down with pots and pans and things. When they get full, she empties them. Then she puts them down again, over and over, like she's scared the house will sink if she doesn't. As if the threat's coming from below. Anyhow, the thing outside had nothing to do with the roof, it was a helluva show the NP was putting on here in Triomf for the election. That's what he calls a last-ditch attempt – in a fucken crane, can you believe it! He feels like declaring tomorrow his own personal holiday and fuck the rest. He's already told them, if only he had the money, he'd fuck off to the Lost City and spend a few days there, they've got bed and breakfast on election special over there. Then he could have settled himself comfortably in those artificial little waves and forgotten about everything else. The whole business is working badly on his tits. He has to drink himself almost paralytic every night just to get some sleep.

He rubs his jerking shoulder. He sees Toby looking at the candles on the tins, inspecting them one by one as Pop puts them up. Must think it's Christmas all over again, the poor dog, like he's in a time-warp or something. He's been completely mad recently, barking at fuck-all half the time. Must be the bombs going off all over the place, and the shooting in the middle of the night. More and more bombs going off by the day. And now it's guns with hand-pump action, he reads in the papers. When Toby hears those things going off at night he runs round the house like he's got a Guy Fawkes movie in his head. Not to mention all the cars that race and crash and the sirens and things on Ontdekkers, a wailing and a gnashing of teeth. The dogs feel it the worst. This afternoon again, when that thing came wheeling down the street, the dogs thought it was coming for them. A monster of a yellow crane with a small head and a long arm. You just saw dogs barking and teeth snapping at those tyres. The wheels were half a house high. So he decided to let Toby out so he could also blow off some steam.

And guess who was sitting up in the cab, along with the kaffir who was driving? None other than those two little lapdogs from RAU. Waving their little white hands from a dizzy height behind a tinted windscreen, as if they were fucken royalty or something. Colour-combined too, like Christmas trees – margarine suns on her ears, and him with a fig-leaf tie in NP colours. Underneath the tie, his stomach was sticking out like a plump white pumpkin.

They all went down to the oak tree at the bottom of the street. The crane stuck out its arm a little further, 'bzzzt!', with Jannie White-Pumpkin strapped into a little chair at its tip. He stretched a big banner right around that tree's crown. It looked like a bad joke, like an ancient creature with a sore head. The banner said, in big, fat letters: THE TIME HAS COME TO CHOOSE BETWEEN THE BUILDERS AND THE BREAKERS! Underneath, someone had written in, just for the occasion, in slanted writing: F.W. LOVES TRIOMF. FORWARD WITH OUR MINORITY! KEEP OUR NEIGHBOURHOOD CLEAN! Pop asked him what he thought it all meant, but all he said was, no comment. He was listening out for his stomach.

So, that was diversion number one. And, he must say, they needed a little break after the shock this morning when they got home and found the house looking like a ghostbuster had ripped through it. Not that he was surprised after all that build up. He'd promised Lambert he'd bring the girl, and there was no way he could go back on his word. He was too deeply dug into the whole story. That's how it goes in this place. You plug one hole with a story and then the story blows up in your face. Then you're left with an even bigger hole. Now even the lounge window's got a fucken hole in it. Well, it keeps him busy, that's all he can say. Deeper than a hole you can't go.

Then it was time for diversion number two. Mol again. They must come see, she says, here comes Miss South Africa. But it wasn't her, it was soft-serve with a difference, 'cause that ice-cream kaffir was covering his backside – the Ding-Dong was decorated with every flag under the sun. From the NP's flag right through to the DP, the ANC, the PAC and the AWB. And, just for luck, he chucked in a zebra flag from Trek Petroleum, as well as a Vierkleur, a Red Cross, a flag with the Malawian rooster on it, and a Toyota horse. The works. On the aerial, of course, he had a blue peace-flag with little doves on it. Yes, he said, that was the only way. A kaffir couldn't take chances with ice cream on a day like this, especially in Triomf. That man had a very good nose for business, not to mention a grand sense of occasion.

The only flag he hadn't seen on that Ding-Dong, he told them, was the flag of the New South Africa, thank God. Then of course Pop wanted to know why, 'cause Pop's a sucker for adverts. As long as it's new. So he told Pop he hoped to heaven that he, Treppie, would be six feet under when the New South Africa started to see its arse, 'cause he'd been forced to watch the old South Africa go down the drain and he couldn't bear to see the new one dying on a life-support system while it handed out golden handshakes left, right and centre. With the bugles of the last tattoo in its ears and a Y-front flag blowing at half-mast in the wind of its last breath. Thank you very much. Two nationalistic fuck-ups, he told Pop, would be too much for a finely tuned and constipated mortal like himself to handle.

491

All this time Pop just stood there, looking at him like he wanted to start crying. He mustn't go and start blubbering now, he told Pop, 'cause he could see what was going on in his head. Pop must just understand, he said, a life-support machine was a lie against the truth of death. It didn't save you from your unavoidable end. He was fed up with this whole show just for Lambert's sake, he said, and that's why he'd let the cat out of the bag this morning. Lambert must take the whole fucken lot now and get finished. If he was good enough to inherit all that they still had of any value, namely his fridge book and his fridge tools, then now was also the time for him to inherit the secrets of the fathers, so he could seek his own salvation with open eyes, like a man.

Then Mol echoed him, of course.

'Yes, fathers,' Mol said. 'That's right. Lambert actually had two fathers, the good father who tried to keep him on the straight and narrow all his life, and the bad father who fucked up every inch of that road, as far as he went.'

Well, what can a person say? Who does she think she is, anyway? So he asked her, in that case, what did she think of a house with no mother? But of course you have to say everything twice before Mol understands, and this time she was really looking for it. So he told her, maybe he was in fact the vital ingredient in their story, and Pop the saving grace, but she should just realise that she was the joy of their desire, in other words the queen bee, and if it hadn't been for her, then Lambert, club-footed cretin that he was, would never have seen the light of day.

That shut them up. The sun was almost down and Pop said, well, maybe they should have the driving lesson now. In Flossie, he said, just in case. Why not in Molletjie? he asked. Then it would be Mol-on-Mol violence. But no one else thought his joke was funny.

To tell the truth, it wasn't funny, but these days he can't help himself any more. It's his stomach that's jammed so badly. No one believes him when he tells them it's enough to make a person write a whole book full of cheap one-liners. And it's been like this ever since he can remember. What goes in, must come out. And what won't come out of the one end has to come out the other end. Top-dressing, that's what he calls it.

Anyhow, then it was a whole palaver again to get Mol into Flossie, 'cause she'd seen in the past how the petrol pedal got stuck when Lambert played go-cart around the house, and how he bumped into things – so hard he sometimes fell right out. There weren't any seat belts in that thing, either.

So Pop first had to take her for a ride, up and down the lawn next to the house, around Lambert's rubbish dump at the far end and down to the postbox again, just to give her the feel of it. And when she eventually got into the driver's seat, Toby went 'whoof' and jumped right over her on to the bricks at the back, which Lambert had packed there for weight. There was no more back seat after that fire he made for Guy Fawkes. Toby's breath on her neck made Mol feel more relaxed, and now Pop could show her exactly how the gears worked. First, second, third, fourth, reverse. Over and fucken over again. Later, Pop even made a drawing to show her how the gears went, 'cause the gear stick no longer had its knob with that diagram on it.

And eventually, there she went. 'Oo-eee! God help me!' she shouted. Slowly, she lurched over the molehills in first gear. Pop was treading like mad with his feet, letting the clutch go and trying to find the brakes. It looked like he was in a paddle-boat or something.

The next exercise was to go from first to second and to work the pedals. It looked like a paddle-boat for two. Mol lost her bearings and almost went right through the gate. Then she just wanted out of that car, clutching on to Pop like she was about to drown or something. Well, he supposes the past few days must have been a bit too much for the old thing, 'cause she suddenly started blubbering, and he saw Pop's hanky come out to wipe her tears. First her tears and then his own. And then he put his arm around Mol's shoulder. She, again, put her hand on his leg. Not exactly driving off into the sunset, but there they sat, on the lawn in Flossie, with its bumper against the pole holding up the postbox. They sat there, staring at that backside-front postbox, and the postbox looked back at them through its receiving end, twisting its head.

What Pop told Mol to make her feel better, he doesn't know. All he could see was Pop pointing his arm this way, that way, and then up into the air. Maybe he was pointing out all the places they were still going to visit. Heaven help them. And Toby too, he kept following Pop's hand. This way, that way, up into the air. Man's best friend.

It was then that he began to hear the sound of old pianos. At first all he heard in that bit of late-evening silence was the nervous traffic of cars beginning to drive faster and faster around Triomf as the election approached. But then, coming right out of his centre, he heard those old pianos, handfuls of old chords. It was so bad he felt like his heart wanted to combust. So he took a little turn past the fig tree at the back of the house. The autumn sun was shining so brightly through those leaves he could see every vein. And the light shone through the holes in the rust spots. The late figs looked as though they'd been preserved in golden syrup as they hung there, so sweet, so sweet. His gills contracted with tears.

Not enough sleep over the last few days. That must be his problem. So he came back to the front and drowned those terribly sad pianos with a few neat shots of Klipdrift. Then all that remained of the combustion were a few hissing and spitting coals in his insides, and a shoulder jerking like it wanted to shoot right off its socket, arm and all, so it could bugger off somewhere on five fingers. But he can't fuck off from here, neither he nor any of his parts. He's just going to have to see this one through to the bitter end.

He told Pop he should rather leave third and fourth for another day, 'cause he doesn't have the time tonight to cure damaged Mol-skin. But all Pop wanted was to fuck off into the street with that Triomf-turbo of theirs after they'd finished their crying and comforting.

So now it's dark and Flossie's ready for the last round. Not for spare parts, but for geriatric training in parallel parking. The candles are burning on the Dogmor tins, one car's length apart from each other. That's how Pop set them out. Christ, if you didn't know them, you wouldn't believe your eyes tonight. It looks like a church. Half-holy, kind of beautiful, the dogs on the tins smiling with their mouths open through patches of rust in the candlelight.

He sees Pop flick on his lighter to show Mol where reverse is. She can't find it. There goes her lighter too. The light from the little flames shine through their hair as they bend forward to look at the gear lever: through Pop's white tufts and Mol's loose strings next to her face. From her bun that's been unravelling for the past two days. Woe is me!

There she starts now. Into reverse. Pop gets out. She must go slowly, backwards, he calls out to her, he'll show her. Pop has to shout hard 'cause Mol's revving Flossie to hell and back. Pop's holding a lighter in each hand. With large circles he motions to her, now she must turn the steering wheel, now she must let go of the clutch, slowly, now she must give petrol, just a little.

Mol's sitting with her neck twisted around. Here she comes. Well, he must say, for someone who can't even open a Tic-Tac box she's learnt very quickly. Here she comes now, here she comes, steady does it. She reverses slowly, towards her goal, with neither a roof nor a mirror.

'You've got the angle, Mol!' Pop shouts. 'Just perfect, old girl, just carry on like that! Now swing her nose in! Turn the wheel the other way! No, the other way. Slowly, look in front of you, Mol, there's a tin in front.'

Mol looks. She bumps the Dogmor tin, just a little. The candle doesn't even fall over. Just the flame nods up and down and the Dog laughs once, a flash of red tongue showing. Just a little more, a little more, Pop shows her, with a lighter in each hand. Like he's conducting a big Jumbo on to a landing strip in the middle of the night.

'Hold it now, hold it just there!' he shouts with his hands up in the air. The glow from the lighters falls over his face and over the back of Mol's head. Happy landings! She stops. Hic, off! goes the car – she forgot to step on the clutch and put the car back in neutral. But she's done it. Parallel parking! Bull's eye, first shot! Who'd ever have believed it! Just look how she's smiling as she gets out of that driver's seat, between two of those tins with candles on top.

Chord upon chord, there's the piano again. Take another swig.

'Put out, put out the ancient psalm
lest the holy notes combust
in the smoking fire of the heart'

Why's Pop telling him to shuddup now? He must stop singing and go to sleep, Pop says. He must let this day come to an end now. He mustn't stand here and make himself sick for nothing. It's all over. They're still alive and Mol has just parked Flossie. Does Treppie want to borrow his hanky? Not a hanky, thanks, he says to Pop. What he needs is a fucken sheet.

'Come, Mol, it's bedtime!' Pop calls out.

'I'm coming now,' Mol shouts back. 'I just want to sit here a little. Rest a bit. Pass my lighter.'

'Blow out the candles,' Pop says as he goes inside.

'Yes, put them out, put them out
before the Milky Way goes to sleep.
What you sow you also have to reap.'

Treppie stays on the stoep for a long time, watching Mol light a cigarette and smoke it all up from beginning to end, there in her victory chariot. And all the while her other hand plays the giddy goat with the gear in neutral.

WONDER WALL ⁓

Pop's sitting in his chair in the lounge. He came and sat here 'cause it was the only place he could still find in all the commotion. He was so tired and everything suddenly looked so strange and far away, as if he was in a different country. It was all he could still do for himself and his chair. They were both out of their depth. The chair had hardly found its way back from the den when it was shifted again, this time on to a heap along with everything else in the lounge; and he himself felt like his flesh was about to start falling off his bones.

So he squeezed his way between the sideboard and the crates, his knees knocking against the sharp edges of things. Now he's sitting here and letting it all wash over him. In the end, everything passes anyway, then it's over and it turns out to be totally meaningless. Even if it felt bad when it was happening.

They got back from voting at about half past eleven this morning. At the Westdene Recreation Centre. In the end it wasn't at RAU after all, where they'd gone to vote Yes the last time. He was glad it was just around the corner 'cause he really wasn't in the mood for a whole to-do all over again. As it was, they had to stand in a long queue while the police and officials and other people walked up and down, shouting that the boxes were full and the stickers were running out. By the time they'd all got their right hands sprayed with ink and put them into that purple gadget for the umpteenth time, they weren't even sure any more whether they'd voted or not.

And those ballot papers, like entrails with such a lot of stuff written there, he couldn't read further than the first four. So he made a wild cross just anywhere. Everyone in the long queue outside the hall was confused and in a hurry.

Anyway, when they got back home, they saw a white lorry plus another two trucks standing in front of their house. And their whole yard was full of workers in white overalls. On the other side of the road, a different lorry was loading up those two women's stuff.

What now, he thought, stopping in the street outside to see what was going on. Who was this coming to fetch them?

'Whiter than snow,' Treppie began singing before they even lit up cigarettes, and only then did he realise, but of course, this was the painting team here at their house. It was the big paint prize they'd won, the one Lambert made him sign for. The one Treppie also signed for, afterwards. At the time he'd wondered if they weren't signing themselves into a fix, but he'd let it go 'cause Lambert was in such a bad way.

And then, when they didn't want to paint on election day, Treppie went and said he'd take them to court, so they said in that case, okay, it was the owners' risk and they reserved the right to paint any time of the day, even

497

if the owners were out. It was going to be a day full of unpredictability, they said.

The painters were busy unpacking their equipment. He must look, said Mol, there on the front lawn. That white flag hanging on a long, thin pole, with the painting company's name written on it in red letters. Red and white spells what? he thought, but Treppie had already read between the folds: WONDER WALL. If you ask him, Treppie said, it looked more like rescue workers at a disaster site than jasper workers from the New Jerusalem.

Treppie's trying to be terribly nice again, telling jokes and things after his doings on the koppie, not to mention his terrible tormenting of Lambert. And on his birthday, too.

This morning, as they stood in the queue, he had no choice but to cut Treppie short again. Treppie was standing there in the middle of the queue, talking at the top of his voice about how it was a disgrace that the officials had to do all this dirty work. It was the NP's duty to put those stickers on. That would be poetic justice, he said. After all, they were the ones who wanted to offer Mangosuthu for sale, first under one label and then another. You could actually call him a many-branded Buthelezi, Treppie stood there saying, standard on the one rump and prime on the other. Ja, that Treppie. He'll just have to learn in his own time to control his mouth. People with his kind of talent face terrible temptations. It's a great struggle for them to choose the straight and narrow path. Treppie has the character. He just lacks the will.

Anyway, Treppie was right, as usual. It looked more like hell than heaven around the house. Big blood-red rectangular machines stood all over the place, with fat, red muzzles stretching out as if they wanted to pump the house full of air. With shiny ladders against the walls, stretching up high above the roof like fire-engine ladders trying to reach a fire in the sky somewhere. At the front door, a silver trolley full of folded sheets.

Shame. And all Mol could say was: 'Sinkhole!' She was terribly disturbed by all the broken stuff in the house and Treppie's stories in the den, and then this voting business on top of everything else – soldiers and low-flying helicopters and waiting ambulances. And, believe it or not, a friendly little piccanin came up to them at the voting station to ask if they didn't want to help swell the peace fund, taking a handful of blue paper flowers from a big basket, each flower on its own stem with a ribbon and two little plastic doves. Then Mol just wanted to go home. But with all the painting going on there was no peace and quiet to be found here either. And Mol's always been so scared of machines and things, too. She was in a complete state.

He explained nice and gently about the paint prize and how she must just keep calm. Just now she could go and see if there was any Oros inside. It was hot and the painters would be thirsty. Then she'd have something to do, he thought, something to occupy her mind.

About Treppie's salvation he really can't do anything. Treppie was busy embroidering again, about things that had nothing at all to do with painting. 'Rescue the perishing, care for the dying,' he began singing loudly in their faces. And he kept bugging Lambert, telling him to listen. If he, Treppie, didn't get out of the car right away and go to the toilet, he was going to shit his pants full. It was a whole week now that his guts had been as solid as a rock. But, he said, now that Lambert's lubrication service was behind them, and now that he'd voted for that mad woman from the Keep it Straight and Simple Party, the one who says she can kick a hole in any government's drum, and with their house on the point of being painted white, he at last felt something was giving way in his insides.

Yes, he said, Lambert should take note, this was what he'd meant all along about the shit flying after the election, and Lambert should get ready for a shitstorm, or, as it was written, the fulfilment of the law and the prophets.

He must say, the way those paint people were carrying on it really did look like they were getting ready for a storm. They covered the windows with heavy, shining screens of aluminium. Flossie got a thick plastic sheet and they draped the fig tree with something that Treppie said looked like a thermal blanket, red on the inside and silver on the outside, which they pinned to the ground with tent pegs. They even pulled a white bag around the overflow and a little red sail over the TV aerial on the roof.

With all those bags and sails and sheets and flags and stuff stirring and rustling in the breeze, the house began to look exactly like a ship lying ready to sail. He said as much to Mol, but Treppie overheard him and then of course he had to make his own little contribution. That ship, he said, was on its way to a country where the citrons were still blossoming. Mol said he was talking bull, and she said it with such conviction that it sounded like she wanted to shut Treppie's mouth once and for all. A vain hope, of course. Treppie said, okay, if that wasn't good enough, then the ship was sailing to the shore where love did last eternally, and would that make her feel better?

Shame, then the poor thing broke into a big smile, sitting there without her tooth and all. Pop's heart wanted to break he felt so sorry for her. She sometimes reads to him from her library books about people who're in love. Under the circumstances, he thinks, he's done the best he could. It will just have to be enough. And with good faith they might yet reach those eternal shores, in their own kind of way. It's just a matter of time.

He would have been happy to remain sitting outside in the car, but the foreman came over and asked them to unlock the door. It was hardly open before lots of workers in white overalls started getting the house ready for painting inside. They worked fast. It must be something they do every day, and maybe they were in a hurry to get finished so they could still have some of the holiday for themselves. Not that it feels like a holiday. It feels more like a war or something, with all those army lorries and little bursts of gunfire every now and again. Celebration shots, Treppie says, but he can't say he's seen any ribbons or balloons.

They started at the back, pushing each room's things into a heap in the middle and covering everything with those white sheets from the trolley. Hell, all their old stuff looked so little, covered like that in the middle of each room. But he must say, the Wonder Wall people showed respect for their belongings. They took the brick out from under the sideboard and clamped a length of iron there before moving it away from the wall. And they first re-glued the loose joints before moving his chair, tapping the little pegs back into the arm-rests with a silver hammer. Now his chair's sitting nicely again. Now it'll be good for a while again.

Maybe this is a good time to take a nap. The workers are taking everything off the wall. They're even wearing gloves to do the job – the calendar picture of Jo'burg, the answers to Treppie's multiple choice, the advert for Cochrane's security fencing, Treppie's poem about peace and the portrait of the three of them with roses. The works. The wall looks bare. White squares where the stuff used to be. As it comes down, gloved hands place the items one by one into a big, white, double-carton, as if they're fragile antiques or crumbling old masterpieces.

And here comes a soft, white bag made of felt. He hears a dull rustle as the china cat from Shoprite is carefully lowered into the bag. The distributor cap with the old and the new NP flag goes in too, plus a few of Flossie's ball-bearings in a saucer. What else? The moon and the stars and the sun that must shine on everyone who remain behind. Three more panfuls of loose floor-blocks from the dark passage. Everything into the bag to make sure that nothing will be lost. Not him either. Now they're throwing sheets over everything. All is white. White for the crossing over.

High above the roofs of Triomf, the roads and the towers and the flat, yellow mine dumps. The chimneys that smoke and blow fire to one side, as if in a salute, beyond the earthly city's limits. Higher and higher, a seed in a white husk. Cries and psalms from other windborne souls.

And then again, from far off, the ground approaching at long last, rocking to and fro, the horizons tilting from side to side. To one side, a small, white house, its doors and windows tightly shut, where he can finally come to rest against the clean, sun-warmed walls, nothing but the whisperings inside as if his ear were pressed to a shell, throughout the bright and endless winter.

FAMILY SECRETS ⁓

Lambert stands in the lounge, watching the painters. They're busy on ladders all over the house, as if they're not even aware of him standing there. They dip their big, fluffy rollers into wide, flat pans, painting the walls in brilliant white with quick strokes. Where they haven't painted yet it looks dirty. Their mouths move as they talk but he can't hear them. He can hardly hear himself thinking. It feels like a silent movie inside his head. The house shudders from the sandblasting. He can make out a fine hissing sound as wet paint-flecks splatter against the aluminium screens. Inbetween he hears the dull thuds of people working on the roof.

He's alone. When those big machines began zooming and revving through their cycles, from warm-up to stand-by and ready to blast, his mother took Toby in her arms and shouted to Treppie she was going to wait outside in the car until it was all over. By then Treppie had been on the toilet for a long time already. He saw him go in there with a stack of newspapers, enough for a week's reading. Even before the noise started, Treppie had begun swearing and growling. Now, he said, he was officially withdrawing from Operation Whitewash. And he wouldn't mind if the bathroom didn't get painted either, 'cause then at least there'd be one place left in the house he could still call home.

Fuck, the noise is so bad now it's hurting his ears. And the paint fumes make him want to choke. But he has a very good reason for being here. When they were throwing sheets over the wardrobe in Treppie's room just now, three little keys fell on to the floor. The workers brought the keys to him; he was the only one they could still find in the house. The key to the trunk, the key to the cupboard and the key to the sideboard, which his mother had wanted from Treppie just two days ago so she could take out the stag bowls. That key also opens the top drawer – forbidden territory for as long as he can remember. The only time he's ever seen it slide open has been when Treppie decides that *he* wants to open the drawer. And Treppie hides that key in a different place every time, to make sure 'curiosity won't kill the cat'. The only thing he's ever seen coming out of that drawer is Old Pop's mouth organ. Each time, Treppie asks Pop to play a song 'from days gone by'.

But there's more than just a mouth organ in that drawer. Without a doubt.

Whenever he's begged Treppie to look in there, Treppie just says: What the eye doesn't see, the heart can't grieve for.

It's a double bind, he always says, 'cause what lies in that drawer is the key to his, Lambert's, existence. But he's convinced that if he, Lambert, were to see what's inside there, he'd fit himself to death on the spot. So what's the use? It's not the kind of information that a dead fit can put to any good use, neither for himself nor for anyone else. That's always been Treppie's last word on the topic, and after that all he would do was give a whole long string of devil's winks.

But it hasn't been Treppie alone who's stopped him from breaking open that drawer, many times over. What really stopped him, in the past, was Pop's face when he put that old mouth organ to his mouth, cupping his hands around its sides as if he were trying to suck some sweetness out of a thing with a red peel, although what he got wasn't exactly what he was looking for. It was almost as if he wanted to taste something different, something beyond bread and polony, beyond their house and their car, beyond the whole of Triomf. Ambrosia, as Treppie would put it. It's as if Pop wants to say: I'll taste what I want to taste, it's not of this world and I don't give a damn about the after-taste.

Whatever it is inside that drawer, it's always felt like the part the Witnesses read about the stuff inside the Ark of the Covenant. You never know what it is. All you know about are the cloths and the rings and the sockets and so on. And the girdles outside and the candlesticks with seven arms and all the carrying across the desert.

That's why he's kept a distance from the drawer all these years. If he ever finds out what's inside there, he's always schemed, then he'll have to carry it through the back-streets. On his shoulders in Triomf, for the rest of his life.

But today he couldn't give a shit. Not after his birthday. Not after that whole fuck-up.

So when the man in the white overalls held out the keys to him, and said, 'These fell from somewhere,' he replied, 'Hey, thanks, man, they fell from heaven, I've been looking for them all my life.' And when the man asked, 'So, can I leave them in your safekeeping?', he answered, 'But of course, they are the keys to our family treasures, I'm in the shit if I lose them again.'

Then that man laughed a strange little laugh which he very quickly swallowed again. He must've seen it was no fucken joke to be holding the key to your existence in your own two hands.

So, today's the day he's going to unlock this drawer. All around him the painters are busy on their second coat. Wonder Wall's paint is 'quick-drying', the papers said, 'matt-white' and 'quick-drying'. Like pistons in white sleeves the arms of the painters go up and down as they paint. He looks at the things under the sheets in the middle of the room. He knows them by their shapes: Treppie's crate, his crate, Pop's chair, his mother's chair, the TV, the toolbox. And then there's the sideboard, with its riffled edge in front.

Lambert works his way in amongst all the stuff. The little key sweats in his hand. It's the flat one with a round head and a little hole in the middle. He opens his hand and sniffs it. The iron smell is still there, right through the paint fumes. The other two keys he's put in his shorts pocket. Treppie must just keep shitting for all he's worth now. But if he does come out, then he'll see him right, just like that. He's not scared of Treppie any more. After forty there's nothing Treppie can say to make him feel small any more. Treppie's tools and Treppie's book and Treppie's keys are all his now. Treppie's a dead duck.

It's only Pop. He can feel Pop's eyes on him somehow, but Pop's not here. He must be outside, sitting with Mol in the car. Pop's become very touchy lately. Must've found the noise in here too much. At the voting this morning, when the man took Pop's right hand and pulled it across the table so he could spray his invisible ink, Pop's arm came out of his sleeve in such a strange way – like the hand was coming right off his arm.

Nothing but skin and bone. The point of his nose was white and he was shaking, too. His mother said Pop took so long to vote she started thinking he'd given up the ghost right there in his little booth. Treppie said she was worried for nothing. The whole Transitional Executive Council had Pop by the short and curlies. He knew he had to vote for volk and vaderland.

He lifts the sheet covering the sideboard. Chairs and things stick into his back, but he doesn't want to shift too much furniture around now. He just gives Pop's old boots a bit of a shove. They're sticking out from under the sheet. Jesus, but they're heavy.

He unlocks the drawer. The little fitting around the keyhole came off a long time ago and where it used to be the wood's discoloured. He notices he's short of breath. He rubs behind his neck. What ghost is breathing down his neck now? No, he mustn't think about that kind of thing.

The mouth organ is lying right in the front of the drawer. He knows it well. It was his grandfather's mouth organ. Old Pop, they call him.

He remembers, once, how Pop sat and played 'The Yellow Rose of Texas', but then Treppie came and messed around with him again. He said Pop mustn't sit there like that and tell lies with a straight face. And he mustn't start imagining all kinds of things about his family tree, either. Pop's family tree, he said, was a tree full of hillbillies without any music in their bones. He said Pop might be the musical one in the family, but that was only 'cause Pop's father hadn't hit him the way Treppie's father had hit *him*. And if Pop didn't believe it, he should ask Mol – she still remembered how their father had disciplined him, out of the love of his heart, so he'd at least achieve more in life than to sit and play 'The Yellow Rose of Texas' over and over again.

Well, now he's going to find out what goes for what in this house, and whose father is whose father and what's a hillbilly in a tree with music in his bones.

'Cause if there's one thing that has to come to an end now, then it's Treppie's fucken bullshit-stories. He says he lies for the sake of truth, the shit. He says it's a paradox. He once heard Pop say to Treppie that whatever it was, para-this or para-that, if you couldn't convey the truth with a pure heart, then it didn't count for the truth, anyway. Then of course all hell broke loose. Treppie said Pop was mixing up truth with goodness, and if there were two things under the sun that were further apart than chalk and cheese, it was those two, and did he, Pop, want Treppie to start telling lies now, just to spare people their pain and sorrow? Pop said if he wanted to put it that way, then his answer was yes, and he, Treppie, would be terribly dirtied and infected by sin if his own answer was no.

'Infected! Infected!' Treppie shouted. Was Pop trying to tell him God was a bath full of Dettol-water for washing off the germ of being human?

When those two start on God and stuff, it doesn't take long before Treppie goes completely berserk. He starts swearing and performing up and down the passage. But it's not just for show, like when you can't get the lawn-mower started or the postbox won't stay on its pole any more.

Then it's for real.

He's already seen how Toby, and Gerty too, when she was still alive, used to hide behind the bathroom door with their ears flat against their heads. And his mother would sink on to her knees, right there where she was standing on the loose blocks in the lounge, or on the lino in the kitchen.

Pray, Treppie would shout at her, conceited fucken old cunt, who did she think she was? Did she think she could talk to someone and he'd listen? That almighty tinpot of a God sitting up there welding time together all by himself? Hearing deaf, that's what he was! 'Bang! Bang! Bang!' There he sat, slamming the moon and the sun like pot lids over our heads. Did she think he had a beard and saucer ears like Father Christmas or someone? Forget it, Mother Superior, forget it! She should listen to the way her heart beats in her chest. 'Bang! Bang! Bang!' Buggered by Lucky Strikes! That's what He sounded like! Just look what God's Providence had wrought over time, creasing the wattles on her throat, weighing down her old gut and cracking the soles of her old feet – being one of the chosen had worn her out good and proper! The whole lot of them in this house, first they were young with God and now they were old with God. God-infested to the back of their teeth! Meanwhile, up there He just kept running down like a king-size bobbin, back and forth like a shunting train. Like the ants, up and down, up and down. If you stepped on him he'd stink like a Parktown

Prawn. All he could do was kick up heaps with his back paws. Molehills! Molehills! Molehills!

One day, when things were going like this and Treppie was shouting and screaming, Pop took a swing and connected him a shot just under the chin. Treppie went down like a bag of cement. Out like a candle on the flat of his back, in the passage.

That was the only time he's ever seen Pop cry. Pop's tears come very easily, and he's always got that drop hanging from his nose. The essence of life, Treppie calls it. But that day, when Pop took hold of Treppie under the arms and dragged him away to his room, Pop was folded over double from crying. His tears were dripping on to Treppie's face, so it looked like Treppie was also crying as he lay there, lights-out.

Pop had tears for Africa, his mother said. Then she looked at him and said he, Lambert, was born in tears and received in tears, never mind sin, and maybe one day she'd tell him what was what, otherwise he'd never understand why they were the way they were in this house.

Well, she waited too long. Now it's tickets with 'one day'. One day is today. Today he'll know what's what.

The paint machines suddenly sound louder outside. Something falls 'bam!' on the roof.

He puts the mouth organ down on top of the sideboard, on the folds of the white sheet. His legs have gone to sleep from sitting in front of the drawer. He gets up. It's hot. Must be all the closed windows. He pulls the drawer further out. Something sticks. He gives it a hard pull. The thing comes out, with a dent on the one side. It looks like a pair of goggles made from a thin piece of tin with a little arm in front. Here's a little handle sliding on a groove in the arm. He can shift the handle. He shifts it up and down. What the fuck? He reads the letters on the goggles. *Viewmaster*.

Where's he heard that before? He's heard his mother say it: Viewmaster. But she's like that, she says funny stuff at odd moments. Light blue, my beloved, she said to the postbox one day. Or was that Pop? Soft in the head, both of them. When she sees a moth she says TB butterfly. Must be thinking of the J&B butterfly on the whisky advert. She can't tell TV apart from real life any more. He's told her so, but Treppie says it's a highly justified attitude, that, 'cause what else is the world if not one huge sitcom? Then Treppie tells one of his stories about corpses. Like when the Germans put dead babies into their BMWs so they could crash-test them to see if they were sufficiently roadworthy and people-friendly. Some things never change, Treppie says, but after the BMW story, 'post-mortem' is a completely new concept to him. Then he kills himself laughing and his mother says she really doesn't see what's so funny.

Lambert sees how the painters all around him are starting to climb down from their ladders. He'll have to start hurrying up now. But then he sees them tying hankies over their mouths with little strings, like doctors before they do operations. Each one clamps a big spray-can on to his back. They climb back up their ladders and start spraying a fine, white mist on to the walls. That must be the matt of the matt-white. In the drawer he sees a pack of pictures held together with an elastic band. Old and faded black-and-white pictures. Underneath each one it says *Viewmaster* and something else that's too small to read.

He puts a picture into the groove and moves the handle up and then down again until he can see what's what through the magnifying glass of the goggles. Now what's this got to do with the price of eggs, he wonders. *Buckingham Palace*, he reads. *The Changing of the Guard.* He tries another one. *The Queen Mother, with Windsor Castle in the Background.* He looks through them quickly, till he gets to *Royal Picnic at Balmoral*, where the queen sits on a blanket among her dogs, holding a boiled egg in her hand. No, fuck! This is definitely not the key to his existence! He puts the Viewmaster down on the sideboard, next to the mouth organ.

He scratches deeper in the drawer. Lots of old papers and other rubbish. Their IDs fall out from a plastic bag. He saw Treppie putting them back in here after the voting this morning. That must have been when he left the little key out, and the other ones too. He was in too much of a hurry to go catch his shit! That's what comes from being in a hurry to shit. Quickly, he pages through their IDs. Lambertus Benade, Martha Benade, Martinus Benade. That's Treppie. Once or twice, when they all go to fetch their pensions, and him his disability, he's asked them how come Pop's also a

Benade. And each time Pop explains that he's from the Cape Benades and Mol and Treppie are from the Transvaal Benades. Their forefather must've been the same old Dutchman or Frenchman, but if they were family, then it was very distant family. And in any case, Pop said, it made things easier, like getting the house in Triomf, 'cause in those days families used to get slightly bigger houses than other people. So they lied a bit, saying they were two brothers and a sister plus her illegitimate child from she doesn't know where any more. But that was all just a lie for the sake of a roof over their heads. He, Lambert, was really Pop and Mol's love-child, the one she was already expecting when they got married in Vrededorp in nineteen-whenever. And then Pop always tells the story about Treppie's speech at the wedding, when he talked about the holiness of matrimony and sowing the seed of the watermelon.

Love-child! You wouldn't say it if you saw how they treat him! If he gets iron, it's scrap iron. If he gets a girl, it's a darky. If he gets meat, it's polony.

Lambert feels his tail-end starting to jerk. He wonders if it's his conscience that sits there, 'cause it's not just them, it's him too. He knows he treats them roughly sometimes. But he supposes once a Benade always a Benade, as his mother says. They're past praying for, as his father says. Same difference.

Lambert scratches around in the drawer among all the papers. His hands touch a wooden frame somewhere at the bottom. An old family picture. It shows the outside of a house, with a wire gate and bricks at an angle lining the garden path. A man and a woman and a youngish man are standing there, and then there's a girl and a small boy. The woman's wearing glasses and a hood. She looks tired. The man's in a boiler suit. He looks fed up. The little boy's holding a little toy whip. He looks like he's pinching his mouth closed. The girl looks sly. She's got black rings under her eyes and she's wearing a bonnet, like her mother. The young man's wearing a waistcoat and a hat with the brim turned up on the one side, with feathers in the band. And a white scarf tied into two silly points under his chin. Looks like he's on his way to a fancy-dress party.

He taps the underside of the portrait. Then he screws up his eyes, peering through the white fog that fills up the whole lounge. What is it that looks so familiar about this picture? He looks closer. But this here is Pop! In his Voortrekker clothes, like that story he always tells when he rode with Johanna on the wagon. Johanna with her twenty-one stab wounds! When he smeared grease on his scarf, for luck!

He turns the portrait around. The paper at the back's old and brown. There's writing on the paper from a pen with real ink. The writing's badly faded. He traces the letters with his fingers as he reads.

Sweat breaks out on his face. Suddenly he hears that song in his ears, right through the noise of the painting, the song that Treppie always sings when he wants people to open their eyes and pay attention:

> It was written on an old sow's ear
> It was a little grey
> But to everyone the news was clear
> It was the monkey's wedding day

Over and over he reads what it is he must understand now, but his head just doesn't want to get it straight.

Vrededorp 1938, it says. And in brackets after that: *(The year of the ox wagons)*. And then: *Mum and Dad and Treppie – 10, Little Mol – 14, Lambertus Jnr, in front of our little house.*

Further down, the writing gets smaller and more crammed, as if there wasn't enough space left to fit in the whole story:

> With love from Pop to you all, my flesh and blood, in memory of a big moment in the history of our volk. Given for safekeeping to Treppie (Martinus), the apple of my eye, so he'll never forget from whence he comes.

Lambert feels dizzy. He fumbles behind him for somewhere to sit down. He's trying to sit, but he's already sitting. It feels like he's sitting on a bag full of sharp things. God, no! It can't be true. Then Pop, not Treppie, is the biggest liar of them all. Then it was Pop who used the truth to lie when he asked Community Development for a house. It was the truth, all along! He's no fucken distant Benade. He's fucken dirt-close! They're all the fucken same, the whole lot of them! Treppie and Pop and his mother!

Lambert rubs his eyes. It feels like he can't get enough air. He wants to get up, out of the chair. Christ, no. He feels like something that's already dead, here among all these sheets. He gropes in the air in front of him as he tries to get up. His feet keep catching on Pop's shoes under the chair, like he's tripping over them. He feels like he's fucking out from the inside. Things that have been said, pieces of stories, falling inwards inside his head.

Treppie! That's him standing there with the pinched mouth! *One* Old Pop, *two* sons!

Suddenly light streams into the lounge. It's dead quiet. The workers are taking the screens off the windows.

Lambert gets up. He stands in front of the sideboard. His eyes feel rigid. Jesus, now some sense must come into all this crap.

He supports himself with his knuckles on the sideboard. He feels like he wants to burst out of his seams as the truth plunges down into him. About his people, their house, their dog, in their street, here in Triomf.

He shakes his head. It feels like there's loose stuff inside his head.

When he's in a bad mood his mother sometimes looks at him in a funny way, and then she says, God help her, she wonders whose child he really is.

And he always thought it was just her way of talking. Like when she says he's full of the devil or something. He always knew he was Pop's child and that the story of his being illegitimate was a lie for Community Development. But if he is his mother's child, and if his mother says her one brother's a devil, and the other's an angel, and he, Lambert, takes after the devil, then Treppie could be . . . Then his mother doesn't know which one . . . then . . . then . . .

He turns around. His ears are zinging from the sudden silence. The sun shines sharply through the window. All the curtains are down. All he sees is white, white, white. Outside on the lawn they're folding up the covers.

His birth certificate, that's what he must find! He turns back to the sideboard. Now he's going to scratch till he finds the thing.

If Pop's his mother's brother and he can sleep with her, and if Treppie's also his mother's brother, then . . . who the fuck's his father, then? Whose fucken child is he?

He shuts his eyes. There's too much white in the room. It makes him see black spots. He digs through the black spots in the drawer. Too many papers here and not enough time. He hears them taking down the sheets in the back room and shifting things back up against the walls.

He finds a piece of paper that's brown around the edges and worn from being handled a lot. His eyes catch at the words:

> *. . . can't carry on any longer . . . make an end . . . failed you and the children . . . Dear God . . . forgive . . .*

Then his eyes stick on Treppie's real name:

> *The business about Martinus not wanting to talk to me any more is breaking my heart. Make peace with him for my sake, I beg you, Mol. I did it because I love him more than I could ever say and because I want him to grow up decently.*

Lambert quickly reads further: *. . . dog's life,* he reads, *kaffirwork . . .* and about the Railways that will look after them. *Widows' fund* and *not much of an estate.* He glosses over the next few lines until he comes to the last paragraph:

> *I know you're sick in your lungs, Mol. Look after yourself. Don't let the kaffirs take over your job. Be careful, the Jew Communists will undermine you. They're heathens, the whole lot of them. A person has only one life and one soul but mine is finished.*

He reads about the hope of a reunion with them all one day between the walls of jasper, in the streets of gold.

Underneath is written: *Your loving husband, Johannes Lambertus Benade. (Pop.)*

The postscript is underlined:

> *Give Treppie my mouth organ. Lambertus plays better but Treppie needs it more. Try to keep them off each other's bodies, Mol, in God's name*

send them away to different places if you can. So an end can come to
you know what. Only a monster will be born from this sort of thing. I've
heard from the others, more and more such cases are happening among us
Railways people.

Slowly he folds up the letter again. He looks at his hands. Skew, full of
knobs. He looks down at his legs and his feet. He wishes he'd kept on his
white pants that he wore to the voting this morning, if only for this one
moment. He wishes he hadn't felt so hot and got back into his shorts
so soon. Now he sees his large knees, his hollow shins, his knobbly,
swollen, monster-ankles, his skew, monster-feet, and his monster-toes.
Ten of them! All different shapes and sizes. Dog-toenails! He feels his face.
A monster. A devil-monster. No wonder! No fucken wonder he's such a
fuck-up. No wonder he can't even fuck a Hotnot bitch! No wonder only
his mother's good enough for him! It's all in the family! The plague!

With one rip he pulls the drawer right out of its casing.

'Family secrets!' he roars.

His eyes feel like they're spinning wildly in their sockets. He feels
himself breaking the drawer with a cracking shot over the chair's covered
back-rest. He sees a man in white overalls looking at him with big eyes.
Then he hears himself shouting at the man to fuck off. The man runs
out the front door with a bundle of sheets in his arms. He hears the man
shout at another worker trying to come inside: 'Take cover, the nutcase
has lost it!'

He storms down the passage.

'Get thee behind me, Satan!' he roars at a white overall here in front
of him. 'Take cover!' He rams the man out of his way. With one kick,
he knocks the bathroom door off its hinges. Then he grabs the door and
throws it into the bath.

In front of him, Treppie sits with his pants around his ankles. He's holding an open newspaper in his hands. Treppie's smiling at him. The shit!

'You!' That's all that comes out of him.

'Tut-tut. Showing me the door, are you?'

As if it was all just a fucken little accident.

GUY FAWKES ～

Mol stands on the little stoep in front. She's listening to the crackers as they go off, one here, one there, close by and then far away again. Not so many before, in other years.

Shame, last year she and Pop still shot off some crackers together, right here, in their hands. It was quite jolly. And then they bathed together. Shame, Pop was so gentle with her that night.

She feels Toby rubbing against her leg.

'Yes, old Toby, so it goes, hey?'

She bends over and scratches him between the ears.

Ever since Pop went, they've never really managed to be jolly again.

It was all 'cause the house was supposed to be painted white. Inside and outside. Everything covered with sheets. That's where the trouble started. She said all along it was going to cost them dearly. *Dearly*, and how!

The account wasn't even the worst of it. They found the account in the postbox when they got back from the hospital, that night after the painting. It was for twenty-five thousand rand less the discount of three thousand rand, so it came to twenty-two thousand rand. That 'prize' was never a prize, after all. It was a discount.

From then on they got a letter every month with a red sticker saying they must pay, otherwise lawyers would sue them. Treppie tore up the letters every time. Then one day the sheriff came to see which of their things he could take away to sell, but he left almost immediately when he saw none of their stuff was worth anything. He still said something about people like them thinking the New South Africa meant they didn't have to pay their debts to the Old South Africa. Next, they got a letter from Wonder Wall saying they could pay the account off. Thirty rand a month plus a terrible amount of interest. Now Lambert and Treppie are paying it off, half and half, every month. Treppie says this is now what you call Triomf-debt – by the time they finish paying it off, their matt-white will have cost them ninety thousand rand.

But the account wasn't even the worst of it. The worst was that no one kept an eye on Lambert that day. So he took his chance and scratched around in the sideboard drawer. Lambert doesn't know what's good for him. But it was bound to happen some time or another. Then he went and broke the drawer in half over poor old Pop's head, right there where Pop was sitting under the sheet. Dead quiet, without bothering anyone. Where she said they must leave him so he could sleep where he always slept.

She found him still sitting there. She took the sheet off to tell him he must please come and do something, Lambert had kicked Treppie right out of the house and now Treppie had no pants on and the NPs had arrived to see if they'd voted right.

Yes, when she looked again, there was Treppie lying starkers on the lawn with Lambert stomping on his fingers. He broke them all, one by one. 'Crack! Crack! Crack!' she heard as those little bones in Treppie's hands broke. Such bony little birdy-hands, too.

And those two from across the road stood there with their mouths open, staring at them. That was their day for moving out. Going to live somewhere else. The same day. No wonder.

It never rains but it pours, Treppie still said when they got back from the voting. They saw, across the road there, a few crock lorries and some lazy, slackarse-movers with red noses trying to move the dykes' stuff. She must say, she looked at them and thought the lorries in front of their own house looked a damn sight better, just for a change. And their painters looked like angels from heaven compared with those wash-outs on the opposite side.

Anyhow, then Treppie said he hoped they knew what they were doing. Those movers looked like a bunch of cheapskate rehabs to him. Must have been all the dykes could find on voting day, as if they really had to go and move on a day like that.

All they seemed to be loading on to the trucks were plants.

One table, two chairs, one bed, and for the rest, just plants, plants and more plants. After a while it looked like the Hanging Gardens of Babylon on wheels.

That's what Treppie said.

He said some people painted their walls white and others moved to greener pastures, but in the end everyone, without exception, just looked north and fucked forth, as if their lives depended on it. Delicious monsters.

Well, yes.

Sometimes there's truth in Treppie's jokes.

But that wasn't even the beginning, that day of the 27th. Lambert was so wild after he'd finished with Treppie, he came for her next. She was walking around, shouting, 'Pop's dead! Pop's dead!', when he came and stabbed her in the side with Treppie's pocket-knife. Just like that. In front of all those people. That's when the painters dropped their sheets and ran for their lives.

Toby thought it was fun and games again. He tried to bite Lambert's backside as Lambert ran amok there on the grass. With the knife still open, like he wanted to slaughter a pig or something.

Lambert turned around to give Toby a kick under the arse, but Toby wasn't there any more and Lambert kicked the prefab wall instead. Broke his leg. A bad break, right at the ankle. And there he lay, roaring on the green, green grass of home, as Treppie said later. She stood around, holding on to her side where the blood was pouring out. And Treppie just lay there, crying from laughing so much. Broken fingers and all.

'One dead, three injured!' he shouted. 'One down, three to go!

'Aid us, aid us, afflictions abrade us!' he shouted for all to hear.

Abrade.

On the very day Treppie appears before the heavenly gates he'll still think of an impossible word to say. He's always called himself an occasional speaker. Shame, and Pop used to say he shouldn't waste his talents so, he was capable of doing so much more. And then Treppie would say he couldn't help it, that's what the people, meaning them, wanted from him. A story for every occasion, and who was he to say they must listen, he could also tell classic stories. In any case, that would be casting pearls before swine.

Classic.

Treppie says a piece that's classic, whether it's a piece of music or a piece of furniture or just a piece of house, is something that lasts forever, something everyone will like. The rest are just May-flies.

Well, if you ask her they're not even May-flies, let alone classics. May-flies are complete in themselves and they fill the whole world, even if it's just for one day. But the Benades were crocks from the moment they first saw the light of day. Pieced together and panelbeaten, not to mention screwed together, from scrap. Throw-away pieces, left-over rags, waste wool, old wives' tales, hearsay, a passing likeness from the front and a glimpse from behind. That's how they found themselves here on this earth. Things that get thrown away. Good for nothing. Write-offs.

She's getting morbid now out here on the stoep. It's not really so very bad, after all. She just thinks like this so she won't have to think about Pop, but actually she does want to think about Pop. She wants to remember Pop. That's what she wants to do. She wants to honour his memory on this Guy Fawkes night.

Shame, and there they stood at the JG Strydom hospital, at midnight of the same day. Treppie said come hell or high water, he wanted a post-mortem. A family like theirs couldn't brave the future with a dubious cause of death in their midst. That's now after she said Pop was blue and his nose was white and she thought it was from lack of breath that he died, sitting there and sleeping under the sheet and everything.

Never mind what she really thought. That's what she said. She knew Pop would've done the same, to preserve the peace. And now Pop wasn't there to do it himself any more.

And Lambert said, yes, he agreed, Pop couldn't get enough air, 'cause apart from that sheet over his head, there were all those fumes and the spray from the Wonder Wall paint, too.

But when Treppie saw the drawer broken in half like that, he began to smell a rat.

Ja, and then Toby stood there and went 'ee-ee' next to Pop's shoes, the ones he was still wearing. Most of the time Pop used to kick them off before he fell asleep in his chair, but now they were shoved so strangely under the chair, you'd swear they didn't have feet in them any more. Toby's face also looked like he had an idea or two about that pose of

Pop's there in his chair, with his knees pointed together in front like a Parktown Prawn's.

Anyway, she and Treppie and the painting foreman managed to get Pop into the car, and then Treppie drove them to the hospital, broken fingers and all. Lambert changed the gears for him. By now, Lambert's foot was swollen the size of a rugby ball. She'd taken off her housecoat to wrap around her middle and she was holding on to her side where it was still bleeding so much. What else was she supposed to do?

If she hadn't been stabbed, she said to them as they stood around outside trying to make a plan, she would have driven the car herself. But they didn't even hear her. Neither of them took her driving lesson seriously. Lambert didn't even know about it. He had been sleeping that afternoon, after his shooting practice. And Treppie had such drunken blues that night, he stood there playing piano in the air. First in the air and then on the edge of the stoep, as if their whole yard was a concert audience, and he was on a stage with an entire orchestra behind him.

Eventually they were all bandaged and plastered up and at last they stood there, next to the doctor, who had to write out the death certificate for Pop on the trolley.

'Heart attack,' the doctor said. 'And multiple thrombosis.' She saw Lambert take a deep breath through his mouth as he stood there on his crutch.

'Lambert,' Treppie said, 'shut your mouth, you look like you've just seen a ghost.'

'Multiple skull fracture,' the doctor said next, prodding Pop's head with his hand so they could see the pieces of his skull moving back and forth.

Lambert shut his mouth. And the doctor looked at each of them, one by one. Right into their faces.

'We were painting,' said Treppie. 'The house, I mean, and I saw him clutching his chest.'

'And then he took a dive off the ladder,' said Lambert. 'Boom! On his head.'

'Took a dive?' asked the doctor.

'That's right,' said Treppie. 'That's what happened. We all saw it.'

Then she also rather said yes, Pop fell on his head.

'Like a warhead,' Treppie still said, 'but no bang, just a puff.'

'Of dust,' said Lambert.

'Of dust,' she said.

Were there any other relatives? the doctor asked. They said no, and the doctor said well, in that case he thought a police statement was perhaps unnecessary.

'Superfluous,' he said, and that's what they all three said, as if they'd practised it all their lives, just for this moment.

'Superfluous!' As if in one voice.

'Shame,' said Treppie, 'but at least he still had time to exercise his vote.'

'And to see the house painted white,' said Lambert.

'Exercise in white,' she said, and then she felt, no, her head was giving just a little more. Almost the same feeling as a piece of tooth chipping off. First the chip washes around a little in your mouth, then it gnashes between your other teeth, and then you take it out to see what it is. Oh, it's a tooth, you think, throwing it away. Wear and tear. But now there's another chip gone. In her head.

They laughed at her about that 'exercise in white', all of them, not that she could see what was so funny, but she didn't care. Everything had gone off well at that post-mortem.

She was still in bandages the day Pop was cremated. Treppie's fingers were in plaster and Lambert was on his crutches.

She insisted: no coffin. And no hole in the ground, either.

Ash.

Ash is light.

First she said they must throw out the ashes next to the Brixton tower where they'd gone to eat their take-aways that time, when they watched the lightning. The day Pop got so lucky with his scratch-cards. When Gerty was still with them.

Treppie said fine, that was also where he remembered Pop the best after that sermon Pop gave him about the high current and the dead earth. But he couldn't very well scatter ash with his fingers in plaster now, could he?

A week or two later, Treppie took off the plaster with a screwdriver, right here in the lounge. All you saw were plaster-chips flying everywhere. Lambert's foot was another story. It didn't want to get better in the plaster. Had to be amputated. And all the time that box of ashes just stood there on the sideboard. Then one day she thought to herself, no, now she was going to make a plan before that ash got cold and forgotten. So she dug a hole in the yard, next to Gerty, and threw the ashes into the hole. Not even three hands' full. And half of it blew away, too.

She added to the writing that was already there on the wall, with a ball-point. They didn't have any yellow left:

> *Here lies Gerty Benade (and now also the ash of Pop ditto)*
> *Mother of Toby Benade*
> *and sweetheart dog of Mol ditto (and beloved by Mol ditto).*
> *(Both) dead from lack of breath.*
> *they're*
> *Now in dog's heaven*
> *where the dogs are seven eleven.*

There was some new space underneath, where Gerty's grave had sunk down a bit, so she added:

> *Just the way Pop dreamt it.*

Mol looks up into the sky. Now her tears mustn't start running down her cheeks.

Last time there were even roses for fireworks.

'What you looking at, Mol?'

It's Treppie. He's come out on to the stoep.

Here comes Lambert, too. In his wheelchair. His other ankle's also giving in, the one that was always so weak.

Lambert's much calmer 'cause of the stronger pills the doctor put him on. Patty-something.

He's boss of the house now, he thinks. But that's okay. He can't corner her anymore like he used to. Now she's faster than him. And she's glad, 'cause when he doesn't take his pills he's especially full of shit.

Ever since Wonder Wall painted over his paintings, and since he's been in the wheelchair, he doesn't paint any more. And he doesn't dig his hole either. Now he sits and watches TV all day. There's just about nothing left of that big heap he dug out for his hole. Most of it got rained away and then things started growing on it. Last year, on Christmas Day, Treppie threw that watermelon on to the heap, the one they were too full to eat after Lambert's braai. The watermelon went rotten, right there on top of that heap. Then, would you believe it, the other day she looked out of the back window and saw shoots growing all over the heap. And before long the heap was full of big, green leaves with watermelons sticking out like bums in the sun. Treppie says it's a miracle. He says it wasn't exactly seed that fell on fertile soil. But then again, he said, watermelons were like that. Very grateful plants. They grew from fuck-all, anywhere, any time. That's why there was a song like 'Sow the seed of the watermelon'. A folk song, said Treppie, was something that became popular 'cause everyone understood it, and in this case everyone ate it, too. He said he'd never heard of anyone who hadn't enjoyed watermelon at some time or another. He hadn't thought of it before, but that would really be a good idea for the NP's flag, if they ever needed a new one, 'cause that little sun and those stripes hadn't fooled anyone. That's in the election, of course. Not that she can be bothered. The ANC party after the election looked a lot more jolly. At least they sang and danced, even old Mandela, though he took just one tiny sip of his champagne. And guess what, someone had taught that Niehaus how to dance. Treppie said it just showed you, you'd never think a dominee would be game for such high kicks. If FW wanted to get anywhere he'd have to take dancing lessons from the ANC. Marike too. It was good for frowns, Treppie said.

They spent whole days in front of the TV, watching all the parties after the election and listening to the speeches and things at the Union Buildings. If Pop had been here he would've wanted them all to go to Pretoria together, just for the occasion. That's what she told them.

521

But Treppie said they'd be able to see everything much better on TV. And, they should remember, there wouldn't be any bullet-proof glass for the likes of them. But as far as she was concerned that wouldn't have been necessary. Heathens, Jews and Mohammedans were gathered there together, and everyone was quite jolly, without bullet-proofing. Even the aeroplanes didn't shoot. They flew over with rainbows of smoke coming out of their tails. The cannons were shot off, yes, but that was just into the sky for the new president. And, mind you, if she had a cannon she would also have shot off a cannonball here out of the heart of Triomf for old Mandela, 'cause he walks so upright and he took everyone's hands and he said, what was past was past, everyone must roll up their sleeves and look to the future now.

Treppie said, ja, well, no fine, with or without rolled-up sleeves, but he wasn't so sure about Marike. She looked even more like a missionary in Africa now with that bandaged hat of hers. If she didn't watch out, they'd throw her into a three-legged pot and make pot luck out of her. But that wasn't the most important thing, Treppie said. The most important thing was that they should never again say the word 'kaffir'. Not in their own house and also not outside. What was past was past, he said, and it applied to them too. Lambert said he wasn't so sure about that, but it was fine with her.

Black people are living across the road now, too. And they're okay on the whole, except they grow mielies on the pavement. Treppie says it's an excellent development. He says he wishes those two dilly dykes would come and see their old house so they could take a lesson or two from its new inhabitants. In times like these no one can afford to buy fertiliser for sweetpeas.

Ja, Treppie. He also just stays the same, except now he's unfit for work, 'cause of his fingers. He doesn't work at the Chinese any more. So, no more toilet seats or free crackers for them. And just one bottle of Klipdrift a month. Lambert's in any case not allowed to drink so much any more. It doesn't go well with his new pills.

Just look at all the stars. Big, wet, runny stars. Old stars. And now she's also almost a whole year older.

After Pop's ashes were put to rest she took the rose bush that Pop bought for her on her birthday last time, shame, and she planted it on top of his and Gerty's grave. It was Treppie who said it would be a good place. Ash is supposed to be good for roses. She told them that's where she also wanted to be buried one day. Scattered under the rose.

'Hey, Ma, stop staring into the sky like that, or next thing you know a Martian pisses into your eye,' says Lambert.

'I'm looking at Orion. Look, a man of stars with three jewels in his belt.'

'Where?' asks Lambert.

'There,' Treppie points for Lambert to see.

'Light blue, my beloved, for ever and ever. Orion washes my feet.'

'What shit you talking now, Ma?' says Lambert.

'It's not shit, it's what you said last time, when you fitted out so badly and you were lying there in the den with a matchbox between your teeth. Pop also heard it. If he was here he would have told you.'

'Lack of breath,' says Lambert.

'Multiple skull fractures,' says Treppie.

Let them think what they want. He was her warhead, through thick and thin.

'Pheeew-doof!'

She sees Lambert and Treppie look at each other. She knows what they're thinking. They think she's losing her marbles. But they can think what they like. And she thinks what she likes. And it's okay that way.

'In Orion,' she says. That's all she thinks about.

'What?' says Lambert.

'I think Pop's taking a rest up there, in Orion's belt, in a hammock that hangs from the two outside stars.'

'And look, Toby,' she says to the dog, who's come outside now to see what everyone else's doing. 'Look, Gerty's resting between the two stars on the other side. All you can see is her tail sticking out.'

'Ma, do you think you're a whatsitsname or something who can see what's going on in the stars?'

'Astrologer,' says Treppie. He's smoking a cigarette with his crooked fingers. The bones grew back all crooked. Now he looks even more like the devil.

'You think Pop checks his postbox every day?' she asks. 'I send my letters express, every night, in my dreams. Nice fat letters. Dear Pop, were you in the Spur today, and how was your T-bone? And did you and Gerty enjoy playing ball? The one that tastes like sherbet in your mouth? Now you're out of the beast's belly, hey, Pop, and you're not looking from afar through a hole in his head any more. Now you're nice and jolly, every day, hey! Not much longer, Pop, then I'll be with you. Then I'll feed you pieces of toast with honey. You and Gerty!'

She shows them with her thumb and index finger how big the pieces will be.

'And you needn't worry, Pop, I won't forget my driving lesson. Flossie's over the hill now, but I practise the gears every night in Molletjie, here under the carport while the others watch the news. First, second, third, fourth, reverse. So I won't be stranded one day if there's a crisis here. For my head, so it won't go rusty. And for my eyes, so they'll stay sharp, okay?'

All three of them look at the stars. They look at the big aeroplanes flying overhead, and the small ones too. Treppie points to a sputnik. It dips, on-off, on-off, through the sky. They talk about this and that. She talks along, with them, even if it is about other things. They've learnt by now to leave her alone.

They stay there for a long time as the crackers get fewer and fewer.

Until Orion tilts over to the west. He begins to dip, head first behind the roofs of Triomf. After a while you can't see the jewels in his belt any more. All you can see are his heels sticking out above the overflow.

Treppie points.

'No more North,' he says.

Before heaven's gates. As she predicted.

North no more.

~

GLOSSARY

Aikona – South African vernacular for 'no!', 'not on your life!', 'forget it!'

AKs – AK-47 automatic guns used by ANC guerillas during the liberation struggle.

Ampie – name of poor-white, backward character from the *Ampie* trilogy by Afrikaans writer Jochem van Bruggen (*Die Natuurkind,* 1924; *Ampie: Die Meisiekind,* 1927; and *Ampie: Die Kind,* 1942). Van Bruggen received the Hertzog Prize a record four times.

AWB – Afrikaner Weerstandsbeweging ('Afrikaner Resistance Movement'). Extremist militant and right-wing movement known for its struggle for territorial autonomy for the right-wing sector of the Afrikaners.

Backvelders – poor Afrikaner whites of rural descent or who still live in the country.

Beeld – name of a daily Afrikaans newspaper published in Johannesburg.

Biltong – dried, salted and spiced fillet of meat (mutton, beef, venison, either in strips or grated); South African delicacy first developed by the Boer pioneers.

Boer – white farmer; denotation for white farmer male; vernacular for police; a pejorative label.

Boerewors – spiced sausage, usually barbecued on an open fire.

Braai, braaivleis – (n) barbecue; (n) barbecue meat; (v) to have a barbecue. Common element of South African lifestyle.

Brood van Heerden – former Apartheid security operative. 'Brood': 'bread'.

Bywoners – tenant farmers; pejorative denotation for rural poor whites.

Cattie – a home-made catapult.

Dagga – South African vernacular for cannabis.

Daisy de Melker – (hist.) name of notorious woman poisoner, who murdered three husbands and was sentenced to death in 1932.

Droëwors – dried spiced sausage.

Drommedaris – name of the ship on which Jan van Riebeeck, the Dutch pioneer who arrived at the Cape in 1652, sailed when he arrived at Table Bay.

Eugene Terre'Blanche – leader of the AWB (see entry above).

Harry the Strandloper – the 'strandlopers', or the 'watermen', were a band of fifty-odd hunters, herders and outcasts of various kinds in the vicinity of Table Bay in the seventeenth century. These 'watermen' received small gifts in return for serving as postmasters, guides, refreshing ships and supplying intelligence about rival fleets. 'Harry's real name was Autshumato (1611–63) and he was the most important of the group. He was imprisoned by Jan van Riebeeck in 1658, but escaped from Robben Island in 1659.

Helpmekaar – (hist.) exclusive white nationalist charity organisation founded in 1917 to assist poor whites.

H.F. Verwoerd – famous leader of the National Party (see below); architect of legislative Apartheid.

Horries – psychological condition, being 'strung out', derived from the word 'horrible'.

Hotnot – pejorative, racist label for Coloured person. Derived from 'Hottentot' (Khoikhoi), indigenous tribes found at the Cape by the first colonists.

Ik heb gezegd – old Dutch expression used in Afrikaans to lend emphasis; 'I have said it'.

Inkatha – nationalist Zulu cultural and political organisation and political party.

Ja – yes.

J.B.M. Hertzog – leader of the National Party in coalition with the Labour Party, 1924–39.

J.C. Smuts – leader of the South African Party, supporter of the allied war effort during World War II. Periods in office 1919–24 and 1939–48.

Johanna van der Merwe – (hist.) Boer folk heroine who is reputed to have been stabbed nineteen times, and survived, during one of the famous Blauwkrantz 'massacres' in the conflict between the Zulus and the Voortrekkers (see below).

Jopie Fourie – Boer folk hero of the Anglo–Boer war.

Knobkierie – a stick with a round, carved head, used in sparring rituals by the indigenous people of South Africa and as a walking stick by the whites.

Koevoets – name given to a notorious South African reconnaissance battalion during the war in Angola against SWAPO in the eighties.

Kofifi – black vernacular for Sophiatown.

Kombi – a South African word for a Volkswagen eight- or twelve-seater minibus.

Koppie – rocky hill. Afrikaans word generally used in South African English for low stony outcrop.

Larnies – South African slang for people from the upper classes who behave in snobbish ways.

Lekker – 'nice', 'delicious'.

Lost City – a luxurious theme park based on a kitsch African legend of an ancient kingdom situated in the former homeland of Bophuthatswana.

Magnus Mauser – pejorative name for Magnus Malan, former minister of defence in the repressive Apartheid cabinet of former president P.W. Botha.

Mielies – corn (maize) on the cob.

Muti – African term for medicine or magic potion dispensed by a traditional healer.

NG Church – short for 'Nederduits-Gereformeerde kerk', Dutch Reformed Church. This is the most important church of the Africaans-speaking community. During the Apartheid years it supported the National Party leadership and gave legitimacy on religious grounds to all aspects of state ideology regarding race, gender, nationhood and political authority.

NP – National Party. White Afrikaner political party in power from 1948–94.

Oranje-blanje-blou – colours of the old South African flag: orange, white and blue.

Paardekraal – a historical site where there is a monument to commemorate the Boer War.

Pap – stiff porridge made from maize meal and sometimes eaten with sauce.

Parktown Prawn – AKA the King Cricket; a common insect in South Africa, notoriously tough and difficult to kill.

Pik Botha – long-time minister of foreign affairs in various Apartheid cabinets. 'Pik' is Afrikaans for 'peck'.

Racheltjie de Beer – (hist.) Boer folk heroine known for protecting her siblings during the Anglo–Boer war.

Reddingsdaadbond – exclusive white nationalist charity organisation founded in 1940.

Sjambok – a whip with a wooden handle and a plaited flail made from thin strips of leather.

Slang van Zyl – former Apartheid security operative. 'Slang': 'snake'.

Stoep – veranda.

Tsotsi – pejorative, vernacular for urban black male person of a criminal bent.

Tuisgebak – an old-fashioned bourgeois word for home-made biscuits, tarts and cakes.

Vaderland – 'fatherland'.

Vierkleur – old Transvaal flag.

Vleis Visagie – former Apartheid security operative. 'Vleis': 'meat'.

Voetsek – 'bugger off!' Slang used to chase away dogs and people.

Volk – nation; carries particular weight of feeling with reference to pseudo-fascist Afrikaner nationalism.

Volksie, Volla – Volkswagen Beetle.

Volksmoeders – 'mothers of the nation'.

Voortrekkers – denotation for the first Dutch colonists who pioneered the land of South Africa in their characteristic ox-wagons, purportedly to escape from the unfair and interfering practices of the British government during the British rule at the Cape.

Vroue-Landbou-Unie – women's agricultural union,